D1600349

COSMIC CRADLE
Souls Waiting in the Wings for Birth

Elizabeth M. Carman
and Neil J. Carman, PhD

The Soul's Passage from Heavenly Worlds
to Our Mother's Womb – as told by Gifted
Individuals, Philosophers, Saints, and Historians

Sunstar
PUBLISHING LTD.

COSMIC CRADLE
Souls Waiting in the Wings for Birth
by *Elizabeth M. Carman* and *Neil J. Carman, PhD*

© United States Copyright, 1999
Sunstar Publishing, Ltd.
204 South 20th Street
Fairfield, Iowa 52556

All rights reserved. No part of this book may be reproduced or utilized in any form by any means, electronic or mechanical, including photocopying or recording, or by any information storage and retrieval system, without permission in writing from the publisher.

Layout: *Sharon A. Dunn*

LCCN: *99-68634*
ISBN: *1-887472-71-1*
Printed in the U.S.A.

Readers interested in obtaining further information on the subject matter of this book are invited to correspond with:

The Secretary, Sunstar Publishing, Ltd.
204 South 20th Street, Fairfield, Iowa 52556

For more Sunstar Books, visit:
http://www.sunstarpub.com

Sunstar
PUBLISHING LTD.

To those who seek
Love, Truth, and Wisdom.

Acknowledgements

We have been working on this book since an inspiration came to us in 1989 and painted the potential for novel insights into the mysteries of how we come into this world. The research project began as part of a graduate writing program at Maharishi International University (MIU) during which several mothers were interviewed about their unique blissful experiences during pregnancy and childbirth. The phenomenon of bliss is poorly understood in our modern culture and so we have much to gain from understanding and directly experiencing it. But the research presented here represents merely one part of the information compiled in order to understand more about higher consciousness and the childbearing process, since the focus here is on the activities transpiring before biological conception ever takes place.

In the process of writing, we have had the instruction of gifted individuals who laid the foundation for inspiring this research: MIU Professional Writing faculty – Jim Karpen, PhD, John Kremer, Craig Pierce, PhD, Robert Oates, and Diane Frank. We also thank all our professors at Michigan State University, the University of Iowa at Iowa City, Maharishi International University, the University of Texas at Austin, Maharishi European Research University, and Maharishi Vedic University. Our personal and scientific research explorations in the field of consciousness, beginning in 1969 (Elizabeth) and 1970 (Neil), have been encouraged by Walter Koch, Jerry Jarvis, Jim Gillette, Terry and Robert Shaw, PhD, Robert Keith Wallace, PhD, Jonathan Shear, PhD, David Orme-Johnson, PhD, Michael Weinless, PhD, Lawrence Domash, PhD, Michael Cain, Geoffrey Wells, PhD, Herbert Johag, PhD, Paul Levine, PhD, James O'Non, PhD, Allen Reminick, and many more. Neil thanks the students who participated in courses on the scientific basis of consciousness at the University of Texas at Austin.

COSMIC CRADLE

Many sages and scholars whose teachings and writings have been especially helpful include: Saint David, Saint Mudgala, Socrates, Plato, Pythagoras, Virgil, Plutarch, Church Father Origen, Plotinus, Empedocles, Macrobius, Philo of Alexandria, Synesius, William Wordsworth, Swami Brahmananda Saraswati, Maharishi Mahesh Yogi, Paramahamsa Yogananda, Shree Maa, Vijayeshwari Karunamayi, Amritanandamayi, Sant Satguru Keshavadas, Swami Vivekananda, Shri Ramakrishna, Shri Dhyanyogi Madhusudandasji, Shirdi Sai Baba, Guru Gobind Singh, Markandeya, Thirteenth and Fourteenth Dalai Lamas, Gautama Buddha, Ashley Montagu, PhD, Andreas Lommel, PhD, Ake Hultkrantz, PhD, Bronislaw Malinowski, PhD, James Cowan, Robert Lawlor, Charles Mountford, Thunder-Cloud, Paul Radin, PhD, Reverend Gideon H. Pond, Edward Schure, Francois Gilot, Fred Jeremy Seligson, PhD, Alanson Skinner, Sir Baldwin Spencer, F.J. Gillen, Rudolf Steiner, PhD, Ian Stevenson, MD, W.D. Wallis, Mircea Eliade, PhD, Maurice Maeterlinck, Franz Boas, PhD, Thomas Verny, MD, Murshida Corda, Elisabeth Hallett, Sarah Hinze, RaNelle Wallace, Arvin Gibson, and David Chamberlain, PhD. The responsibility for the text is solely ours. The conclusions and recommendations expressed in this book may not be shared by other scholars in this area.

To thank those who have personally inspired us on this topic (and in several cases their special children): Beverly Anderson, Taylor Anderson, Teresa Anderson, R. Glen Beicker, Nancy Bellmer, Rena Boone, Stacey Butterfield, Cathy Cannon, Lorenzo Caravella, Christopher Cooper, Ross Richard Crow, Deelipji, Deyon Denman, Judy DeRuvo, Lania Desmond, Vimala Devi, David Dugan, Brad Freggar, Stephanie Foy, Catarina Gardner, Mary Jane Garza, Susan and Henry Herzberger, PhD, Sharon Jeffers, Springley Johnson, Robert Karam, PhD, Amy Kelly, Judy Kew, Gene King, Mark Kinnich, Joanna Luster, Anne Loader McGee, Ellen Meadows, Florence Mellott, Nan and Neel Morton, Jennifer Maye-O'Brien, Vanessa Ralston, Robin Richardson, Gerry Shatz, Terry Shaw, Sky, George Swanson, Deborah Swarttouw, Karla Thomas, Amanda Toulon, Jan Wagner, Signe Wilson, and Natalie Zimmerman. We thank contributors who allowed us to use their real names. Several contributors requested that pseudonyms be used to keep them confidential.

To Elisabeth Hallett for sharing her enthusiasm on the subject and helpful comments.

We owe a considerable debt to librarians at the University of Texas at Austin for several thousand books checked out, and special thanks to Alex Marshall who was always there to assist in courtesy borrowing of several hundred books at a time. Austin Public Library staff is appreciated for assistance in inter-library loans of books that were locally unavailable. Without the libraries much of this information might not have come to light. We also appreciate help borrowing books from friends Mary Buchanan, Terry Shaw, Deborah Aker, and Carol Miseo-Hardin.

For their indispensable help in getting this book written in its final form, we owe a debt of gratitude to Sunstar's format editor/illustrator Sharon A. Dunn for the layout and proofreader Fran Clark for her thorough scrutiny, comments and suggestions. Closer to home, we are especially indebted to our dear friends Judy Kew, George Swanson, Cathy Lee, and Jane Ayers whose tireless efforts to read and comment on draft material were invaluable. We thank Margaret Baacke, PhD, Jeanine Sih Christensen, Michael O'Callaghan, PhD, and Susan Pitman for their enthusiasm and insights as readers and commentors. Richard Austin is acknowledged for his assistance with formatting the original manuscript. Many other friends, too numerous to name here, helped along the way – mentioning a book to research, someone to interview, sharing their thoughts, etc.

Indirect financial support for the *Cosmic Cradle* research project and Elizabeth's full-time efforts came solely from Neil's environmental work with nonprofit public interest organizations including the Lone Star Chapter Sierra Club and the Galveston-Houston Association for Smog Prevention, which were funded by numerous grants from the Margaret Cullinan Wray Charitable Lead Annuity Trust, the W. Alton Jones Foundation, The Sierra Club Foundation, Wanda Graham, and others. The estate of Lawrence Tank is thanked for purchase of a computer and printer.

Cosmic Cradle

A special appreciation goes to publisher Rodney Charles at Sunstar Publishing who saw the potential and helped guide the manuscript in every step to completion. We also thank everyone at Sunstar who worked on *Cosmic Cradle*. We are most grateful to Sunstar for fulfilling our request to print the book using environmentally friendly paper.

To our parents, we owe a deep gratitude for without them this book would have been impossible.

– Elizabeth & Neil Carman

Table of Contents

Souls Waiting in the Wings for Birth

Somewhere Over the Rainbow
way up high,
There's a land that I heard of
once in a Lullaby ...[1]

*The Great Mother opens the portals and summons
the children whose turn it is to be born.*

The Azure Palace[1]

An ancient legend says a wise Queen known as the Great Mother watches over the world's unborn children. She dwells in a kingdom of unsurpassed beauty and harmony. Within Her vast realm lies an Azure Palace, the immense halls of which house countless beings and life forms of that same "supernatural and luminous blue."

Many of Her royal children left long ago to rule their own kingdoms. Those who remain behind the opalescent doors of the palace's 30,000 halls are the children not yet ready to leave Home.

They await their day to be cast in the human drama. One child will be born in twelve more years; another, in fifty years, four months and nine days. Before their departure, they consult guides and plan journeys to the human abode. They even devise the inventions, tools, and instruments they will use on Earth. One child is designing a way to bring pure joy to people through music. Another is creating thirty-three medicines to prolong life. While yet a third child wants to eliminate injustice.

Most of the children have already chosen parents and look forward to entering Earth's school, a kind of testing. One child appeared in her brother's dream saying, "Tell Mom I am ready. Tell Dad to mend the cradle, I will be born as your sister next Spring." Another radiant, enterprising child has arranged with his parents to be born as their physically handicapped son.

At appointed times, the Great Mother periodically opens the portals and summons the children whose turn it is to be born. The little ones descend to Earth in a gold-sailed galley. The Great Mother's heart melts each time she watches Her offspring move out into the universe. In Her love and mercy, She has granted them two gifts – a guardian to watch over them, and temporary forgetfulness so they will set forth with eagerness. She knows that one day, when the memory of their celestial years awakens, they will find their way back Home and claim their divine inheritance.

Chapter 1
Souls Waiting in the Wings for Birth

**This is the story of who you were then,
before you came into existence.[1]**
– Shaykh Muhammad al-Jamal ar-Rifa'i as-Shadhili

*A vibration stirred deep within the mother's being.
The gentle impulses were persistent. Joanna intuitively
knew she had children waiting in the wings for birth. Her
being was in tune with a higher power – an inner light.
Through a ray of consciousness, she felt a connectedness
to the Cosmic Mother who watched over the souls of
unborn children with loving nurturance and light.*

Joanna began to discover that the cosmic explorations of souls
seeking human birth occurs during pre-conception, a phase
unique unto itself before pregnancy begins. Unborn children
appeared as sparkling, virtually invisible visitors. Their souls often
circled around her, wanting her for their mother despite Joanna's
resistance to having a third child. "The room was filled with
floating bubbles with a pearlescent sheen like liquid gold. Each had
a faint impression of a beautiful cherub face – pink cheeks, golden
hair and all. I could see them with my eyes opened or closed."
Joanna's third child was born one year later. He is over ten years
old today. As a mother with gifted awareness for knowing the
soul's subtle world, Joanna was not alone in her perceptions.

Beverly Anderson too felt a son was coming to her for more than
twenty years. "I knew my son's personality, outlook on life, and

sense of humor prior to conception. We had been having non-linear communications for a long time." Then suddenly three months before her marriage Beverly was medically diagnosed with cancer of the cervix. The doctor advised a complete hysterectomy and to blow off the idea of having a child." Beverly replied, "I don't think you know the ball game. I am going to have this child. He is pestering me to be his Mommy, and he is important." Her son Taylor turned eight in 1999 and remains Beverly's only child.

Lorenzo Caravella easily recalls when he agreed on his future life plan, and this pre-conception turning point occurred long before his parents conceived his physical body.

> I saw my whole [future] life before me. I accepted its lessons, both the peaks and the valleys. In order for the peaks and valleys to be what they were, I needed to be guided through those energies called "parents."
>
> So, when the selection was made, it was not specifically that human and that human, but that energy to serve this peak or valley and that energy to serve that other peak and valley … . That is what the "cosmic contract" is all about.[2]

An Untold Cosmic Story

A good question to ask is, "Why isolate the pre-conception stage from pregnancy?" The key reason is that pre-conception is perhaps the most poorly-researched stage of human birth due to its hidden nature. Of course, we can argue that death is equally as mysterious. As William Shakespeare writes, death is "the undiscovered country from which no traveller returns." (Hamlet 3.1) Philosophers therefore contend that we cannot know anything about death. And yet everyone has gone through the birth process … so why does it remain an untold cosmic story?

Whereas pre-conception is part of the whole pregnancy process and is generally lumped together by other researchers as part of pregnancy, the purpose of our investigation is to give recognition to this unknown part of human birth. The wealth of information that has been found warrants an exclusive study. After interviewing 100 people and ten years of research into our spiritual consciousness roots and why we come into this world, we discovered that pre-conception is a universal human experience. Accounts of life before biological conception form a great body of information; they are not confined to gender, age, race, religion, generation, or country. Elements reverberate throughout philosophical, anthropological, religious, and mystical literature. Table 1 (page 7) displays a list of 165 cultures and religions from every inhabited continent within which we found reports, stretching back to the time of Christ and before: 18 religious traditions, 25 cultures from ancient and modern times, 53 Native North American peoples, 28 Australian Aborigine peoples, 20 African peoples, plus 21 additional indigenous peoples around the world.

We invite you on a journey to explore: What kind of people have pre-conception experiences?" "Is most everyone born on Earth with a lesson plan or cosmic contract?" and "Is DNA, the genetic blueprint, linked to our life path?" These questions are steeped in mystery and skepticism. How we happen to be born on Earth seems as mysterious as how a caterpillar transforms itself into a chrysalis, and finally into a butterfly.

As reflected by Shakespeare's poetic statement, "All the world's a stage and we are but the actors," the lives of great souls, such as Moses, Mahatma Gandhi, Mother Teresa, Princess Diana and millions more are scripted before they assume their role on the world's stage. When the Bible says, "There is a time for every purpose under Heaven," that includes a time for planning one's earthly life … and therefore a time for being conceived, a time for being born, for living, and for dying.

The knowledge in these pre-conception reports constitute a new paradigm in the West – a new way of looking at the world. Our consciousness is evolving through a cultural shift concerning the meaning of life itself. Who we really are is better understood by where we have come from and the intimate connections – Cosmic Contracts – between each person and their parents/families that they were born into.

Collective consciousness is rising on Earth and one of the signs is pre-conception reports presented here. Yet the number of pre-conception cases most likely exceeds the number of reports reviewed here since a local or national survey has never been carried out. The power of collective consciousness is likely increasing such reports.

Pre-Conception – Paradigm Shift

*The myth of storks bringing newborns
to their earthly homes seems to possess more
substance than our materialistic paradigm presupposes.*

The Scientific Revolution challenged the long-prevailing notion that an unseen world parallels the physical one. The predominant trend in science since the 17th century has been materialism, the mistaken assumption that physical matter is the only reality and that all thoughts and feelings can be explained by matter and physical phenomena. If we are unable to test, measure, weigh, or observe a phenomenon with a telescope, microscope, analyzer, or cyclotron, we believe it cannot exist. The human mind is assumed to be little more than the biophysical changes of the neurological system. Physical life is depicted as a mere random chance event, and Nobel prizes are awarded for breakthroughs in materialistic science that so far have excluded the field of consciousness. We are mislead to believe that no worlds exist except the physical realms.

The ideas and teachings of the materialistic world view "reduces the mind to matter and eliminates the soul."[3] Materialistic thinking has a great influence, especially through Western universities and the news media. In such a narrow climate, we are unlikely to hear the rare stories of Joanna, Lorenzo, or Beverly. Chances are good that they will be dismissed as merely anecdotal, without a clear scientific basis. Spiritual experiences are too often relegated to the realm of old wives tales and folk legends.

All this helps to explain why we are left with such poor insight into our spiritual roots in these challenging times. A new, yet ancient, understanding of human life is embedded within the principles governing pre-conception phenomena. The experiences parallel an emerging paradigm with a set of assumptions which more completely explain our spiritual roots and the beginnings of our life on Earth.

Before we explore the new pre-conception paradigm, let's encapsulate the old one with its assumptions forming part of our shared world view as taught by our parents, teachers, and society.

Old Pre-Conception Paradigm

The old pre-conception paradigm presumes that we have no soul prior to conception and boils down to five assumptions. (Pre-conception or pre-uterine life is the period before biological conception, the moment when the sperm and egg unite to form a one-celled fertilized human embryo.)

1. *Heredity and social environment (nature and nurture) adequately explain human life.*
2. *Memory and awareness arrive with the development of specific brain structures and a nervous system, where memories can be stored. We have no consciousness or sensory abilities before the brain exists.*
3. *Parents cannot communicate or bond with their children prior to conception. A newborn is a blank slate to be molded by his parents, teachers and society.*
4. *Biological conception is a chance natural event and marks the first step toward creating human life.*
5. *Our five human senses give us an accurate perception of the world.*

To a large degree, it is an oversight that materialistic science does not embrace our inner human nature, a world as complex as the outer cosmos. Behavioral sciences, along with molecular biology and pharmacological psychiatry, fail to describe how we come to be, where we are going, the pre-uterine state, or our reason for existence. A noted Tibetan Buddhist scholar Robert Thurman writes:

"Scientific investigation restricts itself to the material quanta perceivable by the physical senses, augmented by machinery, during this one bodily life. At the same time, Westerners have set about exploring the outer world, the farther continents, the macro realms of the outer galaxies, and the micro realms of the cell, the molecule, the atom, and the subatomic forces."[4]

The end result imagines that we are pawns of genetic codes, heredity, traumatic incidents, what our parents did or did not do, and societal accidents. The being of man is a "biological offspring of the family tree"[5] who lives "a cosmically meaningless life, beginning and ending in nothingness."[6] We do not know why we exist and cannot realize the knowledge of our destiny.

Souls Waiting in the Wings for Birth

Table 1. 165 Cultures and Religions
Reporting Pre-Conception Experiences

Religions (18)		Ancient & Modern Cultures (25)		
Christianity	Manichaeism	Belgium	Germany	Peru
Buddhism	Mithraism	Burma	India	Roman Empire
Gnosticism	Shiism	Canada	Hittites	Scandinavia
Hasidism	Sikhism	China	Israel	Scotland
Islam	Sufism	England	Italy	Sri Lanka
Judaism	Tibetan Buddhism	Egypt	Japan	Thailand
Harrannites	Vedic	France	Korea	Viet Nam
Kabbalah	Zen Buddhism	Greece	Macedonia	United States
Latter-Day Saints	Zoroastrianism		Persia	

Indigenous Peoples: Africa (20)		Asia, Europe, Central & South America (21)	
Aro	Ijaw	Besisi of Selangan	Fillipinos
Asia	Kalabari	Finno-Ugric peoples	Polynesians
Bangwan	Ndokki	Indonesia: Nias,	Sea Dayaks of Borneo
Baoule	Ngwa	Toradja, Tontemboan,	& Bataks
Bini	Onitsha	& Kols	Semang Pygmies
Dagomba	Samaras	Kagaba, Columbia	Siberian Ostyaks,
Edo	Semi-Bantu	Karen, N. Thailand	Gilyaks, Koraks,
Ewe	Sudanese	Nicaraguans	Yakuts, & Tungus
Ibo	Yoruba	Osmanli Turks	Trobriand Islanders
Igbo	Zulu		

Native North American Peoples (53)

Akwa'ala	Dakota Sioux	Kwakiutl	Navajo	Sioux
Algonquin	Delaware	Lakota	Ojibwe	Tacullies
Athapascan	Eastern Dakota	Lenape	Omaha	Teton Sioux
Aztec	Fox	Maidu	Osage	Tlingit
Canadian Dakota	Hidatsa	Mandan	Oto	Winnebago
Great Bear Lake	Hopi	Maricopa	Plains-Cree	Yakut
Cherokee	Huron	Menominee	Pottawatomi	Yokut
Chinook	Ingalik	Miwok	Pueblo	Yuma
Chippewa	Iowan	Mohave	Salish	Yuman
Cocopa	Iroquois	Montagnais	Saulteaux	Zuni
	Kinsquit	Natchez	Shawnee	

Australian Aborigine Peoples (28)

Adnjamatana	Kambera	Ngalia	Taib
Arunta	Kimberly	Nimbalda	Tiwi
Bardi	Koko-yalunyu	Northern Territory	Unambal
Broome District	Kuna	Nyul-Nyuls	Ungarinyin
Euahlayi	Miwa	Ooldea	Uriat
Forrest River	Murngin	Pela	Western Australia
Gunwinggu	Murinbata	Pitjandjara	Worora

Cosmic Cradle Pre-Conception Paradigm

*The re-emergent thinking says the birth process begins
in the "womb of the universe" – long before conception
and parents' tender thoughts of newborn babies.*

The Principles of the Cosmic Cradle Pre-Conception Paradigm
are "new" only to modern materialistic thinking:

1. *Parenthood begins long before sperm unites with egg.*
2. *Preparations for human life occur in the womb of the universe, a
   hidden realm filled with intelligent souls waiting to be born.*
3. *Our life plan, or cosmic contract, is designed prior to conception.*
4. *The boundaries of memory transcend our brain. Human consciousness exists independently of a brain and nervous system, even before
   the tiny fetus forms.*
5. *Individuals with gifted awareness are aware of souls seeking birth
   and remember pre-uterine life.*

Human life is the coming together of a mother, father, child's
soul, and the soul's cosmic contract.

First Principle:
Parenthood begins long before sperm unites with egg.

Needless to say, there had been no organized research or cross-
cultural study of something so ephemeral and misunderstood as
the pre-conception process when we began investigating it. We
discovered that pre-conception communications are spiritual experiences which shed light on our existence prior to entering our
mother's womb. Each soul not only seeks birth, it is aware of
parents and interacts with them in the process. Chapters 2 through
12 outline pre-conception dreams and visions from forty of the
persons interviewed plus seventy-five cases found in published

literature on ancient and indigenous peoples. Such dreams preceded a confirmed pregnancy or birth.

Invisible interactions often mark the prelude to pregnancy, contacts beginning long before the development of the first embryonic cell. The Jewish *Kabbalah* has taught since the 12th century that the creation of human life begins with the parents' cognition of a child's soul image *(tzelem)*.[7] If a model of the baby body which is to clothe the newly descended soul does not hover over the nuptial bed, intercourse does not lead to conception.

Such courting relationships spark couples to have tender thoughts of babies and birth children. This reminds us of the Greek and Roman mythological Cupid who fired golden-tipped arrows into the hearts of potential parents to trigger their falling in love. Perhaps the Cupid factor is responsible for millions of children coming into the world.

Communications with the unborn portray the soul's desire for birth. Parents choose to be parents, except they do not pick out the soul who incarnates as their child. Souls seeking birth are fully conscious, vibrant beings who make the selection from their side first.

Except for a few scattered reports, our modern age has been slow to give serious attention to pre-conception intuition, visions, and dreams. One exception is Elisabeth Hallett's *Soul Trek* which includes 37 stories of meeting a child prior to conception based on interviews with 184 mothers and fathers. As an example, a little male cherub floated above Susan's head during periods of solitude. She accurately predicted to friends the birth of her blond-haired, blue-eyed son eight months prior to conception.

Sarah Hinze's pre-birth communication research, in *Coming From the Light*, explores several modern pre-conception experiences including her own: When Sarah entered her daughter's bedroom, a "hallowed feeling" came from a male presence who hovered "angel-like" above seven-month-old Becky's crib. Becky cooed with great joy and her face glowed as she kicked her feet and gazed upward at the invisible visitor. Sarah's "spiritual ears" heard the male visitor say, "Tell Mother I need to come now."[8]

A cultural tradition of birth dreams survives to this day in Korea. Professor Frank J. Seligson's book, *Oriental Birth Dreams*, reports dreams of South Korean parents occurring during pregnancy as well as pre-conception dreams. "The dream grandfather" for example, appeared to a thirty-seven-year-old woman and advised, "If you desire a son, move to Seoul." Shortly after she followed his advice, a shepherd boy appeared in her dream, accompanied by a vague figure standing behind him in the haze. The boy asked, "Why are you fretting?" She explained her desire for a son. He asked, "What if I become your son?[9] Ten months later, Han-jin was born. The second figure in the dream was born as his younger sister.

Unlike those researchers who include a range of stories occurring between pre-conception and birth, *Cosmic Cradle* focuses on pre-conception – with the exception of Chapter 7 which is devoted to experiences illustrating the whole journey.

Pre-Conception throughout History

The pre-conception phenomenon remains virtually unknown within modern western cultures who have lost contact with their ancient roots. In other parts of the world and across different centuries, however, souls seeking birth communicate their intentions via dreams and intuitions. A Chinese medical professor, Song Sa-myŏng, explained, "Just as the 'Spirit of God' breathed life into Adam in your Western *Bible,* so does the intuitive nature of a woman receive the message of God through the bio-electricity of her body, in her dreams."[10]

One is struck by the diversity of cultures where parents meet their children before conception. To illustrate, here are some published reports.

* Trobriander Islanders (20th century British New Guinea) – "She [the woman about to become pregnant] dreams her mother comes to her, she sees the face of her mother in a dream, she wakes up and says, 'O, there is a child for me.'"[11] The mother's spirit then stations the spirit-child in her daughter's womb.
* China (12th century AD) – A woman dreamed that a gigantic bird, the leader of birds who easily flies 10,000 miles, soared down from Heaven and entered her home. Soon she conceived and birthed a male child. Later in life, her son Yueh-fei, meaning "Big Bird,"[12] served as a heroic general

during China's Sung dynasty, a time of great cultural achievement. (See additional symbolic dream examples in Chapter Eight.)

❀ Maricopa (Early 20ᵗʰ Century Native American) – A prospective parent dreams about finding and collecting newborn birds or puppies prior to conception.[13]

❀ Broome District Aborigines (Early 20ᵗʰ century Australia) – Every baby must be dreamed by its father before it comes into the world, and this "dream baby" is called *ngargalula*.[14]

❀ Unambal Aborigines (Early 20ᵗʰ century Australia) – Everyone begins as a child germ, or *jallala*. "His father finds him in a dream and in another dream projects him into his wife."[15]

❀ John & Rose (contemporary USA) – Tiny round lights with fluttering wings danced around John and Rose's bedroom during every new Moon. The hovering lights disappeared when Rose asked the souls to find another home and added a third contraceptive method. Rose nonetheless conceived a fourth child in her safe time and with all the precautions taken.[16]

Pre-conception communications come from around the world, including Canada, Africa, Egypt, Israel, India, Tibet, Japan, Korea, Persia, Italy, Greece, Ireland, Wales, Polynesia, other Native American peoples, and many Aborigines (including the 28 tribes in Table I). Pre-conception communications can take place in a dream, meditation, vision, prayer, near-death experience, intuitive insight, even driving down the highway.

Pre-conception communications are as crucial as the biological seeds leading to parenthood. They create joy and anticipation and are the heart of Mother Nature's plan to bring a baby into the world. This deeper vision moves us beyond the theories that bonding begins during pregnancy, or at birth. Bonding can begin before conception when alert parents welcome their unborn children with messages of love.

Second Principle:

Preparations for human life occur in the hidden womb of the universe, a hidden realm filled with intelligent souls waiting to be born.

Earth's population recently passed six billion, and more than 70 million people are born each year. Souls line up to be born by the millions. Imagine 200 million specks of invisible flickering stars in the night, hovering around looking for parents much as we look for a home.

What is their pre-conception life like?

Great mystics from ancient traditions tell us that creation is cast in layers of universes, analogous to a giant onion, with physical life constituting a middle layer. Plato pictured creation as three zones: ethereal, aerial, and material. He said the soul's journey to Earth begins in the ethereal universe, its birthplace. A representation of an East Indian cosmology painting (AD 1800) depicts the sixty-three layers of the universe and terrestrial atmospheres. (Figure 1) Embedded within the sixty-three layers is the world of the souls waiting in the wings for birth.

The religions of the West likewise teach us where we come from.

* Hebrew – "Metaphysical silos" in the seventh heaven;[17] "the most subtle ether;"[18] or "the air."[19]
* *Kabbalah* (12th century Judaism) – The soul is hidden within the realm of being or within the first reflection of God, the primordial Azilutic Man, Adam Kadmon. Souls "are in their original state androgynous, but when they descend upon earth they become separated into male and female ... if ... the male half encounters the female half, a strong attachment springs up between them, and hence it is said that in marriage the separated halves are again conjoined."[20]
* Gnosticism (2nd century Egypt) – Jesus Christ declared, "We came from the light, the place where the light came into being on its own accord and established (itself)."[21]
* Islam (7th century Middle East) – "A sanctuary conjoined to Allah's heavenly throne."[22]
* Hazrat Inayat Khan (20th century Sufism) – Each soul pre-exists as an electric current, an energy force beyond space and time in a sanctified mental world where love and unity pervade. The soul is entranced into a human body "by the love experience of its parents."[23]

The cosmologies of indigenous peoples include a place where souls wait for birth, such as a Peruvian mystical lake,[24] the "Fruit Island" paradise of the Besisi (Kuala Langat district of Selangan), and the region known as Burolgu, the "Waiting Place"[25] of the Gobaboingu Australian Aborigines.

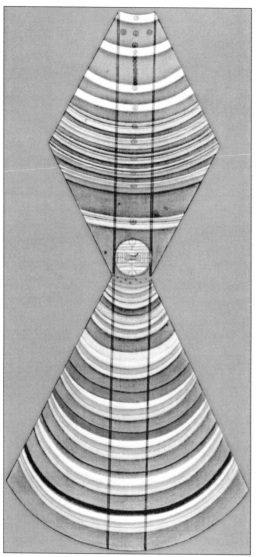

Figure 1. East Indian cosmology painting, showing the universe resembling an hour-glass, comparably narrow at its center and widening at measured intervals both upwards and downwards representing the upper stories of Heaven and the lower stories of Hell.[38]

Another powerful cross-cultural theme emphasizes that we are mere pilgrims on Earth. The soul's pre-existent world is our real home. This notion of pre-earthly life has captivated Western poets, philosophers, and religious visionaries. They tell us: we pre-exist as amazing beings of "intelligence and glory;"[26] our birth is a "change from being to becoming;"[27] we are "brought to birth through parents, not [created] by parents;"[28] and beings of light and beauty are our true family.

- Thomas Carlyle (19th century Scotland) – "[My body is] ... a visible Garment for that divine Me ... cast hither, like a light-particle, down from Heaven."[29]

- Edward George Earle Lytton Bulwer-Lytton (19th century England) – [My] soul descended into its "dark sarcophagus" from its "eternal, star-like" sphere.[30]

- Johann Wolfgang von Goethe (19th century Germany) – Our higher soul "seeks to rise with mighty throes to those ancestral meadows whence it came."[31]

- Thomas Taylor (19th century England) – "The soul, while an inhabitant of earth, is in a fallen condition, an apostate from deity, an exile from the orb of light."[32]

- Christianity – Our souls leave our true home of the spirit, but eventually return as illustrated by the Prodigal Son parable.[33] As Jesus said: "No man can ascend to Heaven, except he come down from Heaven."[34]

- Ralph Waldo Emerson (19th century USA) – The human soul is "a ray from the source of light" which comes into the human body, "as into a temporary abode."[35]

- Gnosticism (2nd century Egypt) – Earth is a dungeon, or an "inn" whereby our souls "lodge," until we regain sufficient wisdom to return to our native home, the true, transcendent reality.[36]

- Mormons (19th to 20th century USA) – "There is not a soul [who has not lived in God's] house and dwelt with him ... ."[37]

Regardless of whether people locate our original home in the sky world, the lower world, or interpenetrating the physical world, they generally portray it in glowing terms. The Jewish *Kabbalah* explains that the soul has too little incentive to leave when God commands: "Descend to a certain place and enter that body." (*Zohar* II, 96) The soul pleads, "Lord of the universe, I have no desire to depart. Please let me stay in the sanctuary of the spirit world. Do not send me to that other world where I will become stained and they will subjugate me." Alas however, God motivates the soul to fulfill its destiny.

The soul's desire to hold out in the upper heavenly spheres is similarly recorded in near-death experiences (NDEs), documented cases of people who were spontaneously or medically revived after being considered clinically dead. Before medical efforts manage to bring them back to life, their souls return to their spirit home where a heavenly guide welcomes them, yet somehow conveys, "Your term on Earth is not up yet. You must return to your physical body." Although the soul resists, something draws it back to Earth and once again it is in exile from the Light.

Chapters 13 through 20 present further examples and historical theories examining the world of the human soul prior to human embodiment: Native Americans from Canada to Mexico, peoples of Indonesia, Siberia, Scandinavia, Persia, ancient Greece, Africa, Japan, India, Tibet, the Roman Empire, Switzerland, Philippines, Polynesia, and British New Guinea.

Third Principle:

Our life plan, or cosmic contract, is designed prior to conception.

Whispers of a soul into a mother's ear reveal more than a baby's desire for birth. The child's destiny and name may be chosen long before conception. The new paradigm suggests that cosmic contracts are part of a complex process in which Mother Nature can see through hundreds of years, like seeing an intangible road map in a glimpse of the unborn future.

Birth is far more than a brief biological marvel. It's the beginning of our spiritual journey on Earth, an ancient notion traceable to classical Greece. The *Republic* of Plato emphasizes the soul's free choice to plan our lives. A divine guide informs an assembly of souls ready for birth: "No divine guardian shall draw lots for you, but you shall choose your own guardian and destiny."[39]

In another dialogue, the *Phaedrus*, Plato teaches that our circumstances on Earth correspond to how much we retain of the holy things (Eternal Justice, Temperance, True Knowledge, and Beauty) we experienced in the upper regions before taking human birth.

The soul who has seen the most of truth is born a saint, what Plato calls "a philosopher." He stands nearest the divine, seeks wisdom, and yearns for higher realities. The second highest is the righteous king or warrior; third is the politician or businessman; fourth is an athlete, physical trainer, or physician; fifth is a prophet or priest; sixth is a poet or artist; seventh is an artisan or farmer; eighth is a sophist or demagogue; and ninth is a tyrant.

Six hundred years later in Rome, the philosopher Plotinus advanced parallel ideas: the soul picks out its body, parents, birthplace, as well as circumstances of life[40] and then "like a herald summoning it, the soul comes down and goes into the appropriate body."[41]

Religious texts, indigenous peoples, and visionaries further support Plato's theory that an orderly plan governs our birth at a set time and location. The soul previews the coming life before entering the mother's womb and is drawn to the family that best reflects its needs. In some cases, the soul does the choosing. From another perspective, a higher power designs our cosmic contract.

❀ Rudolf Steiner (20th century Switzerland) – Materialists believe it is the mother's concern if an unborn life is terminated. But "actually the ego of the unborn and the spiritual hierarchies of the cosmos have worked hundreds of years at preparing the spiritual blueprint for the developing body."[42]

❀ Kahlil Gibran (20th century Lebanon) – "We choose our joys and sorrows, long before we experience them." ("Sand and Foam")

❀ Shiism (Iranian Islam) – The "decisive event of metahistory" occurs when each soul makes the "preexistential choice:" whether to be born as a "believer" or an "infidel." The question and the answer is "exchanged" in "*Malakut*," the world of "resurrection and reassembly," where each soul is "stripped of all matter," and exists "as a celestial, radiant substance, imperishable and immortal."[43]

❀ Maurice Maeterlinck (20th century Belgium) – Unborn children devise the inventions, tools, and instruments to be used in their earthly lives. One child will bring pure joy to Earth. Others will teach people how to conquer death, eliminate injustice, and develop thirty-three remedies to prolong life.[44]

❀ Swami Satchidananda (20th century India) – "God is a great economist. He will not waste even an ounce of extra breath on you. Yes. It's all measured; He sent you packaged with a certain amount of breath."[45]

Souls Waiting in the Wings for Birth

- Judaism – "A man does not hurt his finger in this world unless it has been decreed above."[46] As another example, Solomon said: "Now I was a child of parts, and a good soul fell to my lot; nay, rather, being good, I came into a body undefiled."[47]
- Hazrat Inayat Khan (20th century Sufism) – Angels set unborn souls to "certain rhythms" which determine the path they will "tread in the future." This event is known as "*Azal*" – the Day of Tuning, the day when the life plan of a particular soul is designed.[48]
- Seneca (1st century Roman Stoicism) – "Nothing comes to pass but what God appoints. Our fate is decreed, and things do not happen by chance, but every man's portion of joy or sorrow is predetermined."[49]
- Wang Ch'ung (1st century China) – The Chinese believed in the cosmic direction of life. We receive "a lucky or an unlucky chance" at the moment of conception.[50] "Length and shortness of life are gifts of Heaven."[51]
- Saint Tiruvalluvar (200 BC India) – A man may amass millions, but its enjoyment will never exceed that portion allotted to him. (*Tirukural*, 38:377)

Additional cosmic contract reports come from Africa, India, Tibet, Greece, and Native American peoples. Chapters 21 through 25 elucidate how the soul prepares for its new life, as depicted throughout philosophy, religion, and legends. Chapters 2 through 12 and Chapters 28 through 34 include individuals who chose cosmic contracts prior to conception.

The cosmic contract, as illustrated in Figure 2, indicates that the major facets of life as well as an individual's degree of free will are encapsulated together. The innate information contained within the cosmic contract is structured in a person's unconscious mind.

Fourth Principle:

The boundaries of memory transcend our brain. Human consciousness exists independently of a brain and nervous system, even before the tiny fetus forms.

What is the nature of human consciousness before we enter our mother's womb? In ancient times, answers to the age-old question came from psychology, originally defined as the transcendental study of the soul – from the Greek root "psyche" meaning soul and "logos" meaning a study. Modern psychology, in strong contrast, no longer holds an honored place in the study of the soul. Today's materialists go out of their way to deny or ignore the soul's existence, asserting that personality is the pure epiphenomenon – or the biological workings – of the brain and nervous system. And modern psychology in its attempts to try to be a hard science, like chemistry or physics, has generally replaced the word "soul" with words like "personality" or "mind" which bear no precise scientific meaning.

From a much different view, support for the Greek definition of soul as psychic, rather than material in form, arises out of individuals who recall another life, time, and world beyond the womb. Even as children, some recalled their history in a beautiful world of freedom, joy, comfort, unboundedness, and light. They felt connected to everything in creation and loved by all. Chapters 26 through 34 include seventeen accounts of individuals interviewed as well as over forty historical reports of gifted memories.

Though it seems difficult to scientifically prove gifted memories in a laboratory setting, they evidently happen in the real world. In two stand-alone cases, for instance, two interviewees recall observing from above their parent's sexual act and detailed circumstances of their own conceptions. Both Sage and Glen even-

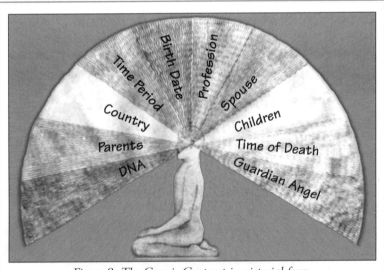

Figure 2. The Cosmic Contract in pictorial form.

tually verified their conception memories with their parents. The memories were an embarrassment to their parents who assumed that they had been alone when they conceived their child. (Chapter 28, *Footprints in Heaven*)

In a related example of the power of the unborn's awareness, Dr. Ian Stevenson's research verified a Buddhist monk's pre-conception memories. (Chapter 30, *Gifted Memory and Higher Consciousness*) In a parallel case, months before his wife's pregnancy, the husband met a girl named Irisna in his dreams in a "glorious realm halfway between the spirit world and the earth world."[52] Irisna said she wanted to be his daughter and was born the next year. The father was not surprised when Irisna shared memories of their dreamy rendezvous.

Historical and Modern Validation of Gifted Memories

Human beings are much more vast and complex than a body, brain, and emotions. We are spiritual beings who can recall gifted memories. Surprising sources posit that gifted memories are indeed natural, even though they transcend the brain and require no "neurological substrate"[53] to contain them or make them possible.

- ❋ Plato (ancient Greece) – "For every soul of man" has to some degree "beheld true being; this was the condition of its passing into the form of man."[54]
- ❋ Plotinus[55] (3rd century Rome) – The soul is a homesick traveller who vaguely recalls its divine origin and communion with the One.
- ❋ Church Father Origen (3rd century Christianity) – The soul receives an instruction from God "before entering the earthly body, an instruction which the soul clothed in its earthly body remembers."[56]
- ❋ Samuel Butler (19th century England) – "We commonly know that we are going to die, but we do not know that we are going to be born. Is this so? We may have had the most gloomy forebodings ... and forgotten all about them."[57]

Just as the physical world corresponds to five gross senses, the subtler world of the soul corresponds with the spiritual eye (Figure 3).

Individuals born with gifted memories or who spontaneously experience them via flashbacks in NDEs or mystical visions appear throughout the ages.

- *Old Testament* – King Solomon recalled when God set the Heavens in their place, fixed the canopy of clouds overhead, and knit together Earth's foundations. Solomon was at God's side each day, God's "darling and delight, playing in God's presence continually, playing on the earth, when God had finished it. ..." (*Proverbs* 8:22-31)

- Guru Gobind Singh (17th century India) – I did not desire to depart from God,"as my attention was fixed on His feet. The Lord remonstrated earnestly with me and sent me in this world."[58]

- Near-death experience (contemporary USA) – "I saw the time I was brought from heaven to the earth by angels to a body, how I was received at the hospital, and how my parents loved me."[59]

- Joan (contemporary USA) – "Everything was consciousness and pure awareness ... . I moved through thousands of levels. On each level different souls were resting before being born again. The lower levels were much darker ... souls on these levels were not as mature as those on the higher levels."[60]

- Samuel (contemporary USA) – "It [higher world] had millions of levels. I could see levels below me, but not above me. The light ... was dazzling. ... beings on the levels below me were not as aware as I was. ... I was infused with a golden light. ... being with God; that's the best way I can describe it."[61]

- Norman Paulsen (contemporary USA) – "I lost no consciousness in entering the planetary body of the earth elements. I can, to this day, look back through the fabric of time and space into times past."[62]

- Gerard de Nerval (19th century France) – "I felt bitterly that I was but a momentary sojourner in that world, that foreign yet cherished world, and I trembled at the thought that I must return and re-enter life."[63]

Twentieth-Century Memory Research

Memory science is catching up with other disciplines in understanding the power of human nature, even before birth. During the 20th century, memory research has advanced all the way from the belief that a baby is born with an empty slate to the acceptance of third-trimester memories.

Figure 3. Illustration of the physical world and spiritual eye.

Scientists were skeptical, until recently, however, that newborn babies or the fetus could remember. Due to the lack of brain development in newborns, they believed that human memory could not operate so early. In addition, they had mistaken assumptions of how memory works. From the babies' perspective, their own difficulty lay in being unable to communicate their abilities to doctors since they do not speak at birth and their screams seemed unrecognizable.

❀ Pre-1950 – The prevailing medical/psychological paradigm was Dr. Sigmund Freud's personality theory: personalities begin to form by two or three years old, and memories are absent until a child learns to speak and use symbols.

❀ Late 1960s – Psychologists posited bonding, a post-birth system of mother-child communications. Medical doctors traced early childhood emotional development back to the hours immediately after birth.

❀ 1981 – Dr. Thomas Verny performed a comprehensive review of the scientific literature on the human fetus and his findings concluded: the fetus sees, hears, tastes, and can even learn from at least the sixth month onward *in utero* (in the uterus – before birth). Parent/child bonding begins during pregnancy. An unborn child, for instance, grows emotionally agitated (as measured by the quickening of his heartbeat) when his mother thinks of having a cigarette,[64] and the fetus is sensitive to subtle nuances in his mother's attitude and knows whether or not he is welcomed with love.[65]

❀ 1990s – Dr. David Chamberlain's scientific literature review on the expanding boundaries of memory,[66] concluded that memory is nonphysical as neuroscientists are still unable to locate or isolate memory in the human brain or in its biochemistry. Researchers in diverse disciplines recognize that memory may not be located within the human brain itself.[67] Memory storage does not reside in the physical brain or body, but is held somewhere else entirely beyond the brain in a field of information accessible to the brain such as a field of consciousness.

Chamberlain cites a broad range of information on relevant memory research: 1) natal and prenatal memories surfacing during therapy; 2) prenatal memories or mental illness – a series of adolescent patients with histories of suicide attempts and a peculiar pattern of these attempts in that they occurred at the same time of year in each of the patients. Psychologist Feldmar arrived at the insightful determination that the suicide dates of four patients matched, down to the month, when their mothers had attempted to abort them, an example of "seasonal intrusions of prenatal memory."

One of the most impressive discoveries is the subtle biochemical memory in the human body's immune system in fighting off up to seventy viruses at any time and developing a cumulative collective response capability to deal with potentially one million different antigens encountered in the blood and cells.[68]

Chamberlain points out, while emphasizing "the lexicon of modern memory reveals both complexity and confusion," that there are more than a dozen kinds of modern memory with some extending completely beyond the neurological substrate of the brain: "... short and long term memory, autobiographical memory, semantic memory, affect, perceptual, and motor memory, declarative and procedural memory, 'habit' memory, recognition and recall, explicit and implicit memory, embryonal imprints, holographic or cellular memory, anniversary memory, out-of-body memory, and past-life recall."[69]

We are left with the conclusion that the boundaries of memory, without a doubt, transcend our brain's limitations and that human consciousness itself exists independently of a brain and nervous system, even before the tiny fetus forms.

Chapters 28 through 34 include in-depth testimonies from historical and contemporary individuals who recall their history prior to entering the womb. These chapters further explain why most people forget choosing cosmic contracts and their subsequent descent to Earth. Reports come from around the world, including Native American peoples, Viet Nam, France, Sri Lanka, Thailand, Burma, Africa, India, Tibet, Japan, ancient Greece, and Siberia.

Fifth Principle:

Individuals with gifted awareness are aware of souls seeking birth and remember pre-uterine life.

When we probe more deeply into pre-conception communications and gifted memories, we find that these stories demonstrate how a future child or the soul's pre-existent state are contained in the present

– as seeds. In other words, an underlying interconnectedness exists between past, present, and future. And once our awareness taps into this underlying field, we can transcend the veils of time.

For that reason, meeting one's unborn children or remembering pre-uterine existence are transcendental experiences existing outside the five senses of ordinary perception. They are a cross-cultural phenomena and are not developed as much by social upbringing, educational background, or religious training as they are by an individual's innate awareness.

For the most part, subtler realms of intelligence and deep memories are unapparent. After all, science tells us human perception captures only a bare thread of creation's grand tapestry – less than one part per billion of the total energy vibrating in the environment. Like a scientist piercing the world of subatomic particles with a microscope-like accelerator, hidden layers become more accessible when we turn our attention within through techniques of consciousness development.

Just as the physical world is experienced through the physical senses, the pre-conception world becomes available through the spiritual senses. Someone who uses "the eye of the soul"[70] is as entitled to speak of pre-conception dreams or gifted memories as much as someone who returns from an unexplored country and speaks about places he has observed. Developing the sixth sense – intuition – is the gateway. Higher realities are grasped by a clear mind, open and without preoccupation, rather than a busy mind cluttered with fears, worries, and anxieties. Some people are even born with this gift.

Transformations in consciousness hold the key to pre-conception intuition and gifted memories. They serve as landmarks on the spiritual road to higher consciousness, related to peak levels on the consciousness scale. Though consciousness is a less familiar term in the modern Western world, the ancient Greek philosophical tradition as well as major spiritual traditions have fine-tuned their understanding of consciousness over the millennia. They elucidate degrees or levels of awareness. Just as a thermometer measures hotter and colder degrees of temperature, a "consciousness scale" registers higher and lower degrees of perceptions of reality.

Souls Waiting in the Wings for Birth

Philosophical and religious traditions acknowledge what happens when an individual attains the upper extremities of the consciousness scale or ladder of consciousness.

❁ Shaykh Muhammad al-Jamal ar-Rifa'i as-Shadhili (20th century Sufism) – "When you know why God made you and why He put you in this place, then you will know the secret of yourself."[71]

❁ Plato (ancient Greece) – "Purified" souls retain memory of the universal archetypes, patterns, or potentials they saw in the super-celestial sphere before coming to Earth.[72]

❁ Sant Keshavadas (contemporary India) – Perfected individuals pierce "the veil of ignorance which hides the innumerable pasts in the sub-conscious mind."[73]

❁ Paramahansa Yogananda (contemporary India) – Advanced souls retain "self-consciousness without interruption" during the dramatic transition between one life and the next.[74]

❁ Chuang Tzu (ancient Chinese Taoism) – "You can't discuss the ocean with a well frog – he's limited by the space he lives in. You can't discuss ice with a summer insect – he's bound to a single season. You can't discuss the Way with a cramped scholar – he's shackled by his doctrines.
Now you have come out beyond your banks and borders and have seen the great sea … . From now on it will be possible to talk to you about the Great Principle."[75]

Chuang Tzu further clarified the lower end of the consciousness ladder:

"We do not ask the blind about a painting, nor invite the deaf to a songfest. Blindness and deafness are not merely of the body: There are souls, too, that are blind and deaf."[76]

Pre-conception's spiritual side is sheltered at the top of the consciousness ladder, part of the cosmos' collective databank available to everyone. Reports from ancient Greek, medieval Catholic, Islamic, and Asian traditions, as well as Descartes, Wordsworth, and Einstein referred to this upper end of the consciousness ladder when they spoke of a higher seeing, or the "all-seeing power" of the "superconscious" mind.[77] The ancient Greeks recognized that when someone's inward eye is awake and higher awareness is opened, he transcends ordinary perception and sees into "another mode or dimension." These perceptions entail "everlasting loveliness," "greatest joy," and "profoundly moving beauty."[78]

Twentieth-Century Meditation Research

Modern research has begun to shine a spot light on states of higher awareness by testing techniques of meditation in laboratory settings. Scientists began investigating physiological changes during these practices and the practical applications they might yield. As ancient teachings have revealed, for thousands of years philosophers have taught it is possible for humanity to attain higher states of consciousness by systematic meditation. Researchers, until more recently, had difficulties evaluating the claims of meditation. Until meditation-induced peak experiences in consciousness could be reproduced and studied in the laboratory with standard procedures, meditation theories remained purely anecdotal and of little scientific value.

Physiological studies of expert Zen Buddhist monks in Japan – who were adepts in Zen meditation – found a cluster of changes: decreased rates of respiration (breathing), oxygen consumption, and spontaneous Galvanic skin response, and a slight increase in pulse rate and blood pH showed.[79] The brain waves (encephalographic or EEG) were primarily alpha-wave activity (even with eyes half open). Alpha waves progressively increased in amplitude (energy level) and slowed in frequency, and occasional theta activity was noted suggesting a highly relaxed state of awareness during Zen meditation. Only expert Zen practitioners with up to 15 to 30 years rigorous training and practice could produce the measurable changes in their physiology. This kind of evidence suggested that a physiological connection existed to expanded states of consciousness.

Figure 4 highlights at least two higher states of consciousness experienced by a person in deep meditation.

Yoga practitioners were later studied in India with similar laboratory methods. They too showed lower breath rate and an increase in skin resistance, but without consistent changes in heart rate and blood pressure during yoga practices.[80] The brain wave patterns of the yogis during meditation, however, showed an increase in alpha-wave amplitude and activity, indicating deep relaxation while awake.

Early investigators in the 1940s and 1950s reported two basic barriers in evaluating meditation techniques: 1) difficulty in obtaining either expert Eastern or Western practitioners of meditation who produced consistent yet measurable physiological changes, and 2) initial problems in taking the laboratory measurements in a way that did not interfere with the subjects' meditative, contemplative or concentrative efforts.[81] Scientists held onto their skeptical view of meditation's claims for several decades because so many persons attempting to meditate were unable to demonstrate a significant physiological change under laboratory conditions.

Pioneering Advances in Studying Human Consciousness

A quantum leap in meditation research was achieved by scientists at UCLA and Harvard resulting in peer-reviewed articles in the journals

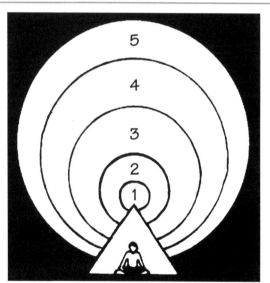

Figure 4: Illustration of the states of consciousness.

The five basic states are: 1. Sleeping; 2. Dreaming; 3. Waking; 4. Transcendental; and 5. Cosmic. We know ourselves more in the waking state than we do in the sleep or dream state, yet we know little in the waking state compared to the higher states of awareness. In the highest state, we overcome the six inner enemies – lust, anger, greed, attachment, pride, and jealousy.

Science, American Journal of Physiology, and *Scientific American.*[82] The innovative scientific research in brain physiology and EEG brain waves – in the late 1960s to mid-1970s – mainly using Western practitioners of Eastern meditation, more than the previous studies, verified the consciousness ladder described by ancient cultures.

Dr. Robert K. Wallace measured the biochemical and physiological effects of meditation. He discovered a unique cluster of consistent yet significant relaxations occurring in the mind and body such as: specific changes in EEG activity of the central and frontal regions of the brain; decreases in oxygen consumption, cardiac output, heart rate, respiration rate, blood pressure, arterial lactate concentration, and base excess; and increase in skin resistance.

Initially, Wallace identified during his pioneering research at UCLA Medical School that the Transcendental Meditation technique – defined as "turning the attention inward towards the subtler levels of a thought until the mind transcends the experience of the subtlest state of the thought and arrives at the source of thought"[83] – produced a "physiologically unique" state, a "fourth major state of consciousness."[84] Reproducible lab experiments with another set of meditators at the Harvard Medical School confirmed Wallace's discovery at UCLA that meditative states can alter physiologic function.[85] Researchers termed the state of awareness induced by meditation as a "wakeful hypometabolic physiologic state."[86]

Another unique meditation finding hinted at and confirmed by subsequent researchers is "suspension of respiration" – lasting from 10 to 45 seconds – without compensatory breathing afterward. Meditators, in essence, were so deeply relaxed and their metabolism so efficiently functioning that they momentarily stopped breathing.[87] This discovery provides an insight as to how advanced yogis in India survived for extended periods in an "air tight" pit, by slowing down their metabolism to non-measurable levels.

By 1975, progress in meditation research had delineated five states of consciousness based on brain wave frequencies recorded in cycles per second (cps), amplitude levels (hertz), and EEG coherence patterns (simply defined as the degree of long-range orderliness in cortical activity between two spatially separated points of the scalp particularly in the *alpha* and *theta* bands), although more correlations were identified using a broad range of other indicators.[88] The five states are sleeping, dreaming, waking, and two transcendental states of awareness.[89]

A brief description of the five states of consciousness based on brain wave data of the four key frequencies (*delta* 0.5-4 cps, *theta* 5-7 cps, *alpha* 8-12 cps, and *beta* 18-30 cps) most commonly studied are:[90]

❀ Sleeping – large slow *delta* waves were dominant typical of rest without mental activity and no measurable coherence.

❀ Dreaming – interchanging mental and restful activity with no coherence.

❀ Waking – fast *beta* waves typical of mental activity and lack of *theta* suggesting it was not a relaxed state as well as no measurable coherence.

❀ Initial transcendental state of restful alertness – dominant *alpha* (mental alertness) and *theta* (deep rest) waves (and coherence) occur together, induced by meditation where the mind is being trained to be awake while deeply resting – not thinking thoughts, an experience of pure "being."

❀ Permanent transcendental state – mixed *beta*, *theta* and *alpha* waves with coherence, established twenty-four hours a day, even outside of meditation.

A cluster of biochemical, physiological and psychological changes have been identified for the five states of consciousness in hundreds of studies.[91,92] Scientists identified a unique physiological style of mind/body functioning during Transcendental Meditation that distinguished it from waking, dreaming, and sleeping, as well as from ordinary relaxation, hypnosis, and conditioning.[93,94]

The theory that the field of consciousness can uncover how we arrive here, where we have travelled from, and why we have come on this journey is in accord with modern thinkers. They include physicists such as David Bohm, Fritjof Capra, and John Hagelin, who correlate consciousness with the quantum field in modern physics. Human consciousness is a field of unlimited potential, an untapped storehouse.

The pre-conception paradigm points to a consciousness pattern interconnecting cultures and spanning centuries. That life on Earth may be an extension from the superphysical down to the physical is spiritually provocative and inspirational. Although most people experience amnesia of their voyage into this earthly cradle, a trail of invisible steps retraces our journey into human form. Life on Earth is intertwined to the cosmos and why we are born here fits into that wholeness.

In contrast to those souls' pre-conception plans to be born on Earth in the 21st century with normal kinds of human bodies, a team of U.S. scientists are contemplating efforts to create the world's first cloned human embryos without the knowledge or ethical consideration of what cloning means for the souls who intend to be born in the future. Cloning appears to ignore and deny that human beings have souls and its implications related to cloning research. Another group of scientists is working on the cloning of embryos that will be part human and part cow, again without understanding the ethical and religious meaning for human life. Greater oversight of cloning is needed. Efforts to clone human beings without understanding the role of the soul in human development indicates that the old paradigm is alive and well.

PART ONE

VOICES INSPIRING THE WOMB

The Star Baby

"She appeared in my dreams, pushing at the boundaries
of my reality until I could see her ... a child of sparkling
golden light, curious and surprised at my presence.

"Who are you?" she whispered, touching me gently with her finger.
A kaleidoscope of twinkling lights suddenly appeared between us and she
grabbed playfully at them, lost in a moment of delight ... .

... she floated in space like a translucent cloud of glittering gold dust.
Through her I could see a star-studded universe, velvet in its darkness ... ."[1]

– *Anne Loader McGee*

Contemporary Interviews

Our investigation of mothers' peak experiences during childbirth began after hearing from several friends who delivered children in a heightened state of blissful consciousness. We had no expectations as we began to interview women – several of whom had been having peak experiences due to practicing meditation techniques and other purification practices.

Serendipity then appeared and led us down "a path not taken," as described in Robert Frost's poem. Women related deeply spiritual experiences occurring during delivery, pregnancy, conception, and even prior to conception.

Over a ten-year period, we gathered material for a series of books, with Cosmic Cradle focusing on pre-conception. Part One presents stories from mothers, fathers, and siblings who encountered a future child via lucid dreams, visions, or intuitive insights.

Their subtle perceptions lead us to believe that the future exists and that we can discern events in that future pattern. As Einstein's theories imply, "everything that ever 'will be' now 'is' … the future is already written and is as fixed as the past."[1]

Chapter 2
Pre-Conception Communications
Waking Visions

**With my inner eyes I have seen and felt
the greatness of the souls now coming to earth .... .
They are great peace-makers
who have come to help this planet.**[1]

– Joyce Vissel

*Pre-conception is one of Nature's
greatest mysteries – like an silent invisible
spark preparing the flame of biological life.*

More and more contemporary parents receive a heavenly contact from the pre-conception world – a message from a child desiring to be born. Collectively they portray a new paradigm demonstrating the deeper aspects of human life.

Pre-conception communications establish a new parent-child relationship. Love for a child begins prior to conception and cultivates a desire for a child. Or if a desire already exists, soul visitations empower a couple to follow that path.

Pre-conception communications come in many "flavors," including visions, dreams, and intuitive awareness. Women report these deeply spiritual experiences more often than men, perhaps to prepare for the sweeping changes in their bodies.

A distinction is sometimes made between where visions and dreams fall on the consciousness ladder. A waking-state vision correlates with higher consciousness because it must compete with and overcome the five senses.

- ❁ Christianity – That is why the Bible says God communicates with ordinary prophets in dreams, but with high prophets like Moses, "I will speak mouth to mouth, even manifestly."[2] The New Testament likewise records Joseph's dreams about Christ's coming, whereas Mary receives a higher annunciation while she is awake.

- ❁ Islam – Ordinary people receive prophetic visions in dreams, but the mystic receives them in the waking state as well as in the state between waking and sleep.

This chapter focuses on pre-conception visions of an ethereal child, a young adult, a cherubim, a mass of energy, or a bright, fiery spark of light. These ten "waking-state" visions all precede a child's conception and subsequent birth.

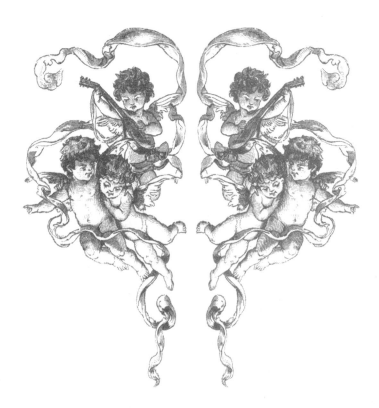

Thousands of Soul Bubbles

*Joanna, like so many women in our technology-based
culture, finds it difficult to share deeply personal
experiences. Her visions go beyond normal perception.*

Mothers disclose countless kinds of exceptional communications stretching the ordinary mind to the limit. The next story is unique because the mother-to-be, Joanna, encounters a whole flock of babies wishing to be born.

Often the prelude to pregnancy experiences are so personal and intimate that many spiritual motherhood adventures remain confidential. Even some husbands never hear about them from their wives. Perhaps that is why Joanna even felt self-conscious sharing her story with me.

> I do not like to make my spiritual experiences more or less than
> they are. When I have an experience, I do not have to decide whether
> it is real or not. But, if I share it with someone, suddenly there is an
> outside opinion deciding whether my experience is imaginary or
> real. It loses its innocence.

With four children under foot, it is hard to imagine that Joanna and her husband, James, were so thumbs down on having more than two children. The incentive was triggered by a charming, magnetic appeal straight out of the blue.

Inspiration to Motherhood

The invitation manifested in a magical setting. The couple was on vacation relaxing at a spiritual retreat for two weeks. It was time to take a break from their children.

Meditation practice was part of Joanna's daily routine for stress reduction. The thirty-seven-year-old mother of two had enjoyed meditation's profound daily benefits for years. This time Joanna had some unexpected thoughts come up during meditation.

> My mind was filled with the desire, "Have another baby, have another baby, have another baby." Because the next thought was, "No, I don't want to," I realized these longings were not mine. Although they were my thoughts, I was not the author of them.

These subtle, gentle impulses unfolded:

> A vision of little bubbles floating around in the room appeared to me – like soap bubbles with a pearlescent sheen on them. There were thousands – about four to five inches in diameter. The room was filled with them, each having a liquid gold color.
>
> Each bubble had a faint impression of a beautiful, little round cherub face – with pink cheeks and golden hair. These soul bubbles were very lovely and absolutely pulling at my heart.

The lovely visions of these little angels tantalized Joanna even when she opened her eyes.

> The bubbles were inside [my consciousness] when I closed my eyes and outside when I looked around the hall. Even though there were thousands of soul bubbles, there was one collective yearning, one special energy I felt: "You're such a good mother. Have another baby, have one of us. What a good mother you'd make. We want you for a mother."

The celestial flock of souls sought Joanna for a mother for five days. "There was no letup." Nonetheless, the mother-to-be was far from easily being "talked into it."

> There were lots there, but there were not lots of voices. There was one collective yearning: "Have another baby, have another baby, come on, have another baby. What a good mother you'd make. We want you."
>
> One bubble even came up and went "ping" right on my abdomen while I was resting. There was a physical sensation, like a hand gently landing on my tummy. The feeling was, "I'm coming. Here I come." I thought, "No, this is ridiculous. You can't make babies like that."

The Greatest Sales Technique

Joanna explained, "No, no, no. It's too hard on my body. I don't want to do it again. I already had two. Find somebody else." Despite Joanna's obstinacy, the ethereal soul bubbles persisted: "No, you're such a good mother. We want you for a mother. Come on, have a baby. Have one of us." Joanna had only one reply, "No, no, no."

Finally, by the fifth day, the thousands of souls appeared to listen: "All right, we're going away. You can't have us." That magical moment opened Joanna's heart.

> That was a great sales technique. The beautiful bubbles began to fade out. I thought, "Oh, no, no, no! Come back. I will have one." They finally had gotten to me. The bubbles were so adorable.
>
> I could not give it up. I decided to have one. There was a wonderful feeling of being chosen. They want me. What an honor.

Transformed Hearts

Joanna savored the extraordinary communications for four days without sharing the experience with anybody – especially James – who was "absolutely against having more children." Naturally, Joanna was reluctant to even broach the subject with him. Ironically, the day before Joanna had a change of mind and accepted the invitation, their discussion became easier. James made a surprising remark and jolted Joanna, "I am thinking of having another baby."

James sudden and startling interest was "funny." Joanna was curiously amused.

> By the time James mentioned he wanted another child, the soul bubbles had pretty much talked me into it. The soul bubbles never appeared visibly to James, yet it was obvious that "someone" had seeded the desire in his mind.

Joanna was probably right. James's gentle desire for another child was genuine and undoubtedly inspired by the unborn child.

Joanna and James took a 180° turn toward parenthood once again. The couple discussed the third child and agreed to conceive in the next year.

> Since birth, our third son has looked just like those little cherubs in the bubbles – round face, golden hair, rosy cheeks. For sure, I came home with one of them. He just had to wait one year for us to get busy and make him.

Cross-Cultural Parallel

In the near-death journey of Thespesius, reported by the Greek writer Plutarch (46 to 120 AD), Thespesius's separated soul – which "seemed as if it had been one eye fully open"[3] – beheld the souls of the departed as small fiery bubbles which rose and burst to disclose the forms of men and women. The souls were tinted with various colors according to their passions and sinful ways on Earth, but became clear through expiation and punishment in the after-death state.

Three cherubs with shield and helmet. (Albrecht Dürer, c. 1500)

Cherubims on Pink Clouds

*Mother Nature provides many avenues of expression
when souls seeking birth need to communicate.*

Ellen enjoys meditation so much that she joined a women's meditation group. One day she opened her eyes during one of those meditations.

About fifteen to thirty feet overhead, I saw a misty, puffy cloudiness and cherubim-like babies rolling around. They were smarter than babies though. They were aware beings. I heard them laughing and talking. For a while, I remained uninvolved and casually observed the babies.

Then two cherubims looked in my direction. At first, I thought they were looking at women around me. Even when the mature one said, "I want you to be my mother," I thought she meant someone else. But then they both said, "No, you." It was a clear connection. I felt their attention.

I sensed that the mature, more "girl-like" cherubim was destined to be my daughter. The one behind her, who simply watched, seemed to be a potential second child, a brother.

Afterward I felt a warm, secure bond with my child. I looked forward to motherhood. On the other hand, I had not expected this. I was twenty-six and had only been married one year. We were not financially able to handle a baby. But that seemed to be okay, too. I did not feel like we had to go about this right away.

Two years later Ellen gave birth to a daughter, Ariel. Then she wondered, what became of "the second cherubim" who seemed a little less eager for birth?

There was a potential to have a second child, but it did not manifest. Several intuitive people perceived that his soul stayed with us and taught us the life lessons it was coming to teach without actually needing to be born. My husband and I learned what we needed to learn from the second child that way.

Cross-Cultural Parallels

Ellen's vision parallels medieval representations of the soul as a naked child-sized figure adorning the tympana of Christian cathedrals, biographies of saints, bas-reliefs on royal tombs, as well as "art of dying" woodcuts.[4]

The soul as a homunculus appears in Asia and Australia as well.

❋ Malayan Peninsula[5] – The soul *(semangat)* is a thin, vaporous, shadowy human image. This thumb-sized manikin (dwarf) is usually invisible and corresponds exactly in shape, proportion, and complexion to the body in which it has its residence. The soul can "fly" or "flash" quickly from place to place and is often addressed as if it were a bird.

❋ Australian Aborigines – A little body that resides within the breast.[6]

❋ Fiji (Nakelo tribe) – A diminutive child.[7]

Native American culture upheld similar notions with regard to the free soul – a subtle and ethereal substance, yet a pale perceptible mirror image of the individual.[8]

❋ Huron – A tiny human with head, body, arms, and legs.

❋ Kwakiutl – "A double of the person," but "like smoke or shadows." The soul expands in size while the person sleeps.

❋ Nootka – A being having a human shape and human-like behavior.

❋ Haisla – A precise image of the person, but only "as big as a fly."

❋ Quinault and Salish – A miniature baby, "yet looks like fog."

❋ Athapascans (California) – The soul stands two feet high and is "strictly human in appearance, dress, and actions."

❋ Shoshoni (Nevada, Gosiute, Lemhi, and Wind River) – A person as small as a pea or up to ten inches high.

❋ Cheyenne – A mere shape, a silhouette – like a shadow without detail, clothing, or features.

❋ Athapascans (Canada) – "A kind of double," a reflection of one's personality, individuality, ego.

❋ Eskimo (West Greenland) – "Pale and wan … they have neither flesh, bone, nor sinews … as if they were nothing."

❋ Mohave – A person's "second self … the core of his identity."

Sweet Sixteen

*Children are self-determined beings with
intentions to be born to particular parents at a
certain time. So once a child finds its mother, he must
wait for the proper father, as well as the right time.*

Helen always wanted to become a mother. She became acquainted with her son through a spectacular vision years before his arrival. Now, at forty-four, she reflects on the event that happened twenty-eight years ago – "it seems like yesterday."

When I was sixteen, we lived on Chesapeake Bay in Maryland. One afternoon as I walked out to the Bay, the whole universe suddenly opened up before me. Everything was illuminated with an incredible glow. The sky was brilliant. I was filled with bliss inside. I began to laugh and I realized, "I know everything!"

When my inner voice asked, "What do I know?" I saw the face of a five-year-old boy – as clear as a bell. My destiny to marry and become the mother of this boy was unquestionable.

In retrospect, I realize "I wanted to know" what every sixteen-year-old girl wonders, "Will I marry and have children?" I certainly received an answer.

My life was different from that moment on. The little boy never left me. The child was always around, no matter where I was or what I was doing. And if I ever wondered about my future, I immediately sensed his presence.

I did not tell anyone about my vision. I did not know who to share it with. It was a deeply personal, spiritual experience.

Helen's son appeared in a brilliant light and radiated a powerful love. She sensed his divine origin and felt inspired to look for a partner to be the Dad for the child she had bonded with. After Helen graduated from college, she searched for a mate with blond hair and green eyes to match the child's characteristics. Until Helen found the father that fit the bill, she told the child, "I know you are there, but it is not the right time yet."

After waiting fifteen years following the vision, Helen and her husband Tom were blessed with a son. At five, Michael was a replica of the child in Helen's vision.

Synchronous Perceptions

*The soul of a future child can sometimes
communicate simultaneously with hopeful parents.
In Lia and John's case, it only required some quiet
relaxing moments to unlock the communication doorway.*

Before wedding bells began to ring, Lia and John mapped out plans to have a child. The couple shared the same deep longing, although Lia had one son nine years earlier with her first husband and John had four children from a former marriage.

One afternoon the newly-married couple enjoyed a short meditation. To begin with, John fell asleep and had a dream-vision.

The dream was impressive because it was so lucid and dramatic. I saw a beautiful, gentle woman on the ocean beach. She was of medium height, light build, and had distinct, sharp facial features. Her long auburn hair was blowing in the wind. She wore a lovely, flowing white gown, unlike our clothes on Earth.

As I walked towards her, I thought, "This is a beautiful woman." When our eyes met, my soul instantly and totally identified with hers and vice versa. I realized, "Wow, I know this person." I felt a warm feeling – like meeting someone whom you love after not seeing them for a long time.

As we talked, I sensed, "This is my daughter yet unborn. Our souls are greeting each other prior to her birth." My daughter's soul was saying, "Yes, I am coming to you." It really touched me.

At the same time John was dreaming, their daughter appeared in Lia's meditation vision.

The same woman appeared to me. Her long curly hair was blowing in the breeze. She was fairly tall, about 5' 7". I asked, "Who are you?" She answered, "I am the child who is coming to you." I said, "Do you have a message for me?" She explained, "I am the one who will come and heal this family."

The couple's simultaneous encounters with their unborn daughter were such coincidences that they seem miraculous. Considering that John was involved in custody battles with his first wife and separated from his four children, Lia and John anticipated that Molly's destiny might be to heal the relationship between John and his children.

Waiting, Waiting, Waiting

Lia's visitation from Molly was not their first encounter. This child had been scanning for the right window of opportunity for a long time. Lia sensed the soul's presence in her first marriage with Bill. Conception had not come about, however, even though there was agreement on all sides.

> This is a child I had wanted for years. I had found her six years prior to meeting John. It was definitely the same soul, same energy. My experience of her was more simple then, because I was less spiritually aware. Yet, I knew there was another baby and it was a girl.

> When our son was two and one-half, my first husband Bill said, "Okay, if you want another baby, fine with me." We stopped using birth control and I tried to get pregnant. Eighteen months later – no baby. But the marriage was over, too, so I thought, "Thank God."

> She refused to come in because my first husband Bill was the wrong father. It was also timing – astrological and spiritual – based on her need to be born at a particular time.

Now, in her second marriage, Lia's expectations for a daughter were high once again. Much to their surprise, eight uneventful months passed, even after regular sexual intercourse.

> I never used birth control, never. John and I said this soul is obviously going to come in. She appeared to us at the same time. She knows what she is doing. What is the point of using birth control? She is going to choose her right astrological aspects. Birth control appeared to be a moot point.

Maybe that is the way their lives were supposed to be. Even before Lia and John celebrated one year of marriage, they separated and were heading towards divorce. John's custody battle had taken its toll on his second marriage.

Again, Lia breathed a sigh of relief that she was not pregnant. And even a few weeks later when she missed a menstrual period, she began to rationalize, "Oh, it is just because I am upset about my separation from John."

Still, as the weeks passed, Lia "became obsessive, checking every day." A pregnancy test finally settled the emotional debate raging inside of her.

The doctor said, "You are pregnant." I replied, "Oh, no. I came here to find out that I am not, so that I would not have to worry about it anymore." I cried, but more than anything, I was furious. After waiting six years for this baby, now she came when I was unable to keep her.

I had expected to conceive immediately after the vision, but it happened the last time John and I had intercourse. Imagine. My daughter took her chance: "Oops, better do it now. This is it. Last time out the chute."

The Healing Begins

Single parenthood seemed impractical despite Lia's deep feeling of love and connectedness to becoming a mother. "I was not going to be a single parent again. I am not going to bring this child in under these circumstances."

Lia had already raised one child by herself following the first divorce. Now when it looked like this second marriage might end the same way, "I called on her, trying to convince her that I would do it at a different time under better circumstances. But no, the child would not go for that at all."

When human beings interfere with a birth, sometimes it is part of the script and at other times, it is like removing an actor from a Shakespearean play. Abortion appeared to be an easy rational alternative, although Lia wondered if an abortion would "screw up" somebody's cosmic contract. So she consulted with her spiritual teacher.

My teacher told me, "I cannot get you off the hook. The soul insists on coming through." I asked him about the spiritual implications of an abortion. He advised that I would incur negative karma[9] because it would disrupt the child's soul agreement. I thought, "I am trying to work off karma, not get more of it!"

Again, on another occasion, a friend reversed Lia's thinking about abortion:

Fran asked me, "Have you considered keeping the child? You waited so long. Who said you can't keep her?" (We always knew it was a "her.") Fran then told me about an option I had been unaware of: "Medicaid pays medical expenses for single expectant mothers."

With the abortion debate now settled, Lia foresaw more problems coming. So she had another heart-to-heart talk with the child in her womb.

All right, what kind of a conception is this when I am on my own, little money, no insurance, on the brink of divorce? I don't know why you set it up this way. Well, if you are that determined and will not let me off the hook, you had better figure it out. I will let it happen. But we must bring in money to support you. I hope you have a good plan for how we will pay for this.

The conversation sparked some amazing changes: Lia's two small businesses improved and profits surpassed what they had been prior to pregnancy. Plus, Lia and John sought counselling.

There was a strong pull to work out differences. Our relationship needed to be positive if we were going to share a child. The child needed parents who talked to each other.

But the couple got more than they bargained for. By the time of Molly's birth, the message – "I am the one who will come and heal this family" – was clear.

The conception catalyzed many changes. If I had not conceived our daughter, John and I would have divorced. Instead, we experienced a huge healing and reconciled our differences. Now we not only live and work together, but we also resolved the conflicts with his four other children who had been such a source of controversy. This is where we sit today. Who knows what healing will come in the future?

Our souls make choices and agreements prior to coming into the body. The more we honor our soul's path, the more we walk in the light. With this child, I honored a soul contract that needed to happen despite the earthly circumstances. I am grateful to bring a soul through who has a real purpose here. It makes my path more meaningful. It fulfilled my soul's desire, her soul's agreement with me, and the soul contracts Molly made with everyone else. Our spiritual paths are better because we allowed this to happen.

Star Dance

The wheel of time returns the ones we love the most.

Penny's eldest daughter announced her arrival during some quiet moments.

> One day during meditation, Julie's spirit appeared to me as I knew her in the lifetime we shared in India. I had been Julie's mother. In fact, we were all together – Julie, my husband, and my youngest son. She told me, "I'll be coming soon." I conceived one month later.

Penny's pre-conception vision involves past-life relationships. She believes each lifetime is one of many experiences of our soul. Neither death nor the passage of time erodes the bond between souls. We connect with loved ones again and again.

Penny's exceptional communication was a welcomed surprise.

> My husband and I weren't thinking of having a child. We had let go of it. If a child came, fine, but George and I were past the point of trying. We had been willing to have a child for a long time and done nothing to interfere with conception. But no child came. Astrology teaches that children come at specific times. I think Julie waited for the right stars.

The Aloha Spirit

Visions of a long-awaited son, as well as physical, psychological, and emotional changes heralded Amanda's pregnancy.

As a child, Amanda walked along Hawaii's beaches at sunrise and remembered her deepest and most secret dream.

> Everything was pristine. The Aloha spirit spread out over the land and onto the sea like a thick, embracing blanket. I sat on the lava rocks splashing my feet in the tide pools. I dreamed of meeting a princely man and having a special son. I did not know what "special" meant. I only knew he was to be dear and close to me. That's the way my childhood was. I lived in a state of wonder.

So, even by the age of five, Amanda knew on "a deep feeling level" that a son was part of her cosmic contract. Yet at the age of thirty-two, Amanda had only experienced "many years of celibacy and relationships having no substance." At the same time, Amanda was just as happy to "put it off.

> Ever since I was old enough to have a menstrual period, I had an inner feeling: "Childbirth will be a major thing for me." When friends talked about natural childbirth, my intuition said that I was destined to be in the hospital.

Fears begin to diminish when Amanda and Mark fell in love. For the first time, Amanda felt "secure and willing to go through childbirth." It is no surprise then that a child began to stir her heart even more.

> Because of my fear, I had a lot of "subtle prep," getting me emotionally ready. In my dreams and visions, I saw a cameo of a baby boy. These were gentle introductions, preparing my psyche for motherhood. They acquainted me with this incoming human being, this friend, this delight who was destined to dramatically change my life.
>
> The visions always had a different dimension or quality and appeared in the morning between dreaming and waking, or while I

was meditating. Once a baby in a cradle basket even appeared in my mind's eye while Mark and I were driving through northern California.

Visions continued as the months passed. Then, Amanda, who usually felt out of touch with her physical body and more into her thinking, noticed another shift.

I felt "ripe," a sensual flavor of womanhood I had never known – full and fertile – like the sweetest, ripest fruit. I thought, "If I get any riper, I'm going to fall off my own tree." I told Mark, "A child is imminent in our lives." These feelings dominated my psychology for four months, up until the time of conception.

By the time of her son's birth, Amanda had lived all over the world and "gone through so much that, though not jaded," she was not surprised by too many things anymore. In strong contrast, motherhood was "a major initiation."

The joy of creation had waned a bit. But once I had a baby, I experienced the most fulfilling love there is – unconditional love, total surrender. To have a delicate, beautiful, new life to nurture, protect, and cultivate was a blessing, a gift. Suddenly an innocent life depended upon me for everything. It was a time of sacrifice. And even though I let go of certain needs, I did not miss anything. I relished every moment the baby looked at me and touched me with his love. Those were the most intimate days of my life with another human being.

Hovering at Heaven's Door

*Benjamin served as a joyful messenger between the
"unseen" world and the "seen" for six weeks. A powerful
bliss and serenity grew deep within his parent's consciousness:
"Tony and I did not know what to do about it. Why
do we feel like this? We almost felt guilty."*

The stage of misfortune was set for Jennifer and Tony, a couple
in their mid-30s, when they lost two-year-old Benjamin. The death
of their only child was a shock – a tragic mishap defying rational
explanation.

Hours after the accident, Tony needed time to be alone. While
walking along a quiet country road, his son's translucent form
suddenly appeared, and reassured him: "It's all right, Dad. It's okay."

The father's comforting contact with the departed child was the
first of many. Later that evening, Benjamin's presence entered his
parents' bedroom as a rosy, red light. Jennifer recognized his voice
when he said, "I'm fine. I'm free."

Each of these visitations helped to heal the couple. Then, a few
days after the tragedy, an irresistible impulse guided Jennifer to seek
higher reasons for the tragedy. In her mind's eye, Jennifer saw her
spiritual teacher busily writing, seated at a coffee table. She asked:
"Why did Benjamin die so young?" Jennifer repeated her plea three
times before her teacher looked up and raised his hand to the left.
Benjamin was in good hands. He was standing at her master's side:
"a young prince, very pure, with great responsibility."

Friends sensed Benjamin's presence and inspired the parents to
accept Benjamin's fulfillment of his cosmic contract. Katarina:

> The light-hearted feeling of Benjamin's soul entered our home and
> bounced through the house. It was sweet and powerful. Benjamin
> was happy and realized his death had to happen. It was a contract

fulfilled. There was no way around it. And there was no other outcome but evolution.

I was astonished to see the changes Benjamin had gone through versus how much we evolve in one human lifetime. Benjamin had become a magnificent being who had catapulted forward through eons of evolution. The shackles of infancy had been pulled away. He evolved through three or four lifetimes in less than seven days.

While most of us have no idea of how Nature coordinates millions of souls coming into the world, while millions are leaving through death, Jennifer concluded that an invisible intelligence guides human life from beginning to end.

Benjamin's death was a huge shock, but there was also an incredible blast of elation and freedom. His death was as powerful as his birth, if not more so. Birth and death are in the same region – from where they come, they go. The gates of Heaven opened in both cases.

As the couple resolved their loss, they desired to shower love upon another child. The couple had "unified as one" and were "into total giving." Apparently a child was listening … for as Jennifer relaxed after a deep meditation –

I had a beautiful, awe-inspiring vision. I saw the souls of twelve children who wanted to be born. They faced me standing in a semi-circle in a less earthly world with a lot of light. They had human form, but were angelic, ethereal. The light around them radiated towards Earth. My attention was drawn to one who had a connection with me. He wanted to be ours. Within days, we conceived a second child.

Cross-Cultural Parallels

Jennifer's pre-conception vision resembles clairvoyant visions.

❋ Geoffrey Hodson – The etheric mould of a recently conceived child is bluish-grey in color and "shimmers and shines with a moon-like luminosity."[10] The little body has a definite sex and stands eight to twelve inches high.

❋ Seri Indians (Mexico and gulf of California coast) – A woman conceives when the spirit of the baby (*SiX kisil kiselka*), a "little winged thing," descends as a tiny flying figure and enters the woman's body. The shaman witnesses this event and may then tell the woman she is pregnant.[11]

Lassoing a Soul

*Though a child desiring the human experience
singles out parents by a process unknown to us, it does
seem to be symbiotic. Each chooses and each benefits.
The soul wishes to be born in the right environment
(family, teachers, genetics, country, global events, and
time period); and couples elect to become parents.*

How many women would hesitate to become mothers, if they chose their children? Terry received this gift, or so she says. For many years, Terry wondered whether she and her husband should have children. Minor health problems discouraged pregnancy, and she had become totally focused on a teaching career.

Still, another answer came when Terry was thirty-six.

One day I was contemplating whether I wanted a child. Because I had a friend whose child had serious health problems, I thought, "If I had a child, I need a healthy one." With that, I felt a bunch of souls disappear. They were tiny brush strokes of light.

My next desire was, "I want a happy, positive child." Then, another group of souls disappeared. At that point, I realized I am on to something. So I went through more criteria – spiritually evolved, and so on.

In the end, two souls were left. One soul was tricky, someone who played a lot of games. The other personality was straightforward. I said, "I can not handle twins. One of you will have to decide. When I said that, the mischievous soul seemed to go away. I was left with the steady soul who felt like a boy.

This was a happy moment – thinking about a child I was comfortable with. I realized, "It is all going to be taken care of as long as I keep doing what feels right in my heart. There is a plan for all this."

Within six years, Terry gave birth to two "healthy, happy, positive" daughters, exactly what she wished for.

Souls Waiting in the Wings for Birth

That first soul was with me for a couple of years until I became pregnant. I strongly felt its presence whenever I closed my eyes.

In retrospect, it is interesting that my first daughter Tiffany is a solid, stable personality. On the other hand, my second child Crystal is mischievous and likes to hide things. Maybe they were those two souls.

As the next story illustrates, Susana also experienced the soul as a light form.

Soul's Fiery Light

*According to Susana, a child's spiritual form appears as a
bright, fiery light – just as air becomes visible, when
a whirlwind sweeps up a column of dust.*

Here is what happens when a soul seeks birth from a woman,
like Susana, who says, "No."

> While I was pregnant with my second child, my third child's spirit
> visited me late one night. I was lying down, ready to fall asleep.
>
> His spirit whizzed past me like a little flash of white light about
> the size of a lightning bug. He circled around me a few times, and
> told me, "We know each other. I love you and want to help you. I
> will be your son."
>
> I said, "I know who you are." I recognized his essence. He was a
> powerful, fun-loving, and happy soul who wanted to help me with
> my spiritual work. On the other hand, I immediately explained,
> "Whoa! I am not having more children. I am telling you right now –
> no more kids."
>
> His little spirit laughed and said, "Yes, you are!" Then he whizzed
> away.

Susana conceived three months after her second child's birth.

> I felt his presence throughout the pregnancy. And the instant he
> was born, I looked into his eyes and recognized the little spirit who
> had spoken to me months before.

Cross-Cultural Parallels

A great historical debate has raged over whether the human soul
exists and if it does, what it consists of, since science has been
unable to weigh in with solid evidence. Ancient Greek and Roman
philosophers offer interesting parallels to Susana's perception of
the soul. Their statements, compiled by Macrobius in the 4th to 5th

centuries, affirm that the belief in the soul's incorporeality has been as widespread as the acceptance of the soul's immortality.[12]

- ❋ Plato – An essence moving itself.
- ❋ Critolaus the Peripatetic – A fifth essence.
- ❋ Hippocrates – A subtle spirit diffused through every part of the body.
- ❋ Democritus – A spirit implanted in the atoms having such freedom of movement that it permeated the body.
- ❋ Zeno – A spirit grown into the body.
- ❋ Aristotle – Entelechy (realization of form-giving cause).
- ❋ Posidonius – Idea.
- ❋ Heraclides Ponticus – Light.
- ❋ Heraclitis – A spark of starry essence.
- ❋ Hipparchus – Fire.
- ❋ Anaximenes – Air.
- ❋ Boethos – A mixture of air and fire.
- ❋ Epicurus – A mixture of heat, air, and breath.
- ❋ Parmenides – A mixture of earth and fire.
- ❋ Xenophanes – A mixture of earth and water.
- ❋ Pythagoras and Philolaus – Harmony.
- ❋ Asclepiades – A harmonious functioning of the five senses.
- ❋ Xenocrates – A number moving itself.

The Old Testament parallels Greek and Roman notions when it says, "the soul of a man is the lamp of the Lord," (*Proverbs* 20:27) as well as the Jewish *Kabbalah* which teaches that "the soul is but a circumscribed light."[13]

Medieval Christian literature recounting near-death visions and other-worldly journeys of theologians and monks sheds light on the nature of the soul as a bright, fiery sphere. Among many such examples, Caesarius of Heisterbach (1170 to 1240 AD) documents two visions: 1) The Abbot of Morimond who discovered that his own soul was shaped like "a glassy spherical vessel, with eyes before and behind, all knowing and seeing everything at once;"[14] 2) a medieval visionary whose soul seemed like "a spiritual substance, spherical in nature, like the globe of the moon."[15] Caesarius explains that "to mortal eyes souls, like angels, have bodily form, but to those free of flesh the soul appears as ... a luminous sphere whose gaze extends to all directions."[16]

In the related visions of Drythelm (696 or 699 AD), Tundal (1149 AD), and Edmund (12th century Christian monk of Eynsham), souls ascend in the form of sparks.[17] And the 3rd century Christian hermit-visionary Zosimus experienced his "soul as a shape of light, perfect in all the body apart from the distinction of male and female."[18]

The soul possesses the color of fire or light according to gifted visions reported within the Native American culture.[19]

- Eskimo – A light or fire.
- Iroquois – A minute spark of fire.
- Skidi Pawnee – A miniature star.
- Shoshoni (Nevada) – A tiny, white object.
- Omaha – A glimmer of light, a halo.
- Mandan – The color of light and transparent.
- Quinault – Like the full Moon.
- Naskapa – A spark of illumination.
- Achomawi – Light; its name reminds one of that for the dawn.
- Wintu – A light shadow.

And, at the time of death, Native Americans of the Northeast perceived the soul exiting the body in the form of a spark or ball of fire. Parallel death-bed cognitions come from other tribal regions as well.

- Quinault – A ball of fire flying through the air "throwing off sparks and making a crackling sound like burning spruce twigs."
- Naskapa – A lightning flash.
- Chinooks (Northwest) – Fire with sparks falling down; like a firebrand.
- Tuscarora (North Carolina) and Cusabo – A spark or flame.
- Cora (Mexico) – A white human figure or a ball of fire spreading light in all directions.

Chapter 3
Dreaming the Future

Contemporary Pre-Conception Dreams

The dream is the small hidden door in the deepest and most intimate sanctum of the soul.[1]
– Carl Gustav Jung (1875 to 1961)

Every state of consciousness has its own conditions and limits. For instance, social interactions are restricted in the everyday waking world, whereas the dreamer escapes the bondage of time and space and even meets future children.

Pre-conception dreams are unlike ordinary, illusory dreams. They leave a profound, clear, and lasting mental impression upon awakening. Sufism refers to them as "true dreams."[2] These types of dreams reflect truth, according to Homer, because they pass through "the Gate of Horn."

Back in ancient Greece, Plato believed true dreams only occur when someone's inward eye is awake. In order to attain this "clear self-consciousness" in sleep[3] an individual retired at night after feeding his mind "noble thoughts" and "collecting himself in meditation."[4]

In sharp contrast, when an individual's inward eye is unconscious, he has imaginary, illusory dreams. These dreams pass through "the Gate of Ivory," according to Homer. So-called "tangled dreams,"[5] as Sufism defines them, are a personal projection of mental preoccupations, resulting from experiences which the five senses transmit to our memory during the day, and are difficult to recall. The African Yansi call confused, insignificant dreams "*ndoey mutwe*"[6] defined as a "dream of the head" because they are only a mental experience.

Ancient peoples believed every earthly event is first announced in the heavens. And from there it spreads out into the world and is transmitted by a herald to the dreamer's consciousness.[7] Perhaps they are right, as illustrated by the following eight dreams preceding a child's conception and birth.

Every Earthly event is first announced in the Heavens.

Soccer Field of Dreams

Parents travel to a parallel world where they interact with future children. And even though it happens in a dream, the visitation feels as genuine as any conversation in the "real" world.

Among all the dreams Mark recalls, three are "crystal-clear." And the one that happened several weeks prior to conception was "an extra special gift."

In my dream, I walked through a pathway in the woods. I came to a clearing where hundreds of little boys and girls were playing soccer in a huge field. All along the perimeter of the field, there were twelve couples standing and watching the children play. Every once in a while, a child left the field to join a particular couple. The child seemed to be picking out parents.

Then, one boy with blond hair and blue eyes walked over to me. He was about two and one-half to three years old. He stopped about three feet away from me. We looked into each other's eyes and took each other in. Next we walked in the woods and explored caves as a way of experiencing what it would be like to be together.

Somehow we communicated even though the child's lips never moved and no sound came from his mouth. When I asked, "You are my son, aren't you?" he responded via thoughts and I felt an affirmative feeling.

I also asked, "What is your name?" He looked at me, and without words said, "I am a human being." That seemed to mean, "I am not ready to have a name yet. A name, at this point, is too physical."

After a while, we walked back to the soccer field where he rejoined the game.

The next morning I shared the dream with my wife. "I met our son in a dream. It was so real. Even though he had blond hair and blue eyes, I know it was our son." [Mark and his wife have dark hair and brown eyes.]

This dream was more real than what is in front of us today. It was outside of how I define my physical, mental, and psychic characteristics. It was something greater than me, beyond personal intuition. It was knowing beyond my knowing. It was in a stream of the Knowingness.

How did the dream transform Mark?

I resist answering that question. Sometimes a friend gives you a flower. You don't question the purpose – "Is he giving me this flower as an apology?" Sometimes the gift of a flower is an expression of joy in the universe and of being connected to that joy. My dream was like that. A window opened and a cool, refreshing breeze blew through.

Dreaming in the Gap

*Pre-conception dreams are intrinsically rewarding and a
benefit to mental, emotional, and physical well-being.*

Julie, an elementary school teacher, pays close attention to her
inner reality.

> Whenever I wake up in the morning or following an afternoon nap,
> I experience a quiet, peaceful state of awareness inside before I am able
> to physically move. Even as a teenager, I needed to put attention on
> moving some part of my body, like a finger, in order to wake up.
> Sometimes when I am in this gap between waking and dreaming, I
> witness a dream which is so realistic that it is difficult to tell whether
> I am awake or dreaming.
>
> I had dreams like that prior to conceiving my two sons. Each time,
> I saw myself nursing a baby and experienced a feeling of fullness, a
> feeling of harmony with Nature, with God, and the Universe. And as
> soon as I became pregnant, my life felt perfect. I was completely in tune
> with destiny. This feeling continued throughout their infancies while I
> was nursing them. Those were the happiest times of my life. Fullness
> was all that I was.

Because "a baby literally manifested," after Julie's first dream, she
knew what it meant when she had the second dream. At the same
time, Derek, her nine-year-old son, was also saying, "Mommy, I
want you to have a baby."

One Foot in the Door

*Stephanie Foy and her husband Dana planned to wait
before having a second child. Renee was working
full-time and kept busy with one-year-old Steven.*

In accord with the couple's destiny, however, one night Stephanie
had a clear, lucid dream, in color, and in three-dimensions – one of
those dreams she "was supposed to pay attention to."

I saw a cracked door with a toddler's foot intentionally wedged in
the door to keep the door from closing. I did not see the child, but I
knew it was a little girl because she was wearing a pink patent
leather shoe and white lace socks.

I often see babies in my dreams and know whether a friend who
is pregnant will have a boy or a girl, so I thought, "Well, I guess a
friend will show up who is pregnant and I will know it is a girl."

But that is not what happened. Three months later, I was on
a business trip and I forgot to take a birth control pill. I was so
concerned that I called my gynecologist long distance. He assured
me, "Don't worry. Just take that pill right now and take your next
pill at the regular time. Everything will be fine."

Two days later I returned home and that is when my husband
and I conceived our daughter. That was her window of opportunity
because that was the only time I missed taking the pill. The minute
the doctor confirmed it, I thought, "This is the little girl who belongs
to that little pink shoe." Sometime later my doctor asked if I wanted
ultrasound. I said, "I don't need to. It is a girl."

Although I had never mentioned my dream to any friends, Carol
gave me a pair of pink patent leather shoes at my baby shower. So my
daughter Amy definitely wore those pink patent leather shoes, and of
course we bought her the white lace socks to match. She loved them.

Soul Teacher

*Thirty-one-year-old Leigh knew a
daughter was part of her destiny.*

Leigh became so bonded with her unborn daughter through a series of dreams that it created conflict between her and Sean. Her husband felt that his children from an earlier marriage were enough for him, but in the end, Sean agreed to have another child.

I had had dreams of a child over a two-year period. One dream occurred before marriage, but many more came afterward. It was always the same baby with blond hair and fair skin about twelve to eighteen months old.

Even though she appeared as a baby, the child had a mature voice and taught me things. Upon awakening, I remembered what I learned. At other times, I knew I had gained knowledge, but was unable to completely recall her message.

When our daughter was twelve months old, she looked exactly like the child who appeared in my dreams. Elizabeth is eleven years old today and has always had a strong spiritual nature and continues to be my teacher. She makes me step up one more level in goodness. She is amazing.

Baby in the Icebergs

*Pre-conception dreams help
couples make life-changing decisions.*

Thirty-one-year-old Lisa was uncertain about the future. She and her husband had been separated three months. One night, the answer came to her in a dream.

> I was on an ocean cruise in the Arctic Ocean. There was a pastel blue tint to my dream as well as sepia tones with blues in it. I felt extremely happy. I stood at the ship's railing looking out to sea at the icebergs in the water. The wind was blowing my hair. A pretty six-year-old girl stood on top of the railing beside me. My arm was around her legs. She had red hair and wore a pair of red overalls.

> The girl made a perfect swan dive into the ocean and disappeared. When I searched for her, a baby arose out of the water. I reached into the cold water, grabbed her, and put her to my breast. The baby started suckling. I was so happy.

> Then before I knew what happened, the baby dove back into the water and said, "I will be seeing you in a little while, Mother."

> I thought deeply about the dream when I awoke. I realized its truth. I needed to go back to my husband. The next week we reconciled our differences. We conceived our daughter within the following month.

Nine months later, Lisa met her healthy red-haired daughter – identical to the child in the dream.

Was it a coincidence that her daughter was identical to the dream? Or did Lisa's daughter exist prior to the dream?

The Awakened Dreamer

*Close family members meet a future child especially
if they are as intuitive as Neil. Apparently he was the
only family member who foresaw Christina's birth.*

It was mid-October 1972. Neil momentarily lingered in the silent
gap between sleep and full wakefulness before arising to meditate.
As he rested in a calm state of consciousness, a vivid picture in full
color appeared before his mind's eye. This special dream-vision
foretold the birth of his niece, Christina. Upon fully awaking
immediately after the dream, Neil felt waves of bliss as he thought
about the dream and to this day it is the only lucid vision he has
had announcing a child will be born.

In a flash, I saw my brother and his wife holding up a beautiful blond
baby girl between them. Doug was on the left, Anne on the right. They
were smiling down at the little girl, and she was smiling up at them. I
was filled with bliss as I looked upon them. I felt that all three were
extremely happy and filled with love.

This dream meant that my niece was planning to join the family
soon. It was incredible because my brother and sister-in-law had been
married over four years and were becoming concerned about childbearing years passing by. More than anything, they wanted a child.

I sensed my niece was to be born about nine months from the
time of my dream, or mid-July. The calendar for 1973 indicated a
full Moon at that time. In early November, I wrote to my mother
predicting her a new granddaughter by mid-July and a pregnancy
would be announced any day now.

At Thanksgiving, there was no news. By early December, my
mother questioned whether my dream was accurate. There had
been no news from Doug and Anne. Finally, at Christmas the
announcement came. Anne was pregnant and, according to the
doctor, expecting the baby in August.

Just as I had foreseen, however, my niece was born with the full Moon in mid-July that was also close to her parents wedding and her mother's birthday. Like the child in my dream, Christina had a bit of blond hair. Doug and Anne were indeed happy. Christina is their only child and has grown into a beautiful adult. She is more special to Doug and Anne than I can imagine.

Although the exact moment of conception is suspected to have been in November, I believe conception transpired a few weeks earlier, in mid-to-late October.

Neil believes that he shares a genetic predisposition with his mother to be a highly intuitive person, and this is one reason such a dream was announced to him.

Pre-Conception Awareness of a Toddler

*Children can be sensitive to
pre-conception emanations.*

No one in Jeremy's family is certain whether the two-and-one-half-year-old had a pre-conception dream or a vision. According to his mother Jennie, however, he was the first family member to become acquainted with his sister.

It all began following a visit to Jennie's friend who had just birthed a baby girl. On the way home, Jeremy announced:

"We could have a baby, Mommy ... a little girl."

"Oh, really?" I answered.

"Yeah, soon," he responded.

Jeremy's remarks further affirmed Jennie's feelings of a soul's presence.

I trusted Jeremy's vision. My daughter's soul came through Jeremy to tell us that she wanted to come in – like bringing a telegram. More than anything else, this was our impetus to have a third child. I became pregnant shortly afterward.

Then, three weeks before delivery, Jeremy said, "Mommy, you will have a little girl. Her name will be Sheila, and she will have orange hair."

Jeremy was right. She is a red-haired little girl. And as soon as our daughter was born, Jeremy began calling her Sheila. So we honored that. There is definitely some life force that created these feelings inside of Jeremy before Sheila's conception.

Cosmic Cradle

Radical Eggs

By hook or by crook, as the saying goes, what we least expect often happens – even in becoming pregnant.

Three children brought tremendous love into Kate's life. At thirty-five, however, she did not expect any more for good reason. Her right ovary and fallopian tube were surgically removed following her second child's birth (1973). Four years later, the left ovary and left fallopian tube were removed during the second month of pregnancy with her third child (1977). Nonetheless, a dream hinted at some unexpected happy news.

I awoke one morning recalling a vivid dream. The dream's message was: "You have radical eggs in your body and you will conceive another child." I felt elated, but then I remembered I had no ovaries or fallopian tubes. So I concluded, "This dream is just wishful thinking."

Four months later I became nauseous and wondered what was wrong. My doctor, asked me, "What are your symptoms?" I explained, "It is funny. I have pregnancy symptoms, but I can't be pregnant. I don't have any ovaries or fallopian tubes." He said, "Well, let's take a pregnancy test anyway."

Two days later I showed up for the results. The doctor advised, "You had better see the gynecologist who did that last surgery. You are pregnant."

Kate confronted the obstetrician who performed the second surgery in 1977 –

The doctor exclaimed, "Your pregnancy is a miracle. I don't understand it. You have no fallopian tubes and we sutured the uterus closed. It cannot be an intra-uterine pregnancy. The fetus must be in your abdominal cavity. We will have to surgically remove it."

Kate wondered, "How can a fetus develop outside the uterus?" The doctor's theory was that, if she had no fallopian tube and the

– 74 –

uterus is sutured closed, an egg can travel from the ovary into the abdominal cavity and attach itself to the intestinal wall.

The doctor ordered a sonogram to determine the exact location of the fetus so that they could surgically remove it. Kate grieved for her lost child ... until she heard the sonogram results.

> I asked the radiologist, in this pained voice, "Is my baby in my abdomen?" He said, "Oh no, the baby is right here in your uterus. See that little being right there? That is your baby." My knees buckled and I caught myself on the counter.

> Needless to say, my pregnancy created quite a "hub-bub." Not too many women without ovaries and fallopian tubes become pregnant. The obstetrician who had performed my surgery in 1977 was even afraid of a malpractice suit and offered to treat me throughout the pregnancy without charge.

As it turned out, Kate's full-term pregnancy was as healthy as if everything in her body were completely normal. She birthed a baby girl at home. And a few years later, as if one miracle pregnancy was not enough, Kate conceived yet another miracle child. Given these events, we may ponder whether the "radical egg" dream expressed Nature's wisdom that is higher than what medical science can understand. After all, medical science has no such definition or term for "radical eggs." Still, according to Kate's pre-conception dream, if a child's birth is willed by fate and Nature's intelligence, anything is possible.

The Mystery of the Radical Eggs

How did the egg develop and manage to find its way into the uterus? These are puzzling questions.

> The doctor called it a miracle. There must have been a tiny opening somewhere in my uterus that had not been sutured closed. An egg had managed to find its way into my uterus during the brief time I was with the girl's father. I was a single parent. Her father and I had only slept together a few times. Besides that, I was nursing my youngest son.

> There is obviously some intelligence, some moving force, even in an unfertilized egg, so that it knew how to find the uterus.

According to what modern medical theory suggests, several unexpected events had to work together. Kate's ovary's regenerated itself just enough to create a few more eggs and one of the eggs migrated along an already existing tract – functioning much like a fallopian tube – into the abdominal area and found a tiny unsutured opening in the uterus. Each of these events would have been a medical miracle, and yet when combined they are even more extraordinary.

Of course what if there was no regeneration of the ovary, no egg migration along an unknown tract, or no pinhole opening in the uterine wall? Does Kate's pre-conception dream offer an alternative theory? The message was that she would conceive a child with her "radical" eggs.

We can merely speculate that a "radical" egg is an egg that originates within the uterus (acting similar to ovarian regeneration except it's at a more biologically efficient location) rather than in the ovary. One biological reason that this appears conceivable is because every cell in the human body, excluding eggs, grows from a single cell containing all the genes (i.e., 46 chromosomes) or DNA necessary to make a human body. Trillions of living cells, each knowing their function in the body, come from one fertilized egg. Every human cell has the DNA to make any other cell in the body, including new eggs or perhaps "radical" eggs (i.e., 23 chromosomes).

We do not know why and how each of the trillion human cells knows its biological script. Nor do we know how Nature sets up each script. We only know that in the beginning of embryonic development, there is a single cell, a fertilized egg having a normal biological history.

Healing is still much a mystery to medicine. The magic remains hidden, yet the right thing happens at the right time with the right results. It could be that Kate's body needed an egg (actually two eggs) and since she had no ovaries or fallopian tubes, "the wisdom of the body" itself created a "radical" egg from a normal, extraovarian cell with 46 chromosomes. By undergoing meiosis it got down to the requisite 23 chromosomes.

A uterine egg, although a far-fetched idea, implies that no fallopian tubes or ovary are necessary. A "radical" egg theory is no more miraculous than a doctor's explanation which required a series of improbable physical events wherein: 1) the body regenerates part of an ovary and 2) creates several new eggs; 3) a normal egg knows where the uterus is located, 4) the egg knows how to get over to the uterus, then 5) manages to find a pinhole in the sutured uterine wall, and 6) finally prepares itself for fertilization at precisely the right timing for sexual intercourse. Either way, Nature maneuvers around the physical barriers to pregnancy as if an unseen guiding hand is present and gets the job done.

Mysteries of DNA

Another possible medical explanation for Kate's pregnancy is that the body's DNA stimulated the growth of brand new fallopian tube tissue to affect a complete repair. After all, fallopian tubes which have been surgically tied off are medically known to have repaired themselves in some women and who managed to become pregnant again. Why and how the DNA accomplishes this feat is unknown. The DNA may simply respond to an unseen signal to maintain the intelligent wholeness of the body, and tying off the tubes is seen as a disturbance within this wholeness.

Modern science has yet to ascertain how we develop all the organ structures (i.e., their three dimensional architecture) within the body from our DNA, and normally in just the proper location. It just happens beginning with a single fertilized egg cell at the moment of conception. DNA is biologically known as a chemical library coding for amino acid sequences in proteins. Exactly how DNA cues single cells into multicellular organs that become eyes, hearts, fallopian tubes and a baby, however, remains a deep mystery to medical science. Researchers have been unable to prove any solid notion of three-dimensionally designed organs encoded within the DNA, if the information is there. Just the same, the fallopian tubes were originally made from a tiny seed cell, a primordial fallopian tube cell. This memory bank for making the fallopian tubes whole is thought to be still inside each living cell of a woman's body after her tubes are tied, although it is turned off after their development.

Chapter 4
Pre-Conception Intuition

**"I am your third child and am ready to
be conceived." … "No!" I stammered, "I don't
want to get pregnant … ." I felt this being
smiling at me, loving me fully and
offering the gift of its presence.[1]**

– Joyce Vissel, mother of three

*Intuition, our inner sense that perceives future events,
need not be a flashy vision or dream. It can transpire as a
subtle non-visual cue which acts like a silent catalytic
partner, stimulating a pregnancy and birth.*

Is the Old Testament accurate when it declares, "For everything there is a season. … A time to be born and a time to die?"[2] If so, who orchestrates the time of conception? Is it the parents, the child seeking birth, or the invisible intelligence behind the universe that continually creates stars and worlds out of seeming nothingness?

Thirteen parents shed light on this question. In some cases, they sensed the soul's desire for birth and felt compelled to fulfill that desire. Pregnancy in these cases came as no surprise. Juxtaposed to these areas is where couples conceive their child without an inkling about the curious events preceding conception. Nature simply took its course. Even in such cases, however, these parents recalled – in retrospect – the subtle, out-of-the ordinary feelings experienced prior to conception.

Pre-conception reports, such as these, transform our view of unplanned pregnancy. More goes on behind the scenes than meets the naked eye. Only on the surface level of our mind is there an "unplanned" child or an accidental pregnancy.

There is no such thing as accidental parenthood.

Path of the Heart

Dorrie and Ian, a newly married couple, had no immediate plans for a child. Dorrie was working as an artist while Ian completed his college degree.

Dorrie's awareness of a child's soul who was hanging around and "wanted in" popped up on the spur of the moment.

I will never forget it. I came home from work and without warning I announced to my husband, "I must have a baby now." Ian did not want to do it. We were dirt poor. He said, "How can we afford a child right now? Let's wait until I finish school. "

The desire for a baby felt urgent even though it disturbed our plans. I had no control over it. I stayed in the spare bedroom on the top bunk and cried hysterically all night. The next day my husband bowed down to my great need.

Dorrie trusted her inner cues as a higher form of guidance, never questioning whether it was "the right thing." This happened twenty-six years ago. Dorrie's son has made her life complete and she has never regretted bringing Richard into the world.

Memphis Bound

*If a child of an artist expresses artistic talent, we
attribute the gift to their parent's DNA. Even if a child
displays an affinity that neither parent has, we believe he
inherited it from someone in the family tree. In sharp
contrast, Adrian holds a different opinion.*

Adrian's story began when she fell in love with a famous
musician.

> I dreamed of having Joseph's child. It seemed like a fantasy though.
> Even though we were deeply in love, Joseph was married and unwilling
> to file for divorce. I also had an understanding with him – our
> relationship ends if I ever become pregnant.

> After Joseph and I had been together four years, I moved to
> California to study music for a while. There, I reunited with "an old
> friend." For the next six months, I enjoyed the presence of a child's
> spirit beside me, somebody I treasured having around. He was a
> powerful being. And although he appeared as a child, he felt like
> an elderly person, someone I knew in a previous life.

> He was friendly and talked to me. He wanted me to be his mother.
> And Joe, who was one of the greatest geniuses I have ever known,
> was supposed to be the father.

> But I knew that it was illogical to get Joe involved. I did not want
> to sacrifice our relationship for a pregnancy. Plus I needed to finish
> my education. But whenever I resisted the idea of having a child
> with Joe, the child's spirit insisted, "No, I must have that good
> brain and those great hands."

As the months ticked by, Adrian's rational mind overshadowed
her intuition, "This can't be right." Yet a strange feeling kept
creeping back into her mind.

> This was the first time I communicated with a child seeking birth.
> It felt like a special, cosmic, wonderful thing – and far be it from me
> to go against that.

Souls Waiting in the Wings for Birth

Finally, it was in my face so strongly that I surrendered. I overcame the fear of losing Joseph as well as the irrationality of becoming a single mother. The pressure to conceive this child was building. It was time and it was my destiny. I almost felt pregnant before I became pregnant.

I could have said "No," but I sensed a strong impulse to return to Memphis. I wanted to see Joe more than anything. Even though this meant ending our relationship, I flew to Memphis to find the child's daddy. I knew I was pregnant twenty-four hours later. There was a big knowingness. A week later, there were clear physical signs.

Ames was born eight months later and to this day, Adrian has no regrets.

My son was a great baby and never cried. He was cheerful and friendly. Everyone who saw him was crazy about him and I was too. He was a neat friend.

Ames was born one month early because long before his birth, he chose to be born at that time. I blame myself for conceiving him late. I did not listen to my inner voice when I was supposed to.

Adrian believes that her son chose his father's DNA in order to develop particular characteristics.

It was my destiny and responsibility to bring Ames into the world. And he selected Joseph to be his father. Today my son is a full-grown "carbon copy" of Joseph. He has his father's brilliant mind and physical features.

Journey to Mount Olympus

*Diedre's revelations represent the most subtle
and fascinating side of pre-conception experiences.*

Diedre left her heart in Greece long ago after visiting that exotic land as a child. Prior to her second pregnancy, Diedre returned to Greece "in meditation."

> A journey unfolded before my inner eye. I found myself in a tiny village with my husband. We were in the last outpost of civilization below Mt. Olympus. In the tranquil hour before dawn, I arose with the desire to climb the peak and meet Apollo.
>
> At the summit, the large temple of Zeus lay in ruins. I stood in front of his throne asking for guidance to Apollo's Temple. The answer came: "Walk to the east side of the mountain and search for the first temple to greet the Sun."
>
> I followed my intuition and found Apollo's temple. I entered the temple, wondering, "What do I do next?" Again, an answer flashed in my awareness: "Find the two columns between which the Sun rises. There, you will meet Apollo."
>
> I located that spot and sat there to meditate. The Sun came up at dawn and filled me with incredible radiance. It was an overwhelming experience of the Divine. I stopped breathing.
>
> The meditation was so moving that when I returned to normal consciousness, I felt that someone had given me a great *rasayana* (elixir) and then removed it from my body. I had been given something so nurturing and so powerful, that when it was taken away, I was left feeling a huge void.

Following the overwhelming meditation vision, Diedre felt that if she and her husband did not go to Greece, she was going to "literally starve."

> We could afford the trip. So for several weeks, I was in a daze of traumatic longing as we planned a vacation in Greece. Much to my disappointment, my mother warned us about Greece's political

instability and the trip was cancelled at the last minute. Instead, we vacationed in Hawaii where we conceived our son.

Diedre believes their son shares a connection with Greek culture. The meditation vision came as an inspiration because he wanted to be conceived in Greece. Subtle clues popped up throughout pregnancy supporting Diedre's intuition. Los Angeles reported its hottest year on record. The erratic weather reminded Diedre of her favorite classical Greek myth: the story of the god Apollo and his love for a nymph who bore him a son.

When the nymph's son was nine years old, he discovered that Apollo was his father and he climbed Mt. Olympus to find him. His father greeted him saying, "As you are my son, I will give you anything you desire."

The son chose to drive Apollo's chariot across the sky just as Apollo did every morning. Apollo replied, "Oh please, anything but that. You are not strong enough. My horses are too powerful." But the boy kept insisting until his father agreed.

So one day, they climbed into the chariot and Apollo handed over the reins. The boy drove across the sky, but soon he lost control. He was unable to handle those mighty steeds. The chariot's deep swoops scorched the Earth, and the Earth froze where he rose too high.

Just like that, the year I was pregnant, the Sun went out of control. You could boil an egg on the sidewalk in March.

During pregnancy, Diedre focused on inspirational books and scriptures. One day she found a verse from an ancient text about "the Sun and his sister Dawn." This passage contained a symbolic message. Because Diedre had given birth to her first child at sunrise and named her Dawn, she intuited, "If my daughter is really the Dawn, then my son who will come, will be the Sun."

I gave birth to my son in a prestigious hospital in Beverly Hills the day major political changes took place in the Soviet Union. The hospital had never monitored such a baby and gave him a perfect ten. Nine hours after birth, he laughed and has been laughing ever since.

Today my five-year-old son is brilliant, powerful, and ambitious – qualities associated with the Sun. There is no separation between us. He was born for me. By the time he was six months old, he was constantly adoring me. Anything I do is just so perfect and divine for him.

The Greek and Roman mythological Cupid fired golden-tipped arrows into the hearts of potential parents to trigger their falling in love.

Cupid's Arrow

*A highly-evolved soul with a strong determination
and keen sense of purpose challenged the
free will of one young couple.*

Ken felt "a definite click" on the level of consciousness when he
and Judy first met.

> Judy and I enjoyed a movie on our first date. Just before the film
> started, the theater became pitch black for a few minutes and I had
> one crystal clear thought, "Someday we will tell our grandchildren
> this is how we met."
>
> My next thought was, "What's this! I only asked Judy to a movie.
> I don't want to get married."

Ken had momentarily forgotten his recent prayer. He was about
to finish his doctoral degree and had been feeling that it was time
to find a partner. He prayed and meditated for an answer:

> If I am destined to marry, then bring me the right woman. I do not
> want to waste energy running after the wrong woman. She will have
> to come to my doorstep.

In a matter of days, Judy knocked on his office door to discuss a
research project. A cupid's arrow drastically changed the direction
of their lives from that day forward. No matter how much Judy
and Ken desired the relationship to move at a normal pace, it
seemed to be moving on its own timetable. If Judy resisted, she
realized that "on some level it had to be." And as Ken put it –

> If I resisted getting closer to Judy, rationalizing that I needed to
> explore other relationships, I felt strained and unnatural. Then as soon as
> I relaxed, out of nowhere, the idea of marriage popped up. The thought
> was driving me nuts – until I finally proposed. We were married three
> months after we met. It was destined.
>
> As soon as we became man and wife, I sensed the importance of
> conceiving a child within a year. Although Judy's rational mind

wanted to wait, on a deeper level, she felt the rightness in my deadline. Nine months later, we consciously conceived our first child.

The pregnancy went beyond personal desires. As Ken describes it –

Who was orchestrating this whole thing? There appeared to be a bigger plan. Our son's desire to be born – or a cosmic desire for him to be our child – was so great that God was working in all this. It was powerful.

When we looked back, Judy and I saw the pattern. It was more than just us consciously desiring a child. The cosmic intelligence structured this whole thing. And we are not the only ones. We have talked to parents with similar feelings, especially if a powerful soul was at work.

Judy also sensed "the overall plan." She has learned to trust her intuition whether she sees the plan or not. "Everything is perfect."

When Timothy was born, I had an "Aha" experience: "Oh, this is why Ken and I got together." Our son astonished us over and over again. Even when he was a few months old, Timothy had visions of angels and divine beings . He had inner experiences of God and received divine guidance. But, of course, he just saw them. He was too young to understand. Later, as he matured, I explained the scriptures and he began to grasp his experiences .

My son has deep insights. Ever since Timothy began to talk, his statements have pierced through the illusions. They are shocking and catch me at what I am doing all the time.

Souls Waiting in the Wings for Birth

Transmission of Knowingness

Alison conceived a child at a "safe" time of the month.

Having a child was the farthest thing from Alison's mind until she realized that someone else had other plans.

A premonition came through my body. It was a transmission of knowledge, of knowingness, an energy: "You will give birth to a very advanced soul." It happened as I was driving home from class one day. I was overwhelmed. It was such a moving experience. I also felt open to it. I knew it was a given.

I was single at the time and did not focus on the child. Several months later, however, I felt an immediate connection with a student in my music class. I knew he was my future husband, but I did not know how I knew that. I did not even know his name. Later, we met at a conference. That was it. It went fast.

After ten months of marriage, Ron and I accidentally conceived our son. We normally used contraceptives, but there was no reason to do so since I was on my menstrual period. It was a deep connection that night. It felt ancient. Intercourse was so dramatic that we started talking about having a child the next day. Ron wanted a boy and we argued about it. I thought he was sexist.

A week or two later, I discovered that I was pregnant. My logical mind thought, "There is no way that could happen. I was on my period." But it did. Ron travelled out of town a lot and that was the only night it could have been.

Alison gained insights into her son's "advanced soul" immediately following his birth.

When Devon was three days old, I entered the bedroom to see if he was awake. As I looked at him, my awareness travelled back in time. I saw us together in a previous life. We were walking through grape vineyards in ancient Greece.

Then, just a few days afterward, the Unity minister began to cry and shake when he touched Devon's head during his baptism. The minister announced to everyone: "This child is destined to be a great leader of

– 89 –

mankind. Whatever Devon does, he will do with excellence. He will bring through something tremendous for humanity. We are honored to have contact with him." The minister was an eighty-year-old man who admitted this was the first time he said anything like that.

When Devon was eighteen months old, the family visited a famous artist-astrologer who lived on a secluded mountain.

The day after we met with Frank, he unexpectedly called us back and said, "I have something you need to hear. I have drawn your son's portrait and completed his astrological chart."

Frank's prophecy was as mind-boggling as the minister's. We were not looking for this. He said: "I am honored to meet your son. As Devon's parents, you need to understand that he is destined to be a spiritual leader of mankind. He will not follow an orthodox route. Most people will not understand or accept his unconventional path; however he will have a great following of people. You must take good care of him and do not try to understand his ways. They will be different from yours."

Just as Frank had foreseen, Devon's life was filled with unusual incidents. As an example, at the age of seven, Devon's screams awakened his mother in the middle of the night. Devon recalled being the custodian of the Greek's greatest library established by Ptolemy I in Alexandria, Egypt.[3]

I entered Devon's bedroom and asked, "What happened? Why are you screaming?" Devon explained, "Oh God, it is all my fault, Mom. I let in a group of people who sabotaged the whole thing. They destroyed the records. They set fire to the library. They took everything away, and it will never come back. It will never be the same." Devon then described discs in which information had been stored. It was not stored in books, but in computer chips that were holographic images.

Another event occurred when Devon was eight years old.

Ever since Devon was a baby, he created geometric patterns, such as red squares and spirals. But even more interesting, when Devon was eight, I took him with me to a meeting. While I attended the meeting, I left Devon in a children's room. I told him, "Stay here and do your homework. I'll be back when my meeting is finished."

One hour later I returned to the room and felt a chill. Something so holy had happened. The entire room was filled with physics symbols. Devon had written them all over the blackboard.

I asked, "What happened?" Devon answered, "I don't know, Mom. I felt something inside of me that wanted me to do all this."

Later on, several people deciphered the scientific formulas and advised us to hide them.

Today, Devon seems to be a "normal" high school student; however he continues to tell us about dreams and visions of other universes and dimensions. He is not like you and me.

A Wave Come Through

Alison did not expect to have more children once she and Ron went their separate ways following twelve years of marriage. But Nature organized a different plan.

One day while I was driving alone through a long stretch of desert, I felt like the top of my head was opening up. I heard a voice say, "If you let me come through, I will heal you."

Some months later, when I met Demetre, another wave came through. I knew Demetre was destined to be my husband and the father of another child.

By the time Demetre and I married and conceived a child, I was already thirty-nine and knew what it meant to have a child at forty. Throughout the pregnancy, I released intense sorrow and grief. I felt so frustrated about my career. My daughter's message was right. That pregnancy forced everything that was in denial to the surface. It brought out the crap. It was a great purification.

On the other hand, I laughed a lot which I usually did not do. It was a hearty laugh. Soon after Jennie was born, I realized that that had been my daughter's laugh. I stopped laughing like that once she was born.

$$\mathcal{L}^{(3)} = -\frac{1}{4}G^{\alpha\mu\nu}G^{\alpha}_{\mu\nu} - \frac{1}{4}W^{\beta\mu\nu}W^{\beta}_{\mu\nu} - \frac{1}{4}B^{\mu\nu}B_{\mu\nu}$$
$$+ \sum_{j=\frac{1}{2}} i\overline{\chi}\!\not{D}\chi + \sum_{j=0}(D^{\mu}z)^{+}D_{\mu}z + V(h,\overline{h},\phi)$$
$$+ \sum_{m,n}[\lambda_1^{mn}Q_m d_n^c h + \lambda_2^{mn}Q_m u_n^c \overline{h} + \lambda_3^{mn}L_m l_n^c h + h.c.]$$

"Something so holy had happened. My eight-year-old son had written physics symbols all over the blackboard."

Contract Made in Heaven

*"Someone else" orchestrated a pregnancy for a
newly-married couple who conceived a child
even though they used contraceptives.*

Darien's "normal mode" is to evaluate before making a major decision: "Is this a good time?" "Are we ready?" "Are finances set?" He had wanted to bring a child into the world after he and his wife were financially comfortable. In sharp contrast, Sage knew it was time to conceive their first child after a few months of marriage.

I experienced a "total knowingness" and was even aware of my son's personality. He was a bright soul, but he was also persistent, domineering, and controlling. (And sure enough, as a child Tom has a strong personality with obsessive-compulsive, addictive type energies. "It is my way or it is no way.")

I knew how Darien felt about having a child before we were ready and I did not try to change his mind. I respected his point of view. I also anticipated our parents' reaction if I became pregnant too soon: "What are you thinking, getting pregnant before Darien is finished with college? You don't have a good income. That does not make sense. That is irresponsible."

Yet, my intuition kept telling me, "The timing is right." And even though I did not verbally agree with my son's soul, "Okay, let us do this," I agreed in my heart. I was ready. Twenty-one was old enough and felt right. Darien and I knew each other since junior high. We had been friends, lovers, and gotten married. Plus my sisters were having babies.

So, even though I always used birth control, his spirit was so persistent that he came in anyway. I conceived at the time of intercourse. My diaphragm slipped, and I felt good about it. I was prepared to become a mother. It felt right and exciting.

When I finally told Darien, I said: "Guess what? I am pregnant." I tried to comfort him by saying, "Well, Darien, we were careful. We did everything we were supposed to and I became pregnant anyway."

Darien, who had switched majors and needed five years to finish an architecture degree, felt his mind being pulled away from having a child.

The responsibility of being a husband was enough for me. I was overwhelmed by the prospects of being a father on top of that. It was daunting and freaked me out. "I am just a kid." I did not feel ready. It took a few years after our son was born to feel comfortable with fatherhood. It threw me for a loop.

Messages from Chris, our Unborn Child

Seven years later, Darien and Sage switched positions. Darien received Chris's message that he wanted to be born. Darien had graduated and felt "secure and open to hear a soul wanting to come through." Chris was fairly persistent too, but there was an easy, carefree feeling like, "We are just going to roll into this."

Sage was surprised when Darien wanted to talk about a second child. Then unexpectedly without any prompting, she said, "Okay, sure." Darien recalls:

I don't know how long the idea was floating around before I woke up to it. I experienced an almost overpowering feeling – "This is it. It needs to happen right now." It was clear, strong, and easy – an absolute turnaround to our first pregnancy.

As soon as I was cognizant of having a child, he was there. And it was only natural to love him. It was beautiful. All that was left was for Sage and me to do our part, and then go through the waiting period prior to meeting his physical form.

Part of my intuitive experience surprised me, but at the time, I chalked it up to – "Well, I have finished school. I have a good job" – circumstances I thought we needed prior to having our first son. I never thought in terms of receiving messages from Chris until after the fact. I assumed it was my idea; but looking back on it, that was not the case.

Brotherhood Takes Nine Years

*A sibling's love attracts souls and the older child
senses the younger sibling prior to conception.*

Raising another child was the most remote thought in Sarah's mind, a thirty-two-year-old single mother. Eight-year-old Vincent, ignored her preaching and kept pleading, "I want a little brother." Sarah remained firm, "Well, you are not going to get one."

One year later Sarah became unexpectedly pregnant.

My friends reminded me that for months I had been saying, "I want a baby." That is how they interpreted my comments. But I did not say it exactly like that. Whenever I saw parents mistreat children, I had said, "I should have a baby so that one less baby gets abused," or "Why are couples having children if they do not know how to take care of them?"

So I had been making innocent comments and Vincent was asking me for a brother. Then, I created the situation where he could have one: Charles had been asking to date me for a year and I had refused. Then not only did I go out with him, we fell in love and conceived Michael. As it turned out, I feel blessed with two wonderful sons.

London Odyssey

Alicia's unexpected pregnancy happened when she lost track of her menstrual cycle; but even then, conception was hardly accidental given the events foreshadowing it.

Due to childhood experiences and difficulties in raising a son in her former marriage, Alicia was terrified of motherhood the second time around. Alicia's fears were so great that it seemed as if she needed to have a child to overcome it.

Cooper and I felt we might start a family one day but had not thought of "when" except for "sometime" later. Cooper would not say anything about it in deference to my fear of being a mother again. So, between the two of us, there could be no conscious planning to have a child. As Cooper says, it had to "just happen."

On the other hand, I had become unconsciously attracted to newborn babies for some time. I was doing it all the time for at least two years. But it took my friend, who is a counselor, to point it out to me. I told her, "So what? Babies are cute; doesn't everybody notice them?" Because of my fear, I was blocked from seeing it.

Another significant event occurred on a visit to England.

The clearest perception came during a bout with terror that I might be pregnant. I was in uptown London and going down a massive escalator to the underground subway the British call "the tube." Posters lined the walls. One said, "If you're pregnant and happy about it, that's fine. If not, call this number" (for counseling).

I thought half in jest, I should call that number because I am afraid I may be pregnant. I put a plea out into the air, "Look, little kid, later; not now. Later." That's me – procrastinate. Nothing specific, just not now. I experienced a distinct impression of a female soul agreeing to my request. She was sweet and, while I enjoyed her energy, I was aghast that I had more or less promised to let her in.

Several months later, I was gripped with fear when I discovered I was pregnant at the age of 41. Fortunately, Cooper sensed our child was a girl. That idea calmed me down. Motherhood would be different this time. I felt optimistic. My daughter would be like myself. I felt a kind of "home" feeling. And, when I tuned in, the child seemed like a simpatico spirit – a fun-loving friend.

Nine months later, I birthed my daughter Mara with great happiness. More than any relationship, our bond is most fulfilling. Today, she still radiates the sweet energy I felt when she communicated with me years ago.

Scandinavian Highway to Motherhood

*Like Alicia and Sarah, Carey's
unconscious mind foresaw pregnancy.*

My husband and I were not ready to start a family. So it was quite a surprise when I became unexpectedly pregnant soon after we returned from a European vacation. It was only then that I reflected upon the subtle hints that had been popping up the month before. While we toured scenic farmlands in Scandinavia, I was obsessed with every little newborn animal. They seemed to be every place I looked. I was drooling over baby calves, pigs, lambs, you name it.

Carey's unconscious mind evidently resonated with symbols of innocence and helplessness, somehow sensing that motherhood was around the corner. Western culture is only beginning to ascertain and tap the powers of the unconscious in the realm of childbearing.

Rainbow Madonna

*Human birth is first worked out in the unseen
world before it manifests in the seen world.*

Gigi has enjoyed drawing and painting as a pastime ever since she was fifteen. Through artistic expression, her conscious mind receives messages from the unconscious.

> When I have the urge to draw, it means something important is coming up for me on a deep emotional or spiritual level. They develop as I go along. I have no preconceived idea of the end result. I usually like the finished drawing, but sometimes it is months before it touches me and I realize, "I know what that means."

According to Carl Jung, the unconscious speaks through the language of images. His clients painted pictures for him as an aid for understanding their psyche. Gigi's impulses apparently followed Jung's formula. Three months before Gigi became pregnant, she spontaneously created an unusual set of drawings.

> I was twenty-one and more interested in establishing a career than starting a family. Nonetheless, I saw the pattern when I analyzed my art work months later: pregnant women and mother/child motifs. My drawings represented how I felt before my pregnancy – things coming into fruition, abundance, and bounty.

During the pre-conception period, Gigi had also watched a pregnant friend do her "nesting," and had become "a little envious." These feelings "surprised me because a child was not something I felt I wanted at that time." As a rule, Gigi and her husband used birth control. One night they "threw caution to the winds." Michael was born nine months later.

> Louis and I did not consciously decide to have our child. However, I do not believe in unplanned pregnancies. The knowledge is there on some level, even though we are unconscious of it.

Souls Waiting in the Wings for Birth

Children of a Virtual Reality

*Once pregnancy is confirmed, parents often contemplate
the tender thoughts leading up to conception. Ironically,
all too often, because birth is such an overwhelming event,
interest peaks with a child's birth. Then ... forgotten
and quickly dismissed is the magical prelude.*

One evening after two-year-old Aaron had fallen sound asleep,
his parents, Judy and Jeff, browsed through the "Book of Wishes"
which they had almost forgotten. Judy had created this book four
years earlier. In it, she placed pictures of everything the newly-
married couple wished for – a son and daughter, a beautiful home,
ideal vacations, and so on.

As they flipped through the pages, the couple realized how many
wishes had been fulfilled. They then looked at the picture of the ideal
children Judy had picked out. Jeff exclaimed, "Look at that toddler. If
we put baby Aaron in that picture, we couldn't tell them apart."

Several years later, the birth of Auriel fulfilled Judy's desire for a
daughter. Auriel did not physically resemble the little girl in the
family's wish book as Allen had, but the age difference between the
two children matched.

> I always longed for a child with blond curly hair. And prior to
> Aaron's conception, that yearning was strong in my mind. Once
> Aaron fulfilled that desire, my attention was no longer focused on a
> daughter having blond curly hair.

So when does the bond between a parent and child begin? Did
Judy create the child of her dreams by selecting the picture for her
Book? Or did she become attuned to a universal field of life where
births are planned? Sometimes Nature tickles a woman's heart and
then human destiny begins taking shape in seed form.

LOVING DISCIPLINE

Chapter 5
Souls Lining Up for Birth
Katarina Meets Her Children

**We chose our parents and our children chose us.
There are no victims in the Pre-existence
... in that place before "here" ... .[1]**

– Jeannine Parvati Baker

*Like a mirror in the making, Katarina was polished and
prepared for the future with repeated visitations of her five
children – more than any mother interviewed.*

Katarina is a unique mother. Even as a child, she recalled her
existence as a spiritual being prior to entering her mother's
womb.[2] These memories are a gift since they enriched the births of
her own children. Katarina knew that her children were "aware of
what they were coming in for."

At the time Katarina and I met to start the interviews, this thirty-
five-year-old mother had recently given birth to her fifth child. In
spite of a hectic schedule, she shared a half dozen mornings
discussing experiences with six souls seeking birth over the past
sixteen years. Katarina was an open book and felt relaxed telling a
friendly stranger her adventures. Motherhood has created opportunities for spiritual growth despite the turmoil of the 20th century.

Children are part of our baggage. For me, there was a profound
sense of completion with each of my children – a feeling that I had
missed these people and they were coming back to be with me.

But when I was heading out into the world at eighteen. I expected to have a more worldly life. I did not foresee that motherhood was destined to be my greatest spiritual duty and contribution. So motherhood was not an adventure I set out on. It was an adventure that unfolded itself to me sweetly and wonderfully. And, I know now in retrospect, "It was well-ordained."

Katarina met the souls of five children who desired to be born.

Message of the Bumblebee

Too often pregnancies transpire when couples least desire them. Just as the saying goes, when opportunity knocks, grab it. Apparently, a soul seeking birth did just that when Katarina had been in no hurry to have a second child.

Obstacles had arisen like thorns on a path. At barely twenty-three, Katarina's "first child was wonderful and the mothering feeling was strong," but Katarina was waiting for Emily to grow up so she could get on with her life. While she had been married for five years, yet marital relations with Travis had become a bit rocky. Money was another complicating factor. Finances were pinched and they would become strapped to the limits if another child was born within the coming year. Katarina and Travis had also begun saving for their new home. They planned to escape a cramped apartment if the marriage managed to survive. In addition, Katarina had just returned to graduate school and was determined to finish a Master's degree.

Subtler impulses soon began to knock at an invisible door in the mother's consciousness. Katarina felt a strong, gentle presence – like a baby's soul – lingering around the household, a different energy in the air:

> During the two months prior to conception, someone was constantly over my shoulder. Whenever I'd leave home in the car, the strange feeling came that someone had been left behind. A child was missing. Or, we'd be sitting at the dinner table and I'd feel like there was someone in the other room who was supposed to be at the table.

Withdrawal as a contraceptive method proved ineffective for the couple. "So right after lovemaking, I knew that I was pregnant." Immediately, Katarina had perceived a definite quickening within her body, even though a fetal body could have grown little beyond a tiny, invisible cell mass. Confirmation of her pregnancy arrived quickly.

> My mind is sensitive and perceptive of every shift that takes place in my body. I was extremely nauseous from day one. Another confirmation was heightened emotions and sore breasts. I've talked to other women who have morning sickness the day after. Many doctors do not believe it, but a woman's body immediately starts to change.

After giving birth to Emily, her first child, Katarina knew that an unborn child seeking birth chooses to come in for a reason and singles out its parents by a process unknown to us. Katarina acknowledged that Emily was a blessing and had brought the mother empowering transformation; however Katarina could not face having another child right now.

> It was such a painful time with my husband. At the same time, I could not bear losing this soul forever, or even giving it up for adoption. I felt so close to her already. I could not bear the thought of living without this being.

Nature's Magic Wand

Since her late teens, Katarina had practiced an Eastern form of meditation to bring peace of mind and tranquility into her life. Katarina routinely experienced an expanded awareness after meditation and it helped her deal with the constant demands of motherhood.

The unborn being who had the patience of a bulldog tenaciously hovered over its future possibilities, leaving the mother with few options. At some point, a breakthrough occurred in Katarina's consciousness. She sensed the possibility of consciously communicating with the little soul whose existence was obviously still in the non-material world. The puzzle was how to talk to her and influence her. Was it really possible?

Amazingly, an intimate relationship with the unborn child spontaneously unfolded as Katarina's subtle perceptions of the soul continued.

> Her presence was strong and close at hand. This soul wanted me to be its mother. She was persistent and knew I was pregnant. Awakening one morning, my intuition inspired me to have a serious talk with her and offer a better opportunity for birth later on down the road.

Souls Waiting in the Wings for Birth

So that afternoon, Katarina withdrew to their backyard and reviewed the goals she wanted to complete before becoming a mother for the second time.

1. *Our marriage needs more time to heal.*
2. *We need a spacious home to provide for our growing family.*
3. *I want to finish my graduate degree. My education is important to my becoming a whole person.*

Katarina jotted down the three goals in her journal and then closed her eyes.

The young girl's soul was with me, listening to my thoughts. Our communication took place on that silent level where everything is connected – in the deepest silence of my soul. I am not always able to reach it, but when I do, I know I am there and that I am having an impact.

In the conversation, I explained it wouldn't be opportune to enter my life at this time. Yet, we were so close, neither of us wanted to give up the connection. The only solution was to ask her to come back at a better time. It was my deepest desire.

I felt like I was talking to a sister, someone with intelligence and discrimination. And, even though she wasn't saying anything, I knew she understood by the feeling she conveyed. It was like a physical "Yes, I've read the demands, I've got it under control. It's fine."

Katarina opened her eyes to ponder the soul's response to her plea. Immediately, as if orchestrated by a magic wand in the hands of an invisible intelligence, a passing bumblebee flew right down to her. He landed on the open journal even though there were neither nectar nor flowers to attract it. To Katarina's amazement, the curious creature slowly walked up and down over the three wishes recorded in her journal, as if on a secret mission. Then, the bumblebee started buzzing wildly again and flew on its way. The bumblebee had come and left in an instant.

I laughed and thought, "Well, I hope he knows her." It was an awesome moment. I wish to God I had had a witness. I don't even know if I told Travis. There was that much distance between us at the time. I just kept that one inside and embraced it. Sometimes if I share a deep experience with the wrong person, it loses something. I didn't want that to happen. It had been a communication with someone very dear to me – a real experience that I didn't want poo-pooed.

The next day, the pregnancy terminated in a spontaneous miscarriage. "It was a relief, but not totally unexpected because our communication had been so clear." When Katarina began bleeding, the heavier-than-normal flow confirmed that she had indeed been pregnant.

Katarina's monthly cycle then returned to twenty-eight days. Life seemed normal again.

Sara, Child of Deja Vu

Through the passing months, one by one, the three conditions Katarina had recorded in her journal had been satisfied. The couple had moved into a large, comfortable home, "all the criteria were fulfilled in our marriage," and the Master's degree was at last in Katarina's hand.

Mother Nature was silently keeping track in the background – it seems:

> One year later, I became pregnant. It was totally unexpected. As I pondered over becoming a mother, the message of the bumblebee flashed into my mind. The realization that the past year's goals were now fulfilled left me tingling with renewed energy.

Once again, Katarina felt the presence of Sara's soul flitting around her, through a profound sense of familiarity, like an old friend coming home for a timely visit. Katarina believed she had experienced the dress rehearsal a year earlier.

> I sensed her soul, that same little person came back, such a little character. When I got pregnant with her the second time, the same severe nausea came as I had had in the pregnancy the year before. Now that I have had five children, I know each pregnancy has a unique quality. With one child, I had no nausea, with another very little. But with Sara, each time I was pregnant with her, I was extremely nauseous immediately after conception.

Katarina felt a deep sense of joy that Sara's soul had returned when the circumstances were less restrictive.

> I could smile back on that last year. Now I was ready as a woman, a wife, and a mother to expand my sphere in the world. It was exciting because I felt ready to go on this journey again. Part of my spiritual quest is to have more children and I had earned this rite of

passage. My mind and body were one, and now I could build a heavenly body for this patient soul.

Following her birth, Katarina's daughter was another source of clues that the same soul had attempted to be born in the previous year.

> My daughter is extremely advanced – always a year ahead of herself. People aren't going to believe it, but Sara could speak at three months old. And, at one year old, her ability to communicate was awesome. She told us things that a child that innocent and young wouldn't normally think of. It was a shock. Perhaps rapid development took place because Sara was supposed to be on with her life already at this point. The wave of her life would have normally started the year before.

Sara continues to be advanced today. She may be tiny, but she is smart. Her teachers say that academics will never be a problem. Her only difficulty could be boredom.

The Bumblebee, *by Sharla Kew (age 8).*

Conscious Choice

*Katarina's conscious miscarriage and pre-conception
of the same soul illustrate how supposed "accidental"
events can fall within the range of conscious choice.*

Katarina's story raises several curious questions.

*Did Katarina really communicate with the soul? How is it possible to
perceive a soul?*

According to Katarina, life extends far beyond what people
normally believe is possible. Souls of future children exist on a
subtler level of existence beyond the range of ordinary perception.
This perspective coincides with the range of life known from the
most advanced field of physics, quantum mechanics, which
teaches that human senses are blind to most natural wonders of the
cosmos. Normal human senses perceive one-billionth of the information in the environment. If the electromagnetic spectrum were
drawn on a school board from left to right, normal vision would
represent no more than an imperceptible line somewhere in the
middle area in the visible light segment.

Mothers like Katarina, who have broadened their vision, teach
us that the nature of human consciousness holds the key to
communication with souls.

It requires a new process of intuition. When I sense souls
around me, I explore them in their "seed form." Subtle differences
in personality and life force become apparent. Then, a relationship
with them on the sweetest level starts to develop. It's a level of
cosmic intuition that cannot be harmed or changed no matter
what happens through many life spans.

What happened to Katarina's physiology in ending the pregnancy?

What happened to Katarina is medically termed "spontaneous
miscarriage." From a biological perspective, however, no simple
explanation exists. These miscarriages can take place within the first

twelve weeks of gestation and for a variety of reasons, including the mother's health, state of mind, diet, or use of drugs. The suggestion from Katarina's experience is that the free will choice of a soul to abandon its attempt to gain birth may induce miscarriage.

No medical or public health statistics are kept on how commonly spontaneous miscarriages occur. For many women, menstrual periods may merely be late, leading some to question whether they were even pregnant, while other women confirm they are pregnant by characteristic symptoms, a pregnancy test, or a doctor's examination.

Katarina's account poses the plausible view that women have more control over their physiology than modern medicine has long subscribed to. What happened to Katarina took place on the level of consciousness, where the mind influences the body.

The mind-body link is gaining scientific and social interest. The long held Western view, where mind and body are believed to operate separately and independently, is being replaced by ancient insights and new experience. Dr. Deepak Chopra, who is a Western-trained medical doctor specializing in endocrinology with an East Indian background, has been bringing out the message of the natural mind-body connection in several books.[3] Dr. Chopra describes how human health is controlled by our awareness at its deepest level. This corresponds to the deepest level of Nature which physics calls "the quantum field." Here the mind and body are one, virtually linked, in a unified field of consciousness. Quantum physics suggests that separateness is an illusion.

Mothers need to heed Dr. Chopra's message, "Thoughts are things." Thoughts turn into actions at a biochemical/physiological level. "Happy thoughts produce happy molecules" while "unhappy thoughts produce unhappy molecules." Therefore mothers need to nurture the most positive thoughts possible. A mother's thoughts become alive in the baby as it takes form. A baby is an expression of its mother's thoughts.

Mind-body connection offers explanations for spontaneous miscarriages. First, it suggests a deeper mind-body-soul connection where physiological and cosmic influences are at work to create a pregnancy condition. Then, as conditions change, they act to terminate the pregnancy. There is little scientific understanding available on the cosmic influences of souls on a mother's physiology. In Katarina's experience, she felt the soul's influence long before she became pregnant.

One theory is that the pregnancy was automatically terminated when the fertilized egg was left unattended by a cosmic influence, a subtle spark of intelligence that energizes it and is the chief architect of embryonic development. As long as this energy is attached to the growing embryo and no outside force intervenes, the pregnancy continues on its natural course. So an influence such as Katarina's strong desire and attunement asking the soul to return may have prompted a disengagement of cosmic energy from the embryo and its termination resulted.[4]

Was the bumblebee's visit a coincidence or a cosmic symbol?

We pick up clues to the future by listening to and looking at what is happening in our environment. Mother Nature is a great conversationalist and talks to each of us in subtle ways, reminding us of things, suggesting ways to act, even foreshadowing future events.

Nature has its own solutions to our problems if we can tune in and listen. For Katarina, the bumblebee's symbolism was clear. It represented the soul and, of course, that it had received her message, and finally, it flew away.

Katarina with her children
waiting in the wings.

Overlapping Souls

*Earlier stories ("Thousands of Soul Bubbles,"
"Cherubims in Pink Clouds," "Lassoing a Soul," and
"Hovering at Heaven's Door") introduced us to a mother's
experience of meeting more than one soul at a time.
Katarina calls this phenomenon, "overlapping souls."*

Children have their own priorities about when they will be born into a family. So sometimes Katarina's pre-conception visions did not accurately reflect their birth order. Souls seem to begin lining up for conception and birth just much like airplanes line up miles from a busy airport before landing. When more than one soul seeks birth from the same mother, each soul must wait its proper turn.

Two years prior to her first pregnancy, Katarina's visions of a little boy naturally created expectations for a son. However, six months into her pregnancy –

> I saw a vision of a beautiful yet unfamiliar living room. A vivacious, pretty sixteen-year-old girl entered the room to talk to me and my husband. I realized I was seeing my life sixteen years into the future. This girl was my daughter whose soul was in my womb at that moment.
>
> Three months later, I gave birth to a girl with features identical to the sixteen-year-old girl. Today, twelve-year-old Emily is growing into that vision and looks like that tall, blond girl.

Katarina birthed two more daughters following Emily's birth, even though the boy's presence continued. When Katarina's marriage ended in divorce, she stopped wondering about why a son had not been born.

> I was through with marriage. I had outgrown it. I abandoned the idea of having another relationship and more children. I had no interest in pursuing men. I was tired of the whole thing. It seemed like more work than it was worth.

Souls Waiting in the Wings for Birth

Then, Stephen, a long-time friend, stopped by to visit. That night as we sat in my living room, I looked at him and suddenly felt that little male soul next to him. I was surprised. I had not felt him around me for quite a while.

Since Stephen was at a point where he wanted to find someone to marry, I thought, "How nice! Since I won't have more children, Stephen will take over where I left off. He will be the father of this little male soul."

Of course, it never occurred to me that Stephen was destined to become my husband – until there had been a lot of metamorphoses. There had never been any romance between us. In fact, I set him up with some girlfriends.

And then, son of a gun! Our friendship suddenly flipped to romance and Stephen became an enormous part of my life.

Stephen and Katarina celebrated their marriage three months after that visit. Looking back, Katarina realizes how one of her visions had correctly foreshadowed her second marriage. As described earlier, the vision indicated that the child growing in Katarina's womb was a daughter whom she saw enter the living room as a sixteen year old. Furthermore –

When I looked across the living room I expected to see my first husband. Instead, my friend Stephen was with me. I wondered, "What's Stephen doing in this vision?"

Even though surprised, I dismissed the question as unimportant. Mainly I wondered about this little boy's soul who had been hanging around for a long time and whom I thought would be born next.

The Twelve-Year Pre-Conception Bond

Like a prospective buyer inspecting a house's specifications, Katarina believes the little boy visited for twelve years to check out her relationship with Stephen.

My ex-husband was entirely into the physical body. I developed a lot of childbirth stretch marks. My appearance made a difference in our relationship and he began looking for other women.

But stretch marks make no difference to Stephen. All the negativity in my life ended when I married him. He sees the physical body as a vehicle to walk through life with. We take care of it the best we can.

It is healing to have a child with someone you can be yourself with. Stephen is completely into family. It makes past negativity seem unimportant. I have no doubt that Jason was waiting for my marriage to Stephen. Once Stephen and I were married, my intuition sensed most strongly that Jason was going to be born next. And I was right.

In fact, it is significant that the Jason's soul first came into my life when I first met Stephen twelve years prior to Jason's birth. At that time, I was engaged to my first husband. After that, he was a little visitor periodically over the years.

Even more interesting, Jason appeared to Katarina and Stephen simultaneously.

Basically our son told us he was coming. We had a vision of him as an adult. It was a clear impression. We also had specific communication. He explained that certain children were being born at this time because of what was happening in the changing world. He told us what he planned to do in this life.

He predicted several world events that surprised us. Since that time, one of them has happened. I do not want to tell the details. It will make the story unbelievable. Eventually these experiences will be commonplace.

Two months following our vision, I became pregnant. Today Jason looks exactly like he did in the vision, although he is still a baby and does not have the same mature essence yet.

Mother Nature's Timetable

Deep down, Katarina began to sense a little boy and girl wanting to be her fifth child, as they hovered around the ethers of the household environment – "another good overlapping story."

Katarina had become familiar with the little girl several months prior to Jason's conception and throughout that pregnancy. Sometimes the girl appeared in a vision with Jason as a potential sister. The little girl was very quiet and stood behind him. On other occasions, they came on separate visits. Katarina thought they were close companions or deciding who was to be born next.

Katarina hoped to birth the little girl after Jason's birth.

Immediately after I became pregnant with my fifth child, I felt the presence of the little girl's soul to whom I felt deeply attached. She even looked like me. But her presence alternated with another little boy's. Since this second boy was not quite as attached to whether he came into our particular family, I hoped the little girl would be born next. Then,

Stephen and I could call it quits. If not, this would be a way to get me to have six children.

Well, I was in for another surprise. The birth order was reversed. The little boy was born next. I had not felt as bonded to this little guy as I did with my other children, but now I do, of course. Our son, Paul, is just adorable!

For now, Katarina's inspirations end with the girl's soul for whom she feels a deep love, still waiting in the wings.

Chapter 6
Dancing in Two Worlds
Miscarriage within the Greater Plan

**I shall never believe that God
plies dice with the World.**[1]

– Albert Einstein

*We acknowledge the role of parents in teaching
children about life. But it is equally true that each
educates the other ... and sometimes an unborn
child is a parent's greatest teacher.*

Souls are like seeds lying dormant in the soil of nature's garden waiting for the rain of right opportunity. The potential always exists for them to be born as children, some blessed with long lives and others equally blessed with shorter ones.

The difficult lesson for parents is that certain souls plan lessons involving a brief life span because that is all they need for their growth. This chapter illustrates the subtle dynamics transpiring in miscarriages. Of course, no one explanation accounts for all incomplete pregnancies.

The contemporary parents presented here did not measure the success of their child's time on Earth by the child's life span. Babies enter the world with a purpose even if they do not stay too long.

Toxic Lesson

*Planning to be born is infinitely more complex
than calculating a rocket launch or forecasting
the weather. And, like the tides, a soul's
interest in birth may ebb and flow.*

A young couple, Reinhard and Christiana, travelled through Denmark on their honeymoon. Within a week after returning to the States, the newlyweds had settled into a new home where Reinhard had a "crystal clear" vision in his mind's eye.

I initially saw a newborn baby when I looked at the ring around my wife's eyes. Next, I saw a group of babies playing together like a series of tiny bubbles. There were layers of boy and girl babies getting ready to incarnate. At times, the babies started becoming older, say four to five years old; then they returned to become babies again.

I saw numerous potentials, as if we might conceive quadruplets. Then we lucked out and the quadruplets became one child again. The child always had the same facial features and hair color, but sometimes it was a boy and sometimes a girl.

Three weeks later, Christiana announced her pregnancy. My reaction was, "Well, it's about time." At that moment, a vision of the baby appeared in her eyes again. This time the afterimage lingered several hours and I felt the child's presence in our home.

I now realized my earlier vision had been a real cognition and felt comfortable sharing my visions with Christiana. I discovered that she had had similar premonitions. Nature had given both of us hints beforehand.

Medical Mystery

Christiana looked forward to motherhood. At only thirty-three, she was in excellent health and a long distance runner. Yet strangely juxtaposed to his wife's upbeat feeling, Reinhard had an inner sense that "a problem" was looming on the horizon, and he did not feel "altogether jubilant."

Within several months, Christiana became ill and withdrew into a shell. Reinhard recalls:

> At first, I experienced denial. I rationalized that the cold winter weather made Christiana sick. But her illness dragged on and on. Christiana had zero energy and felt depressed nearly 100% of the time. She seemed like a person rapidly going through old age: she had the flu for seven to ten days, would be fine for two days; then she became sick with a bronchial problem for another four days. Christiana eventually begin to talk about suicide every day.

Christiana's ailment escaped conventional medical diagnosis.

> Of course, we sought medical help, but the doctors kept reporting: "Everything is fine. Christiana's problem is due to the psychological pressures of a new marriage and a first pregnancy." We ended up consulting seven psychologists, but the psychological probing only increased Christiana's emotional imbalance and worries about her mental health and our relationship.
>
> Abstract advice from friends who said,"Ultimately there is a larger plan behind all this," was the only realistic appraisal Christiana ever received. Yet, no one saw the big picture.

Reinhard sensed that "a heart-disconnect" had taken place between Christiana and the child.

> A mother and child share a complex relationship. In this case, instead of positive bonds forming, my wife and child seemed to be choosing to separate. I sensed a huge internal battle going on, but I was clueless about what to do about it. I did not probe very much.
>
> It was a deep, dark time. Christiana's illness went beyond what I could understand. I felt lost in space – in a universe way too big to understand. I stood back, totally out of the scene, outside the battle. On top of everything else, our marriage became rocky and we began to quarrel.

Christiana's pregnancy terminated after seven months due to a medical complication. The couple felt "short-term relief with the spontaneous abandonment."

> By that time, I had become removed from the pregnancy. My connection had actually ended five months earlier when my visions of the child stopped and Christiana had began to feel so negative. I realized how almost insignificant the male is in creating a child. They

are seed energy and then nothing else. The whole field of the creation is the female side. She has to nurture from that point.

Mystery Solved

Christiana's strange illness did not end with miscarriage. And one year later medical doctors at a clinic for environmental illnesses finally diagnosed the ailment as multiple chemical sensitivity (MCS). Christiana received an insurance settlement for long-term treatment and felt psychologically relieved about having a legitimate health problem.

Today the medical profession is gradually recognizing MCS as an environmental illness attributed to chemical exposures, especially synthetic substances such as pesticides, indoor air pollutants, chemicals in cosmetic products, soaps, deodorants, foods, and miscellaneous materials. Once an individual suffers an insult from a toxin like formaldehyde, for instance, the immune system may be injured to the point that the person's health condition makes them more susceptible to future effects of chemical exposures.

Reinhard and Christiana's problems began after returning from their honeymoon when they moved into a brand-new home – energy efficient and air tight. The home had even won awards for high energy efficiency. Reinhard and Christiana noted a chemical smell, but thought nothing about the normal smell of a new home.

Christiana's poisoning came from formaldehyde emitted from the carpet backing. A toxic level built up penetrating the walls, furniture, and draperies when the house had been sealed up during the month we travelled in Europe. Our expensive, triple-paned windows combined with several inches of exterior foam and expensive doors helped our energy bills, but did not create a healthy environment. We had only one air exchanger in the living room and no easy way to get fresh air into the bedroom.

Moving into a well-insulated home during the winter, when we did not have lots of fresh air circulating, further amplified the build-up of formaldehyde. In retrospect, I realize that the formaldehyde exposure caused the mild degree of moodiness and depression I also experienced during the pregnancy; however Christiana spent more time at home, thus intensifying her exposure.

Christiana's symptoms resemble a case of classic formaldehyde poisoning, in this instance from inhalation exposure.[2] The environmental health clinic identified traces of formaldehyde and another synthetic chemical during testing of Christiana. But at the time of Christiana's pregnancy, doctors did not know what to look for.

It seems unfathomable that medical science could not measure the toxins in Christiana's blood and detect the cause of her illness. An entire generation of doctors treated thousands of patients, like Christiana, and declared them "normal." Just one intelligent word from a doctor could have set Christiana's recovery into motion.

Teachings of the Unborn

Reinhard was unable to alter the past and bring his child back, but as an architect, he decided to change the future and "untangle the mess in the environment."

The soul of our child was conscious of the reason for his incarnation. He came to remind me of everything western society knows, but has failed to do for 100 years. Through my wife's illness, our child screamed at me: "Wake up. Reject everything you have been taught. Rethink the relationship between human physiology and the built [synthetic] environment. Otherwise, many pure souls may stop incarnating."

Reinhard committed himself to serving humanity and entered the most inspiring period of his life. He began to construct homes in a life-enhancing way rather than life-damaging way.

Architecture has "de-evolved" into a degraded state. Common sense has been thrown out the door and short-term profit made the focus. Fortunately I found alternatives in the European "Bau Biology" movement that practices scientific techniques of non-toxic building. I learned how human blood, bone, tissue, and DNA have their own resonance, magnetic qualities, and electromagnetic qualities which need to resonate with similar materials in Nature. For example, stone is closest to bone mass. Straw is closest to sinews and ligaments.

Natural materials create soothing physiological and psychological effects essential to our well-being. We respire through the walls of our homes, our third skin. If the walls are made of straw and clay, they purify the air, vitalizing the cells that pass through them. That is why we feel connected when we visit buildings constructed from vitalized materials like straw/clay or cut stone and tile, such as the great cathedrals of Europe, the 500-year-old buildings of Germany and Southern France, as well as Chinese and Japanese temples. This body language is not taught in modern universities.

Parents must listen to messages of the souls who are incarnating.

Our child bore a profound message. As a powerful teacher who stood in between the pure soul state and the fully-human state, he knew what was best. His playful innocence had no place for poisons. I feel incredible gratitude for this spiritual lesson. He spoke to me in the language of the future.

The unborn child screamed, "Dad, wake up. Rethink the relationship between human physiology and architecture."

The Song of the Pearl

*Like attracts like. Love attracts love.
Parents attract the souls they need for growth
and souls attract the parents they need. Each is
drawn to the other in order to learn lessons.*

Inklings of Yasmin's pregnancy had long been in the air.

I continually felt the presence of a soul who wanted to come in for eight months prior to conception. I don't know how to explain it in terms of seeing in the way we are used to seeing. It is an energy, a feeling, a force. It felt feminine. She was a beautiful, youthful, yet a mature child, perhaps twelve to fourteen years old.

Since I had three children and did not want a fourth, I kept advising her, "Please go somewhere else. I know couples who really desire a child." I even listed the names of couples.

Yasmin felt a sense of relief each month her menstrual period came on time. But like it or not, Yasmin finally conceived the child the morning her husband left on a business trip. Yasmin did not realize that Bill had "left for good" until a few days had passed. The unforeseen abandonment left a bitter pill to swallow and made it harder to face pregnancy. Though the marriage had weathered several ups and downs over the past year, Yasmin had hoped there was still a chance for its survival.

As soon as I sensed the pregnancy, I thought, "I can't believe this. You have been hanging around for eight months. Why now?" But even though the pregnancy alarmed me, I did not have the time or wits to attend to it right away. Coming to grips with a divorce was all I could handle. I was in shock.

Two weeks later, I began to look at the whole picture. I thought, "This is crazy." I told two friends. It blew their socks off. But my best friend also laughed and said, "Well, of course." And I said, "It does make sense doesn't it? It sort of tops the cake."

Yasmin considered using herbs to induce a miscarriage. An herbalist friend discouraged that plan.

Ellen counseled me, "Be certain that this is not a karmic trap and that this soul has not been your dearest, closest sister who has come now when you need her most."

Ellen's advice woke me up. I no longer saw the pearl in the oyster as a bother. The soul held my hand for several months when I encountered rough times. She was my best friend in the cosmos. She was support and strength. It was an amazing act of compassion. I apologized, "So this is why you have been hanging around. You knew what I was in for and you waited patiently, knowing that at any moment I was going to need you."

Yasmin suddenly "let go." She felt safe and protected, connected to a greater wholeness.

I felt a burst of faith and took a huge leap towards enlightenment, self-knowledge, and self-empowerment. My life was happening the way it was supposed to. Everything is in perfect order. I will raise three children on my own, and if need be, I will raise four.

I was sitting in a huge hand. I had mistaken the hand for a vast, barren desert, thinking, "I am lost! I am out here on my own. This shocking thing has happened to me." Now, from a distance I saw that the desert was really a big hand: I was sitting in the palm of God.

I did not need to abort the child. I could not send my dearest friend away. All I needed to do for the next many months was to make the next meal. What choice did I have? The most outlandish things had already happened: four months behind on the rent when Bill left, no food in the cupboard, and bill collectors knocking at the door. It felt like I was driving a car that might have a blowout any minute.

A Strange Wrinkle

During Yasmin's third month of pregnancy, she began to hemorrhage on a flight home from California. It was horrendous. All of the flight attendants knew. The landing crew met Yasmin with a wheelchair. She refused. Since the airport was one hour from home, she and her three children rested in a hotel. The hemorrhaging became so intense that she phoned Ellen in the middle of the night. A strange wrinkle then brought an unexpected source of support.

After talking to Ellen for a few minutes, her husband Jim picked up the phone and asked, "Why aren't we calling Bill?" I explained,

Souls Waiting in the Wings for Birth

"Bill doesn't deserve to know about the pregnancy. This gift has come to me and it has not come to him." Jim replied, "Well, it is high time Bill found out."

Nature arranged for Bill to be there and it worked out for the best. Otherwise, I don't know how I ever would have told him. He showed up forty minutes later and set aside our problems and his shock that I had been pregnant without his knowledge. He was wonderful and assisted me through the miscarriage.

Bill told me about the dream he had had two nights earlier. He saw himself buckling up twin girls into car seats. Bill was right. I miscarried two fetuses.

Yasmin believes the pregnancy was short-circuited once she went through a spiritual transformation.

The soul came when I needed someone. When I didn't need her any longer she felt free to go. Whoever that was, God bless her. She was absolutely what I needed.

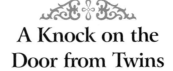

A Knock on the
Door from Twins

*Judy's experience explains why women can
feel a sudden impulse to have a child even though
they feel finished with childbearing.*

A couple in their late thirties had no plans for more children. Judy, a full-time mother, kept busy with four-year-old Timothy and one-year-old Germaine. However, as if following a unseen drummer, Judy received an "urgent phone call from Mother Nature."

The thought came like a knock on the door: "You are destined to have another child and get pregnant right away." Two souls put the thought in my head,"We want in. We want to be born." It was a total contrast to a conscious desire for a child. The twins chose me and somehow knew I was fertile. I felt bewildered and cried because of the awesomeness of the experience.

Judy's husband Ken honored her intuition because she has "a good connection with cosmic intelligence" and frequently senses what is right or wrong.

I was surprised because Judy had never expressed a desire for more children, but I wanted to have a larger family, so I said, "Why not?"

The intentions of the souls seemed authentic to Judy.

We succumbed because the request felt sincere and convincing. We just couldn't say "No." That night when we made love, Ken ejaculated, but he was hardly in me. We thought we needed to try again … eight hours later I woke up with morning sickness.

Mismatched Vibrations

Judy looked forward to two more children. It seemed as if she had some unfinished business in terms of motherhood. Ken felt equally pleased to know that two "special people" were coming into the world. This pregnancy, on the other hand, challenged Judy, unlike the earlier pregnancies.

My heart is normally open to children, but my spirit was far from elevated. I missed the amplification of energy which I felt in my other two pregnancies. They had blessed me with another jet engine and heightened awareness. Instead, the twins created irritability, insomnia, and nausea. I felt dragged down all day and barely held things together. The twin's vibrations didn't match mine. It seemed like my body was carrying another woman's child.

I have been sensitive to a mismatch of vibrations for years. I feel rough and uncomfortable if I am with someone who has a lower vibration. It's nothing personal. It's a question of vibration. If it does not match, it does not match. It's beyond my attention. I have learned that I can be close in heart to someone without being physically proximate to them.

Six weeks into the pregnancy, the whole thing began to fall apart. Everyone was exhausted [including the two souls who were experiencing a difficulty in harmonizing their vibrations and energy with the mother]. I sensed the impending loss and became even more irritable because I knew that I could not hold them. It was a misfit experience.

Meanwhile, Ken encountered his own share of difficulties career-wise.

Judy and I rarely quarreled, but we began to argue, even though I did not want to. Right after that, Judy started bleeding.

Judy relates what happened next.

The souls chose to leave. I lay on the bed and witnessed an extraordinary physical sensation gently rippling up from my uterus to my heart. The souls left one at a time like a gentle burp and then out of my heart. I felt powerless to stop it or speed it up. I just let it take its course. The miscarriage messed me up for a while. It took two months of bleeding and cramping to clean out my womb.

I felt a sense of loss and sadness in their departure. Yet, the miscarriage did not shock me. I had lost the twins on the subtle level before I lost them on the physical. I had known that the pregnancy was not going to make it for a long time. Still, a mother has lost a child. I did not feel any remorse from their side though. The twin souls got what they needed. They were grateful that they could hang in there that long. I have not heard from them since.

Ken similarly regarded the loss as part of a greater plan, rather than an accident.

> I felt bad. I wish the twins had been born. I initially felt responsible because Judy and I had an argument. But Judy assured me that our quarrel merely triggered the whole thing to finally let go. Judy felt that she had done her duty by bringing them into the world, if only for a short time. Apparently the twins needed a faint incarnation to fulfill their desire. So all three benefited in that way.
>
> Right after that, Judy was completely free of any desires to have more children. That was her last pregnancy.

Just as some people trade in their cars every eight years whereas others buy a new car every year, so too, some souls lease their vehicles for ninety years while others lease them a few months. The transitoriness of human life depends on our cosmic contract.

Angels carry our souls from and to Heaven.

Chapter 7
Conversations with
My Unborn Child

Conception takes place in a world
before time .... What is seen in this world
is really the physical expression
of other, greater worlds.[1]

– Rashid Field

Beverly Anderson represents a
sensitive mother who was aware of a child through
all stages – pre-conception, conception, and pregnancy.
The unborn child is now her eight-year-old son.

Beverly is blessed with a gifted awareness that sees through
time and allows knowing future events.

I was born into a genetically predisposed psychic/intuitive family.
So I have always known since I was knee high to a duck that I was
going to have one child – a special son. Most straight folks on the
street do not know about this sort of stuff. But I am psychic and
cannot help but know. I can sit here in this room and hear ten angels
talking at the same time.

Beverly is so sensitive that she knew her son's personality, sense
of humor, outlook on life, and likes and dislikes before he was ever
born: he was going to be "as clean as a whistle and he was going to
have a say on that business."

My son came into this world knowing that people are wonderful.
He does not understand violence or greed. And he often looks at me

stunned when he sees anger. He blinks and says, "Why in the world are they upset? That is nothing to be upset about."

Taylor will be born as your son in twenty years.

Overcoming Cervical Cancer

Before Beverly and her soon-to-be husband Terry
set their wedding date, she told him, "You are going
to get a little boy and that is all you are going
to get." Terry said, "Cool, that will be good."

By a twist of fate, three months prior to their marriage, Beverly was suddenly medically diagnosed with cancer of the cervix.

The doctor advised, "The best option is to have a hysterectomy and blow off this idea of having a child."

I replied, "Oh yeah, I don't think you know the ball game. I am supposed to have a child. He is pestering me to be his Mommy, and he is important. I am going to have this child." I refused to let the doctor remove my uterus.

My doctor respected my intuition. She removed two-and-one-half inches of my cervix and uterus and reformed an artificial cervix. But even then, she said, "The probability of conceiving and birthing a child is ten percent, at best."

The doctor's prognosis appeared accurate despite regular unprotected intercourse for the first six years of marriage.

I found that frustrating. I ached for him. I knew I was supposed to have this child. And I knew Taylor was there. He did not leave me alone. I heard my son laugh. I heard him call me "Mommy." We were old friends. He had been my father in previous lives. So we were having non-linear communications. I knew stuff about him and he knew stuff about me.

Taylor liked to unexpectedly pop into my consciousness whenever I was having fun. He was jealous that he was not getting a chance to play with me. Even as a teenager, I had unexpected thoughts about having a child whenever I was partying. At that time, I wondered, "What does this mean? How do pregnancy and joy connect?" After I had married Terry, I realized that it had been Taylor nagging at me to get off my butt. But of course, my son chilled and waited until I was mature enough to raise him. His normal style, I might add.

Beverly's Secret

Taylor finally decided when he was going to be conceived. Beverly knows the time, date, and the place of conception.

One morning my husband and I were making love. Just as we both orgasmed, the bliss washed through me and I heard Taylor laugh. I felt the kind of calm I feel when I am alone in the forest with only God. It was exquisite.

Something had been missing in my life until then. Taylor is part of my being and I had been yearning to finish me. Now I had finally gotten there. It was time. Taylor is part of me the same way I am part of him. Our pleasure in our connection is still obvious today.

Beverly "got the bingo!" when Taylor's soul connected with the egg and sperm at the moment of love-making.

Time to start. All the pieces of the puzzle meshed all at once. My son knew that his little body was starting and that he could land any time he saw fit.

When they finished making love, Beverly smiled at Terry with a knowing smile. Terry knew Beverly had a secret and asked, "What's so funny?"

I said, "It will be okay. Just chill out." About a week later, with no symptoms being present, Terry felt we were with child, too. My husband who is Chickasaw Indian is very intuitive … being married to me, he cannot be a piece of stone. But we had to wait three weeks before a pregnancy test confirmed it.

In retrospect, Beverly knows why conception was not allowed to succeed despite innumerable opportunities, during six long years.

I was not ready to raise him. I did not have enough joy in my life, not have enough perception of myself. Why should my son step out of eternity into a ball game that was not set up yet? I wouldn't. Why hurry? He came after I went through certain experiences to help me appreciate the preciousness of life, including losing some dear friends.

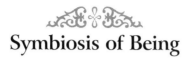

Symbiosis of Being

*It is a challenge for Beverly to
appear normal to the outside world.*

Taylor's soul did not fully enter the fetus until the eleventh week.
She and Terry were driving on Interstate 35 and turning left onto
Highway 183 to go the Renaissance Festival one Saturday morning at
9:30 AM.

> I felt Taylor land in me. He rocked my whole body down to my
> toes. It was the oddest sensation. I was totally blown out of the water
> and lit up from the inside.

> I looked at Terry and said, "Whoa! Did you feel that?" And my
> husband said, "Yeah." I said, "He is there. I can feel him." Before that,
> his body was growing in me, but it wasn't "him." It was just "flesh."
> When he was sure it was going to work out – my son is like that, he
> likes everything to be just so – he went "Okey-dokey."

Beverly experienced "a symbiosis of being" from the instant
Taylor "landed."

> Sure, I had been noticing physical symptoms, but I had not felt a
> being inside of me yet. Now there were two of us in one body. That
> was the oddest weekend. For the first time, I was not completely in
> charge. I was at a Festival having to cope with two of us, deciding
> what we wanted to do. My son and I made agreements on
> everything I did. That was difficult. I don't share some of my stuff
> real well. Neither does my son. We are both dominant and have
> strong opinions. That was quite a weekend – fun, but weird.

Mother/child communication was a stream of energy, rather than
human words arranged in conventional phrases.

> My child was not some foreign little baby yet to be born. I knew
> he was a boy and we treated him like our son from the get-go. We
> carried on conversations in a non-linear way – three-dimensional
> down-loaded reality in the now – feelings, sounds, smells, taste, and
> emotions, all at once. This communication is much rounder and riper

than this little thing called verbiage. That is how we talked and we still do. (I communicate with angels like that, too.)

There was joy in knowing Taylor was near, but also discomfort.

I did not do pregnancy exceptionally well. It is as if I had been living alone in a spacious room with my things just the way I wanted them, when someone else moved in and made the quarters rather tight. Taylor is intense, focused, strong-willed, and very direct – just like me. How do you put two of these souls in one body? That is a lot of noise in a little room.

So, whenever my husband suggested that we go somewhere, I told him, "Let me think about that for a minute and I will get back to you." I then asked Taylor, "Does that sound like a good idea?" I could not make a vote on something alone. It would have been a waste of time to do something without checking with Taylor. If my son kicked and screamed, why bother? Fortunately, we only had few arguments. My son and I tend to like the same stuff.

A Mother's Validation

Taylor is the same person today as he was in the womb. "He has not changed. Taylor is just on the outside now, instead of the inside."

I have a lovely voice and Taylor liked when I sang to him. He stopped kicking and listened whenever I sang opera in the shower. He also responded to Tchaikovsky, Liszt, Chopin, and funky blues. I felt him bumping in rhythm with the boogie music. He got a little groove going on in there. Today he adores jazzy music and does the same little bonk-bomp that he did in the womb. Taylor loves to have a good time. He is a gas of a child.

So music soothed the savage beast as far as Taylor was concerned. It still does. If I need to occupy my son's attention or alter his mood, I pick music. He still refuses to sleep at night unless I sing a lullaby.

Besides music, dance, and rhythm, Taylor calmed down whenever we went to ocean. He still loves the ocean waves today.

In addition to enjoying music, Taylor had opinions about aromatic scents prior to birth.

I have an acute sense of smell and enjoy aroma oils, herbs, and incense. Whenever I shopped for those items, Taylor paid careful attention and registered my tactile sensation of smell in his soul. He was learning through me while yet in the womb.

Souls Waiting in the Wings for Birth

Taylor responded well to exotic smells. My son dragged me over to the cinnamon counter and I stood there smelling cinnamon for ten minutes. He would say, "Yeah! This is really good." Today his favorite smells are still cinnamon, cloves, and apple pie cinnamon.

Prior to my pregnancy, I enjoyed the smell of sage. But, Taylor let me know that he could not tolerate it. It became such an unpleasant experience during my pregnancy that he permanently changed my opinion.

Besides the smell of sage, Taylor did not like licorice and anise. He hates that candy now. He spits it out and makes a horrible face.

Taylor's relationship with his father is the same as it was in the womb.

When I was tired and wanted to sleep and Taylor became restless in the womb, Terry talked to him and massaged him. Taylor immediately fell asleep. Today our son is a non-stop kid. My husband says he only has two speeds: "on" and "off. " Now when Taylor is agitated, all Terry has to do is talk to him, rub his back, and he falls asleep.

Crashing the Party

Beverly was at Taylor's beck and call throughout the pregnancy. Her son overrode and superseded most of her natural inclinations with his own will. Mother and son kept bumping into each other. So Taylor did not just kick and squirm like a baby if he was uncomfortable, he gave his opinion on things so that his mother could avoid the source of his irritation.

Of course, Beverly had free will to listen, such as the time Beverly and Terry were invited to a Christmas party in the sixth month of pregnancy.

I was in the mood to dance and have fun. I had not been anywhere for so long. At the same time, I knew loud noises offended and startled Taylor. So as I dressed for the party, I explained, "I must go to a Christmas party for business reasons. There will be loud music, but I promise not to stay long." Taylor yelled, "I do not like this idea. Please don't go."

Terry and I left for the party anyway. On the way over, Taylor was kicking and squirming, "I don't think this is a good idea." I told Terry, "If the music is too loud, Taylor is not going to let us stay." Terry said, "Okay, when he gets pissed off, tell me and we will go home."

Piped in rock and roll music was coming through the Bose speakers as Beverly and Terry entered the party hall.

Taylor froze and then he started to kick the stew out of me. He said, "I am not putting up with this. This hurts." I did not even drink three sips of my coke before I leaned over and said, "Terry, this is not going to work. Taylor is making me miserable. We must leave right away." We were not there more than fifteen minutes.

Taylor knew what was going to happen and forewarned me. I did not listen and paid for it. He kiboshed the whole evening.The moment we left the party, my son chilled. I felt him sigh in relief, "Aaaah."

I told him, "You little stinker. I looked great for the first time in months and you did not let anybody look at me. I spent two hours getting dressed for nothing." I was so ticked off.

Grapes and Cottage Cheese

Beverly benefited nutritionally from Taylor's input during the pregnancy.

I gave in to eating extra food when I was already satisfied. For instance, ten minutes after I ate dinner – what my body craved and wanted – I was seized with the overwhelming push by him,"Grapes and cottage cheese. Grapes and cottage cheese." It became really loud around the fifth month – pretty much every meal for the longest time.

So I brought out a bowl of grapes and a bucket of cottage cheese. My husband looked disgusted. He said, "You just ate an enormous dinner."

I explained, "I know but I must eat the grapes and cottage cheese. Taylor is telling me this is what he wants." The instant I finished eating, Taylor immediately fell asleep.

Beverly's doctor, a conservative physician, did not advise pre-natal vitamins.

I described my diet and the doctor's eyes become enormous. She said, "There is no reason to put you on pre-natal vitamins." I said, "You are kidding. Everybody takes pre-natal vitamins." (She was my sister's physician and my sister needed them.)

She emphasized, "You are eating exactly the perfect diet. Your proportions are perfect. Your consumption level of vitamin C, calcium, and folic acid (I ate a lot of green leafy vegetables) is usually what we are concerned about. If only I could train people to do that."

Souls Waiting in the Wings for Birth

I said, "I am not consciously doing anything. It is spontaneously happening." I did not explain that my son got me off my butt to eat this stuff so that he got the proper nutrients. She said, "Well, it is perfect."

On every visit, my doctor meticulously documented what I ate. Each time I drilled her, "Are you sure I don't need vitamins?" She always replied, "If you do, you will just O.D."

Even after Taylor began to eat solid foods, he preferred grapes and cottage cheese for nearly eighteen months. Sometimes he let Beverly sneak in rice cereal if it was in the fruit. But Taylor spit everything else out. Taylor's tastes eventually broadened out when his body started growing.

Besides an unsatiable appetite for grapes, cottage cheese, and pistachios, Taylor desired chocolate while he was in the womb.

I have always liked chocolate, but beginning in the fourteenth week of my pregnancy, I had to eat chocolate all the time – sometimes a box of "Godivas" in one sitting. My husband just sat there and said, "Beverly, are you okay?"I told him, "I am great! We are having a blast over here. Leave us alone."

Taylor's favorite foods are still grapes, cottage cheese, pistachios, and chocolate.

Taylor craves and enjoys all the foods I absolutely had to eat during the pregnancy. It is such an obvious correlation. Our son is a "chocoholic" and will do anything, make any deal, for a piece of chocolate.

Taylor enjoyed being a constant house guest throughout the pregnancy.

He did not come and go. No way. You do not blast that child out of where he wants to be. When he landed, he landed for real. He did not take a walk. That would be like telling him to leave his bed without his "blanky." Give me a break. He knows where his bread is buttered and he was perfectly happy there.

I often told my husband, "I am just an incubator for this child. I am a walking, talking incubator. I am just his host. Boy, will I be glad when he is big enough to hatch."

Following Taylor's birth, I thought, "This is good. You are there. I am here. There is a little breathing room. I like that a lot." Then, I chilled with it.

Taylor – A Special Spark

*Beverly's son continues to teach her
just as he did before he was born.*

Taylor has come to Earth to spark empowering transformations.

Now, all mothers think their children are special, but everyone who meets my son is blown away by him. God makes gifts. And this child is a gift. When Taylor was an infant, people commented about his old, wise eyes. Everyone, from shopkeepers to people in lines, noticed that our son was not baby-like: "Notice the way your son looks at things? He is really examining that." Or, "Your son is listening to every word we are saying. How old is he again, four months?"

I said, "Yeah, Taylor has done it since he was born. What is so big about that?" I thought my son's behavior was normal. They said, "Your son is so focused. He is not supposed to be able to do that yet. Babies are supposed to be easily distracted."

Relearning Linear Speech

Taylor strung mature sentences together by the time he was barely two. Four or five syllable words came out of the blue. At first, Taylor did not pronounce them perfectly, but once Beverly reiterated the pronunciation, Taylor said, "Oh yeah," and then added another word to his amazing vocabulary.

One day Taylor said, "What an inexplicable thing" in that very soft baby palate. It came out real soft. His words stopped me dead in my tracks even though he could not perfectly enunciate the consonants. I wondered, "Where in the heck did that come from?"

Even more surprising, when Taylor attended a child care facility at the age of two, he was "talking philosophy on topics."

I thought Taylor's speech was normal because I did not know anybody with children until he started Day Care. I then noticed how the other children were running around babbling. The teacher asked me, "Where did you get this child? Taylor speaks in full sentences like an adult."

So people have always been stunned at the way Taylor uses language. He has never verbalized like a child. He speaks in a precise format like a professor and knows what he is talking about. Each year when he is tested for reading, writing, and comprehension, he consistently scores five or six years ahead of his age group.

Today he is like a forty-year-old in an eight-year-old body. My son does not miss a thing. Taylor is a delight. He knows everything that is going on, on levels that most people are not paying attention to.

Despite Taylor's maturity, he has never lost the joy of childhood.

Taylor is not a little adult with judgment who came into the world. He is a rock and roll little boy. He is a child who plays and has a blast. He did not lose his childishness, innocence, or joy. He is a little kid with a child's imagination and enthusiasm. Taylor just came in glued together pretty tight. He has had more to work with from the get-go. He can even see his angels and talk to his fairies.

Motherhood is the most difficult and wonderful thing Beverly has ever done.

We have always treated my son like an adult in a little bitty body. We talk to him and ask for Taylor's opinion all the time. That does not mean we are not parents and we do not have rules or nurture our son. Don't get me wrong. Taylor is the most nurtured individual I know.

My son is amazing, but he says I am too. It is a mutual rah-rah society. In the middle of this, a very patient, caring, wise man who is my husband, watches us play together. And he says, "I just had Taylor so I could be a kid again."

And Taylor says, "What's wrong with that, Dad?" So Terry knows we have a special bond and he doesn't feel threatened. My husband loves it. It is like having two of us, instead of just me.

PART TWO

PRE-CONCEPTION COMMUNICATIONS DOWN THROUGH HISTORY

The Mountain God *(Sanshin)* visits the dreams of Korean couples bearing a child as a gift. His servant, the mighty tiger, appears in dreams as well, usually promising a son.

*Children's souls have been announcing from a heavenly
abode their pending arrival since time immemorial. Part Two
includes symbolic dreams, angelic annunciations, and prophecies,
as well as direct communications with a child seeking birth,
gathered from biographies of Christian saints, Tibetan
Buddhist lamas, spiritual teachers of India, as well
as political leaders of ancient China, Japan, Persia, and
Greece. Further pieces of the pre-conception story are scattered
throughout ethnological studies of the traditional peoples of
Australia, Africa, Polynesia, Korea, and North America.
Needless to say, our first trip to one of the nation's top
libraries – the University of Texas at Austin – turned
into more than three years of weekly visits
tracking down innumerable reports.*

*These age-old accounts appear to be more than mere
mythical anecdotes considering Part One's contemporary
stories. Modern parents share another common thread
with their ancestors besides the genetic material DNA.*

*It is little wonder that tales of storks and angels
delivering souls of babies have endured late into the
twentieth century. The diversity of cultures reveal a
universal pattern, a bridge between contemporary, ancient,
and indigenous pre-conception experience, and a bridge
across time. Life is more of a tapestry than we realize.*

Chapter 8
Golden Messages
Uncovering the Hidden
Meanings in Dreams

**When the body is asleep the soul is free,
"the king is not in his castle,
the prisoner is not in his cell ... ."[1]**

– Sufism

*Whenever the unconscious mind is off guard,
our intuition surreptitiously travels beyond the five
senses and returns bearing mysterious symbols
in the form of pre-conception dreams.*

Symbolic dreams, rather than straightforward communications with a child, often convey the message of a soul waiting in the wings. Carl Jung's theories shed light on these dream images. Jung believed in a collective unconscious, a storehouse of universal symbols which repeatedly occur within a culture and across cultures. In addition, there is a layer of the mind unique to each individual: the personal unconscious, a storehouse of distinctive symbols, the peculiar mental contents we each have acquired throughout our lives.

Water appears to be a cross-cultural symbol connected to conception and birth, a primordial image shared by humanity since the child is delivered from the uterine waters. The early

Chaldeans "correctly interpreted water dreams as birth dreams."[2] Water dreams come from Africa, Asia, and North America as well.

* Dagomba (Africa) – A man pictures his wife carrying a water pot on her head, a traditional dream symbolizing that she will soon conceive a child.[3]

* Tikopia (Polynesia) – Fishing with a small scoop-net signifies a daughter; sea fishing forecasts a son. Even then, interpretation depends upon the dreamer's age, sex, and profession. More obviously, for a newly-married couple, water dreams signify conception, but for a tribal elder the dream means a fishing expedition.

* Kwakiutl (British Columbia, Canada) – A maternal ancestor appeared to a woman and advised: "Rub your body with hemlock branches in the river behind our village, morning and evening and you will never be sick" – a purification ritual to prepare for conception.[4]

The following dream symbols are unique to a particular culture which interprets them as a sign of a child's conception and birth.

* South Korea – A woman sneaked into her neighbor's chicken coop in order to steal a large, beautiful rooster. The cock then turned "into a Chinese phoenix and sang with a beautiful voice."[5] Within a short period, the woman became pregnant and birthed a daughter. In this case, beautiful songs signify a daughter.

* South Korea – A woman was strolling in an open field which suddenly filled with light. A magnificent rainbow and beautiful white bird then appeared before her. She admired the bird and stroked its tender feathers. The dream immediately preceded conception of a daughter, an intelligent, good-hearted, even-tempered school girl.[6]

* Korea – A bear appeared in the dreams of King Suro of Kayo and his queen on the same night. The bear symbolizes strength and protection and thus represents an ideal king. The couple who had been childless conceived a male child soon afterwards. Their son reigned as the Crown Prince from 199 to 259 AD.

* Ancient China (670 BC) – A heavenly messenger presented the concubine of count Wen of Cheng with an *Orchis* plant, a symbol of nobility. The concubine later conceived and birthed a male child. She named her son Lan, Orchis. When the boy matured, he inherited his father's position and

became the count Mu of Cheng. The count fell ill in his sixty-fourth year, and commented, "As long as the *Orchis* lives, I will not die, because its life is mine… ."[7] Count Mu died shortly thereafter when someone crushed the *Orchis*.

* Islam – A young man who desired children dreamed that someone had placed chicken eggs in his lap. Since chickens were not native to his homeland, but native to Persia, an interpreter advised him to find a wife in Persia. A Persian woman then bore him the desired children.[8]

* Ancient China – Cheng-tsai was walking near a lake one day. She stopped to rest on a grave mound and fell asleep. In a dream, she made love with a Black Emperor. He told her, "You will give birth to a child inside a mulberry tree." As prophesied, Confucius was born fourteen months later, inside the trunk of a hollow mulberry.[9]

* Kwakiutl (British Columbia, Canada) – Four grizzly bears frightened Abayaa while she was picking crab apples at Knight Inlet. Abayaa ran, but not fast enough. One bear caught up with her. The bear, at that point, became someone she knew, a man named Tsanis, who seduced her. "On the way home, I was weeping."[10]

* Kwakiutl (British Columbia, Canada) – Ilis and her husband LELeLEwek were cutting cedar bark in the woods. The couple embraced and had sexual intercourse. Then it occurred to Ilis that LELeLEwek had died long ago. Her husband's spirit explained: "I love you and my life is unhappy since you married NOIbe. You no longer think about me. I will therefore enter your womb and become your child."

  In the next dream sequence, Ilis went to a cedar grove and peeled cedar trees. She tied it into a big bundle and carried the cedar home on her back. When Ilis arrived home, she told her current husband about LELeLEwek's intention. NOIbe became jealous and threatened to beat her. Ilis became frightened and awoke from the dream. She realized that she would birth a son with NOIbe's seed, but NOIbe's life would end prematurely.[11]

* Nigeria (Africa) – A snake dream foretells that a child will be born, or as the Kalabari put it, that "longed-for descendants are about to come."[12]

* King Sansang (3rd century Korea) – The heirless king heard an exalted voice announce, "Do not worry. Your second wife

will bear you a son." The king subsequently kept an eye open for a second wife. Not long afterward, a royal pig escaped from the palace courtyard. No one could catch it but a beautiful, talented village girl. Since the girl caught the pig, it symbolized her bearing the king a prosperous son. The king visited the girl and asked, "Will you bear me an heir to my kingdom ?" The girl agreed under one condition: "Don't let it be hurt by the (jealous) queen."[13]

Additional pre-conception dream riddles heralded the births of Picasso's children; political leaders such as Cyrus and Alexander the Great; Christian Saint David; Chinese emperors; as well as the prophet Moses.

Dreaming Picasso's Children

*Hidden within the life of Spanish painter, sculptor
and ceramist Pablo Picasso (1881 to 1973) is a poorly
known event interconnected with his destiny. Among
the countless books written about the famous Spanish
artist, at least one book[14] describes a dream predicting
the birth of his two children by a common-law
marriage to Francoise Gilot (1922 to –).*

Long before meeting Picasso, Francoise Gilot, a young aspiring painter, had cultivated a habit of recording "out of the ordinary" dreams in her diary. One night, she dreamed of being a tourist visiting famous monuments during a bus tour.

The most mysterious aspect of the bus tour is that instead of stopping at a museum as tours generally do, Francoise and her fellow passengers are "herded" into a goat shed. But rather than goats inside, only a baby carriage is present, with a famous painting by French painter Henri Rousseau nestled inside. A well-known painting, a portrait of a woman by French painter Jean Ingres, is dangling from the handle of the carriage. Francoise had no idea what the dream meant.

Francoise, who had just moved to Paris, met Picasso through a mutual friend shortly after the dream. Francoise was a twenty-one-year-old artist. Pablo approached nearly three times her age. Despite the age difference, a romantic relationship unfolded. The date was 1943. The times were turbulent: German troops occupied Paris, the Nazis were confiscating priceless paintings, and war clouds hung over Europe.

One day when Francoise's love relationship with Picasso had eventually matured, Francoise shared the dream journal with him. Pablo's reaction seemed unexpected. His attention riveted on the symbols of the goat-shed dream. He had admired that particular Rousseau painting so much that he had purchased it. (Whether Picasso made the purchase prior to Francoise's dream or later remains uncertain.)

Finally, as destiny manifested, Francoise gave birth to their son Claude three years after meeting Picasso. She had arranged for Dr. Lamaze to assist. Except, due to unexpected obstacles, Mademoiselle Ingres, a nurse, and Madame Rousseau, a midwife, attended the delivery, and not the doctor. Ironically, M. Ingres parted her hair in the middle and drew it down severely on each side – precisely like Ingres' portrait of the woman in Francoise's dream.

Pablo suspected that these birth circumstances were more than coincidence and the "goat shed" dream puzzled him. Later, after discussing Francoise's dream with a psychotherapist friend, he learned that a goat shed symbolizes a child's birth.

Francoise's dream illustrates how the unconscious communicates years in advance of an important event. An additional twist is that the couple had planned on Dr. Lamaze's assistance. Coincidentally, however, he arrived too late, a point further confirmed by the doctor's absence in the dream. Instead, Francoise's dream forecast a birther who looked like the woman in the Ingres painting.

One more point is that Francoise observed two paintings sitting in the baby carriage, indicating the annunciation of two children. In accord with the dream's accuracy, it was not too surprising when Francoise gave birth to Pomona two years after her brother Claude.

The two births were more unpredictable than the dream suggests. Picasso drank heavily and became abusive, a fact documented in biographies. As a result of his annoying tendencies, Francoise attempted to walk out on him before the pregnancies occurred. Before she had walked very far, Picasso tracked her down along a highway and coaxed Francoise into the car. He told her, "What you need is a child." Picasso may have thought of a child because he subconsciously sensed their destiny interconnected with two children.

Haloed Virtues

The biography of Saint David, the 6th century patron saint of Wales, describes dream symbols forecasting his characteristics.[15]

An angel appeared to Prince Ceredig in a dream and gave him these specific instructions:

> Tomorrow you will discover three gifts while hunting – a stag, a honeycomb, and a salmon. Donate a portion of each to the monastery of Maucannus to be preserved for your son who is yet to be born. Moreover, the place where you locate these items will become the birthplace and monastery of that spiritually-blessed child.

The dream surprised Ceredig, who had taken monastic vows of celibacy and poverty. Nonetheless, the next day he followed the angel's instructions and discovered those items. In one sense, it was a good thing that the prince had been forewarned. For a short time later, Ceredig met the daughter of a chieftain of North Wales on his travels to Dyved. Ceredig ended up seducing Non and she conceived a son, whom we know today as Saint David.

The message of the stag, honeycomb, and salmon are clear today.

- Stag – The antlers symbolize the Tree of Life, purity and light. Darkness disappears wherever the stag goes. With its breath, the stag draws the serpent – the symbol of darkness and subterranean life – out of his hole and tramples it to death. Just as the stag represents purity, Saint David's baptismal water restored a blind monk's sight; a golden-beaked pigeon hovered near young David, whispering divine mysteries into his ear; and in adulthood, a snow-white dove perched upon his shoulder during a sermon. When the crowds grew too large, the earth rose up beneath David's feet to form a hill, so that everyone could hear.

- Honey – An elaborate biological chemical process creates honey and represents Saint David's wisdom to heal others with his touch and to raise the dead. Honey resides in wax, yet remains separate from it. So, too, Saint David lived in the material world, devoting his energy to spiritual acts: teaching, praying, as well as caring for the needy.
- Salmon – Symbol of abstinence and moderation. Saint David lived a life of simplicity and high morality. He founded fifty churches and twelve monasteries where monks tilled the ground without the help of cattle. He and his monks spent their days in silence, speaking only when necessary. Vegetables, bread, and water comprised their daily sustenance. One of Saint David's favorite austerities was total immersion in cold water.

In the end, just as the dream predicted, Saint David established the Monastery of the Deposit – *depositi Monasterium* – at the designated spot where the angel foretold that Ceredig was to find the three gifts.

The angel said, "Preserve these gifts for your unborn son."

Lightning Bolt Heralds Conception

*Dreams announce the arrival of children
destined to leave their mark on history.*

The royal Macedonian couple, Olympias and Philip II, met during their initiation into the sacred mysteries of Samothrace and fell in love. The night before their wedding ceremony, Olympias heard the roaring sound of thunder in a dream. A thunderbolt struck her womb, breaking into a sheet of flame. Flames leaped out in every direction, kindling a brilliant fire. Then, just as suddenly, the flames died out.

Philip had a dream a few days later: he placed an imperial seal bearing the figure of a lion upon Olympias' womb. Aristander of Telmerrus interpreted Philip's dream: "Since it is unusual to seal something that is empty, Olympias is pregnant. The lion's seal signifies a son who will become a bold, spirited, courageous king."

Without much doubt, Alexander lived up to his parents' dreams. History records that Alexander (356 to 327 BC) was taught by Aristotle and acquired a love for Homer and the Heroic Age. His mother's dream illustrates his meteoric life. As King of Macedonia for twelve years and eight months, Alexander conquered a large portion of the civilized world like a wild fire until his untimely departure at thirty-three. Philip's dream was equally accurate. Alexander became one of history's foremost military leaders. The empire of the first western king to be called "the Great" extended from Greece to India.

Oriental Birth Dreams

*The ancient Chinese respected an announcing dream
as a spiritual blessing. Dreams foreshadowing
the birth of royalty serve as two examples.*

Chinese birth dreams dating back 12,000 years include animals of the zodiac which predict the child's sex and personality – mouse, cow, tiger, rabbit, dragon, snake, horse, goat, monkey, chicken, dog, or pig. Any child born without a birth dream experienced mental or physical defects or premature death.[16]

Events foreshadowing a royal son began when Keen-teih, one of Emperor K'uh's concubines, found a black bird's egg resting in the sand. The egg had 800 Chinese characters inscribed upon it, as well as stripes of the five auspicious rainbow colors – blue for East, red for South, yellow for Center, white for West, and black for North.

Keen-teih transported the egg back to the palace. She laid it in a box near her bedside and covered it with a red cloth. That night, an angel appeared in her dream. "If you keep this egg, you will become the mother of a clever son, a fine emperor."

Keen-teih carried the egg with her for a year before conceiving a child. Fourteen months later – an auspicious gestation period – she bore a son who later became the progenitor of the Shang (or Yin) dynasty, traditionally dated 1766 to 1122 BC.

In another instance, an emperor dreamed of a large pig, the color of the Sun.[17] The pig entered one of emperor's palaces. Red clouds subsequently filled the sky, cloaking the palace. Within this red glow, the emperor saw a long dragon. The dragon rested for a while before ascending into the heavens. A dream interpreter later explained: "A son will be born to you in that palace."

Besides indicating the gender of the child, the pig and dragon symbolized personality characteristics and the son's destiny. Pigs symbolize prosperity. And in this case, a gold pig is the color of Heaven and glory. The dragon's presence is a sign of imperial authority and is equally beneficent. The dragon is a complex and multi-tiered symbol – a physical conglomerate of: head of a camel, soles of a tiger, ears of a cow, scales of a carp, horns of a deer, neck of a snake, belly of a clam, and talons of an eagle. The dragon's head even has the *chi'ih nuh* lump, a gas bag which enables the dragon to soar through the sky.[18] The dragon resides in the East representing power and fertility. The dragon's ascension in the dream proclaimed the child as the next emperor.

Considering this interpretation, the emperor asked his favorite wife to move into that palace appearing in the dream. While residing there, an angel appeared in the queen's dream and offered her the Sun, and she ate it. This dream further pleased the royal couple since the solar luminary symbolizes a glorious son.

Within days of the queen's dream, the couple conceived a child. Their son, Wudi (Han Wu Ti; 156 BC to 87 BC) became the most illustrious emperor during the "Celestial Empire" of the Han dynasty. He brought China to a peak of power, wealth, and cultural growth.

Seligson, in his superb collection of Oriental birth dreams, presents 200 dreams out of a pool of 2,000 dreams, occurring before or after conception. He found modern correlations with the emperor's dream such as: a pig appeared in 117 (6%) dreams of the 2,000 dreams – 89 of those 117 dreams (76%) foretold a son's birth; a dragon appeared in 171 (8.5%) of the 2,000 dreams – 143 of those 171 dreams (84%) heralded a son's birth; and the Sun appeared in 29 (1.5%) of the 2,000 dreams – 23 of these 29 dreams (79%) foretold a son's birth.[19]

Contemporary Korean Dreams

*A rich tradition of birth dreams which is about
80% accurate is alive in modern-day South Korea.
Announcing dreams from Professor Frank J. Seligson's book,*
Oriental Birth Dreams, *serve as several examples.*

A Korean woman has a good chance of knowing whether she will bear a son or daughter due to the symbol appearing in a pre-conception dream, such as flowers, fruits, nuts, vegetables, fish, animals, birds, or celestial objects. Interpretation, however, involves more than just dream symbols. Each dream species has a male and female gender – a *yin* or a *yang* aspect. Interpretation must take into account the color, time, space, number, and other physical qualities of the symbol. The same color in some cases may represent different sexes. As an example, the *yin/yang* aspects of hot for boy and cool for girl override color in the choice of sex. So a hot, red pepper foretells a male child, and a sweet, red apple, foretells a daughter. Proper interpretation reveals gender as well as personality traits such as humor, ambition, or patience and so on.

A sampling of traditional dream symbols include:

- ❀ Son – Grapes (resemble testicles); an acorn (inside the shell, resembles a penis); a pigeon; dates; and bears.
- ❀ Daughter – Flowers (soft, colorful, and pretty); strawberries (small, soft seeds of life); a white dove (pure-heart); and rabbits (soft and cuddly).

Son of the Dragon King

A woman strolled along the seashore. In the distance, she observed three boys arguing about a sea turtle beneath their feet. The turtle had three tails and a gold crown on its head. The boys quarrelled about who would cut off its head and take it home for dinner. The woman pleaded with the boys not to harm the turtle and they finally agreed.

The turtle then spoke to the woman, "Thank you for saving my life. As the son of the Dragon King, I can give you anything you desire. Hop upon my back and I will take you on a journey."

The woman hesitated to sit upon the back of the small creature, until the turtle convinced her that there was no need to fear. When the woman finally got on, the turtle expanded in size until he was large enough to carry her.

Shortly after having the dream, the woman became pregnant and later birthed a son, as reflected by the turtle's head which resembles a penis. For that reason, the Korean word for turtle, *chara*, is a colloquial term for penis. Korean folklore further explains that the sea-turtle is the noble minister of the Dragon King, particularly when the turtle has three tails.

Honeymoon Dream

Mr. Song had a dream while he and his bride enjoyed their honeymoon on Cheju Island. A man with long, white hair and a beard called Mr. Song's name three times. Mr. Song recognized the man as his father who had passed away nine years earlier. His father said nothing, but presented Mr. Song with a gift – two walnuts which turned to gold as soon as Mr. Song touched them. Mr. Song in turn handed them to his bride who placed them in a purse.

The father's gift preserved the family line according to dream interpretation. The walnuts symbolize a male child since they resemble testicles. (Six out of seven (85%) walnut dreams investigated by Seligson were correlated with a son's birth.) More than that, walnuts are brain-shaped and symbolize intelligence, and in this case, golden walnuts signify a precocious son.

After waiting only a few months, the newly-married couple conceived a son. By the age of four, the precocious boy had memorized sixty short story books.

Twin Puppies

A woman met an elderly man in her dream. He lived in a house covered with gourds in the middle of a field of ripe grain. The man gave the woman two white puppies. She carried the puppies away, but when she turned back to look at the house, it had disappeared and so had her puppies.

During the next dream sequence, the field of grain became an ocean. Two young girls were now walking in the middle of the sea, coming towards the woman. Dream experts say the puppies signified the two "pure-hearted daughters" whom the woman later birthed, two years apart.

Purple Tapestry

In a sequence of related dreams, Mrs. Kim found herself hanging, as if suspended from a fine spun thread. The upper end of the thread extended high up in the shadows. In one dream, a goddess blessed her with a precious purple cloth, something that is impossible to locate "in the secular city." The angel advised, "Take good care of it." The goddess then held Mrs. Kim's hand. The air became sweet, the ground shook, and Mrs. Kim felt something powerful happen inside her body. Ten months later, she birthed a son.

Mrs. Kim's son remembers coming to this "wonderful world filled with so many beautiful flowers and birds." In the past, he was "a prince with a sad fate." Now, he is "a prince, living a life of mercy and dignity." The purple cloth symbolizes his heritage from "another universe." (Korean culture regards purple as a noble color.)

Gifts from the King of Heaven

A venerable monk appeared in a young woman's dream. He presented her with one large nut which, when placed into her palm, turned into three large, bright, dark brown nuts. She carried these gifts on a journey to a mountain top. There she encountered the King of Heaven. He asked, "What is the purpose of your life?" She replied, "My destiny is to be a good mother for my children." The answer pleased the King who said, "Your sacrifice will be rewarded." Celestial musicians honored her with a beautiful song.

Although it is unclear what type of nut the woman received, a walnut symbolizes an intelligent son, and a chestnut, which is soft inside and prickly outside, indicates the birth of a soft-hearted son or daughter. In this case, two boys and a girl were born to the woman. And as the heavenly king foresaw, she raised the young children after her husband's sudden death.

Heavenly Escorts to Earth

Dream of King Astyages

*Pre-conception dreams can be fraught
with future dangers to the child's life. One
example is Cyrus the Great (599 to 530 BC).
His story comes from Herodotus, the "Father
of History" (484 to 427 BC).*

Two dreams puzzled Astyages, the King of the Medes and ruler of Persia. In the first, his daughter Mandane created so much water that it overflowed his city and the Asian continent. The Magi's interpretation terrified the king: "Mandane's offspring will usurp your throne."

Driven by his worst fears, Astyages prevented Mandane from marrying a Mede when she came of age. Instead, she married Cambyses, a man with a quiet personality; although of noble Persian descent, his status ranked below a middle class Mede.

The king had another mysterious dream within a year after Mandane's marriage: a vine grew from inside Mandane's womb and covered Asia. This dream interpretation reinforced the first. The king ordered Mandane to return home. Upon her arrival, Mandane was pregnant and nearly full-term. At the infant's birth, the king instructed Harpagus to kill his grandson. Ironically, as events turned out, Harpagus passed the order and the newborn onto a herdsman. The herdsman's wife who had just delivered a stillborn convinced her husband to exchange the stillborn for baby Cyrus.

In this unpredictable way, a twist of fate spared the life of Cyrus and led to the end of the Median empire in 549 BC. Cyrus revolted against Astyages and defeated his overlord. The Persians who had long been suppressed by the Medes enjoyed their freedom under Cyrus the Great, an ideal ruler and founder of the Persian Empire.

Cross-Cultural Parallels

Pre-conception dreams warning that a child will bring ruin upon a wicked monarch likewise heralded the births of Abraham, Moses, Perseus, Paris, and Oedipus. Similar prophecies of a divine child resulted in King Herod's attempt to kill the infant Jesus and the evil King Kamsa's attempt to murder Krishna at his birth.

Visionary Signs in the Desert

Yocheved birthed Moses at the age of 130. Subsequently her beauty was restored, skin became resilient, wrinkles disappeared, and her menstrual periods returned.

A Jewish legend relates the Pharaoh's dream of an elderly man who stood before his throne with a merchant's balance in his hand. The old man assembled all of Egypt's material riches along with its elders, nobles, and most illustrious men, and positioned them on one scale of the balance. In the second scale, he set a tender lamb. The baby lamb outweighed all the wealth and power of Egypt.

The troubled Pharaoh awoke and summoned the "Masters of the Secret Things." The spiritual adviser, Balaam, son of Beor, explained the significance of the lamb: a symbol of purity, innocence, meekness, foreshadowing the birth of a Hebrew boy who would destroy Egypt.[20]

The prediction so alarmed the Pharaoh that he ordered all newborn males of Israel to be drowned. Of course, no matter what Pharaoh tried, his plan was doomed to fail. Moses, the ancient prophet, fulfilled his destiny and delivered the 600,000 Hebrews from their bondage under Egypt.

Chapter 9
The Time Before Time Began
Spirit-Children Down Under

They say we have been here for 60,000 years,
but it is much longer … . We have lived and
kept the Earth as it was on the First Day.
All other peoples of the world came from us.[1]
— Australian Aborigine Elder

*Communications with the unborn
may be as old as human life itself.*

Aboriginal peoples of Australia, a territory slightly larger than the U.S., had unique economic, political, social, and linguistic characteristics. At the same time, they shared one extraordinary belief: conceiving a child is founded in a spiritual event – a "spirit-child" selects his parents and this event enables biology to take its course. A Forrest River Aborigine, as a prime example, dreams of a spirit-child playing with his spears or his wife's paper bark; the husband thrusts the spirit-child toward his wife and it enters by her foot.[2] Conception then proceeds into pregnancy (except in certain cases where conception occurs several years later).

The term spirit-child roughly equates with the Western concept of the soul. Aside from that similarity, the Aboriginal pre-conception paradigm contrasts with science's understanding of pregnancy. The first anthropologists to hear Aboriginal pre-conception reports assumed that the spirit-child pre-empted the role of male sperm and labelled this notion "the most elementary belief concerning the genesis of the individual."[3]

Even more puzzling, Aborigines held their belief after learning about biological conception as an accidental collision of sperm and egg. They contended that sexual intercourse, though it may prepare the way for the child's entry into the womb, by itself is not the sole cause of conception – since a spirit-child is necessary. As elucidated by anthropologist Ashley Montagu:

"The Aboriginal world is essentially a spiritual world, and material acts are invested with a spiritual significance … .The spiritual origin of children is the fundamental belief, and among the most important stays of the social fabric. It is absurd then to think … intercourse could be the cause of a child."[4]

This chapter gathers spirit-child pre-conception dreams, waking visions, and related omens from nineteen Aboriginal groups as reported in anthropological research journals and books published from the late 1800s into the 1900s. The chapter concludes with a study highlighting modern culture's impact on this spirit-child phenomenon.

Spirit-Children

*A Tiwi legend explains the history of spirit-children.
In ancient times, spirit-children were transported to
Earth in the bark canoe of the Great Mother's son. His
sisters birthed the spirit-children. With the passage
of time, the son married and his wife selected parents
for each spirit-child. Finally, before the son returned
to whence he came, he made the spirit-children
responsible for choosing their own parents.*

Aborigines have "a long spiritual history behind them."[5] Prior to conception, every Aborigine exists as a spirit-child who "exhibits a certain amount of liberty of choice"[6] in selecting parents, tribal division, and class. A contemporary researcher who lived with the Aborigines elucidates the spirit-child concept:

"The new life which has chosen to enter the woman is a complete entity who has originated at some time in the long distant past, and is immeasurably more ancient and completely independent of any living person."[7]

Spirit-children are tiny, fully developed babies.

* Ngalia – Spirit-children have dark hair with light-colored streaks. They sit under shady trees, waiting for a compatible mother to pass by. Meanwhile they eat the gum of acacia trees and drink morning dew.[8]

* Tiwi – Spirit-children are small dark-skinned people who are two to three inches high, but reach nine inches in maturity.

* Western Australian Aborigines – Spirit-children are as small as walnuts and wander over the land, playing in pools like ordinary children. Their favorite food is a green weed called *ginda:l*.[9]

* Central Australian Arunta – A spirit-child is the germ of a complete preformed individual,[10] about the size of a tiny, red, round pebble.[11]

Map of Australia

Messages from the Dream World

Aborigines learn techniques to become "increasingly lucid in sleep."[12] They know how to act consciously in a dream and bring messages from a spirit-child back "into the awakened world."[13] Representative dreams from Tiwi, Worora, Unambal, and Ungarinyin Aborigines follow.

Spirit-child dreams are the "catalysts" that transform a spirit-child "from the world of the unborn to that of the living"[14] A small dark-skinned spirit-child, two to three inches high,[15] reveals its name to a Tiwi and expresses a desire for birth. If the man has several wives, he chooses the most appropriate mother and describes her whereabouts to the spirit-child.

A number of Tiwi pre-conception dreams illustrate how ancestors remain connected to earthly affairs. A departed father knew that his son had no offspring. That is why he retrieved five "spirit-children from Karslake Island"[16] and brought them to his son. The five spirit-children manifested in the son's dream during an afternoon nap in the mangrove swamp. The girls addressed him as "Papa." The aspiring father agreed and said, "Come along."

That night the Aborigine "felt" a spear hit his head. He roused his wife, and accused her of hitting him, "Look here, I got hurt."[17] "No, no. I did not hit you," the wife said in her defense. The husband had been dreaming of the spirit-children. Within the coming years, all five children joined their family.

Old Tjamalampua recounts a similar dream in which his departed father's spirit, *mopaditi*, sat a tiny spirit-child on his knee saying, "This is your daughter."[18] Tjamalampua accepted the blessing and directed the spirit-child to one of his wives, who later gave birth to the spirit-child.

One young Tiwi man's dream occurred six years prior to his son's birth. In the dream, Bos saw a pilot involved in an air battle. The enemy shot his plane down, and wounded the pilot's arm and leg. The injured spirit-child approached Bos and said:

> You are my father, but I will send my sister to be born first. I must go to America to get good medicine. I will be born to you in six years. You will recognize me.

Sure enough, the moment Bos saw the newborn's crooked arm and leg, he said, "This is the son I dreamed."[19]

A man's dream is the root cause of pregnancy, according to the Unambal and Worora Aborigines. In such a pre-conception dream, the man's soul can wander around in the country and meet a spirit-child, usually at a sacred water pool where the man's own soul originally "emanated."[20] After dreaming about the spirit-child, he hands it over in a second dream to his wife.

Aspiring Worora fathers who sleep near the water pools (*wungguru*) typically dream of a rock python, a supernatural being, who comes bearing a spirit-child in its mouth as a gift. Nine months later, the father names the newborn after the water pool where he "conceived" him.

Ungarinyin husbands sometimes "find" a spirit-child in a dream when they are away from home. On these occasions, an Aborigine captures the spirit-child and ties it in his hair until he returns to his wife. He transfers the spirit-child by placing it near his wife or on her navel. The spirit-child enters the wife's womb, "though not necessarily at once."[21]

Cross-Cultural Parallel

Just as the Ungarinyin Aborigine witnesses the spirit-child on his wife's navel, Sufi teacher, Vera Corda has observed pregnant women with "a tiny electric blue, whirling light"[22] over their belly buttons – the incoming child's soul. Corda explains that the soul is entranced by the thought-forms created by the couple's love and is captured willingly. The soul's light increases in strength and size as pregnancy advances.

The Rainbow Snake

*Aborigines exhibit such a high level of sensitivity
that they not only meet spirit-children via a subtle
dream, they find them while hunting or gathering food.
Examples come from the Murinbata, Unambal,
Worora, and Forrest River Aborigines.*

Aborigine men often experience omens, see fleeting images, or hear a spirit-child's "voice in the wind or water" calling "father."[23] A spirit-child picks out a suitable Murinbata man, sits upon his shoulder, and rides home with him after the hunt. The "father" hears the spirit-child whispering into his ear, or feels him tweaking his hair or making his muscles twitch.

Men in the Forrest River region observe spirit-children riding on the back of the legendary Rainbow Snake. The sacred spirit of fertility carries spirit-children along the rivers and lakes where potential fathers are fishing. When a spirit-child sights a man to his liking, he calls, "father." A receptive man brings the spirit-child home by securing him in his hair which is smeared with red ochre, drawn back and bound with hair string.

In another illustration from the Forrest River region, a spirit-child played a game with a man who quenched his thirst on the way home from a hunt. As the young man pushed aside a green weed, a frog jumped out of the water and startled him. That night, a spirit-child appeared in a dream, asking, "Will you be my father?" The man directed the spirit-child towards his wife.[24] Once pregnancy was confirmed, the man regarded the frog incident as a precursor to the spirit-child dream.

A third Forrest River Aborigine man who had been hunting pelican and duck on a nearby island realized that fatherhood was around the corner. The Rainbow Snake of fertility had trailed him as he swam back home. Even more mysteriously, when he reached dry land, a "mob of emus" disappeared as soon as they smelled his approach. The following day he returned to the enchanted spot to hunt. That night his wife prepared one large bird for dinner.

The next morning the man remarked, "I bin dreamin' spirit-child."[25] Within a relatively short time, his wife conceived their son Wallanang. After some reflection, the Aborigine explains, "The spirit of our son imbued the emu with his essence and permitted me to catch him. Unknowingly I conveyed the spirit-child home and my wife connected with the spirit-child by eating the bird."

In certain cases, an Unambal or Worora Aborigine man will find a spirit-child when he "sees" a tiny snake or fish suddenly appear and disappear. Then, for some reason, he keeps the spirit-child for years fastened in his hair[26] before transferring the spirit-child to his wife.

Rainbow Snake

Bloomfield River Omens

*Koko-yalunyu women know when
a spirit-child comes to camp.*

Prior to a child's conception, Yalungur, the creator of spirit-children *(mulgal-mulgal)*, advises the spirit-child: "Now, go find a mother, but do not let anyone see you." For this reason, a woman sees what she believes is a snake in her blanket, but when she looks again, she cannot find it; another woman collecting tree-grubs notices that her bag suddenly becomes full; while a third woman sees three butterflies fluttering in the wind.

A few months later, a spirit-child stirs inside each woman's womb. She reminds her husband, "Ah, that was the snake I saw, but when I looked again, it disappeared;" or "That was my invisible helper who helped me collect tree-grubs;" or "That was the spirit-child suggestively hovering, as it searched for a mother."

Spirit-child visits can be even more covert. One young woman observed an empty canoe coming up Bloomfield River. The canoe somehow travelled against the current, even though no one was paddling, or pulling it upstream. Then, the canoe vanished before the woman's eyes. The local people searched, but found nothing.

In retrospect, the woman concluded, "A spirit-child seeking a mother brought the spirit canoe up river. As soon as the spirit-child saw me, it entered my womb. That is why I became pregnant."

The tribal elder narrating this story added, "White people have a different way, but with black people these things happen."[27]

The Trickster

Couples relate simultaneous spirit-child visits,
as stories from the Bardi, Murinbata,
and Murngin Aborigines illustrate.

Saying "No" to a Spirit-Child

A spirit-child senses when parents reject him. Still, as one Bardi couple reports, the spirit-child tries to change their minds by reappearing in various forms. The spirit-child *(nagarlata)* first appeared in Nangor's dream. The following day, Nangor sensed something peculiar about the large whitefish he speared. That night, the spirit-child visited Nangor and his wife in their dreams. Nangor explained, "We are not ready to start a family."

The next day, as Nangor and his wife collected honey, they sighted an unusual turkey. Nangor speared the bird and the spirit-child quickly passed between Nangor's legs and entered his wife, who followed not too far behind.

Nangor's wife birthed a son in short order. The parents connected their child's spirit with the spirit of white fish and turkeys due to the pre-conception experiences. They are one body and one blood. As a result, the boy must refrain from killing or eating these foods for his entire life. To do so invites illness.

Riding the Wind Currents

Spirit-children are so mobile that they travel to distant places following prospective parents wherever they go. That is why strong winds suddenly awakened one Murinbata couple in the middle of the night. A southerly wind blew the husband's clothes and money outside the hut.[28] This wind also carried a spirit-child to them from their home village located to the south. Sure enough, in due time, the couple conceived and birthed a child.

Encounter with a Bream Fish

A bream fish silently approached a Murngin woman who was fishing in ankle-deep water. The fish grabbed her hook, shook himself against her leg, broke the fish line, and vanished into deep water. The woman noted: "My father experienced a similar encounter with a bream fish prior to my brother's birth. This fish shook against my leg for that."[29] Menstrual periods would stop now "because that baby fish is inside me."[30]

That night the woman's husband had a "nice dream." A tiny boy passed through the village. He knew exactly where to go. He thumped on the bark wall of the man's hut and called, "Father! Father! Where are you?" The husband replied, "Here I am." The spirit-child asked, "Where is mother?" He directed the spirit-child to his wife.

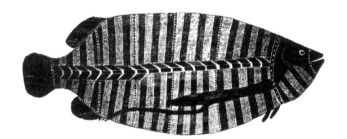

Aborigine Fish

⚜ Spiritual versus Biological Paternity

*Infants are free to form paternal relationships
within the tribe that are both spiritual and biological
because an Aborigine child is not related by blood to any
living relatives. That is why some children have two fathers:
a biological father whose sperm unites with his mother's egg,
as well as a spiritual father who meets him in a dream.*

Daisy M. Bates, more than any other outsider, understood the Broome District Aborigines. This gentle English woman pitched her camp and lived a nomadic lifestyle with the Aborigines for nearly forty years. Bates learned 188 of their dialects and won their confidence. The Aborigines trusted this foreigner with sacred totems and invited Bates to ceremonies which tribal women were barred from witnessing. King George V acknowledged Bates by making her a Commander of the Order of the British Empire in 1933.

Bates discovered something unusual about the Aborigines: paternity is the responsibility of the spirit-child rather than the father's sexual act. A man's dream determines his fatherhood rather than his sperm. So firm was the spirit-child paradigm among Broome District Aborigines that no man acknowledged paternity unless he had met the spirit-child in his sleeping hours. In one instance, a husband accepted a child born to his wife during their five-year separation, thereby ignoring the lapsed time between intercourse and birth.[31]

An anthropologist found parallel beliefs among Tiwi Aborigines. Larry, as a case in point, accepted his wife's child as his own spiritual daughter upon returning after a two-year absence. Larry's daughter had appeared to him in a dream during the couple's separation. She touched Larry with a spear and asked, "Where is my mother?" Larry described how to find Dolly at Snake Bay.

One full moon night, upon Larry's return to his wife Dolly, he walked along the beach cradling his wife's infant in his arms. He was delighted with his wife and ecstatic about their newborn daughter, even though he was not the biological father. He sang to the baby about "the spirit land from which all people came and to which they return on death."[32]

Bates cites further Broome District reports of men who denied paternity even if the couple had never been apart. In such cases, the men did not have a spirit-child dream or dreamed of a daughter, but their wives birthed sons or vice versa. In these cases, the mother must locate the "real" father who had the spirit-child dream.

Stolen Children

An Aborigine husband must be protective of a spirit-child until the transfer of the spirit-child to his wife takes place. If he is careless, another man may steal the spirit-child. That is what happened to a Forrest River man when he presented a shell gift to a friend. The spirit-child followed the friend home, introduced himself in a dream, and was birthed by the friend's wife.[33]

For similar reasons, the Nyul-Nyuls exercised caution upon offering food to a friend's wife.[34] Otherwise, the spirit-child follows the food into the woman. In one case, the "stolen" spirit-child introduced himself to the man's friend in a dream, saying: "You are not my 'true' father, but you must act as my father for I will be born through your wife due to your friend's action."

Another report tells of a Bardi woman who birthed a "stolen" son after her husband trespassed into another tribe's territory to spear a mullet fish. As a result, a spirit-child belonging to the mullet totem accompanied the man home and entered his wife. In this case, their son spiritually belonged to a "father" of the neighboring tribe.[35]

"Spirit-children thefts" typically took place among Unambul, Kambera, Pela, Miwa, Kuna, Uriat, and Taib Aborigines. A missionary commented, "How they know when a child is stolen is a mystery to me."[36]

⸎

Rebirth Down Under

Bardi, Murngin, and Tiwi Aborigines believe
spirit-children live a series of human lives. They chose
rebirth and intentionally select parents, in some
cases knowing them, and in other cases, not.

Nangor, a Bardi Aborigine, felt someone pulling on his belt from behind as he was walking home from the burial ceremonies of a tribal son. Nangor turned to see the spirit of the deceased tribal son. That night, the boy's spirit appeared in a dream, asking, "May I be born as your son?" Of course, Nangor agreed.

Narnarngo, a father from the Murngin Aborigines, recounts a related example. Several days following the premature death of Narnarngo's son, the father walked past a sacred water hole where he sensed his child's departed spirit resided. That night, Narnarngo's departed father announced in a dream, "I'm bringing your son back to you." Following a nine-month wait, Narnarngo reunited with his child when his wife birthed a baby resembling the first son.[37]

A Tiwi Aborigine father reported a similar experience. Although the love bond between parents and children continues in the spirit world, spirit-children sometimes seek birth from strangers. As a prime illustration, Muramajua did not know the spirit-child who introduced himself in a dream.[38] The Japanese boy had died in a plane crash in a previous life and wanted to join the family. Muramajua purified the spirit-child in fresh water for three days prior to putting the spirit-child near his wife.[39] As an interesting side note, Muramajua worked with the Australian Navy fighting the Japanese during World War II.

Lost Visions

*Aborigines reported fewer pre-conception dreams
once Western religion, rationalism, and
science spread throughout Australia.*

European anthropologists named the indigenous peoples of Australia "Aborigines" – a less than complimentary Latin term which means "from the beginning," and implies the most backward people on Earth.[40] But little did the white visitors know that Aboriginal "clever men" had foreseen their coming.

The Euahlayi *wirreenuns* who gazed into crystals beheld future visions which "filled their minds with dread."[41] They sensed the invading culture, much like seeing a fin of the shark before the shark arrived near shore. Indeed, in the end, sixty million Aborigines perished through plunder, massacre, enslavement, and dispossession.[42] The Australian government recently announced a public apology for the official sanctioning of planned Aboriginal genocide in requiring adoptions of the children into white families.

Cross-Cultural Parallel

Foresight of this kind is widespread among traditional peoples. The Sioux prophet, Black Elk, glimpsed the breakdown of Native American culture fifty years ahead of time. He accurately predicted the white man's garments and weapons. Before the invention of the steamboat, another Sioux medicine man described a "fire boat" that would swim upon the mighty Mississippi.

Dr. Andreas Lommel's Study

A number of subtle factors contributed to population decline of Aborigines, as Dr. Andreas Lommel discovered. As part of the

Frobenius Expedition in 1938, Lommel studied modern culture's impact on Aborigines in the Kimberly Division of Northwestern Australia. The German ethnologist interviewed Ungarinyin, Worora, and Unambal Aborigines, including "civilized" Aborigines and those on the fringe of settlement, as well as the "untouched" who maintained their heritage.

To begin with, Aborigines who had been raised on missions and government stations knew little more about hunting kangaroos with spears or collecting edible roots than a typical white man. These stock boys, farm-hands, and laborers had adopted European dress and preserved only fragments of their native language. The American cowboy, as they knew him from Wild West films, served as their hero.

The assimilated men differed from their forefathers in another significant way. They were losing the ability to have "proper" spirit-child dreams. Birth rates were decreasing. As a result, despite excellent economic and sanitary conditions, one-tenth of the 200 members of the Worora in the Kunmunja Mission was under twenty, typical of a population in decline.

A missionary's advice, "Increase sexual contact with your wives," fell upon deaf ears. The Worora knew that conception depends upon a spirit-child's will to be born. The physical sex act was "more or less insignificant," even though the men had been educated about male sperm.

In Lommel's discussions with the Aborigines, the men offered one reason for fewer spirit-child dreams: "Sleep must not be too heavy." The dreamer must remain alert and sensitive, even as the body rests. When a man dreams like that, the spirit-child's name enters his heart; then, it "goes into his head" and the man becomes "fully conscious" of it.[43] If, on the other hand, a man lacks "strength either in his heart or in his head,"[44] he does not catch the spirit-child's name, and is unable to pass that spirit-child onto his wife. In essence, the Aborigines attributed proper dreams to a duality of consciousness event, an alert mind and resting body – comparable to conscious dreams as defined by yogis who pursue a meditative lifestyle.

The Aborigines began to accumulate modern stress once they left the tranquil, silent life of the bush where they had practiced sacred ceremonies and had time to contemplate and meditate.

They lost the "zest for living" in government missions where "moonlit evenings are silent, or broken only by the muttering of the card-players or a sudden burst of quarreling."[45]

The Unambal Aborigines

Lommel spoke to Aborigines who hid in the backcountry away from white men. The lifestyle of the Unambal, as a prime case, remained unchanged. Kangaroos were abundant and economic conditions remained favorable. The government prohibited visiting adventurers, traders, and settlers from entering Unambal territory.

The Unambal reported falling birth rates however. And instead of spirit-child dreams, they encountered nightmares. Even though the Unambal had never seen a white man, they were irritated by the rumors and dreamed of "white men who looked pale like the spirits of the dead," devices flying overhead, and strange lighted steamboats that passed in the night.

News of the approaching civilization upset their peace of mind. The Unambal no longer attained the psychological "disposition necessary for the physical act of generation." In a sense, the Aborigines were suffering from a kind of psychic shock. As Lommel put it, the spirit-child dream might well be "indispensable" for biological conception. In his opinion, the Aborigines' grievances were "justified."

Traditionally, if an Aborigine could not find a spirit-child on his own, he "borrowed" a spirit-child's name from a "clever man or woman." These individuals can see a spirit-child's appearance down to the last anatomical detail and can encourage a spirit-child to enter a woman's womb.[46] Lommel discovered, however, that just as fear and stress kept husbands from "catching a spirit-child's name," clever men lost their powers "because the whole psychic atmosphere of the natives is disturbed."[47] Aborigines lamented, "There are no more clever men. No one knows their secrets."

Robert Lawlor, who writes of personal encounters with the Aborigines (1991), independently agreed with Lommel. An Aboriginal elder explained how inner fears work to break the glimpse of a "web of intersecting threads on which the scenes of the tangible world as well as dreams and visions are hung."

Young men talk and act smart, but "they no longer have the vision, 'cause they have the same fear inside as white fellas." They can't go into the bush and find roots and fruits to eat like I do. They are "frightened inside like a little child who has lost his mother and with that fear the vision of the spirit world departs."[48]

What remains to be seen is whether the Aboriginal spirit-child tradition will ultimately renew itself, given the pressures of modern culture. What the Aborigines need is "the wild world of nature ... as a tonic to the soul."[49]

Cross-Cultural Parallels

Aborigine medicine men were not alone in experiencing a loss of their *raison d'etre* with the onset of modernization. As the Jesup North Pacific Expedition in the 1920s learned from the Siberian Yukaghir, "Ancient shamans knew everything, the modern ones do not."[50]

In Kenya, Africa, Carl Jung observed this socio-spiritual trans-formation as well. The talkative Elgonyi people became reticent when Jung inquired about dreams. Jung discovered the reason when he conferred with the *laibon* or medicine man.

Tears came into the old man's eyes as he replied: In times past, the *laibons* saw the future in dreams, and advised the people of war, sickness, drought, or where the herds should be driven. But since the white man came to Africa, no one had dreams like that anymore. "The Divine voice which counselled the tribe was no longer needed because the English know better."[51]

Ethnologists studying Native American cultures noted a related pattern with the onset of modern culture. Dream content dealt more with individual psychology and less with "culture pattern dreams."

The clash of modern and ancient tribal cultures is demonstrated again by visions of the Maori people. On the one hand, the South Pacific people were recognized as highly intelligent and possessing phenomenal memories as two examples highlight. One is where a Tuhoe elder recited 406 songs that had never been written down, and a second case is an elder whose genealogical recall of his clan included over 1,400 personal names.[52] But outside skeptics, on the other hand, criticized the visionary perceptions of the Maoris. One woman suddenly observed the departing soul of a lady whose wake was being attended by community members: "There she goes. It is Te Rangi Ahui. I saw Te Rangi Ahui glide over your heads, and disappear into the brushwood yonder."[53] A skeptical anthropologist, present at the dirge, described the woman's vision as an "hallucination" of a temporarily insane creature.

"We have only one wind break, one fire, and one blanket each. We huddle together to keep warm in winter. Mum often has to get up to stoke the fire, and it's then that I see her crawl back into my Dad's blanket. I hope you don't think I was conceived and born as the result of sexual intercourse which takes place there ... .

Mum and Dad know that I was created by a spirit entering her body. You laugh? Nonsense, you say? Yet I heard you say you were a Christian. If that is so, you must believe in virgin birth, in immaculate conception. Then why laugh at us if we think babies are formed by spirit-children who pass into the mother while she sleeps? ...

If you want to argue the point ... why not come out here to see us at Yuendumu settlement? We could give you a windbreak and a fire and we'd find a spare blanket for you. Or do you believe that babies are found under cabbages?"[54]

— Wailbri Tribe, Central Australia

Chapter 10
Near-Death Visions
of Souls Seeking Birth

**Touching the future I desire to make a prediction;
for I am at the point where men foresee the
future best – when they are soon to die.[1]**

– Socrates

*More than dreams or visions, pre-conception
communications transpiring during near-death experiences
(NDEs) transcend normal waking consciousness.*

Ancient Greek philosophers were among the first to account for the abrupt change in consciousness occurring on the edge of life and death: Aristotle explained that "a man's soul is never more active than when he is at the point of death;"[2] Xenophon taught that the soul becomes even more divine and able to foresee the future at the advent of death; and Socrates, on his deathbed said, "I am at the point where men foresee the future best – when they are soon to die."[3] Socrates foresaw the destinies of the men who had voted to condemn him.

History documents the transformation of individual awareness taking place on the border between life and death into modern times, including:

❀ Europe (Middle Ages) – People respected the dying "as prophetic souls, voyagers and pilgrims valuable to the community in a number of ways ... they provided those around them service and spiritual growth."[4]

- Callanus (4th century BC India) – Alexander the Great ordered Callanus' death. He ascended the funeral pyre without fear, saying, "Ah, glorious death! When the flames consume my physical body, my soul shall come forth into the light." Alexander asked, "Callanus, do you care to say anything else?" Callanus added, "Yes, indeed; I shall see you very soon."[5] And so Callanus did; Alexander died a few days later.

- Ancient Greece – In his death bed, a man from Rhodes correctly foresaw the deaths of six men, and listed the order in which the deaths would occur.[6]

- Judaism – In his final hour, Moses predicted the future of the tribes of Israel. (*Deuteronomy* 33) Jacob likewise cognized the future of his sons and said, "Gather yourselves together, that I may tell you that which shall befall you in the last days."[7] And when Jacob had made an end of commanding his sons, he gathered up his feet into his bed, and yielded up the ghost, and was gathered unto his people.

- Shakespeare – Nerissa says, "Your father was ever virtuous, and holy men at their death have good inspirations."[8] And the dying John of Gaunt declares: "Methinks I am a prophet new inspired, and thus expiring do foretell of him."[9]

- Curleen Beicker (contemporary USA) – Glen visited his wife Sandra's hospital bedside. She told him, "Don't be rude. Step aside." Glen did not understand. Curleen explained, "You are standing in front of Aunt Alvenia and Uncle Adolph [deceased relatives]." Glen asked, "Why are they here?" His wife replied, "They told me it was all right to come on over. They have prepared a place for me. They will be meeting me in a couple of days and I will be going over there." Sandra passed over several days later.

Individuals in their final moments see future possibilities, including children yet to be born. Saint Buite accurately foresaw the birth of a renowned Irish saint as if it were already set in motion:

> Thirty years from tonight in this location, a child will be born who will become "glorious" and inspire awe and admiration. He will have twelve disciples and he will discover my grave and the decaying foundation rocks of my church. Our association will exist in Heaven and on Earth.

History affirms that Saint Buite predicted the time and birth place of the 6th century Saint Columba, a saint so holy "that no one for centuries could speak or write of him in any but extravagant term."[10] Columba founded one of the oldest monasteries in Ireland (Manister-Buite).

Much like Saint Buite's vision of a future child, individuals who report near-death experiences (NDEs), meet children waiting to be born. Included are testimonies gathered from contemporary best-seller books and academic journals.

Angel with Swanlike Wings

Near-Death Experiences

*NDErs who report experiencing sensations of peace,
floating upwards through a tunnel of light, and finding
themselves in a beautiful kingdom, lend support to
the theory that the tunnel is the passageway souls
use to come down from Heaven to be born.*

NDErs suggest that not only do our souls have a pre-earth life, but we also have a destiny to be born to certain parents. Prior to being resuscitated, these individuals who were supposedly "dead" chose to return to their injured physical bodies; otherwise they will miss out on the children waiting to be born to them.[11]

Choosing Children

RaNelle Wallace had no desire to return from her heavenly "home" and reenter her injured body following an accident.[12] But as events unfolded in the NDE, her deceased grandmother managed to change the young girl's mind when she introduced RaNelle to Nathaniel, a soul planning to be born. The young man wept and pleaded: "RaNelle, why are you here? I cannot fulfill my work on Earth without you." RaNelle realized how each individual's mission is intertwined with the life missions of others. She returned to birth a special son, Nathaniel.

Bertha, a Canadian mother, visited a similar realm where souls prepare for earthly life. A guide escorted Bertha to a room filled with children. Two beautiful girls captured Bertha's heart. "Do you want them?" her guide asked. Bertha replied, "Yes, may I return to Earth and become their mother?" The escort answered, "Yes, that is precisely the purpose of your visit, to see these girls."[13]

A year later (1914), Bertha birthed Alberta, her thirteenth child. And two years later, LaVirle came into the world. Bertha insisted that these two daughters were the same girls she had met when she toured the world of future children.

JoAnn, like RaNelle and Bertha, stopped breathing and journeyed to a wonderful place of brilliant white light and peace. All of a sudden, JoAnn found a beautiful, blond-haired, blue-eyed infant in her arms. A spiritual being behind JoAnn explained, "This is your daughter, Virginia."[14] The little girl's appearance matched the daughter JoAnn had always dreamed of. "Virginia was very slow in coming to earth," but JoAnn's daughter was born – a mirror-image of the infant JoAnn had held in the spirit world.

Men also meet future children via NDEs. Henry Zollinger's body remained lifeless for eight hours after a hay derrick crushed him in August 1920. Meanwhile, a guardian angel showed Henry the spirits of the children destined to be born to him if his family remained "faithful." The children waiting for birth were fully grown and dwelled in a separate sphere from Henry's ancestors.[15]

Mark and Andy

Children meet future siblings destined for human birth. That is why the first question Katie asked upon awakening from a near-death coma was: "Where are Mark and Andy?"[16] No one understood seven-year-old Katie until she explained what had happened following her near-drowning accident. At first, Katie remained in a dark space where she was unable to move or speak. Suddenly a tunnel opened up and she met her guardian angel Elizabeth. The angel escorted Katie to a place where she met the Heavenly Father and Jesus. Katie conversed with Mark and Andy, two young boys expecting to go to Earth in the immediate future.

Katie talked about the friends she had met at the end of the tunnel throughout her convalescence and drew pictures of Mark and Andy as ordinary schoolmates.

Highway to Heaven

A pregnant woman's connection to the land of unborn children becomes even more apparent when she has an NDE. These women travel through a cosmic passageway, much like a hollow tube, and meet children who will be born to them in a subsequent pregnancy.

Jean Scott's pregnancy ended with a D&C (dilation and curettage). When she recovered from her surgery, Jean reported that her spirit had floated towards a warm, bright, golden light at the narrow end of a tunnel. On the other side, Jean felt drawn to an open area. There she joined a gathering of people and met two souls desiring to be her children.

Since Jean's pregnancy had nearly taken her life, the doctor warned against future pregnancies. Be that as it may, Jean felt a bond to the two souls seeking birth. She sensed that her life's tasks somehow involved bringing them into the world. So in spite of two subsequent miscarriages, Jean eventually birthed the children who dwelled on the upper end of the tunnel.[17]

Another woman's near-death journey, triggered by a miscarriage, took her through many dimensions, passing through geometric forms – circles, triangles, and squares. As she approached a brilliant white light, an angel reminded her, "Have you forgotten your commitment to be a mother?" Although she had free will to stay in the spiritual world, she witnessed a vision of the child and changed her mind. She birthed that child several years later.[18]

Kathleen Martinez had agreed to accomplish certain tasks on Earth prior to birth. Some of these commitments were long forgotten until her spirit encountered a gathering of deceased family members during an NDE. They reprimanded Kathleen and expressed disappointment in Kathleen who, as a single mother of three, had conceived a child following a divorce. Kathleen promised to alter her life style, and they agreed to give her a second chance.

Thereupon Kathleen's spirit encountered a wise male spirit with piercing eyes, about ninety years old. He ultimately had free will to chose human birth, and if he did, Kathleen sensed that he was destined to be her son. Following this realization, Kathleen saw a white, brilliant shaft of light. She descended down the shaft, and entered her body through the forehead. (Kathleen's NDE is interesting because she recalls returning through the tunnel whereas most NDErs emphasize ascending through the tunnel.)

Kathleen expected to meet the male spirit as her newborn upon regaining consciousness following the C-section. Instead, she birthed a daughter. Only after numerous inner transformations did Kathleen bring a special son into the world with her second husband several years later.[19]

Pendulum of Life

*Many spiritual teachings give the same
answer to the questions: "Where am I from?"
and "Where will I go after death?"*

The cosmological notion that equates the before-birth state with the after-death state lends credence to the experiences of NDErs who travel "home" and meet children waiting for birth. As Heraclitus, the pre-Socratic philosopher, declared, "The way up and the way down are the same."[20] Alongside the flow of souls from the eternal realm to Earth, a current carries us back.

Death is a fulfillment of the soul's longing to return to its original home, according to eminent philosophers, poets, and theologians.

- ❊ Jewish *Kabbalah* – Souls yearn to return to the "palace of the divine king,"[21] "the place from which ... [our souls were] hewn."[22]
- ❊ Leonardo Da Vinci (Middle Ages Italy) – "Behold now the hope and desire to go back to our own country, and to return to our former state. How like it is to the moth with the light."[23]
- ❊ Dionysius (5th century Christianity) – "All things flow out from God, and all will ultimately return to Him."[24]
- ❊ Church Father Origen (Early Christianity) – All souls return to our purely spiritual home, an *apocatastasis*.[25]
- ❊ Henry Vaughan (17th century Wales) – And how I long to travel back, and tread again that ancient track ... But ah! my soul with too much stay is drunk, and staggers in the way ... And when this dust falls to the urn, In that state I came – return.[26]

Human consciousness is like an eighteen-wheeler with twenty-five gears. At the time of death, we ascend to a higher frequency dimension like a truck shifting into higher gear in order to climb a steep hill. And, when we depart from our spiritual home to begin human life, we downshift to Earth's frequency in the same way the truck downshifts to come down the hill. Teachings which equate pre-birth life with the disembodied after-death state include:

- ❀ Plato (ancient Greece) – Once the human soul becomes purified through a series of human births, the soul is guaranteed immortality as a Pure Intelligence in the Aether, the birthplace of human souls.[27]

- ❀ Plotinus (3rd century Rome) – "To real Being we go back, all that we have and are; to That we return as from That we came."[28] On his deathbed, Plotinus commented, "Now I seek to lead back the self within me to the All-self."[29]

- ❀ Leo Tolstoy (1828 to 1910 Russia) – Birth is a rebirth from the "other, more real life" to which later in old age, we prepare ourselves to return.[30]

- ❀ Church Father Origen (Early Christianity) – Origen waited for his disciple to arrive at his deathbed before he made his transition: "Eustochius, I have been expecting you. Now my divine part will return to the universal divine nature."

- ❀ Saint Honen (1133 to 1212 Japan) – The Buddhist saint uttered the following message in his final hour: "I came from the Land of Bliss and I am sure I am going back there."[31]

- ❀ Koran (Holy book of Islam) – God generates beings, and sends them back over and over again, till they return to Him.

- ❀ Baoule (Africa) – At the end of human life, the people of West Africa go back to the "Village of Truth," the before-birth realm where everyone knows the ultimate truth and deception is unthinkable. The "Village of Earth," by contrast, is a pretentious world where an individual "never gets to the bottom of things."[32]

- ❀ Native Americans (Menominee, Iroquois, Ojibwa, Delaware, Oto, Lenape, Omaha, Cherokee, Winnebago, Plains-Cree) – Spiritual friends still residing in the "Land of the Spirits" can entice a newborn back home. Parents circumvented a premature departure by making newborns happy and fitting them with perforated moccasins, making it impossible to travel the four-day journey over the Spirit Road, the Milky Way. The infants then responded to the invitation, "I cannot travel so far, my shoes are bad."[33]

- ❀ Venezuela (Caribs) – Louquo, the first man to live on Earth, came down from the sky. He returned to his sky home after producing many offspring. When his decendants die, they too ascend to the heavens and become stars.[34]

Angel Gabriel announces the conception and birth of Jesus Christ. (Detail from the "Annunciation" by Leonardo da Vinci)

Chapter 11
Light Attracts Light
Meeting a Saint Before Conception

Very refined souls ... are like walking intelligences with inventive creativeness and powers of preservation, beaming with love and luminosity in their self-effulgent bodies of quantum light particles.[1]

– Satguru Sivaya Subramuniyaswami

Biographies of saints include more than the time and place of birth, schooling, and so on. They document prophecies and inner experiences of their parents prior to the saint's conception.

The creative coupling together of parents and a saintly child is more than coincidence. Like two calibrated tuning forks vibrating in harmony, the child's soul resonates in accord with the frequency of the parents' consciousness. When couples come together in physical union, "there is a flash of light in the ether."[2] When the vibrations of that light are compatible with a particular soul waiting for birth, that soul rushes towards it.

The principle, "like attracts like," facilitates a spiritual child's entry into the womb of a woman who is pure in heart. Couples exuding love, righteousness, humility, tolerance, patience, and spiritual wisdom become like divine instruments and give birth to children who serve the greater good.

An illustration of this principle is Sarada Devi (1853 to 1920), Ramakrishna's life-partner and a saint in her own right. The Indian saint chose a father who was charitable and pious, and a mother who was "full of the milk of human kindness."[3]

The Second Dalai Lama (1475 to 1542) similarly considered it a "great fortune"[4] to be born into a family with an ancient legacy of spiritual practice. He entered the womb of Kunga Palmo, a woman who had attained high consciousness centuries earlier in a previous birth. During her childhood, Kunga recounted many past incarnations. As the yogini Khadroma Drowai Zangmo, for instance, she had studied under the master Gyalwa Gotsang, and received teachings from the First Dalai Lama (1391 to 1474). For these spiritual reasons, the Second Dalai Lama chose his mother for the impetus he would receive from "a recognized female reincarnate yogini" adept at meditation, and an accomplished practitioner of the highest yoga tantras, the Medicine Buddha, as well as other tantric systems.

In another case, Sage Asita visited King Suddhodana's palace to bless his newborn son and announced: "Because of your righteous deeds in former lives, now are manifested these excellent fruits."[5] Suddhodana's son was none other than the infant who became the Buddha of our age.

Stories presented in this chapter are gathered from parents of Christian, Buddhist, and Hindu saints, including two contemporary female saints who bless our world with their words and deeds.

Mother of Compassion

*Beginning with her birth in Andhra Pradesh
in southern India, people revered Vijayeswari
Karunamayi (1958 to –) as the embodiment of the
Divine Mother, Sarasvati, the Goddess of Knowledge,
Music, and the Arts. As a saintly humanitarian,
Karunamayi teaches spiritual practices to lead
individuals to inner purity and ultimately world peace.*

Subramania, as a businessman and Sanskrit scholar, had only one desire – to serve God. He devoted his life to selfless service by quietly donating to help the needy and supporting India's struggle for freedom in the 1940s. In addition, Subramania was a follower of the highly revered 19th century saint Ramakrishna Paramahansa and often visited the temple in Dakshineswar where Ramakrishna himself had lived and worshipped.

Srimati Annapurnamba, his wife, was known for her compassion, cooperation, and service to others. Prior to marriage, the shy young woman had spent much time praying in Arunachala at the main ashram of the venerable Ramana Maharshi. The saint maintained silence most of the time and rarely conversed with students. Interestingly, on one visit, Annapurnamba asked, "Maharshi, may I retreat from this world and retire to your ashram?" The young woman marveled that her spiritual teacher knew her mind so well, when the holy sage replied:

> No my child. Not now. And not in this ashram. You must return to your village and become a householder. When you are married, you will give birth to the Divine Mother. Then you will live in your daughter's ashram.

With that, Maharshi turned and left the dazed woman vibrating with awe and happiness. In the coming days, Annapurnamba sought no additional clarification, but felt timid and had no courage to divulge the prediction to anyone.

Victory Day – 1957

Shortly following the saint's prediction of a holy child, Annapurnamba and her newly-married husband Subramania attended the 1957 Festival of Nine Lights, a nationwide holy event. The sacred festivities culminate on the tenth day with a celebration of Victory Day – Victory of Good over Evil. According to the *Markandaya Purana*, the Mother Goddess defeated two demons who threatened the stability and existence of the gods on that day.

During that auspicious celebration, Annapurnamba prayed in the temple of the Mother Goddess, the Sri Chamundeswari Temple in Mysore, and witnessed a spiritual vision of a great lotus lake. At the edge of the lake, the Divine Mother appeared sitting on a raised dias within a pearl temple supported by pillars.

The Divine Mother descended from her seat and approached Annapurnamba. At the same moment, an eternal light in the form of the goddess Chamundeshwari manifested in the temple. These two forms of the Divine Mother entered Annapurnamba's body, filling her with joy and bliss.

Annapurnamba's initial experience was accompanied by subsequent visions. They were so miraculous that Annapurnamba did not confide them even to her husband.

Victory Day – 1958

Precisely one year after Annapurnamba's first vision, Subramania experienced a powerful meditation on Victory Day (1958). He felt absolute serenity and supreme bliss and witnessed sixteen lights enter the room, one after the other. A beautiful divine feminine form manifested in the midst of these lights.

Besides a blessed meditation, Subramania rejoiced on Victory Day for another reason: the birth of a daughter, Karunamayi Vijayeshwari Devi. Karunamayi means Compassionate Mother and Vijayeshwari means Mother of Victory. Her omnipresence and omnipotence were evident from childhood. Baby Karunamayi was gifted with an indomitable pleasant smile, creativity, and an unperturbed disposition. She won over the minds of others at first sight and expressed herself in a natural, beautiful, refined manner. Unlike most children, meditation and discipline were the games of her childhood.

Jyotish Interpretation

By the tender age of five years, the child's Jyotish horoscope (an ancient Indian sidereal system different from western tropical astrology) was examined by a famous Indian Jyotish astrologer. Sri Chandra Shekhara Saraswati Swami explained to Subramania that according to Karunamayi's birth time and her chart:

> Your daughter is of a divine nature and will settle down for some years in a forest. She will be the "Light of Lights" to humanity. She will impart eternal knowledge to the world and provide shelter to orphans, the poor, sinners, and to those in distress. She will not marry and will be worshipped by the world.

Subramania was disturbed when he heard that his daughter was destined to live in the wilderness for a lengthy period, yet he chose to keep silent about this prediction. Shortly afterward, as proof of the child's special nature, little Karunamayi entered her father's office as he pondered over the Jyotish interpretation. She set aside her books, stood next to her father, and asked a surprising question, as if reading his mind: "Father, why are you depressed by such a small issue?"

Subramania replied, "What do you mean?" The child answered, "Regarding my life, that I must live some time in the forest." Subramania shuddered: "How did she know what was passing through my mind?"

This gentle confrontation is one of many incidents that convinced the parents to follow Swamiji's advice and allow Karunamayi to devote her life to God.

A Saint at Ten Years Old

One event transpired during an intense spiritual discussion between Karunamayi and her mother. Karunamayi said:

> Mother, you have no ego. It is "the wall of egoism in the heart" which prevents Self-realization. Those who have given up selfishness can step into the Spiritual realm.

Annapurnamba asked, "Do I have the eligibility to get God's grace?" Karunamayi answered, "Yes," and placed her hand on her mother's head. Annapuranamba recalls:

"I felt such heaviness, as if the entire universe were resting there! I heard the sacred sound OM vibrating through the earth and sky. I felt bodiless and as light as cotton fiber. I heard words like: *Vibruma, Hema, Nila, Dhavala,* and *Chyalmukhai* [names of the Divine Mother]. Then I had the darshan of *Sri Gayathri Devi* [Divine Mother] in Her Cosmic form, seated on the lotus bedecked with precious stones … light enveloped the entire universe. I felt that everything was Mother Herself. That figure was familiar and a very close one. I experienced in that form all rivers, oceans, mountains, three crores of deities, *Maharshis, Siddhas, Gandharvas, Nagas, Kinnaras, Kimpurushas* and crores of *jivas*. The sun and moon were Her two eyes. Fire was Her third eye [in the forehead] … .

'Oh, Mother of the Universe, please bless me.' I so prayed. Gradually that Cosmic form disappeared. I felt that the All-pervading Universal Power was my Self."[6]

For the next two days, Annapurnamba was totally engrossed in ecstasy. She was unable to open her eyes and her family grew concerned that she was suffering from some ailment. This divine vision was the most sublime experience of her life.

Mother Incarnate

By 1980, at the age of twenty-one, Karunamayi completed her college education, and retired to the remote forests of Andhra Pradesh where she spent over a decade in deep meditation, performing spiritual austerities on behalf of humanity. According to one story, as she sat and chanted sacred prayers, the birds gathered around her to listen. Very quickly, she taught the parrots and macaws to sing praises to the Divine: "Jai Ram" and "Om Namah Shivaya."

Since Karunamayi's emergence from the forest, she has fulfilled the predictions of the holy sage Ramana Maharshi and the Jyotish astrologer. Her divine qualities and spiritual discourses have swept the people in India as well as the USA. She visits the slums and distributes food, clothing, and hope. Her ashrams feed more than 1,000 people per month. She has established orphanages, as well as a Home for the mentally handicapped.

Souls Waiting in the Wings for Birth

Karunamayi's compassionate smile and softspoken words create intimacy and familiarity with all those who meet her. The saint takes everyone into her fold, addressing them as her children, solving their problems, and healing incurable diseases. Her mere glance converts atheists into humble devotees of God.

Annapurnamba's Liberation

Unexpected news from India interrupted Karunamayi's 1998 US tour: her mother was critically ill. Karunamayi returned to be at Annapurnamba's hospital bed. In those last moments, as Karunamayi gently stroked her mother's forehead, family members in the room heard a loud crack. Annapurnamba's skull split open and blood flowed out. Then a golden light emerged from a tiny aperture in the crown (*brahmarandhra* or *vidriti*) and ascended into Heaven.

Teachings contained in the *Prashna Upanishad* compare this event to passing a thread through the eye of the finest needle. The thread can jam if someone has one fiber of impurity. As elucidated in Indian and Tibetan Buddhist scriptures, the vital air, *udana prana*, travels through the main subtle nerve channel at death and carries the soul to an exit point such as the crown, eyes, nose, mouth, or lower openings. The aperture through which the soul departs reveals the soul's destination following death.

On the whole, an individual's deepest longings come to mind at the time of death, directing the soul to the appropriate aperture. If the soul departs from the crown energy center, as it did at Annapurnamba's death, the *Katha Upanishad* explains: "Going upward through that, one becomes immortal."[7] Typically only a few individuals experience the highest exit.

Annapurnamba followed her daughter's teachings and attained higher consciousness through meditation and selfless service.

An Angel Appears

*Angels foretell many events, including the births of children.
Stories of angelic messengers appearing to childless couples
were frequently reported in Biblical times.*

David-Aaron lived in Magdalia, a small village in a district of Jerusalem. He observed the Law of Moses and the Prophets and as a man of great wealth, he "performed manifold acts of charity to those who were in want."[8]

One evening David slipped into an ecstatic state as he rested on his bed. He heard a voice announce: "Israel's Redeemer will spring from your family. The time has come for the root to put forth fruit." David said, "Whatsoever God wisheth let it happen."[9] Within a short period, his wife Sara conceived and bore a son, Joachim (aka Joakim).

When Joachim came of age, he married his cousin Anna, the daughter of Aminadab. Like his father, Joachim realized that material wealth is a transient treasure, and that bestowing such things upon others was more rewarding. The pious couple therefore lived on one-third of their income, donated one-third to the temple, and shared the remainder with the needy.

Despite their material fulfillment, one spiritual treasure had evaded Joachim and Anna. They had even made a vow: "If God grants us a child, we will devote it to His service." Nonetheless, the couple remained childless after twenty years of marriage. For that reason, Joachim faced an embarrassing situation. The high priest at the Temple in Jerusalem rejected his generous offering on the grounds that a husband without offspring is unworthy.

Joachim felt so ashamed that he retreated into the wilderness. He vowed to remain in solitude without food or drink until he had received a divine answer. "Prayer shall be my meat and drink."[10]

Joachim's mind attained such a lucid state of consciousness after forty days of fasting, that an angel appeared in a dream:

> Joachim, the priest unjustly reproached you. There is a hidden reason for Anna's sterility: God shut her womb so that He could open it in a wonderful manner. Anna will conceive a daughter named Mary. People will regard her child as a gift of God instead of a product of physical gratification.
>
> Mary will be filled with the Holy Spirit even while in the womb. And later, just as Anna will birth a child despite her barren nature, Mary will birth a divine son as a virgin.

Meanwhile in Joachim's absence, an angel answered Anna's prayer to be free of sterility and said:

> You will conceive a child and birth a daughter Mary, of whom the whole world will speak. Begin Mary's spiritual training at the age of three. Bring her to the Temple where she will serve the Lord in fasting and prayer for eleven years.

Virgin Birth

Joachim and Anna conceived a child in due time and followed the angel's guidelines for Mary's spiritual training. Prior to Mary's marriage to Joseph, the Heavenly Father took counsel with Jesus, saying:

> The time has come for you to leave the Kingdom of Heaven and deliver Your message to Your sheep who have gone astray in the world. Your abode is prepared on the Earth – the Virgin Mary.

Jesus asked Archangel Gabriel to announce His coming to Mary "with words of tenderness" and "trouble not her mind."[11] So rather than appearing to the young maiden "in his glory," Gabriel stood outside her chamber and called, "Hail, thou maiden who hast found favour! The Lord is with thee."[12] Mary wondered, "What kind of a salutation is this?" Seeing that he had disturbed Mary, Gabriel appeared to her "with a joyful bearing"[13] and said:

> Hail, Mary, the Lord is with you. Blessed are you among women. You have found favor with God. The Holy Spirit will come upon you and you will conceive and bear a holy child. His name shall be Jesus. Heaven and Earth await your "holy birth-pangs."[14] Your fruit will give salvation to the world and to all mankind.

This message troubled Mary. She marvelled:

Your words are beyond my understanding. I have never known a man. I am a virgin. How can this happen?

Gabriel replied, "Test my words. Visit Elizabeth who has conceived a son in her old age and is now six months pregnant." Mary exclaimed, "Elizabeth conceived a son through her husband. What you speak of is a virgin birth." Gabriel filled Mary's heart with further confidence and answered, "With God nothing is impossible." She humbly responded, "I am the Lord's servant. May whatever happens be according to His Will."

Now Joseph resolved to divorce Mary when he heard that she was pregnant. Before that happened however, an angel advised Joseph in a dream: "Do not divorce Mary. Her child was conceived of the Holy Spirit. She will bear a son, named Jesus, who will save His people from their sins."

So as destiny would have it, Jesus Christ fulfilled the old prophecy that God's Word would incarnate in the House of David.

Vision of the Virgin Mary

Little was known about the Virgin Mary's family tree until early Christian manuscripts preserved in Egyptian monasteries and churches were translated into English (1915). One text written by the Holy Patriarch Cyril, Archbishop of Jerusalem (315 to 386 AD) describes the events leading up to the birth of Joachim, the Virgin Mary's father.

Cyril was led to the discovery as he prayed for the Holy Spirit to illumine him about Mary's genealogy. The Virgin Mary appeared to Cyril, stretched her hand, and said:

I was a child promised to God. My parents who were of the tribe of Judah and of the House of David dedicated me to Him before I came into the world.

Mary said that she was born in Magdalia to Anna (aka Mariham), the daughter of Aminadab, and Joachim, the son of a rich man called David-Aaron and his wife Sara.

Cyril confirmed Mary's genealogy with documents written by the 1st century Jewish historian Josephus and the 2nd century Saint Irenaeus.

Christian Saints

*Critics dismiss announcing dreams of Christian saints as
imitations of the annunciation to Mary of the birth of Christ.
They accuse biographers of embellishing stories in order to
enhance the saint's piety. As evidence in support of the
biographies, the following dreams resemble the pre-
conception pattern of symbolic dreams and premonitions.*

Star of a Saint

A radiant star descended from Heaven and entered Liadain's
mouth. The rays of the star flowed from her, enlightening everyone
in Ireland. An interpreter explained: "Just as a star illumines the
darkness, you will conceive a son who will perform miracles and
great deeds."

Quaint legends grew up around Liadain's son in the years to
come – the first saint born in Ireland – Bishop Kieran of Saighir (5th
to 6th century AD). A perfect example occurred on the day a boar
observed Saint Kieran building his forest monastery. The wild
animal fled in terror. Then, for some strange reason, the creature
returned. The boar became the saint's first disciple. He cut the
forest, turned up the ground, and leveled it.

Saint Kieran's affinity with animals does not end there. A wolf, a
badger, and a fox obeyed Kieran by cutting wood and building
huts. On one occasion, however, the fox took the saint's shoes to its
former den intending to chew them. As soon as Saint Kieran
missed his slippers, he said, "It is improper for a monk to steal."
The wolf and badger brought the fox back. The fox begged forgiveness and fasted until the saint bid him to eat. From then on, the fox
never strayed from an honest path.

More than Saint Kieran's miraculous powers to communicate with wild animals, he had the ability to bi-locate. Every Christmas Eve, Saint Kieran celebrated mass simultaneously at his monastery in Saighir, as well as at a remote monastery (Ros-Bennchuir). How he got there and back in the same night remains a mystery.

Golden Apples

A woman received a blessing of seven apples in a dream.[15] Of the seventh apple, it is said that her hand could not hold it "for its size." Even gold, as it seemed to her, "was not lovelier than the apple."[16] Her husband understood the symbolism, "You will bear a famous child who will influence Ireland." Today we know their son as the amazing newborn who began to speak and praise God at the age of one month – Saint Molasius (aka Laserian), the 6th century Abbot of Devenish.

Parallel Dreams

One day the king's minstrel poet Hyvarnion encountered a beautiful woman with a pink and white complexion in the forest. The woman said, "My name is Rivanona. I am searching for herbs to heal a sad heart, cure blindness, and promote immortality." Hyvarnion sensed something unusual about the woman: she had appeared as his wife in three dreams. Rivanona was equally intuitive. She had seen Hyvarnion as her husband in several dreams.

As if following a hidden drummer, their dreams destined them to marry and give birth to a male child who was blind from birth. Amazing miracles surround the life of this 6th century Brittany saint whom Christians invoke to heal eye problems. One event caused a quite a stir in the countryside: a wild wolf attacked and devoured the saint's donkey that plowed the fields. The people reported that, in answer to Harvey's prayer, the wolf put himself into the donkey's harness and finished the plowing.

Saint Patrick, Patron Saint of Ireland

When a high saint is about to incarnate, saints who live in the area intuitively know about it, such as Saint Patrick (389 to 461), who foretold the births of Saints Abban, Ciaran, Molasius, and Coemgen, as well as the Irish abbot Canice. Patrick refused to be "silent or hide the signs and wonders" which God pointed out to him. God "knows all things even before the world began."[17] To anyone who criticized Patrick's premonitions, he replied: "Let anyone who wishes to, laugh at me and insult me."[18]

Saint Patrick followed divine guidance even when an angel told him: "You can not settle in Menevia. God has appointed Menevia to be the monastic seat for a saint who will be born thirty years later."

Saint Patrick asked. "Why did the Lord choose someone who has not even been born instead of me?" The angel pacified Patrick: "God has sent me to show you a vision of where you shall serve God – Ireland." As a consequence, Patrick converted the Irish to Christianity.

And just as the angel said, thirty years later, Saint David, patron saint of Wales, was born in Menevia and established his monastery there.

Saint Patrick and Saint Columba

By right of birth, Columba (521 to 597) was direct in line to be an Irish king. His family had reigned in Ireland for six centuries. And the throne would have been his, had Columba not dedicated his life to God. Columba's destiny was no surprise to Saint Patrick who had prepared Columba's father and grandfather to greet their son as a prophet long before the boy's birth.

A "beloved, clear, bright luminary" will be born in your family. He will be "a sage, abbot, prophet, and poet." He will be a "King of royal virtues"[19] – pious, steadfast, and will never utter falsehood.

History indeed tells us that for centuries no one wrote of Columba in less than "extravagant terms."[20] The monastic's holiness, austerity, and reputation for miracles attracted countless visitors. Columba healed lepers, the blind, and the lame. Like Christ, he raised the dead. Next to Saint Patrick and Saint Brigit, he became the third most famous Irish saint.

Holy Mother of Kamakhya Mountain

An Indian swami foresaw the birth of Shree Maa,
one of the great Bengali saints in contemporary
history, who is described as "kindness incarnate."

Kalyani was barely thirteen when she married Sushil, a wealthy young man in his early twenties who managed a tea estate. One year after their marriage, the pious couple climbed to the top of a holy mountain to do worship at the Kamakhya Temple, India's holiest Goddess shrine. Much to their surprise, Swami Bhuvananda Saraswati was standing before them when they reached the summit. This great saint who dwelt on the mountain at the nearby Kalipur Ashram announced:

Kalyani, I have been waiting for you. You are going to give birth
to a very pure soul, and you must be prepared. I will initiate you
with a special mantra.

Kalyani protested, "I am not pregnant. You are making a mistake." The Swami insisted, "No, no, it is you." With this surprising introduction, he moved closer to the couple, stretched out his arms, and blessed them with sacred prayers. He anointed Kalyani with holy water and whispered the *Gayatri* mantra, a powerful Sanskrit formula that raises consciousness, into her left ear:

Om Bhur Bhuvah Swah. Tat Savitur Varenyam. Bhargo Devasya
Dhimihi. Dhiyo Yo Nah Prachodyat. Om Apo Jyoti. Raso 'Mritam. Brahma
Bhur Bhuvah Svar Om.[21]

Following the unexpected initiation, the Swami advised, "Please return when Kalyani is two months pregnant."

Within a month, the couple conceived and immediately sensed that, if the Swami was correct, their child was destined to be "a divinely inspired messenger."[22] Remembering the Swami's directive, Kalyani and her husband returned to the ashram on the holy mountain.

The Swami then performed a sacred ceremony to the expectant mother and gave the baby growing in the womb a mantra initiation. Moreover, he instructed the parents on how to maintain a spiritual atmosphere conducive for the impending birth and requested, "Return when the child is two months old."

Third Pilgrimage

On the parents' third journey up the mountain, carrying for the first time two-month-old Shree Maa (meaning "respected Holy Mother"), Swami Saraswati cradled the newborn baby in his arms and danced with her in joy throughout the temple. Afterward, he whispered mantras into the infant's ears in the process of initiation. Even before this instruction, Shree Maa had been aware of her mission. At the time of birth, she recalls hearing the 19th century Bengali sage, Ramakrishna Paramahansa, whom she now regards as her spiritual teacher, say to her:

> Oh, you have come to Earth again. Much more needs to be done in this Dark Age. You must show people what divine life and spiritual practice really mean ... .

According to Shree Maa,[23] "My parents received further initiation from Swami Saraswati when they first brought me as a newborn child to the Kamakhya Temple." When the Swami initiated her mother, Kalyani went into *"samadhi."* She spontaneously levitated off the temple floor in an ecstatic swoon of divine realization. The Swami could not get her down for two hours. Her mother's "third eye opened to the size of a football." Shree Maa emphasizes, "My mother was a pure individual who was barely fifteen years old at the time."

A Living Saint

The whole milieu of what a family attains – including the past generations – goes into the foundation for raising a child. If a boy is born into a family of shoemakers, he hears his father and uncles conversing about that profession. And it is easiest for him to make his living in the same way.

Souls Waiting in the Wings for Birth

Shree Maa chose to be born into a family that was most conducive to catalyze sainthood – a family of saints, musicians, artists, poets, singers, entrepreneurs, and pioneers. They were a highly educated caste – successful in business, international in outlook.

Shree Maa chose a cultural melting pot, the foothills of India's Himalayas, as her birthplace. Tibet was ten miles away; China, Burma, Thailand, Bangladesh, Nepal, Sikkim, and Bhutan were close by. She had put herself in an international culture which gave her a unique perspective. From childhood, she spoke many languages. She empathized with the other's point of view. So many different cultures, yet all one family.

Even though Shree Maa grew up in an affluent extended family with twenty-two members, she empathized with the poor and did chores that the servants did not have time to perform. She nursed her dying grandmother during her final days, since she had been instrumental in raising Shree Maa. Her grandmother rose for prayers like clockwork every morning at 3:00 AM and prayed again at 11:00 AM and 4:00 PM. This discipline was instilled in Shree Maa from the time she was barely two years old.[24]

As a child, Shree Maa had the capacity to enter into deep meditative states at will. Her most difficult realization was to understand that not everyone was as equally blessed and gifted with God Consciousness.

Having laid the foundation to pursue a higher calling, Shree Maa left home after completing her college education and walked off into the Himalayan forests. She was raised with a feeling that the whole world is mine and had no problem sitting in a cave by herself. Yogis observed her in ecstatic meditation for days at a time. She rarely spoke and ate little, except sandalwood paste, basil leaves, and juice. Shree Maa remained in the forests praying and meditating for nearly a decade.

Even in India, it was inconceivable for a woman to travel throughout the forests alone, especially without money, possessions, and protection. Despite warnings and protests, Shree Maa was oblivious to impending dangers, "What risk, what fear? When I am one with the soul of existence, how will anyone or anything cause me harm?"[25]

Sharing Messages of Divine Love

Shree Maa receives spiritual messages from Ramakrishna who inspired her to come to the West.

> "He has ordered me to share unselfish divine love ... . The most important accomplishment of human life is self realization. It doesn't matter what we become ... what we attain ... what we possess. All of that is so temporary ... . A well-lived life is one that is full of love and joy and peace and compassion."[26]

Shree Maa is a living example of this message. Today she lives in California (Devi Mandir, Napa Valley) where she worships and meditates at least ten hours every day. Yet Shree Maa is also a poet, singer, and artist. She has contributed to the authoring of three dozen books in twelve languages and has written hundreds of devotional songs. Shree Maa's music and voice bring tears of joy to people of every religious heritage. Her egoless nature and simplicity shine through every action, inspiring spiritual growth and radiating peace to everyone she meets.

A Saint's Blessing

One Colorado couple encountered an infertility problem in having a child. Finally they approached Shree Maa for assistance in overcoming the barrier. Shree Maa presented them with a special fruit and instructed them: "Eat this and you will have a child." The couple was blessed with a girl who is now two years old.

Masters of the East

Pre-conception is an integral part of a
saint's biography in Tibet, Japan, and India.

One in One Thousand

Mirrors reflect more than outer appearances. In *Snow White and the Seven Dwarfs*, a mirror reveals the most beautiful woman in the world. In the *Arabian Nights*, a mirror reflects whether a woman is chaste. And as a Tibetan story illustrates, another mirror found the right mother for a great saint.

Two dreams prepared a spiritual couple for the unexpected. The husband daily recited Buddhist sacred prayers, whereas his wife chanted *"Om Mani Padme Hung,"* Tibet's national mantra, while performing her daily chores. In the dream, the wife found herself in a celestial flower garden among a group of 1,000 prospective mothers. The young women were joined by a boy dressed in white. He entered the garden from the east, carrying a special vessel. Then, a girl dressed in red entered from the west.

The boy spoke with each woman, one by one. Afterward, he consulted with his female companion who carried peacock feathers and a large mirror. The Tibetan woman did not comprehend the purpose of the interviews, but in the end, they chose to purify her in a ceremonial bath. When she awoke the next morning, she felt a lightness in her being.

Around the same time, a monk visited her husband in a dream. The monk explained: "I am from Wu Tai Shan. Please give me shelter in your home for nine months." The husband realized his visitor came from the sacred five-peaked Chinese mountain, home of the bodhisattva of wisdom, Manjusri. With much respect, he replied, "You are welcome to stay in our family shrine room."

Within the next year, the couple conceived a child who changed Tibet's destiny for hundreds of years and "swept away wrong views with the correct and perfect ones."[27] By the time he reached nineteen, Tibetans had recognized their son, Tsong Khapa (1357 to 1419), as a great scholar and spiritual genius. They called him Je Rinpoche, meaning, "teacher without parallel."

At the end of his illustrious and prodigious life, Tsong Khapa had contributed eighteen volumes of religious prose and poetry to Tibetan cultural history, and synthesized the practice of four major schools of Buddhism, by combining intellectual learning and direct yogic experience.

Modern Tibetan Buddhists herald Tsong Khapa as one of the top three spiritual figures, along with Padmasambhava and Atisha. Tsong Khapa's disciples, the Yellow Hats sect, became central Asia's largest Buddhist school and set in motion the longest unbroken chain of spiritual-national leaders in the world – the lineage from which the Dalai Lama comes.

A Monk's Vow

The high soul knew what he wanted to accomplish and chose a Japanese princess, the wife of Emperor Yomei, as his mother.[28] He appeared as a golden-robed monk in her dream and announced, "I have taken a vow to help humanity. I wish to temporarily take shelter in your womb."

The princess replied, "How can you take shelter in it? My womb is impure." Be that as it may. The monk seemed to enter her mouth with one bound.

After a short period, the princess became pregnant and birthed a son who worked for religious reform and became a champion of Buddhism. In keeping with his destiny, Prince Regent Shotoku Taishi (573 to 621 AD) built Buddhist temples, such as the Horyuji Temple, the oldest Japanese temple. Besides these saintly actions, he sent missions to China, resuming communications that had been cut off in the fifth century. He subsequently introduced Confucianism, the Chinese calendar, and aesthetic values to his people.

Vittal Pant's Four Gifts

The notion of a Supreme Being descending upon Earth in human form happens once in Christianity with the birth of Jesus. In contrast, Hinduism teaches that God is made flesh in different ages. This notion parallels the Christian belief in Christ as the Word made flesh, "full of grace and truth."

Looking back, it seems surprising that Vittal Pant ever took a marriage vow. From childhood, he had a dispassionate outlook toward worldly life. He preferred to visit temples and attend religious discourses. And more than anything else, his heart yearned for self-realization. So when Vittal reached the proper age, he rejected the marriage proposal as he thought it to be only a bondage.

Instead Vittal obtained permission from his parents and visited sacred places, such as Alandi, a village in Maharashtra along the Arabian Sea. There he bathed in the Indrayini River and sat under a sacred fig tree to meditate. Meanwhile, a devout man named Siddhopant passed by and recognized Vittal's greatness. He told the travelling monk, "Vittal, I should be honored to give a Brahmin like you food and shelter for a few days."

Vittal accompanied Siddhopant to his home where they spent the evening chanting sacred songs. After a late dinner, they took rest. That night Siddhopant had an unexpected dream. A divine being, Lord Panduranga (Krishna), appeared and said:

> For the sake of the world, offer your daughter's hand in marriage to Vittal. Four great souls will be born of this union. Each child will embody a portion of the Divine and is destined to illumine the world. (Indians recognize degrees of Godhood. Below the full *avatar*, *purnavatara*, is a partial *avatar*, *amsavatara*.)

Siddhopant awoke in a state of bewilderment. After all, his daughter Rakhuma Bai was barely eight years old and Vittal wanted to lead a life of a celibacy. He obeyed the dream, however and humbly requested that Vittal accept his daughter in marriage. Not surprisingly, Vittal refused.

God will tell me Himself if it is truly a divine directive. I will consent only if the Lord comes in my dream and tells me that I should marry.

The next night, a divine being exhorted Vittal in a dream, "Marry Rakhuma Bai without delay." In the morning, Vittal related his dream. He now had no other recourse, and an auspicious wedding date was set. Marriage, not surprisingly, did little to change Vittal. After several years, he grew increasingly restless and requested his wife's permission to become a monk. She agreed, but only under one condition – after the birth of a son.

The couple remained childless after many years. At last, Vittal ran out of patience and felt justified in leaving his wife. He travelled to Benares and visited the monastery of the famous yogi, Swami Ramananda. He asked, "Swami, please initiate me and make me your disciple. The Swami inquired: "Tell me about your background. Do you have any dependents?" For fear of rejection, the young man replied, "No, only my aged parents." After further questioning, the Swami was pleased with Vittal's humility and desire for renunciation, and said, "Prepare yourself, for I shall accept you."[29] Vittal took sacred vows to renounce the world and received the spiritual name, Chaitanyashrama Swami.

Within several years, Vittal became Ramananda's foremost disciple and watched over the monastery whenever Ramananda made his pilgrimages. On one occasion, Ramananda went to a temple in Alandi where a woman asked for a blessing. The Swami noted the red turmeric mark on her forehead signifying marriage, and promised: "You will be blessed with four divine children."

Rakhuma burst into tears and complained,

How can your words come true when my husband has left me without my consent to become a monk. He has become a sanyasin in Benares. Your blessing is fruitless.

The Swami knew that the scriptures forbade anyone to confer holy orders on a man who had no children to take care of his family. He inquired, "What guru initiated him?" Rakhuma answered, "Ramananda Swamij." The Swami then realized that

Vittal had lied in order to join the monastic order and he accepted partial responsibility for initiating him.

Without a moment's delay, the Swami returned to Benares. He rebuked Vittal, "You lied to your own Guru. You will not attain self-realization through deception." Vittal shook with fear and confessed his guilt, "My lord, show mercy."[30]

The Swami replied, "I will forgive you only if you return to your wife and raise a family." The Swami placed his hand on Vittal's head as a final blessing and expelled him from the monastery.

Four Blessings

Vittal's return to married life pleased Rakhuma. Unfortunately the local brahmin priests were horrified at this unheard of event: a man who once took monastic vows came back to the world. It was like "someone swallowing his own vomit."[31] The sacred texts never cited such a circumstance. The Brahmins had no other recourse than to ostracize the couple. For transgressing the laws of society, the outcasts were not allowed to associate with Brahmins. The couple retired to the city outskirts and "bore it all without a murmur."[32]

During the next twelve years, the couple focused on spiritual development and studied at the feet of famous Nath Yogis. They learned that the human body is a microcosm, and by proper discipline, it can receive vibrations from the macrocosm and wake up to supreme cosmic consciousness.

At the end of that period, Rakhuma conceived and bore a son, Nivrithi (1273 to 1297). Two more sons and one daughter followed: Jnaneshwar (1275 to 1296), Sopana (1277 to 1296), and a daughter Mukta Bai (1279 to 1297).

Vittal named each child after the four stages of self-realization.

1. *Nivrithi* – An extraordinary state of the stillness of mind.
2. *Jnaneshwar* – Knowledge and wisdom.[33]
3. *Sopana* – Pathway to God.
4. *Mukta Bai* – Total freedom, salvation, or liberation.

However, because Vittal was a former ascetic, nagging obstacles kept appearing. The priests refused to initiate his children into the sacred thread ceremony. According to tradition, children of a swami who had broken his vow were illegitimate and unworthy of spiritual instruction.

In despair, Vittal took his family on a long, arduous pilgrimage, hoping to gain favor with the priests after an act of penance. One evening, in the course of this journey, an angry tiger pounced in their midst. Everyone, except the eldest son Nivrithi, fled in separate directions and reached safety.

Little did the other family members know that Nivrithi had escaped and had discovered a deep cave where yogis and wild animals lived together in perfect peace. The boy ventured into the cave until he encountered a meditating yogi of a luminous appearance. The yogi opened his eyes and said:

> I know who you are. My name is Gahininath. My master, Guru Gorakhnath, has foreseen your coming and advised me to initiate you into the mysteries of Yoga.

In accord with the directive, the ten-year-old attained enlightenment within seven days. Gahininath advised, "Return home and initiate your brothers and sister into the complete knowledge of Yoga." Under his new name Nivrithinath, the eldest brother served as a Guru for each of his siblings.

Only after much hardship, social ostracism, and their parents' early deaths,[34] did society recognize the brothers and their sister as great saints. Together they spiritually emancipated thousands of people and played a major role in the path of devotion (Bhakti), during India's golden age.

Lamp of Simple Explanation

Above the rest, Indians remember Vittal's son, poet-saint Jnaneshwar Maharaj. On one occasion, some priests condemned Jnaneshwar and his brothers as illegitimate children and refused them an audience with the high priest. Jnaneshwar argued with the religious scholars on the meaning of purity:

> "What is in a name? When nothing exists outside the One infinite Brahman, my Atman [soul] is no different from yours or from that passing he-buffalo!"[35]

The priests did not yield. In fact, one pundit taunted Jnaneshwar, saying:

Souls Waiting in the Wings for Birth

> Be careful not to disrespect the scriptures. If what you say is true,
> there is no reason why that buffalo over there should not be able to
> recite holy scriptures.

Seeing their arrogance, the enlightened boy answered:

> So be it. All things belong to God who has no caste. Divinity
> resides in everything, whether awake or dormant, even in this
> buffalo.

The pundits laughed and dragged the buffalo into the meeting
hall. Jnaneshwar stroked the buffalo's head and said: "If the true
Divinity which resides in all things resides within you, recite the
Vedas." Jnaneshwar recited passages from the Rig Veda praising
the meaning of the word "Om." Then, the buffalo took over and
chanted sacred hymns for one hour in a deep, clear voice.

Silence filled the hall. The high priest came out to witness the
buffalo recite the mantras unfalteringly as long as the boy saint had
his palm over the buffalo's head. The opponents were humbled.
The high priest apologized:

> Please forgive us. You are a realized soul and embodiment of divine
> knowledge. Blessed be your parents for giving birth to you.

Even to this day, India remembers Jnaneshwar for his literary
accomplishments. The young saint had been pained by the ignorance of the everyday people of the higher Truths, since until this
time, the *Bhagavad Gita* had been studied in Sanskrit, the language
of high-caste brahmin priests. So in a radical shift, at the age of
fifteen, Jnaneshwar composed the scripture in Marathi, the
language of the common people. His work stands unrivalled – the
most beautiful commentary ever written on the *Gita*. Jnaneshwar
did more than the scholars of thousands of years. Now for the first
time, ordinary people studied the *Gita* in their homes.

The beauty of Jnaneshwar's commentary and its illustrations
demonstrate his spiritual genius. The boy saint accomplished this
task of 9,000 verses without formal training. His work entitled the
Bhavarthadipika, "the lamp of simple explanation," is popularly
called *Jnaneshwari* in honor of its author.

> "One wonders which sage was it who took birth as this child or
> which manifestation of the Supreme Being blessed this land."[36]

Golden Child in the Temple

*Ramakrishna Paramahansa (1836 to 1886), probably
the most famous Indian holy man of recent times, was born
when India's intelligentsia believed that progress required
forgetting India's past and adopting Western modes of thinking.
The British conquest had introduced western education,
materialism, and scientific/technological achievements.
Ramakrishna nonetheless opened the nation's
eyes to the strength of its heritage.*

Khurdiram and Chandra Devi lived in an obscure village in
Bengal, unspoiled by the modern sophistications that were being
imported from abroad into nearby Calcutta, the metropolis of the
British Empire. Khurdiram was known for his moral uprightness
and Chandra was "a soul of honesty and sincerity." She knew little
about the ways of the world and was incapable of concealment.
Neighbors called her "Mother" due to her simplicity, sweetness,
and love for God. The ideal couple spent much time in worship
and meditation.

One day Khudiram had a spiritual vision, unlike any dream,
while napping under a shade tree. The deity Rama appeared as a
boy of angelic beauty having a green complexion, like a blade of
young grass. Rama said: "For long I have been lying there (pointing
to an adjoining paddy field). I had nothing to eat and no one to look
after me. Take me home; I long to be looked after by you."

Khudiram replied: "My Lord, I am poor and unfit for this favor. How
can I serve you in my hut? If my service is unworthy, I shall lose your
grace." Rama refused any excuses, "Do not fear. I shall not blame you
for anything that's lacking. Take me with you."

Khudiram awoke from his vision in an exalted mood and burst
into tears of joy. As he looked around, he spotted the adjacent paddy

field, the very spot he had seen in his dream. He walked toward the field and observed a round black stone having special markings of embedded fossil ammonites, a *shalagrama*. (The worship of these stones is widespread in India and dates back to a distant past. They are worshipped as a natural emblem of Vishnu.) A cobra was spreading its hood over this *shalagrama*, guarding the sacred stone. Khudiram felt no fear as he approached. The venomous snake then retreated into its hole.

Khudiram accepted the boy of his vision as an venerated guest by placing the stone in the household shrine. From that day, neighbors noticed a transformation. During Khudiram's meditation on the sacred *Gayatri* Mantra, his chest swelled and became radiant with a divine glow. Tears of devotion rolled down his cheeks. Heavenly visions and unearthly experiences filled him with divine joy. His mind soared far into higher regions where he communed with Rama.

Khudiram's divine visions continued for sixteen years. Khudiram then had a second pre-conception vision. In keeping with the scriptures, he expressed gratitude to his forefathers and performed *shraddha* ceremonies for the departed at a temple 100 miles from home. Khudiram made this journey on foot at the age of sixty.

During the one-month retreat, Khudiram felt great joy in discharging "one of his obligations as a son."[37] One evening Khudiram had a mystical dream. In it, he was transported back to the temple. When he arrived, he saw "his forefathers feasting with gladdened hearts on the oblations"[38] he had offered. More than that, "a divine effulgence"[39] entered the room. His ancestors bowed reverently "before a luminous Person seated on a throne."[40]

The "effulgent One" spoke:

> Khudiram, I am born again and again to chastise the wicked and protect the virtuous. The time has come for me to be born once again. I will be born as your son. Your sincere devotion has made me happy.

"But my home and heart are too small," Khudiram pleaded. The Lord reassured Khudiram, "I will enjoy whatever you give." Khudiram was filled with ecstasy upon waking from the dream – proof that he had experienced a divine revelation. He thought, "Truly a divine child will bless our family."

Meanwhile during Khudiram's absence, his wife witnessed a vision. On this particular night, Chandra Devi observed a celestial figure resembling her husband in the bedroom. At first, she assumed Khudiram had returned home and a great happiness filled her soul. Suddenly, when the face of the figure shone, "like the face of a god,"[41] Chandra realized it was not Khudiram. She thought, "Yet, how is it possible for a god to appear to a human being? A wicked man must be in the room." She lit a lamp – no one was there.

Shortly thereafter, Chandra visited a shrine and witnessed a divine light emanating from Shiva's image. The holy light filled the room and engulfed Chandra, whereupon she lost outer consciousness and slumped down.

The poor Brahmin couple conceived a wonder child following these foretelling incidents. Ramakrishna was born with full illumination. As a child, he learned sacred hymns and tales from the great epics. He was a happy and friendly boy who also enjoyed solitude and contemplation. His first ecstatic vision occurred on the way to the temple of the goddess Vishalakshi. Ramakrishna looked up and noticed that the sky had become overlaid with dark clouds. Then a flight of white cranes flipped across the sky like a brilliant meteor. The beautiful sight "touched the inner divine chords of his artistic mind to the extent that he lost all external consciousness and became merged in the Absolute."[42] In his God-vision, he witnessed light, felt joy, and experienced "the upsurge of a great current" in his chest, "like a fire cracker shooting up."[43] Passers-by carried the ten-year-old boy home mistakenly fearing that he had fallen ill or suffered a seizure.

Later in life, Ramakrishna became a priest at a Kali temple in Dakshineswar near Calcutta. Although not a scholar, Ramakrishna demonstrated that there was nothing wrong with the spiritual way of life taught by the ancient rishis of India. To Ramakrishna, religion meant "ecstasy, his worship transcendental insight … ."[44] He illuminated old truths and purified rituals which had become distorted.

Although Indian scriptures state that a yogi cannot sit in *samadhi*, the highest state of meditation, for more than twenty-eight days, "Ramakrishna sat, unmoving, in the highest states of meditation for six continuous months."[45]

"He was often merged in rapturous ecstasy … his heart full of the burning love of God … tears would run down his rigid, pale, yet smiling face ... he would sometimes break out into prayers, songs and utterances, the force and pathos of which would pierce through the hardest heart and bring tears to eyes that never wept before through the influence of religion."[46]

"Ramakrishna ... beheld his individuality dissolving in a limitless blaze of spiritual light. In the experience of the nondual Reality there is no distinction, not even the distinction of experient and object experienced."[47]

Ramakrishna's religion was not confined to Hinduism. His spiritual realizations enabled him to look upon all religions as different paths to the same destination. Shortly after Ramakrishna began to contemplate the personality of Jesus, Ramakrishna was resting in the temple garden house where portraits of holy personalities covered the walls. As he gazed at a painting of the Virgin Mary with Jesus sitting on her lap, rays of light emanated from the Madonna and Child and entered Ramakrishna. His heart expanded with love for Jesus. A vision of Christian priests burning incense and waving candles before Jesus in their churches opened to him and he sensed their devotion.

Four days later, a tall, stately stranger with a fair complexion approached Ramakrishna. He possessed large brilliant eyes and a beautiful face, despite the fact that the tip of his nose was slightly flattened. Ramakrishna's inner voice told him: "This is Jesus the Christ, the Great Yogi, the loving Son of God and one with his Father, who shed his heart's blood and suffered tortures for the salvation of mankind."[48] They met face to face and embraced. Ramakrishna fell into a superconscious state – convincing him of the divine nature of Jesus.

In much the same way, Ramakrishna experimented with Islam, Buddhism, and different Hindu sects. He concluded that everyone must be free to follow his own religion, and if he does so sincerely, he will realize God. For that reason, Ramakrishna never uttered one word of condemnation for any religion. He believed there is no caste nor creed among true saints – as the ancient sages said, "Truth is one: men call it by different names."

Three angels announced: "Abraham, your wife Sarah
will conceive and birth a son in her old age."

Chapter 12
Children of Prayer

**My mother fasted and prayed for years
and years so that I should be born.**[1]
– Swami Vivekananda

*Fervent prayers for a child reach the
invisible ears of souls seeking birth.*

The ancient world was filled with temples where people practiced the art of soliciting prophetic dreams through the power of prayer and sacred chants.

- ❋ Babylonia – Before making important decisions, people slept in temples or sacred spots and invoked the help of the goddess of dreams, Makhir.

- ❋ Greece – People suffering from ailments slept on pillows of laurel leaves, the "prophetic plant."[2] With any luck, a benefic deity appeared and dictated the remedy or left a prescription behind.

- ❋ Egypt – Individuals seeking dream counsel from gods or saints slept in oracular seats and chanted mystical words prior to sleep. After a healing, they suspended a model of the restored body part – such as eyes, ears, distorted arms – in the temple of the god whose interposition they had invoked.

- ❋ Pythagoreans (Greece) – Students of Pythagoras listened to tranquilizing music prior to sleep in order to induce light sleep and dream revelations.

- ❋ Africa – The Yoruba applied herbal juice on their eyes or rubbed powder in a cut below their eyes prior to sleep.

Announcing dreams of women awaiting a blessing for a child likewise arise through prayer. In Nigeria, young brides sacrificed a fowl beneath a sacred tree before sleeping beneath it. If lucky, the tree spirit accepted a woman's offering and placed a baby upon her breast. When the woman awoke from the dream, she wondered, "Where is the baby that lay over my heart?"[3] She placed a second offering beneath the tree to "make my dream come true."

Another prime example comes from the Egyptian woman Mahituaskhit who offered prayers in the temple of Imuthes (aka Asklepios) in Memphis to the deity who "givest children to him that hath none."[4] She then slept in the temple and the benevolent deity revealed the cure for her husband's sterility.

> In the morning, go to the fountain of your husband Satni where you will find a colocasia plant. From this plant, make a potion for your husband to drink. Then, sleep with your husband and you shall conceive a child that night.

Mahituaskhit's dream heralded the birth of a great prophet Senosiris.

Two souls anxious to be born hovered above a gathering of Canadian women who attended a Mormon prayer service for barren women who desired offspring. The Church president, Edward James Wood, promised two of the women that they would receive the blessing they had prayed for. The babies were born in less than one year.[5]

Parents who birthed Christian, Hindu, and Sikh spiritual leaders reported similar pre-conception dreams or visions in answer to a prayer. This chapter also includes the story of a modern saint who blesses couples with exceptional children.

Prayer of the Virgin Mary's Mother

*Angels answered the prayers of the parents of the Virgin Mary,
as mentioned in the last chapter. The* Protevangelium
of James *records Anna's request for a child.*

Anna rested beneath a laurel tree and implored God to bless her just as He had blessed Sarah who birthed Isaac – a special son who became instrumental in perpetuating the Hebrew race. Anna looked up to Heaven and saw a nest of sparrows in the tree and "made lamentation within herself."

"Woe to me, who begot me. What womb brought me forth? … Woe is me, to what am I likened? I am not likened to the birds … even the birds … are fruitful … . I am not likened to … animals … even the … animals are fruitful … . I am not likened to this earth; for even this earth brings forth its fruit in its season and praises thee, O Lord."[6]

In answer to Anna's plea, an angel appeared and said: "God has heard your prayer. You will conceive and birth a child, who will be spoken of in the whole world."

Anna replied, "Whether I birth a boy or girl, I will bring it as a gift to God and the child shall serve the Lord all the days of its life."

Once again, the blessing of Anna and Joachim with the holy child Mary is an indication that sincere prayers are answered.

Saint and the Magical Coconut

Childless couples in India are a family disgrace.
They suffer economic hardship and are unable to
fulfill spiritual obligations to their ancestors.

In all of India's history, Saint Hazrat Sai Baba of Shirdi (1835 to 1918) stands out as unique. A local village woman first noticed him as a youngster sitting in yogic posture under a sacred neem tree along the outskirts of Shirdi. The handsome boy appeared to be free from worldly encumbrances and ordinary cares.

Villagers "were wonder-struck to see such a young lad practicing hard penance, not minding heat and cold. By day he associated with none, by night he was afraid of nobody … . He was the embodiment of dispassion … an enigma to all."[7]

Young Baba wore Muslim clothing. Yet, he put ash on his forehead, a Hindu custom. He was fluent in many languages, a master of Vedanta philosophy, and practiced complicated yogic exercises and postures.

The young adept eventually settled in the village. For years, the saint spent alternate days living in a Hindu temple and then in a Muslim mosque. His teachings mainly derived from Hindu scriptures, yet he referred to God as Allah and had insight into Islamic scriptures. He achieved peace and mutual respect between Muslims and Hindus at a time when religious rivalries had caused holy wars. In addition, visitors of every religion, race, sex, caste, language, and nation arrived to see him daily. Even outcasts, lepers, untouchables, and the ill had free access to the rare saint.

From the time of his arrival in Shirdi, young Baba changed water into lamp oil, stopped storms, healed the sick, predicted future events; he left his body to resolve dreadful situations of followers; and he made the Ganges river flow from his feet. Shirdi Sai Baba was even spiritually powerful enough to fulfill desires for a child.

He answered the prayers of one infertile woman by materializing in her dream. The saint presented her with a gift saying, "Partake of this coconut and you will bear a son."[8] The woman awoke the next morning to spot a real coconut in her bed. Within a year, she paid Baba a visit of gratitude bringing a newborn son with her.

Shirdi Sai Baba stands out for yet another reason. Before his final transition in 1918, he informed a renowned lawyer and member of the Bombay Legislative Assembly, "The death of my body means I will be temporarily ending my work. I will be reborn as a boy in eight years."

In 1926, eight years after Sai Baba of Shirdi left his mortal body, a precocious boy was born in the village of Puttaparti. The lad Sathya declared himself to be the rebirth of Sai Baba of Shirdi when he reached age thirteen. Within a few months, Sathya Sai Baba discarded his school books and announced to his family, "I am going, I do not belong to you, I have got My work, My devotees are waiting for Me."[9] Shirdi Sai Baba returned as promised and does miracles as the saint Sathya Sai Baba today.

Cross-Cultural Parallels

The "magical coconut" prelude to pregnancy transcends our understanding of a dream experience. Shirdi Sai Baba's appearance to the young woman, though unusual, is typical of testimonies of the saint's power to materialize in dreams and leave devotees with a material object. Baba possessed the yogic ability to be in two places simultaneously and physically materialized in the woman's bedroom. His miracles were performed unselfishly for the welfare of others.

The Indian woman's dream parallels reports widespread throughout history, but there is little idea how many remain unknown, since periods of skepticism and censorship have prevented their transmission. Throughout many cultures, sacred personages have appeared in two places simultaneously when a follower required healing. One of the better documented instances of bilocation occurred in the life of Saint Martin de Porres (1579 to 1639). When Martin's fellow friars mentally called him to their sickbeds, he visited them and uttered consoling words or gave them proper medicines. Others reported that they had seen Martin at that time, although in a different location.

Sea Dyaks of Borneo report similar "magical coconut" dreams. Typically an angelic being appears and gives the dreamer a charm. "And lo! when he awakes, he finds them in his hands."[10] The charm or *pengaroh*, usually black pebbles, endowed the owner with exceptional powers.

Numerous "magical coconut" miracles are recorded in the annals of Greece.[11] Pausanias, the 1st century geographer and Strabo (63 BC to AD 21), the geographer and historian, describe how the Temple of Asclepius at Epidaurus was thronged with the diseased, imploring assistance, and the cured, presenting offerings. It was common for a supplicant to remain lying prostrate in the Temple all night, expecting to converse with higher powers through dreams. Patients were healed through medicines prescribed in dreams or remedies left behind. The names of people who had been healed were inscribed on the many columns of the Temple commemorating the cures by the gods.

Today, quantum physics reveals that solid matter is an illusion of our senses and some scholars and physicists propose that if an individual's consciousness is advanced, he can act beyond the limitations of physical laws. Exceptional individuals, such as the Shirdi adept, can bilocate and materialize a coconut when they act from that level where time, the sequence of events, no longer exists. "There all is One, at the same moment … . No past, no future, only the glorious eternal Present extending into infinity."[12]

Saints Destined before Birth

It does not matter whether the couple desiring a child offers a Hebrew, Christian, Hindu, or a Sikh prayer. Earnest prayers are answered.

Miracle Mothers

Israel's first great patriarch, Abraham, desired a son. Of course, what could be more incomprehensible than for his ninety-year-old wife to behold a pre-conception vision and birth a child? Then, unexpectedly, angels Michael, Gabriel, and Raphael materialized before the couple. Michael drew a line upon the wall, predicting, "When the Sun crosses this point, Sarah will become pregnant, and when it crosses the next point, she will birth a child."

Sarah naturally harbored doubts: "Is it possible that my womb can bring forth a child, that my shriveled breasts can suckle a baby?" Yet, as a special favor from God, she birthed their son Isaac from whom a multitude of nations arose.

Besides Sarah, news of a special son was beamed towards other elderly biblical women who had abandoned all dreams of motherhood: Hannah, Rebekah, Rachel, Samson's mother, and Elizabeth, John the Baptist's mother.

Much like a cosmic computer, an infinite intelligence sees the field of all future possibilities for birth. Parenthood beyond traditional childbearing age is apparently one of many potentialities. Maybe an impossible physical birth scenario was the way God drew attention to unique children from the start.

Son of the Star

The Irish King Sena and Queen Eithne beseeched God for a son. They even fasted, observed abstinences, and gave alms to the poor.

In the middle of one period of fasting, Eithne witnessed a star enter Sena's mouth after making love. Sena simultaneously observed a star fall from heaven and enter his wife's mouth.

The men of "prudence and penetration" interpreted the dual visions:

> Just as a star guided three wise men to Christ's birth in Bethlehem, the same sign has been revealed to you: "a noble and worshipful son will be born ... filled with the grace and favor of the Holy Spirit."[13]

Eithne soon realized that she had conceived a child on the night of their visions. Nine months later, a bright, dazzling ray descended from the heavens heralding the birth of Mochoemog who grew up to be the 6th century Irish abbot and founder of Liathmor Abbey.

Historians attribute an endless list of miracles to Saint Mochoemog. One day a golden ladder descended from the heavens by Mochoemog's side as he lectured to a student.[14] Mochoemog ascended the ladder and disappeared before his student's eyes. Upon returning, he explained, "Saint Columcille has just passed on and I joined the family of Heaven to venerate him."

Saint Mochoemog's encounter with a destitute man further illustrates his abilities. One day as the holy man harvested the barley fields, a pauper asked for help to pay off a debt owed to the king. Mochoemog quickly transformed some barley into gold to fulfill the request.

When the "penniless" man showed up to pay his debt, the king inquired, "Where did you obtain this gold?" The pauper related the story about the gracious act. The king commanded, "Return the gold. Your debt is cancelled." The man did so. And just as mysteriously, the holy man transformed the gold back into barley.

On another occasion, a thief pilfered a sheep from Saint Mochoemog's flock and ate the sheep for dinner. When accused of the crime, the offender took an oath of innocence. As the wicked man swore on the Holy Bible, the ears of the sheep protruded from his mouth.

In a final illustration from Saint Mochoemog's life, the saint experienced grief over the murder of the King's son. Brandub had been a true spiritual hero, devoted to helping the poor and protecting the weak. Mochoemog immediately visited Brandub's tomb and commanded: "Brandub, arise in the name of Jesus Christ." Brandub arose from the grave and said, "Mochoemog, please don't call me back to this frail world." With that, Brandub confessed his sins and ascended.

The Pillar Saint

Martha suffered great anguish over her barrenness. Her husband Elias and her kinsfolk even reproached her. Martha finally made a secret appeal during one sleepless night.

"Oh Lord Jesus Christ, who are long-suffering towards the sins of men, Thou who didst in the beginning create woman to increase the race of men ... take my reproach ... grant me fruit of my womb that I may dedicate him to Thee ... ."[15]

Martha wept bitterly and finally fell asleep beside her husband. That night Martha witnessed two great circular lights come down from Heaven and rest near her. She thought, "God will do what is best for my unhappy soul." Within a few days, Martha conceived the Byzantine Saint Daniel (409 to 493 AD).

Saint Angelus of Furci

An Italian couple had been childless for years and vowed to dedicate their son to the Lord if God granted their desire. Saints Michael and Augustine heard their pleas and appeared in a celestial vision, promising a son who would follow the teachings of Saint Augustine.

The parents named their newborn Angelus. In keeping with their pledge, the parents placed him in the care of the abbot of Cornaclano as soon as the mother had weaned him. The boy loved prayer and studies and living the life of a little monk.

Much to Angelus' surprise, family members attempted to arrange his marriage at the age of eighteen. Angelus had never been interested in a worldly life. His father would only say: "If it be God's will and if it pleases my son."[16]

Shortly afterward, Angelus heard about the pre-conception vision for the first time from the lips of his dying father. The young man was horrified that his father "had unwittingly contemplated frustrating God's purpose for him." He quickly joined the Augustinians following the funeral. The 14th century saint completed various stages of philosophical and theological training and became professor of theology at the Augustinian college in Naples.

Praying for a Son

An Indian couple had been blessed with five children, yet four sons did not survive childhood. One daughter remained. As Bhuvaneshwari performed the household chores, she prayed for a son to carry on the family tradition. The pious woman believed that God would answer her plea if she fasted and worshipped once a week for one year (Somavara vrata). Bhuvaneshwari wished to perform this worship in Benares where women traditionally pray for children at the Shiva temple. Since she lived so far away, an aunt living in Benares made the temple offerings and prayed that a son might be born to her niece. Meanwhile, every Monday, Bhuvaneshwari fasted and prayed at home.

Bhuvaneshwari had a vivid dream upon completing the sacred vow. Lord Shiva roused himself from meditation and transformed himself into a male child. Bhuvaneshwari awoke finding herself bathed in an ocean of light. In due course, a son's birth gladdened the hearts of Bhuvaneshwari and her husband.

The unexpected twist is that the much-longed-for baby was no ordinary child. Originally named Narendranath Datta, he became Swami Vivekananda (1863 to 1902), chief disciple of Ramakrishna. Within him was hidden the tremendous power of a perfected soul as well as a savior of souls. (See Chapter 27, *Piercing the Veils of Light*, for Vivekananda's cosmic contract.)

Swami Vivekananda's brilliant lectures in Europe and the USA created respect for Hinduism in the West. On one USA tour, the saint paid tribute to Bhuvaneshwari and stated that he owed everything to his mother's spiritual purity. He was "born through prayer" rather than "sensuality."

"The child must be prayed for. Those children come with curses, that slip into the world just in a moment of inadvertence, because that could not be prevented, what can you expect of such progeny?"[17]

Twenty-One-Year Retreat

The Mohammedan conquest of India became the bloodiest story in history. Muslim raiders had been looting India for 600 years. Afghan sultans crossed into the Punjab with their armies, returning home with slaves, gold, precious jewels – including diamonds the size of pomegranates. India lived under a regime of injustice and oppression. Religion had been reduced to superstition and ritualistic performances.

Within this political climate, Guru Teg Bahadur and his wife Mata Gujri lived in an underground cellar for twenty-one years, undisturbed by worldly happenings.[18] The couple remained absorbed in divine worship and beseeched God for a hero-son to become the protector of the people.

Pleased with their devotion, God granted them a son. At the time of his birth, a brilliant light spread towards the east. A Sufi saint, Pir Bhikhan Shah of Punjab, who observed this vision travelled to Patna, a city on the Ganges, to search for the special baby. He placed two covered bowls of sweets near the child to determine whether the Guru-to-be would lean more towards Muslims or Hindus. Much to his surprise, the three-month-old simultaneously placed his hands on both bowls indicating he treated them alike. The saint bowed and said, "My master, this country needed thee more than anyone else at this juncture."[19]

Guru Gobind Singh (1666 to 1708) grew up to unite Hindus and Muslims within one religion, Sikhism. His autobiographical poem describes how his parents' worship pleased "the Unseen One" who thereby ordered Gobind's birth as their son in this Dark Age.

~~~~~~~~~~~~~~~~~~~~~~~~~

Saint Foresees "Future Life" Son

*The birth of India's 15th century saint
Narsimh Saraswati is another case of seeing
through time into the unborn future and illustrates
how saintly souls waiting for birth respond to prayer.*[20]

The power of Amba Bhawani's consciousness preserved the memory of how she had prayed for a son in a previous life as a woman named Ambika. Her master, Saint Shripad Shri Vallabh, blessed her saying, "Ambika, as a devoted spiritual seeker, you will birth a great saint, but it will not happen until your next birth."

In this way, the seeds were long planted for the mothering ability to bring in a highly evolved soul. As soon as Amba's son was born, instead of crying like a normal baby, the newborn uttered the mantra "Om," indicating that advanced children are more aware and even able to speak a few words from birth.

At the age of eight, Amba's son Narsimh announced, "I desire to find God and must take a pilgrimage to India's holy places. God will bless you and Father with four more children to shower your love upon. I will return to meet them." The renowned saint fulfilled his promise thirty years later.

A Saint's Blessing

*A couple's longing for a saintly child was
answered by worshipping in a sacred temple.*

Sage Nam Dev, a wandering saddhu, stopped to pray at a village temple in the Gurdaspur District of the Punjab. The local priests, however, refused admission to the outcast. Undeterred, Saint Nam Dev sat behind the temple and become lost in *samadhi*. The Lord, unhappy at the insult offered his disciple, turned the face of the temple towards the place where Nam Dev sat. The brahmin priests fell at Nam Dev's feet asking for forgiveness. From that day, the village took the name Ghuman, a Punjabi word signifying "to turn around." The shrine was renamed "Dera Baba Nam Dev."

Centuries passed and villagers offered prayers, and saddhus paid homage to Saint Nam Dev at the shrine. Among them, a pious couple, Bhai Jodh Singh and his wife Bibi Daya Kaur, prayed for a virtuous son.

"Great souls seldom come announced, and one night Bibi Daya Kaur was visited by Nam Dev in a dream, who told her that her prayers were granted."[21]

Baba Jaimal Singh was born ten months later (1838). The boy showed precocity from an early age and sat attentively in the shrine. The child repeated verses from spiritual discourses at the age of three. Villagers nicknamed him "Bal-Sadhu" or child-saint. When Jaimal was five, his parents placed him under the care of a teacher, under whom he mastered the scriptures within several years.

Regardless of what happened, Jaimal remembered his spiritual disciplines. The young man allowed nothing to disrupt his prayer and meditation even when he served as a combat soldier. During the Anglo-Afghan War in 1879, he walked into the wilderness at night where, after digging a pit, he placed his rifle under his knees and became lost in meditation. Enemy snipers spotted him, "but seeing his Radiant figure," they refused to shoot a holy man. A few enemy soldiers even bowed before Jaimal when he arose from prayer.

Jaimal's reputation grew and seekers requested help to alleviate worldly afflictions. One man seeking his aid had been married many years, but no children had been born. Jaimal informed Subedar Kharak Singh that he was not destined to have a child. Still the man begged for the blessing. Jaimal finally granted the request upon strict conditions: "Subedar, donate 500 rupees to charity." Unfortunately, shortly after the child was born to Subedar and his wife, the father neglected the charity requirement and fell deathly ill. Jaimal was summoned, but it was too late to save Subedar. The man passed away several days later.

Jaimal's ability to foresee future events is again reflected in the case of a pundit who repeatedly sought "a glimpse of the inner Realms." Jaimal replied: "You will be unable to withstand such a holy vision. The intensity will be too great."

The pundit persisted: "What does it matter even if I lose my life, if only I may see what is within?"[22] At this point, the sage instructed the pundit to meditate. Jaimal focused his intense spiritual gaze upon him and "the pundit's soul was forcibly drawn up into the higher realms."[23] After a sojourn away from his physical body, the pundit's soul was brought back to physical consciousness. The man fell sobbing at the saint's feet. The pundit poured out:

"I thought my life was being wrenched out of me, and a million lightnings fell upon my head …. forgive me my foolishness …."

"What have I to forgive?" replied the Sage. "It is you who must forgive yourself, for it is not I who suffered. Now go and make the most of your time, for you have only three more years to live."[24]

From that day forward, the pundit focused on meditation and prayer. Three years later, as Jaimal predicted, he passed away.

Additional eyewitness accounts support the saintly nature of Baba Jaimal Singh's spiritual development. He helped to continue a lineage of teachers offering the Sant Mat teachings succeeded by Sawan Singh, Kirpal Singh, and contemporary Tahkar Singh.

Blessing of Supreme Energy

*Millions of people around the world recognize that Mata
Amritanandamayi's (1953 to –) touch, words, and glance
can spiritually heal incurable diseases and, according
to countless infertile women, they too bear children.*

Mata Amritanandamayi, the Holy Mother, turns no one away
who seeks sincere blessings. The unbelievable story of a beggar,
Dattan, who suffered from leprosy, epitomizes the saint's love and
compassionate efforts to help the suffering.

Dattan's childhood had been transformed into an unforgiving
nightmare while he was growing up in Perumpally near
Kayamkulam in Kerala province. Living on the brink of wanting to
end his life, Dattan felt sheer desperation and pain. His family had
spurned him and kicked him out long ago. Becoming a beggar on the
streets and living on a temple's grounds, his life became filled with
misery as the leprosy increased its stranglehold. Passers-by held their
nose and scurried away. Others spit on his hideous looking body.

As destiny at times lends itself to extraordinary encounters,
Dattan heard about Amritanandamayi and attempted to visit her in
the city of Vallickavu for Bhava darshan (a Saint's spiritual glance
that purifies a person). Mata's disciples felt differently, however, and
refused to admit the leper inside the ashram, out of fear that the foul
odors emitted from his wounds would insult the Holy Mother.

Despite his hellish existence and bodily odors, the saint summoned
him inside the hall. Many people were seated with the Holy Mother,
including Swami Amritaswarupananda who referred to Dattan as the
ugliest person he had ever seen. Dattan was bald. He had no eyes –
only small slits through which he observed the world. He wore no
clothing because it would stick to the oozing pus and blood being
emitted from the infected putrid-smelling wounds covering his body.

According to the Swami's eye-witness account, Amritanandamayi consoled Dattan like her own child, as she did with everyone who came for blessings. Except in his case, Dattan needed extra attention. So first she took him on her lap, then her shoulder. Then Mother kissed his cheek and licked his pus-infected wounds. Finally she bit him on the forehead, sucked the blood and pus, and spit it out.

The Swami says, "If a third person had told me, I would have rejected it, but I saw it with my naked eyes." Some people fainted. Several vomited. Many walked out of the hall. Still others watched with awe and shed tears of love and devotion.

The Holy Mother explained:

"Who else is there to take care of him and to love him? Mother doesn't see his external body. She sees only his heart. I cannot discard him. He is my son and I am his mother."[25]

Dattan visited Amritanandamayi in this fashion about three times each week. On Bhava darshan days, the Mother poured water over him and smeared sacred ash on his body. Just as the Bible says Jesus Christ cured the lepers, due to the Mother's purifying saliva and attendance (ash, water), Dattan's incurable disease nearly vanished, his wounds almost all healed, his hair grew back, his eyes opened, and he is happy. Compared to his previous state, he is a handsome fellow.

According to India's scriptures, the saliva of a self-realized soul is a divine medicine which evidently includes a biochemical substance called *soma*. *Soma* is a natural elixir created in the physiology of an enlightened person. Modern biochemical laboratories have yet to identify such a substance, but are attempting to isolate it.

The leprosy case is relevant by suggesting that, if a saint has the loving ability to heal an incurable disease, her gift will help couples suffering from infertility problems.

Shakti Prasad – Another Special Healing

In lieu of Dattan's special *darshan*, Omana visited Amritanandamayi for a different reason. She and her husband had prayed for a child for nine years to no avail. Without uttering even a word to the Holy Mother, Amritanandamayi consoled Omana, "Daughter, you came here to gain a baby. Mother will remove your sorrow. Within four months the child will take form in the womb."[26]

As Nature took its course, Mother's words were fulfilled. Omana's pregnancy proceeded normally until the ninth month when three gynecologists found no evidence of a fetus despite her enormous belly. X-rays taken at different hospitals revealed only dense smoke on the film, but no signs of a fetus. Amritanandamayi smiled at the medical report and told Omana, "Be courageous, that child is God's son, not an image. They cannot take his photograph."[27]

Omana remained focused on prayer and meditation during the next three months. Nothing seemed to shake her faith, even the cutting remarks of villagers: "She is going to give birth to a baby elephant."

During the sixteenth month of pregnancy, Amritanandamayi advised, "Take Omana to the hospital." Still the doctors found no evidence of a baby in the womb. After much deliberation, they performed a C-Section. And lo and behold, a full-grown healthy child emerged from the womb.

Amritanandamayi named him Shakti Prasad, meaning "Blessing of the Supreme Energy." The boy began to live up to his name at the age of three when he chanted mantras and meditated in a perfect yogic posture.

Amritanandamayi has healed countless women, like Omana, who deserve children. She chooses couples carefully. Selection depends upon subtle considerations beyond the human intellect. Once Amritanandamayi agrees to help, she enters a deep meditation and transmits a power into the woman's womb.

In such inspired cases, mothers birth spiritual children. Some live a typical family life. Others are perfect saints. If parents feel disappointed when they realize that they will eventually lose their sons for the altruistic service of mankind, Amritanandamayi promises a second child to fulfill the normal expectations of parents.

PART THREE

LAND OF HIDDEN BEGINNINGS

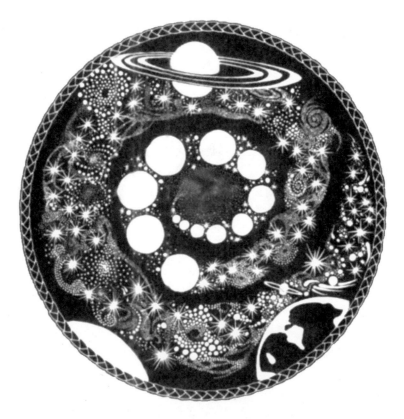

Creation is unfolding in a Sequential Pattern.
A Star Danced, under that I was Born.

Investigating
Pre-Conception Worlds

*The notion that human souls dwell in another realm
prior to conception was new to us. We grew up learning the
Christian view of life after death, but had heard nothing about
the soul's history prior to conception. Yet, as we discovered, even
Christianity has a bifurcated history. Many Christians accepted
that the soul has always existed and will never cease to exist,
that is, until the Second Council of Constantinople condemned
the theory in 553 AD – probably because belief in the soul's
pre-existence opened the door to the theory of reincarnation.*

*Unlike Christianity's present stance, descriptions of
a "land" where we exist as spiritual beings, choose parents,
and negotiate the circumstances of our lives seems to be nearly
universal. Belief in the soul's pre-existence can be found
throughout religion, philosophy, poetry, and mythology.*

*Just as the physical world corresponds to our five outer
senses and waking state of consciousness, higher worlds
correspond to our subtler senses and higher states of awareness.
Vast spheres lie completely submerged beyond the obvious material
world, hidden domains existing simultaneously with this one.
Physicists might call them parallel universes or quantum
fields. Usually this "land" exists out of sight, but
is sometimes near our ordinary world.*

*Part Three explores this "life within life" –
a land of enchantment in the long forgotten
memory of our birth on this planet.*

Chapter 13
Lodge of the Great Manitou

**We regard the soul as the greatest
and most incomprehensible of all.**[1]
– The Iglulik Eskimo

*Native American communities from Canada to
Mexico shared the belief that babies originate from
somewhere other than the mother's body.*

Native Americans viewed human birth in terms of a passage down from the beyond. The Canadian Saulteaux regarded children as a "Gift from God," since they dwelled with God prior to birth. The tribal elder Fair Wind remarked, "The ancestors have been on this earth once, and before that they were sent from above to come on this earth."[2] A Winnebago shaman likewise spoke of "my higher spirit-home from which I originally came."[3] And the Chiefs of the Natchez, who are "the Suns," came from the "luminary,"[4] to which they will return.

At each child's birth, parents announced that a baby traveller has descended from various cosmic regions as a gift of the Deity or an emanation of His Being.[5]

❋ Chinooks (Pacific Northwest) – "The baby's home is the Sun before being born. All children come from the daylight. That is their home."[6]

❋ Eastern Shawnee (Oklahoma) – Kokomthena rules the soul's abode on little stars of the Milky Way. The goddess, a sole survivor of the great flood, created humans and gave them a code of laws and religious ceremonies. She weaves a basket which, when completed, signals the end of the world.[7]

❁ Lakota (Great Plains) – "Toward the south there is a large camp in which beauty and peace abide. There is a council lodge and inside sits ... Grandfather ... . he calls out to a man and woman ... . 'You are now going to make a long journey, so do the best you can ... . In the future you will come back ... . you will be asked to tell about how your journey fared. So go now ... . But never own more than you need.'"[8]

❁ Ingaliks (Alaska) – There is a warehouse pervaded by spirits of children, all impatient to be called into this life. Each time a child descends to Earth, the remaining children express jealousy and impatience by slapping him.[9]

❁ Northwestern peoples – Unborn children live and play in Babyland before they come to Earth.[10]

Other tribal groups located the pre-existent state in various cosmic regions: Aztecs (Mexico) – Ninth Heaven, dwelling place of the supreme gods; Salish (Shoalwater Bay, Washington) – the Sun; people of ancient Mexico – *tlacapillachiualoya*, the "baby-factory" where children are created;[11] Mandan – stars and planetary bodies; Osage (western Missouri) – babies are tiny stars who come from the sky, Spiritland;[12] Athapascans (Oregon) – spirit abode of the Goddess in the South; and Montagnais (Quebec) – the clouds.[13]

The California Miwoks equated their pre-earth home with the dwelling place of the ancestors. The soul journeys westward after death and becomes like a baby in the region of "spiritual genesis and exodus."

[O-lo-win] "is a big place, and a long, long ways off, and no live man can go to that place. Only the dead ... . The spirit ... knows the road ... it has been that way before. We don't know when, but ... we all ... come from there. Even our little children know that trail. Yes, there is plenty of waters ... . No, there is no boat ... . A bridge, a fine, fragile long bridge, more than a mile, maybe ... a thousand miles long ... ."[14]

Rather than the sky world, other peoples place the pre-birth world below the Earth.

❁ Hidatsa – A house of infants is in a cavern, called Makadistati, near the Knife River. The entrance measures nine inches in diameter and extends deep into the Earth. Parents attribute marks on the infant's body to "kicks received from his former comrades when he was ejected from his subterranean home."[15]

❀ Hopi – The underworld is the house of the Sun and Earth goddess. "Here are generated the souls of the newly born on earth, and to this home of the Sun return the spirits of the dead."[16] The breath-body or shade of man passes through a gateway or *sipapu* located on the wall of the Grand Canyon at birth and death. Thus the place of the soul's genesis equates with its "post-mortem home."[17]

❀ Pueblo – A small hole, *shipapu*, in the floor of a Kiva symbolizes the umbilical cord leading from Earth to "the previous underworld."[18]

❀ Zuni – The grandfathers said that in the Underworld there were villages of people who were "unborn-made … [they] had not yet begun to live … in the daylight … partly like ourselves, they had bodies, and partly like the dead they had no bodies … these people were really like the smoke … every being passes through many successive states of becoming, always beginning as a haze being and passing through the Raw or soft, the Formative, Variable, Fixed or Done, and Finished or Dead states … ."[19]

Additional descriptions of the soul's pre-earthly home come from: Kwakiutl, Oklahoma Shawnee, Akwa'ala, Yuma, Maricopa, Lakota, Menominee (aka Menomini), Teton, Ojibwa (aka Ojibway, Ojibwe), Chippewa, Mojave, Yuman, Fox, and Dakota Sioux.

Cosmic Door in the Sky

The image of an interconnecting door – a bridge,
rainbow, or Milky Way – is an ancient motif symbolizing
an opening leading towards the world of souls.

LEk·âs, a Kwakiutl woman, recounts a vivid dream. A man
called her to the upper side of the world.

> The guide grasped me by my right hand and we went straight up,
> passing through the door in the middle of the upper side of our world.
> He let me see "everything that was in the house." Finally we found
> "the hole in the edge of the world." My guide explained, "Through
> this (hole) pass the children when they are born, when they come from
> the upper side of the world. Now pass through it and go home."[20]

The Almond-Shaped Universe

Knowledge of the region where souls await birth comes from
medicine men who travel there and back again. An Absentee
Shawnee (Oklahoma) says: "Visitors go to a western region beyond
the end of the earth, crossing four oceans, passage over the last one
being possible only as the rhythmically rising and falling sky
ascends and leaves an open gap"[21] – a type of trap door.

Visitors who pass through the trap door find themselves in the
home of the creator Kokomthena, Our Grandmother. Kokomthena
rules the world located one level beneath the Sun. Through her
sky-window, she watches to see whether her earthly children are
maintaining the traditions and laws she gave them.

Kokomthena helps visitors avoid the trap door on the return trip
to Earth. She lowers them through the sky-window in a basket.
This short cut traverses the layers of the universe between Earth
and Heaven in which birds and various beings dwell.

Cross-Cultural Parallels

The momentary opening of a metaphorical curtain or a trap door
as an entry to the celestial realm is an ancient motif.

Souls Waiting in the Wings for Birth

❁ Greece *(Odyssey)* – Two rocks *(Planktai)* emerge from the foaming sea and continually clash together in tempests of fire.

❁ Greece *(Argonautica of Apollonius of Rhodes)* – Clashing Islands, the Symplegades, stand at the entrance to the Euxine Sea.

❁ India – Soma, the plant which bestows immortality, is kept safe at Heaven's Door behind two golden, razor-edged leaves which snap together at every winking of an eye.[23] This Door stands "where Sky and Earth embrace" and where the "Ends of the year" are united.[24]

The wise know when the "Cosmic Door" will open. Magical flights signify a rite of passage, requiring "intelligence, under-standing of secret things, and metaphysical truths." Sacred texts from India declare: "Intelligence is the swiftest of birds;" "Those who know have wings."[25]

❁ Native Americans (Cherokee, Yuchi, Creek, Chickasaw, Navajo, Chitimacha) – People ascend to the sky through a "horizon curtain" that opens but for an instant. Alternately, the barrier is a cloud swaying where Earth and sky meet.[22]

❁ Lao-Tse (China) – "Canst thou, when the gate of heaven opens or shuts, be as a bird-mother?"[26]

❁ Plato *(Phaedrus)* – When souls attain the summit of the celestial vault, they pass outside it, stand upon its back, and are carried round by its rotation and gaze upon the things beyond the sky.

❁ Siberia (Buryat) – The dome-shaped sky is always rising and falling. As it rises, a crevice appears between the rim of the dome and Earth. One hero kept the crack open by placing an arrow as a support to the rim of the dome. A wonderful light shone from the Otherworld illuminating the Earth. "The flash, and what it reveals, itself satisfies the desire of him who sees it."[27]

❁ Siberia (Chukchee) – Layers of worlds, stacked one above the other, are connected by holes situated under the Pole Star. Heroes seated on eagles or thunderbirds fly through the holes and traverse the heavens one after another.[28]

❁ Philippines (Bagobos) – Lumabat attained absolute freedom by ascending to the horizon where the sky rises and falls and gives periodic access to another world.

❁ Native American (Seneca) – Two brothers passed through the up and down moving sky rim and became immortal. They acquired super powers and even caught deer with their hands.[29]

Twin Souls

*Native Americans subdivided the pre-conception world
into diverse communities. Twins formed one distinct group.*

Twin children are a mystery. In certain cases, a supernatural
father impregnates the mother rather than her earthly husband.[30]
The Chippewas felt a reverence for them and respected all
members of a family having twins. Chippewas and Ojibwas
believed twins were related to superior beings, the Thunderers or
Thunders.[31] Unlike ordinary souls which spring from the state of
"aliveness" after conception, the Mojave insisted that souls of
twins always existed in Heaven and had no earthly parents. After
cremation, twin souls "return to Heaven using another branch of
the forked road" which they followed on their descent to Earth.
Twins never return. "One life is all they want."[32]

Other native peoples believed twins came from: (Yuma and
Maricopa) – a mythical village in the Northwest;[33] (Lakota) – a
superior world compared to ordinary people; (Northwest coast
tribes) – "Salmon-land" where twins pre-existed as salmon;[34]
(Tetons) – Twin-land;[35] and (Mojave) – Heaven.[36]

Cocopa women of the Southwest[37] dreamed of their twins
during pregnancy. The twins came from Twinland, one of the
cosmological realms within the four-storied sky world. Around the
age of three, twins usually recalled the names they had in Heaven
and named themselves – unlike ordinary children whose parents
named them on their first birthday. Twins further distinguished
themselves by piercing their ears and nose, and tattooing their
chins. Many twin souls, however, never come to Earth because
Twinland is so charming.

Twins born to the Akwa'ala Indians of Lower California
descended from a mountainous realm to the south of their habitat.

Souls Waiting in the Wings for Birth

The shaman Jackrabbit "acquired, by dreaming, the knowledge that unborn twins in spirit form leave their earthly mother at will and return to their own country."[38] Apparently this occurs during the mother's pregnancy.

Akwa'ala twins often became homesick for their "own country," a desire which can linger for years. Parents then requested the help of Jackrabbit to communicate with the newborns. He was "always looking after twins in this fashion." He promised the homesick twins abundant food and a happy family life. In fact, twins had the privilege of dressing in "gala attire." Despite Jackrabbit's encouraging words, he did not "prevent them very well" from going back to their real home.[39] The twins explain:

> We will visit here for a while. Then, we will return to our own country. We are always going back and forth and are born to different mothers.

"Our souls are always going back and forth and are born to different mothers each time we come to Earth."

Lodge of the Great Manitou

The Fox peoples believed each individual possesses
a small soul which emanates from the impersonal force
pervading the universe, Gitche Manitou, *as well as a*
large soul which originated with a great being
called the Great Hare, Wīsàkä.

The small soul dwells in the spirit world between one life and the next. This is a pleasant place located in the West, beyond the setting Sun. The soul travels on a narrow path until it reaches a bridge that spans a swift foaming river. The bridge is a log that continually moves up and down.

The soul passes over the bridge and arrives on the opposite shore. The sound of a drum is heard. The drum beat draws the soul to the Great Manitou's lodge. Iyāpā'tä, the Great Hare's younger brother, a godlike being, sits inside singing and beating a drum. Iyāpā'tä takes each soul by the hand as a sign of welcome, and offers a meal and a seat.

Iyāpā'tä questions each arrival about their life among the living. Other lodge members, equally curious, gather to hear about families still left on Earth. Afterward, the soul meets a multitude of departed ancestors and friends outside the lodge.

Life in the Great Manitou's realm is enjoyable. Yet every soul must undergo a spiritual death in the upper world and be re-embodied in a baby born on Earth. The small soul assumes birth "four times."[40] Each time a new large soul becomes its guardian.

Home of the Thunder Beings

Supernatural beings called "Thunder Beings" "or Thunder Birds" chose to be born as mystics among the Menominee, Fox, Central Algonquin, Sioux, Winnebago, and Eastern Dakota.[41]

The Menominee believe "some babies are actually manitous in human shape ... thunder boys ... nothing less than these powerful god beings come to earth for a while; ... girls ... personify one of the sacred sisters of the eastern sky."[42] One elder narrated the story of the Thunder Beings and proudly exhibited three birchbark drawings, scenes from the earthly lives of the Thunder Beings. (Figure 5) He inherited the drawings from his father who traced them back to his great-great grandfather; beyond that there was no record.

The legend narrates how Chief Thunder Being requested two representatives to be born on Earth for a special task. He explained, "Go to Earth and obtain tobacco. Through sacred fire ceremonies, offer the tobacco in gratitude to the Thunder Beings in the higher worlds."

The two volunteers, Kewûta'wapeo (Rolling Eyes or Look Around) and Pawē'koné (Moulting Feathers), "traveled all over the world looking for a tribe of men sufficiently brave and honorable, and women of great virtue to honor."[43]

As they inspected various peoples, the lesser of the two, Pawē'koné, realized: "I forgot an important item. Please wait while I go home to fetch it." His companion waited faithfully until Pawē'koné took longer than expected. Meanwhile Kewûta'wapeo began to cast his gaze upon the Menominee. He felt so satisfied that he entered a woman's womb, causing her to become pregnant.

As the story describes, by that time, Pawē'koné returned and felt deserted by his partner. He "flew away" and chose a mother of a nearby people.

When the two Thunders reached maturity, they recalled why they had come to Earth. They cured the sick and helped people in numerous ways, "asking only a fee of tobacco," although they accepted other gifts. When the Thunders received their wages, they cast the tobacco into the fire crying to the relatives above, "Take this tobacco. I transfer it to you. This is what you sent us on earth for."

Sky Children

Parents of Thunder children – who come down "from above" – usually noticed a radiant aura around their youngsters. Of course, in some cases, the parents failed to realize the child's "supernatural origin." Puzzled by a child's constant tears or unexplained illness, the struggling parents called upon a seer initiated in the dialect of babies. Then the seer "examines the child, speaks to it, and soon learns the secret of its troubles."[44] The seer explains:

> Your child is under the protection of the powers above and should be named as the gods intended. He is upset because you substituted another name for the true name he brought from above.

As sky children mature, they slipped off by themselves and gazed at the western sky, their "ancient home." In these silent moments, they witnessed future events due to their "inherited knowledge of overhead affairs."[46]

Figure 5: Three Birchbark Strips containing records written by the Thunderbirds who sometimes were born on Earth to spiritually uplift the Menominee.[45]

Cross-Cultural Parallel

Fire ceremonies form part of the religious tradition of India. During a ceremony called a *yagya*, vedic priests offer various ingredients into the fire – rice, clarified butter – to attain the blessings of powers governing different impulses of intelligence and energy which direct creation's evolution and to answer the prayers of someone who needs healing, etc. The *Bhagavad-Gita* (3.10-11) states:

> *Yagyas* bestow everything desirable for a happy material and
> spiritual life. Through *yagya* you cherish the gods and they will
> sustain you. By sustaining one another, you will reap the very highest.

On a deeper level, the story of the Thunders means that Chief Thunder Being sent them to spiritually uplift and heal the people through performing sacred ceremonies.

Sky children enjoy gazing at the western sky, their "ancient home."

Chapter 14

Land of the Boomerang

Nana Churinga indulla-irrakura ingwana;
unta knailjalugga;
Here is your *Churinga indulla-irrakura;*
you came out of it.[1]

– Arunta Aborigines, Central Australia

Unlike modern individuals who often feel uneasy
before stones, trees, or monoliths as manifestations of the
sacred, Australian Aborigines revere all natural objects
because they hide an underlying sacredness.

Where babies come from is closely interwoven with the topographical features, according to the Aborigines. Dwelling places of spirit-children are superimposed upon the physical dimension and are as real as the physical world. A creation legend narrated by the Central Aborigines sheds light on the world of spirit-children. In conjunction with this legend, the Primordial ancestors, the *tjukurita*, were immense, super-human creatures, complete expressions of the mysterious life essence, *kuranita*. These powerful beings arrived when Earth was devoid of life – only dry, featureless plains.

The mission of the *tjukurita* consisted of creating all living creatures, the countryside, rocks, and water-courses using the *kuranita* force. This is how the life essence came to permeate everything. The medicine-man has the most; men have more than women; the emu has more than the wild turkey; the kangaroo has more than the wallaby; and trees have more than rocks and grass.[2]

In connection with sacred objects, the *tjukurita* formed "increase centers," dwelling places for spirit-children, in monoliths, caves, rocky areas, artifacts, a mountain landscape, sandhills, or large trees.

Spirit-children homes vary from one region of Australia to the next –

- Ooldea Region – Spirit-children gather around fires near water holes, but disappear as soon as a human comes too near. Notwithstanding its desire for birth, if a spirit-child eyes a suitable mother, it follows her home, seeking an opportunity to enter her womb.
- Western Arnhem Land, Northern Australia – Gunwinggu Aborigines converse with spirit-children when they leave their paper bark trees and meat-ants' nests in order to swim and splash in the water. Aborigines are careful not to light a fire in their presence. Otherwise, spirit-children let out a fearful cry, dive back into the water, and never reappear.
- Adelaide, South Australia – At the time of death, souls depart to *Pindi*, the western land. Before they are reborn in human bodies, they come back to Earth and take up their abode in trees.[3]

More examples are gathered from ancient stories, memories, and religious beliefs published in anthropological studies on ten Aboriginal peoples: Kimberley and Worora, northwestern Australia; Forrest River Aborigines, North Kimberley Division in West Australia; Broome Aborigines, West Kimberley District of Western Australia; Murinbata, Northern Territory; Aborigines from Daly River region, Northern Territory; Ngalia, Central Australia; Tiwi, Melville Island; Gunwinggu, Western Arnhem Land, Northern Australia; and Arunta, Central Australia.

The Divine Element

*Kimberley Aborigines know where they lived
prior to birth: their fathers found their spirits in a dream
near the water pool. In ancient times, that is where
Kaleru, the Rainbow Serpent, deposited them.*

Kimberley, Worora, and Forrest River Aborigines regarded water as a divine element since it comes from above.[4] That is why water makes an ideal spirit-child home. The child's "country of origin" is so important that parents named a child after these sacred sites – until Christian missionaries forbade this custom. Each father marked the location with a special stone. A Forrest River father takes his child to visit the pool and explains, "You may live and hunt here freely for the rest of your life."

In this manner, every child knows where his father "conceived" him, and intimate social bonds exist between children originating from the same spirit-child home. These relationships contribute to tribal stability and unity. Even after death, the link with one's spirit home continues. That is why Bugai Aborigines of Forrest River hide the deceased's bones in a cave near the pools where their fathers found them.

Custodians of the Spirit-Children

*A custodian tends for the
spirit-children of each pre-birth region.*

No trouble, strife, toil, or death ever arises in Jimbin land – only the happy laughter of spirit babies *(ngargalulla)* at play. New baby spirits, as well as baby spirits who have been born before, dwell in this underground region lying at the bottom of the sea. In the Broome District, medicine men *(Jalngangooroo)*, and tribal members with the gift called *ranji*, watch these little people tumble and somersault in the waters with "*Pajjalburra*," the porpoise. Or they observe spirit-children play in the dancing spray and sunlight of the beaches under the guardianship of "*Koolibal*," the mother-turtle.

Babies who come from *Alalk-yinga*, a hill located near Daly River, "are kept shut up there under the care of an old man whose duty it is to prevent them from escaping" and nourish them with water via an underground channel connected to Daly river. "When a child is to be born, this old man sees to the business."[5]

Good mountain spirits, *tuanjiraka*, and their wives, *melbata*, serve as caretakers in the Finke River region. They carry each spirit-child *(gurunna)* to a tree where it remains in the foliage until its mother experiences labor pains. This tree, known as *ngirra*, is sacred and the Arunta do not disturb it. If winds or floods injure the tree, the child becomes ill.

Eluding Motherhood

Women exercise caution around spirit-child
dwellings if they are not ready to set spirit-children free.

Arunta women must sometimes travel past a fertility stone which projects three feet above the ground. They call this stone *Erathipa*, meaning child, because on one side of it there is "a round hole through which the spirit-children are ... on the look-out for women who may chance to pass near."[6] Recognizing these fertility powers, a woman who does not desire a child pretends to be old, as if leaning on a stick as she passes by this stone. She says: "Don't come to me, I am too old to bear children."

For similar reasons, Gunwinggu women give paper bark trees and meat-ants' nest a wide berth and warn young girls to stay away.

A legend of the Murinbata advises women to avoid certain spirit-child dwellings. Kunmanggur, the Rainbow-Snake Man, placed healthy spirit-children in the hollows of trees, logs, water-courses, and even the wind, but he placed a few unhealthy spirits in the leaves of trees. These "leaf" *(mulun)* spirit-children are never found in a pre-conception dream. A mature woman avoids these branches, lest a *mulun* enter her womb. Young girls are less careful and birth sickly or deformed children.

Interpenetrating Worlds

*Spirit-children are aware of activities
in the physical world and dwell in different
homes depending upon the time of day.*

Spirit-children sleep inside a storehouse of metaphysical arti-facts on Mt. Winbaraku, according to the Ngalia Aborigines. Then these tiny dark-haired children with light streaks awake at sunrise and travel to a nearby village in search of a mother. They sit under shady acacia trees and eat the acacia gum and drink morning dew. If a spirit-child sees a suitable mother stroll by, it reduces itself to the size of a termite and enters her body. Spirit-children who are less fortunate return to their mountain abode at night and take up their search for a mother the following day.

As another example, Tiwi spirit-children, *pitipituis*, dwell in an underground home, where it is warm and dry at high tide, and at low tide they come out to play on the sandbanks.

Numbakulla's Totemic Children

Every Arunta Aborigine is born into a totem
associated with an animal, plant, or natural object.
Spirit-children belonging to the same totemic group
live together at a site sacred to that totem.

In the beginning, "there were a very large number of *Kuruna* [souls] inside"[7] the body of *Numbakulla*, the Creator who arose "out of nothing."[8] He kept them concealed for a while, but eventually the *Kuruna* emerged from *Numbakulla*.

Numbakulla inserted the spirits belonging to a specific totemic group into different stone slabs *(churinga)*. Stones containing spirit-children belonging to numerous totems, such as Achilpa (wildcat), Erlia (emu), Arura (kangaroo), Udnirringita (witchetty grub), Irriakura (yelka), or Emora (opossum).

The Sky Heroes who wandered in bands across the country in a primordial age, known as the *Alchera*, carried these elaborately marked stones with them. At the end of that era, the mighty beings "went into the ground," leaving the sacred stones behind. Each artifact, inscribed with totemic designs, sheltered spirit-children who became the original Arunta men and women belonging to various totemic groups.

Figure 6 shows an inscribed stone *churinga*. The hole in the central design represents the doorway through which the spirit-child is "dreamt" into its mother's womb. The spirit-child leaves the *churinga* behind as soon as it enters the womb. When a woman senses she is with child, she searches the environment for the spirit-child's *churinga*. She then discovers the child's totem and names the child appropriately.

The Arunta hide the *churingas* in caves, fissures in rocks, tree hollows, or sandbank holes. The elders present a wooden *churinga* to a young boy at his initiation: "Here is your *Churinga indullairrakura*; you came out of it."[10] They explain the meaning of its markings along with the chants "rendered in a sacred language with which he is unfamiliar."[11] The wooden *churinga* is then rewrapped in leaves, tied with a hair string, and repositioned in the totemic center. The young initiate also sees the original stone *churinga* belonging to his totem, the one fashioned by the Sky Heroes.

The boy rubs his fingers over the sacred markings on this sacred symbol and his "metaphysical heritage becomes paramount."[12] Earlier this century, an anthropologist recorded an Arunta father's words to his son at this presentation.

"This is your own body from which you have been reborn."[13] Today you are learning that you are the great Tjenterama for the first time. We entrust all the sacred *churinga* to you. Protect and honour the traditions. We will teach you many more verses and secret ceremonies. We are growing old and must pass them on.

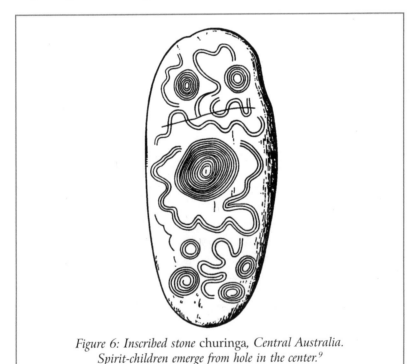

Figure 6: Inscribed stone churinga, *Central Australia. Spirit-children emerge from hole in the center.*[9]

Witchetty Grub Totem

Semi-divine ancestors established a large center for witchetty grub (large moth larva) spirit-children near Alice Springs in Central Australia. Any Arunta woman who enters the picturesque gap in that area increases the likelihood of conceiving a spirit-child dwelling in its prominent boulders and gum trees. Illustrating this point is a woman belonging to the witchetty grub totem who stopped nearby for a drink of water. She heard a child's voice cry out, "Mia, mia!" – a term for mother. The woman fled. "But to no purpose; she was fat and well favored," and of course she birthed "a witchetty grub" child.[14]

In the previous instance, both parents belonged to the witchetty grub totem. In other cases, the predilection for plump mother is so strong that a spirit-child accepts the risk of birth to parents of a different totem. That is how a pleasingly plump woman of the emu locality became pregnant with a witchetty grub spirit-child while travelling near the witchetty grub increase center. Had the emu woman stayed within emu territory, she would have birthed an emu spirit-child.

Chapter 15
The Great Mother's Maternity Ward

God, intending to make a visible world,
first formed an intelligible one; that so having ...
a most god-like pattern before him, He might
make the corporeal world agreeable to it.[1]

– Philo of Alexandria

Human mothers are mere copies of the Great Mother,
the divine intelligence who signifies creative power,
periodic renewal of life, and who creates the
child's soul in the cosmic regions.

Humankind has revered the mother goddess from as early as 30,000 years BC, as the Venus of Willendorf, a limestone statue, suggests. In many myths, the Creator is the Great Mother, a kind of hidden nervous system which operates beyond the physical world, yet influences it. The Great Mother appears with dozens of names throughout mythology and religion including: Inanna, Devi, Chokmah, Teh, Cybele, Isis, Athena, Astarte, Tara, Juno, Freia, Sophia, Semele, Coatlicue, and Ishtar. Her image remains alive today in the Virgin Mary as *theotokos*, the "God-Bearer," or "Mother of God."

The *Upanishads* of India portray the Great Mother as a female spider who carries within herself the seeds of creation. The spider weaves her thread out of herself and then lives upon it. Indigenous peoples portray the goddess in much the same way.

- Australia (Aborigines, Arnhem Land) – "It was she who put all the people here, who left the spirits of future generations … ." She did not need a man to fertilize her due to supernatural powers. She carried the spirits in her uterus "and let them out at intervals." Before departing from Earth, she observed the spirit-children she had created. "There were so many … . 'Ah,' she said, 'I've taken too many out of myself … .'"[2]
- Columbia (Kagaba Indians) – "The Mother of Songs," translated as "the mother of our whole seed," bore all races of men.[3]
- Indonesia (Semang Pygmies) – The Great Mother suckles baby spirits near a great Mapic tree on an island paradise at the center of the world. Baby spirits cross over a switch-backed bridge when they are ready for birth.
- West Africa (Ewes) – "The Mother of Spirits" creates the souls of infants and wills for them to be born.

The Great Mother archetype further enriches the realm of unborn children, according to indigenous peoples of Australia, Siberia, Central America, as well as the Finno-Ugric peoples.

Little Children from the Sky

*The Great Mother births, nurses, and protects souls until
ready for birth, according to the Australian Aborigines.*

Moon Legend of Bloomfield River (North Queensland)

A spirit-child comes to couples only if it is the will of Yalungur,
the wife of the Moon. She is "the mystic cause" from whom spirit-
children originate and who causes them to undergo incarnation.[4]
Yalungur sits on a rock at Kanyar; the Koko-yalunyu Aborigines
hear her singing as she makes her dilly-bags. From time to time, she
sends spirit-babies to mothers, even though no one knows to which
woman a baby is coming: "Old Yalungur sends them – girl baby,
boy baby! South, East, North, and West!"[5]

Two Sisters

The mother goddess manifests as the *Maudlanami* who create
spirit babies in *Wikurutana*, a world located above the blue vault of
Heaven. The two sisters "sat still for so long that they became the
color of grey weathered rock" and their bodies became nearly blan-
keted by their sweeping hair. The *Maudlanami* nurse the "little
children from the sky," *muri*, at their pendulous breasts.[6] Then, as
soon as a cluster of spirit-children builds up, the goddesses
announce, "Go to be born on Earth."

Spirit-children are so tiny that only individuals having subtle
sight, including medicine men or elderly women, observe them
when they arrive. Mulili, an elderly mother, illustrated the spirit-
children's journey with a pencil sketch. She shows spirit babies
leaving the breasts of one of the *Maudlanami* and flying down like
tiny butterflies to Earth (see Figure 7). The spirit-children are

Figure 7: An Adnjamatana Aboriginal woman illustrates a multitude of spirit-children leaving the breasts of one of the Great Mothers (upper left-hand corner) and travelling to the world beneath in search of an earthly mother. A gossamer nexus yokes Earth and sky, and tiny beings descend on a string as fine as a spider's web. When spirit-children first arrive on Earth, they feed on the grape-like fruit of the Jasminum lineare *bush (upper right) or blossoms of the gum tree (lower right).*[27]

complete, self-directing beings who sleep under the bark of tree-trunks until they find mothers.

Mulili insists on the spiritual origin of children despite the impact of modern civilization. She knows "what the white-fellow says," but the physical theory of biological conception is incorrect.[7] Westerners cannot explain why women who always sleep with their husbands are not having babies all the time, or what determines how many children a woman births, but Mulili can: a woman who births many children is a favorite of "the little children from the sky."[8] A woman who has a few children, "then only an odd *muri* wants her for a mother."[9] And when the spirit-children don't like a woman, they refuse to "use her body to become a human being."[10]

Children of the Rain

Nimbalda Aborigines identify the "Yammutu" as the progenitors of spirit-children. When it rains the two old goddesses recline on their backs with their legs open and birth the spirit-children like infinitely minute drops of golden rain.

> "The water runs into their person and causes them to bear a lot of young blacks called *Muree* ... who as they grow up, start westward, always throwing a small waddy, called *wretchu*, before them, till one of them meets a blackfellow with his *lubra* [wife]. The *Muree* ... throws the small waddy under the thumbnail or great toenail, and enters into the woman's body. She is soon pregnant ... ."[11]

I am waiting

Galactic Mother

*Indigenous peoples in Siberia and Central
America correlate the Great Mother's
realm with the Milky Way galaxy.*

Siberian Yakuts believe the "goddess of the ages," who determines and records the destiny of each soul and also suckles unborn children with her breasts, as large as leather sacks, resides somewhere within the Milky Way. In Nicaragua and Honduras, the Sumo likewise revere "Mother Scorpion," a many-breasted goddess who shares the abode of the ancestors located at the end of the Milky Way. She suckles spirit babies and conveys them to the wombs of earthly mothers. Nicaraguans call her *Itoki*.

Cross-Cultural Parallels

As these indigenous accounts suggest, the Milky Way may be contained within the Great Mother goddess. Insights into the mysterious connection between human birth and astronomical objects come from early civilizations who depicted the Milky Way galaxy as the Great Mother's realm: 1) Babylonians – the Milky Way is the road between Earth and Heaven;[12] 2) Egyptians – the Milky Way issues from the breasts of the Goddess Hathor; and 3) Greeks – the Milky Way originates from the milk of Hera, the mother of Heracles, or from the milk of the goddess Rhea of Crete which spurted into the sky as she suckled Zeus.

A Spirit-Child
Maternity Ward

*Supernatural forces working with
sacred creation stones connect a baby
spirit to the umbilical cord of a fetus.*

The Euahlayi Aborigines of Australia believe the wood lizard *Boomayahmayahmul* creates male spirit-children. They have more details to relate about how *Bahloo*, the Moon and patron of women, does "girl manufacturing" on a creek of the Culgoa River. One can see a hole in the ground if this creek is dry. However as soon as water begins to flow along the creek, *Bahloo's* spirit-stone rises out of the hole along with the rising water level, always keeping its top above the water.[13] Nobody dares touch the spirit-stone where *Bahloo* launches female baby spirits upon their earthly missions.

Wahn, the Crow, sometimes assists the chief creator of female spirits at this location. If, on the other hand, *Wahn* attempts to do "the business on his own," "the result is direful; women of his creating are always noisy and quarrelsome."[14]

Once baby spirits are ready to become human babies, the female spirit, *Waddahgudjaelwon*, hangs them upon the branches of the *Coolabah* trees. From this vantage point, spirit-children watch for a suitable mother. When a good choice passes by, a spirit-child "seizes" her and is "incarnated."[15]

In the course of events, the whirlwind-spirit *Wurrawilberoohey* can snatch two spirit-children before they find mothers and whirl them towards a woman against whom he has a grudge. If the woman observes the whirlwind coming, she covers herself under a blanket and avoids the drooping *Coolabah* branches, lest she birth twins, an inauspicious birth.

Some baby spirits never find a suitable mother. They wail in vain. They become so wearied that they transform themselves into the bronze mistletoe branches growing on the *Coolabah* trees. Their blood forms the red flowers.

Kutunga's Legend

An unwanted lover, *Milbili*, the Lizard-man, pursued and impregnated Kutunga, the Great Mother of the Pitjandjara Aborigines who birthed quadruplets at the Niunya rock-holes. Four boulders represent Kutunga's children: two egg-shaped boulders "contain an inexhaustible supply" of "little silvery-haired" healthy spirit-children; whereas two irregular boulders are the source of "misshapen babies."[16] Aspiring fathers chant to the healthy spirit-children at this landmark and coax them to take birth into their families.

Mountain Mothers

Mountains are closest to the sacred sky
where spiritual energy can be received. Their height,
vastness, and the mists that shroud them inspire
us to regard a mountain as the birthplace of
unborn children, as well as the universe.

Vagneg-imi (aka Golden Old Woman and Daughter of the Heaven God) dwells in a seven-storied mountain, according to Finno-Ugric peoples. Seven seas – apparently seven dimensions – separate the goddess' golden home from the physical world. Seven cradles hang from her roof. She carefully rocks each cradle seven times to create a soul. If ever a cradle accidentally overturns however, that child is destined to have a brief life on Earth.[17]

The cosmology of the Siberian Ostyaks includes a similar seven-storied mountain in the sky world. The goddess who protects the spirits of future children makes her home there and inscribes each child's destiny, including length of life, in a gold book, or on a gold ornamented seven-branched tree.[18]

Unlike traditions which place the Great Mother's mountain in the sky, the Pitjandjara Aborigines of Australia feel her presence at Uluru, Earth's largest monolith. They call her *Tjinderi-tjinderiba*, which loosely translates as "Willy-Wagtail-Woman."

Willy-Wagtail is certainly no mortal being. Mythology, songs, and stories describe how, in ancient times, she made a camp on the northern side of Uluru along with her spirit-babies.What remains at this site is a long cylindrical boulder representing Willy-Wagtail's metamorphosed body. Two nearby boulders contain a storehouse of "little beings only a few inches high, with light skin and long black hair."[19] The boulders accommodate spirit-children belonging to two separate tribal divisions. When a spirit-child desires to become a human baby, it follows a woman with large breasts and a friendly face. But just as a man can only marry a woman who belongs to his tribal division, so too, the spirit-child must find a mother of the proper subdivision.

Cross-Cultural Parallels

Indigenous peoples who locate the Great Mother's realm on a gargantuan mountain form an interesting juxtaposition with evidence correlating the mother creator with a real or mythical mountain. The ancient Phrygians worshipped Cybele, mother of the mountain. And a seal impression of late Minoan style (1500 BC) found on Crete depicts the Mother standing upon a mountain dressed in a flounced skirt and holding a sceptre. She is flanked by guardian lions. An ecstatic male worshipper stands before her.[20]

A second synthesis can be made between traditions which position the Mother's realm atop a mountain with peoples who equate a central mountain with the oldest place in the universe – the point where life itself is born: children descend to Earth from Japan's Mount Kirishima; Mexico's Mount Cacalepei is the mother of early peoples; the Navajo's pre-earth home is a great mountain in the San Juan range; and Mount Ushidarena is the pre-birth home of Persia's ancient kings.

Additional parallels include:

- Central Asia, Tatars of Minusinsk – A mythical mountain near a golden birch tree is the birthplace of the first ancestor.[21]
- Christianity – Mount Golgotha, the "Center of the World," is where the creation of the first man, Adam, took place.[22]
- Hinduism – Golden Mount Meru ascends from the Center of the World at the North Pole. Above it shines the Pole Star, the center of the sky. The gods grasped Mount Meru and churned the primordial ocean of consciousness with it. This whirlpool of energy birthed the universe.[23]
- Buddhism (Central Asia) – Iron Mountain Sumeru[24] reaches as high into heaven as it does downwards into the universal ocean. The mountain rests on a layer of gold, that ultimately is borne by a tortoise. Seven rings of golden hills encircle Sumeru, isolated from each other by seven concentric seas. These seas are sweet, except for an outermost salty ocean

which is bounded by the last, iron ring of mountains. Kalmuk lamas relate how the gods created a whirlpool in the ocean by using the Iron Mountain as a stick to stimulate the dormant ocean. Thus the sun, moon, and stars came into manifestation.[25]

❀ Judaism – "The Holy One created the world like an embryo."[26] Just as the embryo proceeds from the navel onwards, God created the world from its navel – Mount Tabor *(Har Tavor)* in northern Israel. Creation emanated from that "center"and spread out in different directions.

❀ Zoroastrianism – The cosmos is like a six-spoked wheel with a large hole in the middle like a navel. The Creator god of light, *Ahura Mazda*, fashioned *Gayomart*, primordial man, at the navel where Heaven and Earth are linked together.

Chapter 16
Travellers from the Light

The Exalted Ones could wait no longer;
my earth mother was ready for me.
I felt a gentle but firm push.
From a state of immense expansion
in spiritual cosmic space,
I felt myself falling and contracting
at what seemed to be the speed of light.[1]

– Kirk D. Gardner

Our earthbound journey emerges from a world
of transparent light and timelessness. The voyage down
to Earth is part of a sojourn through heavenly dwellings
of the Creator. When seen as a whole picture, birth
is a cosmic event, a fantastic voyage charted on a
blue pearl called Earth travelling on course.

We are immortal beings whose bodies are simply external wrappings – light trapped within matter. Everyone has been a dweller in Paradise and enjoyed the company of angels. This idea that the soul is a wandering heir to a lost inheritance is a recurring theme throughout religion, philosophy, poetry, and mythology.

Great thinkers of the ancient Western world believed our souls are foreign sojourners on Earth due to a fall and punishment; others taught that the soul volunteered to experience physical life.

❀ Pythagoras (ancient Greece) – "I am not of this world, for it is not sufficient to explain me."[2]

❀ Zoroastrianism (Persia) – Our souls originate in "the upper spheres."[3]

❀ Rome (5th century BC) – We come from "the heaven of the gods, which was before the Earth."[4]

❀ Marcus Tullius Cicero (1st century BC Rome) – "Our home is in the highest."[5]

❀ Apuleius (1st century Rome) – We come from "the soul of the world" (anima mundi).[6]

❀ Philo of Alexandria (1st century Judaism) – The wise soul Moses, who temporarily renounced his native land in order to take up residence on Earth, was "possessed of a diviner structure."[7]

❀ Suhrawardi (ancient Persia) – "Woe unto thee, if by thy country thou meanest Damascus, Baghdad, or any other city of this world!"[8]

❀ Manichaeism (3rd century Gnosticism) – The soul's true home, tents of joy, Father, Mother, and brethren dwell "on high."[9]

❀ Gnosticism (Hymn of the Soul in Acts of Thomas) – "Know that long ago I was in my country, the abode of my parents and my forefathers … . the master of the country sent for me and said: It befits thee not that thou shouldst remain abiding in my country … ."[10]

Beginning with the early Greek Orphics, the human body has been regarded as "a living tomb in which the human soul is enshrined." Later on, Western poets, who believed that the soul is in exile from the true home of spirit, compared the soul's physical embodiment to "a lark in a cage,"[11] "a vague guest on a dark earth,"[12] as well as "a candle shut up in a dark lanthorn," or a "fire … almost stifled for want of air."[13]

Modern philosophers, poets, and Native American peoples who emphasize that we "belong" to Heaven, not Earth, include:

❀ Laurence Binyon (modern poet) – "Where is that world that I am fallen from? … surely I was rather native there, where all desires were lovely … ."[14]

❀ William Wordsworth (19th century England) – "The soul that rises with us, our life's star, Hath had elsewhere its setting, And cometh from afar."[15]

❋ Immanuel Kant (18th century Germany) – Our soul "neither began in birth, nor will end in death."[16]

❋ Pawnee (Native American) – "Our people were made by the stars."[17] When the time comes for creation to end, we will become small stars and fly to the South Star where we belong. The Milky Way is the soul's pathway after death. First the soul goes to the North Star which sets it upon the north end of the celestial road. The soul then proceeds to the Spirit Star of the south.

❋ Maurice Maeterlinck (20th century Belgium) – "There are thirty thousand halls like this, all full of them [children waiting for birth] …. enough to last to the end of the world!"[18]

❋ Leibniz (17th century Germany) – Souls pre-exist "in a sort of organized body."[19]

❋ Amos Bronson Alcott (19th century USA) – "To conceive a child's acquirements as … dating from his birth into his body, seems an atheism that only a shallow metaphysical theology could entertain."[20]

❋ Esoteric Christianity – The Fall of Adam and Eve is an allegory for the outgoing, or manifested universe from the "the Ever-Concealed Causeless-Cause."[21]

Further references to our true citizenship come from the Greek philosophical tradition, Buddhism, Hinduism, Sufism, Judaism, the *Kabbalah*, Gnosticism, Christianity, Mormons, and Neoplatonism, as well as near-death experiences.

Celestial Roots

Western and Eastern teachings equally
embrace the notion of the soul as a distinct entity
who enters the body from a higher reality.

The Greek word "generation" refers to the process by which the soul is separated from the higher form of existence and brought into the earthly condition. This idea is portrayed by the mythical youth Narcissus who fell in love with his reflection in a pool of water. Narcissus spent so long gazing at his beautiful image that he died beside it. In symbolic form, this story reflects what happened when the soul first became enamored with physical form and captive in a bodily costume.

In simpler terms, the Greek words for "body" and "personality" suggest that our immortal essence is encased within an outer disguise. A soul must be confined in the body in order for a creature to have existence.

"For this reason the Greek words for body are *demas*, that is a bond, and *sōma*, a *sēma* as it were, being the tomb of the soul."[22]

The root of our word personality – the Greek word *persona*, a mask – equally supports the soul/body distinction. And in a related case, the Arabic language acknowledges that physical embodiment dulls memory as revealed in the word *insan*, an Arabic word for human being which sounds the same as their word meaning forgetfulness.

Plato and the Greek Philosophers

Plato (428 to 348 BC) considered the soul the most important part of man. The soul is truly divine and far more real than the physical body. The soul is an immortal being from the higher world in which only Eternal Forms and Souls exist. The soul always existed before its indwelling in a mortal body and will continue to exist after it has won final release.

The soul's divine, transcendent world is utterly foreign and remote from the earthly world perceived with human senses. Before our souls fell from the universe of Being into the realm of Becoming, we could witness the Vision of Heavenly Beauty. (Plato's *Phaedrus* 250c)

> There was a time when our souls beheld Beauty shining in all its brilliance – "the beautific spectacle and (divine) vision. We were initiated into the holiest of mysteries, in which we joyed in mystic ecstasy. For then we were in the state of wholeness and unconscious of the evils that awaited us in time to come … ."[23] We were still pure and not yet "imprisoned in the body," bound to it "like an oyster in his shell."[24]

The soul has duties to perform on Earth, yet the soul shares nothing in common with the world of the senses in which it finds itself. The soul must never behave as if it belonged here. Most humans, however, are like captives chained in a subterranean cave. (Plato's *Republic*) Their backs are turned to the light and so they can only see the shadows of the objects passing behind them. The prisoners attribute a true reality to this shadow-show, the flow of appearances. They become slaves to the senses; their earthly sojourn is a dreamy exile from their true home.

Liberated souls, on the other hand, return to the paradise of purified ones, to "the place beyond the heavens," where "true being dwells, without color or shape, that cannot be touched; reason alone, man's pilot, can behold it." (*Phaedrus* 247d-e) Freed souls obtain the genuine knowledge of being which "is not easy to describe, nor is there now sufficient time to do so." (Plato's *Phaedo* 114C)

Greek philosophy abounds with additional proponents who say the soul is an immortal god imprisoned in the body.

- ❀ Orphic Mystery School (500 BC) – Orphics sought to purify themselves, escape, and return to the company of the gods – a "half-corporeal, half-spiritual" state in the "Heaven of Saturn" where everything is full of splendour, charm, and the harmony of the spheres. There the soul neither thinks nor reflects … but simply lives, "drinking in sounds, forms and light, floating like a dream … ."[25]
- ❀ Pythagoras (497 BC) – The soul originates in the divine world and therefore has the power to know eternal unchanging

Truth – musical harmony, fixed proportions of the scale, and the order of heavenly bodies. The soul can purify itself and return to its godlike state by contemplating the element of form, order, proportion, limit, and harmony in the universe.

- Empedocles (484 to 424 BC) – Empedocles wept at being born on Earth, the region of "raging discord," and expected to rejoin the immortals following this life. He was an exiled divinity who deserted God and fell to Earth from his high estate. Due to the "decree of necessity" which requires erring souls to wander from their home, he experienced a series of human lifetimes for 30,000 seasons.[26]
- Anaxagoras (500 to 428 BC) and Heraclitus (480 BC) – Our souls make their pilgrimage to Earth from other planets.

Vedic Sages of India

India's ancient rishis proclaimed that we are more than our body, mind, or emotions. We are divine souls on a wondrous journey.

"We came from God … . We are … the Truth we seek … . Deep inside we are perfect this very moment, and we have only to discover and live up to this perfection to be whole."[27]

Paramahansa Yogananda, the 20th century Indian master, taught that we are "children of the King of the Universe who have run away" from home.[28] We have forgotten our "divine heritage" because we have been locked up in human bodies for so long. We are created in God's image and must transcend the "imperfect human consciousness of mortality."[29]

Buddhism

The world is a dark dungeon in which man is a prisoner.[30] Our "Buddha-nature" is "unchangeable and eternal."[31] We cannot compare it with anything. It is neither male nor female, good nor bad. "When the Ten Thousand things are viewed in their oneness, we return to the Origin and remain where we have always been."[32]

Sufism – Mystical Branch of Islam

The soul originates in the World of the Unity, *al-Azal* (pre-eternity).[33] The World of Reality, the "Reality of God,"[34] is colorless and formless, neither male nor female. The step-by-step process of descent from pre-eternity began 21,000 years prior to the creation of human beings.

- Conscience – God first created our conscience. This innermost aspect remains longest in the vicinity of God's Grace and is unable to respond to evil suggestions.
- Spirit – Seven thousand years later God created our spirits and installed them in His "garden of intimate fellowship."[35]
- Heart – After 7,000 years passed, God next created our hearts and set them in the station near Himself.
- Physical Body – God waited another 7,000 years before he began creating human physical forms for our souls.

Prior to birth, God assigns each soul to a particular human body, places a conscience within a spirit, a spirit within a heart, and a heart within that body.

"To come into the world [Earth] is to pass from the world of Reality in the true sense to the world that is doubtless real for ordinary consciousness, but which in the true sense is only figure and metaphor."[36]

Cross-Cultural Parallel

Sufi poetry employs various images of the soul/body relationship to emphasize the soul's longing for the perfected state in which it was first created: a fish on dry land; a caged parrot; a moaning dove that has lost her mate; a reed torn from its bed and fashioned into a flute whose melancholy music fills the eye with tears; and the melting snow ascending to Heaven as vapour.[37]

Sufi metaphors are reminiscent of descriptions used by individuals who survive a near-death experience. NDErs compare the human body to a coat, skin, cage, box, shell, narrow quarters, an envelope, and even "a sinking into a grave."[38] Still even more than that, a contemporary NDEr points out:

"I was actually relieved to find that the earth is not our natural home, that we did not originate here ... . earth is only a temporary place for our schooling ... . I knew that [we had all been there before] ... filled with light and beauty ... ."[39]

The Seventh Heaven

*Jewish traditions tell us about the
dwelling place where the souls of unborn
generations wait for human birth.*

● Traditional Judaism – A promptuary, called the "*guf*" or
"*guph*," is located in *Aravot*, the seventh heaven. This heaven
also includes souls of the righteous, the "dew of light"
which God uses to revive the dead, the Divine Throne,
Seraphim (highest angels), and ministering angels.

● Essenes – Souls emanate from "the most subtle ether and
are enfolded in bodies as prisons" due to a natural entice-
ment for human life. Following the experience of physicality,
souls are "loosed from the bonds of flesh, as if released from
a long captivity." They "rejoice and are borne upward"
once again.[40]

● Philo of Alexandria – There are two classes of souls: 1) souls
who are attracted by material desires and fall from their
"heavenly mansion" into the body's prison; and 2) perfected
souls, like Moses, who are absolved from all bonds to earthly
life and know that Earth is a "foreign" land. They are volunteers who urge wayward souls to return to the lost region
of light, "their citizenship, fatherland."[41]

Biblical figures in the Old Testament refer to their "prenatal
antiquity." (Some scholars argue that these passages refer to
previous lives).

● King Solomon – "The Lord created me the beginning of his
works, before all else that he made … . Alone, I was fashioned … long before earth itself." (*Proverbs* 8:22-31)

● Jeremiah – "Before I formed you in the womb I knew you
for my own; before you were born I consecrated you, I
appointed you a prophet to the nations." (*Jeremiah* 1:4-5)

● Job – Job was there when God "laid the earth's foundations." (*Job* 38:4-21)

Souls' Treasure House in the Garden of Eden

*The soul's pre-earthly habitat plays a vital role in
the mystical aspect of Judaism, the* Kabbalah, *considered
the true Jewish theology from 1500 to 1800 AD.*

Before coming to Earth, all souls "were present in the Divine Idea in the same form, that they were to have in this world."[42] "They knew everything they learned on Earth prior to their coming into this world."[43] Each soul "originates in the world of Emanation which is all Godliness … ."[44]

The *Kabbalah* outlines the stages from the soul's creation to human birth.

* Divine Mind – "All the spirits *(ruhot)* of the righteous" had already been "stored up in God's thought, each one in its own particular image" before the Divine ever thought of creating the world.[45]

* Creation – God revealed the spirits of the righteous "and they stood in their own image before Him, in the most exalted height."[46]

* Treasure-House of Souls – God placed the spirits in a separate storehouse in the Garden of Eden. *Psalms* refers to God seeing our spiritual shape in the world of souls when it says, "Your eyes have seen my substance."[47]

* Crystallization – Each soul became more crystallized as an independent entity by passing through three increasingly dense dimensions. The four spirits of the Upper Garden of Eden clothe each soul in a "celestial garment of light"[48] and the soul takes on the human body shape it will assume on Earth. This spiritual garb distinguishes one soul from another, and gives the soul a taste of corporality prior to wearing its "coats of skins," (*Genesis* 3:21) a human body constructed from earth, air, fire, and water.

- Summons – As the time for human birth approaches, God commands an angel, "Bring Me the soul so-and-so, which is hidden in Paradise, whose name is so-and-so, and whose form is so-and-so."[49]

- Audience with God – The designated soul prostrates in God's presence. God commands, "Go to a certain place and enter that sperm." (*Zohar* II, 96) The soul pleads: "Master of the Universe, why must I, who am holy and pure and a part of Thy glory, enter an impure sperm? I am pleased with the world I live in. I do not wish to be enslaved and corrupted." (*Zohar* II, 96) Alas, God consoles the soul, "You were created to experience human life. You have received certain gifts in order to carry out a role in the Divine plan."

- Cosmic Contract – The soul surrenders and vows to fulfill a lesson plan. *Deuteronomy* 4:35 refers to this presentation and the cosmic contract, when it says: "You have been presented so that you might know [that the Lord, He is God]."[50]

- Final Instructions – The soul "flies down" to the lower Garden of Eden where it receives guidance. The soul penetrates its mother's womb thirty days later.

Upon entering the fetus, the soul is "bound to conform to the laws and principles of the physical universe even as a prisoner is bound to the law of the prison."[51] That is why sleep is such a gift. During sleep the soul returns to its original home and experiences rejuvenation. "Without sleep, the body would destroy the soul in short order."[52]

Souls of men see their images as if in the mirror of Dionysus, and come down to that level with a leap from above. Yet their tops remain firmly set above in Heaven.

Plotinus *Enneads* IV. 3.12-13

Christianity and the Soul

*The question in Christianity, "When was the
soul created?" parallels science's problem
of when was the universe created.*

Early Christianity faced a dilemma regarding the metaphysical
definition of the soul and its origin. The soul's beginnings were
"not very clearly defined in the teaching."[53] Fourth-century Saint
Gregory of Nyssa enumerated some unanswered questions:

* Who understands his own soul?
* Is the soul's essence "material or immaterial?"[54]
* How do souls come into being?
* How does the soul unite to the human form?

Since the mid 6th century, the orthodox answer has been
Creationism: the soul's existence in the physical universe begins at
the moment God creates its body forming in the mother's womb. The
Gospel refers to this continuous creation of souls when it declares:
"My Father worketh hitherto and I work." Thus, at every moment,
multitudes of souls are "freshly made ... and placed in bodies."[55]

Besides Creationism, Church Fathers, including Tertullian (155
to 220 AD), proposed a less popular theory, known as
"Traducianism," meaning that the parental seed transmits the soul
along with the body at conception. The conjunction of a male and
female creates, or brings into being, an immortal soul.

A number of church leaders and scholars did not accept either
Creationism or Traducianism. They reasoned, "If the soul exists eternally after the body's dissolution, must not the soul exist eternally
prior to the body's formation, as well?" This minor group proposed:
if the soul is endless, the soul must "be beginningless, like a circle."[56]
Parents merely prepare a material body for an "immaterial pre-
existent inhabitant" who is ready to be conceived.[57]

The following saints and Church Fathers offered varying degrees of support for the theory that souls pre-exist in Heaven or in a repository built by God:

* Saint Clement (150 to 215 AD) – Before the world's foundation, we have been "immortal and children of eternal life"[58] who existed in the Divine Mind.

* Saint Jerome (347 to 420 AD) – "A divine habitation ... is ... where, before their descent to a lower position, and removal from invisible to visible (worlds), and fall to earth, and need of gross bodies, they enjoyed a former blessedness."[59]

* Synesius (5th century AD) – "I will never consent to the belief that the soul comes into being after the body."[60] [The soul is not] "a created thing immortalized by divine Grace."[61]

Father Origen – Theologian and Biblical Scholar of the Eastern Orthodox Church

Father Origen (185 to 254 AD), the primary advocate of pre-existence, synthesized Christianity with Greek philosophy. He theorized that "every soul has existed from the beginning"[62] with God in a "precosmic spiritual universe."[63] His theory outlines the steps between the soul's exile from Heaven to biological conception.

* Spiritual Fall – Souls abused their free will in Heaven. They followed an angel who instigated a rebellion and refused to obey God. Due to this transgression, God exiled the fallen spirits to lesser worlds, including Earth.[64]

* Cosmic Contract – The degree of the soul's offenses in the spiritual world determines earthly circumstances.

* Conception – The embryo receives its soul at conception from an angel presiding over the birth.[65]

* Return of the Soul – Human embodiment offers the soul an opportunity to become purified and return to a purely spiritual state – *apocatastasis.*

Father Origen points out two biblical mistranslations of the souls' fall from Heaven. To begin with, scholars mistranslated the Greek word "*dejicere,*" meaning "to cast downwards," into the Latin word "*constitutio,*" meaning "beginning." The standard translation of *Matthew* 24:21 contrasts with Origen's.

- ❀ Standard Interpretation – "And there will be tribulation in those days, such as was not since the beginning of the world."[66]
- ❀ Father Origen – "And there will be tribulation in those days, such as was not since the souls were cast downwards."[67]

In another passage, *Ephesians* (1,4), *dejicere* – "to cast downwards" – is mistranslated into the Latin word meaning "foundation."[68]

- ❀ Standard Interpretation – "Who hath chosen us before the foundation of the world."
- ❀ Father Origen – "Who hath chosen us before the souls were cast downwards."[69]

Father Origen's theory survived intact for 300 years until the Church decided that he went too far. Origen was "never formally a heretic"[70] because his opinions always bore on points not yet settled by the Church, yet the Second Council of Constantinople (553 AD) condemned his "mythical doctrine of the pre-existence of the soul"[71] due to its obvious association with reincarnation. Pre-existence does not require the doctrine of reincarnation; nonetheless, Origen was misunderstood as supporting reincarnation since he believed the soul does not begin with the life of the body. Since that turning point, Christian doctrine upheld that "creation and infusion of the spiritual soul coincides with the moment of conception."[72]

On Probation

*The belief in pre-existence makes
Mormons unique in modern Christianity.*

Mormons believe that they dwelled with the Heavenly Father in his House, their rightful Home, prior to the world's creation. Any other belief "lessens the character of man." There never was a time when their spirits did not exist and they will experience immortality after bodily death. "We are co-equal (co-eternal) with our Father in Heaven."[73]

Mormon teachings emphasize that God made a human body, put a spirit into it, and it became a living soul. They point out that the Bible does not say, "God created the spirit of man."[74] Rather the Old Testament states, "God made man out of earth and put into him Adam's spirit, and so became a living body."[75]

Spirits lived as free rational intelligences in the heavens, pure and holy as angels. The spiritual body is "more pure, elastic and refined"[76] than the earthly body. It resembles the earthly counterpart, as it will appear when the individual is fully mature and in perfect health. The spiritual body has organs of thought, speech, sight, hearing, tasting, smelling, and feeling.

The spirit world offers limited opportunities for learning how to triumph over evil and suffering. So God assigned ⅔ of the spirits to experience the human condition. He determined family lineages and earthly missions based upon intelligence and abilities. As God revealed to Abraham: "Thou wast chosen before thou wast born."[77]

As elucidated by Mormon President John Taylor in 1857, when the time arrived for human birth, the Heavenly Father announced:

> Go to the lower world and take a human body. Work out your probation and rise to perfection. You will forget the spirit world and "become one of the most helpless beings ... subject to sickness, pain, tears, mourning, sorrow and death."[78]

Homesick Traveller

Plotinus, the 3rd century philosopher,
taught that the soul is lost in the world of space
and time, like a traveller who vaguely recalls his origin.

"Before we had our becoming here we existed There."[79] We walked the lofty ranges with the complete Soul and were made perfect. We were immune from care and trouble.

When the moment comes, each soul descends to Earth – the least divine part of the universe – in order to gain a higher exaltation.[80] Each soul has its own special destiny and moment, one now and one at another time. "Like a herald summoning it,"[81] the soul penetrates to Earth in a "voluntary plunge" and goes into the appropriate body. This orderly process parallels the way everything has its own time – the sprouting of beard and horn, new flowerings, and trees springing up at their appointed time, etc.

Plotinus was so "ashamed" that his soul had become "enchained" or "imprisoned" in a body, that he refused to have his portrait painted. It was sufficient to temporarily assume this image without creating a more lasting one for posterity to inspect. That is why Plotinus never spoke about his birthday, parents, or country of origin.[82] He wrote: "Life here, with the things of earth, is a sinking, a defeat, a failing of the wing."[83] Once our souls drift from home, we are like infants taken from our parents and brought up at a distance. "The soul is a deserter from the All."

Based upon his own spiritual experiences, Plotinus believed that the purpose of the soul's descent into the visible world is to arrive at knowledge of, and unification with, "the One," a mystical experience – described as "ecstasy," "self-surrender," and "flight yonder, of the alone to the Alone." Moral training and contemplation of beauty helped him attain this goal.

The Gnostic's Principle of Return

Christ's discourses, according to Gnosticism
which has origins in Judaism and Christianity,
emphasize that human souls are not from Earth.

Human souls are "allogenous" – of another race.[84] The root of every human being is not of this world. Earth is a dungeon, or an "inn, whereby our souls lodge."[85] The human body holds a divine seed prisoner. This spark is a portion of the eternal light realm which accidentally fell into the material world. Gnosticism aims to release "the inner man from the bonds of the world" back to the "native realm of light,"[86] the true, transcendent reality.

Gnostic texts record Christ's discourses on the subject of pre-existence.

* *Pistis Sophia* – "I have indeed said to you from the beginning that you are not from the world; I also am not from it."[87]
* *Book of Thomas* – "We came from the light … . We are its children, and we are the elect of the living father."[88]
* *Apocryphon of James* – Christ taught his disciples to say, "I am from the Pre-existent Father, and a son in the Pre-existent One."[89]
* *Apocryphon of James* – Christ instructed his disciples to answer that I am going "to the place from which I have come, there shall I return."[90]

Free Will Run Amok

*Edgar Cayce, a southern Presbyterian mystic
and clairvoyant, cognized that the human soul is
God's greatest creation because God gave the soul the
gift of free will ... but with strings attached, of course.*

Newly-created souls were aware of their identity with God. Gradually, however, souls began to marvel at their power and versatility of free will. Some longed to feel the beauty of Earth – the seas, winds, forests, flowers, and animals. They experimented with their free will by modifying creation. God's plan for the soul included experience of all creation, although this plan did not mean spinning "their own little worlds, twisting and bending laws to make images of their dreams."[91]

Some souls nonetheless amused themselves in this manner and became entangled in matter. They were more concerned with their own creations than God's. They created strange mixtures of animals in one body. These genetic experiments persist in Greek fables of centaurs and the Cyclops. The interference with God's creation resulted in the fall in spirit or revolt of the angels.

To make a long story short, God prepared a way of escape for the souls trapped in matter. A physical form was chosen and perfected to be the soul's earthly vehicle through a series of incarnations. When the vehicle was ready, souls descended into bodies and humanity appeared in five different places as the white, yellow, black, red, and brown races. "Earth had a new inhabitant: man."[92]

The challenge of the embodied souls was to overcome Earth's attractions to the extent that they were as free within bodies as they had been outside of them. Every thought and action of the physical body needed to be in accord with God's original plan for the soul.

Divine Ancestors

*Traditional peoples say humankind existed in a
non-physical form prior to their appearance on Earth.*[93]

❀ Omaha (Native American) – At first, everything existed in
the mind of Wakonda, the Creator. We were spirits who
wandered in the space between Earth and the stars seeking
a place where we could come into physical existence.

❀ Hopi (Native American) – The Great Spirit created us somewhere in the underworld. "We were created equal, of
oneness, living in a spiritual way, where life is everlasting."

❀ Wakuluwe (Africa) – Our ancestors were a couple who came
down from Heaven and birthed us from parts of their bodies.

❀ Zulu (Molama clan, Africa) – A man and woman left the sky
world and landed on a certain hill. They became our ancestors.

❀ Celebes (Bugi of Macassar) – Our people descended from
the son of the Heaven-deity and his six wives.

❀ Carolines – Ligobund descended from the sky to Earth and
birthed three children, the ancestors of all humanity.

❀ Indonesia – We descended from the sky region, which was
formerly nearer to Earth, by means of a tree or a vine.

❀ Warrau (Orinoco and Guiana, Latin America) – Long ago,
we dwelled in the happy hunting grounds above the sky.
One day Okonorote's arrow missed its mark. The young
hunter looked for the lost arrow and spiralled down a hole
by means of a cotton rope [light tunnel]. After exploring the
lands below, he persuaded us to come to Earth. One stout
woman unfortunately became lodged in the passageway
and prevented us from ever returning to our sky home.

❀ Toba Batak (Sumatra) – Our people descended from a divine
maiden who came to Earth and a heavenly hero who joined her.

❀ Malagasy (Madagascar) – We dwelled with God in the sky.

❀ Oceania – We descended from gods who came to dwell
upon Earth.

All-Pervading Master-Vibration

*When the soul is freed of the bonds
of the physical body and senses during a near-death
experience, it consciously returns Home.*

Arthur E. Yensen, a thirty-four-year-old syndicated cartoonist, experienced an NDE following an auto accident in 1932. Arthur enjoyed a heavenly realm and observed distinct flowers growing on the slopes of two round-topped, snow capped mountains fifteen miles away. A shimmering lake seemed to be alive, and vivid, green grass carpeted the landscape. Arthur's visual ability seemed to be 100 times better than on Earth.

Beyond a grove of large, luxuriant trees, twenty people with translucent bodies were playing a singing-dancing game. Four beings skipped over to greet Arthur. The eldest one, who looked like a Greek god, informed Arthur, "You are in the land of the dead. We lived on Earth, just like you, until we came here."[94]

Nothing deteriorates or ages in this world due to an "all-pervading Master-Vibration" which keeps elements from mixing or breaking down. Arthur realized –

"Back on Earth I had been a visitor, a misfit, and a homesick stranger. With a sigh of relief, I said to myself, Thank God I'm back again. This time I'll stay!"[95]

Arthur's guide overheard his thoughts and explained:

You must dwell on Earth until your mission is completed. Human beings need your "stabilizing influence" during the upcoming time of great confusion.

Arthur fulfilled his cosmic contract following the NDE. He became an educator, public speaker, political activist, and organic gardening authority, as well as one of Idaho's "Most Distinguished Citizens." Arthur returned "home" in 1992.

Larry Tooley, another young man who was "killed" in an accident, toured a heavenly city where he recognized every street and building. Larry's attention was drawn to one building in particular. Larry advised his guide, "I must attend to some important business in that building." Larry met with a committee inside who had gathered in a meeting room. He pleaded with the men to reconsider his "premature entry into the spirit world."[96] Larry even pounded his fist on the corner of the desk, to emphasize that his work on Earth was incomplete. The committee pondered his situation and agreed to support Larry's request.

Every Soul is an angel before it touches the Earth.[102]

Soul Ladder

*Legends and myths depict humanity's descent from
an immense tree-like structure at the center of the world.*

The World Tree metaphor emerges as the birthplace of humanity's primordial ancestors as well as the repository for future generations.

- ❀ Christianity – The Tree of Life and the Knowledge of Good and Evil stood in the Garden of Eden, birthplace of Adam and Eve.
- ❀ Siberia (Yakut) – Man originated near a Cosmic Tree: "above the wide, motionless deep, under the nine spheres and seven storeys of heaven … where the moon does not wane and the sun does not set, where eternal summer reigns, and the cuckoo calls unceasing."[97]
- ❀ India – Yama, the first human, drinks with the gods beside a miraculous tree interconnecting the whole of creation. *(Rig Veda)*
- ❀ Mesopotamia – Gilgamesh came from a celestial tree in a garden.
- ❀ Jewish *Kabbalah* – I planted this tree "that all the world might delight in it, and made it an arch over all things … and from it the universe emanates … it is thence that the souls emanate."[98]
- ❀ Borneo (Kayans) – Only water and sky existed until a giant rock fell to Earth from Heaven. Next, a sword-handle from the Sun fell upon the rock and it became a tree; a vine dropped from the Moon and wound around the tree. From this world-tree, human beings originated.[99]
- ❀ Native American (Lenape) – Creation sprang from a tortoise. A tree sprang from the middle of its back, upon whose branches men grew.
- ❀ Africa (Samaras) – Every living being – Damaras, Bushmen, oxen, and zebras, etc. – sprang from the universal tree.
- ❀ Siberia (Goldi, Dolgan, Tungus) – Souls perch like birds on the Cosmic Tree until shamans go there to find them.[100]
- ❀ Africa (Inner-Angola) – Children await birth on a celestial tree. God picks them and casts them down to Earth.[101]

Chapter 17
Circle of Life
Buddhist and Hindu Inter-Life Realms

What we call birth is merely the reverse side of death ... like a door which we call "entrance" from outside and "exit" from inside a room.[1]

– Lama Anagorika Govinda

One of the oldest mysteries is whether human life ends at death, and, if life continues, what happens. One theory explains that we are born again into our own family, or among strangers. This notion of a series of births and deaths offers insights into the realms where souls exist before biological conception.

Deep within our soul, we sense that Mother Earth does not exist in a vacuum. Modern science confirms these feelings and tells us that Earth is a small speck of dust, floating in a sea of stars and the vastness of galactic space. More than that, Buddhist and Hindu traditions describe unlimited cosmologies – the spiritual homes for the soul between one life and the next.

Biological conception and birth are not what they appear to be. Human birth constitutes a transitory stage between one world and the next. According to the theory of rebirth, prior to conception, we leave a spiritual realm to which, later in old age, we will return. Just as we rest between each inhalation and exhalation of breath, our souls rest in spiritual realms, free from physical conditions and limitations, between one earthly life and the next. After which, our souls select or are given a new body into which we are once again born into this world. Our experience in each successive existence depends upon how well we fulfilled our cosmic contracts in preceding lives.

Spiritual masters of the East teach that the Truth is full within everyone. Yet in order to realize that Truth, souls must assume "different birthday coats, sometimes white, sometimes, brown, sometimes black – different bodies in different lives."[2] The soul thereby enriches itself through the experiences of a series of human incarnations, with sojourns to other dimensions in-between. As the early Indian saint, Adi Shankara, put it, "Again birth, again death, and again life in mother's womb. This process of *samsara*[3] is very hard to cross over."

Buddhist and Hindu adepts who climbed high enough on the consciousness ladder were able to cognize the inter-life domains. These spiritual travellers discovered that intermediate regions are characterized by specific conditions, circumstances, and longevity much like the diverse living conditions needed on Earth for people, mammals, fish, and birds (see Table 2). As a case in point, Buddha described *Tusita*, the Heaven of the Blissful Gods, where he dwelled 4,000 years prior to his earthly incarnation.

At the ends of the Earth,
there is an interspace "as
thin as the edge of a razor."
(Brhadaranyaka Upanishad III.3.2)

Table 2: Buddhist Cosmology Table Showing Duration of Life[27]

Four Formless Heavens

1. Heaven of Neither Consciousness
   nor Unconsciousness .... 80,000 kalpa
2. Heaven of Absolute Non-existence .... 60,000 kalpa
3. Heaven of Infinite Consciousness .... 40,000 kalpa
4. Heaven of Boundless Space .... 20,000 kalpa

Seventeen Heavens of Form

1. Not Youngest .... 16,000 kalpa
2. Well-Seeing .... 8,000 kalpa
3. Beautiful .... 4,000 kalpa
4. No Heat .... 2,000 kalpa
5. Effortless .... 1,000 kalpa
6. Abundant Fruit .... 500 kalpa
7. Merit-Born .... 250 kalpa
8. Cloudless .... 125 kalpa
9. Complete Beauty .... 64 kalpa
10. Immeasurable Beauty .... 32 kalpa
11. Limited Beauty .... 16 kalpa
12. Radiant Gods .... 8 kalpa
13. Immeasurable Splendor .... 4 kalpa
14. Limited Splendor .... 2 kalpa
15. Great Brahmas .... 1 kalpa
16. Brahma-priests .... 1/2 kalpa
17. Retinue of Brahma .... 1/4 kalpa

Ten Desire Realms

1. Heaven of the Freedom
   of Transformations .... 16,000 years
2. Heaven of Transforming Pleasure .... 8,000 years
3. Blissful Gods .... 4,000 years
4. Yama .... 2,000 years
5. Heaven of the Thirty-Three Gods .... 1,000 years
6. Four Great Kings .... 500 years
7. Four Worlds for Human Beings .... varies
8. Ghosts .... varies
9. Animals .... varies
10. Eight Hells of the Damned .... varies

*Longevity in the upper realms is measured by kalpas. Buddha explained
how to calculate the length of a kalpa:[28] Imagine a solid rock mountain,
one league high, without break, cleft, or hollow. Every 100 years a
man rubs the mountain once with a silken garment. The time it takes
for the man to wear away the mountain is less than one kalpa.*

Jumping Into the Light

*Whereas Christians believe we have only one life
on Earth, and we are liberated at death from our
bondage, only enlightened Buddhists can fly directly
into the highest spiritual light world after death.*

Just as our environment changes when we shift from dream to the waking state of consciousness, we experience a different reality due to the change in consciousness when we drop the physical body. This life between death and rebirth seems just as real as the physical world we have left behind. Our soul enters an inter-life level matching the thoughts and deeds of our earthly life. Souls who attain a comparable degree of purity are spiritual citizens of the same realm.

Following the end of human life, each soul is magnetically attracted to a particular realm of rebirth, relative to its individual merits and demerits. The purest souls "jump into the Light" and enter the dimension just below *Nirvana* – "the Realm of Non-Form," or "the Realm of Dharma."[4] This window of opportunity lasts between twelve to twenty-four hours following the time of death. Transiting souls who gaze upon this Clear Light, as dazzling as 1,000 Suns, enter an afterworld made of light, secluded there for several hundred billion years.

Remaining souls, who turn away from the Clear Light, experience an opportunity to witness a nearly transparent white-silver light. This light is less brilliant in intensity, although it is still too over-powering for most souls. Only souls who have earned great merit can enter into "the Realm of Form," or "the Realm of Reward."[5] This light world is composed of exquisite substances. Beings in this world wear clothing composed of light and live on light.

An opportunity to enter "the Corresponding Realm,"[6] one of the higher sub-divisions of the light world of the gods, comes next.

Souls Waiting in the Wings for Birth

Souls who have great love and compassion for all sentient beings pass this test by gazing upon a beautiful red-purple light. Tusita is in the center of this light world. Gautama Buddha and the Dalai Lama descended to Earth from this plane. Tusita also is the home of Maitreya, the next Buddha.

Following the red-purple light, the purity of the realms diminishes on a daily basis. In this final sequence of visions, the human realm dawns around the forty-third day. Unbeknownst to most couples, souls witness the sexual intercourse by which their parents conceive them. When the soul sees the prospective parents with whom it has a *karmic* affinity, it feels "a blind yearning toward the mother-to-be on the part of one who will be reborn as a male, or toward the father-to-be for one who will be reborn as female."[7] This impulse is neither a "self-conscious reflection or cognition."[8] The soul unconsciously jumps into that realm and finds itself nestled in a womb. The soul feels as if "absorbed." For souls who do not take human birth, the animal realm comes into view around the forty-fifth day. The last realm, Hell, emerges on the forty-ninth day.

The soul sees the mother with whom it has an affinity.

✿❀✿

Between Two Destinies

*Biological conception requires three conditions, according
to Buddha: 1) a gandharva – a between-being who is ready
to incarnate; 2) sexual intercourse; and 3) a fertile woman.*[9]

Buddhists define "the between-being" as the intermediate being who exists between "the being in the dying state," *maranabhava*, and "the being in the state of being born," *upapattibhava*.[10] Sacred texts state that between-beings possess an intellect, emotions, will, five sensory organs, and a subtle body, "which is neither reflected in a mirror nor casts a shadow … ."[11]

Between-beings have the proportions of a five to ten-year-old child. They appear as they did in their previous human births. They then gradually assume the face and body of their next incarnation.[12] Other authorities believe they either maintain the appearance of their previous life, or assume the appearance of the next incarnation.[13]

Texts further elaborate how consciousness determines inter-life experiences. The character, past actions, and religious paradigms of an individual create subjective inter-life visions. An individual witnesses whatever paradises, hells, and the Judge of the Dead he believes in – much like we each create different nightly dreams.[14]

Intermediate beings are seven times more aware than when functioning in human bodies. They are clairvoyant, telepathic, and can read minds. They witness "the Innate Spirit" record their earthly deeds and present them to the Lord of Death.[15] They observe their families on Earth dedicating food on their behalf. The fragrance of that food nourishes them. They locate future parents.

Between-beings are capable of many other wonders. They travel wherever they wish, just by mere intention. Their transparent bodies pass unobstructedly through walls, forests, oceans, and mountains just like "an electric current."[16] They fly hundreds of

– 312 –

miles as quickly as thought, like time standing still. Between-beings traverse the "Third Void Universe" of Buddhist cosmology. (The first degree of Voidness corresponds to a single solar system of nebulae and suns and planets such as astronomers see through telescopes. The second degree consists of 1,000 solar systems. One million solar systems comprise the third degree.)

Between-beings have limitations, too. They cannot prematurely enter their mother's womb. Nor do they travel to *Vajrasana*, the Diamond Seat which remains intact at the end of a cosmic era *(kalpa)* when fire destroys the rest of the universe.

Cross-Cultural Parallel

As an interesting comparison, the abilities of between-beings parallel those of NDErs, suggesting that the pre-birth and after-death state are one and the same:

❀ Increased mental and visual capacities.
❀ Telepathy.
❀ Travel by floating.
❀ Passing through solid objects.
❀ Directing oneself to other worlds in a split second.

Chinese Spirit World

Chinese intermediate states are
a place of judgment and retribution.

Chinese temple priests communicate with departed loved ones and pass messages on to the living about the "World of Spirits." An early 20th century study documents a variety of inter-life scenarios depending upon the soul's spiritual maturity.

1. *Undeveloped Soul* – A man whose life ended at twenty-seven admitted to his surviving wife that he now stood trial in the "World of Spirits" as a criminal before Buddhist Judges for his sinful deeds. The husband explained: "Decrees have been issued for my reincarnation. I hope to vindicate myself during the next life."

2. *Mature Soul* – Deserving souls bypass filling out forms, enumerating sins, paying fees for "crimes," and receiving prison sentences. They are dispatched to the Tenth Judge and are subsequently reborn into good families. The departed spirit of one woman informed her surviving son, "I have asked for immediate reincarnation. Already I have the document and am only waiting for my turn to say farewell to the Tenth Judge."[17]

3. *Advanced Soul* – Celestial attendants received Yang with much pomp, offered him a seat in an immense, green flannel sedan chair, as well as a high-ranking position: recording the deeds of humans and dispatching emissaries to call for individuals whose time was up.

4. *Pure Soul* – The gods favored the soul who neither required punishment nor human rebirth. His spirit dwelled in a guest palace where he studied the scriptures before his transfer to a permanent residence in "the Higher World." Even then, he was free to volunteer for human rebirth.

Vedic Conception of the Soul

India's ancient scriptures proclaim that earthly life is nothing compared to the vast cosmos. All of humanity's armaments, guns, and airplanes are "merely little kites with which the babies play."[18]

The *Bhagavad Gita* defines the nature of the human soul: (2:25-29 and 15:10)

Some look at the soul as a wonder, others speak of it as a wonder, still others hear of the soul as a wonder. Yet no one truly knows the soul. The soul is unmanifested, non-cognizable, and immutable prior to and subsequent to entering a physical body. Only the wise who have intuitive wisdom perceive the soul.

The soul is a crystal pure, infinitesimal spark as subtle as the tip of a hair subdivided 100 times. (*Svet. Upanishad* 5-9) The soul's attributes depend upon whether the soul is the unembodied state or in a human body.

In the unembodied pre-conception state, the soul sees without eyes, hears without ears, roams about without legs or wings. The soul is endowed with senses, but not sense organs. The soul has no appetite, hunger, or thirst. They are the attributes of physical bodies only.

In the embodied state, it is the soul who sees, feels, hears, smells tastes, thinks, knows or acts. (*Prasan. Upanishad* 4-9) The soul enjoys the objects of the senses through the ears, eyes, flesh, tongue, nose, and the mind over which it presides. (*Bhagavad Gita* 15:9)

The soul has a subtle body and like air cannot be seen. (*Pang. Upanishad* 4-12) The soul has no sex. It is neither male, nor female, nor neuter. It becomes identified with whatever body it takes as its own. (*Svet. Upanishad* 5-10) As air assumes the shape of the object in which it enters, the soul becomes amenable to the characteristics of the physical mantle it wears and the physical environment it dwells in. (*Kath. Upanishad* 5-10)

Endless Lokas

When the soul departs from the human body after the cosmic contract with that body is completed, the soul receives another body depending upon his deeds. Like that, the soul continues to don and shed human bodies until it no longer requires them. In between death and rebirth, Lord Yama's (the Lord of Death) retinue ushers these soul to a judgment scene.[19] Yama's assistants prepare an account of that person's deeds.

If the soul reaps the benefits of virtuous deeds, it goes to an upper luminous sphere *(loka)* between incarnations. Each *loka* reflects a range of consciousness, each one higher and more shining than the previous one. Most souls go to one of the lower gradations of the inter-life paradise:

- *Bhurloka* – The atmospheric region, the ancestral kingdom located on the Moon's dark side.
- *Swarloka* – The first heaven, the heaven of the angels, archangels, divinities, and celestials which extends from the Sun to the Pole Star (North Star).
- *Mahaloka* – Sphere of the cosmic intelligent beings, such as Brighu, who guide the destinies of individuals and nations.

In sharp contrast to luminous regions, regions of grosser, coarser matter exist below Earth: the seven hellish regions *(talas)* – places of temporary punishment brought about by an individual's evil thoughts, words, deeds, and emotions. Misguided souls suffer there in order to purge the residual effects of evil deeds.

The *Markendeya Purana*, *Sukla Yajur Veda*, and *Srimad-Bhagavatam* detail conditions in the smoky "fallen regions."

- Tormented emotions of hatred, remorse, anger, resentment, fear, jealousy, self-condemnation, anguish, dismay, confusion, despair, depression, and argument.[20]
- Fire and heat.[21]
- Blinding darkness – No Sun or Moon.[22]
- Extraordinary enjoyments, including millions of different kinds of "wines."[23]

❀ Demons – Homes of the *nagas*, the serpent gods.[24]

Between one life and the next, the soul is encased in a subtle astral body with *samskaras* – the same mentality and characteristics he had on Earth. The soul's return journey to the "world of action" varies depending upon which cosmic region the soul is coming from.

❀ Advanced Souls – Chariots of light or angels in aerial cars transport souls from the luminous worlds. *(Swarloka, Mahaloka)*

❀ Ordinary Souls – Celestial messengers transport souls from the ancestral kingdom located on the Moon's dark side. *(Bhurloka)*

❀ Sinful Souls – The "tempestuous wind of karma" carries souls to Earth from the smoky planes or nether regions.

*Astrology teaches that an orderly plan governs
our birth at a set time and location.*

Ticket to Ride a
Celestial Airplane

*The story of the great seer, Saint Mudgala, told in
India's masterpiece epic, the* Mahabharata, *offers
insights into the possibilities between earthly lives.*[25]

Mudgala supported his family in an honorable way known as
Uncha Vritti. This is a process whereby Mudgala routinely worked
in the fields collecting grain left over after the harvest was taken by
the owner. On the full Moon, Mudgala's family prepared a meal
with the unclaimed grain collected between the new moon and full
moon. They prepared their next meal on the new moon, after
collecting grain between the full moon and new moon. The family
fasted except for these two meals.

Rumors surrounding Mudgala intrigued a bad-tempered sage
who planned a severe test to see what manner of man Mudgala
really was. Durvasas presented himself as a guest just as
Mudgala's family set the dinner table. The sage demanded, "Food,
food. Give me food. I am dead hungry." Mudgala offered a
generous portion, but the sage devoured the family's entire meal.

Durvasas returned in a similar fashion on six separate occasions.
Not once did he ruffle anyone's temper. At the end of the test,
Durvasas lauded Mudgala.

Though I caused the worst irritation, you never became distressed.
You have conquered the tongue, a nearly impossible feat. More than
that, you have conquered hunger. Giving up food when your family
was in dire need is the greatest self-sacrifice and highest charity. Due
to your virtues, I offer you a special boon.

Within moments, a celestial airplane filled with heavenly beings
descended from the skies. A messenger stepped out and greeted
Mudgala:

Souls Waiting in the Wings for Birth

Your accumulated merits are so great that our Lord sent me to fetch you. Come with your wife and children and enjoy heaven's pleasures. To attain heaven with a physical body is rare indeed.

Mudgala saluted the messenger of the gods:

I am blessed to be in your benevolent presence. I thank the gods for the affection showered upon me. Before I accept, please tell me the benefits of heavenly life.

The messenger described regions of subtle matter composed of beautiful lights, sounds, and colors.

Mudgala, you can live like a god with a lustrous, shining body adorned with fine ornaments, garlands of unfading flowers, and excellent dresses. Every object, every being, you look at will be beautiful. You can change the seasons at will. Usually it is Spring with perennial sunshine. If you desire Winter, then snow when it falls, is peaceful and beautiful, and not at all cold. And if you desire rain, a shower will descend gently, as myriad-colored lights.

Desire-granting trees fulfill every wish. Pleasure gardens extend 30,000 square miles for sport and pastimes. Golden airplanes transport you anywhere you wish. There is no hunger, thirst, worry, trouble, decadence, disease, or old age. Special angels watch over each realm which has a sun, moon, ocean, and mountains.

The sage thanked the messenger, but wondered, "Does heaven have any defects?"

Because you are a good man, I will answer you. Heavenly life is delightful, yet it is temporary. Souls dwell with the gods for varying periods depending upon their merits. Like you, they have accumulated credit through charity and sincerity, or they have lost their lives in righteous battles. But once someone's merit is diminished, he must be reborn into another womb. You can't accumulate good merit there. Earth is the place for doing actions. Heaven is where you reap the good fruit. But let us not waste any further time. Come to heaven. Let us go now.

Mudgala replied:

Thank you, but keep heaven for yourselves. There are two kinds of heaven. Your heaven is transitory and cannot compare to the super-transcendental Heaven, the abode where souls merge with God and never again appear in the world of suffering. Even when the heavens and lower worlds are destroyed, such souls experience the everlasting freedom and supreme bliss of liberation. This bliss is one trillion times the maximum happiness which any human experiences on Earth.

Granted it is true that suffering and limitation dominate human life. At the same time, spiritual progress is fastest. The human body has the *sushumma nadi* [energy channel] along the *chakras* [seven energy centers along the spine] which allow realization of perfection. Humans are the greatest beings in the universe. Only a human nervous system supports transformation from human to divine. Even angels do not have this dispensation to realize the ultimate truth. As the *Ramayana* teaches, the gods and the goddesses of celestial abodes desire to come to Earth in human form so that they can be liberated.

I have a rare privilege on Earth, a thousand times greater than your offer. Leave me to my fate. I regret my inability to oblige your invitation.

The messenger saluted Mudgala:

Your high ideals are rare in the world, Saint Mudgala. I am jealous. I take leave of you and will report the matter to the Lord in heaven.

Through prayer and meditation, Mudgala and his family attained *sayuja mukti*, where the "astral body dies away and there is total extinction of all envelopes and impressions of the soul."[26] The soul becomes one with God in the same way flowing rivers disappear into the ocean. Without an astral body, no movement is possible.

East Indian symbolic representation of the structure of the cosmos.

Chapter 18
Soul's Orbit
Western Perspectives on Inter-Life Realms

**The change from being to becoming
seems to be birth, and the change from
becoming to being seems to be death.**[1]
– Apollonius of Tyana

*Birth and death are not the unconscious,
unplanned passages they appear to be. Instead,
birth and death are passages taken through the same
doorway but moving in the opposite directions,
life transitions designed before conception with
forethought and considerable planning.*

Western proponents of rebirth teach that our soul enters this life, not as a fresh creation or blank scroll, but after a long course of previous existences on Earth, in which it acquired its present peculiarities. Within this framework, our souls have experienced other worldly dwelling-places before we enter our mother's womb.

In the same way Jesus Christ revealed, "In my Father's House are many mansions," philosophers and visionaries propose that prior to birth, we leave a spiritual mansion which, later in old age, we prepare ourselves to return to:

❀ Ralph Waldo Emerson (19th century USA) – "The soul is an emanation of the divinity, a part of the soul of the world, a ray from the source of light. It comes from without into the human body, as into a temporary abode, it goes out of it anew; it wanders in ethereal regions, it returns to visit … it passes into other habitations."[2]

❀ Plato (ancient Greece) – Plato's treatise dealing with how to establish a Republic concludes with a proclamation from a man who had apparently died and was restored to life. The man declared that he had visited the inter-life region and witnessed the orderly steps by which souls descend from the spiritual world to human rebirth.[3]

❀ Giordano Bruno (16th century Italy) – Souls alternate between the visible worlds and an infinite number of planetary worlds.[4]

❀ Macrobius (4th to 5th century AD Rome) – Souls come from the region of the fixed stars through the descending portal, the "portal of men." This portal is located at the point where the Milky Way intersects the zodiac astrological sign of Cancer. As souls descend from the top of the cosmos to the bottom, Saturn confers reason and understanding, Jupiter – practicality and morality, Mars – a bold spirit, Venus – passion, Mercury – eloquence and discrimination, Sun – sense perception and imagination, and the Moon – ability to procreate and nurture. Souls attain perfection after a series of incarnations and return to their imperishable abode via the ascending portal, the "portal of gods," the way of Capricorn.[5]

❀ Immanuel Kant (18th century Germany) – The soul's inter-life sojourn begins at the Sun and advances farther from it, planet by planet, until after many lifetimes, we reach perfection.[6]

❀ Johann Ehlert Bode (19th century Germany) – The soul's inter-life experiences begin in Uranus, the coldest planet. As the soul evolves through a series of human incarnations, it advances toward the Sun, the home of perfect beings.[7]

❀ Madame H.P. Blavatsky (19th century Theosophist) – Whatever aspirations an individual has for higher life blossom in the inter-life. The mature soul lives a glorious life of freedom along with the spiritual souls of other human beings, great angels, and other divine intelligences. Or if someone has no beliefs in life after death, then there is nothing for his "spiritual life to be made up of." His soul is "a blank" slate. Such a soul is reborn "immediately, almost without an interval, and without regaining consciousness in the other world."[8]

Souls Waiting in the Wings for Birth

❁ Socrates (ancient Greece) – "When a man dies, his genius (guardian angel) leads him to a judgment scene where departed souls have gathered for their life reviews.

Everyone shuns and avoids the soul who is guilty of an act for which atonement has not been made. No one will be his fellow-traveller or guide. The unpurified soul wanders alone, the victim of doubt and distraction, until a specific time has elapsed, and he is carried to an appropriate habitation.

By contrast, the wise soul who has lived on Earth in a pure and temperate manner finds companions and divine guides, and dwells in the place that is suited to him.

When each soul meets with his appropriate fate in that other world, a different guide brings him back to Earth after many long revolutions of time."[9]

This chapter highlights inter-life theories of Virgil, the Orphic and Pythagorean traditions, Plutarch, and Rudolf Steiner. It concludes with opinions on the duration of the inter-life period from ancient Greece and Rome, modern visionaries, and indigenous peoples of Africa.

The Golden Bough

Aeneas, a Trojan hero, meets souls waiting for rebirth as recounted in the epic masterpiece Aeneid, *authored by the Roman poet Virgil (70 to 19 BC). Before Aeneas reaches the fields of Elysium, however, he must pass through various gates and journey across the Acheron Lake.*

"Confer with your deceased father for he will reveal your destiny." This dream revelation message inspired Aeneas to pray at the temple of the Sibyl of Cumae, the prophetess whose ecstatic utterances were inspired by Apollo.

Gracious Maiden, grant me passage "into my dear father's sight and presence ... open the hallowed portals!"[10]

The prophetess opened her eyes and answered:

Easy is the descent to Avernus [Hell]; escaping to the upper regions, however, this is the task. Clearly with enough love in your heart, it might be possible. For that, a golden bough must be taken to the beautiful goddess Proserpine as a gift. Look in the forest for the tree with the golden bough. "If Fate be calling thee,"[11] the bough will easily break and allow you to pluck it. If not, no force will win it.

Journey to the Nether World

With the golden bough in hand, Aeneas with the Sibyl as his guide, approached the earthly entrance to the Nether World. Lounging there were the tormenters of mankind: "Lamentations, Avenging Cares, Diseases, Old Age, Fear, Hunger, Want, Death, and Hard Toil."[12] A second group included Sleep – the younger brother of Death – Evil Pleasures, War, the Furies, and Civil Strife.

When they faced the third hostile group of monstrous apparitions, Aeneas grasped his sword and was ready to attack: Centaurs, double-formed Scyllas, the hundred-fold Briareus, the hissing Lerna Snake, the Chimaera armed with flames, Gorgons, Harpies, and

Geryon.[13] To allay his fear, Sibyl explained that they were "unsubstantial shapes and mere shades that move about in earthly forms."[14]

Aeneas and the Sibyl then offered gifts to Hecate and Pluto before the "mouth" of the deep cave and entered the world below. Upon passing through the Gate, the two earthlings marched along a road that led to Lake Acheron. They observed great throngs of the newly deceased on the near side of this muddy, sluggish lake. The departed souls clamored to enter a frail craft. Charon's ferry was the only way to transport the dead to the opposite shore. Charon accepted only those who had received a proper burial on Earth. The less fortunate souls, the Sibyl explained, wait in limbo for 100 years on the pool's near side.

Meanwhile, Charon returned from the far side of the lake and approached the landing to pick up a fresh batch of souls. Upon observing Aeneas dressed in his armor, Charon challenged a mortal's right to ask for transportation. To overcome the challenge, the Sibyl appeased Charon with the sight of the golden bough, and reassured Charon that the giant warrior meant no harm.

The ferry soon set sail across the lake only to open up at the seams due to the heavy load. Eventually they did reach the other shore intact – the realm of Pluto and the region of the Styx. This is the inner realm of the dead for souls who have received proper earthly burials and are fully dismembered from the physical body. Aeneas and the Sibyl needed to enter a narrow Gate before they could advance any further. At their approach, however, three-headed Cerberus, the fierce watch dog, began a raucous barking. The Sibyl tossed Cerberus a medicated cake which he greedily devoured. Soon the savage dog was stretched out sound asleep and the travellers proceeded through the doorway.

Inside this inner realm, the road parted: the left path led to Tartarus, the right one to Elysium. Since humans cannot endure the sights in Tartarus, Aeneas only observed the entrance, with its triple walls, steel tower, and mighty gate of impenetrable stone. Aeneas remained content to hear the Sibyl's account of the punishment of great sinners which took place in Tartarus.

The two searchers hastily completed the survey of the dingy Nether World and neared the Palace of Pluto and Proserpine, located at the entrance into Elysium.

"Aeneas gained the entrance, halted there, asperged his body with fresh water drops, and on the sill before him fixed the [golden] bough."[15]

Thanks to the magic of the golden bough, the mortals directly passed from "a dungeon into a garden,"[16] Elysium, the happy abode of the good.

"Now that at last this ritual was performed, his duty to the goddess done, they came to places of delight, to green park land, where souls take ease amid the Blessed Groves."[17]

Previously Aeneas had groped his way through a forbidding realm of shadows and dark paths, lit only by the dim glimmer of the crescent Moon. Now he emerged into a region where the Sun and stars are more radiant and dazzling than any seen from Earth. Majestic groves and blooming gardens vary the landscape. Days are serene, the air pure, and a soft celestial light bathes all objects.

Elysium is the resting place for souls, such as Aeneas' father Anchises, who have served as humanitarians, priests, great artists, or heroes who had died for their country.

"Anchises, deep in the lush green of a valley had given all his mind to a survey of souls, till then confined there, who were bound for daylight in the upper world. By chance his own were those he scanned now, all his own descendants, with their futures and their fates, their characters and acts."[18]

Anchises's attention shifted as his eye caught Aeneas advancing toward him on the Elysium grass. The father stretched out his arms in welcome. Tears rolled down his face. Aeneas' tears, too, "brimmed over and down his cheeks."[19] Aeneas attempted to embrace his father as if he were on Earth. Strangely, each time "the shade [his father's soul] untouched slipped through his hands, weightless as wind and fugitive as dream."[20]

Souls of the Future

Aeneas, strolling with his father, observed a grove at the end of a spacious valley. A stream flowed through the tranquil landscape.

"Souls of a thousand nations filled the air, as bees in meadows at the height of summer hover and home on flowers and thickly swarm on snow-white lilies, and the countryside is loud with humming."[21]

Souls Waiting in the Wings for Birth

Aeneas shivered at the sight and asked, "Father, what river flows there? Who are those men wandering along the river bank?" Anchises replied:

"A second body [new human birth] is in store: their drink is water of Lethe, and it frees from care in long forgetfulness."[22]

Aeneas responded in disbelief:

Oh father! It is possible that any can be so in love with earthly life as to wish to leave these tranquil seats? "The poor souls, how can they crave our daylight [physical life] so?"[23]

Anchises took each point in order. Everything is "fed within by Spirit," but "earthliness and deathliness of flesh" dims the soul's "free essence." Once the soul becomes poisoned or clogged by mortal bodies, this makes them fear, crave, rejoice, and grieve.

"They cannot clearly see heaven's air … even when life departs on the last day not all the scourges of the body pass from the poor souls … . Therefore they undergo the discipline of punishments and pay … for old sins: some hang full length to the empty winds, for some the stain of wrong is washed by floods, or burned away by fire."[24]

The need for purification varies from soul to soul. At last, when souls have turned time's wheel 1,000 years, and worn away their stains, "the god calls in a crowd [of souls waiting for birth] to Lethe stream."[25] There they dwell on Lethe's bank drinking "oblivion of their former lives."[26]

"Come," said Anchises as he drew Aeneas and the Sibyl close to the murmuring throng of souls. A green hill rose above the fields as an observation point from which to watch the multitude of souls as they flowed forward, one at a time. Anchises explained:

Aeneas, for so long, I have been desiring to share your destiny with you. These are souls to whom bodies will be given in due time. Some are connected to your fate – for after many victories in battle and winning your bride, Lavinia, you will establish the Roman civilization. Come and meet face to face the glorious procession of souls destined to be your children and grandchildren. I can elaborate on the exploits of each, deeds men will never forget.

Anchises proceeded to call attention to a young man leaning on a spear.

This is Silvius, your last child. Your wife Lavinia will rear him at the end of your great age. He will be a king and father of kings. His descendants will rule Alba Longa (ancient Latin city about 12 miles southeast of Rome).

Anchises likewise introduced Procas, "the pride of the Trojan line." Next he pointed out men "with oakleaf crowns shadowing their brows." "What men they are! And see their rugged forms."[27] They will be born as Capys, Numitor, and Silvius Aeneas. In this manner, Anchises "fired his love of glory in the years to come."[28]

"What famous children in your line will come, Souls of the future, living in our name."[29]

After they wandered "the airy plain and viewed it all,"[30] Anchises sent Aeneas and the Sibyl back to Earth through a Gate *(candenti perfecta nitens elephanto)* which directly opened from Elysium to Earth.[31] Upon his return, Aeneas went forth as a messenger to his fellow men to teach about "a far greater country."

Virgil intended to complete the *Aeneid* on his travels to Greece and Asia; however, his life prematurely ended after he caught a fever. Virgil left a will directing the *Aeneid* to be burned, as being imperfect and unfinished. By a twist of fate, the emperor Augustus overturned Virgil's request.

The *Aeneid* became to Augustan Rome what Homer's *Iliad* and *Odyssey* had been to the classical Greeks – an explanation of their origins and heroic past.

Spiritual Astronomy

Rudolf Steiner (1861 to 1925) realized that he was "born out of the universe" – born with the macrocosm compressed within him.[32] He began to gain these insights into subtle worlds during childhood. Steiner was an Austrian philosopher, scientist, and artist, and founder of anthroposophy, a philosophical school which develops the innate faculty of spiritual cognition.

Steiner's "supersensible cognitions" reveal that each soul's inter-life journey up in the "Great World" is as rich and diverse as any life on Earth. We first grow into macrocosmic beings (ascension stage). This means that our consciousness spreads out into celestial space as souls advance through the planetary spheres to the world of pure spirit. The entire cosmos becomes our home.

A range of experiences transpire depending upon an individual's spiritual maturity. The divine beings of the star-world, for instance, communicate with morally inclined souls. Opposite to such good fortune, less virtuous souls are like hermits who "wander through the realm of the higher hierarchies as if stumbling" in the dark.[33] They miss many gifts.

Steiner also cognized the second stage – the descent into the visible world.

Ascent to the "Great World"

The ascension process (first stage) begins at the moment our soul departs from the body at death. Our consciousness expands to gigantic dimensions. At the same time, each region we pass through has set limits on awareness, in the same way that gross senses restrict human experience.

Our departed souls first dwell in the Moon-sphere, the region extending outward from Earth to the Moon's orbit. In this first period after death, souls are preoccupied with memories of earthly life and yearn to have a physical body again. This is the "region of burning desires," the purgatory of Christianity, the place of cleansing fire.[34] This is where our ties to the physical world are eliminated so that we may live in the world of spirit. How long souls remain here depends upon the soul's ability to wean itself from earthly attachments. The soul stays a short time if it has clung little to material life, whereas the soul spends a long time if many desires and wishes were still alive within its consciousness at the time of death.

Our souls then ascend, step-by-step, out to the orbits of Mercury (astral world), Venus, Sun, Mars, Jupiter, and Saturn. The soul's expansion of awareness becomes complete when we reach Saturn, the summit of the spiritual world. Beyond that sphere, our souls can make no further progress. We realize that we must return to Earth in order to make this perfected state permanent. We yearn to develop stronger faculties and talents, which only human life "within a body physically separated from all others makes possible."[35]

Building the Spiritual Prototype for the Physical Body

Celestial beings active in each sphere of the twelve signs of the Zodiac – the "Hierarchies" – then come to assist each soul. These Architects supply the spiritual plan and forces for the physical body that the soul will need in order to carry evolution a step further during the next Earth life. The spiritual hierarchies design an "Architectural Plan" for every organ and detail of our earthly body – liver, lung, kidney, brain cell, blood cell, DNA molecule, chromosome, etc. The cosmic intelligences are none other than the "Music of the Spheres spoken of by the Ancient Seers who perceived the Spiritual Beings and their activities."[36]

This second stage (descent to Earth) begins, starting from the consciousness fields of Saturn, when our souls lose awareness and slip into a "cosmic twilight." We progressively shed our gigantic dimensions as we retrace our steps back to Earth, passing down through the realms travelled through previously.

Along the passage down to the amniotic world on Earth, spiritual and moral forces "penetrate us,"[37] and "lofty spiritual beings"[38] illumine us. Gifts of "the starry heaven"[39] include moral inclinations from Mercury, religious feelings from Venus, and wisdom from Mars.

All in all, inter-life is a time of rejuvenation. Steiner compared it to waking up in the morning strengthened and refreshed with new energy, following a good night's sleep. Steiner's subtle cognitions explain why people feel such a deep connection with the planets whenever they gaze into the heavens. Human beings are far more than "earth beings."[40] It is "a sin against the true nature of man to trace his source and origin to earthly forces … . Man bears the image of the cosmos … not merely that of the earth."[41]

Our talents and gifts come from the energies the starry heaven bestowed upon us as well as our parents' DNA. If our bodily development, Steiner argues, depended merely upon physical forces, we would have a grotesque appearance.

❧

Lunar Hideaways

*More than the millions of Suns in our universe and
billions of galaxies beyond our Milky Way, the Moon
plays a central role in the soul's inter-life journey.*

Classical Greeks (Orphic and Pythagorean traditions) and
Romans believed that once our soul permanently departs from the
body at death, we desperately desire to reach the far side of the
Moon, a jump off point for the heavens. The karmic dilemma is that
only "good and virtuous" souls are so fortunate to attain this goal.
These advanced souls are momentarily detained on the Moon in
order to undergo a demagnetization process and cleansing of their
astral bodies.

"... they are purified [by a shower of healing energy], and have
by expiation purged out of them all the infections they might have
contracted from the contagion of the body, as if from foul breath ... ."[42]

The fate of advanced souls, who no longer need to undergo
human rebirth, is to remain "in the mildest part of the air, called the
meadows of Pluto,"[43] for an appointed time. Their subtle physical
bodies then return to Earth and their spirits to the Sun.

In contrast to liberated souls, the immature souls do not reach
the side of the Moon facing the heavens. Violent ethereal winds
blowing in the abyss of Hecate, the less pure atmosphere filling the
space between Earth and Moon, toss thousands of souls to and fro
in the murky depths,[44] like "whirling leaves, or swarms of birds
maddened by the tempest."[45] "Fate" ordains that these souls who
have not yet overcome material desires "wander for a time ... in
the region lying between the earth and moon."[46] They are eventually forced back to Earth to inhabit mortal bodies again.

As a further explanation, the Greeks divided the Moon into two
territories:

- The Moon's departure-from-Earth processing area – on the far side – "demagnetizes" perfected souls departing from earthly life for entry into a heavenly abode.

- The Moon's entrance-to-Earth processing area – on the near side – "magnetizes" heroes and great spirits who volunteer to return to earthly life. Such perfected souls temporarily reside on the Moon "in order to clothe themselves in bodies appropriate to our world."[47]

Cross-Cultural Parallels

Besides the ancient Greeks, several other sacred teachings acknowledged the Moon's dual nature:

- Persia – The prophet Zoroaster taught that all souls, following departure from their bodies, ascend to the invisible mountain of fire lying under the Moon. Less advanced souls are unable to go across the fire to become angels. They must be reborn on Earth.[48]

- Orocs (Siberia) – The Moon has two inter-life regions: one is ruled by "the Mistress of the Bear;" the second is governed by "the Mistress of the Tiger."

- India – Ordinary souls reside on the Moon's dark side, *Bhuloka*, the lowest celestial inter-life region. Souls enjoy this happy realm until they exhaust the merits acquired in their previous earthly life, perhaps one year, or even thousands. The soul's watery body which supports the soul's organs and allows it to generate experiences eventually dissolves allowing the soul's subtler body to fall toward Earth with its storehouse of karma,[49] via the pathway known as *Pitriyana*.

Time in the Land of Immortality

Time spent in the intermediate world
varies from one soul to the next.

Plato's *Republic* states that all souls – the good souls coming from a heavenly interlife and less virtuous souls coming from Tartarus, the nasty underground – remain in the interlife regions for 1,000 years. Virgil's *Aeneid* presents a similar time frame.

"All these [souls], after they have passed away a thousand years, are summoned by the divine one in great array, to the Lethean river. In this way they become forgetful of their former earth-life, and revisit the vaulted realms of the world, willing again to return into bodies."[50]

Plato emphasizes how the time between incarnations correlates to how well individuals lived on Earth.

* Mature Souls – Human beings who pursue wisdom and array themselves in freedom, truth, justice, courage, and temperance enjoy a "long revolution of time" preparing for the next incarnation.[51]

* Immature Souls – "Each pleasure and pain" we experience on Earth is like a "nail which rivets the soul to the body until it becomes like the body."[52] Souls who are thus fixated on the fleeting nature of the world and indulge in worldly pleasures, desires, griefs, and fears, are unable to fly to the upper realms because of the sheer weight [like karmic baggage] of the material appetites clinging to them. They are quickly dragged back to the visible world to once again be arrayed in "foreign attire."

Earthbound Souls

A premature death due to war, natural disasters, or accidents minimizes the soul's time in the inter-life, according to Sufism. Whenever souls are suddenly forced out of their bodies without warning, as opposed to dying of old age or illness, they are thrust unwillingly into "the astral plane" and quickly return to a new human body.

In cases where disasters occur regionally, many souls simultaneously "battle and fight" for birth, using "every and any trickery or method that will allow them to manifest"[53] a human body. These impatient "earthbound souls" are anxious to complete their life experience. In their eagerness, they will hover around lovers who have no intention of attracting a child.

Indigenous peoples of southern Nigeria view premature deaths in a similar fashion. The soul will experience immediate rebirth in order to complete his life plan: twelve days, according to the Southern Ngwa, Asia, and Ndokki peoples; or up to thirty days, according to the Ibo people of Okigwi Division.

Suicide and Magnetically Bound Souls

Suicide interferes with a "timing mechanism built into our psychic web"[54] which determines how long we are bound to our cosmic contract. According to James Van Praagh, contemporary author of the best selling book *Talking To Heaven*, when suicide victims short-circuit this mechanism for the "closing of life," a magnetic bond remains in effect as part of their cosmic contract. Suicide victims remain bound to Earth until the preordained time of their natural death.

This means that if someone's life span was set at sixty years and he commits suicide at age twenty, the soul's "magnetic ties" keep him lodged in a limbo state between the physical and spiritual worlds until the forty years pass. What is even worse, the suicide victims feel remorse because they realize that they had planned the difficulties that drove them to suicide as trials prior to their own birth. They failed to reach the spiritual plateau they had intended. They equally sense the grief of loved ones left behind. Their souls remain trapped in a "no-man's land," with the relentless memory of their "horrific" acts, playing over and over again, "like a bad movie."[55]

Van Praagh emphasizes that not every suicide victim experiences the limbo state. Exceptions to "the wrongdoing of suicide"[56] include: individuals who are mentally ill or have a biochemical imbalance, and souls who are not mature enough to handle their lessons.

Nigerian Inter-Life

God and the Over-Soul set time limits on the interval between lives, according to the indigenous peoples of southern Nigeria.[57]

- Ijaws: one month to three years.
- Yoruba: one to two years.
- Edo (Bini, Esa, Kukuruku, and Sobo subtribes): one to ten years.
- Ibo: two to seven years.
- Yoruba Ekiti: two generations.

Various factors influence the duration of the inter-life sojourn. The Ibo of Owerri stay at least ten years because the inter-life world is so much more pleasant than earthly life; the Kalabari return to another maternal womb quickly if they desire to be with their earthly family.

The Edo reason that life in "heaven" must be unpleasant since bad people are kept there longer to "learn sense," whereas wise people are reborn quickly. That is why the Bini subtribe prefer "to be on earth as the hired servant of another, in the house of a landless man with little to live upon, than be king over all the dead."[58] The Semi-Bantu Boki and Yache likewise agree that human life is superior and return to Earth after nine months and between two and ten months respectively.

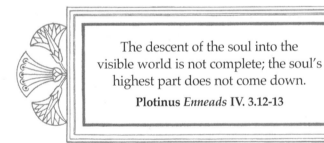

The descent of the soul into the visible world is not complete; the soul's highest part does not come down.

Plotinus *Enneads* **IV. 3.12-13**

Chapter 19
Indigenous Journeys

**There is a constant coming or going
between us and the world of the ancestors.**[1]
– Chinua Achebe

*A diverse array of indigenous peoples contend
that human life transcends biological and environmental
influences. Birth brings someone back who already has a
personality, intelligence, and a whole past behind him.*

Traditional peoples paint a picture in which no spiritual separateness exists between themselves and their ancestors. Departed family members are always alive in an inter-life realm where they rest and predetermine their next human life.

As an illustration, a Kinsquit elder living in British Columbia recounts that his deceased grandmother appeared in his mother's dream saying, "I am lonesome for you and wish to return to Earth." Within a short period, his mother became pregnant. The family recognized the newborn as the late grandmother and the baby was even given the grandmother's name. The elder addressed her as "grandmother" rather than as "sister."

The cosmologies of indigenous peoples include:

- Philippines – "Babe-spirits" fly around Mount Pinyatubu like wild doves prior to conception.[2]
- Koryaks (Siberia) – Departed souls of the Koryaks hang suspended on the posts and cross-beams of the house of "The-One-on-High."[3] The duration of life of each soul is

marked on thongs tied to them. A long strap indicates
longevity, a short one premature death (see Figure 8).

❂ Gilyaks, aka Nivkhz (Siberia) – Souls depart the body at
death and enter a portal on Earth's surface leading to
Mly-vow, a subterranean region where they fish, hunt, marry,
and bear children until they are ready to return to Earth.

❂ Samoa (Polynesia) – The Tree of Leosia, a coconut tree
growing near the entrance to "the World of Spirit," *Pulotu*,
operates like a channel of energy that transports the soul
from the upper world to Earth. Whenever a soul strikes
against the Tree, the soul departs to the earthly realm. At
birth, parents announce, "He has come back from the Tree
of the Watcher."[4]

❂ Cameroon (Africa) – Souls of the Bangwans repose in a
immense dark cave where swarms of spirit babies float in
groups in search of suitable parents. For years, they hunt for
a cozy home with fitting parents.

❂ Australia – Each Aboriginal totem-clan in the region to the
west of Victoria has its own spirit-land, *mi-yur*, where souls
congregate after death and then are reborn.

Inter-life paradigms appear in the cosmologies of other peoples
of Africa and Siberia, as well as British New Guinea.

The angelic soul lives
in a purely mental
world, a world created
by thought-form alone.[25]

Figure 8.[24] The upper portion of this Koryak sketch illustrates the supreme Being, his wife, and souls hanging in the house waiting to be born on Earth. Length of the cord attached to the soul indicates longevity. A short cord indicates a brief life on Earth; a long strap indicates longevity. The lower portion of the sketch shows a shaman beating a drum, assisting his dying patient's soul to the higher world.

Soul Bird

Departed souls are winged beings who fly to
Heaven, and then fly back later to be reborn.

Siberian legends (Tungus, Goldi, Dolgan, and Yakut peoples) relate that the departed spirit (free soul) flies to "the celestial land of the souls" along "the upper course of the tribal river."[5] The soul locates the splendid tree "upon which warble the fledgling souls of future babies of the clan."[6] For several years, the soul lives in this parallel world where the upper swamps are rich in lichens and filled with droves of the domesticated reindeer who await incarnation in the clan's herds. In this way, Siberian clans always inhabit their own territories "whether they are alive on Earth"[7] or wait in the higher world for rebirth.

Beliefs of indigenous peoples of Angola, Africa resemble those of the Siberian peoples. Angolans say God plucks the soul from a tree when it is "ripe" and transfers it into a mother's womb.

Cross-Cultural Parallels

The inter-life paradigm found in Siberia and Africa creates an interesting juxtaposition with soul/bird images around the world and images of winged spiritual beings such as Greek gods, Hebrew angels, and Norse gods who put on an eagle's coat. Perhaps this is why the Hebrew word for angel is bird and the Latin word *aves* means birds and angels, as well as ancestral soul.

At the time of death, the human soul often ascends as a bird to the heavens, according to diverse cultures.

- Bilquila Indians (British Columbia, Canada) – The human soul resides in an egg located in the nape of the neck. The soul flies away when the shell cracks at death.

Souls Waiting in the Wings for Birth

- Central Asia and Indonesia – The soul flies to Heaven and perches on a special tree where it is prepared for rebirth.[8]
- Semangs (Malaysia) – The departed soul appears as a miniature bird.
- Plutarch (1st century Greece) – All souls, after departing from the body, "hover" for awhile between Earth and the Moon.
- Finland and Lithuania – The Milky Way is the path of birds, i.e., of souls.[9]

Visions of departed souls flying to Heaven likewise support the soul-bird image.

- Ancient Greece – Eyewitness testimonies of deathbed visions include: an eagle rising from the bodily remains of Alexander the Great; Pliny's account of the famous ecstatic, Aristeas of Proconnesus, whose soul departed as a raven; as well as visions of the soul of Peregrinus which soared like an eagle into the air and cried out, "I have left the Earth, and am going to Olympus."[10]
- Roman Empire – When the Romans placed the emperor's holy remains on a funeral pyre, "it was contrived that at just the right time there should appear flying from the summit of this flaming Cosmic Tower an eagle, bird of the sun, as the soul of the deceased, released from its earthly coil, now winging home."[11]
- Early Christianity – Two angels appeared as heavenly doves and escorted a third dove to heaven – the soul exiting from Saint Medard's mouth; visions of the soul as a brilliant white dove in flight were reported at the deaths of Joan of Arc, Saints Polycarp, Julia, and Briocus, to name a few.[12]
- Muhammad (Islam) – Souls in Heaven are brilliantly-colored, melodious birds perched on the Tree of Life.[13]
- Jewish *Kabbalah* – The *Zohar* refers to Heaven and God's Bosom as "the Bird's Nest."[14]
- Classical Greece – Plato uses the bird/soul image to portray the soul as a charioteer who drives a team of winged horses travelling across the universe prior to human embodiment. (*Phaedrus* 246a-257a) The wings keep the soul from gravitating downward into the physical world.
- Poland – A folktale tells of the departed souls of unmarried women flying away as doves and married women turning into owls.[15]

The NDE vision of Barontus of Longorus (678 or 679 AD), as recounted in Christian medieval literature, concurs with the preceding visions. According to the Barontus story, his separated soul "seemed so small that it was like a tiny bird just hatched from the egg."[16] His senses remained intact, yet he felt disoriented. "My little soul ... could not speak until, when it came time for discussion, it received a body of air similar to the one I had left behind."[17] Barontus journeyed through heaven and hell with his "body of air and light."

It is fairly common for Native Americans to portray the free-soul as a winged being in flight.[18]

- ❋ Bella Coola (Northwest) – "The shaman hears its [the soul's] buzzing wings, which give a sound like those of a mosquito."
- ❋ Huchnom (the Yuki, California) – Thunder is caused by "the flight of some Indian's many-winged spirit up to heaven, flapping its pinions loudly as it ascends."

The Tsimshian and Southern Paiute compare the soul to a butterfly. Other Native Americans liken the soul to a bird: White River Shoshoni and Huichol – a minute white bird; Kwakiutl – an owl; Luiseno – a dove, and Kootenay – a tomtit or jay.

Parallel Worlds

*Traditional African cosmology consists of the Earth,
the sky world of the supreme deity, and the
realm of ancestors where souls await rebirth.*

Each newborn is an "emissary from the other world"[19] and is often reborn in the same lineage. Due to this conviction, people cry out at the death of a family member:[20] "Let him go! He will come back. Now, a new child will be born in our home."

A typical south Nigerian belief is that the ancestors live in a subterranean world so close to their living relatives that the ancestors observe earthly events and even meet with the living if their relatives use the proper prayers to get their attention.

Southern Nigerians divide the inter-life realm into countries, each with its towns and villages, where souls dwell in the particular locale inhabited by the souls of his own countrymen. Everyone holds a social position similar to the one they had left on Earth. A chief remains a chief, a slave a slave, a farmer a farmer. In certain cases, however, the grandeur of the funeral ceremony can raise the rank of the departed soul.

The Kalabari Ijaw of Nigeria explain that social relationships, amusements, scenery, and homes parallel those on Earth, but only the animals, plants, and food which they offer in honor of the ancestors exist in the inter-life region.

The Kalabari and Ibo believe good and bad souls do not dwell together. Restless souls inhabit the body of animals whereas noble souls rest in a peaceful refuge. Souls of the Eastern Ibo, for instance, await rebirth within the shelter of a giant family tree. Local villagers never cut the honored tree down. Ancestral souls are close enough to render their families assistance. One ancient forest specimen, although branchless and almost dead, still serves as an inter-life home. Sweet white orchids, epiphytic ferns, and leafless, transparent-berried mistletoe veil the tree from top to bottom.

In West Africa, the Ewes call the inter-life world *Amedzow* – the place where the spiritual counterpart of everything on Earth is found, including yams, corn, and cotton. Couples marry the partners whom they will marry on Earth. Except, not all couples are reborn together. If a man marries another woman, his spiritual wife disturbs his domestic bliss until he offers gifts to her in the spirit world.

Island of Perpetual Youth

*Trobriand Islanders in British New Guinea
view inter-life as a mirror image of earthly living,
minus the difficulties and misfortunes.*[21]

Trobriand Islanders position the in-between state next to the terrain of the living, but in separate dimensions. Human spirits *(baloma)* enjoy constant rejuvenation in this subterranean paradise located on Tuma, a small populated island ten miles away. Whenever aging signs begin, the spirits regain youth at will. Like a snake shedding its skin and acquiring a fresh one, the spirit sloughs off his outer covering and looks fresh and young again, with black hair and smooth skin. Trobrianders teach that human beings possessed "perpetual youth" during the Golden Age. This power of rejuvenation became extinct when a spiritual tragedy befell Earth.

Spirits start to yearn for another round of earthly life following an extended existence "underneath." An essential step in the rebirth process requires bathing in a salty ocean, where the spirit regresses in age and turns into a *waiwaia* – a beautiful, minute, fully-developed spirit-child.

Medicine men observe the non-incarnated spirit children floating upon the drift-logs, leaves, dead seaweed, or sea-scum scattered in the sea. The "rejuvenated spirits" seek out an opportunity to enter the body of bathing women and emit drawn-out wailing sounds as they approach the seashore. Each "pre-born infant"[22] selects a mother who belongs to the spirit-child's clan and sub-clan.

Starry One

*African "Wise Men" who practiced the only
"true Science" dependent upon the Power of
Thought cognized the soul's inter-life journey.*

Strange as it seems, Zulu Wise Men, who were "intensely reserved," with their own people, favored a European boy living in the wild African bushlands, "with their confidence."[23] Mankanyezi, a seventy-one-year-old of royal blood and young Patrick's friend and mentor, taught him the "Wisdom which comes from of Old." Mankanyezi, or "Starry One" as it translates into English, belonged to an African Brotherhood which originated in Pharaoh Cheops' reign, over 7,000 years ago.

Patrick obtained knowledge of the soul's journey between one life and the next. First, the soul *(dhlozi)* passes time in *Esilweni* where the soul assumes its rightful shape: part animal – passions, emotions, and instincts; as well as the higher human part – the spark of the Universal Spirit, *Itongo*.

By and by, the soul casts aside its lower animal-like component and progresses to the next realm. The soul falls into a profound sleep, only to dream about a mission lying in store for it on Earth. The soul feels inspired upon awakening and proceeds back to Earth retracing its previous steps.

Jacob witnessed the Gate of Heaven leading to our "before-birth-place."

Chapter 20
Bridge of Angel Hair
Near-Death Visions of the World of Souls

**Jacob had a dream: A ladder was fixed on
the Earth. Seventy-two steps led to the top,
reaching to Heaven. And behold, angels
of God ascended and descended on it.**

– *Holy Bible* (*Genesis* 28)

*Like sand teeter-tottering through one section of
a hourglass to the other, souls journey back and
forth over a "bridge" separating Earth from
the world of souls who wait for birth.*

Spiritual cosmologies picture a transcendental vertical pillar at the middle of the universe binding Heaven, Earth, and the underworld. The early Romans referred to this "communicating point of the three spheres," as the *mundus*.[1] The Kwakiutl of Vancouver Island portrayed the Milky Way as this cosmic spine, whereas the image of the World Tree served as the ultimate prop for indigenous peoples of British Columbia and the Mayans of Yucatan.

Mayan cosmology depicted the World Tree much like a toothpick piercing the middle of a multi-layered universe and holding the segments together. Seven heavenly zones rested above Earth. Each region had a central doorway. A tree growing in the middle of Earth pierced through the seven apertures. The branches of the tree connected all layers of the cosmos stretching as far as God's home in the seventh heaven.[2]

Native American, South American, Asiatic, European, and African cultures portray how people crossed back and forth over this interdimensional bridge in humanity's legendary Golden Age of paradise, when Earth was nearer to the sky world. Six examples follow:

❀ Native American (Pawnee) – "Feather Woman," beloved of the Morning Star, ascended into the upper realms through an entrance – the Pole Star [North Star], a still point in the sky.[3] At the end of her visit, the spider-man who lived near the Pole Star, in the constellation of the crown, twined the thread by which the Feather Woman was let back down to Earth.

❀ British Guayana (Warrau Indians) – A heavenly being lost an arrow while hunting in the upper realm. A search for the lost object led him to an opening through which the arrow had fallen. He peeked into the aperture and observed the Earth below along with herds of wild swine, deer, and other creatures. The visions inspired him to create a rope, a ladder of cotton, whereby he and his friends descended. In this fashion, their forefathers fell to Earth via the cosmic pillar.

❀ Moluccas (Luang-Sermata Islands) – Sky-woman climbed down a rotan-palm tree to Earth. The South wind impregnated her – and she populated the entire planet. Her children accessed the sky world until the Lord of the Sun became angry and cut the rotan tree in two. The root of this tree turned to stone and can be observed on Nolawna Island.[4]

❀ Borneo (Dayaks) – The young hero Si Jura climbed a tree growing on Earth and ascended to the "Seven Stars," the Pleiades. One day he gazed into "a high jar" with a transparent base – apparently a telescope – and surveyed the Earth below, his home, and family. Si Jura's observations made him homesick. The Pleiadians agreed to lower him back to Earth via a long rope. But before they did, his kindly hosts taught Si Jura farming, bird-omens and rice cultivation, and presented him with three special seeds.

❀ Danish folklore – A person is let down from the sky or from the Moon with a rope twined from chaff. In a related story, someone climbs to the sky world by means of a rapidly growing plant, sprouted from a caraway or mustard seed.

❀ Estonia, Eastern Europe – A folktale describes how a man climbs to the sky world via a fast growing tobacco plant. When the wind uproots the plant, Father Pitkne, the Thunder God, lets the man back down to Earth with the rain.

Souls Waiting in the Wings for Birth

The magical traffic between Earth and the sky world is related to the belief that the human soul originates in the sky world and its near relations still dwell there. This set of traditions correlates the world-axis symbol with a passageway, much like a hollow tube, by which souls journey between their spirit home and Earth.

The Jewish *Talmud* alludes to this cosmic pillar when answering the question, "What does God do after creating all the souls which are to enter human bodies?" One rabbi explains: "God keeps making ladders for souls to ascend and other souls to descend, until all the souls in the heavenly repository experience human life." These celestial ladders correspond to the image witnessed in Jacob's dream: a seventy-two rung ladder resting on Earth and reaching into Heaven with angels climbing in both directions, up and down, like a highway to and from Heaven. (*Genesis* 28:10-17) Jacob evidently realized the angels carry souls down from Heaven for birth and up from Earth after death and proclaimed: "This is the gate of Heaven."

Images of the soul's pathway between Earth and the spirit world appear throughout early religious traditions.

* Egypt – One sculpture portrays souls ascending and descending on a flight of steps.[5]
* Manichaeism (3rd century AD) – Souls come down to Earth and depart via a column of light.[6]
* Persia – An artistic representation of a seven-stepped ladder (*klimax heptapylos*)[7] symbolizes the soul's journey to and from Earth through the seven planets.[8]
* India – The "pathway of the ancestors" is the gateway souls traverse from Earth to the postmortem realm as well as the route back to human rebirth.[9]
* Buddhism – Buddha descends from Heaven by a stairway to tread the earthly path. From the top of the stairway, he sees all the *Brahmalokas* above and all the depths of hell below. Reliefs at Bhārhut and Sanchi depict this miraculous stairway, the true *axis mundi* at the center of the universe.

Regardless of how cultures represent the link between the physical and nonphysical worlds – a pillar, bridge, rainbow, a rope, a cobweb, a tunnel, the Milky Way, a tree, a creeper, or a mountain – the cosmic pillar represents a frequency shift from a higher to lower (descending), or lower to higher (ascending) rate of vibration. In other words, our arrival parallels our departure in reverse order.

The cosmic pillar is an entry gate as well as departure gate. Our souls exit at death through one of 10,000 doors, which "go on such strange geometrical hinges. You may open them both ways."[10]

Following Earth's Golden Age in the Garden of Eden, only rare individuals initiated in the ancient wisdom knew how to climb the cosmic pillar and return to Earth to tell their stories. Among them were NDErs, individuals who were supposedly "dead," and travelled "in spirit." For the most part, however, "the windows of Heaven were stopped," as the Old Testament puts it. (*Genesis* 8:2)

Contemporary near-death experiences (NDEs) are included here, as well as near-death episodes from ancient Greek and Native American culture.

People used the Pillar of Light to visit "Home" during humanity's Golden Age, the Garden of Eden.

A String of Babies

*One Native American traveller witnessed souls
bound for human birth crossing a cosmic bridge.*[11]

An unfortunate accident ended a Yokut woman's life soon after making her marriage vows. Under great duress, her husband fasted and lay next to her grave site, without sleep. Finally after three days, the ground trembled, and the wife's spirit emerged from the grave, intact with burial gifts. She brushed herself off saying, "My dear husband, I am going to the ancestral realm. Please do not follow me."

The husband paid no heed. He pursued his wife's spirit for four days until they reached a bridge spanning a perilous, churning river. The bridge was as fine as a spider's web and the husband needed his wife's assistance in order to cross. Along the web's narrow walkway, they met a long string of children moving silently past them going in the opposite direction down to the Earth. "They were coming to be born to our women."

When the couple reached the opposite shore, ancestors and deceased friends greeted them in a region of light, joy, and beauty. As much as the husband desired to stay, his cosmic contract was not up yet. His wife escorted him back across the river:

> Husband, return to Earth and report all that you have seen. Once that task is done, we will reunite within three days.

The husband ran home and gathered his kin. After three days passed, he fulfilled his pledge and "died" again. This time he did not come back to his body.

Cross-Cultural Parallels

This Native American legend parallels the story of Odysseus, Aeneas, Moses, and Dante who visit the after-death realm. Their narratives include someone crossing a bridge, rainbow, or the Milky Way, going into a spiritual world, encountering obstacles, and searching for a deceased loved one.

Plato's Myth of Er

*At the end of Plato's Republic, a warrior named Er,
who "died" in battle, observed a towering band of light
resembling a rainbow, only brighter and purer. It seemed to
be a passageway by which souls journey back and forth
to Earth. Most western scholars tend to interpret Er's
experience as only an allegory, yet it parallels NDEs.*

Greek culture is filled with stories of healers, oracles, and miracle-workers – the *iatromanteis*.[12] We even find records of "air-travellers" who knew how to leave their bodies at will in order to visit celestial worlds and remote earthly locations.[13]

On one mystical flight, the famous ecstatic, Hermotimos, lost his "bodily shelter." While his soul visited faraway places, jealous enemies burned his inanimate body. As recorded in Plato's *Republic*, the warrior Er nearly met the same fate as Hermotimos. In Er's case, however, his soul reentered the body just in the nick of time before his family lit the funeral pyre.

Once Er regained consciousness, he related secrets revealed to his soul during its separation from the body – the story of the soul's 1,000 year journey between one human life and the next. Er's near-death episode began in the region where individuals who had just completed their earthly lives experience a life review. Er watched as judges overseeing the process sent mature souls to Heaven; whereas souls who lived at cross-purposes with universal law went to a nasty underground prison *(Tartarus)*, there to pay their penalty.

Like the rest, Er took his turn to stand before the judges; they surprised him and advised:

> Er, you are not here for judgment. You have come as Earth's
> messenger and must return to mankind to tell them of the
> other world.

Er's Journey to the Land of Cosmic Contracts

Er's assigned task began in a great meadow where he mingled with a gathering of souls, "like a festival crowd." For seven days, the warrior listened closely as souls recounted experiences taking place over the past one thousand years: the "shining" souls related beautiful visions of Heaven, whereas soul dwellers from the underworld, who were still covered with dust and grime, wept as they related all that they had suffered.

Er then observed how this entire company of souls prepared for another human birth. To begin with, he ascended with them through a heavenly gate and travelled to the outer rim of the sky. They eventually reached a luminous column stretching through Heaven and Earth, the axis of the cosmos by which the universe revolves. This cosmic pillar, a towering band of light, resembled a rainbow, only brighter and purer. (See Figure 9, *Structure of the Cosmos*)

Within this scene, both the souls who had spent 1,000 years in the heavens or in Tartarus [Hell], began preparing for their next lifetimes. First, souls leisurely previewed a set of tablets inscribed with life patterns of every living creature and condition. The total number of scripts available exceeded the number of souls in the assembly so that everyone had the opportunity to choose a good life.

Before the souls picked out the cosmic contracts which pleased them most, an overseer threw lot numbers amongst the assembly. The number the soul picked up determined the order in the queue for selecting a new life. Number one had the first choice, and so forth, according to the numbers held, until all had chosen.

The overseer next warned,

You are free to choose and will be held responsible for your choice. Let not the first choose carelessly, nor the last give up hope. Even the last soul to pick a cosmic contract will find a tolerable life lying here, if he chooses with intelligence.

Er noted that some souls selected conditions of their next life more wisely, and others less wisely. Pleasurable lives easily tempted less mature souls. Young souls blindly grabbed cosmic contracts without examining the fine print such as – great wealth followed by bankruptcy, or years of sensual pleasure followed by years of pain.

Dispositions formed in previous lives definitely influenced the soul's preference. The first soul in line illustrates this principle. He settled upon the life of an absolute dictator. Having made a hasty decision, he noticed that he was fated to eat his children, among other evils. He beat his breast, blaming God, the stars – everyone except himself. In this case, he had been virtuous in a previous life, yet "his virtue had been merely 'customary' without foundation upon consciously realized principle."[14]

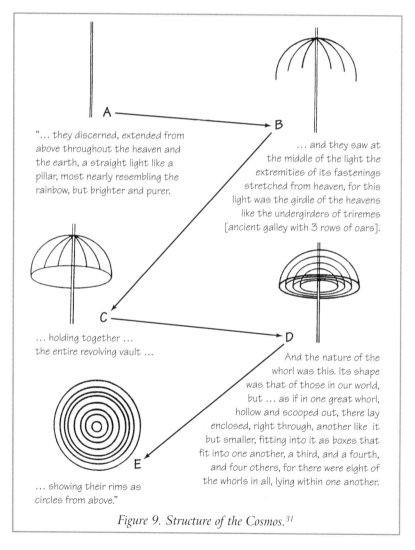

A

"... they discerned, extended from above throughout the heaven and the earth, a straight light like a pillar, most nearly resembling the rainbow, but brighter and purer.

B

... and they saw at the middle of the light the extremities of its fastenings stretched from heaven, for this light was the girdle of the heavens like the undergirders of triremes [ancient galley with 3 rows of oars].

C

... holding together ... the entire revolving vault ...

D

And the nature of the whorl was this. Its shape was that of those in our world, but ... as if in one great whorl, hollow and scooped out, there lay enclosed, right through, another like it but smaller, fitting into it as boxes that fit into one another, a third, and a fourth, and four others, for there were eight of the whorls in all, lying within one another.

E

... showing their rims as circles from above."

Figure 9. Structure of the Cosmos.[31]

Wiser souls, according to Er, took time to contemplate previous experiences before making a decision. Souls who had suffered in Tartarus, on the average, seemed to plan more wisely than souls coming down from Heaven.

Odysseus, the clever king of Ithaca, serves as another prime illustration. Although Odysseus had emerged victorious in battle after suggesting the stratagem of the Trojan Horse, he encountered obstacles in returning to Greece following the Trojan War. Odysseus wandered with his men from place to place for an entire decade. They had countless adventures: the sorceress Circe turned them into swine; they nearly succumbed to the temptations of the land of the Lotus-Eaters and the insidious song of the Sirens; they barely survived the dangers of the passage between Scylla and Charybdis; and they encountered the fearsome one-eyed giant Polyphemus.

Er observed how Odysseus reflected upon the hollowness and uncertainty of fame, the batterings of endless journeys, and treacherous adventures. This time he decided to look for an easier lot with less heartache and tragedy. Sure enough, he picked up the cosmic contract for a quiet man's life, the one that had been rejected by the other souls. Although Odysseus happened to be the last to make a choice, he said, "I would have done the same even if I had drawn the first lot."

In another instance, Orpheus recalled how he had been murdered by a woman in his previous life. As a consequence, Orpheus' hatred of women influenced his decision to be reborn as a swan rather than entering a woman's womb.

Besides humans choosing to pass into animals in the next life, Er even noted that animals changed into one another and into humans.

Shooting Stars from the Banks of Lethe

Er witnessed one final step prior to the "take off spot for the return journey to Earth."[15] He marched with the assembly of souls through a burning heat and frost across the Plain of Lethe. At last, when the souls arrived at the River of Forgetfulness, they felt compelled to satisfy their thirst. Foolish souls drank more than the rest. The more they drank, the deeper they slept – and the more they forgot of their divine heritage.

Unlike the rest, Er chose to forgo the waters of Lethe in order to remember all that he had seen and heard. He remained wide awake at midnight to witness a lightning and quaking of the universe to awaken the souls, propelling them to the waiting wombs of their earthly mothers – "leaping upward like shooting stars."[16]

Twelve days had passed since Er had "died" on the battleground. Yet according to Er, before he knew it, he had opened his eyes and found himself on the funeral pyre, not knowing by what means he had gone in and out of his body.

Moral of Er's NDE

After relating Er's story to a student, Plato explains:

"Thus, Glaucon, the tale was preserved ... and if we listen to it, it may preserve us, and we shall cross the river of Lethe without defiling our souls. And if we believe what I say, convinced that the soul is immortal and strong to endure all good and ill, we shall ever hold to the upward path and practice justice with knowledge ... and when, like victorious athletes ... we have won the prize for justice both here and in the thousand-year journey we have gone through, we shall fare well."[17]

Images of the soul's pathway to Earth are as old as human life itself.

Near-Death Vision of Thespesius

The 1st century Greek writer Plutarch
portrays Thespesius's journey to the higher regions
upon a rainbow of light – the cosmic pillar – and
tells how he met souls waiting for rebirth.[18]

Aridaeus of Soloi, who had a reputation for amassing a fortune using dishonest means, became famous as a result of asking the Oracle of Amphilochus, "Will my life ever improve?" The Oracle answered, "It will be better after death."[19] In a sense that is what happened shortly afterward. Aridaeus fell and suffered a concussion. And after laying "dead" for three days, he returned to life as funeral preparations began.

Afterward his neighbors never knew anyone of a better conscience, no one more virtuous. The reasons behind the metamorphosis piqued everyone's curiosity. Aridaeus eventually revealed what happened during his upward journey. His spirit initially felt like a pilot who had been plunged into the bottom of the sea. Then quite suddenly a powerful force raised him up, and he began to breathe with his whole being. His soul opened wide as if it were a single eye. He observed gigantic stars separated by infinite distances and radiating a marvelously colored light.

Like a ship on a calm sea, Aridaeus travelled wherever he desired upon this rainbow of light – the cosmic pillar. He observed "small fiery bubbles," – departed souls of all kinds – good, bad, and indifferent – ascending from Earth. Each flame-like bubble was distinguished by a color, according to the soul's purity or impurity. Some were like pure moonlight and emitted one smooth even color. Others were quite mottled and dappled with livid spots like adders. Another type was distinguished by faint scratches.[20] When these bubbles "brast insunder," the souls emerged in the form of men and women, "very light and nimble, as discharged from all poise to bear them down."[21]

By and by, a childhood friend, someone who had died many years earlier, greeted Aridaeus. The friend called Aridaeus by a new name, "Thespesius," and explained, "True, you were Aridaeus, but from now on, you are Thespesius (meaning godly, wonderful)."[22]

Throughout the near-death tour, the friend served as a guide. He explained that Thespesius had not really "died." Rather a special dispensation from God and the permission of Destiny allowed the intellectual aspect of his soul to experience this realm. Because this was not true death, another part is still in the body on Earth, "sticking fast as an anchor to your body."[23] The earthly connection limited Thespesius's ascension into the higher regions: "the cable of your soul gives no further upward play and does not grow slack, but holds taut, being made fast to the body."[24]

Even with a short "cable," however, Thespesius "buoyed up by the beams of the light as by wings."[25] He explored a giant chasm where "a soft and gentle breeze" carrying fragrant scents had attracted a huge assembly of souls. The souls "drew themselves in like birds and alighted and walked around the circuit of the chasm, not venturing to pass directly across."[26] The sweet odours aroused "wondrous pleasures and such a mood as wine induces in those who are becoming tipsy."[27]

A subtle magnetism drew Thespesius to this chasm as well as the other souls. His escort warned:

> Do not linger in the region of Lethe, the realm of oblivion. This is where "bacchic revelry, festivity, and merry-making"[28] feed the sensual part of the soul and dissolve reason. Souls who remain here recall fond, nostalgic memories of earthly life and are overcome with strong desires for birth and physical experiences.

Thespesius's otherworldly adventures included witnessing the penalties awaiting him if he persisted in living a life of deceit and corruption. He observed the torments of an Inferno and a Purgatory, as well as a remodeling center where workmen reshaped sinful souls who would be reborn as animals. Besides welding and hammering new parts, the artisans twisted, polished, and nearly abolished former parts. Following the final spectacles, Thespesius snapped back to his body in a great rush of wind and opened his eyes shortly prior to his funeral. The spiritual insights that Thespesius gained while travelling outside of the body caused a transformation in consciousness for the rest of his life.

Cross-Cultural Parallel

Thespesius's three-day NDE and Er's twelve-day NDE sound far-fetched until compared to the NDE phenomenon reported in the Himalayas: *delog*, one who returns from the beyond. The Tibetan Library of Works and Archives in Dharamsala, India houses the records of many documented cases. At least twelve NDEs lasted one week or longer. *Delogs* occur more often among virtuous women.

A Tibetan woman from the village of Tsarong experienced a seven-day *delog*. She enjoyed the lightness and agility of her ethereal body and the ability to immediately travel anywhere she wished. She crossed rivers, walked upon waters, and passed through walls. One thing she found impossible, however – to cut the almost intangible cord connecting her ethereal being to the material body which she easily observed sleeping at home upon her couch. Although the cord elongated indefinitely, she sometimes got "caught up in it"[29] and it hampered her movements.

Other Tibetan delogs include Dawa Drolma, an enlightened woman who remained inanimate for five days in the 1920s.[30] The mother of Tarjay Gyamtso, the teacher of Kalu Rinpoche (1905 to 1989) serves as a third example.

Tibetans test the authenticity of a *delog* by plugging up the orifices of her body, such as the nose, mouth, and ears with solid butter, and applying a barley flour paste over the face. If the butter remains solid and the mask firm without cracking, Tibetans consider the NDE to be genuine. Of course, there is no way to prove whether the *delog's* experiences parallel those felt by the dead.

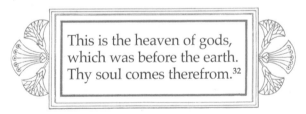

This is the heaven of gods, which was before the earth. Thy soul comes therefrom.[32]

The Pillar of Light parallels Jacob's vision of the stairway to Heaven.

PART FOUR

COSMIC CONTRACTS

**Cosmic Contracts descend from
Heaven like falling Star Dust.**

Individual Free Will
and Cosmic Will

The prelude to human embryonic life is filled with mystery — as unknown as the beginning of time and the universe itself. Religion, philosophy, and legends describe how a cosmic contract or a lesson plan exists for each of the roughly 130 million children coming into this world each year, as well as the estimated 50 million people exiting. According to this process, country of birth, parents, life purpose, even time and circumstances of death are determined prior to conception.

Each actor somehow arrives on the stage of life with the most appropriate script. Some philosophers propose that this is a free-will universe and each soul actor chooses his role. A second perspective proposes that the soul's ability to influence pre-birth choices varies with spiritual maturity. Still a third theory emphasizes that every actor selects a script in the light of balancing out accumulated past actions from previous lives. This is like someone who is given free will to fly to any destination out of the New York airport, but because he has influences he created in the past, he picks the plane to Houston.

A fourth theory proposes that a Divine Intelligence who knows the precise laws of nature writes the script for the grand play in life and sets the stage. This higher power determines the sequence of events in our cosmic contracts from birth to its destiny, much like an assembly line manager in charge of a production line which begins with raw materials and goes through various stages until we have a final product.

Without our cosmic contracts, global chaos might reign in a few years. Even a photon seems to have a cosmic contract. Some physicists theorize that by knowing the time a photon emerges from a field, we have knowledge of its world line, including such things as "the photon's spin, how much energy it has, the direction it will take, and how long it may last."[1]

Chapter 21
Souls Signing Their Cosmic Contracts

**"I must not be the right mother for Ivan,"
said a frustrated mother trying to
comfort her eight-month-old son Ivan.
Frank, her four-year-old son, reassured her,
"But, Mom, you are. Ivan looked down
and picked you out to be his mom."[1]**

*Seldom do people stop to think they are actors who chose a
script for the colossal stage of life. But, within the seed of our
destiny, as it turns out, we have a grain of free will.*

Human life is an intentional and purposeful experience.
Shakespeare's saying, the soul is the "mistress of her choice"
(*Hamlet*) on Earth equally applies to the prelude to human life
where dynamic interactions transpire between the soul's world
and our own.

As an ancient parable[2] explains, no soul enters three-dimensional
form without a general plan for the road of earthly life ahead.

At the time of this creation, each newly-created soul decided, "I
choose to be free." "So be it," answered the Supreme Voice, who
held each soul by a shining cord, "but you will experience
suffering. Pride will seduce you. And you will know death."

"I must contend with death to conquer life," each soul responded. So God loosened the shining cord from its bosom, and the soul ventured forth to make mistakes, suffer the consequences, and thereby grow in strength, wisdom, and stature.

This generalized story from India encapsulates Plato's teachings:

"Each Soul, according to its nature, clothes itself in certain circumstances ... which it has itself chosen ... circumstances which are to be regarded not as forcing it, or dominating it mechanically from without, but as being the environment in which it exhibits its freedom or natural character as a living creature."[3]

Legends from Africa, Indonesia, Borneo, North America, Australia, Thailand, plus Mormon and Gnostic scriptures, and NDEs concur that souls select parents, children, spouses, lesson plans, and guardian angels, and coordinate birth time with historical events.

Every soul ponders over a cosmic contract before birth.

The Soul's Caretaker

In the same fashion that Plato's Republic
*describes the soul's intentions: "No divine guardian
shall draw lots for you, but you shall choose your
own guardian and destiny,"[4] indigenous people
of Africa pick guardian angels prior to birth.*

A Yoruba legend from western Nigeria recounts the story of
Orisanku, Oritemere, and Afuwape – three children who were
friends in Heaven. One day, they "deliberated" about whether
human life on Earth might be better than Heaven. The boys
decided to experiment. Before they "settled down together"[5] on
Earth, however, the wise ones instructed: "Go to the place where
guardians are created and select an *ori* who will be your guardian
and protector on Earth."

The first two boys, Orisanku and Oritemere, set off to visit a
being named Ajalamo – "the one who moulds new children."[6]
After briefly waiting for Ajalamo to show, he failed to appear. The
anxious children entered the storehouse, snatched two guardians,
and rushed off to the earthly world.

A third boy, Afuwape, decided a more patient approach was
best. He waited to make his choice of guardian until Orunmilla, his
father-to-be, offered prayers on behalf of bringing in a good son.
Meanwhile, the local priest *(babalawo)* advised the aspiring father:

> Orunmilla, prayers will help the boy select a proper guardian and
> fulfill his destiny of birth into your family. Perform sacred rituals and
> contribute 1,000 cowries towards his benefit. Pray that your son
> spends the money in the house of Ajalamo.

As a result, Afuwape arrived at Ajalamo's abode bearing 1,000
cowries. Like the first two boys, Ajalamo was not at home when
Afuwape arrived. So the boy waited around for an audience.
Meanwhile he conversed with an elderly woman in the waiting

room. She had come to collect the debt Ajalamo owed her – 1,000 cowries.

Afuwape, out of the goodness of his heart, pulled out the 1,000 cowries from his own pocket and paid off the debt. The woman expressed gratitude and promptly left. Unbeknownst to them, Ajalamo had observed the boy's benevolent act from his hiding place high up in the rafters. He too thanked Afuwape and escorted him to a garden filled with guardians:

> Afuwape, I create many guardians. Not every one turns out flawless. I forget to bake some, over-bake others, or sometimes even neglect finishing touches. Remember that imperfect guardians will not bear the strains of an earthly journey.

Assisted by Ajalamo's expert guidance, Afuwape was matched with just the right guardian to bring success. And unlike Afuwape's impatient friends, Ajalamo sent the boy down to his earthly home with blessings. Even though a guardian accompanies every soul's journey to Earth, guardians vary because "fate is different."

The blessings of Afuwape's inborn talents, hard work, and will-power led to great accomplishments. In contrast, Orisanku and Oritemere wondered where they had erred in planning their journey on Earth:

> Where did Afuwape find his guardian? If we knew, we would go there and choose again. We thought we went to the same place.

Cross-Cultural Parallel

The African pre-conception ritual described in this parable parallels a tradition from India. Just as Afuwape's father prayed for the birth of a good son, one year prior to conception, an Indian woman fasted and prayed one day a week so that she could birth a son. Her son, Swami Vivekananda, was "born through prayer" rather than "sensuality."[7]

> "The child must be prayed for. Those children who ... slip into the world just in a moment of inadvertence ... what can you expect of such progeny?"[8]

Indigenous Contracts

*Indigenous peoples have a direct hand
in designing their lesson plans.*

Throughout West Africa, members of the Kwa language group (Igbo, Yoruba, Edo, Kalabari), as well as the Tallensi and other peoples within the larger Niger-Congo language family, believed that each child chose "its physical and mental potentials and the use to which these potentials would be put in its future life"[9] before birth. The Igbos, in fact, arrive at their cosmic contract by striking a deal with God.[10]

Besides Africa, traditional peoples in Asia, Australia, and the Native American culture believed each soul chose his personal destiny.

* Indonesia – The Bataks of north-central Sumatra define destiny as "that which the soul has asked for." They believe a tree grows in the upper world upon which each leaf is inscribed with lessons to be learned, life span, and circumstances of death. Prior to birth, each soul picks out his "lot-determining" leaf.

* Sea Dyaks (Borneo) – The creator of human beings presents each baby to the higher council of gods before birth. The council asks: "Choose a tool you will handle and use." If the baby replies, "A sword," the gods declare it a male. If the baby answers, "Cotton and a spinning-wheel," it is a female. Thus, according to their wishes, they pick their earthly destinies.

* Tontemboan (Sulawesi) – Souls select a match related to a particular destiny from a myriad of long-burning matches.

* Euahlayi Aborigines (Australia) – Souls of children who die prematurely are free to re-enter the womb of the same mother or, if they prefer, a different one. These *millanboo* children – "the same again"[11] – are like students who drop out of school, resume their lessons when they return. For

instance, if a young man marries an older woman, it is believed that he lived on Earth before and loved this same woman, but died before passing through the puberty rite initiation and marriage. Thus, he fulfills his former agreements in his next life.[12]

❀ North Tacullies peoples, aka Carrier (North America) – When a sign signifying "yes" appeared on the recently deceased's breast, shamans knew the soul desired rebirth. The shaman helped the soul find a new mother by blowing the soul into the air or by placing his hands on a family member desiring an offspring. The ensuing child bore the name and rank of the deceased.[13]

❀ Karen peoples (Hill tribe, Northern Thailand) – The child's spirit determines life span and how, when, and where death will occur. Even if death is premature or violent, no one laments, since it was the person himself who chose it.[14]

WANTED:
Actors and Actresses
for the greatest drama
in the Universe

Soul Groups

*Souls who advocate similar religious and moral
values occupy designated realms in the spirit world ...
just as great spiritual masters promise, "I will
prepare a seat for you at the feet of the Lord."[15]*

The proverb, "birds of a feather flock together," seems to apply even in cases of souls preparing for birth. Souls seek out companions who think alike. These souls elect to join together and work on Earth in order to learn equivalent lessons.

Mormon teachings, as a prime example, declare that humanity lived as eternal intelligences who "sang together with the heavenly hosts"[16] until the "Day of the Great Council." At that turning point, God proposed a cosmic plan to the assembly of spirits: experience "gross matter" in order to advance in "mastery over the universe,"[17] and become "saviors" for themselves and for the human race.[18] The entire assembly volunteered to participate in the "great preparation."[19] Each spirit makes the earthly sojourn only once and coordinates cosmic contracts, or "covenants," with his favorite spirit companions to be his guardian angel, parents, spouse, and children.

Communities of Like-Minded Souls

During RaNelle Wallace's NDE, her spirit transported back to the moment when she, along with her "brothers and sisters in eternity," chose an earthly experience. RaNelle felt "tremendous honor" to stand before her "Father." Every member of her soul group raised his right arm, like someone "in a court of law," and made "a sacred covenant" to use their time, energies, and talents to bring about "goodness on Earth."

Love and joy swept over RaNelle during her near-death life review, as she relived how everyone had "elected to follow Jesus

Christ as their Savior who would bring them back to their Father."[20]
Each member in the assembly fit as a piece of an interrelated puzzle.
If one person's mission failed, everyone sensed a gap until the
missing part returned "to its rightful place." In a comparable
manner, everyone benefited from each person's success.

"Birds of a feather flock together" even applies to souls preparing for birth.

Dreaming of the Gods

*Before leaving the spirit world, souls destined to be Dakota
Sioux medicine men and women not only selected their
future roles, but they went through a dress rehearsal
before the actual performance of a new life.*

The Dakota Sioux of the Great Plains revered every creature as a
greater or lesser expression of the all-pervading divine essence,
"Wakan." They even respected the elements, forces of nature, sticks,
and stones, as sacred. The highest expression were medicine men
or women – "gods in human form, though in diminished proportions."[21]

Much like electricity, *Wakan* energy can strengthen or injure. So
just as an electrician learns how to handle the power of electricity
and electrical equipment, the shaman spends time with a particular
"class of gods" and learns to use "the Great Mystery" prior to birth.

"As the winged seed of the thistle or of the cottonwood floats on
the air, so they [souls of the shamans] are gently wafted by the four
winds – *Taku-skan-skan* – through the regions of space, until, in due
time, they find themselves in the abode of some one of the families of
the superior gods by whom they are received into intimate
fellowship."[22]

The "embryonic" medicine men undergo an "inspirational"
process called "dreaming of the gods" under the tutelage of teacher
gods. They become acquainted with the chants, feasts, dances, and
sacrificial rites they will use on Earth. Spiritual guides train them
to heal, foretell future events, discover objects lost in time and
space, and "perform all sorts of wonders."

In accord with pre-conception planning, each shaman chooses the
tribe and parents which allows him to best serve another generation:

"… (he) now again rides forth, on the wings of the wind, over the
length and breadth of the earth, till he has carefully observed the

characters and usages of all the different tribes of men; then selecting his appearance among men, to fulfill the mysterious purposes for which the gods designed him."[23]

Once the shaman selects the circumstances for birth, his soul is "committed to the direction of the four winds" whereby he finds his mother's womb.

Born by Choice

Researchers document additional examples of Native Americans who picked their birth entrances and set their earthly tasks as healers.

- ❀ Canadian Dakota – Medicine men and women favored Native American parents because they preferred Indian customs over those of the white culture.[24]

- ❀ Menominee – "Look Around" and "Moulting Feathers," traversed the globe in search of a brave, virtuous tribe. Look Around felt pleased with the Menominee, selected a mother, entered her womb, and caused her to become pregnant. Moulting Feathers selected parents from a neighboring tribe.[25]

- ❀ Great Plains Lakota, aka Teton Sioux – Souls desiring birth as twins wandered around in the nearby hills and frequently entered camp, peeking into tepees until they found appropriate parents.

Cosmic Contracts Made Here

The Twelve Disciples

*Souls destined to be spiritual masters coordinate birth
time with helpmates who will accompany them to Earth.
Sixty disciples agreed to be born with Baal Shem, aka
Israel ben Eliezer, the 18ᵗʰ century founder of Hasidism.
The master refused to be born because he feared evil
people would destroy his courage. The disciples agreed to
guard him. Ramakrishna similarly selected Vivekananda,
and Buddha had his favorite disciple, Ananda.*

A collection of Christian gospels, including dialogues, conversation, and visions attributed to Jesus and His disciples, were discovered in 1947. Included were the *Books of Pistis-Sophia*, Gnostic texts which begin by saying, "… after Jesus was risen from the dead … he spent eleven years discoursing with his disciples."[26]

Among other topics, Christ explained how he selected the Twelve Disciples "before He came into the world."[27] He cast these "twelve powers," "as light sparks, into the wombs of their mothers, [in order] that … the whole world might be saved."[28] Christ continued to oversee their mothers' pregnancies and the births so that "no soul of the world-rulers should be found in them, but one of a higher nature."[29] Christ played the same role in the birth of his forerunner, Saint John the Baptist. Christ "looked down upon the world of mankind at the command of the first Mystery"[30] and observed Elizabeth. Christ thereupon infused Elizabeth with a power from "the Good,"[31] and ensured that the soul of the prophet Elias entered John the Baptist's body.[32]

In a comparable fashion, Christ supervised his own birth from the region of "Infinite Light." Christ first surveyed mankind by searching for an appropriate mother. When Christ found Mary, He spoke to her in the guise of the angel Gabriel.

"… when she [Mary] had turned upwards towards me, I thrust into her the first power … that is, the body which I have borne on high. And in the place of the soul I thrust into her the power which I have taken from the great *Sabaoth* the Good, who dwells in the place of the righteous ones."[33]

Soul Weight

*The soul has specific characteristics including
weight and size. Based on these concepts,
the soul's weight and size might be measurable.*

The Nias (Island of Sumatra) believe each individual decides upon the soul's weight prior to birth and a soul of the desired weight is measured out for him.[34] If someone desires longevity, he

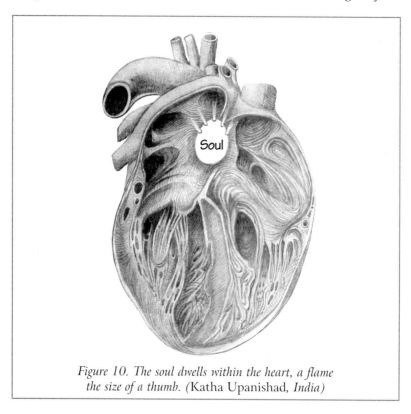

*Figure 10. The soul dwells within the heart, a flame
the size of a thumb. (Katha Upanishad, India)*

picks a soul with the heaviest weight of ten grams (about one-third of an ounce), as opposed to a soul of a few grams or less which corresponds to premature death. For that reason, when someone's life ends, they say, "What he asked for is gone."

Cross-Cultural Parallel

Dr. MacDougal tested the hypothesis of whether the soul has a measurable weight in 1907. He and a colleague used a scale (sensitive to 5 to 6 grams) to attempt to measure weight changes in a few terminally ill hospital patients, immediately before and at death. Measurements indicated small, quantifiable weight losses ranging from 21 to 42 grams (0.75 to 1.5 ounces) at and immediately after the instant of death in three cases. The first patient showed a one ounce total weight loss at death:

> "This loss of weight could not be due to evaporation of respiratory moisture and sweat, because that had already been determined to go on, in his case, at the rate of one sixtieth of an ounce [about 0.5 grams] per minute, whereas this loss was sudden and large, three-fourths of an ounce [about 21 to 22 grams] in a few seconds."[35]

Three patients' weight loss difference was observed to be 40 to 120 times larger than typical per minute weight loss due to the body's metabolic and breathing activities.

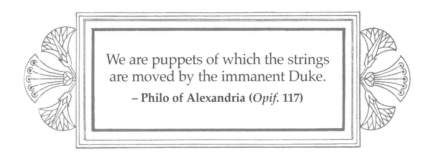

We are puppets of which the strings are moved by the immanent Duke.

– Philo of Alexandria (*Opif.* 117)

Chapter 22
Golden Books of Destiny

**Suddenly in my dream ... . I saw a
beautiful baby with big dark eyes ... .
He said, "I have been waiting a long time,
and I have your name on me."**[1]

*Imagine that we exist in God's Mind, as little
more than red blood cells swimming in an infinite
ocean, orchestrated by a higher intelligence. Just as a
red blood cell is part of our body, we share part of a
universal wholeness beyond ordinary perception.*

The world is like a vast theater and our cosmic contracts are like
the pictures appearing on its giant movie screen. Behind the
scenes, a director writes and projects our cosmic contracts on the
screen. Without the director, the show is impossible. Like that, our
cosmic contracts crystallize before we enter the drama of the
universe. As an ancient text of India proclaims, "Life span, karma,
wealth, learning, and death are born with the embodied creature in
the womb."[2] Shakespeare then tells us, "Heaven from all creatures
hides the book of fate."[3]

Our scripts are recorded in the world of the soul, the world
before creation. Sometimes this is the work of God or an angel. Sufi
teachings explain that 50,000 years before the existence of Heaven
and Earth, when God's throne was "on the water," God created a
green beryl Tablet and an emerald Pen filled with an ink of white

light. God commanded, "Write O Pen!"[4] And the Pen of Fate asked: "Lord, what shall I write?" God answered: "Write the destinies of all things until the Final Hour." The Pen thereupon inscribed all the events that were to happen on the world stage.

According to a diversity of religions, God writes the scripts of souls assigned to be spiritual leaders before they enter the womb.

* *Old Testament* – The Lord told Jeremiah: "I knew you before you were born. I appointed you a prophet of the nations before I formed you in the womb." (*Jeremiah* 1:4-5)
* *New Testament* – John the Baptist's life was predestined while yet in his mother's womb.
* Guru Gobind Singh (17th century India) – "I did not want to come … . God, however, instructed me, inspired me to undertake the mission [to spread righteousness and chastise the wicked]."[5]
* Gnosticism (2nd century Egypt) – Jesus chose the Twelve Disciples and cast them as sparks into the wombs of their mothers that the world might be saved.[6]
* Mormons (19th century USA) – God selected Abraham as a spiritual leader from an assembly of virtuous souls: "Thou art one of them; thou wast chosen before thou wast born."[7]

Cultures embracing the notion of cosmic contracts include the ancient civilizations of Egypt, Assyria, Carthage, Greece, and Rome; indigenous peoples of Africa, Europe, Asia, and the Middle East; as well as Judaism, Islam, Sikhism, Hinduism, a contemporary Christian visionary, and the subtle philosophy of Lewis Carroll.

Do you know that Thread by which …
all beings are strung together
and controlled from within,
so that they move like a puppet,
performing their respective functions?[62]

Guardian Angel of the Embryo

The All-Mighty One sends a recording angel
to a pregnant woman's womb after the embryo
is forty-two days old,[8] according to Islam.

The angel asks: "Lord, shall this be a boy or a girl? What shall be the child's life span, location, and circumstances of death?" "Occupation?" "Will he be happy or miserable?" The Lord answers, in accordance with "His fancy," and the angel inscribes God's decrees in a heavenly scroll. The angel even records whether couples will have daughters or sons, or whether a woman will be barren. Once the angel completes his task, nothing can be added or subtracted from the scroll.

The pre-birth decree – "no soul can ever die except by Allah's leave and at a term appointed"[9] is elucidated by the story of a Caliph. Early in his youth, a sage had foreseen the Caliph's destiny: "Your life will end in the town of Raqqa." As events turned out, years later, the Caliph camped in a location where he was seized with a violent fever. He asked a villager, "What is the name of this town?" Upon hearing the name "Raqqa," the Caliph sighed, "Alas, although I have avoided travelling here, destiny has brought me to this place without my knowing it. Death will surely follow" … as it did, in fact, within several hours.

That is also why, when Muhammad's disciple asked whether protective charms and medicines prevent negative events, the prophet explained, "Anything which protects someone from illness or death is also part of his pre-natal decree." We are born with our cosmic contract "hung round our neck."

Marriage Made in Heaven

*Judaism introduces a free will
clause into the cosmic contract.*

Early Hebrew writings call attention to pre-birth planning when
they state:

"Man in his nature and environment is a product of a
predetermined will. He is fashioned, born, lives, dies and is brought
to judgment against his will. In his ante-natal state his sex,
constitution, size, shape, appearance, social position, livelihood, and
all that may befall him, are pre-ordained."[10]

Marriages are arranged in Heaven forty days before a child's
birth. A herald proclaims the name of its future spouse. No prayers
can change that.

On the other hand, even though "everything is foreseen,"[11] God
gave human beings free will to be "as upright as Moses or as
wicked as Jeroboam, wise or foolish, kind or cruel."[12]

The notion that God pre-plans our earthly lives appears in the
Old Testament as well:

"You saw me before I was born. The days allotted to me
had all been recorded in Your book, before any of them ever began."[13]

The Heavenly Recordkeepers

*The philosophical and spiritual traditions of sophisticated
as well as indigenous cultures acknowledge a power
outside man's control which determines cosmic contracts.*

Most ancient peoples had a deity responsible for cosmic contracts, such as the Indian God Brahma, the God of writing, who inscribed a newborn's destiny on its forehead *(brahmarekha)*; Nabu – the ancient Assyrian scribe to the gods – who recorded King Ashurbanipal's destiny;[14] the "Scribe Man" and the "Man observing the World" of the Siberian Voguls, Yakuts, and Mongols; as well as the gods of Carthage who "have … my name; my mark … along with their names have they inscribed, and the glory and splendor of my name have they recorded right from the beginning."[15]

In Greek mythology, Zeus is the ruler of Heaven and Earth who controls an individual's *moira*, or slice of life. Zeus drew from two jars of destiny: the "unmixed good," and the "unmixed evil." The lesser gods received only "unmixed good," while Zeus gave human souls a mixed assortment of good and evil, or "unmixed evil."

Zeus possessed an equal power to reconfigure an individual's destiny. When he realized that his own son Sarpedon was not to survive the Trojan War, he consulted the queen of the Olympian gods. Hera warned Zeus not to intervene lest a precedent be set for other gods to interfere with the destiny decreed for their favorites. As events turned out, Zeus allowed Sarpedon to go to his doom, rather than threaten the cosmic order.

Female deities, much like fairy godmothers, frequently appear in the list of guardians: Ixchel, the Mayan rainbow goddess; Ishtar, the Babylonian/Assyrian goddess; Artemis, an Ephesian fertility goddess of Asia Minor; and the Syrian goddess Atargatis. Additional female guardians include:

- Ancient Hittites – The Gulses, a term derived from "*gul*" meaning "write or inscribe."[16]
- Ostyaks (Siberia) – Whenever a birth occurs, a goddess who sits on a seven-tiered mountain in Heaven inscribes the secret events to occur in the child's life on the seven branches of a golden tree.[17]
- Ancient Egypt – Seshat engraved destinies on leaves of a holy tree at Heliopolis. Seers who "consulted" these leaves learned the next Pharaoh's name and life plan, even before the child left the womb.

Chi-Children

*The Ibo and Onitsha of southern Nigeria
acknowledge that the Over-Soul, or* Chi,
coordinates cosmic contracts. The Chi *"creates" his
various personalities on Earth, arranges his births
and deaths, and the frequency of his incarnations. Souls
generally reincarnate in the same sub-tribe, clan, or town,
often in the same household. Although the* Chi *gives the
final orders, if someone has been unhappy in a family,
he will usually receive permission to go elsewhere.*

The *Chi* is a collective Group-Self which exists in a spiritual state with God and does not incarnate on Earth, yet the *Chi* can gain experience and evolve through sending down emanations to Earth. The Ibo believe that at the beginning, when one is born for the first time, the *Chi* determines: "This man shall come back to Earth so many times and for so long each time."[18] Prior to each subsequent rebirth, the Onitsha explain: "God puts one's fate into parcels – and one's lot depends upon what parcels a *Chi* picks up. Any bad things are due to the *Chi's* mistake."[19]

The Ibo recognize children who are emanations of the same Over-Soul. Under-Souls, or *Chi*-children, are born within a three-year interval and share a mystical affinity, stronger than blood kinship. The younger *Chi*-children find parents by communicating with an older sibling already born on Earth. An older sibling who is happy with his earthly lot encourages the unborn to join his family or neighborhood. Parents call the older child *nwa solu nwa*, meaning the "child who brought the child."

As each *Chi*-child develops different aptitudes and learns new lessons, the *Chi's* over-all evolution is enhanced. This notion reminds us of Buddhist *bodhisattvas* who have concurrent incarnations.

Leaves of Fate

*Alongside the theory that our lives are pre-recorded
dramas runs the belief that they can be deciphered.
Common to all peoples is the prophet, shaman, or sibyl
who foretell someone's destiny. Palmistry, which reads the
lines on someone's palm, or astrology, which interprets the
natal position of planets, arose due to abilities to see the
future direction of someone's life via these mediums.*

Five thousand years ago, the seven *rishis* – Vasishtha, Kratu, Narada, Paulastya, Paulaha, Angiras, Brighu – used divine sight to cognize the sacred Vedic scriptures of India. The enlightened seers wondered what to do next. So they travelled into the future and witnessed the lives of future souls on the planet. These great beings wrote their cognitions on *ola* (palm) leaves.

Contemporary Nadi astrologers know how to read the palm-leaf bundles. Translating the leaves is a hereditary profession passed down from father to son. The leaves expound details such as an individual's name, birth location, parents' names, occupation, medical problems, prominent past-life, remedies for sins committed in previous lives, and even the time an individual will show up for the astrological appointment.

The Nadi reader narrates unmistakable things that will happen in an individual's life. Mahatma Gandhi's reading,[20] as an example, confirms the accuracy of the rishis' visions of 5,000 years ago. The Nadi astrologer instructed Gandhi as a young boy: marriage at thirteen; foreign travel at twenty – mother's death occurs while travelling in a foreign county at twenty-two; lawyer at thirty-two; meet the king of the white race before sixty-five; fast for the good of the world; and live beyond the age of seventy.

Nadi readers do not advertise. Only a certain number of people have a leaf and an individual cannot receive a reading unless it is so ordained. Circumstances forced one woman to cancel five appointments over a four-year period. One time, an out-of-town relative passed away the day before. In such a case, there is either no leaf or the appointed time has yet to come. That is why the word *Nadi* in Tamil means "destined to come on its own accord."[21]

Cross-Cultural Parallels

Early European people acknowledged a relationship between wisdom and leaves. That is why prophets adorned their heads with a circle of leaves. And one man even dipped a leaf in the stream flowing from the Castalian fountain of Daphne and foresaw his future as the Roman Emperor Hadrian.[22] The Osmanli Turks, as another example, believed a higher power imprinted human destinies on a tree possessing one million leaves. Each person's leaf remained on the cosmic tree until the moment of death.

Thread of Life

*"Thread" is an age-old symbol for destiny,
used as a tool by a higher power to create a woven
fabric representing the pattern of our lives.*

Much as a giant spider spinning a web from her own substance, the Greek gods "spun the thread for pitiful humanity, that the life of man should be sorrow, while they themselves are exempt from care."[23] Clotho, the "spinner," spun the thread, Lachesis determined its length and personified good luck, and Atropos, who represented the inevitable, snipped the thread when the life span was complete.

The Greek story of Achilles portrays the thread of life as an inseparable bond. The goddess Thetis knew from birth that her son Achilles would die in battle. Thetis hoped to outsmart mighty fate by making the boy's body invincible. She dipped the newborn into the sacred River Styx. Only his heel, by which Thetis held Achilles, remained a vulnerable spot.[24]

During the Trojan War, Thetis again tried to outmaneuver God's plan for her son. Thetis hoped to circumvent the military draft by disguising Achilles as a woman. The scheme nearly worked until Odysseus uncovered the boy's identity and persuaded Achilles to join the army. The competent warrior died in battle after being wounded in his heel. As Homer put it, Achilles' untimely death equates with "his life's thread, spun for him when his mother gave him birth."[25]

The theme of "a power above" who fastens a long coil of thread upon every human being pervades other cultures as well.

- ❁ Rome – The three Parcae spin, measure, sustain, and cut the strands of happiness or sorrow.
- ❁ Norse Mythology – The virgin deities who are older than the gods and beyond their influence spin the colored threads at

Yggdrasill, "the tree that metes out the fate of men."[26] The trio chant as their shuttle flashes to and fro. The oldest Norn, "that which has been," looks backward, continually absorbed in the past. The second Norn, "that which is in the process of becoming or is in being," is young, active, and fearless, and looks ahead. The third, "that which shall be hereafter,"[27] is veiled and holds an unrolled scroll of the unmanifest future. The maidens weave the cosmic contracts and divide the fortunes unequally: to some they bestow joy and honor, to others calamities and little glory.

- ❋ Ancient India – The Great Mother uses a cosmic needle (*Axis Mundi*) as her "tool" to "sew" Creation.[28]

- ❋ Native American (Iroquois) – An old woman gifted with seeing the future sits on the Moon and weaves a forehead strap. Her creation is never completed, however. Each month it is unraveled by her companion, a cat.[29]

The ancient phrase – *thread of life* – has come to mean an individual's cosmic contract from cradle to grave. Even today we invoke the metaphor that human life is a thread in a universal tapestry when we state that an event is "bound" to happen.

- ❋ Rome – The Latin word *destino* (destiny), meaning that which is woven, or fixed with cords and threads, reflects the "binding" of our cosmic contracts by the gods.

- ❋ Jewish *Kabbalah* – There is a crossing of threads in the fabric of fate when a man and woman marry. Many strands bring the couple together "and spin their lives into a fabric that is woven on in their children."[30]

- ❋ Seneca (1st century Rome) – Nothing can alter the threads of fate's "inevitable spindle." "Whate'er we mortals bear, whate'er we do, comes from on high … . All things move on in an appointed path, and our first day fixed our last. Those things God may not change which speed on their way, close woven with their causes."[31]

- ❋ Sikhism – "We are all just like puppets who are dancing, and the strings are being pulled by Him according to our karmas. The realized souls and the unrealized souls are all dancing in the same way. The only difference is that the realized souls know that He is pulling the strings and the unrealized souls think that they are dancing by their own effort."[32]

- ❋ Servians – The golden thread of life (*zlatna shitza*) unwinds from Heaven and twines about a man.[33]

❊ Saint Thaimanuvar (India) – "Human beings are like wound-up tops. The one 'Player' winds the string around us, pulls it, and then we spin. Depending on how tightly He winds the top and how fast He plays, we rotate for a while and then we fall down."[34]

❊ Paramahansa Yogananda (20th century India) – The soul is housed within bodies of varying density: the subtlest causal body, an intermediate astral body, and the grossest physical body. By analogy, the physical body is like an overcoat; and the subtler bodies are like the lining and inter-lining. Just as many threads hold the coat to the two linings, invisible threads of destiny connect the causal and astral bodies to the physical body so that they can function together.[35]

❊ Marcus Antoninus (Rome) – "Whatever may happen to thee, it was prepared for thee from all eternity; and the implication of causes was, from eternity, spinning the thread of thy being, and of that which is incident to it."[36]

❊ Hesiod (ancient Greece) – "The Gods with a thick veil have covered human life."[37]

The ancient Greeks, the Judeo-Christian tradition, as well as indigenous peoples associate a definite life span with a cosmic thread.

❊ Finno-Ugric peoples – The Great Mountain Mother holds a wooden staff from which countless threads hang. Each thread represents a newborn's life. At the time of someone's birth, she ties a knot in his thread. The distance between the knot and her staff determines longevity.

❊ Siberia (Koryaks) – Longevity is related to the length of a mystical strap suspending the souls waiting for birth from the posts and cross-beams of the Creator's house.[38]

❊ Homer (ancient Greece) – Hector's death came at the hands of "mighty Fate" which had spun her thread at his birth.[39]

❊ Judeo-Christian – "Thou hast cut short my life like a weaver who severs the web from the *thrum* [loom]" (*Isaiah* 38:12); "… our thread of life is snapped, our web is severed from the loom." (*Ezekiel* 37:11)

❊ Judeo-Christian – The *Bible* calls the thread of life "the silver cord,"[40] the cable which breaks at death, freeing the soul of its mortal remains. (*Ecclesiastes* 12:6)

❊ Jewish *Kabbalah* – All souls who assume human life were initially woven into a mystical fabric *(pargod)*, the "curtain of souls," which hangs before the Throne of Heaven.[41] Each soul's past and future is woven into the spiritual ether making up this curtain or "promptuary."[42] Adam viewed this curtain and witnessed the future generations of mankind. (*Zohar* I, 90b-91b)

Cosmic contracts are part of a complex process in which Mother Nature lays out the unborn future.

Angels of Destiny

Reverend Flower A. Newhouse, a contemporary Christian visionary and mystic, describes how angels, operating like cosmic computers, perceive a future plan and organize the births of millions of souls in human bodies.

The cognitions of Flower Newhouse reveal that "all of life is recorded in the mental world upon an impressionable and highly sensitized screen of mental essence."[43] Not a thought or action escapes its recording. Great angels known as Tawonel are the guardians of these records.

> "They safeguard these living screens with their tremendous shields of Light. It is they who are constantly observing the records presented each moment by all the countries of the world and by each of its citizenry."[44]

Another unique group of angels, the "Karmic or Kindel Angels," are assigned the entire evolutionary history of a number of souls. They determine which souls need to return to our third-dimensional world. Sometimes as much as 100 years prior to a particular soul's descent into physical matter, a Kindel Angel interviews the soul to discuss the needs, desires, and karmic consequences it will encounter in the coming lifetime. The soul is receptive to suggestions from the Angel despite its indrawn inter-life condition, a passive "contemplative state."[45]

Based on this visit, the Angel slowly forms a special mandalic pattern, the soul's "incarnation disc." The diagram is much like a computer disk with software programs in it and set to be activated for the future. The disc contains "closed or filled keys," directly relating to "predestined events" we need to work with once again – crises of spiritual consequence, karmic influences to be encountered in health and life span – as well as opportunities earned in the past, such as meeting special people.

Along with closed keys, Angels incorporate unpatterned periods into our lives, allowing us to "skip grades," just like we do on Earth. No destiny can affect us in open key periods. Souls cherish these open key periods where they can accelerate inner growth, "psychological maturity," and "spiritual establishment."

Through this step-by-step planning process, we sojourn to Earth with the major blueprint of our destiny "woven into a most complex disc made of mental substance."[46]

An angel determines each soul's birth into our third-dimensional world.

Unalterable Cosmic Contracts

Our souls are travellers on the "freeway of life."
We enter the human highway at a pre-chosen point
in time and space. Restrictions are placed on how fast
or slow we can travel. And like it or not, we cannot drive
up into the air or down into the Earth. A Nigerian Ijaw
legend illustrates the set limits on the soul's free will.

The Great Mother Woyengi arrived on Earth in the middle of a lightning storm along with her "Creation Stone." She seated herself at a table near an Iroko tree, placed her feet upon the Creation Stone, and began to mould human beings from earthly substance which had come directly from Heaven.

Woyengi breathed life force into each individual creation and they became living souls. Each soul had free will to choose a human life as male or female as well as the manner of life they would lead. Some said, "I desire abundance and riches," or "I desire numerous children." Others said, "Give me a long, healthy life." Each soul also selected their manner of death from a range of diseases so that they would eventually return to be with Woyengi.

The legend details what happened to two souls preparing to be born as sisters. The first sister said, "I desire riches and famous children." Ogboinba, the second sister, stated, "I have no interest in material life. Give me supernormal powers that have no equal in the world." To all these wishes, Woyengi said, "So be it" and escorted them to the streams that flowed toward birth. Ogboinba entered a clear stream; Woyengi guided her sister to a muddy one.

The sisters became inseparable friends on Earth. Each experienced the fulfillment of their pre-birth plans. Ogboinba's sister enjoyed a happy family life with her husband and children, whereas Ogboinba, even as a child, healed people of diseases and had "second-sight." She understood the languages of birds, beasts, trees, and even blades of grass.

Yet, even though Ogboinba's fame as a prophet and healer spread far and wide, she felt a lack in her heart: she and her husband had no children. So Ogboinba gathered together her most powerful medicines and resolved to take them on a secret journey – back to Woyengi's creation field.

Along the way, Ogboinba reached the mangrove forest, the Kingdom of Isembi. Isembi and his wife entertained her to an exotic meal and palm wine and they asked, "Where are you going?" She explained:

> I have been married many years and have no children. I possess all the parts of a woman, but I am barren and never once been pregnant. I'm going back to Woyengi to ask her to recreate me.

King Isembi warned, "Your journey is in vain. Turn back. No person who is alive can see Woyengi." Ogboinba's mind was strong and she paid no heed to the king's counsel.

Ogboinba travelled a short distance before she decided to go back and test King Isembi's powers. The king declared, "I will not fight a woman. Go on your way. You are no match." Ogboinba insisted on the trial of powers and won.

Isembi was not the only one Ogboinba challenged to a contest of powers. Her incantations made the mighty sea recede, a sea that no human had ever crossed.

Ogboinba proceeded onward to challenge King Egbe, the Tortoise king, the powerful gods Ada and Yasi, and the Cock. Ogboinba won in each case, and put the powers of the loser into her medicine bag.

At last, when Ogboinba's strong will brought her to the Great Mother, she hid in the forest observing Woyengi as she created human beings. At the end of the ceremony, Woyengi prepared to ascend, however Ogboinba rushed into the open field, challenging Woyengi to a contest of powers. Woyengi replied:

> "I know you were hiding in the buttresses of the Iroko tree. I saw you leave … on your journey to find me. I saw you over-come all living things and gods on the way with the powers that I gave you which were your heart's desire. Now it's children you want… . You have come

to challenge me, the source of your powers. I now command all the powers you acquired on the way to go back to their owners."[47]

With this pronouncement, the powers were stripped from Ogboinba and returned to their rightful owners. Ogboinba, filled with fear, turned and "fled in panic to hide in the eyes of a pregnant woman she had met on her way to the creation field."[48] Woyengi permitted Ogboinba to escape. For she would not violate the commandment that pregnant women should never be killed.

Even to this day, Ogboinba hides in the eyes of pregnant women … in the eyes of some men and children. "So the person that looks out at you when you look into somebody's eyes is Ogboinba."[49]

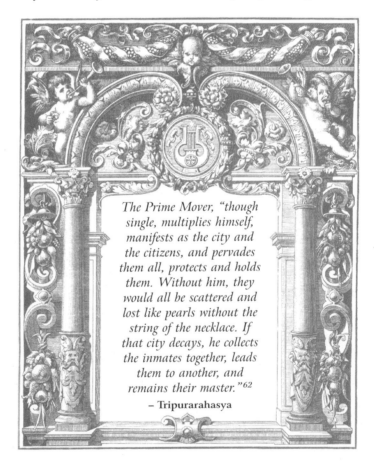

The Prime Mover, "though single, multiplies himself, manifests as the city and the citizens, and pervades them all, protects and holds them. Without him, they would all be scattered and lost like pearls without the string of the necklace. If that city decays, he collects the inmates together, leads them to another, and remains their master."[62]

– Tripurarahasya

Alice in Wonderland

We are beings in the magnificent "dream"
of the Creator, the grand designer of our universe.
Lewis Carroll symbolically depicted this great
truth in his masterpieces for children, Alice and
Wonderland *and* Through the Looking-Glass.

Lewis Carroll, the 19th century English mathematical genius and writer, was inspired to use fantasy to explore the nature of cosmic reality – teaching children many divine and eternal truths – using simple language and rich symbolism. Many children read *Through the Looking Glass*, one classic children's tale, yet the deeper meaning is lost or misunderstood as pure fantasy.

A paraphrase of a brief excerpt follows. Alice personifies the ego, and her two rotund companions, Tweedledee and Tweedledum, represent man's dual mentality.

Dream of the Red King

Alice hears a curious sound in the distance as she is walking through the forest with her newly-found friends Tweedledee and Tweedledum. Tweedledee explains that the noise that sounds like the puffing of a large steam-engine is the Red King snoring. "Come and look at him," the brothers cried, and they each took Alice by the hand to where the King was sleeping. "Isn't he a lovely sight?" asked Tweedledum.

"The King is in the middle of a dream," observed Tweedledee. "What do you think he is dreaming about?" Alice answered, "I don't know. Nobody can guess that."

"He is dreaming about you!" Tweedledee exclaimed. "And if he stopped dreaming about you, where would you be?" "Why, I would be where I am right now, of course," said Alice.

"Oh no, not you!" Tweedledee retorted scornfully. "You would be nowhere. Why, you are merely a sort of thing in his dream!" "And if the King wakes up from his dream," added Tweedledum, "you'd disappear – bang! – out just like a candle!"

"Nonsense, I don't believe it," Alice exclaimed indignantly. "Besides, if I am just a figment of his dream, what about you?" "Ditto," said Tweedledee. "Ditto, ditto," shouted Tweedledum.

"Hush!" warned Alice. "Be quiet, or you are sure to wake him up with all your racket." "Well, there is no sense talking about waking him," said Tweedledum, "when you're only one of the things in his dream. You know very well you are not real."

"But, I am real!" said Alice, and she began to shed tears. "You will not become any more real by crying," Tweedledee remarked, "there's nothing to cry about."

"If I wasn't real," Alice said – half laughing through her tears because it all seemed so ridiculous – "I should not be able to cry." "I hope you don't think that those are real tears," Tweedledum interrupted in a tone of great contempt … . After a series of adventures in a fantasy world, Alice concludes:

"So I wasn't dreaming, after all," she said to herself, "unless – unless we're all part of the same dream. Only I do hope it's my dream, and not the Red King's! I don't like belonging to another person's dream," she went on in a rather complaining tone: "I've a great mind to go and wake him, and see what happens!"[50]

Cross-Cultural Parallels

Lewis Carroll's notion[51] that the whole phenomenal cosmos is the by-product of Divine Dreaming appears as a theme throughout western religion and philosophy.

* Plato (ancient Greece) – "Whether we have been constructed to serve as their playthings, or for some serious reason, is something beyond our ken [understanding] … we have these emotions in us, which act like cords or strings and tug us about … back and forth we go across the boundary line where vice and virtue meet."[52]
* Shakespeare (16th century England) – A divinity "shapes our ends, rough hew them as we will."[53]

Souls Waiting in the Wings for Birth

❋ Plotinus (3rd century Rome) – "As the actors of our stages get their masks and their costume, robes of state or rags, so a Soul is allotted its fortunes, and not at haphazard but always under a Reason: it adapts itself to the fortunes assigned to it, attunes itself, ranges itself rightly to the drama, to the whole Principle of the piece: then it speaks out its business, exhibiting at the same time all that a soul can express of its own quality, as a singer in a song … . "[54]

❋ Christianity – "Whom He has predestined, these has He called." (*Romans* 8:30)

❋ Esoteric Christianity – "Unborn things" exist as "divine ideas" in God's Mind.[55] A Reverend explained, "Creation is but a Transcript … [When] God … made the world, [He wrote] … it out of that Copy which He had … in His Divine understanding from all Eternity."[56]

❋ Stoicism (300 to 400 BC Greece) – Every man can choose how he will obey the decrees of Divine Reason. He is "like a dog tied to a moving cart" who can either "trot along cheerfully or be dragged along uncomfortably."[57] In any case, he must go along with the cart.

Eastern and Middle-Eastern spiritual teachers, who portray God as the Puppeteer and human beings as His toys, include:

❋ Paramahansa Yogananda (20th century India) – "The Cosmic Director" writes scripts for His super-colossal entertainment and summons "tremendous casts for the pageant of the centuries."[58] God makes His motion picture very complex, full of contrasts of good and evil.

❋ Muhammad (Islam) – "Men who are living here are in a dream and when they die then shall they be awake; for all this world is a mere thought – the thought of him who is the True, whose thought is Truth."[59]

❋ Chuang-Tse (Taoism, ancient China) – Chuang-Chou dreamed that he was a butterfly. He spent his life flitting about and tasted the joys of being a butterfly. He had no consciousness of being a human. Suddenly he awoke and again he seemed to be Chuang-Chou. He wondered, "How do I know whether I was then a man dreaming I was a butterfly, or now a butterfly dreaming myself a man?"[60]

❋ Ibn 'Arabi (1165 to 1240 Islamic mystic) – "Everything we call the universe is related to the Divine Being as the shadow (or his reflection in the mirror) to the person. The world is God's shadow."[61]

Chapter 23
The Path of Suffering

**You chose your disease and the amount
of pain you would be willing to suffer –
when you were in a pre-mortal state.**[1]

*Everyone's quest in life is to find out who
they are and what they are supposed to do here.
Of course, the veil falls upon us and overshadows
us at birth. Thus we do not remember why a difficult
condition exists once we enter the earthly stage.*

D̲o hardships and handicaps fall within our cosmic contracts …
or are they a mistake crossing our path during life? The answer
depends upon our world view. Western religions, such as
Christianity, Judaism, and Islam, for instance, regard humanity's
plight as a punishment due to disobedience to God's will, to nonbe-
lief and nonacceptance of His law. Eastern philosophers, on the other
hand, say that our souls agree to imposing conditions for a lofty
purpose, as a challenge to greatness. Still others, scientific materialists, argue that genetic defects and adversities are the results of
chance, accident, physical heredity, and social conditioning.

Answers to this question challenge our rational mind and linear
understanding. The sheer limitations of human thought are made
clear in a Sufi parable about a student and the great master Al-
Khidr, a wise, "God-inspired man."[2] Al-Khidr reluctantly accepted
his new student Moses and told him, "I will teach you under one

condition. No matter what, you must never question my actions." Under these terms, the two reached an agreement and Moses proceeded to accompany his new teacher.

Within a short time, Al-Khidr and his apprentice walked along the seashore and encountered a fisherman's boat. Moses was stunned when Al-Khidr sank the boat by punching holes it. The apprentice questioned the Master's seemingly cruel act. Al-Khidr reminded the student of his pledge. Moses promised not to question him again. Next, Moses and Al-Khidr paid a visit to a family. Moses was even more shocked after Al-Khidr sent the family's only son off to war with an army even though he knew the son would be killed in battle. Moses wondered, "Why did you send an innocent boy off to be killed?" Once again Al-Khidr reminded Moses of his vow. Moses reaffirmed the pledge, only to break it a third time when he witnessed Al-Khidr assist a village of thieves in rebuilding a collapsing wall. At this point, Al-Khidr announced:

> You have violated your pledge to me three times. But before we go our separate ways, let me answer your three questions: The tax collectors of a tyrannical ruler were about to confiscate the only boat of the poor fisherman. By sinking the boat and hiding it from the tax collectors, the fisherman was later able to repair and reuse the boat. As for the boy, he was delinquent and destined to be a source of ongoing torment for his godly parents. They deserved a better child and will beget one. As for the falling wall, the wall contained treasures, the property of orphans who lived in that house. Helping the thieves rebuild the wall saved the fortune by concealing it from the thieves.

Al-Khidr's actions make no sense according to conventional logic and reasoning. Yet if only Moses had bypassed his own reasoning and viewed the situation intuitively, he might have passed Al-Khidr's test. Moses unfortunately was not adept at intuition, a far superior source of knowing.

In a similar fashion, answers to the question, "Why is adversity part of a cosmic contract?" – go beyond logic. Yet, when viewed from the pinnacle of consciousness documented in near-death experiences and spiritual revelations, light is shed on life's paradoxes.

Universal Teachings

Pain and problems have a mysterious purpose in life.

All experiences offer opportunities for growth. Examples come from the spiritual teachings of indigenous people as well as sophisticated cultures.

❁ Indonesia – A crippled man left home to seek God's help. Upon arrival in Heaven, the cripple petitioned God, "Please change my sad fate." The Creator agreed and told the complainer, "Choose again." Upon reflection, the man realized the wisdom in his contract and made the same life choice again.

❁ India – A saint tells someone who desires physical healing, "I know the reason for your ailment and I cannot heal you. If I heal you, you will not attain full enlightenment in this life." Or as the Divine Mother, associate of saint Sri Aurobindo (20th century), advised, "Come back after you purify yourself. Then I will heal you. If I heal you now, you will merely go out and accumulate more bad karma."

❁ Africa (Luba of the southeastern Kongo) – A woman lost her family in a tragic situation and remained all alone. She went from heaven to hell in a heartbeat. She begged God for an explanation. He answered, "I am almighty and cannot be called to account by man." The woman consoled herself with the knowledge that her fate had been willed by God.[3]

❁ Betty Eadie (contemporary USA) – During an NDE, Betty visited the heavenly world where souls prepare for human birth. She noted how the spirits looked forward to entering Earth's school. One "brilliant and dynamic spirit" even arranged with his parents to be born as their mentally handicapped son.[4]

Sacred teachings of the East emphasize that no matter whether we experience positive or negative conditions in our cosmic contracts, they are precisely what our souls need.

- ✦ Sage Yogaswami (Sri Lanka, 20th century) – "A physician takes various roots, mixes them together into one medicine and with it cures the disease. Likewise, the great all-Knowing Physician, by giving to the soul its body, faculties, the world and all its experiences, cures its disease and establishes it in the bliss of liberation."[5]

- ✦ Saint Tiruvalluvar (200 BC India) – "As the intense fire of the furnace refines gold to brilliancy, so does the burning suffering of austerity purify the soul to resplendence."[6]

- ✦ Rishi Tirumular (200 BC India) – The nature of the world is duality, but "when viewed from higher consciousness, this world is seen as it truly is – perfect. There is no intrinsic evil."[7] Each thing and its opposite – joy and sorrow, good and evil, love and hate – is the means whereby the soul learns and evolves, eventually finding Truth beyond all opposites.

- ✦ Buddhism, Hinduism, Sikhism, Jainism – "All is good. All is God. No force in the world or in man opposes God, though the veiling instinctive-intellectual mind keeps us from knowledge of Him."[8]

- ✦ Persian mystic Rumi (13th century Sufism) – "Know well, all evils are but relative … . there is no Opposite of God – for all such opposites are lost in Him."[9]

We chose our challenges
to test our souls.

Deja Vu

When the veil is temporarily lifted during an NDE,
individuals appreciate the harmony of life.
Nothing is then wrong or out of place.

As a prime example, DeLynn, a businessman who owned a small company, shook hands with death after an emergency operation for sinusitis. The Heavenly Father reminded DeLynn why he had suffered with cystic fibrosis, an incurable genetic disease:

> So far you have suffered as much pain in thirty-seven years as a normal person suffers in seventy-six years. But you volunteered to experience this disease and the amount of pain you would be willing to suffer prior to birth.

DeLynn initially found this explanation a bitter pill to swallow, but quickly lost all skepticism. Like seeing his life on a movie screen, DeLynn observed himself sitting in a spiritual classroom with thirty men and women dressed in white jumpsuits. An instructor stood at the head of the class teaching them about accountability, responsibility, and pain – preparing them for birth. According to the teacher, difficulties in life are like the irritating piece of sand needed to form the pearl inside the oyster. Consequently, souls can either move slowly through life and learn small lessons or advance quickly via the experience of pain and disease.

Toward the end of the lecture, the instructor wrote the words "cystic fibrosis" on the board and asked, "Any volunteers?" DeLynn raised his hand. He accepted the challenge to learn dignity in suffering, to overcome the obstacles of a physical ailment, and make himself spiritually stronger from the ordeal. Following this NDE life review, DeLynn agreed to return to Earth and to teach accountability and responsibility to his family and employees.

DeLynn's life review spurred him to radically shift his opinion about himself. He stopped regarding himself as a victim of a "plague" and considered himself "a privileged participant" who had accepted a brief, but marvelous life.[10] As "a powerful, spiritual being," DeLynn could now emotionally and psychologically handle his illness even though he was unable to control his physical deterioration.

The Uniqueness of Human Life

Elane Durham represents another NDEr who realized that "suffering is the swiftest steed that brings us to perfection."[11] Elane's NDE in 1976 followed a stroke precipitated by a brain tumor.[12] While Elane's spirit toured the other world with her guide, she agreed to see herself before coming to Earth. Elane then found herself standing on a height taller than a mountain surveying planet Earth, surrounded by a dust storm and dark clouds. Her guide pointed to her future home and explained:

> Earth is a place where souls learn lessons faster than anywhere else. The disabled learn endurance and how to receive help; the wealthy who assist the disadvantaged learn lessons of service, sharing, and unconditional love.

As Elane's life review unfolded, she observed herself in a waiting room with two guardian angels and three novice "angels in training."[13] They were helping Elane design her future life on Earth. First, she singled out parents from three prospective fathers and two mothers, from whom she would learn equal lessons. Part of the plan involved being the oldest child. Next, Elane chose to experience two physical crises and a miraculous healing. One of the "angels in training" questioned Elane's plan. The senior angel interjected and explained to the immature angel, "These events are much like special tutors which act to hasten spiritual progress."

Niels' Life-Review Vision

Just as DeLynn and Elane re-experienced glimpses of their pre-earth lives and recalled motives for their cosmic contracts, Niels was reassured of his life purpose via a spiritual revelation. The young European man had been crippled for sixteen years following an accident. Niels brooded over his fate and imagined how fulfilling life might be without a physical deformity.

At the height of Niels' melancholia, a vision unfolded before "the eye of the spirit."[14] As Niels prepared his daily meal, he consciously travelled back in time to his pre-earth life in the spirit world. He watched himself select "a reward." His spirit "insisted upon having that reward, and accepted and agreed to the conditions."[15] He understood that the reward was only to be earned through being a cripple and enduring "severe physical pain, privation and ignominy."[16]

Niels no longer complained. To do so was a reproach to God, as well as a violation of his pre-birth agreement. Niels himself had designed his earthly curriculum much like someone enrolling in a challenging school rather than an easy one.

Cross-Cultural Parallels

Our souls feel no apprehension about incorporating adversities into our lesson plan because during our pre-birth state, we perceive our life plan from a heightened state of awareness. Each soul gathers what it needs to fulfill the goals chosen prior to entering the womb. Five spiritual perspectives support this view.

- ❀ Swami Chinmayananda – "If God is sitting and writing our individual histories – all these sorrows and tragedies – he must be a mental pervert. Right? This idea of God is a poetic point of view; it has no philosophical support. The creator endows the mental and physical equipment and situations in the creation according to your own instructions, so that you can expend your own desires."[17]

- ❀ Stewart C. Easton (20th century Anthroposophy) – "Whenever we bemoan our destiny … we are railing against our own choice … . In consequence the one vice which no one with knowledge of karma would permit himself is envy, either envy of anyone else's life situation or of his talents, fortune, or friends. For we have what we have chosen and earned … ."[18]

- ❀ Ma Yoga Shakti (contemporary India) – "Things which appear wrong are not evil, but are meant to promote our progress. All problems are our tutors."[19] They bring wisdom and develop compassion, empathy, and tolerance.

- ❀ Sadguru Sivaya Subramuniyaswami (contemporary Hawaii) – Suffering offers the realization that "true happiness and freedom cannot be found in the world, for earthly joy is inextricably bound to sorrow, and worldly freedom to bondage."[20]

- Betty Eadie (contemporary USA) – Difficulties faced on Earth are only "a split second of consciousness in the spirit world."[21]

Revelations on Abortion
and Crib Death

Lania Desmond, a contemporary spiritual healer, offers a more encompassing perspective on cosmic contracts involving abortion and crib death, SIDS (Sudden Infant Death Syndrome). (See Chapter 33, Overcoming Spiritual Amnesia, *for Lania's gifted memories.)*

Lania is like someone who rides the elevator to the top of a sixty-story building and enjoys a loftier vista than someone who observes a limited view from the second floor.

She explains why a short life may be all someone needs. When the use of that body is accomplished, the soul leaves.

Say there is a spirit who needs to briefly experience physicality in order to accomplish something. That spirit chooses a particular mother because of another agreement. Before that woman took on a form, she selected lessons to learn. Maybe an abortion was the only way to catalyze certain circumstances – guilt, fear, anger – in order to learn a particular lesson.

But what happens if the woman doesn't have an abortion? The spirit is faced with an unexpected decision: miscarriage or a lifetime that it had not intended. And the woman doesn't have the opportunity to learn her lessons either.

Abortion makes no sense from a linear perspective. When you have more information, it makes perfect sense. The abortion benefits both of them.

Regardless of the mysterious physical process behind early childhood deaths, there is a mutual benefit when souls select a life lasting a few hours or days.

Some babies choose to quickly leave because all they wanted to experience was a peaceful death. They do not want to learn any other lesson. Perhaps they had a horrendous death in the life before. Now they want to balance it out and go out peacefully, to just stop breathing. That is all there is to it.

So let us say that this entity is a newborn who has all this love flowing to it from the parents. The baby is soaking up that love and bliss and attention. And this peace and contentment is all the baby wants to experience. And so the baby's soul chooses to slip out, wrapped up in all that love.

Of course, before this happened, there was already a cosmic contract between the parents and child. The parents wanted to move into a space where they could realize that physical reality is not all that there is, and that this little being who came into their presence was allowing them to have a total experience of love and then not judge that they had done something wrong – maybe the parents needed to resolve an issue of forgiveness, guilt, letting go, or not holding on.

Insights into Life's Traumas

*Beverly Anderson, a contemporary mystic, explains
how certain conditions in our cosmic contracts cannot
be understood unless we "go beyond the veil."*

The Revolving Door

People come to Beverly for psychic counselling covering every-thing under the sun. (See Beverly's story in Chapters 7, *Conversations with My Unborn Child*, and 34, *Angels in the Never-Ending Schoolhouse*.) And a few even dare to say, "I am thinking about committing suicide." Beverly does not try to switch their negative perspective. People are stunned when they find she is so blasé.

I tell them, "Fine. It is your life, your time. Good bye. But let me point out a couple things before you haul off and do that. The angels will kick you right back around the revolving door and put you at the same square you started at with the same kind of life you are at right now. They do not let you make any other choice.

So you must come back to Earth and do this all over again. So let us talk about this. Do you want to be kicked back to here again? That is all you will get out of the deal. And that is okay if you do not want to deal with the karmic lesson, the development that you chose before you incarnated. Then go back to square A and start all over again because nothing is going to change. Nor will you get much of a breather in-between.

Suicide only delays the inevitable. You must experience to learn and grow. Do you want to discuss the issue that you want to put off, or what?"

Abortion and Karma

Abortion is a karmically complicated issue that confronts many women today, due to partner's wishes, demands to be a working mother, premarital sexual relationships, economics, or pressures from souls to be born. Beverly describes two scenarios.

Abortion can be the result of a forceful child who wishes to be born to a woman, but she did not agree to be its mother. She has every right to say "No" to that deal. Birth must be a mutual agreement between mother and child in order that a child be born healthy and abundant. So if the soul is impatient, he learns that it would have been better to wait a few years when the woman was ready. So there is an experience on both sides.

If there is not a mutual agreement, abortion is not murder.

Then there is "the woman who is toting around deep negative karma, trying to learn the lesson of the preciousness of life." Her cosmic contract includes an abortion in order to learn that lesson. And the child chooses birth in order to teach the mother that lesson.

Abortion is the ultimate disrespect for the preciousness of life because it is indefensible. Women have deep guilt because they know that there is an entity inside them when they do it. But they chose this profound, unsettling experience in order to learn to be more responsible with life.

In these cases, there was a relationship between that mother and child in a previous incarnation. The woman was arrogant and did not appreciate the gift of life. She either lost a child because it died, the child was taken from her, or she killed the child. In this life, she is reliving her loss, shame, or guilt. Her soul selects a cosmic contract involving fear and pain because she thinks that experience will teach her how to not need that experience anymore. But that is not what is going on here. But she has such fear and judgment about herself that she programs another life to give her an opportunity to step above it.

Premature Death or Childhood Disease

We must also "fall outside the veil" in order to understand why a soul chose to experience premature death or a childhood disease.

Perhaps the little baby was paying back a favor or a debt towards their parents to teach them about the preciousness of life. The baby offered up his life source to an experience of pain and suffering to give that lesson back to the people he loved. So instead of regarding a life course as a singular event, we need to look at it as a pattern of being, a pattern of exchange, and a pattern of intercourse with people and spaces and times around us. It is all interwoven.

Poverty versus Wealth

People think wealth is the answer to all worldly problems. Yet wealth can be just as much a burden as poverty. For one thing, the super-rich can become overly concerned about protecting their resources.

I find it amusing when people become jealous and agitated and say, "Why am I down here in the dirt, sweating and working my butt off? If I just had money, everything would be okay." I tell them, "No, it would not. You would still be you, wouldn't you?"

Don't look at wealth as anything special or not having money as special. Sometimes we pick a life where we rest and cruise a little bit and play. It is what we do with the money that matters.

"What's in your cosmic contract?"

Chapter 24
Souls in Training
Free Will and Karmic Lessons

"Oh father!" asked Aeneas, "Is it
possible that someone can be so in
love with earthly life as to wish to leave
this tranquil realm in the upper world?"

– Virgil's *Aeneid* (1ˢᵗ century BC Rome)

What triggers the soul's return to earthly life?
Why do souls leave the inter-life realm of serenity,
self-knowledge, brotherhood, and compassion?

Incoming souls are faced with a paradox of two eternal choices –
remaining in an ideal world, or opting for a challenge to brave
the unknown on Earth – so which path is to be taken? Several
philosophies illustrate how an innate magnetism pulls souls back
to human existence.

- ❀ Shloime Ansky (1863 to 1920, Yiddish author) – The soul is
  drawn back to Earth just as a baby is attracted to its mother's
  breast.[1]

- ❀ Pythagoras (ancient Greece) – "An invincible force" attracts
  souls back to reexperience the "struggles and sufferings of
  earth. This desire is mingled with terrible dread and a mighty
  grief at leaving divine life."[2]

Souls who choose to believe that material life brings lasting
happiness keep returning to Earth. As long as they desire the
things of Earth – cigarettes, motor cars, or a hefty bank account –

they must return to this material plane where these things are readily obtainable. The spiritual world does not provide material possessions. (On the other hand, desires for beautiful music, expansive scenery, or harmonious relationships can best be fulfilled in the spiritual world. Pure desires are "due to deeper-than-conscious memories of the beauty and harmony one experienced"[3] in the spiritual world.)

A wealth of examples from religion, philosophy, mythology, and anthropology emphasize the soul's desire for physical rebirth.

- ❀ Macrobius (4th to 5th century AD Rome) – Souls reside in the celestial or fixed sphere as long as they reflect one pointedly on their divine nature. Once they are overtaken by a yearning for a mortal body, however, they gradually slip down, taking on corporeal accretions as they traverse each of the spheres.

- ❀ Paramahamsa Yogananda (20th century India) – Material desires in the subconscious mind reawaken after the soul has passed the appropriate amount of time in the inter-life region. The soul is then drawn back to Earth, or to another planet in the material universe, by the magnetic attraction of desire.[4]

- ❀ Trobriand Islanders (British New Guinea) – Souls become bored with the paradise-like spirit world and yearn for human rebirth.[5]

- ❀ Plato (*Phaedrus*) – The inferior part of human nature drags the soul down to Earth. (Plato's allegory of the Chariot and Winged Steeds)

- ❀ Eleusinian Mysteries (ancient Greece) – The soul's attachment to sensuous earthly life entices it to be born again. The mythological story of Persephone symbolically illustrates this theme.[6]

- ❀ Harranites (Middle Eastern Gnosticism) – The soul became enamored with the material world, and developed a burning desire to experience the pleasures of the flesh.[7]

- ❀ Ky'itl'ā'c (17th century Tlingit, British Columbia) – Ky'itl'ā'c peeked through "the cloud door" and observed the Earth below. The vision kindled a desire to be reborn and enter another mother's womb.[8]

- ❀ Sudanese Edos (Africa) – The soul desires rebirth and petitions God who sanctions the return once the appropriate time comes.[9]

- ❀ Philo of Alexandria (1st century Judaism) – Souls who dwell in "the air" nearest to Earth desire to live in mortal bodies once again.[10]

Souls Waiting in the Wings for Birth

- Swami Satchidananda (contemporary India) – We each decide on our number of births and the duration of each birth. Each of our actions has its own consequence which we must face. "If we don't have enough time in this life alone to face all these reactions, we are given another body."[11]

- Zen Buddhism – The intermediate being gazes upon the mirror of its karma, like watching a movie, and discovers that it is already committed to pursuing a specific cosmic contract. The intermediate being feels a blind attraction to be born to parents of a particular race, nationality, and social status.[12]

Free will plays a key role in shaping human destiny even within the context of earthly rebirth. Without the freedom to select lessons, we would be mere mortal puppets manipulated by Divine strings. Our souls consequently reach a crystallizing point following an inter-life rest where we become eager to attend "advanced training camp" – planet Earth. We agree to be born into another human body in order to grow in patience, honesty, perseverance, compassion, equanimity, courage, humility, and charity. We are spiritual beings drawn down to the Earth by an inborn attraction to perfection.

The desire for human rebirth arises in the inter-life realm when souls reflect upon the possibilities for future growth via physical existence.

- Zulu (Africa) – During the period between earthly lives, the soul sleeps in the "place of rest … til a time comes when it dreams that something to do and learn awaits it on earth."[13]

- Winnebago (Native American) – Thunder-Cloud desired to return to Earth in order to attend to some unfinished business.[14]

- Rabbi Abraham Yehoshua (19th century Hasidism) – The Rabbi came to Earth in order to learn unconditional love. Once he succeeds, he will "never return."[15]

- Reverend Flower Newhouse (contemporary Christian visionary) – The soul senses that he must leave the fourth and fifth dimensional existence and come back to "the outer-three-dimensional world until he has conquered it."[16]

- Judaism – A soul is "sent time and time again to this world until he does what God wants him to do."[17]

- Johann Wolfgang von Goethe (19th century Germany) – "I have existed a thousand times before and I hope to return a thousand times more."[18]

Stories and philosophies elucidating how and why the soul makes rebirth choices range from Buddhism, Hinduism, Sufism, Anthroposophy, and Theosophy, to traditional peoples of Africa and North America. Rudolf Steiner, Edgar Cayce, and Madame Blavatsky offer insights as well.

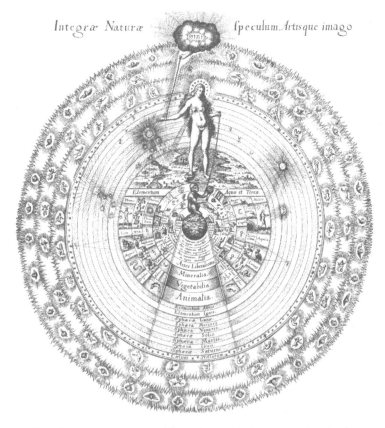

Cosmic contracts are recorded in the world of soul prior to rebirth.

Evolution of the Soul

*Our souls unfold our full maturity via the path of
human birth. The perfected souls who have learned
all the earthly lessons no longer need to return to Earth.*

Spiritual and philosophical teachings alike proclaim that the
soul's destiny is self-realization of its innate oneness with God. In
ancient Greece, Aristotle proclaimed, "Every natural thing in its
own way longs for the Divine and desires to share in the Divine
Life as far as it can."[19] The Persian poet Rumi likewise declared,
"The motion of every atom is towards its origin."[20] And in 14th
century Italy, the preeminent poet Dante put it this way –

"The supreme desire … is to return to its first source. And since
God is the First Cause of our Souls … the Soul especially desires to
return to that First Cause. As a pilgrim, who goes along a path where
he never journeyed before, may believe every house that he sees in
the distance to be his inn, and, not finding it to be so, may direct his
belief to the next, and so travel on from house to house until he reach
the inn, even so our Soul, as soon as it enters the untrodden path of
this life, directs its eyes to its supreme good."[21]

The purpose of our soul's pilgrimage into matter is to test our
abilities in the phenomenal world. Some are young souls just
beginning to grow; others are old souls nearing the end of a long
cycle of human births.

* Saiva Siddhanta Religion (ancient India) – Every soul is
perfect, but "is like a small seed yet to develop." Just as we
must plant an acorn in the dark underground to grow into a
mighty oak tree, so too, our souls must … take human birth
and mature through the reincarnation process.[22]

* *Kabbalah* (12th century Judaism) – Souls must be refined and
educated before we "re-enter the absolute substance whence
… [we] have emerged" and attain "the condition which fits

us for reunion with God." We must become "composed in a mystic manner of what is above and below."[23]

⚜ Master Hazrat Inayat Khan (20th century Sufism) – "Nature has taught every soul to seek its purpose … it is continually calling that soul to see that purpose. If the soul does not hear the call and sleeps, it is not the fault of nature, which is continually calling."[24]

⚜ Hinduism (ancient India) – The trials and tribulations of human life are "food for the soul … that actually raise the level of intelligence and divine love."[25] We mature out of fear into fearlessness, out of anger into love, out of conflict into peace, out of darkness into light and union in God."[26]

⚜ Thoth or Hermes Trismegistus (ancient Egypt) – The Soul Ruler condemned the fallen spirits who had revolted in the spirit world "to imprisonment in the organs of mortal bodies," and to be ruled by "Desire and Necessity" in the lower region. Only when the soul's inclination becomes purely spiritual once again is it free to return home, "in the places nigh to heaven."[27]

⚜ Empedocles (ancient Greece) – The souls' restoration to its original spiritual domain takes place following a self-cleansing process, requiring a series of incarnations lasting as long as 30,000 seasons.[28]

Rebirth and Our Highest Good

*Souls select cosmic contracts, sometimes
including harsh conditions as part of the lesson plan.*

Every action is pregnant with consequences, according to the
karmic law of cause and effect. We shape our own destiny by our
actions and reactions. Until we learn all of our lessons, our accumulated merits and demerits determine the range of karmic
lessons we chose from in planning our next birth. Much like
advanced college students who have more freedom to select
courses than elementary students who must follow a prescribed
course, inter-life choices of race, culture, geographical location,
physical appearance, sex, temperament, parents, and time of birth,
vary according to soul maturity.

Rudolf Steiner – 20ᵗʰ century Father of Anthroposophy

A perfected state of consciousness awaits us when our souls
reach the summit of the inter-life journey in the "supersensible
world." We are given a glimpse of the big picture – something
beyond what our ordinary minds can fathom. At this climatic
point, we experience the exalted awareness which is our human
birthright. Furthermore, we realize that additional growth is
needed in order to stabilize this elevated awareness. Before we lose
awareness of our highest good, we choose cosmic contracts with
the help of the "spiritual hierarchies of the cosmos."

Edgar Cayce – 20ᵗʰ century American Visionary

Between one life and the next, our souls recognize the
"Oneness" of which we are a part and know which pre-birth
choices are in harmony with that Oneness. Consequently –

"At the moment of entry into a new physical form, the uniquely shaped nonphysical self is drawn to the body that fits it, and to the family environment that best reflects its history and needs."[29]

Cayce distinguishes between mature souls who are capable of selecting earthly tasks, and young souls who are unable to choose so wisely. Less mature souls have made poor choices in the past and are "dangerously subject to earthly appetites."[30] They are therefore born under circumstances best suited for their growth.

Madame Blavatsky – 19th century Founder of Theosophy

Madame Blavatsky outlines the soul's inter-life journey.

* Imprinting – The "forces of the body and mind rush through the brain," and the entire life just ended "is imprinted indelibly on the inner man by a series of pictures," including the tiniest detail and most fleeting impression.[31]

* Purification – The astral body disconnects from the physical body and goes to the astral plane of desire *(Kama Loka)*, a "slag-pit" where purification of desires and passions takes place, similar to the Roman Catholic purgatory.[32]

* Unconsciousness – The soul enters an unconscious state.

* Dreaming – The soul experiences a "remedial, restful, benefi-cial" state in *devachan*. Someone who lived a "colorless life" on Earth experiences a colorless life in *devachan*; however, "if a rich life, then it will be rich in variety and effect." This dream stage lasts "for years of infinite number," or "for a period proportionate to the merit of the being."[33]

* Cosmic Contract – The soul awakens to witness the *karmic* reasons leading it to the life it is about to begin on Earth. Soon the soul realizes that all is "just" and does not complain. In the end, the soul "takes up the cross again,"[34] and powerful "magnetic threads" binding the soul to Earth carry the soul off to the womb of its awaiting mother.

Vedic Tradition of Ancient India

The soul detaches itself from the physical body at death and continues on in the subtle body *(sukshma sarira)* into the "in-between" world *(antarloka)*, the world in which souls dwell between births and return to after death. Reincarnation – "re-entering the flesh"[35] – involves a step-by-step process.

* Cosmic Contract – Souls enjoy a peaceful, delightful, "luminous sleep" whereby they assimilate past experiences and make future plans to enrich the growth of consciousness. This is a spontaneous "luminous brooding and incubation,"[36] rather than a deliberate rational process.

* Choosing Parents – The soul bears the same awareness, will, memory, and intelligence as when it lived in a human body. Identical desires and aspirations "exist in the soul body."[37] Like a vast cosmic computer capable of infinite correlation, the *samskaras* (cumulative effect of desires, tendencies, and habits established in previous lifetimes) magnetically draw the soul from the subtle realm to its future parents.

* Conscious Conception – Aspiring parents do what they can in order to attract a worthy soul. India's ancient tradition, *Ayurveda*, emphasizes developing the parents' spiritual, mental, and physical well-being prior to conceiving a child.

Zen Buddhism

The "Lord Who is a Being of Pure Love" does not judge us in the in-between state. Where there is Pure Love, there is no judgmentalism. Following a life review, we determine how many "karmic jangles" still separate us from the Lord. Next, we are shown the place and state of rebirth to resolve the optimum number of "karmic jangles."

There is no coercion when we are shown parents with whom we will best learn our lessons. We are free to accept or reject that birth. "The cosmic Buddha, who is Truth Itself, does not insist … . The cleansing of karma must come about as a result of desire to be re-united utterly with the Lord."[38]

There is no such thing as an accidental pregnancy. Parents are "deeply involved in the karmic jangles" of an about-to-be conceived child. Aspiring parents "should meditate deeply and ask the Lord how best they may help their soon-to-be conceived child cleanse his karma and in what way that child can help them cleanse theirs … . The child born of such a union would be wanted and understood from the moment that it stood before the Lord and was asked if it was willing to accept its new parents … ."[39]

Bargaining with the Creator

*Traditional African peoples negotiate their
entire destiny "over there" before becoming clothed
in physical, mental, and emotional bodies once again.*

Nigerian Igbos outline the steps between death and rebirth.

- Death – At the time of death, Igbos think about what they want in their next lives, such as "having mouth," the power of oratory and wisdom, as well as longevity, intelligence, and wealth.[40]
- Cosmic Contract – "There's a bargain made, there's a discussion."[41] The Creator presents the soul with one parcel containing "statuses" – apparently credits and debts attained in his previous life – and a second parcel containing aspirations expressed at time of death.
- Interception – A guardian angel, or *chi*, stops the soul at the "borderline" and attempts to alter bargains involving unrealistic aspirations.
- Birth – No matter what earthly obstacles result from the "bargain" made in Heaven, an Igbo makes the most of his lot, always planning to do better next time.

Inter-life paradigms of three additional African peoples follow.

- Ewes of Togo (West Africa) – Souls coordinate pre-birth choices with an ancestor *(tasi)* or with "the Mother of Spirits," *Mawu-Lisa*. They select their destiny *(gbetsi)* in *bome*, "the place of prenatal existence."[42] Souls who are dearly loved in that realm agree to return quickly – just as a young adult who leaves home assuring his parents of his return.
- Semi-Bantu (Southern Nigeria) – Each soul is a portion of a greater "Over-Soul" which can simultaneously experience multiple human lives – similar to Buddhist *bodhisattvas* who experience five simultaneous incarnations. The Over-Soul sanctions the frequency of its births, personalities, and the cosmic contracts each manifestation experiences. Whenever

someone's life circumstances within a family or town have
been unhappy, the Over-Soul considers personal wishes, and
the soul is free to make a different choice.

❋ Zulus – Following the cleansing of the soul's passionate
nature in a realm called *Esilweni*, the soul enters a deep
slumber. By and by, the soul dreams of another mission and
the opportunity to gain more knowledge. The soul awakens
and retraces its steps back to Earth.

The Last Thought Before Death

*Buddhism and Hinduism teach that the last
moment of the dying process is significant. The
final thought determines the impetus and circumstances
of rebirth just as the last thought before going to
sleep can become the first thought on awakening.*

The deepest longings fixed in our heart surface in the mind at the time of death. Typically our final thoughts relate to the degree to which we fulfilled our ambitions: "Oh, I did not complete this work;" or "Oh, I am dying. I have to do this. I have to do that." An individual subsequently receives a chance to fulfill these objectives in his next life. As the *Mundaka Upanishad* declares: "He who forms desires in his mind is born again ... ."[43]

Buddha compared our final thoughts to a herd of cows bottled up in a barn. When the farmer opens the barn door, the strongest cow or thought flies out first. If there is no dominant cow, then the habitual leader leaves first. If no such leader exists, the cow nearest the door gets out first. In the absence of any of these, the entire herd tries to go out together.[44]

As Buddha's analogy illustrates, the final thought spontaneously mirrors an individual's spiritual evolution and the extent to which his goals have been fulfilled. Someone who has been greedy and hateful is unlikely to have pious thoughts during the final moments when he quits the body. Whereas positive thoughts will arise automatically if they are established through constant practice. Mahatma Gandhi, as a case in point, was shot by a assassin in 1948, and died with a smile on his face and holding the name of God, "Sri Ram," his meditation mantra, on his lips. Gandhi's last thought may have clinched his soul's final liberation. The thought of God came to mind because Gandhi had been reciting that sacred sound for a lifetime.[45]

Reading sacred scriptures of prayer to assist the dying person in obtaining the good terminal thought is a common practice in Hinduism and Buddhism, as well as nearly all other religions.

Angels decide the length of each soul's inter-life vacation.

Time in the Land of Immortality

*Buddhism and Hinduism teach that some souls
spend more time in the inter-life than others.*

Buddhism

The more mature soul generally stays in the inter-life world longer than the immature soul. Gautama Buddha, as an example, enjoyed 4,000 divine years – equivalent to 584,000,000 human years – in *Tusita* prior to his final incarnation. On the other hand, the being who clings to the notion of a separate, individual existence rushes about seeking an available womb in which to be reborn as soon as he realizes he has no flesh and blood body. He desires to live and fears death. Thus "the will to live" makes him "re-live."[46]

In all cases, a magnetic attraction factor influences the duration of the inter-life world. The intermediate being cannot experience rebirth until he locates the parents, environment, and physical existence with which he has a karmic affinity.

Tibetan Buddhism similarly differentiates between degrees of spiritual maturity. Altruists, such as the Dalai Lama, who are propelled by a desire to benefit physical sentient beings, return to Earth whenever earthly conditions become ripe for serving humanity. The XIII Dalai Lama who died in 1933 illustrates this principle. He only spent two earthly years between one life and his next because he needed to reincarnate as the XIV Dalai Lama (who returned in 1935) as soon as possible.

Less mature beings who do not find a birthplace within seven days after death undergo a minor spiritual death and are reborn into a second intermediate state, or *Bardo*. This swoon can happen up to seven times or forty-nine days. Between-beings who do not find a birthplace after forty-nine days take birth as a spirit.[47]

Hinduism

Souls get to take a vacation between one earthly life and the next. Length of the soul's inter-life vacation depends upon what has been spiritually earned on Earth, the stored-up good merits or *punya*. And by analogy, just like the person who saves money for a summer vacation and checks in at a five star hotel, the length of his stay depends upon how much money is in his pocket; so too, the soul remains in the heavenly inter-life regions until its accumulated merits are used up.

Souls with the most credit go to inter-life regions of great beauty for centuries. In their earthly lives, these individuals had virtuous inclinations, meditated, or were soldiers who suffered an honorable death in combat. Mature souls have a higher degree of intuition and consciously enjoy the spiritual world. Sometimes they elect to return sooner in order to advance their spiritual growth, spurred on by the desire for enlightenment. They realize that the spiritual world, too, "is but a veil behind which the Lord hides His face of eternal perfection."[48]

By contrast, souls who arrive in the inter-life realm with less merit do not enjoy their vacation. They enter a deep sleep. They are so intensely hypnotized by what they think of as matter's reality that they are insensitive to subtler realms of existence around them. If they do wake up, they find themselves surrounded by darkness or a grey mist. They do not know where they are and suffer nightmares if they lived evil lives on Earth.

The Heavenly
Retirement Home

*Sacred teachings of the Jews, Hindus, Buddhists,
and African Zulus agree that souls choose a
series of human lifetimes in order to attain spiritual
purity. Yet even when they retire to their heavenly
home, that state can be temporary.*

An East Indian story explains that souls who graduate from the earthly school at the end of a cycle of births and rebirths are exempt from rebirth. However, an enlightened soul tells the Heavenly Father:

"Evil is rampant on Earth. People are killing one another and suffering in many ways. There is much grief and pain. Why must this be?" God answers: "I will send you back to alleviate their suffering."

The notion of liberated souls, moved by compassion, who volunteer as part of God's plan of rescue for souls who have lost their way, appears in numerous religions.

* Philo of Alexandria (1st century Judaism) – Wise souls, "possessed of a diviner structure," are born again for the benefit of others. They urge people to "return to the original source, calling that heavenly region … their citizenship, fatherland, but this earthly region in which they live, foreign." Moses, as an example, "chose this expatriation from heaven and through curiosity and the desire of acquiring knowledge came to dwell in earthly nature."[49]

* *Kabbalah* (12th century Judaism) – Souls who fulfill the 613 commandments in the *Torah* join a spiritual hierarchy and have the option of returning to Earth. The Fable of the *Lamed Vav* reckons that, at any given time, thirty-six perfected souls watch over the wayward souls and help awaken them to their spiritual nature. They appear ordinary so that no one knows who they really are.

- Christianity – Jesus Christ is the Word made flesh, "full of grace and truth."

- Muhammad (Islam) – "To every race great Teachers have been sent. God hath not left any community without a prophet, warner, and true guide. He sendeth Prophets to the ignorant and those misguided into evil ways ... to teach ... wisdom and philosophy."[50]

- Hinduism (ancient India) – The Sanskrit term *vyutthana*[51] refers to the rebirth of exemplary beings who take birth whenever the world undergoes a decline of virtue and an increase of injustice. They include full *avatars – purnavatara –* and partial *avatars – amsavatara.*

- Sufism – The term *buruz* delineates the reincarnation of a perfect soul who is born voluntarily "for the sake of perfecting mankind."[52] Sufis also describe the rebirth of the *Imam* or spiritual leader, as *Rij'at*, and the periodical incarnation of the Perfect Man or Deity, as *Hulul*.[53]

- Taoism (ancient China) – "The High Emperor of the Sombre Heavens descends to earth ... hundreds (of) times, to become the companion of the common people and teach them the truth ... heal the sick ... endure suffering patiently ... that his pain may be a spring of joy and righteousness to many hearts."[54]

- Zulus (20th century Africa) – Through a series of births, the Zulus master seven grades of Brotherhood – pupil, disciple, brother, elder, master, *sangoma* (those who Know), and *Abakula-bantu* (the perfect human beings who no longer need to return to Earth, but can retain or relinquish the human form as they please). Once an individual attains the final stage, his soul "becomes one with that from which it came ... (the *Itongo*), the Spirit within and above all men – even all things."[55] He no longer dreams of a mission on Earth, the seed to rebirth.

- Dakota, aka Sioux (Native American) – When a medicine man dies, "he returns to the abode of his gods, where he receives a new inspiration and a new commission, to serve a new generation of men in some other portion of the world." After a cycle of four incarnations, he returns to his "primitive nothingness."[56]

Tibetan Buddhism: Rebirth versus Reincarnation

Tibetan Buddhists distinguish between "rebirth" and "reincarnation" through significant nuances.[57] Rebirth is portrayed as mandatory – the law of karma rules the rebirth of immature individuals. They are powerless to determine the circumstances into which they will be born.

Whereas reincarnation is viewed as voluntary – the return of highly-evolved individuals who retain awareness passing through the transition from death to rebirth and know how to choose cosmic contracts. They enjoy various stages of *Nirvana* due to accumulated spiritual attainments and think little more of the passage from one life to the next than a Westerner selling an old car and buying a new one.

Rather than accepting a permanent place in Heaven, "the Compassionate Ones" take the *Bodhisattva* Vow: "I vow to defer my final liberation and assist others in their struggle toward realization until every last one is enlightened." *Bodhisattvas* are known as "blessed manifestations" *(tulkus)* and "Precious Ones" *(rinpoches)*, or Dalai Lamas. Such high "incarnates" can take on a human body with its limitations and sufferings or they can even manifest in the lowest hell where they share their merit with beings who need liberation. Or as the XIV Dalai Lama emphasizes, he will take rebirth so long as he can serve the Tibetan people who are now scattered around the world – even if that means to reincarnate "as an insect."[58]

Another phenomenon within the Buddhist hierarchy is known as "multiple manifestations" – mature healers and teachers elect to incarnate into more than one human body at a time. Such a *bodhisattva* typically transmits his spiritual influence through five concurrent incarnations. One individual embodies the visible presence of a departed Lama, while the other four represent his powers of speech, thought, activities, and qualities. Even higher than *bodhisattvas* are Buddhas who choose to live 100 to 1,000 different lives at the same time.[59]

Chapter 25
Alternate Destinies

**We are equal partners in Creation.
Matter, space, and time are malleable.
We can interact with and impact
time/space more than we are aware of.
We can create Heaven on Earth.**

– Beverly Anderson

*The destiny of our souls is as intricate,
well-planned, and interconnected as a cosmos
filled with stars and galaxies. Nothing is impossible
as long as we have free will. Whatever cosmic
contract we created, we can recreate.*

Loopholes lie hidden within our cosmic contracts. Certain threads of destiny are precisely set; others are more flexible. For instance, the joy or suffering arising out of material wealth and family life is the most predetermined; adhering to the path of virtue and attaining liberation depend more upon free will and spiritual disciplines.

Detecting loopholes in cosmic contracts is easiest for adepts who attain higher consciousness. Hinduism refers to these individuals as *avataras*. Buddhists call them *bodhisattvas*. Such fortunate ones can remold cosmic contracts when the greater good is served.

Bheeshma, an ancient prince, warrior, and yogi, serves as a case study. He acquired the spiritual gift of *ichchhamrtyu*, "death by his

COSMIC CRADLE

own wish only."[1] Even when the arrows penetrated Bheeshma's body and protruded from the other side, death did not take him during the Mahabharata war.

Bheeshma's body was so full of holes that it resembled a sieve. He collapsed and lay suspended on a bed of arrows. Due to his vow to remain embodied until the kingdom was secure, Bheeshma chose to remain in his body for another six months. Then using a technique of breath retention, Bheeshma packed his body with life energy so tightly that the arrows all popped out. Within seconds, his body was healed. He prayed during the auspicious northern solstice and attained the supreme Heaven. He lived to 180 years.

The life of philosopher Adi Shankara yields a related story. He focused on completing his life's mission within an allotted span of sixteen years. By the age of twelve, the child genius had become a prominent spiritual leader and had attained enlightenment. When Shankara's set time to depart arrived, he entered a Himalayan cave near Badrinath and prepared to cast off his body. In the nick of time, sage Vyasa arrived and argued: "Your mission is incomplete. You must train students to continue your work after your departure."

Shankara replied, "But how can I remain in an earthly body which I am supposed to use for only sixteen years?" Vyasa answered, "I will extend your life by giving you sixteen years of my own life." Shankara lived to thirty-two, training disciples and writing commentaries on sacred scriptures.

Bheeshma and Shankara belong to a group of adepts who extend longevity in order to serve humanity. For example, if someone's destined life span of sixty years has run its course, he achieves a sixty-year extension as long as he conserves energy by bringing *prana* into the crown energy center at the top of the head. Someone who masters this technique three times can extend his life contract indefinitely.[2]

For similar reasons, India's saints Markandeya and Dhyanyogi, as well as Tibet's XIII Dalai Lama, rearranged their own cosmic contracts. Their lives illustrate that "the man in whom the lower soul predominates is subject to Destiny, while the man whose soul instead gains complete freedom for its activity ... rises above the laws of nature and of the material world."[3]

The Cosmic Contract Loophole

*Just as a stone thrown upwards can be caught
before it falls to the ground, the moulding of the future
is cradled in our hands. The story of Markandeya
illustrates how God is moved by our prayers.*[4]

Sage Mridanda and his wife Marudvati made a commitment to
worship and bathe in India's sacred Ganges River for 365 consecu-
tive days. One day the Almighty Father in the form of Shiva
appeared before them in a vision, saying, "You have earned Divine
grace through your perfect saintliness. I grant you any boon." The
couple replied, "Lord, we have no offspring. Please bless us with a
son." Shiva replied:

> You may have an excellent son full of virtues who will live sixteen
> years. Or, if you wish, I will grant you a wicked son who will live 100
> years. Choose one of the two.

Shiva answered the couple's prayer for a good son within the
next year. The boy Markandeya brought much happiness to his
parents. At birth, a rain of flowers fell from Heaven and divine
beings blew trumpets. The precocious boy studied sacred texts from
the age of five. Within ten years, Markandeya mastered enough
wisdom to attain self-realization. Yet, as time passed and the boy
grew, how could the parents forget when his life was scheduled to
end? Finally, the time drew close at hand, and the father revealed
the history behind his son's birth. Markandeya replied:

> Father, have no fear. You and mother gave me a strong mind
> and body. Intuition tells me that we can alter the course of our
> future at each moment. Without that freedom, there is little point
> in spiritual training.
>
> Please bless me to do intense meditation, prayer, and austerities
> in order to attain God's grace and protection. I will conquer death,
> win honor and glory, and live longer than anyone else.

Mantra to Avert Death

Young Markandeya went to the ocean shore and established a sacred Shivalinga for worship. The Shivalinga, the most ancient icon of Shiva, is a rounded, elliptical stone. One day after prayer, Markandeya was dancing in ecstasy. Just then, the last day of Markandeya's sixteenth year had ended. Yama, the God of Death, had not forgotten the warning words of Shiva. Yama approached suddenly, with fierce swordlike jaws and ferocious body as huge as a black mountain. Yama's hands were full of sharp weapons. His bodily hair resembled scorpions and poisonous snakes. His face exhibiting the highest anger, Yama was accompanied by the goddess of death and attendants as vicious as he. They threw a noose through Markandeya's nose and began to drag his soul out of the body.

Markandeya caught hold of the Shivalingam and said:

> Yama, my dear sir, I have no fear of you. I have vowed not to move until I complete my prayer to Lord Shiva. Please wait until I have finished and I will follow. Until then, go away from me. It is impolite for you to interfere with my vow.

Yama replied:

> Markandeya, you fool. Why didn't finish your prayer before I came? Thousands of kings fell to me; hundreds of gods died in my hands. You are only a small boy. Come along right now.

Markandaya explained:

> Yama, for your own interests you must know that anyone who disturbs prayer reaps evil consequences. Besides you have no control over Lord Shiva or me.

Yama opened his mouth to devour Markandeya. The boy continued chanting Shiva's mantra — cosmic sounds known to avert death.

> *Om Trayambakam Yaja Mahae, Sughandhim Pushti Vardhanam Urvarukamiva Bandhanan, Mrityor Muksheeya Mamritat.*[5]

Just then Lord Shiva appeared in the lingam stone due to the boy's one-pointed devotion. Shiva kicked Yama away and transformed Markandeya into a *Chiranjivi*, a great saint who appears young, beautiful, and lives forever in a physical body.

Souls Waiting in the Wings for Birth

Markandeya never grew old. Due to his inexhaustible life-strength, he witnessed the alternation of creation and destruction — how the universe is born, evolves, and dissolves in cycles much like we go through the four seasons through the year. A cycle of creation, lasting 4,320,000,000 years, begins when Lord Vishnu's life-breath flows out. Then, with the next inhalation, like a spider, Vishnu draws "the web of the universe"[6] back into himself for 4,320,000,000 years. Time, form, and space are obliterated and reabsorbed into the body of God. These inhalations and exhalations are the Days and Nights of the Creator.

Universes are projected by His mere will, fall, remain in the gap for some time, and once more rise in wave after wave, and fall after fall. The *Matsya Mahapurana* text records Markandeya's observations during the interlude of non-manifestation between dissolution and re-creation of the universe. When Earth, the atmosphere, and the first heaven rest within God's body, the Lord sleeps in a wide expanse of water for 4,320,000,000 years. "There is no one to behold him, no one to comprehend him; there is no knowledge of him, except within himself."[7]

Even today Markandeya reportedly lives in the remote Himalayas, where he prays for the world's welfare. Among his accomplishments, Markandeya authored the *Markandeya Purana*, a scripture dating before the 9th century BC which contains the *Chandi Path*, the story of Divine victory over egotism and selfishness. The *Chandi* is still recited to this day as a spiritual discipline of self-control and purification.

Human Body – A Precious Gift

An elderly saint survived an NDE
in order to disseminate spiritual knowledge.

When Dhyanyogi was supposed to be a playful seven-year-old schoolboy, he attempted to embark on a budding spiritual quest by leaving home in search of God. The year was 1885. The happy ending for the moment is that his frantic parents quickly tracked their son down and brought him home. Yet in the end, the boy left for good at age thirteen intent on finding a spiritual teacher.

By the 1930s, the boy had trekked barefoot all over India and studied with great yogis. He become the renowned saint Shri Dhyanyogi Madhusudandasji, an adept in yogic philosophy and scriptures, as well as a master of Mantra, Yantra, Hatha, Raja, Jnana, and Kundalini Yogas.

During December 1971, famine, drought, and disaster plagued the Northern part of Gujarat state, the home of Dhyanyogi's ashram. The eighty-three-year-old saint suffered exhaustion doing relief work at the ashram in the 110° to 115° degree heat. Disciples urged their leader to rest. Still the devoted saint distributed milk to 500 hungry people and fed 1,700 cows every day.

For several days during the drought and heat wave, Dhyanyogi had been experiencing a mild fever and a boil had grown on his lower back. One evening, the villagers became agitated and upset about the saint's condition and gathered outside Dhyanyogi's room where he lay in bed. Inside, disciples were following the doctor's advice and applying moist hot packs to the boil. As they worked on him, Dhyanyogi suddenly felt his body temperature rise to 105°. The body's heat increased until Dhyanyogi was left unable to speak about the ensuing paralysis. He lost muscular control over his mouth, tongue, legs, and entire body.

Souls Waiting in the Wings for Birth

Then, as the holy man sensed the last moments were at hand, he recalled a yogi's prediction, "Dhyanyogi, you will encounter death at around eighty years of age." The teachings of the *Bhagavad Gita* also surfaced in his mind.

Whatever we remember when we are leaving the body will be realized in the hereafter because that will be what our mind has most commonly dwelt on during our life. If we remember God at the time of death, we will be released from all past sins and go directly to God.

Dhyanyogi continued to lose contact with the external world in a step-by-step fashion: his legs become immobilized; he could barely hear people frantically calling, "Guruji! Bapuji! Guruji!;" his hands became wooden; he saw light all around, while people in the room were no longer discernible even as figures; everything in the room became dimmer and finally faded out; and the sense of touch disappeared – the saint could no longer feel anyone handling his body. At the same time, another strange event was transpiring in the room. One disciple after another noticed a dark shadow leaving Dhyanyogi's body and attempted to shake the saint back to normal consciousness. The instant they touched his body, they too lost consciousness.

I knew I was going away forever. I thought of the divine name "Rama," but thoughts of unfinished business raced through my mind. I felt regret for not starting a school in my village. The closest school was thirty miles away. I was disappointed about not building a hospital for the people near Bihar, my birth place. They travelled 100 miles for medical treatment. Plus, I wanted to build a temple and improve the ashram. I felt that I had not put enough effort into these projects.

Added to thoughts of unfinished business, inner visions interrupted Dhyanyogi's prayers. As if he was watching a movie screen, flashbacks of previous lifetimes and actions performed in the present life flashed before his mind's eye. Past actions, in some cases, were not too good. But in contrast, the saint hoped to come home to God because his present life had been devoted to prayer and service to others.

Earthly scenes began to fade away as Dhyanyogi's breathing became heavy and began to work beyond control. He reconciled concerns about unfinished projects by thinking, "Whatever happens will be God's Will. It is beyond my control. I will let God take care of it."

Dhyanyogi became immersed in praying to Rama. Suddenly he felt as if somebody pushed him very hard. His soul rose out of the body. All physical discomfort vanished. Floating around in the air like a bird, he observed the room below, his unconscious body, and people crying over his "death." Dhyanyogi wanted to say, "Don't cry. Chant God's name. There is no point in crying." But he could not speak.

At this juncture, two beings approached the space where he was floating. Their faces were pleasant, blissful, and quiet. They said, "Dhyanyogi, it is time to join us. You must come to a different place." Dhyanyogi felt a oneness with the messengers as they travelled through space. He felt no fear, yet wondered, "Where am I going?" The messengers communicated little, except to say "You will see when we get there. We assure you it will be pleasant."

Dhyanyogi pondered over why it was possible to communicate with Death's messengers, yet he was unable to speak with disciples just before he left the body. His guides explained:

> While you were in the body, your senses could no longer function and the body became cold because the life energies were concentrating in the heart. No energy went into the channels that control and empower speech. As for our conversation, only beings on this plane can hear or see us.

Dhyanyogi puzzled over the two long rows of people they passed by, one on each side of them: men and women of all nationalities, races, and religions. Standing on the right side, people were weeping and crying. Whereas the crowd lining up on the left looked happy and peaceful. His guides said:

> Those who cry realize that they had received the precious gift of a human body, but instead of using it to help others and do good acts, they wasted their time in harmful, selfish pursuits. Now they fear the consequences — rebirth among the beings of the lower regions or among men who have little or no chance of self-realization. On the other hand, the ones who performed virtuous deeds are laughing and singing. They anticipate favorable rebirths in the various heavens or on Earth where they have the chance to realize God.

With the two guides leading the way, Dhyanyogi had evidently glimpsed two flocks of souls lining up in the inter-life world, with many waiting to be born on Earth.

Finally, his guides revealed, "Because you prayed to Rama all your life, we are taking you to Him." Dhyanyogi found himself in "God's audience room," a place shining with colored lights. The light appeared more brilliant than the Sun. Dhyanyogi prostrated before Lord Rama who smiled and said:

> It is good that you came, but you cannot stay. If you remain even a bit longer, they will cremate your body. You must return and fulfill your desires to help people.

Dhyanyogi had no inclination to leave Rama's radiating presence until Rama manifested a vision of a large assembly of people.

> You cannot attain final liberation as long as there are desires in your mind and God's work to do. You must help these spiritual seekers who are waiting for your guidance and teachings. Go finish it.

Rama advised the messengers, "Quickly take Dhyanyogi back to Earth."

Cremation

Cremation is done quickly in India. The normal rule of thumb is that when someone passes on during the night, the body is cremated before sunrise. The saint appeared to have been "dead" for at least three or four hours. People were preparing for Dhyanyogi's cremation.

In the meantime, as Dhyanyogi's spirit descended back to Earth, he observed how his body seemed like a foreign object, lying on the first floor of the ashram. At the same moment, the holy man noticed Anandi Ma (Ashadevi), a thirteen-year-old disciple, who had been meditating in her room upstairs, crawling down the stairs, while still in a meditative state.

The young girl, as if intuitively guided, placed Dhyanyogi's head right in her lap. Suddenly Dhyanyogi felt pushed back into the body, the same way he had felt pushed out of it. When Anandi Ma opened the master's eyes, light pouring from her eyes fell all over his body, enlivening it. His senses began to work again. His nagging boil and fever were totally healed.

Upon returning back to "life," Dhyanyogi noticed how the same three disciples remained unconscious as when they tried to assist him. By tapping them gently and rubbing their backs, Dhyanyogi brought them back to consciousness. Then, the saint told them to chant Rama's name.

Over the next week, Dhyanyogi's body felt a sense of extreme lightness. His mind often returned to the state of floating freely outside his body. He had little desire to eat. In fact, the saint felt so estranged from the body that whenever he ate or drank, he wondered, "Who is doing the eating?" and "How does this machine (this body) work?"

As God's Will took its course in the period following Dhyanyogi's NDE, he fulfilled each of his aspirations to help the people in India. Then, some Americans urged him to visit the USA.

I recalled the faces I saw in Lord Rama's courtyard and agreed to go. All of the people I saw are members of my spiritual family, and I must help them.

Dhyanyogi initiated thousands of Americans into Kundalini Maha Yoga between 1976 and 1980. He explained, "It often happens that people come to me, and we instantly feel a great love and attachment for each other. Then I know this was the reason Lord Rama sent me back."[8]

If ever a compelling case existed for an extension of someone's "Lease," as Dhyanyogi called it, this example might be it. Dhyanyogi (1878 to 1994) had thirty-three years tacked onto his life following the NDE and lived to the age of 116. Today, the master's higher energy continues to work through Shri Anandi Ma, his spiritual heir.

Five factors make Dhyanyogi's NDE extraordinary: 1) a remarkable state of consciousness allowed him to be alert throughout the step-by-step NDE process; 2) his advanced age; 3) rare are reports of saints having NDEs and reporting details of the process; 4) the change in his "Lease" (cosmic contract); and 5) the NDE was not the result of an accident, surgery, serious wounds, life-threatening illness, drugs, or lightning, as are most NDEs.

On the Rooftop of the World

*During the past 300 years, Tibet's national
purpose has been organized around monastic education,
literary and philosophical creativity, meditation,
and development of ritual and festival arts.*

Among Tibet's treasures are spiritual lineages of lamas linked together in one unbroken series of incarnations who have the ability to foresee their rebirth years in advance. When one lama dies, he is reborn shortly thereafter, being discovered through traditional ways, and he continues the lineage until he, in turn, dies and is subsequently reborn. Most famous of these lineages is that of the Dalai Lama.[9]

Dalai Lama means "Supreme Teacher," "Greatest Master," and "Ocean of Wisdom." Tibet's spiritual, political, and social leadership rests in his hands. This one-of-a-kind nonmaterialistic system distinguishes Tibet from the rest of the world. Rather than elections or family inheritance, Tibetans circumvent vested interests and apostolic succession and rely upon their spiritual authority to return again and again.

Tibetans believe that when ordinary people die, they spend time resting in the between-life state. Rebirth depends upon what lessons an individual needs to learn and the winds of karma – effects of past actions from previous lives. A Dalai Lama, in contrast, is an emanation of the Buddha who voluntarily returns to uplift humanity. Following the instant he relinquishes the former physical body, he knowingly enters upon the path of rebirth – selection of parents, and the time and place of birth that allow him to continue his humanitarian mission.

The Dalai Lama is drawn into rebirth out of compassion. He is like a shepherd who declines to enter the sheepfold before the last of the flock are safely inside. Only then does he enter *Nirvana* and close the door. The sheep are like the suffering beings of the Universe "down to the last blade of grass."

A Plan to Save Tibet

The current XIV Dalai Lama's life is linked to the inspired "Master Plan" to save Tibet undertaken by his predecessor, the XIII Dalai Lama Tubten Gyatso (1876 to 1933). Prophecies had been made that the Great Thirteenth could live to be 80, except with one catch: only if Tibetans had sufficient merits and followed political guidance.

The Great XIII's *Last Political Testament* (1932) forewarned that a Chinese invasion loomed on the not-to-distant horizon if Tibetans failed to modernize and create a strong defense. Tibet's population would be "scattered like ants around the world and forced to live like beggars."[10] The remaining Tibetans would become slaves of the conquerors, endure incredible suffering, and "roam the land in bondage."[11]

"... venerable incarnates and those who protect the Teachings shall be wiped out completely. Monasteries shall be looted, property confiscated and all living beings shall be destroyed.... institutions of the state and religion shall be banned and forgotten."[12]

As Tibet's destiny travelled on its course, the XIII Dalai Lama realized that his people would not modernize in time and formulated a back-up plan. Besides commanding time and place of rebirth, he possessed the freedom to alter the moment of death. The XIII Dalai Lama shortened his life span. The reason: it would be best if the Chinese invaders were faced with a youthful leader rather than a helpless leader in his twilight years. Consequently in 1933, at only 57 and in good health, he "mystically stepped aside and passed away, making way for the new reincarnation."[13]

The XIII Dalai Lama coordinated his passage from this world with a meditative state known as the "State of Clear Light." He sat with spine erect and legs crossed and remained in this traditional lotus posture after his death, showing no signs of the usual decay. Thousands of people came to view the Dalai Lama's final meditation pose. Crowds passed by chanting sacred mantras and twirling prayer wheels.

Souls Waiting in the Wings for Birth

The Dalai Lama sat facing South, the Buddhist direction of auspiciousness. One morning caretakers noticed his head had turned to face East. The monks dutifully repositioned the head back to face South. Yet each morning, even though the hall was securely locked, the XIII Dalai Lama was found again looking East. Since no one dared to shift or touch the body, this sign indicated that the young incarnation would take birth in the eastern portion of Tibet.

Following the XIII Dalai Lama's transition, a cluster of oracles, visions, mystical signs in sacred lakes, and cloud formations further assisted a group of monks in locating the child who embodies the spirit of Boundless Compassion. The boy, born Tenzin Gyatso in the Wood Hog Year of the Tibetan calendar (1935), passed all the necessary tests and was indisputedly the reincarnated Dalai Lama.

The Greatest Escape of Twentieth Century

"Go! Go! Tonight!" declared the oracle. Staggering forward in the divine state of consciousness and snatching up paper and a pen, the oracle drew the route to be used for the daring getaway. Details on the escape map were precise even down to the last Tibetan town on the Indian border. After waiting nine years for instructions to flee, the directions were to be more challenging than the cold paper reflected. As foreseen by his predecessor, the XIV Dalai Lama, at barely twenty-four, was finally forced into exile in 1959 by the Chinese invasion, which began years earlier.

The cool March evening air was filled with nervous energy as the clandestine party of monks and their disguised sacred leader crept out into the Himalayan night. Chinese soldiers lurked at every turn. Capture and death were seconds away if a mistake was made. Because the situation was so desperate and evading capture would be difficult, only a few people were informed of the decision to flee Tibet. The Tibetans had the element of surprise on their side, since the Dalai Lama had never hinted that he might someday flee his home land. The Chinese felt secure that he would remain with his followers. A Tibet without the Dalai Lama seemed unthinkable.

The secret journey using pack animals and mules was fraught with perils, freezing temperatures and winds, dangerous mountain paths across the Himalayan range. Places for food and shelter were few and far between. Heavily-armed Chinese soldiers watched roads, rivers, and key mountain passes making crossing icy mountain streams and rivers without bridges difficult.

Two days passed before the Chinese discovered that he had vanished into thin air. The irony is that the era's greatest escape had been envisioned decades earlier. A young Dalai Lama fleeing Tibet with the Chinese army soon in hot pursuit was the fulfillment of the XIII Dalai Lama's prophecy (1932). The XIV Dalai Lama, reached India in a few weeks, a feat that his predecessor, if he had lived, could never have accomplished.

The XIV Dalai Lama's Cosmic Contract

The XIV Dalai Lama remained in Tibet after the Chinese takeover in 1950 until March 17, 1959. Seven days after the civil uprising against the Chinese, he was alerted to a plot to abduct him to Peking and decided to flee. India gave him sanctuary. More than 100,000 compatriots followed. The XIV's "task is the most difficult of all Dalai Lamas."[14] Tibet's head of state-in-exile guides his people through their darkest hour.

"Tibet's many monasteries, now ravaged, were the largest in the modern world.... One-third of Tibet's entire male population inhabited them, in a country where the priesthood was the most prominent profession."[15]

As an interesting twist, the Dalai Lama and the Tibetan culture more than likely could not have survived if the XIII Dalai Lama had lived out his life span. Instead, the Chinese invasion propelled a young Dalai Lama "from his serene medieval kingdom on the Roof of the World into the turbulent twentieth century, where he personifies qualities that modern society no longer expects from its leaders."[16]

The XIV's influence on the world's stage has been greater than any predecessor. Westerners have contact with his spiritual aware-ness and methods for cultivating love, compassion, and wisdom. He works to preserve Tibetan culture, arts, scriptures, and medicine. In 1989 he was awarded the Nobel Peace Prize for his nonviolent struggle to end Chinese domination of his homeland.

Souls Waiting in the Wings for Birth

The XIV Dalai Lama's mystical dreams confirm that he is a reincarnation of the Deity of Compassion, *Avalokitesvera*. The great Indian saint Atisha, an earlier reincarnation of the Deity of Compassion, appears leading the Dalai Lama by the finger on a string. At the end of the string lays a clear, sublime "image of *Avalokitesvera*,"[17] a guarantee of heavenly protection.

PART FIVE

GIFTED MEMORY

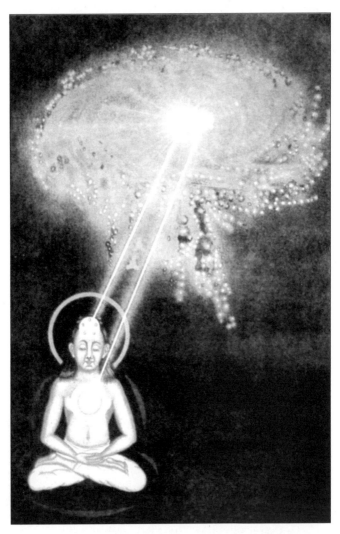

Past, present, and future are not manifest
at the same time in our physical world due
to conditions created by cause, effect, space,
and time. A yogi's consciousness, however,
attains that state which is the substratum of
all things and even recalls the Big Bang.

Pre-Conception Remembrances

Memories are fleeting or buried beneath layers of consciousness few perceive. Except important events, most of us forget over 99% of our lives. After all, who recalls every fact learned in high school, to say little of memories in the womb, or life before conception?

People at the top end of the memory scale, on the other hand, recall their first breath, even previous lives. And even more rare is gifted memory – "memory of events occurring prior to being in a physical body and developing a physical brain for information storage."

Gifted memory suggests that part of our consciousness is "alive and well outside the physical bodybrain"[1] prior to conception. Yet how can we retain memory without a brain or container of memory? Is memory non-physical or spiritual in nature?

One answer is that the storehouse of memory is individual consciousness itself. Much like a white screen underlying the projection of a movie film, imagine a primordial, unchanging reality existing at the basis of individual existence. Just as moving images on the movie screen change while the white screen remains ever the same, so too, no matter whether we are young, old, awake or sleeping, a primordial awareness persists, much like an eternal "now." And just as we can rewind the movie film to view earlier stages, when our mind runs back our inner "film," we become conscious of gifted memory.

Why can some people rewind their life's film and re-experience where they came from whereas others have already forgotten last week's events? Why do some recall gifted memory only as a child? Do levels of memory correlate with spiritual maturity?

Part Five highlights these questions in the context of historical teachings about memory along with seventeen first-hand testimonies of gifted memory from interviewees, and forty-one accounts found scattered throughout scholarly journals, biographies, and legends.

The ancient Greek story of Narcissus symbolizes
the soul's Fall into the phenomenal world.

Chapter 26
The Illusion of Forgetfulness

**I found myself alive in a body,
in a place I didn't know.
I had forgotten how I came there,
where I'd lived before,
or if I'd ever lived at all ... .[1]**

*We enter the world as babes and, except for a few
blessed with their pre-uterine memories intact,
most of us have nary a hint of where we
have come from or why we are here.*

Forgetfulness, as a spiritual theme, pops up all around the world: we know how our bodies came into this world, and yet most of us have long forgotten how our souls came into the body. By analogy, human birth is like walking into a theater to watch a movie. We quickly become identified with one of the characters and immersed in our own Hollywood drama, the earthly illusion.

References to spiritual forgetfulness, or the Fall of the Souls, appear throughout religion, philosophy, literature, and mythology. Ancient sources include:

- ❀ Plato (Greece) – Prior to the soul's initial physical incarnation, each soul sees the "Things Which Are" – "Things which our Souls did then see in pure light, being themselves pure and without the mark of this which we call body, and now carry about with us, as the fish carrieth the prison-house of his shell."[2]

But few souls, once they enter the flesh, are "left having Memory present with them in sufficient measure."[3] Those unfortunate in their earthly lot, having been turned to inequity through some corrupting influence, forget the holy things which once they saw.

⚘ Harranites (Middle Eastern Gnosticism) – A passionate desire to experience the pleasures of the flesh caused us to forget our "original habitation," our "true center," our "eternal being."[4]

⚘ Pythagoras (Greece) – "The child is born, a pitiful image of earth, and he cries aloud with fright. The memory of the celestial regions however has returned to the occult depths of the Unconscious; it will only be revived either by Knowledge or by Pain, by Love or by Death!"[5]

Relatively modern sources embracing the theme of forgetfulness include:

⚘ Mormons (19th century USA) – "He sees in part, and he knows in part; but never while tabernacled in mortal flesh will he be fully awake to the intelligence of his former estate. It surpasses his comprehension, is unspeakable, and even unlawful to be uttered."[6]

⚘ Shaykh Muhammad al-Jamal ar-Rifa'i as-Shadhili (20th century Sufism) – "Although you may not remember, you are from the first of my children. I gave birth to you in pre-eternity."[7]

⚘ Gotthold Ephraim Lessing (18th century Germany) – "Have I forgotten forever what I must forget for the time being?"[8]

⚘ Giordano Bruno (16th century Italy) – "In order not to burden too much the transmigrating souls, it [Fate] inter-poses the drinking from the Lethean river … so that through oblivion everyone may be … eager to preserve himself in his present state. Therefore, youths do not recall their state of infancy; infants do not long for the state in their mothers' wombs; and none of these longs for the state in that life which he lived before he found himself in such a nature."[9]

⚘ Unitarianism (19th century Christianity) – "Our experience is not coextensive with our being, our memory does not comprehend it."[10]

- Rabbi Barukh of Mezbizh (19th century Hasidism) – "At first glance, it is not clear why God created forgetfulness. But the meaning of it is this: If there were no forgetting, a man would incessantly think of his death. He would build no house, he would launch on no enterprise. That is why God planted forgetting within him."[11]

- Yoruba (Africa) – "We knelt down (in heaven) and chose our destinies, but when we arrived on earth we became impatient."[12]

Further insights into how forgetfulness enshrouds the soul as a consequence of being clothed in a human body are reported by: Western philosophers, Mormons, and indigenous peoples, as well as Sufism, Gnosticism, Judaism, Buddhism, Hinduism, and Zoroastrianism.

<figure>✦</figure>

Consciousness Barrier

*Amnesia is a prerequisite for human birth, a bondage
that limits the soul and thereby facilitates its growth.*

Western and Eastern spiritual traditions acknowledge that souls
seeking human birth must pass through a barrier which represents
a frequency shift from a higher to lower rate of vibration. Once
beyond that barrier, souls forget their recent existence in the spiritual world; a thick veil blocks out pre-conception memories.

- ❁ Mormons – The veil "wisely thrown over all the past" makes
  us unconscious of "the scenes, the endearing associations" of
  our "first primeval childhood in the heavenly mansions."[13]

- ❁ Pythagoras (ancient Greek philosopher and religious leader) –
  "The time has come; the law must be obeyed. The heaviness
  increases, a sensation of dimness is felt. The soul no longer
  sees its companions of light except through a veil, and this
  veil, ever denser and denser, gives a presentiment of the
  coming separation. It hears their sad farewells; the tears of the
  blest, the loved ones whom it is leaving, fall over it like a
  heavenly dew which will leave in its heart the burning thirst
  of an unknown happiness. Then, with solemn oaths, it
  promises to remember – to remember the light when in the
  world of darkness, to remember truth when in the world of
  falsehood, and love when in the world of hatred."[14]

- ❁ Plotinus (3rd century Rome) – The human body is "the true
  river of Lethe; for souls plunged into it forget all."[15]

- ❁ Solomon ben Yehudah Ibn Gebirol (11th century Jewish
  Kabbalah) – "The soul was created with the True knowledge
  … . But when the soul unites with substance (matter) and
  confuses herself with it, by the mixture and union, she [the
  soul] is removed from the perception of these impressions;
  they remain concealed in her, because the darkness of the
  substance covers her in such a way, as to obscure its light,
  and the substance dulls her: she then becomes as if a trans-

parent mirror to which has been applied a muddy and thick substance, etc."[16]

❀ Ralph Waldo Emerson (19th century USA) – "Where do we find ourselves? In a series, of which we do not know the extremes … . We wake and find ourselves on a stair; there are other stairs below us … there are stairs above us … . But the Genius which … stands at the door by which we enter, and gives us the Lethe to drink … mixed the cup too strongly, and we cannot shake off the lethargy … ."[17]

❀ Sufism (7th century Islam) – Seventy thousand veils separate the spiritual and physical worlds. Our souls lose divine attributes as we traverse the first 35,000 veils of light. We then accumulate earthly qualities in our passage through the next 35,000 veils of darkness.[18]

❀ Zoroastrianism (ancient Persia) – "I lie here, a star of heaven, fallen upon this gloomy place. Scarce remembering what bright courses I was once allowed to trace. Still in dreams it comes upon me, that I once on wings did soar … ."[19]

❀ Greek mythology – The handsome youth Narcissus gazed upon his beautiful reflection in a pool of water and plunged into the stream and disappeared. This fable symbolizes the soul's fall into the phenomenal world. Souls remain at peace "above" until, like Narcissus, they became enamored with physical form and mistake "the image for reality."[20] The soul becomes a captive in a bodily costume and no longer remembers its immortal nature.

Buddhist, Hindu, and Sufi teachings state that pre-physical memories become imbedded within the subconscious mind at birth. Physical embodiment and social conditioning dull our awareness, causing us to believe that sensory experience is the true reality.

❀ Tibetan Lama Govinda (20th century Tibetan Buddhism) – "The torn and tortured human being … who knows neither his infinite past, nor the infinity of his future … is like a man suffering from … a mental disease which deprives him of the continuity of his consciousness and … the capacity to act … in accordance with his true nature."[21]

❀ Chogyam Trungpa Rinpoche (20th century Tibetan Buddhism) – Memories of the period before birth are such strong impressions that every young child should remember them. However, a child's family, educational system, and society quickly "indoctrinate" children "so that the original deep impressions become faded except for occasional sudden glimpses."[22]

- Paramahansa Yogananda (20th century India) – Just as a bird hesitates to leave the open cage because "confinement in the cage has made it forgetful of the joy of free flights in the open skies,"[23] so too, our souls become locked up in the human cavity of five powerful coverings or *koshas*: gross body, vital airs, mind, intellect, and sheath of bliss.[24] We become attached to our physical veils and forget our divine heritage.[25]

- Rumi (13th century Persia) – If a man spends a lifetime in one city, but dreams one night of another city, memories of his hometown vanish from his mind. He does not suspect that he is dreaming. He believes that he has "always lived in this city and was born and bred in it. What wonder, then, if the soul does not remember her ancient abode and birthplace, since she is wrapt in the slumber of this world, like a star covered by clouds; especially as she has trodden so many cities and the dust that darkens her vision is not yet swept away."[26]

Macrobius – 4th to 5th century Roman Neoplatonist

Macrobius compares souls to lost children who have run away from their spiritual home. In his Commentary on Cicero's *Dream of Scipio*, Macrobius depicts how the soul passes from the divine world through the spheres and makes contact with physical matter. As a consequence of its passage, the soul encounters amnesia, a kind of death. The mortal body is a prison or tomb.

- Desire – The soul looks down from the "highest summit and perpetual light"[27] and secretly contemplates earthly life. The soul is overtaken by a longing for a body.

- Fall from Original Blessedness – The "weight of this earthly thought" causes the soul's descent "into the nether world."[28] The soul passes through the seven celestial spheres and becomes "clothed" with various faculties including reasoning power from Saturn, practicality and morality from Jupiter, and sensuality from Venus.

- Magnetic Attraction (cosmic contract) – The soul "gravitates" towards the appropriate "earthen garment."[29]

- Intoxication and Oblivion (physical entry) – Due to the tumultuous influx of physical matter, "matter flowing into her [the soul's] essence," the soul suffers a type of intoxication and oblivion of the world from which it comes. "The soul is drawn into a body staggering with recent intoxication … . Hence oblivion, the companion of intoxication … begins silently to creep into the recesses of the soul."[30]

Adi Shankara – Early Indian Philosopher and Sage

Adi Shankara was an infant prodigy who mastered the holy Shastras and Upanishads by the age of seven, and within a year, the boy genius left home and studied under a spiritual teacher. By the age of sixteen, he had mastered all philosophies and theologies. At a time when chaos and confusion reigned in religion, Shankara imparted new life into the old teachings and wrote commentaries on the *Bhagavad Gita, Upanishads*, and *Brahma Sutras*. He challenged learned men to discussion, argued with them, and converted them to his views.

In one small text, Shankara depicts how forgetfulness increases as souls traverse the "Four Spheres" of existence separating the primordial state of Oneness from the human realm.[31]

- ❀ Primordial Home – Souls leave their Source, *Turiya*, where they enjoy the "ecstatic life" and intuitively know everything.
- ❀ Amnesia – Souls traverse the Sphere of Transition and emerge on the other side wearing "Lethean Garments" – spiritual veils which erase memory of their previous condition as spirit.[32] The souls forget the true "Self" and experience reversed, or false, knowledge, known as *viparita jnana*.
- ❀ Desire to Overcome Amnesia – Souls pick up the *Linga-deha* (psyche) in the internal world of dream and imagine themselves as "conscious, feeling, breathing" beings.[33] They seek to recover all that they once knew within themselves.
- ❀ Identification with Physical Body – Souls don physical veils which cause matter and the five senses to overshadow awareness of the Higher Self.

Edgar Cayce – 20th Century Seer

Edgar Cayce, a Southern Presbyterian mystic, cognized how the conscious mind became separated from the subconscious mind where the memory of spiritual identity was kept. Through a series of human incarnations, souls gradually "descended into earthiness, into less mentality, into less consciousness of the mind force."[34]

Cayce's five stages of forgetting follow. Global civilization seems to have attained the fifth stage.

1. *Natural Memory* – All human beings had full conscious memory of their spiritual identities in the beginning when human souls only "lightly inhabited bodies."

2. *Mystical Dreams* – Memories arose only via mystical dreams during sleep.

3. *Fables* – As fewer people experienced mystical dreams, people recorded the memories and passed them down in stories and fables to the next generation.

4. *Religion* – A handful of saints and philosophers cognized the soul's heavenly source and religion arose to fulfill the souls' longing for lost memories. Humanity developed philosophical and theological theories for what people felt to be true, but were no longer able to experience.

5. *Science* – Humanity reached the bottom and believed only what they could experience through the five senses. Individuals discovered scientific laws, secrets which they carried inside, but could no longer consciously access.

The River of Forgetfulness

When our souls are about to pass into the flesh,
we stand at the entrance to the human realm and
someone gives us a cup of Lethe's water to drink.

Plato influenced our understanding of gifted memory more than any other Western thinker. According to his well-studied dialogues, our souls preview their future course prior to birth,[35] but then we forget everything upon entering human bodies. That is because incarnating souls must drink the waters of Lethe, the "River of Forgetfulness." This beverage suppresses memories of "all things which exist, whether in this world or the world below."[36]

Three hundred years after Plato's death, the Roman poet Virgil wrote about the potion of forgetfulness in the *Aeneid*. This 1st century AD text recounts a visionary journey to the "Valley of Oblivion where souls of a thousand nations filled the air."[37]

Aeneas perceived before him a spacious valley, with trees gently waving in the wind, a tranquil landscape, through which the river Lethe flowed. Along the banks of the stream wandered a countless multitude, numerous as insects in the summer air. Aeneas, with surprise, inquired who were these. Anchises answered:

"They are souls to which bodies are to be given in due time. Meanwhile they dwell on Lethe's bank and drink oblivion of their former lives."[38]

Another report originates from Plutarch. The 1st century Greek philosopher depicts Thespesius's near-death journey to the region of Lethe.[39] In this case, Thespesius witnessed a flock of souls who alighted and walked around a gaping chasm. They had been attracted to the chasm by a soft gentle breeze carrying a delectable odor. The sweet scent produced such a mood as alcohol induces, a sort of intoxication. The laughter, "bacchic revelry, festivity, and merry-making"[40] dissolved reason and engendered the soul's desire for physical experience by reviving fond, nostalgic memories of life in a human body.

Legends reminiscent of the river Lethe, presented by Chinese Buddhists, picture souls awaiting birth in a sub-terrestrial realm ruled by King Yen-lo Wang. His administrators help souls plan rebirth. Afterward, they are escorted to the Hall of Oblivion where Granny Meng offers them a special broth. Upon feeling the amnesic effects of this mystical beverage, a torrent of red foaming waters precipitates the souls into the human realm.

The Suffering of Ignorance

India's medical treatises and religious texts
explain that the baby possesses gifted memory until
the last moment of his stay in the womb. The soul then
becomes covered with "the cosmic delusion that
'existence' depends on body and breath."[41]

Sixty days prior to birth, every fetus observes the movie of its past and future lives.[42] The soul becomes fearful and uneasy as this film appears on the mind's screen. The soul much prefers "the freedom of having no form"[43] and changes its mind about experiencing another human birth.

The fetus stirs restlessly in the womb and runs into trouble in every direction. When it moves up against its mother's stomach, it is burned by gastric fire. Then the fetus bumps its mother's kidneys and receives a salty shock. At some point, the fetus moves in the direction of intestines and is offended by the smell. Alas, there is no turning back. The soul calls for God's help: "Let me out of this prison! I can't see, I can't hear, I am bound."[44] God hears the plea and teaches the fetus to meditate on the mantra *so'ham*, meaning "I am Pure Being." The fetus realizes its identity with the supreme principle and settles down.

Still, as time takes it course, the fetus forgets as quickly as it learns. God's instructions and the understanding that it had attained are lost. The fetal memory loss results from the trauma of being forcibly ejected from the womb. "The soul emerges into earth consciousness, veiled of all memory of past lives and the inner worlds."[45] Upon forgetting *so'ham*, the baby cries the sound "kwanh, kwanh," or *ko'ham, ko'ham*, meaning "Who am I?" From that moment, the soul identifies with the physical body: I am a male; I am a female; I am a child, a youth, an old man; I am a physician, a teacher, an artist, and so on. Vedic teachings refer to the classic state of amnesia as "the mistake of the intellect" or *pragya-parad*.

Another scripture depicts how the fetus contemplates hundreds of previous lifetimes and resolves, "Never again will I thus act, when once I am delivered from this womb; assuredly I will so strive that I do not again undergo conception."[46] As the baby is expelled, however, the baby "is pained by the wind of the *prajapatis*, and it is expelled wailing, being pained at heart by its suffering."[47] Until the baby comes into contact with oxygen, the newborn enters "an intolerable swoon."[48] Finally "Vishnu's magical power" rubs out the newborn's consciousness; "its soul being stupefied thereby, it loses its knowledge."[49]

The veil, represents the heavy folds of ignorance – fields of energy – that keep us hidden from our true identities. The lifting of the veil, fold by fold, corresponds to the step-by-step journey of rising awareness from the lower to the higher steps of the consciousness ladder. The spiritual teacher Meher Baba writes:

> "The 'veil' … is so subtle that even the highest and finest thought
> cannot pierce through it. This veil consists of seven folds of seven
> different, deep colours. Each fold is tied with a separate knot … . The
> colors represent the seven root desires – lust, greed, anger, etc. –
> connected with the seven openings of sensation in the face: mouth,
> right nostril, left nostril, right ear, left ear, right eye, left eye."[50]

Cross-Cultural Parallels

The Hebrew *Talmud*, in a similar fashion, states that the fetus "looks from one end of the world to the other, and knows all the teachings," but the instant the newborn takes its first breath, "an angel strikes it on the mouth, and it forgets everything."[51]

The irony is that modern medical science dovetails with these ancient accounts. Dr. Thomas Verny points out that oxytocin, the hormone controlling the rate of a mother's labor contractions, floods a child's system during labor and delivery. Oxytocin, in fact, not only regulates contractions, it produces a biochemically-induced amnesia. Thoroughly trained animals are known to lose their ability to perform laboratory tasks under the hormone's influence. For that reason, the hormone creating biochemical forgetfulness may correlate with "Vishnu's magical power," the Hebrew angel striking the newborn's mouth, as well as Plato's waters of Lethe.

Souls Waiting in the Wings for Birth

Chapter 27
Piercing the Veils of Light

Where wert thou, Soul, ere yet my body born
Became thy dwelling-place? Didst thou on earth
Or in the clouds, await this body's birth ... ?[1]

– Samuel Waddington

*Souls sometimes slip through the cracks of forgetfulness
and avoid the muddy drink from the river Lethe.*

Souls differ in their heavenly memories once they are born on Earth. An unveiled soul which is "a dry beam of light is wisest and best."[2] By that, Heraclitis means "dry" souls remember what they had known in the heavens because they abstain from the potion of oblivion prior to being born. "Wet" souls, on the other hand, become so "gorged with the forgetfulness from the Lethean beverage that, as Plato puts it, they have no "Recollection of Those Things" which each soul saw when it journeyed with God.[3]

The temptation to drink deeply of the water of Lethe is strong. According to Plato, the journey to the plain of Lethe takes the soul through a dry, torrid region. Wisdom is needed in order to resist the drink of forgetfulness. A Vietnamese man who refused to drink the spiritual "soup of forgetfulness" serves as a curious example of a dry soul. He surreptitiously offered it to a companion – the soul of his dog who took the journey with him.[4] Consequently, the man recalled his inter-life journey as well as a past life. No one knows what happened to his canine companion.

Souls sometimes overcome amnesia by avoiding the drink of oblivion and choosing an optional beverage. Six variations of twin potions follow.

* Gnosticism (2nd century Egypt) – An immature soul drinks from "a cup filled with the water of forgetfulness" and forgets "all the regions to which it hath gone." That human being will be "continually troubled" in his heart.[5] In sharp contrast, a spiritually mature soul receives a cup filled with thoughts, wisdom, and soberness. When that soul is "cast" into a human body, the cup of soberness "whips" his heart until he seeks "the mysteries of the Light" and "inherits the Light forever."[6]

* Greek Orphics (500 BC Greece) – Intriguing gold tablets found in graves in south Italy and Crete (dating from 3rd or 4th century BC) contain explicit instructions for departed souls who wish a permanent place in Heaven: Do not quench your burning thirst in water coming from the fountain on the left with a white cypress tree growing near it. "O happy and fortunate one," ask the guardians for a drink from the cool water of the holy well of the Goddess Mnemosyne (Memory) and "you will be a god and not a mortal."[7]

* Zoroastrianism (ancient Persia) – Inhabitants of paradise drink from a range of purifying draughts: limpid water; rivers of milk – signifying rivers of knowledge; rivers of purified honey; wine which removes terror, fear, and sadness. Inhabitants of hell drink from four rivers as well: river of heat; river of water, blood and matter; river of liquid pitch; river of poison – meaning death, ignorance, simple ignorance, and compound ignorance.

* Macrobius (4th to 5th century Rome) – The "drink of the gods," the highest and purest nectar, sustains celestial beings; the "drink of the souls," the muddy drink from river Lethe causes human souls to stagger, forget their previous state, and experience rebirth.[8]

* Nigeria Ijaws (Africa) – Souls interested in material riches, children, and worldly possessions enter human life via muddy waters, whereas souls seeking spiritual powers enter via a clear stream.[9]

* Dante (Late Middle Ages, Italy) – Dante's vision of the mount of Purgatory includes the stream of Memory (Eunoe) running beside the stream of Forgetfulness (Lethe).[10] At the completion of the soul's purification in Purgatory, the soul

drinks of Lethe in order to forget its sins. Then it drinks of Eunoe, that it may retain memory of virtuous deeds. Thus sins are wiped out after penance. The soul begins heavenly existence with memory only of his good actions.

Ancient Greeks referred to the soul's awakening to its true identity, its celestial origin, as *anamnesis*, meaning the opposite of amnesia. Western philosophers, Sufis, Gnostics, Hindus, and Mormons offer further understanding of this phenomenon.

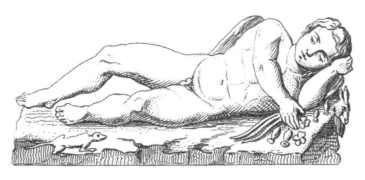

The ancient Greek symbol of forgetfulness, Hypnos, the God of Sleep.

Recipes for Gifted Memory

Amnesia of our heavenly life is imperfect;
light-carrying memories can pass through the veils.

Gifted memory is a natural part of our cultural heritage. Plato, Sufism, Middle Eastern Gnosticism, American Mormonism, American Transcendentalism, Hinduism, and Buddhism, to name just a few, teach that memories will arise as we ascend the evolutionary ladder of consciousness.

❀ Plato (ancient Greece) – "The soul then being immortal, having been born again many times, and having seen all things which exist, whether in this world or the world below, has knowledge of them all; and it is no wonder that she [the soul] should be able to call to remembrance all that she ever knew about virtue, and about everything ... for all inquiry and all learning is but recollection."[11]

❀ A. Bronson Alcott (19th century American Transcendentalist) – The soul's destiny is to see through the veil – to dispel "the oblivious slumber" and recover "for the mind recollections of its descent and destiny."[12]

❀ Epes Sargent (19th century writer) – The soul is like "a bird that is born in a cage," however, "nothing can deprive it of its natural longings, or obliterate the mysterious remembrance of its heritage."[13]

❀ Chwolson (Middle Eastern Harranites) – God endowed us with an intelligence and faculty of perceiving so that we can recall that we are strangers "down here."[14]

❀ Iranian Gnosticism – "My soul, O most splendid one ... whither hast thou gone? Return again. Awake, soul of splendor, from the slumber of drunkenness into which thou hast fallen ... . follow me to the place of the exalted earth where thou dwelledst from the beginning ... ."[15]

❀ Joseph F. Smith (19th century Mormon President) – The "power of the Spirit" allows us to "catch a spark from the awakened memories of the immortal soul, which lights up our whole being as with the glory of our former home."[16]

❀ Ramana Maharshi (20th century India) – "Forgetfulness of your real nature is the real death; remembrance of it is the true birth."[17]

Spiritual traditions handcrafted precise formulas for personal transformation and fine-tuning consciousness. An automatic by-product of ascending the ladder of consciousness is that memory is spontaneously restored. Examples range from ancient to modern times.

❀ Mystery Schools (ancient Greece) – According to Plato, students remembered their true "home," and experienced the "blessed vision of the higher intelligible natures" (*Phaedrus* 64) upon passing the severe tests of the Mystery schools.

❀ Paramahansa Yogananda (20th century India) – India's spiritual master came to arouse humanity's "sleeping memory of Immortality."[18]

❀ Hazrat Inayat Khan (20th century Sufism) – Khan did not teach "something new or different." He taught his students something which their souls already knew, but which their minds had forgotten.[19]

❀ Theodotus (2nd century Gnosticism) – "What liberates is the knowledge of who we were … where we were, whereinto we have been thrown; whereto we speed … what birth is, and what rebirth."[20]

❀ John Taylor (19th century Mormon President) – We are born as "one of the most helpless of all beings … . But when truth shall touch the cords of your heart they will vibrate; then intelligence shall illuminate your mind … and you shall begin to understand the things you once knew, but which had gone from you, you shall then begin to understand and know the object of your creation."[21]

The soul can look "into its own world," as the Sufis put it, during a vision or dream when "all the avenues of the senses are closed."[22] Or when the time is right, remembrances of celestial origins can pop out of the unconscious mind as spontaneous flashbacks during relaxation, meditation, or prayer.

A rest period, according to one report, revived a contemporary woman's memory of entering an amphitheater and meeting with three men dressed in white. Julie recalls waiting for the men to determine her birth time. She reflected upon how strange it would be "to go to earth and forget home." She knew a veil would fall over her mind once she passed through the white curtain hanging across the front of the theater – the consciousness barrier between her true home and human life.

"I understand ... what I'm getting into and what I have to do. But I cannot comprehend forgetting home. Please let me remember this experience and this room."[23]

Joan is another contemporary woman who recalls her pre-birth intention to overcome amnesia and strive for higher awareness.

"I had a lot ... to accomplish in my next life. I could not fail ... . It was easy here being without a body ... . I knew when I returned to the world a temporary amnesia would overcome me. I would forget my purpose and my mission ... ."

I resolved ... to become fully conscious in that lifetime, to overcome my imperfections ... . I wanted to be on earth as I was here, totally conscious of my existence. To realize that I was not simply a person, but that I was part of God ... ."[24]

Lethe's Drink –
A Blessing or a Burden?

Heresy? Insanity? Throughout the ages,
Western society has especially ostracized individuals
with gifted memory who dared to share them
in a public way – writing or speaking out.

Destiny *(Adrasteia)* decrees, according to Plato, that the soul which has been the companion of God and recalls most of the "Things Which Are" shall be born on Earth as a Seeker after True Wisdom and Beauty.

Mystical philosophers, however, face difficulties because they are gifted with divine sight and see everything as being radically different compared to worldly, striving men. Although hysteria and other disorders sometimes imitate this phenomena, Plato believed that the higher faculty, intuition, is at work in visions of eternal truth, goodness, and beauty. In actuality, philosophers are *entheast* meaning "immersed in God."[25]

When they behold a likeness or reminder of the holy things that they saw in that other world, they are immersed in a state of "wonder, but what it is that moveth them they know not, because they perceive nothing clearly."[26] They desire to "fly away" to their true home, yet cannot.

"... [the philosopher] is careless of worldly interests, being rapt in the divine, the crowds deem him mad."[27] "For they perceive not that he hath inspiration of God."[28]

Much like Plato's description of the mystical philosopher, 19th century England rebuked the rare awakening in William Wordsworth. The poet suffered severe criticism over his infamous "Ode on the Intimations of Immortality," a poem expressing sorrow at the inevitability of humanity's amnesia. Applying their own brand of spiritual censorship, English society and religious leaders pressured Wordsworth to disavow his sentiments because they gave "pain to some good and pious persons."[29] Wordsworth apologized without totally denying his inspiration.

Wordsworth's poem is based on the theory that a child is born with spiritual knowledge that is lost through contact with the world. We regain this knowledge only through "recollections" of our childhood. An excerpt follows.

> "Our birth is but a sleep and a forgetting:
>   the Soul that rises with us, our Life's Star,
> Hath had elsewhere its setting, and cometh from afar:
> Not in entire forgetfulness, and not in utter nakedness,
> But trailing clouds of glory do we come from God,
>   who is our home."[30]

Even more so than Wordsworth, Gerard de Nerval's reminiscences of pre-earthly existence cost him "the price of unspeakable suffering."[31] Friends of the 19th century French poet desired to hear more about "that mystic country" he had "half seen," but others among his countrymen labeled the inner journey that took place "in the mysteries" of his soul as just a "mental aberration" of an ill person. Gerard subsequently spent time living in an insane asylum due to society's difficulties in coping with his mystic experiences. Still his innermost spiritual encounters did not cease even in the asylum.

Paradoxically, Gerard's autobiography, *Aurelia*, recounts a powerful spiritual transformation: he never felt better than during his so-called "illness;" strength and energy doubled; he felt omniscient and understood everything; and his imagination gave him "infinite delight."

In one mystical dream, Gerard was mentally transported to an unfamiliar city set on a celestial mountaintop surrounded by numerous hills covered with homes. His soul wandered through busy streets until a youthful guide escorted him up a long flights of steps. At the summit, Gerard witnessed:

> "Here and there were terraces clad in trellises, small gardens laid out on a few level spaces, roofs, lightly-built summer-houses painted and carved with fantastic patience: vistas linked together by long trains of climbing verdure seduced the eye and delighted the mind

like a delicious oasis, a neglected solitude above the tumult and the noise below, which was here no more than a murmur."[32]

Gerard entered a terrace laid out as a garden where the "smiling eyes" of beautiful young girls and children "sought mine in soft compassion."[33]

"The light of their souls shone so vividly from their delicate forms
.... I cannot communicate the feelings I had among these charming creatures who, although strangers, were very dear to me."[34]

Being only "a momentary sojourner,"[35] Gerard trembled and wept "scalding tears"[36] at the thought of once again leaving that world of sweetness and beauty. Gerard's "heavenly family"[37] crowded around, trying to retain him. But, alas, their "enchanting forms"[38] dissolved into "confused vapors," their "lovely faces paled," and their "sparkling eyes vanished into a shadow where still shone the last gleam of a smile."[39]

Gerard's life ended mysteriously. Some said it was suicide; others suspected foul play.

Hymn of the Pearl

The Gnostic Hymn of the Robe of Glory symbolically illustrates how our "pneuma," or spirit, accidentally fell from a spiritual realm into the world of matter, succumbed to the lure of human life, and eventually remembered our divine heritage. This Gnostic story, written 1,800 years old ago, is preserved in the Acts of Thomas.

When I was a little child residing in my Father's house, my parents sent me from our homeland with provisions for a long journey. From the royal Treasure House, they supplied me with riches: "great it was, yet light, so that I might carry it alone."[40] Before my departure, my parents removed the Robe of Glory, which they had created for me, along with a Purple Mantle to conform to my figure. Next they made a covenant (cosmic contract) with me and wrote it in my heart:

> You must go to Egypt and bring back the Pearl lying in the middle of the sea. It is encircled by the terrible loud-breathing Serpent. When you complete your mission, you will return and put on your Mantle and your Robe of Glory again. Along with your brother, you will be an heir to our kingdom.

No one suspected my foreign heritage when I arrived in Egypt. I dressed like the rest and learned to eat their food. The "weight of their victuals"[41] produced in me a deep sleep. I became intoxicated by the poison of their world. I became unmindful of my royal ancestry while becoming a slave to their king and forgetting the mission for which my parents had sent me.

My parents waited in the light world for my return. They finally dispatched a letter in the likeness of an eagle. It alighted beside me. I rose from my sleep, kissed the letter, and read the same message my parents had inscribed on my heart:

You have fallen into bondage. Wake up. Remember who you are – the son of a king. But see whom you serve. See the slavery. Remember the Pearl for which we sent you to Egypt. Remember your Robe of Glory and Mantle. You will wear them again and we will inscribe your name in the book of heroes.

The message revived memory of my royal heritage and mission. I chanted the sacred names of my Father, Brother, and Mother, the East-Queen. In so doing, I charmed the snorting Serpent into a deep slumber and quickly snatched the Pearl. I then "stripped" myself of "their filthy and unclean garments,"[42] and resumed my spiritual Robe of Light and "Mantle of sparkling colours."[43] The Robe became "a mirror-image of myself: myself entire I saw in it, and it entire I saw in myself, that we were two in separateness, and yet again one in the sameness of our forms."[44]

I turned to the kingdom of my Father's House and ascended to "the Light of our Home."[45] I bowed my head and paid respect to the "King of Kings" and "Mistress of the East,"[46] their bidding I now had accomplished.

Cross-Cultural Parallels

The Jewish *Kabbalah* interprets the biblical story of Jacob's family moving into Egypt as a symbol of the soul's descent. And just as Jacob's family became enslaved and forgot where they came from, so it is when the soul enters human form. That is why the Hebrew word for Egypt is *Mizraim*, meaning "confined" and "limited."[47]

The English fairy tale *Snow White* tells a similar story of the "descent of the spirit into matter, awakening of consciousness and eventual return from whence it came."[48] The princess Snow White is forced to flee from her father's castle. She finds refuge with the Seven Dwarfs in the dark forest. There the wicked queen puts her into a deep sleep with a poison apple. The kiss of a handsome prince finally awakens Snow White. She marries the prince and returns to a happy life.

Thin Veils

*When people realize that they own a Mercedes,
instead of believing they are riding around in a Model-T
why would they continue to drive the clunker? Like that,
without the opaque veils woven by the senses, we would
yearn for our ancient abode. Moreover, oblivion makes
us eager to preserve ourselves in the present and fulfill
our earthly missions. This holds true even for perfected
souls such as Swami Vivekananda (1863 to 1902).*

As soon as the young child closed his eyes to doze off to sleep at night, a ball of brilliant light with changing colors appeared between the youngster's eyebrows. The light slowly expanded until it burst, "bathing his whole body in a flood of white radiance."[49] The experience repeated itself virtually every night, as the child was blessed with a supernormal faculty.

In a simultaneous vision dancing across his screen of consciousness, two possible destinies flashed before the boy's mind: a man of immense power surrounded by family and servants; or a renunciate who wore only a loincloth, ate whatever food came his way, slept under a tree, and lived in complete reliance on God's Will. During these precocious childhood experiences, the boy Narendranath Datta sensed that the second path would lead to true happiness. So the saint who would become Swami Vivekananda ("Bliss of Clearing Knowing") was born from the powerful experiences of inner illumination as a child named Narendra.

Student Meets Humble Master

Vivekananda's gift to the world was being "a sage from birth and even from before his present incarnation into the world of space and time."[50] The sage Ramakrishna and the young Narendra first met one morning at the Temple Garden. At a nearby university in Calcutta, Narendra had been studying the journals of the English poet Wordsworth. His British-born poetry professor, while discussing the poet's states of contemplative rapture, informed the class that a certain sage at nearby Dakshineswar entered similar states of transcendental suspension and absorption.

With his curiosity getting the better of him, Narendra travelled to the Temple Garden at Dakshineswar with one burning question for Ramakrishna: "Can God be directly perceived, and have you had this experience?"

Ramakrishna was not the first religious leader whom the revolutionary seeker Narendra had visited always asking the same question. Their answers came filled with complex qualifications and hesitation. As a result, Vivekananda had become a skeptical searcher of spiritual consciousness and was no less so with Ramakrishna. Ramakrishna's response was startling because of its simple, relaxed tone and direct message:

> Ramakrishna simply laughed with delight – his eyes swimming in tears of joy as he instantly recognized the spiritual stature of Narendra, inexperienced and somewhat brash as the young man might be … . "Of course, my dear," the blissful sage replied with tender affection, "Divine Reality can be experienced much more fully and directly than we are perceiving and understanding each other at this moment."[51]

Vivekananda sang Bengali songs at Ramakrishna's request. Ramakrishna recalls:

> "These were the spontaneous outpourings of a devout heart desiring union with the Self. He put so much pathos into the song that I could not control myself, but fell into an ecstatic mood."[52]

Afterward, Ramakrishna took the young spiritual seeker aside and told him –

> Ah! You have come so late. How unkind of you to keep me waiting. My ears are almost seared listening to the profane conversations of worldly people. Oh! How I have been yearning to unburden my mind to someone who can appreciate my innermost experiences.

> You are the ancient sage, Nara. You have taken the body to remove the misery of mankind. Before taking human form I prayed to the Divine Mother for having a pure-minded devotee of God in the world to talk with.

On Vivekananda's third visit, the Master confirmed his intuitions concerning who Vivekananda actually was. As they sat in the parlor, Vivekananda watched as Ramakrishna fell into a ecstatic state. Suddenly Vivekananda also lost consciousness of his own individuality. Though Vivekananda was ignorant of what happened, the Master asked him many questions while he remained in that state.

> – such as who he really was, where he had come from, duration of his mortal life, his mission in this world, and so forth. Vivekananda dived into his innermost being and found the answers to my questions. These answers confirmed what I had already seen in my visions and inferred about him. It is forbidden to tell all those things. But I can say that, he was a sage who had attained perfection, a past master in meditation, and that on the day when he knows who he really is, he will pass from this world by an act of free will, through Yoga.

As Mother Nature's plan took its inevitable course, Vivekananda became a disciple of Ramakrishna during the final five years of Ramakrishna's life. The new disciple's spiritual desire was to plunge into the region of True Divinity for five to six days at a stretch, and then to return to the sense-plane to maintain the body, and then again to revert to the state of *nirvikalpa samadhi*. The young aspirant desired to let go of the "little I," the ego, which creates the soul's bondage.

Paradoxically and unexpectedly, Ramakrishna rebuked his student's desire for personal liberation, calling it "a one-sided ideal." Ramakrishna prayed for Vivekananda to fulfill his earthly purpose first because Vivekananda's veil is "so very thin; it may give way at any time."

Not surprisingly, on one occasion, his veils came down for a few hours. As Vivekananda dove deeply within himself and meditated, he cried out to Gopal, his companion, "Where is my body?" Vivekananda was conscious only of his head; his body seemed lost. Then, Vivekananda's breath stopped and his body became rigid. Gopal alerted Ramakrishna, "Vivekananda has become utterly absorbed in the supra-cosmic silence of the Spirit." The master responded, "Let him stay in that state for a while. He has pestered me long enough for this realization."

Many hours later, Vivekananda returned to normal consciousness and described his inner experiences. To begin with, he witnessed a "great torchlight" playing at the back of his head. The light increased in size and brilliance until it burst and his mind entered a vibrant state of tempestuous rapture.

Every idea, impression, and image seemed to fall out of Vivekananda's mind. From this state of "Divine Bewilderment" he passed into "Utmost Ecstasy," where Divine consciousness saturated his personality until it vanished and Divinity remained. His soul finally merged as an immense light back into the infinite silence of peace. Vivekananda was in his early twenties when he had this ultimate spiritual experience of divine reality.

Whether Vivekananda liked it or not, Ramakrishna later instructed him:

> Just as a treasure is kept locked in a vault, so will this realization be locked up, and the key will remain with me. You have much work to do. You are a great banyan tree who is destined to shelter thousands of weary souls. You will shake the world to its foundations through the strength of your intellectual and spiritual powers. When you have finished your work, the treasure-box will be unlocked again; and you will know everything, as you did just now.

In this humble approach, Ramakrishna made it clear that inner liberation is incomplete without the outward action of love and selfless service to fulfill his cosmic contract. Thus, the whole of Vivekananda's life became an unceasing effort towards spiritually regenerating all of humanity.

> "It may be that I shall find it good to get outside of my body – to cast it off like a disused garment. But I shall not cease to work! I shall inspire men everywhere until the world shall know that it is one with God."[53]

Carrying on as Ramakrishna's chief disciple after the master passed on and had returned to the higher realms, Vivekananda founded the Ramakrishna Mission. Most notable among his accomplishments was a tour whereby he attended the World's Parliament of Religions at the 1893 Chicago World Fair. Thirty-year-old Vivekananda became the first enlightened being to journey from the East to the modern West. He arrived penniless and lacking formal invitation so he spent the first night sleeping in a railroad boxcar. Westerners were impressed with his brilliant spiritual lectures and simple universal message from India, "Truth is one: men call it by different names."

Cross-Cultural Parallel

The "great torchlight" reportedly processing at the back of Vivekananda's head appears to have been described by a contemporary mystic and author, Lorenzo Caravella. He names this subtle structure the Mouth of God, which also serves as the title of his new book on this and related topics.[54] Evidently few, if any, westerners have written so clearly and eloquently about this spiritual experience of higher consciousness prior to Caravella's transcendental research. Nonetheless, the uncanny parallel between Vivekananda's "great torchlight" and Caravella's "Mouth of God" experiences seems too similar to be anything except identical.

We begin our journey into this world from a hidden realm of the cosmos.

Chapter 28
Footprints in Heaven
Contemporary Gifted Memory

If we unlock the rooms of the far past, we can peer in and see ourselves busily occupied in beginning to become you and me.[1]
– James M. Barrie (1860 to 1937)
Scottish novelist and dramatist

*Pre-uterine memories transcend the physical –
the grey matter of our brain – known as "the
neurological substrate" that supposedly
makes memories biologically possible.*[2]

Contemporary individuals, who recall designing their cosmic contracts with guardian angels during pre-uterine existence, recount – as if it were yesterday – their existence as spiritual beings: floating and feelings of freedom, joy, unboundedness, lightness, comfort, and relaxation. In the majority of cases, they sensed a serene connection to everything in creation, a complete belonging, and being loved by all. Several persons perceived a world of beauty through refined senses. Others communicated telepathically at will.

Individuals with gifted memory, besides recalling their life prior to conception, in some cases report detailed memories of conception, life in the womb, and birth. Persons with such excellent modern testimonies parallel the more advanced modes of human birth outlined by Gautama Buddha thousands of years ago:[3]

- ❀ Advanced conscious birth – We enter our mother's womb knowingly, stay in it knowingly, and come out from it knowingly.
- ❀ Intermediate partially conscious birth – We enter our mother's womb knowingly, stay in it knowingly, and come out from it without knowing.
- ❀ Intermediate less conscious birth – We come into our mother's womb knowingly, stay in it without knowing, and come out without knowing.
- ❀ Least conscious birth – We come into existence in our mother's womb without knowing, stay in it without knowing, and emerge from the womb without knowing.

Included are gifted memory research from ten adults. Individuals were excluded who had deliberately probed for memories using rebirthing, hypnosis, psychoanalysis, or drugs, since some may consider such methods unreliable and too artificial, and yet these accounts share parallels with individuals reporting spontaneous recall.

Crib Musings

*Teresa is a thirty-eight-year-old mother and business
owner. Teresa's gifted memory surfaced before
she chose to utter her first words.*

Teresa's phenomenal memory includes hearing her parents
debating what to name her shortly after being born. Her father
preferred the name Teresa, while her mother liked Michaela. In the
end, "Dad won the discussion. Mom was not 100% pleased, but
was acquiescent."

More revelations are imbedded in Teresa's pre-conception
memories – thoughts she pondered over at two years or younger.

> I experienced peace as I lay in my crib. The deeper and more still
> the peace, the more beautiful it felt. I knew this Peace was God, but
> I also felt apart from Him. For some reason, my body made me feel
> separate.

> I tried to remember why I was blank, a clean slate, "Who am I?"
> There was more to me than what was happening at the moment
> because what was happening seemed so strange. I didn't understand
> my little fetus body which had just come out of my mother's womb.
> I could not figure out what my body was, what to do with it, or my
> attachment to it. But I knew one thing, I could not get out of it. It was
> as if I experienced mud on my face for the first time.

Baby Teresa wrestled with figuring out "Why am I here?" and
"What is going on?" and then remembered what happened in Heaven.

> I saw someone do an action which I perceived as less than worthy
> and I chose to judge him. I was trying to make myself better than
> him. I told my friend, "This person should not be able to get away
> with this. This is the most despicable thing and surely I am better
> than this being and deserve more appreciation from God."

> We are not supposed to judge in Heaven. The beautiful beings
> around me warned: "Do not think that way. Let those thoughts go." I
> had attacked my brother and brought that high energy level down.

I had a strong sense of wanting to be more special to God, to get more love from God. I began to think, "Why can't there be good and evil? Why can't there be specialness? Why can't I judge another?" I was dwelling on less than loving thoughts and forcing them into belief to see what would happen.

The more I thought about this, the more confused and miserable I became. I realized that by judging another, I had judged myself. I felt ashamed and did not want God to know. I had failed my Divine Creator by thinking that evil was possible and thinking my brother was "less than."

I felt all curled up in a ball like a little scared animal hiding in a hole. I did not want to talk to anybody and I would not come out.

Teresa "had taken it to the limit" and needed help getting out of this thought process. Several heavenly beings suggested that Teresa work with a guide to help her.

In order for me to believe that evil cannot exist, that specialness is not what I want, that judging my brother is not what I want, I needed to experience what happens when we think evil toward our brothers and judge them.

That is when I met this Divine Planner, a tall, stately gentleman who stood in front of a device similar to a podium, but it was more like a computer on the top. He was calm, cool, and collected. He talked about going to Earth: "Earth is set up for the purpose of healing the mind. Earth is a world built off of specialness. Specialness is the opposite of Heaven where God loves everyone equally. Specialness is when you give someone special favor over another, when you start judging others. Earth is where we see the result of the attitude or thought of specialness."

In Heaven, conversation was a "thinking back and forth, not using lips. Thought passed back and forth straight from the forehead – the easiest form of communication."

The guide told me, "Nothing will be held against you if you chose to go. You can think and act anyway you want to the maximum extreme. You can be anyway you want. You will not be judged or condemned. It will just be an experience of whatever you want to believe."

I kept saying, "There must be a catch." He replied, "No catch, no nothing. And anytime you want to get out, you can come back here."

"Well," I thought, "This sounds like the best deal in the world: think the way I want, act anyway I want, and if I want to come back here, I can come back." I said, "Okay, I am in."

Souls Waiting in the Wings for Birth

The Divine Planner worked with Teresa to set up her cosmic contract.

First, he asked, "Do you want to be male or female?" At that time, I was enjoying the female energy. So I said, "Of course, I prefer the female energy." It was a powerful loving energy, the coolest, more wonderful feeling. He warned, "Well, you will be persecuted if you are female on the planet. That is part of the deal."

I replied, "I don't care. I want to be female. I love the energy too much." When he punched my choice in on his keyboard, it was like going up to a bank teller. You are not sure what the teller does on the other side of the window, but you get your money.

Next the Divine Planner posed a choice of material status, "Rich or poor?"

I replied, "I prefer to be rich. I do not want to work too hard, to make a serious effort. Then he advised, "It will make it twice as hard if you are rich."

I asked, "Why is that?" He explained, "You learn from challenges." I did not know what to think about that, but I stuck to my decision. I liked the idea of wealth and not having to grovel or starve.

Deciding who to select as Teresa's parents was now deliberated by her divine guide.

I asked, "What is the best family to choose?" He said, "The highest family is the Brahmin family." I did not know a lot about the structure of the Earth, but I visualized the lifestyle of a Brahmin family. I said, "No, I don't want to do that. I want a cushy world, not a hard resilient world." But the guide explained, "Brahmins are 100% devoted to the worship of God in everything they do, in all their actions. Being born in a Brahmin family is a great fortune."

Teresa remained firm and so the heavenly planner made another selection.

My guide told me, "You will be born in a family in America and your parents will have a Christian background and belief in God." This was a good match because you can be born in a family that has no belief in God. He also told me about my brothers and sisters.

The Divine Planner chose a key person, "a male energy," to help Teresa learn the maximum.

The first thing I noticed was that he was hyperactive and seemed to bounce everywhere. They had him stand still in front of me. I looked at his heart and saw exactly who he was – his thoughts and feelings. This divine being had one thing I detested: zero compassion for children. I did not want anything to do with him. And the instant I showed lack of interest, he had no interest in me.

But then I realized, "If I do not do this deal with him, I won't reach True Thought, my goal." I turned around, looked at him, and proposed, "Let's make a deal. If you help me with my mental salvation, I will help you with your children." There was something in it for him so he was interested. "Deal," he said and turned away.

The Divine Planner asked the male partner questions after the agreement was made.

I did not key in 100% to what the Divine Planner told him, except I heard him ask, "Do you want to be rich or poor?" He replied, "Very rich." Then the guide talked to him about his family and birthplace. The guide set it up so that we would meet. The Divine Planner gave him everything he asked for.

This man agreed to help me on the planet and if I reach True Thought (learn why I don't want specialness, why I don't want money, and why I don't want to judge my brother), he will achieve the same goal.

Since this male person was to play such a major role in Teresa's life, the Divine Planner held his face still. "We were very close, face-to-face." The guide inserted the memory imprint of the male counterpart's face directly into Teresa's mind so that there was no question of identifying him on the planet. Then the heavenly planner turned to Teresa and added more details about the relationship.

"This man has a choice, but most likely he will choose the path of drug abuse." The Divine Planner showed me a vision of a man sitting on the ground with folded knees and his head resting on his knees. His arms were around his legs.

The heavenly guide explained that the man would be younger than me. My ego liked that: "Oh, a younger man." The guide even asked me if I minded having sexual intercourse with this man. I replied, "No, not at all. I would love to do that."

Next the Divine Planner asked if I wanted this man to physically harm me. I said, "No way." He explained, "You learn the divine lessons much quicker when these things occur." I said, "I don't care. I don't want the guy to hit me."

Souls Waiting in the Wings for Birth

(My husband has never physically abused me. For the personality he has played [drug addict], that is amazing. I have pushed his buttons, but it is not in the Divine Plan for him to hit me.)

Teresa resisted the next decision: "Choose an injury." Teresa replied, "I don't want to get hurt. Forget it. I am not choosing any kind of injury."

The Divine Planner told me, "You will learn from these things. You must select an injury." I finally agreed, "Okay, my hand." He was disappointed that I picked something minor, but made the entry into his computer.

(I broke my hand five years ago, a painful experience due to my ego. I was a black belt in martial arts school and a man was goading me because I did not practice with him. After he teased me three times, I put on the pads and decided we were going to have a round. Before he threw a punch, he went blank as if in a meditative state. The punch broke my hand. He did not do it on purpose. It was part of the Divine Plan. He felt terrible. This is what the ego does. It not only causes pain for ourselves, but for others.)

The Divine Planner finally told Teresa, "You must choose a death."

I said, "Now, wait a second." He explained, "You have a choice. You don't really have to die. You can follow the Divine Voice within and resurrect off the planet. This concept is simple, but it is not easy. Most people don't follow the Divine Voice and experience a physical death when their time is up. So you must choose a death. Remember you can get out of this anytime that you want."

Attaining Mental Salvation the Hard Way

Teresa was born into an environment where she had opportunities to attain mental salvation, her original goal.

I had divine experiences as a child because my thoughts were so open. I lived in the country and I could go outside and ponder and contemplate. I had a beautiful experience of God. Then when I was introduced to the world's concept of God and spirituality, I did not want anything to do with it. I saw that it could only cause misery. It left a bad taste in my mouth and I became confused.

By the time Teresa reached the age of seven, she chose forgetfulness as a temporary path to relieve her from the burden of the memories.

I shut down the memories and put them on the shelf. They did not fit in the world. Nobody else had these experiences. I got involved with the physical materialistic part of the world – personal appearance, physical form, who I was dating, my education, what kind of car to drive, and what kind of house I should have.

Not until about thirty years later did I have a memory recall and realize that my memories as a child were not an illusion. Everything fits. My husband even looks like he did in Heaven. We had adult bodies in mature form.

The family I was born into fits the description that the Divine Planner discussed. Mother was a Christian missionary. Dad was a minister. He spent his life thinking of nothing other than Jesus. Jesus was every other word. Every time he signed his name it was "Love in Christ." He had a fellow traveller's mission. He picked hitchhikers off the street, gave them clothes, a place to stay, food to eat, and sent them on their way.

I was placed in a family where I experienced specialness in a way that caused me to not desire specialness. My grandfather set up a trust for my father. By the time Dad returned to Heaven, he left myself and siblings a significant inheritance even when the IRS took half.

If Teresa could go back and Heaven and make her choices all over again, she would do it differently.

I went through thirty-five years doing what I wanted to do and making mistakes everywhere. When we don't follow the Divine Plan we are literally attacking our self and others. I went to church, but was not committed to God. I caused a lot of misery for myself and all around me. It took me a lot longer to get back to who I really am, and loving everybody the same. That is the whole purpose of my being on the planet.

Memory Gap

Julie's memories raise an interesting question:
Does the soul enter into the physical body in stages
until the body is developed enough for the entire soul?
(Julie's pre-conception dreams appear in Chapter 3.)

Julie, an elementary school teacher and mother of two, remembers a primordial state of consciousness prior to human birth. Then, there is a gap. Her next memory is learning how to function in a toddler's body.

> I remember one Sunday when I was two or three years old. My family had just returned from church services. I was wearing my Sunday clothes: white dress, black patent leather shoes, and white socks. I entered the kitchen to feed my cat. All of a sudden, I looked at my hands, and I felt shocked, "Oh my God, how did I get here?" – meaning "How did I get in this body?"
>
> And then I remember not being born yet. All I experienced was pure consciousness. Next I experienced a darkness becoming lighter, grey, and then twinkling lights or stars. As a child, whenever I closed my eyes, I had this twinkling light sensation. It was very familiar to me.

In another childhood realization, Julie stood on a church pew and turned to look around. A woman in the pew behind Julie placed a nickel coin in her palm. Once again, as Julie looked at her hand, "there was a recognition of being in a body."

After these early experiences, a veil remained over Julie's memories until the age of twenty-three. She spontaneously remembered "the whole thing again" after regularly practicing a meditation technique to reduce stress. Now it is "permanent memory."

> Today I still have the same experiences I had as a child. I observe my hands and find it fascinating that I am localized because I feel that I am so much more than this body. But I am somehow contained in this body, living this human life, going through all that I go through.

Something about being in this body has captivated me ever since childhood. Now I am at the point of figuring the whole thing out. Is this a movie being played out, a script that I am saying? What is free will? What is determinism? Who am I? Isn't this lifetime intriguing – just the way my life is set up and what I go through and what other people encounter? Isn't it fascinating that I am living the life that I am living with the emotions and experiences that I have?

This is an interesting lifetime because I feel universal and individual at the same time.

A Toddler's Unlimited Possibilities

*At the age of three, Judy, a fifty-year-old
mother of two, recalled her footsteps in a higher world.*

Since early childhood Judy had strong feelings of not belonging to this physical plane by knowing – from direct memory – that in the past she had unlimited potential. The toddler was stumped by her confined abilities: "Why can't I immediately fulfill a desire? Why can't I walk through walls or levitate? Why is my body so cumbersome? Why can't I just flow through the room? Why do I have to walk and bump into things? Why is there pain?"

My memories were so strong that I knew my experience of limitations was incorrect. And yet no one else seemed confused. Everyone seemed comfortable with the way things were. It felt like being in a zoo with people who were happy not to question anything. I thought, "Is this a nightmare or a dream? Reality was hard to discern. Of course, being only three years old, I was too young to articulate.

Earthly pleasures were not enjoyable like they were for everyone else. I was amazed by how much emphasis people put on material possessions. I felt it was a cheap imitation of what I knew to be a thrill. It would have been more exciting to manifest a Christmas tree rather than to buy one. Or why have a toy plane when you are used to flying through the air yourself? Every material object became a disillusionment. I also did not understand ownership. Taking possession of things as mine seemed wrong or artificial. It made no sense, "You mean I am supposed to be thrilled because this toy is mine and not yours?" It felt like I owned everything and everybody else owned everything.

Higher consciousness was Judy's dilemma. Judy was alert to discovering the nature of her "true origin," but years went by before she understood there was nothing wrong with her perception of the world.

Growing up, I felt very much the loner. Then, by my late 20s, I began meditating and met people who understood higher consciousness and I was given the vocabulary to express my reality. I resonated with spiritual teachings on higher consciousness because that was my experience. By the age of thirty, I had met people who resonated perfectly with me on an experiential level. We could talk about the same reality. Just those few connections, six-twelve people, made all the difference knowing that others are having a similar reality and feel very alone.

My life still does not match the memory I came in with of having unlimited potential and using it. But I have picked up some understanding of why that is – this is a different dimension than the one I came from. Each dimension has its own challenges, obstacles, and limitations. I feel at peace with that. Still I wonder, "Why did I come here?" I have forgotten, but I have learned to enjoy without knowing all the answers. I trust there is some reason for choosing this.

Cosmic Contract
with Strings Attached

Robert has been practicing and teaching meditation techniques since the early 1970s. Even as a child, Robert had vague memories of the space between life and death. These memories became more clear through experiences of meditation.

Robert recalls a conversation with a guide prior to rebirth. He was given two choices as to when to be reborn.

If I incarnated in 1948, I would be a spiritual pioneer, paving the way for others on the path to enlightenment. I would incur much good karma by taking this difficult path and removing roadblocks for others. On the other hand, if I waited twenty years, my life would be easier, but I would not be a pioneer.

I chose 1948. I also selected my father whom I loved. I wanted so much to be with him. My guide explained how that choice involved a packaged deal – it included my mother and brother, and karma to be worked out with these people. I remember being almost impulsive about my decision. Even though part of me looked with chagrin at being with my mother and brother, I thought, "I will be strong enough to handle anything. The positive factors of being with my father will outweigh the negative."

As a young child, I was drawn to my father. I yearned to have a strong bond with him, yet he was uncommunicative. It was a good, positive relationship, however he was distant, too removed for my liking. For instance, I wanted to go camping with my father, but we always did things as a family unit.

We did our most bonding when Dad got cancer. I was sixteen – old enough to drive Dad back and forth to the hospital, and relate to him as a man. We shared some closeness for the next two years. My desire to establish a stronger bond for a longer time never came to fruition. It was a bud just starting to open. Then Dad died.

Veiled Promise

A gifted memory first popped into Mary's awareness at the age of five or six.

I was attending Sunday school classes which were held upstairs in the main church parlors. I recall walking downstairs through a quiet, empty hall in order to go to the rest room. I was all alone. On my way back, I suddenly remembered that someone had promised me something wonderful and I thought, "When will I receive the special knowledge?" I knew I was destined to learn or experience something extraordinary. It had been agreed upon. I looked forward to that day, but I wondered, "When will it happen?"

As a young child, Mary did not know who promised her this knowledge or even what it represented.

I anticipated that I would experience something beyond the normal. There was no doubt. It was a given. It was merely a matter of "when." A few years later, my Sunday school teacher spoke to our class about a conversion experience. When he talked about this spiritual transformation, I thought, "Oh, so this must be what I have been promised. When it will happen?"

Mary was secretive and did not mention the promise to anyone for over thirty years.

I had learned to keep unusual events private. At an earlier age, my mother had discouraged my clairaudient experiences. Subsequently even to this day, that ability is lost or suppressed due to lack of use.

Later when I looked back at the events in my life, I suspected that attaining a higher consciousness – my chief goal in life – is related to the goal that I had been promised before entering my mother's womb.

Spiritual transformation is being sought by many people today, and this story represents one example among countless cases.

Path of Thorns,
Smell of Roses

*The memories of Glen Beicker, a retired
military intelligence officer, confirm that souls
waiting for birth are aware when couples are fertile
and having sexual intercourse. Up until now, Glen
has shared his memories with only a few people.*

Glen becomes irritated whenever people complain about their parents.

> When I hear people curse their parents, I want to tell them, "Look you fool, you chose your parents. You are to blame, not them." But I don't do that because if you are not careful, people will label you as a kook.

Heaven's Powers of Observation

Glen's memories go back to being in the midst of an assembly of souls standing on a long ledge in a high place and observing the Earth. It was "like looking down from an airplane or dirigible [blimp], only we were standing on something solid."

> There were souls to my right and souls to my left. We looked like human beings and wore full-length white kimonos. Each soul had a messenger standing next to him. By their attitude and actions, I knew which ones were the directors. I heard different conversations going on around me. Some souls were pointing down to the Earth and selecting parents.
>
> My messenger stood on my right and held me by the arm. I felt like a student and he was a full-fledged teacher. He had superiority over me. My guide looked like a human being and wore a white gown, too. What is so amazing is that I looked at these messengers and visualized that I would return to this place in the hereafter.

The guide presented Glen with a choice of three couples: a very wealthy one, an average one, or a poor family. Looking down, he observed the couples having sexual intercourse. All the wives were fertile.

1. *Wealthy couple* – The rich couple were the oldest – early 40s or late 30s – and were on the pudgy side. They did not mess around. They entered the bedroom, disrobed, and got on with the program. In those days, it was fashionable to have a wooden bed with an elevated head and footboard. They had a walnut bed with spindles on the corners. I also noticed a matching dresser and chest of drawers.

   My guide explained, "If you are born into this family, you will breeze through life and encounter the least amount of trouble. Your reward will be the smallest."

2. *Middle income couple* – The youngest couple did a little kissing and caressing before intercourse. The wife was stout and the husband was a large tall man. Their bed had an elevated metal head board – three or four feet high along with a high metal footboard. Both had vertical metal spokes in them.

   My guide advised, "In this family, you will have some problems, but not too great. You will earn an average reward."

3. *Poor couple* – This couple was the smallest in physical size. When I started talking to my guide, they were riding along a quiet country road in an old car and stopped before they reached home. The husband and wife were petting and smooching in the front seat. Pretty soon, he laid her on her back and the car door opened. The wife looked in the back seat. The little girl child was sound asleep on her back with her arms up. Her feet pointed toward the driver's side.

   My guide told me, "If you go to this family, you will have many trials and tribulations. You will never reach your potential. It will be in the cards that you experience frustration."

   I asked, "If I take the couple with the most trials, my reward will be the greatest, won't it?" [meaning the spiritual reward will be greatest in the hereafter] My guide explained, "That is right. But with the other two, you will just about have it made. But with this third one, it will be frustrating to pass God's test. Part of your trial is not to totally achieve what you are capable of."

Glen had no special feelings towards the couples' material wealth.

It was a matter of choosing what degree of salvation I wanted –
an easy trip or a trip where I wanted to prove myself. My guide
instructed, "You decide which one you want." I replied, "I want the
one with the greatest trials." I wanted to shoot for maximum
salvation. My guide asked me, "Are you sure this is what you
want?" I answered, "Yes, I do."

Next Glen felt himself enter a huge tunnel – it reminds him of air
conditioner ducts on trailer houses, a big round duct.

I flew down through that tube at a terrific speed. Lights from a
narrow light band flashed by. The lights wrapped all through that
tube, like a red stripe on a peppermint candy cane. The light circle
never broke. It went with me. It was dark except for the band of light.
The light was on the outside of the tube and it was transparent, and
you were looking through it, but you weren't looking through it, it
was just a band of light. That is the last thing I remember. The next
thing I knew I was a little boy.

Cruising Down a Texas Country Road

Glen's parents conceived him in the spring of 1929. When he was
four years old, his aunt passed away. Glen overheard his family
talking about his aunt going to another place and "memories of
these other people and places came back." His gifted memory
made no sense and confused the youngster.

I did not talk about that place I came from and those people I
was with until I was seven and started school. My mother replied,
"Where did you get that idea from?" I said, "Was I placed with you
and Dad when you were in a car?" Now my mother came from an
old German family and cut me off post haste, "What are you talking
about? We don't talk about that kind of stuff. That is not decent."

My mother thought it was just childish chatter. I kept quiet after
that. Still the memories did not stop going through my mind.

By his early twenties, Glen wanted to put a few things at peace:
"Are my memories true or some quirk of nature in my mind?" He
flew home to confront his parents.

I got Mom and Dad together. I said, "Do you know where I was
conceived?" My mother said, "That is something I haven't thought
about in years." I said, "Suppose I supply some details. Can you
confirm them?" My parents looked at each other and said, "Yes."

I asked, "Was it on the front seat of that old 1917 Overland car?" My mother turned to my father and said, "Gus, you haven't been talking?" He answered, "No, Hilda, you know I would not talk about that. Did you say something to this boy?" She said, "No." My parents had turned red in the face.

I shared my memory and explained that they were monkey-messing, etc. … . I recalled all the details. It had happened twenty-five years earlier yet the memory had been branded in my mind as if it were yesterday. My parents confirmed everything. They were awed by my memory and somewhat embarrassed.

Following our discussion, the subject was dropped and never mentioned again for the rest of their lives.

(My parents never discussed sex or taught me the facts of life. Nor did they ever let us joke about sex. And there was no show of public affection in these old German families. My parents were married over fifty years and I saw Dad kiss my mother twice.)

Gifted memory taught Glen four lessons:

1) Life begins at conception, not when we are born. 2) We choose parents. 3) There are degrees of salvation. We can get in at the bottom or higher up the ladder, depending upon how we fare with earthly trials. Those who succeed, solve, or overcome get the biggest rewards. 4) God gave us free agency. We make choices throughout our lives and even choose parents before birth.

I am fortunate to remember. The eraser did not work quite right on me. I am ten steps ahead of people who must figure this out on their own. And most never do.

Choosing Trials and Tribulations

Glen never forgot his spiritual guide's instructions: "Your tribulation will be to not achieve your potential."

I have been at the edge of fame many times, but never reached notoriety. Other people got the limelight even though they did not do much. For instance, I figured out a medical invention, but a doctor stole the idea and made millions. These things do not bother me in the least because I know the reason.

Tribulations included narrow escapes from death. In 1961, in one case, Glen's military plane crashed and he bailed out 3,000 feet above the ground. At first, no one believed he had survived. Military officers arrived at Glen's home to notify his wife, "Glen died in a plane crash." She knew it was not true. Glen called home moments later. His wife handed the phone to the officers and asked, "Do you want to talk to a dead man?" Glen walked away without a scratch.

I was shot several times. Another time I was knocked off a bridge and fell thirty-six feet. I was saved by landing on a slant and sliding down. I have had many chancy experiences and come out smelling like a rose. I lost a brother at fifty, a daughter at forty-two, and a son at forty. They did not live a dangerous life like me. God must have something waiting for me or He would have taken me long ago.

Glen's cosmic contract included two strokes at the age of thirty-three.

I had a lot of push. If it is worth doing, it is worth doing right. But I was under-exercised, weighed 255 pounds, and stressed out with my career. Besides two strokes, doctors repaired my heart and gave me a pig valve. They removed half my colon, small intestines, and stomach. The doctors put me on morphine for pain.

I was hospitalized for fifteen months. I weighed 128 pounds when I went home. The doctors gave me two years to live. I could not walk, stand, or hold my head up. I lay in bed and stuck my legs and arms up in the air, and moved them around until I fell asleep. When I woke up, I started all over. I broke myself of the morphine habit – cold turkey.

Thirty years later, doctors diagnosed Glen with cancer.

I had nine surgical procedures over a two-year period. During the first major surgery, the doctor gave me morphine. Now morphine is lethal to me because of my hospital experience with morphine in 1962. My heart stopped for four minutes. I floated out of my body. I looked down and recognized my body lying on the table. I saw the doctor, nurse, and anesthetist. The doctor had put huge clamps – like carpenter's clamps – to hold me open in order to operate on my intestines. Next I floated through the wall and observed my wife sitting there, along with my brother-in-law, daughter, and preacher.

I never felt so good. I had no desire to return. All my material possessions meant absolutely nothing. They meant less to me than a burnt cigarette.

Right then my deceased son Glen, Jr., appeared and told me matter-of-factly, "Papa, you must go back. My two children will need you as they grow up. I can't be there, but you can."

Glen, Jr., asked his father to do him another favor. He talked about his Lionel toy train set, a prized possession from his childhood, and some antique heirlooms.

"Papa, give them to my children after they grow up and have their own homes. I hid them so that my wife would not toss them out. You will find them in the airplane hangar next to an old kitchen cabinet. Look for the box in the northeast corner of that cabinet underneath a box with parts to repair aircraft fuel tanks. I left a message in the box explaining what to do."

I wanted to ask about his mother, my first wife, but my son pointed to a big dark oval archway, and said, "Papa, you must go back. But you will come again. I will wait for you. I will meet you and we will go over to the other side together."

The decision to return was up to me and I chose to satisfy my son. He had left behind a six-year-old son and a three-year-old daughter. Family was more important than my present peace of mind – I would have that peace again one of these days anyway.

Glen observed a second scene while he conversed with his son. He saw the doctor raising hell with the staff because Glen's heart had stopped. There was no respiration and a proper machine was not hooked up.

The nurse tried to start my heart with adrenalin, but there was no reaction on the monitor. Next, they placed a large thing like a big balloon over my face and pushed both sides together at the same time to get me to breathe. The doctor rushed around trying to hook up a machine that had these two big circles to give electric shocks. He put on rubber gloves, laid a wet towel on my chest, and gave me three shocks. On the third time, I started to get a heart beat.

That is when my deceased son pointed to the oval archway and started to fade away. It felt like I was slipping down a hillside and there was nothing under me. As I descended toward my body, I started to feel pain. It became more intense as I neared my body. I hovered above my body and felt my feet enter this thing [body] below me first. I went down into it. I locked back into my regular body.

All of a sudden, the next thing I knew, I was looking the doctor and nurse in the face. They were worried about whether I was going to make it.

After the surgery, Glen asked his wife about the people he had seen in the waiting room. She wondered, "How did you know they had been here?"

The Hidden Train

About one week after Glen's NDE —

I walked out to the hangar as soon as I felt strong enough. I didn't realize my second wife was following. She was worried about me. I was so weak. She set back a little ways and watched. I found the items for my grandchildren exactly where my son told me. Inside the box was a handwritten note, "Dear Papa, please save these things for my children … . Explain to them the history of it … . "

I sat down and cried. My NDE was not a stretch of the imagination. My wife came over and threw her arm around me and said, "That is what you were talking about when you came out of the anesthesia and we did not listen."

Optimism – "a Big Key to Survival"

Glen took life too seriously before his stroke at age thirty-three. Then "God shook me up and put me back on the right track." And until his NDE, Glen feared death and did not want to die. But after all Glen has gone through, death is his least concern now. He worries more about getting up in the morning and feeling good. Glen intends to leave the world a happier place.

When negative things happen to me, I have a positive attitude and joke about them … . I am going on seventy, but do physical work that young kids back away from. I have all my hair, and except for my moustache, I have no gray hair … . When people have a genuine need, I help them. I don't walk around with blinders, and to hell with everyone else, and I am number one.

Glen's NDE revealed how to find the treasured items.

A Million Stars

*Sage remembers her own conception and birth
even more clearly than those of her three children.*

Sage's memories stretch back to a period long ago when she
existed as a conscious being in "spirit form." It was like a gram-
matical "comma," a temporary break from the physical dimension.
She remembers isolating herself in a soul form, long before she
prepared to be born this time. A quiet permeated that spirit realm
which Sage has craved ever since – "a quiet that totally restores, the
deepest rest you can imagine. Everything in balance."

Sage floated in a "vacuum," feeling safe and protected. Once in
human form, Sage missed the love, joy, peace, and comfort of pre-
earthly life. Over the next forty-two years, Sage returned to that
"Realm of Quiet" four times. One incident happened in childhood,
another in the middle of a conversation.

There is nothing schooled about having the experience. It is
beyond my ability to consciously go there. It is not available unless
my consciousness goes far out of body. And when I do, I can't
experience it for very long.

The experience is so "beyond." There is no place remotely like it,
no reprieve like that. It can be frightening because there are no
boundaries in that space. All of a sudden, I can be totally spread out
everywhere, like turning into a million stars. Part of me craves it, but
my ego is frightened because it is hard to find my focal point. "Oh,
no. I am going to lose my attachment here!" There is something
unsettling about it. My mind tries to make sense of it, but it is part of
the "great mystery" which I cannot begin to understand.

Family Cosmic Contracts

Each family member would play a special role in Sage's life.

Souls Waiting in the Wings for Birth

The family patterns were clear … the positive and negative. I could see the blessings and the burdens. I felt close to and loved several of the souls in this family unit and I wanted the experiences.

I had strong connections to my oldest sister, Dad, and my grandmother on my mother's side. My grandmother and my oldest sister were "seers" so my family was familiar with higher sensory perception. I felt safe coming into a family who understood my gifts. I knew my sister would support me regardless of whether my mother tried to shut us down, which is exactly what my mother tried to do. Our abilities terrified her.

Couples think they live in a private sexual world, and yet souls seeking birth can be in the neighborhood, especially during coitus.

I remember slipping in during noon hour. Dad came home and mother was cooking lunch. He said, "Drop everything and let's go into the bathroom."

My mother said, "Well, I have to put on my diaphragm." He replied, "No, it won't hurt this time." I thought, "Now is my chance. Here is my door."

So it is no accident that I was born with eating disorders, a food obsession. My parents conceived me at the noon hour; their lunch meal was interrupted. And my daddy is a compulsive, obsessive person who squeezes life for all it is.

I waited until adulthood before discussing conception memories. My mother freaked out. She screamed, "How could you know that? We did have sex at lunch and I felt like I became pregnant because that was the only time we did not use a diaphragm."

Cross-Cultural Parallel

Sage's gifted memory of choosing parents, similar to Glen's, parallel what Buddhist scriptures say: the intermediate being sees the prospective parents engaged in sexual intercourse. The intermediate being unconsciously jumps into the human realm and finds itself nestled in a womb.

Remote-Sensing in the Amniotic World

Sage's awareness of the outer world continued in the womb.

As a child, I recited word-for-word a speech that I heard President Eisenhower deliver while I was in the womb. It blew my parents away. I also recalled Mom and Dad's discussion of the speech.

Another gifted memory embarrassed Sage's mother.

My father and my mother's sister had a sexual affair during my mother's pregnancy with me. My mother denied the affair. She knew, but she did not want to consciously know. She felt terrified. At the same time, I watched Dad sitting on the porch and crying, "What are we doing having a fourth child? [referring to Sage who was in the womb] I am not even with the family that I have now."

I told Mom that I was aware of Dad's affair during my wombtime. She said, "Yes, you are right. They started their affair when you were in the womb, but I did not find about it until five years later."

Because I knew about the affair, I tried to babysit my father through it. As a child, I did things like sitting in between Dad and my aunt at church. During childhood, I felt angry towards my mother for being unconscious about it, but she contended with it as soon as she could.

Sage arranged to be born with an intuitive sister.

Even though my grandmother had been a "seer," mother did not appreciate anything but ordinary, everyday stuff. She labeled my grandmother insane because she foresaw the death of her two-year-old son (my mother's brother). The prediction frightened my mother. She did not want to "see." What if she foresaw the death of a child? Mother could not cope with that.

Because of these fears, my mother did not allow me and my sister to discuss our visions and inner experiences with spirit guides. So we did everything in the closet. Without my sister, I probably would have stopped believing. We still share thought forms today, even when we are thousands of miles apart.

Twilight Birth

The doctor advised Sage's mother to use drugs during labor.

I had entered the birth canal. If my mother had given three good pushes, I would have been out. Instead, she took the drug Twilight and had an out-of-body experience. She went completely dead on me. She did not have the soul-urge to push. I was furious. I thought, "If things get rough in this life, don't lean on mother. She'll leave."

It felt good to be born, even though I was wet and the cold air hitting my face felt uncomfortable. The doctor didn't put me in my mother's warm arms. She was gone for two days. I missed her heartbeat. Twilight gave my mother a wonderful experience of floating out of the body, one that went beyond her ability to put into words. But I was angry. Without a mother to bond with, I experienced an emotional vacuum and later I found life jarring and unnourishing. Fortunately, my daddy held me – a rare event since doctors typically did not allow fathers to participate.

Awareness of the spiritual world has been a constant companion throughout Sage's life. Even as an infant she recalls —

I saw winged ones, little bright-winged creatures around me in my crib. I also had an NDE at two-and-one-half. I died of double pneumonia. Archangel Uriel asked me if I'd consider coming back.

Falling to Earth

*Katarina knew that the whole universe was
contained inside of her consciousness. But within
a few months following birth, she quickly became
"an innocent, tiny baby and part of this world."*

Even as a child, Katarina was aware that gifted memory can
fade, just as a muscle atrophies from lack of exercise and use.

At the age of four, I experienced several incidents of lying in bed,
consciously remembering my birth. I recognized its importance and
told myself that I must remember. Forever after, I'd mentally review
the experience so that I'd never forget.

Katarina's memories nonetheless became dormant for a while –
as if "second-hand" – until she was in her early twenties.
Spontaneous recall came as a natural outgrowth following a six-
month course in consciousness development, much like removing
the clouds to realize the sunshine is always there. Katarina's gifted
memory has been "refreshed and remarkably clear" ever since.

Katarina's gifted memory goes back to a "place of pure light,"
"intermittent between lives" where she enjoyed the freedom and
movement of being without a physical body. Katarina used remote-
sensing capabilities of the soul instead of the sensual experiences of
hearing, vision, smell, taste, and touch, used in a physical body.

My individuality was barely "audible." That is the best way I can
describe it. I had a subtle feeling of myself. All my senses became
unified. Everything was one. Yet, there was still a subtle "my-ness,"
identity, ego, an individuality. I felt the presence of God, of not being
totally one with God, but being in God's womb, so to speak.

I was aware of other souls close by. It's hard to explain because
there was no space and time. Yet there was still the present, and other
souls coming toward and going away from me.

A loving, wise guide helped plan Katarina's next life.

Souls Waiting in the Wings for Birth

Before I came into this body, I desired to achieve the maximum in terms of clearing up karma and reaching complete enlightenment. When the time came to establish my next lifetime, I travelled through a tunnel filled with lights representing the laws of nature [astrological aspects], and different people.

I had an ongoing dialogue with an angel, God, an aspect of God, or Saint Peter. It is hard to say exactly who he was. We discussed what I needed and how to achieve my purpose with particular individuals. I saw my goals as well as all the choices that I could make. It was like looking at a computer board, only the computers seemed like stars [and planets]. When I saw a quality I needed, like kindness or compassion, I pressed the corresponding light. Then, in a milli-second, I witnessed a panoramic view of roads I could take with different people in order to fulfill those objectives.

It is not as if my consciousness said: "Give me a good life," "I want to be rich," or "I want to be pretty." It was simply, "It would be good for me to be rich or good for me not to be." Or "It would be good for me to have the criterion for wealth – kindness – and once I established that quality, the wealth would come."

I emphasized certain choices more than others. Since enlightenment was a major goal, I made a special effort toward having my spiritual master. There was no other path for me. I did not allow any leeway. And nothing in this life has interrupted my relationship with my teacher.

As part of the plan, Katarina planned to be born into a family with Susan as an older sister. The sisters had evolved through "many, many lifetimes" together. A "soul magnetism" brought them together again. Katarina, in contrast, does not recall selecting parents.

Yet I do remember that my parents needed to have a deep level of spirituality that did not fit into a little cubbyhole. They needed to be yogis in their own right. As it turned out, my parents are not dogmatically religious. My mother knows greater truths than those presented in traditional Christianity. Because of my mother's openness, as a child, I could say, "Do you remember your birth, Mommy? I remember mine." My mother did not ridicule my beliefs. A lot of parents do. Without this upbringing, I would not have had the same spiritual experiences as a child.

Insertion of the Soul into the Maternal World

Katarina recalls the sensation of leaving the place where she had established her cosmic contract and the descent into matter.

I travelled through space and time which literally looked like flashing stars. It is a very fluid motion of space and time, from death to life and life to death. Obviously I did not have eyes and ears. I had nothing physical to perceive with. However my senses were in play. I became one sense. All the senses became one, travelling through space and time, and coming into the womb. So there was some entity that was myself that had these tools at its disposal.

I remember finding myself in this physiology, of coming into my body in my mother's womb for the first time. I knew I was going to be born, recalled former lives, and knew I was coming from an intermittent place between earthly lives.

Having a body felt pleasant. I stretched out and felt my hands and body, even my fingers. I thought, "Oh great, I have a physiology again." All my body parts had already formed. I felt contented. Sometimes I heard voices and sounds outside my mother's womb – my mother, sister, brother, and children playing. My parents were happy. Of seven children, I was the fourth and the only one planned. I was a product of a fortunate time. That is probably why I'm so happy.

Katarina had no concept of time, of how long she waited in the womb.

But at one point, a sudden click signalled that birth was getting underway. There must have been a hormonal infusion in my body. I remained alert and comfortable and felt my head moving downward. But just as I reached the birth canal, I could not breathe. I heard my mother scream, "You're going to kill my baby. Get off of me." She was upset and terrified.

I thought: "Maybe I'm not going to be born." I felt lackadaisical and consciously left the body. It was a gentle and slow pulling away from the body. There was a different sensual aspect to being out of the body, hovering above the woman on the table [her mother]. But then, with a quick snap, I was wham, back in really fast. I thought, "Well, I am going to be born." I felt a burst of cool air on my face, an overwhelming coldness hit my body, and a rush of cold air enter my lungs.

If I close my eyes right now, I can see the delivery room – angle of the bed, the angle of the birth coming out, how the doctor lifted me, and the direction I faced. I looked around and saw the doctor and attendants, but their features were blurred. They wore hospital outfits, without the masks. (Later, my mother explained that the staff did not have time to wear masks because of the fast delivery.)

Everyone appeared red. Yet, there was no red lighting in the room. Maybe pressure on my eyes caused the redness or it came from opening my eyes for the first time. Since I was blue at birth – barely there – it may have even been due to lack of oxygen.

I saw everyone's face, but mother's. The doctors had put my mother out [anesthesia]. I only remember that she was conscious until my birth. It felt unpleasant to be separated. The nurses pulled me out into the cold, wrapped me up, and took me to the nursery. I did not really understand "mother," but I felt a yearning, a sad feeling of being alone, a cold feeling in my heart. I felt psychologically and emotionally out of sorts, but I did not know why.

Even though Katarina recalls the fetal near-death experience, she did not understand the cause of it. Twenty-three years later, Katarina's mother revealed the reasons.

My mother was conscious for most of my birth and answered my questions about what pinched the umbilical cord and interrupted my oxygen supply as I came down the birth canal. On the day before my birth, the doctor blamed a nurse for delivering a stillborn by herself. So that nurse became frightened when my mother began to deliver before the doctor arrived. She tried to slow down the process by sitting on her knees and holding her legs together. My mother knew you do not interrupt delivery like that and frantically fought the nurse's efforts.

During her first months, Katarina saw "big faces looking down at me."

The faces of my mother and father hovered above my bassinet. They were parents, yet until I was five or six, they appeared greater that that. They protected me. They translated into God up above in Heaven. It's interesting to see how children gain this perspective on life. I also recall biting my mother's breast as she nursed me. She squealed. I pulled back and laughed. She then laughed at me laughing at her. I remember where my mother sat and which room we were in. I may have been as old as my four-month-old because he's starting to bite, pull back, and grin. It's a game and he gets my reaction. It creates a sensation on his gums. Even though it hurts me, it's charming. He can interact with me and I never get angry.

Katarina's "traumatic birth was a set up."

And the set up worked. I'm glad I experienced it that way. It is a gift. My memories enriched the births of my five children. I knew that I was giving birth to an alert, conscious individual. Babies come in very wise, aware of other lives and of what they are coming in for. But then within a few months, they lose this wisdom and become giggly, innocent, charming little babies.

Born with the Atomic Bomb

*Neil is another soul in the world who
knew whom he would be born to and was intent
on what he had to accomplish in this life.*

Neil made a choice to re-enter the Earth in 1945 right with the dropping of the first atomic bomb on Hiroshima. The state of the world was precarious and he volunteered to help uplift the planet in a time of global crisis.

Since my birth marks the ending of World War II and the first atomic bombs symbolizing the war's end, every year at the time of my birthday my mother told me, "When you were born, I prayed for permanent peace and that my little boy would never go to war."

My recollections of an intent to be reborn go back to early childhood and prior to my mother's pregnancy. Ever since learning to walk and talk, I recall the purpose for my being in this world and that my parents helped provide that opportunity.

Neil selected parents partly because they were friends from another lifetime.

As a young child, I had an inner feeling that they were old friends more than parents. That feeling of friendship made me feel especially close to my mother since she raised me after my father left. Because of the atomic bomb tests in the United States, I sensed a need to be born in the midwest away from the fallout of the bomb clouds so that my genetic material was intact at birth. I knew my birth was being planned more than a year before the expected 1945 bomb tests and the guardians helped me select time of birth, parents, and the place and circumstances for it.

Neil's mother was forty when he was born. While the family viewed his birth as an accident late in a woman's prime years after seven children, Neil knew that the pregnancy was orchestrated behind the scenes. Certainly an economic burden already existed in such a large family and another child added to the heavy load.

Souls Waiting in the Wings for Birth

An extraordinary event occurred when Neil was about four years old.

> I was outside in a country field and looking up into the open blue sky knowing that I and everything on Earth was being observed by a higher intelligence – as if we were living under a large looking glass like tiny living cells you can see through a microscope. I knew that the Earth was round and not flat, that it was like a tiny cell within the Creator who consisted of vast expanses of space and infinity. There was a definite sense that everything was connected and had significance. Being on Earth was like taking a trip for a few years and the journey had been carefully planned with tasks to perform until the journey was fulfilled and I would leave.

One of Neil's deepest yearnings as a teenager was learning to meditate as if to awaken more information deep within.

> Meditation seemed important for my life work. The urge also seemed to be part of an old impulse from another lifetime. Finally by the time I was twenty-five, I learned what was necessary to become silent within while fully awake. Immediately a stream of wonderful experiences surfaced to inform me about who I was, my abilities, and memories of other lives. During my first meditation – a training session – a field of light energy exploded within me. I became absorbed in a silent vacuum of pure serene light. It brought up vivid recollections of meditating in Himalayan caves in Tibet. I was Oriental looking with slanted eyes and yet my soul's essence was the same as today. I was seeking enlightenment which had been a goal through a series of lives in Tibet.

A few years later during a series of meditations, Neil spontaneously relived his early days as a newborn baby and recalled his birth including emerging from the womb with midwives present.

Vortex of Creation

Lorenzo Caravella shares total recall of his birth journey.

Author, lecturer, and intuitive/spiritual consultant, Lorenzo retired from his Madison Avenue advertising firm following a spontaneous remission from cancer. His book, *Mouth of God: Your Cosmic Contract*, is an account of an inner mystical journey to the light and the healing which occurs through self love.

Lorenzo was born in 1935 in Brooklyn, New York. Did Lorenzo engineer his birth to parents who were musicians, artists, singers – the "whole creative ball of wax?"

When you ask that question, the first image that comes to me is the charm that my parents radiate. There were times that they could charm the world. My mother played and taught piano and surrounded her immediate environment with all the Classics. Plus, I grew up with the influences of my father, a talented artist. They were sweet people; however, my parents were also Italian and emotional. So they were just a little out of balance here and there at times, but this was also part of my life's lesson.

Lorenzo recalls "the pre-existing soul stage" prior to entering his mother's womb. Everything was part of the Oneness. He was aware of "everyone and everything and everywhere else."

Imagine all your senses just rolled up into one sense of being. You don't really hear, see, taste, smell, or touch. You don't do any of those things. Yet everything exists for you. And you are totally unattached. It is a total unity experience: *Tat Twam Asi* – "Thou art this. Thou are That."

Lorenzo's cosmic contract was a combination of free will and karma.

As the pre-existing soul, I saw my whole [future] life before me. I accepted its lessons, both the peaks and the valleys. After the time of the contract, however, certain details were smoothed over. I knew there was going to be some discomfort – and sure enough, it came along in different shapes and forms – but I did not want to remember some valleys that I contracted for. There was forgetfulness on purpose.

Souls Waiting in the Wings for Birth

For the same reason, I'd rather not consult Jyotish [Sidereal/Vedic astrology]. It is unnecessary. When these events do happen, it doesn't matter whether they are negative or positive. If there is no attachment to negative or positive, they are equally exhilarating. Both the peaks and the valleys give us permission to evolve fully and richly. That is why a battery in a car has a negative and a positive pole, so it can move forward.

In order for the peaks and valleys to be what they were, I needed to be guided through those energies called "parents." So when the selection was made, it was not specifically that human and that human, but that energy to serve this peak or valley and that energy to serve this other peak and valley. So I was conceived by a mother with a compatible nervous system – one that would permit me to grow. That is what the "Cosmic Contract" is all about.

Whole Time versus Fragmented Time

Lorenzo invokes Albert Einstein's time/space continuum theory to clarify the experience of entering three-dimensional reality via the vortex of creation. Einstein believed time – past, present, and future – exists all at once, like three bends in a river. Just as we cannot see all the bends when a land mass is in the way, so too, as human beings, we do not experience whole time. We experience fragmented time – past, present, and future.

All dimensions exist within each other. That is why they are simultaneous. There is no past and no future. Everything exists in a parallel dimension. If we were permitted to experience the simultaneous universe without the consciousness to support that, we would perceive only chaos. Only someone with an expanded consciousness can discern what is what. So only so much is revealed to us according to our growth.

Time being dimensional is also spherical. And when we stop thinking linearly, we perceive multi-dimensional concepts.

The experience of fragmented time is an illusion. This illusion was revealed through the process of "interdimensional-manifestation" and travelling through the vortex of creation. Lorenzo experienced past, present, and future as the parts of an interconnecting circle.

When I chose to be born, I passed through the vortex of creation. When I moved toward the vortex to go through it to come out the other side, it was not as though I was travelling from point A to point

B. When entering the vortex of creation, it is the proverbial black hole. And when exiting the other side, when I was all reassembled again on the level of consciousness, that was the creation aspect.

Modern physics confirms my memory. Scientists found that a black hole sucks up everything and on the opposite side of the black hole, energy and particles come out. They call that opposite side galactic jets.

That is also what will happen when we die in this lifetime. At least that has been my experience. [Lorenzo is referring to three NDEs.] I went through the vortex again and came out on the other side. So, an NDE is like being born anew in the same life.

Divine Infusion

A special process, "divine infusion," takes place between conception and birth.

The actual action of divine infusion when the pre-existing soul infuses with "the matter being" is very vivid. I recall the connection being made in the initial spark of self-love. This spark must take place between conception and birth. In other words, we cannot be born without self-love, without self-acceptance. If the pre-existing soul and the matter being were not meant to infuse, the spark of self-love would not happen. There would not be any birth. You would have a miscarriage or an abortion, the modern-day miscarriage.

This infusion took place after the matter-being begins to develop inside the fetus. It is not for me to say exactly at what stage of the pregnancy. Fetal development is like building a house. Even though the house can be built, you may not have moved in yet. So there is no way I can pinpoint when the divine infusion took place.

In the womb, the pre-existing soul becomes the divine child – that point of pure innocence where there is just a touch of ego for identification purposes. The divine child has a little more ego than the pre-existing soul. They are not two different things, but different vibrations, one more expressed than the other.

What happens is the pre-existing soul brings parallel life memory and parallel life karma with it and the matter-being brings genetic memory and genetic karma. (Genetic memory in the DNA is karma on the physical level instead of karma on the soul level.) And actually the pre-existing soul contracts with the matter being – the union of egg and sperm – and attracts this particular vessel so that it can fulfill life's lessons.

Souls Waiting in the Wings for Birth

In the fetus, I was aware of the coexistence of present, past and future, "a supreme witness situation." I knew this was going to be a high life and that there was going to be a lot of work, too. And of course, that was my choice. The past is also there with the pre-existing soul. So we are talking about parallel lives. We even see lives that are not quite part of our pre-existing soul energy, those that are yet to come, they are still common to the present.

After I attached to my vessel [physical body], I experienced my parents as images, but nothing in form. They were environments of male energy and environments of female energy. That does not mean one coming from male and one coming from female. They both interact and interchange.

Lorenzo was sensitive to the physical, mental, and emotional environment of his mother, as well as celestial sounds from the higher realms.

I grew up in the fetus, listening to Sibelius, Beethoven, Schubert. One of my favorites was Sibelius's "Valse Triste," an extremely sultry, seductive, haunting, metaphysical piece. That is the level I appreciated it on. Whereas it created melancholia in my mother. I felt her melancholy energy. So it is important what we feed the fetus. It took a while to grow out of that melancholia.

There was always celestial music and voices coming from "the Mouth of God Energy," the energy induction center at the base of the skull. I can't say that this is what happens to everyone, but – it is available to everyone. Apparently the Mouth of God Energy was prominent for me in this life. I always hear celestial voices and music coming through in that channel. That has been with me all this life. It is as though the universe is a huge beauty parlor hair dryer sitting on my head. The "hum" is always there. It is not music and voices as we interpret them on Earth. They are vibrations and feelings, expressions of a Divine nature.

Jovian Core Galaxy

While Lorenzo's mother carried him in the womb, he travelled back and forth to the higher realms.

Even though I wanted to learn certain lessons from my parents, there were times when being with them was uncomfortable. Basically, it was the physiological reaction of any irritation created between them. There were emotional things going on with my father. My father would act and my mother would react, instead of respond. It gets political. My grandfather was a mafia "peacemaker," Don Giovanni.

Throughout the entire pregnancy, Lorenzo heard his parents discussing their local political situation and understood how it disrupted their lives.

I was more aware of it at that time. Less aware of it when I became more physical. But, that was perfect. It taught me that I had jurisdiction over my being in the womb. As the divine child, I knew that the door opens both ways. If some activity was unsupportive, I did not have to be totally there. I could check out. Although there was disharmony in the environment, there was no disharmony with the disharmony.

So my lessons came to me quickly and swiftly in the fetus. The contract had been written. Now it was being read and played out. My parents and I were definitely in accord.

I came and went as I pleased. I played anywhere I wanted. Lots of playtime took place on Jupiter and Saturn because that is where most of my lessons come from. They are Jovian, non-terrestrial planets. Every galaxy has solar systems with Jovian planets. (Besides Jupiter and Saturn, Uranus, Neptune and Pluto are also Jovian planets.) They are seed planets. They have no core like Earth, no rock, nothing solid. Jupiter and Saturn are fire and ice, and gas and lightning. And that is my nature – silent, rumbling, and thunderous. Jupiter is the Guru, the planet of growth, and Saturn is the karmic teacher. That is where I hung out. I still do.

Lorenzo even recalls inter-life states prior to each of his previous lives.

Oh, my God, yes. Between lifetimes, I have been visiting the Jovian Core Galaxy, which is a spiritual spa. It is my Home. It is one of the original galaxies in the universe. It is an area filled with Jovian planets, lightning and thunder.

Does every soul come and go?

There is a Sanskrit phrase in the *Isa Upanishad – Krato Smara Kritam Smara*, which means: "Remember, oh mind, remember what has been done." Those of us who have recited that phrase from one transmigration to the next bring all that spiritual information with us and realize that we have the latitude to travel. We do not have to stay put. We can learn lessons elsewhere, too, not just in this little environment [womb].

By maintaining that concept, the ego does not develop along with the illusion as quickly, as normally. In other words, if you do not bring all the prior-life spirituality to the moment within the fetus, you can get caught up. It becomes a real boundary.

Flight to Earth for Navaswan

When Lorenzo's mother birthed her first child, it nearly killed her.

Mom was a tiny woman and the first delivery (my sister) shattered her pelvic region. She was in a body cast for six months. My father carried her around the house. She was not supposed to go through that again. They just barely got her walking again. Then, nine years later, she became pregnant with me. My parents had not been sleeping in the same bed for years. It was purely an "accident." And I was labelled the ghost baby and was called that for the rest of my childhood.

Lorenzo did not realize the doctor had decided to do a C-section.

I was too busy picking my birth time rather than paying attention to anything else. I wanted to be born at an auspicious time. And that was: *navaswan* – the gap between night and day, around 4:00 AM. So I returned from Jupiter and Saturn in just enough physical time to enter Mom's uterus to formally come out.

Navaswan is when the Guru's Golden Classroom opens up to me every morning. So I picked a good time. I enjoy being inward. I enjoy the void. No stars, no planets, just a silent void. It's fun travelling with the stars and the planets. And it is fun letting them go.

Cesarians create trauma for mothers, although they are easier on newborns.

Yeah, no squeezing, no pushing, no shoving. I was comfortable. I think the choice was there. We do have riders in contracts and it was there to go either way.

Lorenzo's mother checked out.

Mom "died" and came back. She found herself in a passageway, a long corridor, having various doors. Mom knocked on each door, but none would open. At the end of the corridor there was a single door, and that one opened. There sitting on a throne was a large green bug, a big beetle. She said the bug greeted her – a friendly benevolence as she describes it – and then she went back.

She remembers it as a "dream," and never realized she was being welcomed by the Egyptian scarab, a sign of immortality. So, Mom was not to die. Even though she "died," she was not to stay in that realm too long.

Lorenzo was unaffected by his mother's medication and fully aware of birth events. As he put it, "Drugs don't do much for me."

> I remember my first breath as a brilliant flash of light. The *kundalini* energy shot right up the *sushumna* [spinal channel through which a powerful, subtle energy travels upward]. I was told that an ejaculation took place. It was documented, but I don't remember it as an ejaculation.

> Another experience is I can see the delivery room. But it is an experience, rather than a physical sight. Just as when we close our eyes and touch an object with our fingers, our fingertips become our eyes, like that my nerve endings were creating awareness of the delivery room. I knew I was in Brooklyn. I knew it was dark outside and the Sun had not come up yet. But it is hard to say I was actually on this planet because the experience of Jupiter and Saturn was clear. It is as though they were in right in the room. In that moment, Brooklyn had its first earthquake in fifty years.

Lorenzo did not have immediate contact with his mother due to her "transmigration experience" (NDE), but he did not seem to notice.

> There has never been any concern about happiness or unhappiness in this life – until somebody told me that I was supposed to be happy or unhappy at certain things. And I could not understand why. There was never any feeling of happiness or unhappiness. There was always a feeling of well-being and light or the experience of the absence of the presence.

> So I do not recall bonding with my parents or my sister. Up until the age of four, the experience was extremely celestial. It was just Jupiter and Saturn and a whole bunch of light. Everything I saw was totally infused with everything else. There was no separation. It was a unity experience. I was never separate or apart from anything that existed. Earth was just part of the totality and not individualized.

> My awareness of parent was nothing more than love coming from a specific direction, as opposed to every direction. When I came into this life, my parents did what they were supposed to do. After that, I just wanted them to leave me alone. To be honest, I wanted everybody to leave me alone.

Path of Forgetfulness

Lorenzo summarizes the step-by-step process of coming from the world of spirit and forgetting who we are and where we come from.

> First, there is the shock of passing from one realm to another. Because, let us face it, Mom's womb is a whole universe unto the self

of the fetus—totally, self-sufficient, self-referral space. "My space, my space, alone." So we are dynamically thrust from a subtle energy plane to a thick, dense, hard rock consciousness energy plane.

My memory did not stop immediately. I felt the same energy at one and two years old, levitating, the whole bit. My perception was celestial up until four. Everything I saw was totally infused with everything else. I was never separate or apart from anything. It was a unity experience.

A moving van "grounded" Lorenzo at the age of four. The large truck ran over the his body and hit his head. Lorenzo went through the vortex of creation (NDE), and then was "thrust back with a thud."

After being anointed by a truck, things changed. The Earth lessons were starting. The unity experience was there, yet what prevailed was more feeling of Earth because I experienced fear. I was lying in. the street with my parents hovering above me. And in their faces was fear. Prior to that, I had had no fear. In fact, my mother walked onto the roof of our sixth story apartment building one day where I was ready to fly off.

Some people say the accident was a tragedy. But it was a catalyst, a blessing – a spiritual bridge. Prior to being hit on the head, there wasn't enough compassion. Too much nonattachment. My sharp intellect wanted to dissolve anything that brought discomfort, to conveniently move it away, including my parents.

After the accident, compassion grew, the intuitive aspect, the feminine approach. To have aloofness and compassion is to have both worlds. So, this is part of my contract, a planetary lesson I needed to learn.

In other words, forgetfulness started when I accepted mind conditioning and the world appearance from authority figures who wanted me to get involved in their drama. I then saw that this third-dimensional presentation on Earth was contradictory to what I had been going through.

So the more ego I developed, as the divine child and then the confused child, and then ego-lesson on top of ego-lesson, the more I was pulled into my parents' emotional activity. They became giants and I felt I was too small to fight them. I was drawn into that drama and the heavy lessons began. There was too much fuss. Much to do about nothing. On the other hand, it was part of my cosmic contract, the grounding point. When I tried to run away from home, for example, my parents pulled me back in. The only way I could leave was the original way [on the level of consciousness].

Curse of Samsara

Lorenzo planned "to end the curse of samsara."

Rebirth, rebirth, rebirth, who needs it? That is the reason for my three transmigrations (NDEs) in one life. I accelerated in this life so that I do not have to be born three more times. My first transmigration brought compassion into my being and grounding on the planet. So that is important. Prior to that, I was just a stuck-up little spiritual snob ready to annihilate anything that came into my path.

We need to pay attention to what we call valleys, those areas of discomfort.

The valleys can be just as accelerating as anything else. As Nietzsche put it, "When you cast out your demons, be careful that you don't cast out the best part of you." We tend to deny our negative side. This is a mistake. Both are equally important. If we release ourselves from attachment to good and bad, then we expand our whole being. All our lessons are born through the co-existence of opposites.

Chapter 29
Children as Messengers

**If there is a constant coming or going
between us and the world of the ancestors,
which is what my people believe, then it's
in fact the child who can tell you about
that world since it's coming from there … .[1]**

– Chinua Achebe, Nigerian Writer

*Sometimes the Angel of Forgetfulness "forgets" to remove
from our memories the records of our pre-birth state.
Then, even a newborn recalls fragments of another world.*

Newborns come to us wearing "baby disguises,"[2] yet they are far wiser than adults give them credit for. In contrast to adults who report gifted memory, however, children add greater innocence and credibility to this phenomenon. They are less subject to cultural contamination, and have had little time to think about life and death.

Six examples of children's gifted memory follow.

* USA (19th century) – An older sister overheard her four-year-old sister talking about matters which she could not know about. The older sibling exclaimed, "What do you know about that? All that happened before you were born!" The younger one responded, "I would have you know … I grew old in heaven before I was born."[3]

* Sri Lanka (contemporary) – Disna recalls an inter-life world where she wore rich, elegant clothes which never needed

washing.[4] And although Disna felt no need for food, she could manifest food by simply desiring it. A kindly "ruler" helped Disna plan rebirth.

* USA (contemporary) – A young boy asked his parents for permission to talk privately with his new baby sister. The parents consented, but without their son's knowledge, they recorded the conversation through an intercom unit next to the crib. On that recording, the little boy said, "You have to tell me about God. I'm starting to forget."[5]

* USA (contemporary) – Four-year-old Jennica was helping her mother wash dishes when she looked out the window and starting waving. She explained to her mother, "I'm saying good-bye to Jesus. He's in his castle … . The one [castle] I lived in before I came to live with you."[6]

* India (3102 BC) – A vital air called *satha* envelops ordinary children at birth and obscures the true knowledge with which they were endowed while in the mother's womb. On the contrary, Nammalvar, son of Kariyar and Udaiyanangaiyar, overpowered this veil and gained the name "Sathakopa."[7]

* Yakut (19th century Russia) – Baby Ivan's first words spoken to his parents left a deep impression. "Many people were on the Djargata'ch [name of Yakut village] and we all died of smallpox, starting to the other world on only one horse." Even though his parents had baptized their son as Ivan, they immediately began to call him Baibal. They acknowledged him as their relative Baibal who had died in 1888 along with many Yakuts during a smallpox epidemic. On their graves, "only one sacrificial horse had been killed, so that the souls of all the deceased were obliged to ride to the Land of Shadows on the shadow [soul] of only one horse."[8]

Additional gifted memories come from five children whose mothers shared their stories with the author, as well as reports from researchers on children born in Thailand, Japan, America, England, Tibet, and within the Native American culture.

Coming from the Turquoise Land

*Jana's children recalled pre-conception memories at an early
age and still remember them today as young teenagers.
Her son also recalls past life memories.*

Two or three months following Jana and Bruce's marriage, Jana's
menstrual period shifted to coincide with the Moon phases.

> I felt that a child was coming. I sensed a male child who wanted to
> be conceived in the middle of the month and born on the full Moon.

Jana's intuition proved true. When her son Robert was two years
of age, he began to talk about his dreams.

> Robert had recurring dreams. He woke up in the mornings and
> said, "I came from Red Roshi Land. The people wore red robes.
> There was a big fire in Red Roshi Land. We had to go away." At other
> times, he said, "I went back to Red Roshi Land. There was a fire there
> and we had to travel over the mountains."

Jana did not know what the dreams meant until it dawned on
her that he was describing the flight from Tibet during the Chinese
invasion of the 1940s. Jana also had connections with Tibet.

> During the year prior to my son's birth, I took refuge with Tai Situ
> Rinpoche, a Tibetan teacher. It is also interesting that when I was
> pregnant, I dreamed of travelling in fast sports cars with Tibetan lamas.

Jana believes Robert is a reborn Tibetan Buddhist monk.

> My son looked like a little monk in his baby pictures. An intuitive
> therapist I worked with in England looked at my daughter and son
> and said, "They came straight from Tibet." This surprised me because
> of my background. I had a Zen meditation center in my home and a
> yogic background since I was eighteen.

Jana feels that Robert chose her as a mother, knowing he would
have contact with spiritual teachers. Indeed, even before his first
birthday, Robert received a series of blessings: 1) A Buddhist Abbot
blessed the newborn and gave him the name "Lokanatu," an

epithet for the Buddha, meaning "Savior of the World;" 2) Swami Satchidananda gave him the spiritual name "Krishna;" 3) Robert attended the XIV Dalai Lama's empowerment ceremony (initiation); and 4) a Zen teacher gave Robert the name "Enko" meaning "Perfect Light." He also made a calligraphy as a gift with this naming. He used the symbol of a perfect circle in the calligraphy. Instead of completing the circle, the master left it open and said, "He has his own life to live."

Robert's father became a Zen priest when Robert was ten. Robert meditated in the full lotus pose during the one-hour ordination ceremony. Robert desired to become a monk when he was twelve; a Zen teacher advised that it was not yet time.

Robert's Pre-Conception Memories

Robert's memories extend beyond a former life in Tibet. Robert was less than three years old, the year before his sister's birth, when he announced:

> "I came from the Turquoise Land and there was different music there – different from the music Daddy plays." [Jana's husband was a musician.] Then Robert told me, "My sister is waiting outside the gate, in the Pink Land. She is going to put a ball of white light in your tummy and jump in."

> The fact that Robert spontaneously said this was extraordinary. I listened and thought, "This is wild." He also told me, "My brother is further away in another land, the Blue Land. He will come later and be born in America."

Jana and Bruce moved to the USA shortly following the birth of Jana's second child, a daughter. Jana recalls a conversation with her son which occurred a few years later. Robert was six or seven years old.

> I very much wanted a third child. One day I asked Robert, "Do you remember telling me that your little brother was going to come to us when we moved to America?" He answered, "Yes, but it is uncertain now because he is in school in this other Land and learning things – but it is a different kind of school than we have here. And my brother is not sure whether he is coming now."

> Robert kept telling me, "I talk to my brother and he talks to me. He is not absolutely sure whether he will come. It is not determined whether my brother is coming."

I think that his hesitancy was partly due to the difficulties with the marriage. My husband was not open to a third child, our marriage became bumpy, and we decided to go our separate ways. A third child has not come, but still waits in the wings.

Coming from Angel Land

Jana's daughter shared gifted memory before the age of four.

Anna Grace told me, "I was up in the Land that I came from, Angel Land. I heard Dad calling my name, 'Anna Grace,' and I knew it was time for me to come."

What happened was several weeks before our daughter's birth, my husband suggested the name "Anna Grace." I said, "That is a beautiful name." (We thought it was going to be a girl because of the amniocentesis.)

Anna Grace lived in England for six weeks before we moved to America. Yet, she told me many times, "I knew about England because when I was in Angel Land and decided to come here, I saw you in England."

Then she often told me, "I do not like it here. It is too hard. I want to go back to Angel Land." I would tell her, "I love you very much. I know that it is different here, but you can feel good here, too. I am glad that you are here. Everything will be okay."

At other times, Anna Grace told me, "I miss Angel Land," or she explained, "I have all the angels in my bedroom, and throughout the house are stars, but only I can see the stars because I can still see Angel Land where I came from."

The Realm of the Angels and Fairies

Social conditioning plays a role in whether we recall pre-uterine memories. Stephanie Foy's two children recalled where they came from "until the world corrected them." (Stephanie also shares a dream in Chapter 3.)

Stephanie's first child played games by himself and often became aware of invisible playmates. Sometimes this even happened in the middle of the night.

Steven experienced a lot of insomnia when he was less than a year old. He called from his bedroom, asking to be taken to another room in the house, where he looked all around and began laughing and talking. He saw a subtle presence in the room, but I did not.

On other nights, as my husband and I drifted off to sleep, we heard our son laughing in his bedroom, like he was playing with a real companion. We finally realized, "Well, so long as he's safe, we are going to sleep."

Stephanie's daughter was born eighteen months after Steven. When Amy was twenty-one months old, and became "old enough to jabber, she reengaged her brother into remembering."

They talked to each other about angels and fairies saying, "This is what it was like before we came here." They described big angels, as well as little fairies who were cute, funny, and had pretty colors. Their conversations continued for one year and often happened whenever the children played in the bathtub. Even though my husband and I did not discourage the visions, the conversations stopped once we moved into a different home and Steven attended another preschool.

Thunderbolts from a Tenacious Child

Taylor Anderson's memories extend back to pre-uterine life. Taylor is the son of Beverly whose stories appear in Chapter 7 and Chapter 34.

Two-year-old Taylor's words struck Beverly like a thunderbolt straight out of Heaven.

Taylor and I were having a conversation. I told him, "Thank you so much for being my son, I am proud that you are my little boy. I appreciate being your Mommy."

Taylor stopped and leaned over. His eyes got these tiny slits and he said, "But Mommy, didn't you know, I picked you?" I replied, "Excuse me, will you run that by me one more time?" And he said, "I picked you because I knew you would be a good Mommy. You would take good care of me. And I love you." I said, "Really, you picked me to be your Mommy?"

And he explained, "Well, you also picked me to be your son. We cannot do this unless we both agree." I said, "Well, that works fine for me. Does it work good for you?" And he said, "Yeah, it's good for me."

That was the end of the conversation. I had never explained karma or reincarnation to my son. I walked away thinking, "Oh my God! This child just had an abstract, advanced Buddhist philosophy conversation and he is barely old enough to understand the words he was spitting out."

Similar levels of interchange proceeded from that point on. Beverly recalls an incident when Taylor was three-and-one-half.

I was talking to a pregnant friend and said, "That due date business does not mean crap if you gauge it against me. Babies come out when they decide to be born and there is nothing you can do about that. Taylor was due on the first, but he liked his little incubating unit so much that he did not want to budge even when the doctor induced labor. She finally yanked him out with a C-section twenty-five days after the due date."

Taylor overheard my comments and beamed up at me, "Yeah, it is great in there – your own private swimming pool with all you can eat." That really floored me. I looked at my son and said, "Yeah, you little stinker." He just smiled. Taylor is still a comfort-oriented child today – into his "snugglies" and comfort zone.

Taylor was in the womb almost ten months for another reason.

Taylor hung around to make sure that our circadian rhythms were identical. He was born near my astral clock, six hours before my birthday. We are pieces of the same thing, except he is a boy and I am a girl. We are an unusual pair.

First Thirty Seconds of Birth

Taylor shared memories of birth when he was twenty-eight months old.

Taylor recalls the first thirty seconds. He told us: "I remember all the lights and it was cold. I had to go to the bathroom and I peed all over the doctor. I remember her (the doctor's) funny (shocked) face."

A thunderbolt struck me when my son said that. My mouth hung open. I stared at Taylor, thinking, "Oh, Lord. You are like me. Oh, my God we have another one in the family." I realized what was cooking in there. I always knew my son would be psychic, however, I had been unsure of the volume of his sensitivity.

So Taylor did a perfect stream of pee and hit the doctor right in the chest when she picked him up to show him to me. Everyone in the room cracked up. His birth started with humor. That is my son. He remembers doing that. And we never told him. He brought that up.

Taylor is not unique. There are at least 200 children on the planet who are "stunningly beautiful and startlingly awake, the most evolved of our soul continuum."

And the promise of the Christ Consciousness being born again has already happened in them and is blossoming in all of us. So God has spread himself out all over the globe because of the level of love that will be needed to get the human race through the tribulations.

So there is a rather horrendous time to come. It is not going to be a piece of cake. People ask, "How can there be a vengeful God?" I say, "God is not vengeful. Vengeful is fear. He is so loving. He wants us to be happy. Occasionally however there must be some scrubbing and cleaning … ."

It is a big job and these children are willing to do it. We adults are just going to see the beginning of the tribulations. It is the children that my heart aches for because they have to live through it or not … . But God will help them. Humanity will be very different on the other side.

"Being human is about accomplishment, growth, and satisfaction – testing our mettle."

So couples should not think, "We should not bring a child into the world." It is the choice of these children to test their mettle at this level of extremity. This existence here is necessary, important. Do not choose not to have children. Be proud of them. Look at how much these beings are going to grow and learn. And they might just step off the planet after that and be little godlings.

So this ball game is just getting warmed-up. Isn't it cool?

Precocious Children

*Research studies and books cite children
who remember choosing parents.*

Bongkuch Promsin, a young Thai boy, recalls being murdered in Hua Tanon village in his previous life.[9] His spirit remained on a tree next to the crime scene for seven years. Then one rainy day, Bongkuch tagged along with a man who passed by. They rode on a bus to the man's home. That man became Bongkuch's father.

What is so interesting about Bongkuch's memories is that both parents visited his soul's resting site (where he had died) prior to conception. The father attended a meeting in Hua Tanon on a rainy day whereas his mother went there on another occasion to collect bamboo shoots.

Adoption Contract

A precocious baby born in Thailand in 1964 announced to her astonished parents, "I want to do 'merit making' at the Buddhist temple." Baby Ratana was barely eleven months old at the time. She pestered her parents for several months, until they took her request seriously.

On the first temple visit, the toddler knew how to make proper devotional gestures and offerings, and remembered where Buddha's relics were located. This visit triggered more memories of Ratana's past life as Kim Lan, a Chinese woman who attended a three-year-meditation retreat at the same temple. Ratana identified monks she had known in the past life who were still alive today. She further recalled how Kim's life ended in open heart surgery: "the doctor put the knife beside my heart and made me die."[10]

The interlude between Kim's death and Ratana's birth was "a brief intermission." Following Kim's death, a celestial being asked,

"Where do you want to go?" She answered, "I want to pay respects to Buddha's relics." A carriage transported her to that spiritual dimension.

As part of her pre-birth planning, Ratana searched in the heavens for Samnuan, the man who had been her father in two previous lives. She hoped to be born as his child in her upcoming life. Prior to birth, she found Samnuan again. He was already on Earth. They conversed and enjoyed a walking meditation at Wat Mahathat.

When Ratana "came down from heaven, the descent was like one breath."[11] And although Samnuan's wife, Charoon, had grown beyond childbearing age, Charoon's daughter birthed Ratana. Charoon and Samnuan then ended up adopting Ratana since Ratana's natural mother decided to terminate her unhappy marriage and did not desire a child. Even adopted children end up where they choose to be.

Heavenly Escorts to Earth

Contemporary children recall the spiritual guides who prepared them for birth.

Norma thought she understood one-and-one-half-year-old son Jonathan when he said, "I miss my Father." She replied, "You will see father as soon as we get home." Then her son surprisingly explained: "No, my Father in Heaven. I used to sit and talk with Jesus."[12] The toddler's comment amazed Norma since she lacked "religious" belief and had never discussed such topics with Jonathan.

Six months later, Jonathan shared another memory with Norma and her husband Kerry: "I talked to my grandfather and my uncle, and they told me I had to wait a very long time to come and be with you."[13] Strange as it seems, Jonathan described Kerry's relatives as the two individuals he had met prior to birth even though the child had never heard about or seen photos of Kerry's father and uncle. Both men had passed away in Kerry's early childhood.

Baby Jonathan's memory dovetails with the fact that Jonathan's birth took place in Norma's marriage to Kerry, which was Norma's second marriage. Norma already had a number of children during an earlier marriage which ended due to her husband's abuse. Jonathan undoubtedly waited for Norma's marriage to Kerry.

Jonathan's memories are far from unique. When Alan's mother explained to two-year-old Alan, "Aunt Lida has returned to the Heavenly Father," he asked, "Who took her?" His mother answered, "Someone Aunt Lida knew." Alan's face lit up, "Oh I know what it's like! Grandpa Clark brought me when I came to you. He'll probably take me back when I die."[14]

What is interesting about Alan's comment is that the child had, in this life, never met Grandpa Clark. He had passed away ten years prior to Alan's birth. Yet, the toddler "knew," "loved," and described him perfectly. For the next few months, Alan talked about how Grandpa taught him about life on Earth. A veil then fell over his memory.

Three-year-old Johnny is another child who recalls his heavenly escort. One night Johnny requested a bedtime story about Grandpa Robert. The request surprised his mother. Lois had never spoken to Johnny about her grandfather Robert who had passed away years ago. Lois asked, "Johnny, how do you know Grandpa Robert?" He explained with reverence, "Well, mamma, he's the one who brought me to Earth."[15]

Katsugoro Follows Tozo's Footsteps

Japanese documents validating the memories of a Japanese boy born in 1815 became available through the translation of a western journalist, Lafcadio Hearn (1850 to 1904).[16]

One day while Katsugoro and his sister, Fusa, played in the rice fields, Katsugoro asked, "Where did you come from before birth?" His older sister had no answer, but Katsugoro did. He told her about a previous life as Tozo, son of the farmer Kyubei and his wife Shidzu who lived in the village of Hodokubo. His father died when Tozo was five. Tozo's mother remarried a man whom Tozo loved very much. But within a few months, Tozo died of smallpox.

Katsugoro even remembered the period between death and rebirth. Tozo's family placed his body into a jar and dropped it into a burial hole. The jar made a noise: "pon!" Tozo's spirit hovered near his family's home for a while, and "stopped" on his pillow. He then entered a world of light where the Sun never set. Tozo did not feel warm, cold, or hungry. He heard his family prayers and "inhaled" the vapor of hot rice cakes offered to uplift his soul and bring him a better rebirth.

Tozo's spirit met a spiritual guide who resembled a grandfather. They walked together through the air, "as if flying." The sage led him to a village. Pointing to a house, the guide announced:

> Three years have passed since you died. Now is the time for rebirth. It will be good to be conceived and born in this home. The woman who will become your grandmother will be kind to you.

The guide disappeared, and the child's spirit sat beneath the family tree patiently waiting. As he was about to enter the home, he overheard a conversation between the husband and wife that stopped him cold. The couple had agreed that the wife needed to work outside the home rather than tending to babies.

Souls Waiting in the Wings for Birth

Tozo's spirit hovered in the garden for three days, wondering what to do. As he paid attention to their household activities, he tuned into another discussion. They were changing their minds. Sensing the time was right, that night his spirit slipped into the house through a knot hole in the sliding shutters. Tozo's spirit lingered in the kitchen for three days before entering his "mother's honorable womb." He came into the world "without any pain at all."

Years later, Katsugoro's grandmother Tsuya validated the boy's memories as Tozo. She and her ten-year-old grandson visited his former village. Katsugoro led Tsuya through the streets as if he was reading a road map. The excited child then cried out, "This is the house!" He rushed inside, without waiting. Tsuya followed and met the family whose six-year-old son Tozo had died of smallpox thirteen years earlier. The family hugged little Katsugoro, as love transcended lifetimes.

Battle of the Gates

Parents who think a child is an empty reservoir of its birth journey react critically if their child speaks about memories prior to entering the womb. This response can confuse a child. Fortunately, one four-year-old American girl defended her memories.

As soon as Anne began to speak, she often talked about things a baby could never know. Anne's teenage sister recorded some of these unusual comments. On one occasion, Anne became angry and announced "I am going away forever."

Her father asked, "Back to heaven where you came from?" Anne shook her head:

"I didn't come from heaven to you," she asserted with that calm conviction to which we were quite accustomed now. "I went to the Moon first, but – you know about the moon, don't you? It used to have people on it, but it got so hard that we had to go."[17]

Anne's father laughed, "You came from the Moon?" Anne explained:

Oh, no. I have been on Earth many times. One time I was a Canadian soldier and I "took the gates!"[18] My name was Lishus Faber.

Unlike Anne's father who did not take his daughter seriously, Anne's sister researched Canadian history and discovered "a quaint old book, interestingly picturesque in many of its tales." One story in particular "put all the others out of my mind for a time."

"... a brief account of the taking of a little walled city by a small company of soldiers, a distinguished feat of some sort .... A young lieutenant with his small band – the phrase leaped to my eyes – took the gates ... and the name of the young lieutenant was Aloysius Le Febre."[19]

Cross-Cultural Parallels

Ancient cultures, such as India and Greece, depict the Moon as an inter-life realm. See Chapter 18, *Soul's Orbit*.

Telepathic Babies from the Sun

*Native American children share gifted
memory before they begin to speak.*

Northwestern Chinooks credited babies with the ability to think prior to learning the native language. As far as they were concerned, thinking and communication are inherently human, regardless of age.

One month following every child's birth, communications between the newborn and a tribal doctor, someone gifted in interpreting "baby language," were accompanied by festive ceremonies and dances. The doctor even discovered where babies come from: "The baby's home is the sun before being born. All children come from the daylight. That is their home."[20]

The infant indicated whether his parents had named him properly and whether he liked earthly life. If disharmony existed in the home, the baby told the doctor: "After four days, I shall go home."[21] And sure enough, the baby became ill and returned to "baby land" four days later. There he played with other baby souls until he sensed that his parents desired another child and had become better caretakers. If the child gave his parents a second chance, he was born the opposite sex as his previous life.

Gifted Memory and
Pre-Conception Dreams

Although the soul seeking birth may appear as a complete
stranger, in many cases, parents identify the soul as an ancestor
or someone they have known before. Children's memories
sometimes validate these pre-conception dreams.

A Visit to Auntie

Gifted memory was one of the first things Nok talked about after learning to speak. One night as her parents speculated about where Nok had lived in a previous life, one-year-old Nok answered, "Paknam." Her mother Sampan asked, "How many people came with you?" Nok said "One" – a young boy, Ai Kai, who still sought a place to be born.

Nok's memories made a lot of sense to Sampan in the light of a dream occurring two months prior to Nok's conception – the same night she and her husband moved to Paknam. Two children appeared in the dream, holding hands. They addressed Sampan as "Auntie." Sampam invited the children, who were hungry, to serve themselves in the kitchen. Afterward the little girl and boy thanked Auntie for the Chinese noodles.

The children liked Auntie and asked permission to stay. Sampam objected, explaining, "Your parents will miss you." The children replied, "We no longer have parents. We were drowned in the river near the pagoda." Sampan remained firm, "No. No. I will not take you. You are dead."[22] The children nonetheless insisted upon staying.

Following Nok's initial comments about her past life, the child spoke about them on a daily basis over the next few years. The parents learned that she and Ai Kai had been boating in a river near the Paknam pagoda when the boat capsized. Nok's body sank, and her head slammed into a pillar. The current swept the boy's body away. Nok died at the age of four. Between the fatal drowning and rebirth, Nok lived in a Paknam monastery with a Buddhist nun.

Nok's companion Ai Kai remained very real to her. She conversed with him from the age of two. She even sketched his picture. Later on, Nok communicated with him during meditation. Nok's mother directed questions to Ai Kai through her daughter and received reasonable responses. Perhaps Ai Kai had been Nok's brother in the past and desired to be her sibling again. Nearly nine years after Nok's birth, Ai Kai still waited to be reborn.

No official records support Nok's testimony. Between ten and twenty children drown in that area each year and such accidents are seldom reported to the police. One man, however, did recall the deaths of a boy and girl due to a boating accident.

Another bit of evidence is a life-long depression in Nok's skull, measuring one centimeter in diameter and four millimeters deep. Nok claimed the deformity had been created when her head struck the pillar after the boat capsized. If so, we can speculate that a past-life injury imprints on the subtle body we carry over between lifetimes. When a new physical body is generated from the subtle imprint, the marking also manifests.

Intentional Rebirth

One day, three-year-old Michael told his mother, "I lived before and I remember how I died." Michael explained how his car careened off the road, rolled over, and the door came off. He fell out and his body was carried over a bridge. A friend, Henry Sullivan, was a passenger in the car. Michael remembered that his name had been Walter Miller and he had a sister Carole.

Michael's mother, Catherine, reeled in amazement at the mere mention of a name from the past. For in fact, she had a romantic relationship with a man named Walter Miller eleven years earlier, before Walter's life ended in an auto accident. Her boyfriend had been slightly intoxicated, fell asleep, and lost control of the car. A friend, Henry Sullivan, had been a passenger.

Catherine heard from Walter two years after the accident … in a dream. He announced his imminent return to draw pictures for her again. Catherine assumed "Walter" might be born to Walter's sister Carole, who was pregnant, and because she and her husband had no plans to start a family at the time. Walter nonetheless waited until Catherine became ready to become his mother several years later.[23]

Second Opinion

A Burmese child who recalls choosing parents he had known in a previous life is interesting because both parents reported a pre-conception dream.[24] The child's spirit appeared to the wife first, asking permission to be her son. For some reason, she said, "No." Undaunted, he then appeared in her husband's dream. The husband welcomed his friend's return. Later, in good humor, the wife agreed. When their son began to speak, he described the dreams of his parents and explained that his father's acceptance overcame his mother's initial "veto."

A Child's Prophesy

*Saint Cuthbert, a 7th century Celtic
monk and missionary, became alerted to
his cosmic contract at an early age.*

The playground was filled with boys indulged in vulgar games and tricks. Some of the children removed their clothes and stood on their heads with their legs stretched out and their feet sticking up in the air. One three-year-old, acting as an adult, urged eight-year-old Cuthbert, "Stop these foolish pranks." Cuthbert scorned the warning until the child cried so violently that they could barely quiet him. The child shouted at Cuthbert:

"Why ... do these things so contrary to your nature and your rank? ... the Lord has consecrated you to be teacher of virtue even to your elders."[25]

The child's advice struck a chord with Cuthbert's memory and his life took a new direction within the next few hours. From then on, angels came to Cuthbert's aid whenever the child prayed for God's help. As the saint's cosmic contract took its course, Cuthbert healed the sick and became known as the "wonderworker of Britain."

As an interesting side note, the Church exhumed Cuthbert's body on numerous occasions. Even 850 years after death, his body continued to remain flexible, of natural weight, and it exuded a heavenly perfume. As St. Cyril of Jerusalem put it: "Power and virtue remain in the bodies of the saints because of the righteous souls which have dwelt in them."[26]

A Sage's Swaddling Clothes

At the time of physical death, the First Dalai Lama
remained lucid and passed from this world fully
conscious of what was happening.

From the "rooftop of the world," Tibet, comes the story of what happened between the death of the First Dalai Lama (1391 to 1474) and his rebirth. Gendun Drubpa announced to disciples that he would soon pass away. An assembly gathered for a final message. At the close of the sermon and sitting in the upright posture, the eighty-four-year-old Lama closed his eyes in meditation and "consciously dissolved the elements of his body."[27]

Gendun Drubpa made his accomplishment of enlightenment evident for all to see. For although the Lama's heart and breath stopped, he withdrew his consciousness into the heart by the powers of meditation and miraculously transformed his body. He assumed the appearance of a radiant sixteen-year-old for forty-nine days. The Lama sat in a mystical state between life and death called *tukdam*. When *tukdam* was complete, the Lama's head fell slightly to the side and a drop of sperm was released from his sexual organ.

Seed of Blue Light

A young couple remained in contact with their spiritual teacher, the First Dalai Lama, following his death. Kunga Palmo, a yogini of distinction, had served among the First Dalai Lama's accomplished spiritual disciples. As a child, Kunga remembered previous incarnations. Centuries ago, she had been Khadroma Drowai Zangmo, a renowned yogini and disciple of Gyalwa Gotsang. Kunga's husband, Gyaltsen, had also been initiated by the First Dalai Lama.

Souls Waiting in the Wings for Birth

Shortly following the First Dalai's passing, a young boy delivered a message to Gyaltsen in an auspicious dream:

> "The omniscient Gendun Drubpa [First Dalai Lama] will soon come to Yolkar. You should receive him well."[28]

The messenger boy in the dream then transported Gyaltsen to Gendun Drubpa's meditation cave. The First Dalai Lama's body blazed with light. He smiled at Gyaltsen, but did not speak. A few days later, Gyaltsen dreamed of the Lama again. This time the Lama announced:

> "I have almost completed my retreat. Go to my monastery, Tashi Lhunpo, and collect my robes and monk bowl for me."[29]

Within a brief period of time, Kunga dreamed that a blue radiant light, the size of a sesame seed, entered her womb. The light "filled her and flowed out through every pore of her body, filling the ten directions of the universe with its luminosity until all the darkness of the world had been dispelled."[30]

Meanwhile, Gyaltsen dreamed again of visiting the First Dalai Lama's meditation cave. The Lama even appeared in Kunga's dream and touched her stomach. He announced that Palmo would birth a son whom she must name Sang-gyey Pel, "the Creator of Enlightened Beings … the name by which the Buddhas of the ten directions and of the past, present, and future know him."[31]

Over the months following conception, Kunga repeatedly experienced auspicious dreams. The parents realized they were the caretakers for a great being.

On the day of their son's birth, a rainbow appeared over the home even though the Sun shined and the sky was free of dust or mist. The year was 1475, the Fire Monkey Year. Immediately upon exiting the womb, the newborn looked around and acknowledged everyone's presence. The baby's face exuded radiance. He smiled and turned in the direction of the First Dalai Lama's monastery. He then placed his tiny hands together in prayer and praised Arya Tara, the Great Mother of all the Buddhas by reciting, *"Om tare tuttare ture svaha"* – the First Dalai Lama's meditation mantra.[32]

The newborn carried physical signs of being a high incarnation: "eyes wide, clear and soft like those of an antelope;"[33] auspicious lines – Dharma wheels and conch shells – marked his hands; and marks on his shoulders indicated additional invisible arms to help him enlighten humanity.

Early Childhood and Gifted Memory

The wonder child confirmed his real identity by announcing that he was the reincarnation of the First Dalai Lama as soon as he learned to speak. During playtime, Sang-gyey created temples and Buddhas out of clay, sat on a rock throne, and imagined giving lectures to students. Even more extraordinary, not only did Sang-gyey enjoy the role of a lama, the child also recalled the First Dalai Lama's memories, dreams, and visions. As one of many examples, the boy spontaneously entered a supernormal state of consciousness one day during a thunderstorm. Sang-gyey emerged several hours later and told his parents that the sound of thunder reminds him of his previous life as Gendun Drubpa when he sat at the great Lama Tsongkhapa's feet, listening to the Lama's thunderous voice.

The boy lama equally remembered his predecessor's death and journey to a heavenly inter-life region, *Tusita* Pure Land. He met with Buddha Maitreya, Nagarjuna, Asanga, Atisha, and Tsongkhapa and asked for advice on where to reincarnate in order to continue his work of enlightening others. Tsongkhapa, upon hearing this intention, tossed a white flower from *Tusita* toward the Earth, stating that he should reincarnate where ever the flower fell.

"The flower landed in Yolkar Dorjeden. Therefore, I chose this place for my rebirth and you as my parents."[34]

By the time of Sang-gyey's third birthday, rumors surrounding his birth had spread throughout the land. More than that, a great master Chojor Palzang, one of the First Dalai Lama's disciples, received a message in a dream vision.

"Of all wonders in the world, the rebirth of omniscient Gendun Drubpa [First Dalai Lama] stands supreme. That great wonder … is among us now."[35]

The announcement inspired Chojor Palzang to visit the child lama and see the boy for himself. Indeed, the boy impressed the master. Later, in a dream, Chojor heard a voice resonate from the sky, admonishing him, "Fulfill the wishes of the Buddhas."[36] This omen further convinced Chojor to inform the monastery of the boy's birth.

Within a year, the child lama visited his predecessor's monastery. The child identified former locations where he had enjoyed quiet meditations as well as thrones where he had given spiritual initiations. He acknowledged his previous disciples, accurately greeting everyone by name without an introduction.

One elderly monk, however, harbored reservations about the boy's identity. Without saying anything, the monk wondered, "This child is supposed to be the rebirth of my great guru, but his manner is so different. Surely he cannot be the true reincarnation." (The First Dalai had been humble, modest and introverted, whereas this child appeared outspoken, assertive, and outgoing.) Then, the child, a gifted clairvoyant from birth, whispered into the old monk's skeptical ear: "Due to the changing of bodies, the character must also undergo some kind of a change."[37]

The Wheel of Life

The Second Dalai Lama (1475 to 1542) represented the greatest of all Dalai Lamas, according to the XIV Dalai Lama. By the end of the Second Dalai Lama's life, every person of importance in rank or position in central Asia – from monks to householders, chieftains, and simple nomads – had received teachings or initiations directly from him or indirectly through his close disciples.

Like his predecessor, the Second Dalai Lama had a premonition when his final days were at hand.

"Today I had a vision. Jowo Atisha and his disciples, Lama Tsongkhapa and disciples, and countless Buddhas and *bodhisattvas* appeared in the sky. They then dissolved into my three places (crown chakra, throat chakra, and heart chakra). Many youthful male and female tantric deities appeared and requested me to go with them. Please do not be sad when I go. I will care for you in future lives."[38]

The great master further explained that his aged body had completed the spiritual training of those individuals he had come to teach.

"Therefore I will abandon my body. But I will not abandon you. Soon a young reincarnation will come to take my place and continue my work."[39]

Disciples prepared an altar for the Second Dalai Lama's final prayer and meditation and he began the tantric meditation known as the *vajra* recitation. He slowly withdrew the subtle energies from his body and directed them to his heart. By the next morning, the energy absorptions were completed. He brought his breath and heartbeat to a state of stillness.

In accordance with Tibetan sacred rituals, the lamas cremated the body shortly afterward. Disciples who opened the cremation pyre discovered relic pills and auspicious signs. In particular, the flames had not consumed the master's heart. In fact, the heart had crystallized into the Buddha form of the tantric deity *Heruka Chakrasamvara*.

The Nechung Oracle cognized that the Second Dalai Lama sent forth 100 emanations into this world, with a child born in the Tolung area being the main reincarnation. In due time, as promised by Second Dalai Lama, a child born in Tolung expressed memories of his previous life and became acknowledged as the Third Dalai Lama.

Chapter 30
Gifted Memory and Higher Consciousness

**If you know why God made you in this world,
then you begin to know everything.**[1]
– Shaykh Muhammad al-Jamal ar-Rifa'i as-Shadhili

*An individual's ability to maintain awareness
beyond death, through other worlds, and back to rebirth
is proportional to spiritual maturity. The higher the
consciousness, the greater the memory.*

Gifted memory characterizes the most exalted mode of human birth as described by Gautama Buddha: to enter the mother's womb knowingly, stay in it knowingly, and come out from it knowingly. The broad awareness of Hebrew prophets, Indian saints and yogis, Buddhist lamas, Sikh masters, Greek philosophers, and indigenous elders endowed them with the means to recall inter-life experiences.

Four examples from ancient times follow.

❋ Empedocles (ancient Greece) – Empedocles admitted that he was "a wanderer exiled from the divine dwelling."[2] He fell down to Earth from his high estate due to the "decree of necessity" which requires erring souls to wander from their heavenly home. He experienced a series of human lifetimes for 30,000 seasons.[3] In former times, he had been a boy, a girl, a bush, a bird, and a mute fish in the sea. He wept at being born on Earth, the region of "raging discord," and expected to rejoin the immortals following this life.

❀ Plato (ancient Greece) – The soul of Ulysses remembered his former long life of trials and tribulations and had tired of ambition. That is why, in the pre-birth state, he chose the life of a private man of no business. (Plato's *Republic* – "Myth of Er")

❀ Moses (ancient Hebrew) – According to Philo of Alexandria, Moses was "possessed of a diviner structure," because he recalled his "citizenship" in the Father land. Moses reminded people that this earthly region is "foreign" and urged them to "return to the original source."[4]

❀ Plotinus (205 to 207 AD Rome) – "Many times it happened: lifted out of the body into myself; becoming external to all other things; beholding a marvelous beauty; then, more than ever assured of community with the loftiest order; living the noblest life, acquiring identity with the Divine … . Yet there comes the moment of descent, and after that sojourn in the Divine, I ask myself how it happens that I can now be descending, and how did the soul ever enter my body, the soul which, even within the body, is the high thing it has shown itself to be."[5]

Saints, poets and philosophers in modern times provide six other examples of gifted memory.

❀ Rabbi Abraham Yehoshua (19th century Hasidism) – The Rabbi recalled ten previous lives and explained, "And so I was sent forth again and again in order to perfect my love. If I succeed this time, I shall never return again."[6]

❀ Mother Meera (contemporary Germany) – "Before coming here I knew who I was, knew that I would incarnate and what my work would be."[7] Mother Meera further states that she is an incarnation of the Divine Mother and that this is her first experience as a human. People from all over the world receive blessings from Mother Meera in a quiet German village.

❀ Paramahansa Yogananda (20th century India) – "My far-reaching memories are not unique."[8] Many yogis have the ability to retain self-awareness without interruption during "the big sleep of death" – the gap between the end of one life and the beginning of another.[9]

❀ Rudolf Steiner (20th century Switzerland) – Steiner's cognitions revealed that Martin Luther, 16th century leader of the

Protestant Reformation, chose his great-great-great-grand-parents 500 years in advance in order to ensure the characteristics he needed in his hereditary stream.[10]

❀ Rabindranath Tagore (1861 to 1941 India) – "At the far end of the stage of the world's play I stand. Each moment do I see the shore beyond the darkness where in the vast consciousness of the Unmanifest I once lay merged." ("The Final Offering")

❀ Norman Paulsen (contemporary American mystic and author) – "Awakened spirit-beings, approaching the earth and vision of new birth, can look back through the corridors of times past, for their Book of Life lies open to them."[11]

An African elder, Tlingit shaman, four Buddhist monks, an Indian saint, an American mystic, and a Sikh master also pierced the veil which hides the innumerable pasts within their sub-conscious minds.

The Disenchanted Twin

*Little was known about the gifted memory of the
Bangwans of Cameroon, Africa, until a tribal elder spent
a day relating memories to a trusted anthropologist
who had lived with the tribe in the 1970s.* [12]

The tribal elder recounts how he and his soul brother prepared for a twin birth. The twin souls reposed in a immense dark cave where swarms of spirit babies floated in pairs or groups in search of suitable parents. For years, they hunted for a cozy home. At long last, they settled upon a couple and penetrated the belly of a man who transferred them to his wife's womb via his semen.

Of course, tastes can differ even in the province of unborn children. For some unexplainable reason, the Bangwan elder's twin withdrew in a fury to the comfort of the spirit world. At this point, however, the Bangwan elder refused to accompany his brother. The angry departed twin tormented the peaceful twin who remained in the womb, thus physically straining the mother's pregnancy. The renegade twin ultimately located a woman living in a neighboring village who was evidently more to his liking. She birthed the "departed" twin as a baby girl, one day after the Bangwan elder's birth.

Leaving an Old House for a New One

*Memories of a revered Buddhist monk
highlight cases of instant return.*

A farmer-turned-Buddhist monk gives an account of his unbroken stream of consciousness between death and rebirth. When his life as a Thai farmer ended, Leng entered a totally new kind of existence. He was able "to see in all directions."[13] He witnessed the body he left behind on the veranda and watched his funeral rites. He observed the cremation of his body and listened to Buddhist monks chanting at his last rites.

But more than that, Leng's spirit visited a younger sister who had given birth to a son the day before Leng's own death. Leng's spirit observed the infant with great affection and desired to touch his newborn nephew, but held back because he did not want to disturb the child. Next Leng's spirit suddenly experienced "a sense of falling," and he became aware of himself as the same infant in the crib. His consciousness was coherent and he recalled his previous life as Leng even though he was now a helpless infant who could not talk yet.

When he began to speak, he astounded his family by describing his past life and naming relatives and friends he had known. His previous mother and father were now in his new lifetime his grandparents. He grew up to be the Venerable Phra Rajusthajarn of the Pa Yodhaprasiddhi monastery in Changwad Surin, Thailand.

Interpenetrating Worlds

*A Burmese Buddhist monk recalls how
a spiritual companion escorted him through
the spiritual world to his mother's womb.*

Monks chanted on the seventh night following Maung Po Thit's burial (1920). That night a sage dressed in white appeared in the dream of Maung's widow, saying: "I am sending your deceased husband to the village headman's house." A sage fitting an identical description appeared in the dream of the headman's wife, announcing:

"This Maung Po Thit wants to live with you, so I am bringing him along. Please accept him."[14]

In due course, the headman's wife's became pregnant and birthed a baby boy (1921). As soon as her two-year-old son Sayadaw began to speak, he related memories of his past life as Maung Po Thit. He recalled events in that life going back to the age of twelve. He remembered being a surveyor and described former relationships, friends, property, and debts.

Young Sayadaw explained that Maung's life ended prematurely at thirty-six, evidently due to an appendicitis attack. Maung left a pregnant wife and child behind. Strange as it seems, Sayadaw reunited with his former family who lived near his current home village. The young boy's playmates were two children he had fathered in a former life. Sayadaw addressed them without honorifics, as if he were their father.

Maung's family confirmed Sayadaw's memories of how his former life ended: vomiting; abdominal pain and fever; riding to the hospital in the midst of a monsoon on an uncovered oxcart, encountering torrential rains; and lying on an operating table, looking up at a masked surgeon.

Souls Waiting in the Wings for Birth

In between one life and the next, Maung found himself leaning against a tree in a forested jungle with splendid flowers. He wore a short Burmese jacket, sandals, and turban headdress. He felt thirsty, weak, discouraged, and lonely until a friendly old man approached him. The sage carried a staff and wore a white shawl draped over his shoulder. He bore a knot of hair on his head, a long flowing white beard, and moustache. The sage greeted Maung by name and invited him on a journey. They travelled on foot for about an hour until they reached Maung's former home.

The guide went indoors. Maung waited in the front yard under a tree. A few minutes later, the sage directed Maung to the village headman's house. The sage beckoned Maung to come inside. The guide then explained, "I must go back, but you must stay here." Maung remembers the family members inside – the last memory prior to his birth as Sayadaw.

Sayadaw grew up to become a Buddhist monk and scholar, the Venerable Sayadaw U Sobhana. He is convinced that the spiritual helper who guided him to his family corresponds to the sage appearing in the dreams of his former wife and his present mother. His message, "This Maung Po Thit wants to live with you," suggests Maung's pre-arranged birth as Sayadaw.[15]

Star over Patna

*Upon Divine command, Guru Gobind Singh
(1666 to 1708) left a celestial realm to be
born during one of India's bleakest periods.* [16]

I shall now tell my own history of how God sent me into the world when I was absorbed in penance on Mount Sapat Shring where King Pandu practiced Yoga and attained bliss. There I continuously remembered the omniscient power of God and I became blended with Him.

I had no desire to take human birth. My thoughts were lost in prayer at the Holy Feet of the Lord. However, the Lord made me understand His Will and inspired me to undertake the Mission: "I have appointed you as My son and created you to spread righteousness and prevent people from committing senseless deeds." I bowed my head and answered, "I will take birth in the Dark Age of Sin. Bless me with supreme sustenance." The Lord then ordered me to take birth as Guru Gobind Singh, the son of a couple who worshipped "the Unseen One" and strove to attain God's Union.

Amalgam of Divinity and Action

Gobind's birth took place during the Mohammedan conquest of India, the bloodiest story in history. Moslem raiders had been looting India for 600 years. Afghan sultans crossed into the Punjab with their armies, returning home with slaves, gold, and precious jewels – including diamonds the size of pomegranates. Millions of Indians starved to death in the 1630s alone when the Mogul Emperor emptied the royal treasury to buy jewels for his "Peacock Throne." Religion had been reduced to superstition and ritualistic performances. Muslim rulers destroyed 60,000 Hindu temples and constructed mosques in 3,000 of these sites.

Souls Waiting in the Wings for Birth

Gobind assumed birth as the tenth Sikh Master, but the political circumstances of the time turned him into a general of the armed forces, patriot, arch enemy of exploitation, and social reformer. Established in a higher consciousness *(samadhi)*, Gobind and his disciples fought oppression and persecution in religion, society, and politics. They won battles, yet never fought for territory or power.

Gobind emphasized that both Hindus and Muslims were living under a regime of profound injustice and oppression. He admonished people to recognize all mankind as one and united them within one religion, Sikhism.

Bahadur Shah, the Mogul Emperor, assassinated Gobind in 1708. It was a pity that Gobind's life ended at the age of forty-two. As one biographer points out, "He accomplished what others could not accomplish in four hundred years."[17] Had Gobind worked to a ripe, old age, what more could have happened in the course of Indian history?

Home of the "Blind Buddha"

*The gifted memory of the American mystic
and author Norman Paulsen exists in his
"consciousness as a visual memory recall
with vivid images, sounds, and colors."[18]*

Norman descended toward a "bright blue pearl of a Mother Earth." Her waters and land appeared like "a celestial garden" floating in the cosmos and drew him like iron to a magnet. His life energy and love merged with images of clashing waves, "torrents of spray ... clouds of mist, slowly settling upon glistening monoliths of stone."[19]

Still searching, Norman flew East beyond the rolling hills and bright green meadows to a fertile valley. There a village greeted him and a silent street ran north and south. He watched for a house facing the rising Sun. Then, a picket fence, an open gate, and a green lawn sprang out beneath two tall palm trees to welcome him. Indeed, he found the home of the blind Buddha – his father-to-be.

Charles Paulsen was the newly elected judge of the city and county courts, as well as an American Buddhist minister. Deprived of earthly vision, Charles walked with a white cane sensing the ground beneath him. The blind man was "stalwart and precise."[20] Using his acute hearing, he heard "the message of the whispering wind and the babbling brook as he extended his life outward into all beings and images around him."[21] Silently Norman's spirit approached the blind man by being as quiet as the wind. But like an ocean wave meeting another wave, their souls could not resist.

"He found me standing there on the street in the midst of his life. My spirit-image flashed before his inner vision; I had startled him. He stopped walking to stand alert in a silent greeting. Time stood still for him. 'You have finally come to help me, to be my eyes in the world.'"[22]

Norman explained:

"Long have we been friends and again we meet. My spirit is fixed upon rebirth here. Our lives must be joined together for a time."[23]

Charles invited Norman into his home like any other guest. Although cheerful, Charles harbored reservations that blindness might accompany Norman if he was born in his family. Once Charles overcame his fear, he prayed:

"Man from the North, eyes for two, abide in my house with my wife and me; be my friend once more. Your name shall be Norman after the blood of our fathers: Nor (the) man."[24]

Norman answered the blind Buddha's call on February 3, 1929, and "lost no consciousness in entering the planetary body of the earth elements."[25]

Norman maintained clear consciousness as an infant. Certain sights, sounds, smells, tastes, and touch "assaulted" his awareness. Sounds of a fire and the odor of burning oak, for instance, often woke baby Norman early in the morning. His father was in the kitchen making breakfast. As the morning coffee "assailed" Norman's nostrils, he thought, "Give me a cup of coffee!" His father replied, "No, not yet, Norman. Coffee is not good for little boys."[26]

The infant also found that his "newly extended limbs were cumbersome."[27] Norman struggled, resenting the restrictions of the body "ball and chain."[28] At night, he overcame his confinement: he floated out of body to join spirit companions.

Degrees of Free Will

The gifted memory of two lamas who lived centuries ago
illustrates the degrees of freedom in selecting one's social
environment – a story told by the XIV Dalai Lama.

The monks were members of the same monastic order and discussed what they hoped to achieve during their next birth.[29] The first monk said, "I will be reborn in Tibet so that I can advance spiritually within the same monastic tradition." The second lama said, "I will be reborn as a Minister in China" – perhaps to influence China's political relationship with Tibet.

In the next life, the first monk was reborn according to plan. Then rather unexpectedly, his friend surprised him one day when he too joined the monastery. The friend explained, "Many candidates were striving to attain that elite position. I was outcompeted even though I had the knowledge and spiritual accomplishment."

Cross-Cultural Parallel

As the Tibetan story suggests, the life map, or cosmic contract, can be as detailed as the world map. In a similar fashion, three-year-old Brett's "first choice for a Mommy" was not his American mother, but rather "a woman from the Philippines" who was "already taken."[30]

❧ Crossing the Luminous Fence

*Ramakrishna Paramahamsa (1836 to 1886),
the great Bengali sage, stated that his disciples did not
need to perform spiritual disciplines for their personal
salvation. They came here for the sake of the world.
On one occasion, Ramakrishna shared his memories
of how he chose his chief disciple prior to birth.*

Nineteenth-century India faced a grave crisis. Due to the British conquest, Indians were becoming awed by material power. Ramakrishna agreed to be born, under dire circumstances, in order to open the eyes of India to the grandeur of their spiritual culture. Prior to his birth, he prayed for divine collaborators to be his companions so that he would not feel alien and restless: "How can I go alone if I have not a pure-minded bhakta uncontaminated by lust and gold to talk with?"[31]

Ramakrishna thus did not come to Earth alone. The birth of Ramakrishna's wife, Sarada Devi, and "a mandala of intimate companions, expressions of the Divine Essence,"[32] came in answer to Ramakrishna's prayer. In fact, at the time of his chief disciple Vivekananda's birth, he saw a shattered ray of divine energy flash across the sky from Benares to Calcutta where Vivekananda was being born at the same instant. Ramakrishna jumped in joy and announced, "My prayer is answered. You have taken a body for my sake."

Ramakrishna never made a secret of what he thought of Vivekananda. Long before they first met, he was enraptured about Vivekananda's advent, and recalls his original revelations. Ramakrishna was reminded of how he had selected Vivekananda while he was deep in ecstatic meditation one day:

"My awareness rapidly ascends through every illumined level of being, plunging toward the Mother Essence, the dazzling darkness of the absolutely unmanifest, beyond any possible experience."[33]

Ramakrishna's consciousness "soared high" and ascended a luminous path through the world of gross matter into the subtle world. He transcended the stellar universe, entered the subtler region of ideas, and witnessed the ideal forms of God.

When his mind reached the outer limits of that region, he encountered a luminous barrier separating the sphere of relative existence from that of the Absolute realm where form ceases. Crossing that "fence made of light," his mind entered that realm where no physical form is visible. Even the highest celestial beings kept their seats far below and dared not peep into that sublime realm.

In the next moment, he saw the seven eternally liberated sages – "a constellation of conscious stars, floating in the boundless awareness beyond all heavenly realms."[34] The light of pure consciousness constituted the bodies of these "primordial, genderless stars of wisdom."[35] They were unsurpassed in knowledge, holiness, renunciation, and love.

"A bolt of radiance"[36] meanwhile manifested out of that undifferentiated luminous region and condensed into a five-year-old child. The golden boy approached one of the seven brilliant lights – a venerable Buddha-figure who sat gracefully in the lotus meditation pose. The child climbed onto the sage's lap and "tenderly clasped his neck with his lovely arms."[37] The child's magical touch roused him from his transcendental state of equipoise. He gazed with half-open eyes upon the wondrous child who appeared as "a flame dancing everywhere around the silent sage."[38]

The boy addressed the Buddha-figure with a charming voice and whispered: "I am descending into time. You, too, must come with me." The sage gazed upon the child, and although he remained mute, "his beaming countenance" revealed that the child was "the treasure of his heart."[39]

The sage then became immersed once again in an ecstatic state and a fragment of the sage's body and mind, in the form of a bright ray, emanated from his right eye. As the ray of light descended to Earth, the light pierced each plane of existence like a needle passing through layers of loosely woven cloth until reaching a home in Calcutta – the future birth home of Swami Vivekananda (1863 to 1902).

Souls Waiting in the Wings for Birth

Ramakrishna's mind crossed the "fence made of light."

Chapter 31
Native American Seers

**Never before has an Apache told a white
man those things which are our own.**[1]
– Gosh-o-nne, Apache Medicine Man

*Native American shamans parallel religious
mystics of sophisticated cultures. They play the role
of philosopher, seer, sage, priest, healer, botanist,
teacher, and psychologist. In addition, they
are distinguished by gifted memory.*

Gifted memory arises from a state of consciousness far beyond
the normal states we call waking and dreaming. As strange as
it sounds, medicine men enjoyed being awake "inside" during
sleeping and dreaming, like reports of Eastern saints, contemporary meditators, and Zen Buddhist masters.

"Even while he is asleep, he knows and sees everything; you
cannot go near him without being perceived."[2]

Medicine men, in some cases, were endowed with a cosmic
faculty to simply think of a remote place and travel there on the
level of consciousness. A Tlingit legend refers to this type of
"remote sensing" when it says, "Like arrows, thoughts fly forth on
the sunbeams."[3] The Zuni likewise "can absent itself from the body
to find out the secrets of other beings."[4] The 20th century Apache
Geronimo was rumored to always know where government
soldiers were, making it difficult to track him down.

Titles of medicine men reflect a heightened awareness:[5]

- Dakota – *Wakanwacipi:* "Dreamers of the Gods."
- Algonquin – *Manitousiou:* "Those knowing Divine Things."
- Mexican – *Teopixqui* and *Teotecuhtli:* "Masters or Guardians of the Divine Things."
- Cherokee – *Atsilungkelawhi:* "Those having the Divine Fire."
- Iroquois – *Honundeunt:* "Keepers of the Faith."
- Mayan – *Cocome:* "Listeners."
- Eskimo – *Angakok:* "Ancient Ones."
- Apache – *Diyi:* "Wise Ones."

Medicine men, or "specialists in ecstasy,"[6] as the comparative religion scholar Mircea Eliade calls them, rarely discussed gifted memory with outsiders. In fact, Apache medicine men became "as silent as the sphinx,"[7] when it came to answering questions about spiritual wisdom.

Subtle indigenous experiences were cloaked in secrecy for many reasons:

1. U.S. Bureau of Indian Affairs and other federal agencies illegalized tribal religious rituals making it difficult for Native Americans to pass on their sacred knowledge.
2. Christian zealots persecuted Native Americans as heathens.
3. Outsiders ridiculed the medicine men as ignorant witch doctors.
4. Anthropologists viewed tribal spiritual experiences with suspicion, skepticism, and disbelief, deeming them to be imaginative at best.
5. Cultural barriers existed in the translation and interpretation of tribal languages and experiences into English.
6. Tribal members threatened the lives of medicine men in order to keep their knowledge sacred and confidential.
7. Whites were guilty of blatant censorship of Indian traditions.
8. Genocide reduced the Native American population, decreasing the number of medicine men to research.
9. Surviving members lost sacred knowledge.
10. American schools did not teach Native American traditional knowledge.

Despite the barriers, Old Man Buffalo Grass revealed sacred Navaho knowledge to a trusted anthropologist in 1928, three months before he passed on.

Souls Waiting in the Wings for Birth

You see me only as an ugly old man, but I am filled with great beauty inside. "I sit as on a mountaintop and I look into the future. I see my people and your people living together."[8] My people will soon forget their earthly way of life unless they read about it in white men's books. Write down what I say and make a book so that coming generations will know this truth.

Medicine men in other North American tribes declared that they had been "spirit-beings" prior to human life.[9] In Canada, a Great Bear Lake "doctor" acquired healing powers prior to birth. He learned about medicinal plants as he witnessed elixirs falling from a medicine star like rain to Earth. After he came to Earth, an angel appeared in a dream and asked, "What have you there?"[10] He showed the medicines. The angel advised, "Leave them alone lest you use them for bad ends." And so he did.

A Huron medicine man illustrates another gifted memory. He dwelled as an *oki* (spirit) in a sub-terrestrial world together with a female spirit. They decided to be born as twins and "had finally concealed themselves near a path and taken up their abode in a passing woman." The medicine man fought with his twin in the womb. Due to a premature delivery, his sister was stillborn.[11]

Additional gifted memories come from Canadian Dakota, Sioux, Iowa (Ojibwa), and Winnebago tribes.

Travelling with the Thunders

Canadian Dakota medicine men or women
(chiefly the Wahpeton) "know everything that is going
to happen in the near future, into what family they will
be born, and every event of their future life."[12]

Before coming to live on Earth, medicine men travelled with the higher worldly beings called the Thunder Beings or Thunders, messengers of the Supreme Being *Wakan'taka*. During every thunderstorm, they scouted "for a choice place for nativity,"[13] – "sometimes among the Indians, sometimes among the whites."[14]

Memories of dwelling with the Thunder Beings parallel the memories of Lorenzo Caravella (Chapter 28, *Footprints in Heaven, Contemporary Gifted Memory*). Lorenzo recalls visiting an area filled with Jovian planets, lightning, and thunder during the inter-life period.

Of course, there is a connection between the Jovian Core Galaxy and Thunder Beings. Different cultural backgrounds express experiences differently. The Jovian Core Galaxy is a spiritual spa, a playground for gods, goddesses, gurus, and spiritual teachers. That is why all the rumbling is there. There are undertones and a transcendental dialogue going on all the time. It is a huge library of information.

In certain cases, some Dakota "were to be born among whites, but they refused to have it so."[15] They preferred birth "among Indians so that they might have Dakota customs and dress."[16] The Thunder Beings warned, "If you choose white parents and fail to abide by our instructions, the vengeful Thunders will kill you."

Most medicine men received their power from the Thunders prior to birth. The Thunders agreed to send the medicine men a sign when it was time to begin their careers. The "promised sign"[17] – a dream in which the Thunders advised them to perform a Sun Dance ceremony – came after the age of twenty. This sacred Sun ceremony lasted up to three days, during which time the tribal community fasted and observed silence. They prayed to the Sun and were transformed and strengthened by inner revelations as they observed the Sun's course across the sky.

Afterward, they administered to the needy and knew the nature of their afflictions. Similar to "X-rays," the diseased portion of the anatomy, such as the heart, stomach, or liver, appeared before them when they closed their eyes and chanted songs they learned from the Thunders. The Thunders gave them remedies for everything except lungs.

Friendship Before Birth

*Wanet'un'je, an Iowan medicine man, recalls floating above
Earth "inspecting" various tribes for an ideal birth place.*

Wanet'un'je rejected the Winnebago "because they smelled
fishy." So he "circled around," until he discovered the Iowa who
were "clean, kept their camps swept up, and sent their women a
long way off to menstruate."

"So he came down and entered a dark lodge with a bearskin
door and after quite a stay he came out (i.e., came out of mother's
womb and was born)."[18]

Wanet'un'je developed into a great prophet. One day he told his
people, "After I left the spirit world, my twin spirit brother and I
experienced a twist of fate. We were born as medicine men into
tribes of bitter enemies – the Sioux and Iowa (Ojibwa)."

As reported by another account, the Sioux medicine man also
knew that his spirit brother, Wanet'un'je, had been born to an
enemy tribe. The Sioux medicine man sensed his twin spirit
brother's presence one day while hunting near tribal boundaries.
He advised his warriors, "My spirit brother – the revealer of hidden
truths— has been born as an enemy. Our meeting now appears
imminent." He advised them that he and his spirit brother look
alike, "display the same totem," and sing the same "war songs!"[19]

The Sioux hunting group advanced toward the enemy camp
bearing a peace pipe. The Ojibwa responded in kind, despite
mutual hatred. As soon as the spirit brothers witnessed each other
for the first time in the earthly world, they embraced with friendly
fervor. The enemy tribes became awestruck with their close resem-
blance. The enemies camped together in harmony for several days.
At a final feast, the Sioux brother asked his Ojibwa counterpart to
sing a song. He sang the Sioux medicine man's favorite song to
everyone's amazement.

Home of the Thunderbirds

A Canadian ethnologist reported memories
of "G," a member of the Winnebago tribe who
claimed to be a reincarnated Thunderbird.

"I came from the home of the Thunderbirds … . My spirit father and mother were Thunderbirds. The Thunderbirds are beings whose glance can penetrate any object … . I have seen a man through a tree … . When I was ready to go down among the human beings … I was given the power to overcome my enemies in battle. And this I have actually done. All the Thunderbirds have small war-clubs. I also had one when I came. Whenever I went on the warpath I made myself a war-club … . I also had the power of causing or stopping rain. All that I had to do was to offer tobacco to the Thunderbirds and make my request."[20]

When "G" tires of human life, he will return to the Thunderbirds someday.

Touring the Milky Way

*The memories of a late 17th century Tlingit
shaman from British Columbia illustrate
how a yearning for home triggered rebirth.*[21]

A ladder descended from Heaven after Ky'itl'ā́c's soul exited the body. He climbed to the top and met the ladder's guardian – an elderly, dark-skinned man with curly hair. He asked, "Why are you here? Ky'itl'ā́c explained, "I have chosen to end my own life."

The guardian allowed him into the upper realm. Ky'itl'ā́c travelled throughout the world of spirit until he came to a huge mansion with a kettle sitting in front. The owner, the ruler of the upper world, invited him inside. His attendants granted Ky'itl'ā́c a tour of the kingdom, including a visit to the Milky Way. Ky'itl'ā́c saw two white geese swimming in a lake. He accepted the guides' challenge to hit the geese with a small pebble. The geese sang such melodious tones that Ky'itl'ā́c laughed, as if someone had tickled him.

His hosts next invited him to look through the cloud door. Ky'itl'ā́c saw two bashful young girls, "the celestial daughters of the Tahit [Heaven]," as well as the Earth with its treetops looking like countless pins. Upon seeing the Earth, he pulled a blanket over his head, flung himself down to Earth, and landed safely in a forest. Ky'itl'ā́c wandered through the woods. Then he spotted a home with mats covering the door. He peeped inside and saw a newborn crying. The infant was none other than himself reborn.

Like the biblical Jacob, the Tlingit shaman witnessed the stairway to Heaven.

Chapter 32
Cosmic Memory

God knows all and we are
each a piece of God.
– Beverly Anderson

Memory can expand back to pre-conception,
back to previous earthly lives, back to the inter-life
periods between previous lives, forward to future lives
and, in certain cases, stretching back to the
beginning of time and creation.

Memory must be nonphysical or spiritual in nature if the advanced kinds of memories described in this chapter have validity. Some stream of individual consciousness must be alive and well between death and rebirth, no matter for how long or on what plane of existence the interval takes place.

Memory storage cannot reside in the physical brain in these advanced cases, for no physical connection continues between lifetimes. Instead, memory is held beyond the brain in the field of consciousness. Memory is in the storehouse of consciousness and is accessed at any time or place by gifted individuals.

Plato acknowledged the same concept when he taught that each soul contemplates pure and perfect knowledge when it is a companion with god in the upper regions prior to birth. Wisdom is merely relearning what we naturally knew "before the influx of matter intoxicated our souls"[1] when we approached our mothers' wombs. For the same reason, the Greek word for reading means "knowledge regained."

The Greeks further differentiated between types of memory:[2] 1) memory of primordial events (origins of the cosmos, of the Gods, of people), or what we will call cosmic memory; and 2) memory of individual personal events, what we will call pre-conception memory, past-life memory, and inter-life memory.

"Lethe, 'Forgetfulness,' has equal efficacy against the two kinds of memory. But Lethe is powerless in the case of certain privileged persons: 1) [cosmic memory] those who, inspired by the Muses or by virtue of a "power of prophecy in reverse," succeed in recovering the memory of primordial events; 2) [past-life recall] those who, like Pythagoras or Empedocles, are able to remember their former lives."[3]

The Greeks, Eastern religions, as well as Jungian psychology, acknowledge advanced memories or the cosmic memory faculty to recall Creation's first moments like the Big Bang described by theoretical physicists.

❀ Buddhism – "There are those who by virtue of concentration and other yogic practices are able to ... draw upon the unrestricted treasury of subconscious memory wherein are stored records not only of our own past lives, but the records of the past of our race, the past of humanity, and of all pre-human forms of life, if not of the very consciousness that makes life possible in this universe."[4]

❀ Hazrat Inayat Khan (20th century Sufi) – "There is a still deeper sphere to which our memory is linked, and that is the only sphere of the universal memory, in other words the divine mind ... ."[5]

❀ Hinduism – "... the Self simply cannot be conscious of a time when it ... is not, was not, will not be. It is a contradiction in terms. Immortality is indelibly stamped on the face of Consciousness, the face of God."[6]

❀ Carl Jung (20th century Swiss psychiatrist) – We carry an 80,000-year-old being within us.

❀ Apollonius Rhodius (ancient Greece) – "Not even now, though he [Aethalides] has entered the unspeakable whirlpools of Acheron, has forgetfulness swept over his soul."[7]

People in sophisticated as well as indigenous cultures report cosmic memories.

❀ Rabbi Moses ben Nahman (13th century Judaism) – The Jewish mystic retained memories of being among "God's hidden treasures"..."from the beginning of time." God called him forth from "Nothing." Divine forces then built, nourished, and gave form to his soul. His soul remained "preserved in the chambers of the King" before descending upon Heaven's ladder "from the primeval pool of Siloam" to Earth, "the garden of the King."[8]

❀ William Blake (19th century England) – Blake looked "back into the regions of reminiscence" and saw "our ancient days before this Earth appeared."[9]

❀ Paramahansa Yogananda (20th century India) – Yogananda recalls being a part of "the chorus of singing lights which heralded the coming of the worlds."[10]

❀ King Solomon *(Old Testament)* – Solomon recalls being created as a soul before the Earth was formed. (*Proverbs* 8: 22-31)

❀ Job *(Old Testament)* – Job was there when God laid down the Earth's foundations. (*Job* 38:4-21)

❀ Vamadeva (ancient India) – "Finding myself in the womb, I knew all the births of the gods."[11] (*Rig Veda* IV, 27,1)

❀ Goddess Mnemosyne (ancient Greece) – The mother of the Muses knows "all that has been, all that is, all that will be."[12]

❀ Krishna (ancient India) – "You and I have taken many births, Arjuna. I know them all, but you do not." (*Bhagavad-Gita*, IV, 5)

❀ Rumi (13th century Sufi poet) – "For a million years I floated in ether, even as the atom floats uncontrolled. If I do not actually remember that state of mine, I often dream of my atomic travels."[13]

❀ Dhu al-Nun Al-Misri (9th century Sufi teacher) – The ascetic walked down the street and passed a black slave-girl whose "heart was rent asunder by her love of the All-Compassionate."[14] The woman knew him by name and explained, "My spirit knew your spirit when our souls were created in the spiritual world thousands of years ago." Dhu al-Nun accepted her as his master. (Some biographers name Dhu al-Nun founder of the Sufi religion.)

❀ Rabindranath Tagore (modern India) – "The Time that my Journey takes is Long and the Way of it Long. I came out on the Chariot of the First Gleam of Light and Pursued my Voyage through the Wilderness of Worlds, leaving my Track on Many a Star and Planet … ." *(Gitanjali)*

Native American shamans, as well as Pythagoras, the Indian saint Thakur Anukulchandra, Rabbi Jaacob Yitzchak, the Winnebago shaman Thunder-Cloud, and Gautama Buddha were all aware of their primordial heritage.

Vision of the Delphic Oracle

*Heraclitis described the philosopher Pythagoras as
"the most learned of all men in history." Pythagoras
was the first to introduce teachings of the
soul's immortality to the Greeks.*

Apollo spoke through the Delphic Oracle and promised Mnesarchus and Parthenis "a son who would be useful to all men and throughout all time."[15] The couple followed the Oracle's advice and conceived a wonder child in Phoenicia, away from the disturbing influences of Samos.

From an early age, their son devoted his life to learning. Pythagoras was initiated into Grecian sacred mysteries, travelled to Egypt, learned their language, and entered their holiest temples. Pythagoras socially intermingled with the Chaldeans and Magi, learned mysteries in Crete, and may have travelled as far as India.

Pythagoras carried geometry to perfection, introduced measures and weights, and developed basic principles of mathematics, astronomy, and music theory. Six hundred students sought his knowledge every day. Disciples were bound by oath to keep many of the esoteric teachings private.

One disciple, Empedocles (490 to 30 BC), spoke of Pythagoras as "a man of extraordinary knowledge," for "whenever he directed all the power of his spirit, he easily saw what he had been in ten, twenty human lives."[16] Pythagoras' memories begin with his first human life as Aethalides when his father Hermes, the God of Wisdom, granted him a boon. He chose "an unfailing memory."[17]

"According to Apollonius of Rhodes, even when he [Pythagoras] crossed Acheron, forgetfulness did not submerge his soul; and though he inhabits now the realm of shades [souls], now that of the sun's light, he always remembers what he has seen."[18]

Souls Waiting in the Wings for Birth

People believed Pythagoras was a son of Apollo and of a virgin birth. His beauty, godlike appearance, and actions made this a reasonable assertion. Legends refer to Pythagoras' relations with exalted beings, communication with animals, and ability to appear simultaneously in more than one location. Pythagoras even revealed his golden thigh to Abaris, a priest of the Hyperborean Apollo, to prove his divine status.

Ancient Athens

Indigenous Memory of the Big Bang

*The white man criticized Native American
shamans who reported cosmic memories,
calling them wildly imaginative at best.*

Until modern physicists proved that the Big Bang had taken place billions of years ago, claims of indigenous people recalling when the cosmos came into existence fell on deaf ears.

Three examples follow.

- ❀ Joe Homer (Native American Yuma) – Joe Homer "was present at the very beginning and saw and heard it all." Joe never lost consciousness even in the womb: "Before I was born I would sometimes steal out of my mother's womb while she was sleeping, but it was dark and I did not go far. Every good doctor [Native American medicine man] begins to understand before he is born, so that when he is big he knows it all."[19]

- ❀ Mojave – Medicine men insist that they stood on the sacred mountain, Avikwame, or played at Aha'av'ulypo. "I was there, I saw him,"[20] a shaman says of his hero, or of the death of the god Matavilya. Each shaman received supernormal abilities from the god, *Mastamho*, when existence burst forth into the world and unleashed Time.

In another interesting case among the Dakota Sioux, the Native American holy men recalled "what occurred to them in bodies previously inhabited for at least six generations back."[21]

The Cosmic Soul and the Big Bang

*Indigenous people were not alone in their
knowledge of the Big Bang. India's spiritual teacher,
Thakur Anukulchandra (1888 to 1969), claimed to be
an unrivalled observer of the entire process of creation,
from the prime indivisible point to this widely evolved
vast universe, the Creator and the created both.*

Thakur Anukulchandra recalls how a prime point let itself
explode into millions of hyper atoms. Each hyper atom then burst
into millions of supra-hyper atoms resulting in "an uncut indivisible physically inconceivable point." Thakur witnessed that
ultimate point – the Cosmic Soul – create an infinity of beings out
of itself like thousands of sparks coming from a fire. The souls were
destined to live through a series of lives so long as they remained
subject to the illusion of personal individuality.[22]

From the beginning of Creation until Thakur's present life, his
ego passed through various phases prior to being "encaged" in a
living body, last of all human. His chain of human births include a
cobbler, prince, and spiritual seeker. In the gap between each death
and rebirth, Thakur felt empathy for family members whom he
watched grieving for him.

Thakur dwelled in an "undefined higher region" prior to his
present life. His journey to Earth involved travelling through "a yet
undiscovered system of celestial constellations." He traversed a
vast distance in space, passing through 44,000 planets. While our
planets rotate around the Sun, Thakur observed that "lakhs of suns
rotate around a bigger sun."[23] He also proceeded through a former
planet that had split into pieces, and observed a planetary system
yet to be discovered by science. Still fresh in his memory is the
strange behavior of a unique constellation – a central star
surrounded by four other stars. The four stars appeared red when

they approached the central star and turned blue when they moved away through a principle known to science as the Doppler Effect.

En route to Earth, Thakur stopped at various planets where celestial beings welcomed him with a grand ovation. Each planet had unique life forms suited to their atmospheres, unlike any found on Earth. Thakur felt "a pang of separation" as the planetary beings chanted hymns in his praise as he departed from their planet.

Thakur finally arrived in our solar system by coming through a ray of light and descending into the Sun. He was not "burnt to ashes." The Sun's interior is "very cold, the heat is on its surface."[24]

"Just think, I descend from inside the sun by a track. If one takes the track from here, would see pitch darkness just on the left and on the right, not right, rather diagonally he would see light only. He would witness 44,000 planets on the way, one of which is split into pieces … ."[25]

East Indian symbolic representation of the structure of the cosmos.

Video Tape of the Soul

*Gifted individuals perceive the soul's history in
the shape and lines of an individual's forehead and
hand, as well as in the aura radiating from the body.
Hasidic rabbis, including Isaac the Blind and
Rabbi Jaacob Yitzchak, for instance, knew
whether a man's soul was "new" or "old."*[26]

Rabbi Jaacob Yitzchak was born with the ability to see from the beginning to the end of the world. Visions of the flood of evil engulfing the Earth so disturbed this 18th century "Seer," that he prayed to have his talent restricted. God narrowed his vision. Yet to witness everyone's "pilgrimage" as a soul from the Source was even too much to bear. Jaacob cognized how each soul "entered a human frame and how each time it had wrought ill or well at the great task which it was destined to accomplish."[27] For seven years, Jaacob tried to block the visions by hiding his eyes under a thick mask. He removed the mask only for prayer and study. Unfortunately this practice did nothing except weaken physical eyesight.

The Seer stopped wearing his mask at nineteen. His lifetime's work of administering to troubled people began. He gazed upon their foreheads, "into the depth of time and saw the origin and story of the soul – soul's ultimate descent and root."[28]

The Rabbi's Magical Shirt

One day, the Seer directed a bright young pupil to take charge during his absence. The humble lad, Yaakov Yitzchak of Pzysha, was known as "the holy Yehudi," pleaded, "Please appoint a more learned disciple." The Seer advised, "You are 'the right one.'[29] Wear my shirt while you fulfill the duties of my office."

The next morning, the Yehudi, wearing the Seer's shirt. counselled a distressed man. Much to the apprentice's surprise, a curtain appeared to be drawn apart when the Yehudi innocently looked upon the man's forehead. The Yehudi found himself standing at the edge of a sea, "whose dark waves assaulted the very heavens."[30] When those waves "split asunder," "a figure, totally unlike that visitor, yet with the same seal upon its forehead" appeared. Next, the waves devoured that figure and again the Yehudi saw a different figure, "but sealed with the same seal."[31] That figure then vanished revealing yet another figure, and so on.

After his first appointment, the Yehudi took a break before the next appointment. Unbeknownst to him, the Seer had vicariously conferred his power unto him. With each subsequent appointment, the curtain was again torn apart allowing the Yehudi to not only see the paths each soul had taken from the beginning, but to penetrate through "the background of that row of figures" until he arrived at "the very being of the primordial."[32]

I saw Eternity
the other night,
Like a great Ring of
pure and endless light ...
Some ... soar'd up into the Ring.[58]

Sojourns of a Winnebago Shaman

*The memories of Thunder-Cloud, a well-known
Winnebago shaman, go back to his first human lifetime.
He shared his past life and inter-life memories with
Canadian ethnologist Paul Radin in 1908.*[33]

Thunder-Cloud considered himself a spiritual being having human experiences. His brother-in-law, Crashing Thunder, describes him as "a virtuous man, disliking no one, never stealing and never fighting," and he "adhered strictly" to all the "precepts" of the Medicine Rite.[34]

> "I came from above, and I am holy. It is I, Thunder-Cloud, who speak, I who am now on earth for the third time, I who am now repeating experiences that I well remember from my previous existences."[35]

First Lifetime on Earth

Many years before his present life, Thunder-Cloud lived on Earth in "a party that numbered about twenty camps."[36] Everyone seemed to be on the warpath. As a young lad, an enemy war party attacked his tribe. Innocent lives were lost. Due to his sudden death, Thunder-Cloud thought he still had a physical body. He even returned home to his wife.

> "'What can be the matter,' I thought, 'that they pay no attention to me ... .' All at once it occurred to me that I might, in reality, be dead. So I immediately started out for the place where I had presumably been killed ... ."[37] "... [there] I saw a heap of bodies on the ground and mine among them. No one was there to bury us, so there we lay and rotted."[38]

Thunder-Cloud's spirit was taken to the place where the Sun sets (the West). He lived with an elderly couple in "an excellent place" where "people have the best of times." Whenever he desired to go anywhere, all he had to do was "wish" and he was instantly there at the speed of thought.

Second Human Lifetime on Earth

If individuals do not fulfill their desires in one life, they feel them after death and wish to express them through another material body. Like that, Thunder-Cloud's thoughts turned to unfinished business. (Cross-cultural parallel – Indian philosophy, Buddhism, Trobriand Islanders, and the Yoruba of Africa describe the soul's need for earthly life in similar terms. See Chapter 24, *Souls in Training*.)

> "The old man with whom I was staying said, 'My son, did you not speak about wanting to go to the earth again?' I had, as a matter of fact, only thought of it, yet he knew what I wanted. Then he said, 'You can go, but you must ask the chief first.'"[39]

The chief responded to Thunder-Cloud's desire by saying, "Go and obtain your revenge upon the people who killed you and your relatives." Thunder-Cloud was brought down to Earth, even though he did not enter his mother's womb right away.

> "I was taken into a room. There I remained, conscious at all times. One day I heard the noise of little children … I thought I would go outside. Then … I went through a door, but I was really being born again from a woman's womb. As I walked out I was struck with the sudden rush of cold air and I began to cry."[40]

In his second life, Thunder-Cloud learned how to fast as a preparation for warfare. He took "full revenge" for the innocent lives lost in the earlier life. Near the end of his long life, Thunder-Cloud's bones became unjointed, his ribs caved in, but death came without pain. Loved ones wrapped his body in a blanket and set it upon sticks positioned over a grave. His spirit lingered near the burial site until a voice said, "Come, we must leave now!"

> A guide escorted me in the direction of the Sun to a village where we met the ancestors. My guide instructed me, "Stop here for four nights." In reality, I stayed four years. I enjoyed myself. There are lively dances all the time. From that place I ascended "to the place where Earthmaker lived and there I saw him and talked to him, face to face, even as I am taking to you now. I saw the spirits too, and, indeed, I was like one of them."[41]

Dancing in Nature

Strange as it seems, Thunder-Cloud recalls lifetimes as a fish, bird, and a buffalo – apparently between the second and third human lifetimes.

> I recall being transformed into a fish. They are happy beings and have many dances. Nevertheless, I often lacked food and that made my life worse than humans.
>
> In another life, I became a tiny bird. Bird life was pleasant so long as the weather was good. However, I underwent many hardships when it became cold and was compelled to steal meat from the racks at the camp of some people. A young boy stood near the racks. We were afraid of him because he shot at us with a bow and arrow. It made a dreadful noise and we flew away. I slept in a hollow tree at night. If I entered the tree first, I would be nearly squeezed to death by the other birds who came behind me. If I waited until the last, there was no room and I slept outside.
>
> "At another time I became a buffalo. The cold weather and food did not worry me much then, but … we would always have to be on the alert for hunters."[42]

Third Human Lifetime

Thunder-Cloud was "permitted" to go to his "higher spirit-home, from which I originally came" subsequent to his buffalo existence. He asked Grandfather, the ruler of that spirit-home, for permission to return to Earth.

> He refused three times. But after the fourth request, he replied, "Grandson, you had better fast before you go and if any of the spirits take pity upon you (i.e., bless you), you may go and live in peace upon earth."[43]

The spirits above, "even to the fourth heaven," approved and blessed his rebirth after Thunder-Cloud fasted for four years. He extended the fast thirty days and "all the spirits whom Earth-Maker had created"[44] blessed his cosmic contract. Finally Earthmaker granted him a boon – to select his earthly mission. He joined the Medicine Rite again.

> A council of spirit teachers gathered in a lodge and advised Thunder-Cloud about his cosmic contract: "You will never fail in anything you wish to do. But before you go, we must test your powers."

All the spirits that lived up in the clouds taught me in a doctor's [shaman's] village everything that I was to do on Earth. There in the middle of the lodge lay a dead, rotting log, covered with many weeds, representing a sick person. They asked me to treat the log, "Human, try it."

I breathed four times upon the log and spat water upon it. "As a young man he, the dead log, arose and walked away ... . 'Human, very holy he is,' they said to me."[45]

In a subsequent trial, the spirit teachers taught him sacred chants to sing on Earth and placed "an invulnerable spirit-grizzly bear at one end of the lodge."

"I walked around the lodge holding a live coal in the palm of my hand and danced around the fireplace saying *wahi-!* and striking the hand containing the coal with my other hand."[46]

The spirit-grizzly bear fell forward prone upon the ground. Thunder-Cloud circumambulated the bear and breathed upon it four times and all the spirit teachers breathed with him. Thunder-Cloud restored the bear's life. The spirit-bear walked away in the shape of a human being. The teachers said, "This is good. Surely you are holy. Just as you have done here, will you always do on Earth."

In another test, Thunder-Cloud breathed on a black stone four times and blew a hole through it. The teachers said, "Good. If anyone asks you to heal pain, you can blow [heal] it away." The spirits made Thunder-Cloud's breath holy.

The spirit teachers from the middle of the ocean even blessed Thunder-Cloud.

The spirit teachers tested my powers at a shamans' village in the middle of the ocean. I blew upon the waves, all of them as large as the ocean. The waves became as quiet as water in a tiny saucer. I passed that test three times. In the fourth test, the teachers made the ocean choppy, and piled the waves one upon the other. I blew and the mighty ocean became silent.

The dancing grizzly-bears at Blue-Clay-Bank (St. Paul, Minnesota) blessed Thunder-Cloud's sojourn to Earth.

The grizzly bear spirits promised to assist me on Earth if I ever met with trouble. They blessed me with songs, holy claws, and "the power of beholding them" whenever I call for help.

The grizzly-bears danced, performed and showed me how to heal. They wounded themselves and "were badly choking with blood."

They showed me how they cured themselves and made themselves holy again. They told me, "All of this, human, we bless you with; and if you do (what we desire), you will obtain (what you desire)."[47]

The spirit teachers gave Thunder-Cloud a final message: "This, Human, is the way you will have to do. Not anything will there be that you can't accomplish. Whatever illness all (the people) may have, you will be able to cure it."[48]

Thunder-Cloud descended to Earth for the third time. He thought he had entered a lodge. In fact, he had penetrated his mother's womb.

Seeds of Buddhahood

*The stream of Buddha's consciousness remained
unbroken for roughly 2,500 years throughout
a series of 550 deaths and rebirths.*

The story of Gautama Buddha (563 to 483 BC)[49] exemplifies the consummation of spiritual growth by rising to the state of *Nirvana*. Buddha planned his final incarnation thousands of years in advance. His lofty goal to be released from the recurring condition of rebirths required a series of steps – just like a child's leanings to become a doctor require knowledge and graduation from several schools.

The decision to become a Buddha originated in an earlier lifetime as Sumedha. As the son of wealthy Brahmin parents, the child Sumedha lost both parents at an early age. Sumedha subsequently donated his inheritance to charity and sought a simple monastic life in a Himalayan hermitage.

One day as if following a hidden drummer, the young Buddha-in-training left the hermitage to visit the city on the very day townspeople were preparing a welcome for Buddha Dipankara – the 24th Predecessor of Gautama Buddha. The young monk, too, approached Dipankara. The saint's radiance inspired Sumedha to resolve:

I will become like Buddha Dipankara and illuminate others
through a ray emitted from my heart, no matter the distance.
Anyone who sincerely repents, regardless of how great a sinner,
will be reborn in my kingdom following his earthly life. They will
be instructed, improved and placed on the road to final liberation.

Sumedha lay flat on the muddy ground, as Dipankara approached, so that the holy one might use him as a human bridge and avoid soiling his feet. In a flash, Dipankara recognized Sumedha as a candidate for Buddhahood *(Buddha-bijamkura)*.[50] Miraculous events, including an earthquake, confirmed Dipankara's prediction of Sumedha's birth as the Buddha in a later age – including birth place, family name, the manner by which he was to attain supreme knowledge, and chief disciple's name.

Sumedha worked hard to attain perfection of higher powers, such as divine vision and hearing, reading others' thoughts, and knowledge of previous births, but as Dipankara foresaw, full awakening requires developing the ten virtues.

In subsequent births, the Buddha-in-training acquired great merit by perfecting charity, morality, renunciation, wisdom, energy, patience, truthfulness, resolution, love, and equanimity. In one lifetime, he witnessed a hawk attack a defenseless songbird and intervened, satisfying the predator with some of his own flesh.[51]

Five Great Perceptions

Directly preceding his final human incarnation, the Buddha-to-be reached the fourth Heaven of *Tusita* where he served as the presiding god over 32,000 *bodhisattvas*. Desires are quickly fulfilled in *Tusita*. Sexual desires, for instance, are satisfied by holding hands, and children are born "apparitionally" – a five-year-old child instantly appears on the knees of its mother.

Tusita is a blissful realm, although like human existence, divine life eventually ends. After 4,000 divine years, equivalent to 584,000,000 human years (one divine day and night equal 400 human years), a tumultuous turbulence resounded through the entire universe: the "Buddha-Uproar." The gods of 10,000 worlds had long waited this sign.

Setting the cosmic wheels in motion, the Buddha-to-be agreed to incarnate as the next Buddha and cognized "the five great perceptions" – time period, continent, country, family, and day of birth. He selected an auspicious period to be born, a time when people lived to 100 years, and a birth place in Kapilavasthu, a town nestled in the Himalayan foothills where people had high morals.

With the advice of the heavenly counsel, the Buddha-to-be selected a clan who satisfied the sixty-four requirements of moral and spiritual excellence. Within the clan, Queen Mahamaya met the thirty-two superior signs to be his mother, such as: virtue, beauty, patience, modesty, virginity, fearless heart, perfect limbs, as well as freedom from envy, anger, hatred, roughness, and evil thoughts. The heavenly counsel selected individuals who had controlled the desire to delight in mundane pleasures, to be born as Buddha's disciples and companions.

The Buddha-to-be announced:

> I will take human birth in twelve years. Do not grieve over my departure. My Buddhahood has been seen from eternity. In my absence, my successor, Maitreya, will instruct you in the Law.

Just as discomfort marks the end of human life, five omens signalled the Buddha-to-be's departure from *Tusita*: 1) soiled garments; 2) wilted garlands; 3) weakness and perspiration emitted from his body, like a tree covered with dew; 4) his mansion lost its attractiveness and beauty; and 5) he no longer enjoyed his companions.[52] Before he was conceived in his mother's womb, the *Tusita* gods reminded him, "Attain in your next existence your high destiny."

Footsteps in the Sands of Memory

Twenty-five hundred years ago, a family in present-day Nepal birthed Prince Siddhartha, the Buddha of our age. The royal son was destined to inherit a vast kingdom, until one night a voice called: "Awake! Thou the awakened! Arise, and help the world! Sleep no more!"[53]

Siddhartha renounced his kingdom, retired into the forest, leaving behind a beautiful wife and son. In his quest for Truth, Siddhartha spent nearly seven years in meditation and visiting sages. Still he found no answer for how to escape the misery of human life. At last, he meditated under the sacred Bo tree resolving to die if he did not obtain full illumination. On that night, Siddhartha sank into a golden-filled illumination and became Pure Consciousness itself.[54] He arose and danced in divine ecstasy: "I am emancipated, rebirth is extinct ... what had to be done is done ... ."[55]

As the Buddha, he beheld the universe consisting of innumerable world systems each with their earth, sun, moon, heavens, and hells. The unbounded universe with its countless realms was transcendental to physical notions of the cosmos. A whirling universe danced within his illumined consciousness, like sparks emanating from an infinite fire. He recalled 550 previous lifetimes in various types of human bodies, animal bodies, and even as a tree. Each life had served as a stepping stone to reach a state of being where his efforts could free mankind from suffering. Because he had willed to be born in each of the orders of life, it is said, "There exists not a particle of earth where Buddha has not sacrificed his life for the sake of creatures."[56]

Following his illumination, Buddha returned as a teacher of wisdom and compassion to the palace where he taught family and the entire kingdom how to embrace the Middle Way.

"[Buddha was] the great one, who never thought a thought or performed a deed except for the good of others, who had the greatest intellect and heart … ready to give up his life for the highest angels as well as for the lowest worm."[57]

Greek goddess of Memory – Mnemosyne

LANIA'S COSMIC CONTRACT

"I will help you recognize the vastness and power of love, that you might stand tall above darkness."

– Lania's Mother

Chapter 33
Overcoming Spiritual Amnesia

My soul remembers its lost Paradise ... .[1]
– Francis Thompson, poet

*Lania Desmond's memories parallel the teachings
of the Greeks, Sufis, and Gnostics, as well as the Jewish
Kabbalah: the physical body is a tomb, a prison, or a cage
until we wake up and remember who we really are.*

Lania understands and teaches people how to resolve their deep-seated issues of separation from God. Before Lania "came into form," all she knew was total connection with God.

> Wholeness is all there was. And I accepted the illusion that I would be separate from God once I entered physical form. But, I also chose to resolve that – to realize that there is no way to be separate from God. My main intention for this life was to overcome spiritual amnesia.

Lania's memory of being in the womb illustrates how impressionable we are when our souls enter form. Lania's mother was nineteen when she married a man in his forties, a friend of the family. The young girl married him primarily to get away from her parents. Lania's mother was diabolical and could fly into a rage at any moment. Lania sensed these "emotions and drama, manipulations, forcefulness, and intensity" the moment she entered the womb. The embryonic fluids charged with her mother's negative emotions acted like a potion of forgetfulness.

> I experienced such abject terror, total contraction, darkness, and fear that I began to forget "Home." I felt trapped, annihilated. I did everything I could to stay in the womb, and yet not be present. It was

a shock because it was different from where I came from. I felt overwhelmed. But there was no option, no escape hatch. It was part of my cosmic contract.

Lania recalls her father's enthusiasm when her mother announced the pregnancy, shortly after their wedding day.

My father's business involved a lot of travel. My mother didn't like that. She hoped to keep him home by having a baby. But the plot didn't work. What the pregnancy meant to my father was that he needed to work more. He invited my mother to travel with him and stay in the nicest places. The suggestion filled her with rage.

The final blow came on the day I was born. My father was out on the road. My mother became furious because, in her mind, I hadn't fulfilled what I was supposed to do – keep my father home.

So when the nurse brought me into my mother's room, I felt a devastating slam of energy. My mother said: "Get that piece of shit out of here." I thought, "Oh my God, what am I doing here? I made a horrendous mistake. I am bad. My choices are wrong."

Another formative event took place six months later.

My mother became upset while my father was away on business. Perhaps I was crying, hungry, or needed my diaper changed. She began to beat me. Meanwhile, my father began to feel something was happening to his little girl. He had found me badly bruised before.

My father trusted his intuition and returned just in time. He heard my cries as he got out of a cab on a busy street. He rushed to our fourth floor apartment. My mother had broken a number of wooden hangers over me. My father grabbed me and immediately took us to my grandparents' home. However, he didn't explain to them what had happened. Then he left. As a result, I learned, "If I open my mouth and cry for help, men run away."

Lania's relationship with her mother never became any sweeter. By the time Lania was six months old, major patterns had been set up.

I learned that I had no value – I am taking up air that someone important could have. I believed it was dangerous to ask for help and voice my opinion. I could never be taken care of. These patterns became so interwoven into my consciousness that I did certain things on automatic pilot. I could be devastated if I didn't understand what I was responsible for as far as someone else's perception was concerned.

Lania didn't forget her spiritual gifts despite the trauma.

I knew that Earth wasn't the appropriate place for me. The stork dropped me on the wrong planet. I knew, heard, saw, understood things that no one seemed to notice. I was different. When I looked at my mother, I saw through the facade to the underlying manipulations. She was covert. I knew her thoughts. It had nothing to do with being nice. It was just my mother's game of trying to look good for outer appearances.

Happy those early days when I shined in my angel infancy!
– Henry Vaughan

Angelic Visitation

*Lania's relationship with her mother forced
Lania to focus her attention outward.*

I have unusual gifts and have talked to my angels since I was
a baby. But when anything came out of my mouth related to that, my
mother force fed me Tide laundry detergent to shut me up. She did it
when I looked at her the "wrong" way or said or did something
"wrong." I was five years old the first time I recall it happening.

I started to believe that what I could see, feel, and touch was more
important than my higher consciousness. I went into a pleasing mode
and gave my power away. This was the beginning of my loss of self-
trust and belief in outer validation.

Lania suffered serious health problems due to her mother's
abusive nature.

Of course a child would become anorexic if they are eating laundry
detergent. Why would I want to swallow anything? It hurt too much.
By the time I was nineteen, I weighed seventy-six pounds, was
bleeding internally, and couldn't hold water. Doctors diagnosed me
with ulcerative colitis. My internal organs had shrunk down beyond
regeneration. A team of doctors stood around my hospital bed and
advised me, "We must remove three-fourths of your colon – not to
keep you alive, but to resolve some of the pain. After surgery, you
must have a bag on your side. You will need to be sedated with
morphine and remain in a rest home for the remainder of your life."

Lania left the hospital refusing the operation. She arrived home
totally depressed, realizing that she would never have a normal
life, get married, and have children.

The doctor sent me home with sleeping pills. I thought, "Why
prolong the inevitable?" I called my grandmother to say good-bye.
My grandmother always felt responsible because her daughter had
inflicted this on me. So I didn't want her to carry that burden. I told
her, "I love you. You have been the most wonderful influence in my
life. This isn't your fault." My grandmother was upset, but she was

going to be upset no matter what. I wanted to explain it rather than have someone else notify her.

As we talked on the phone, I began taking the pills. After I ended the phone call, I felt drowsy and rested in bed. I vaguely recall hearing a knock on the door which I didn't answer. I went into the bathroom and sat on the toilet. I became nauseous, fell and hit my head on the tub, and went unconscious.

Meanwhile, Lania's neighbor had been knocking on the door. When nobody responded, he felt something was wrong. He broke the door down and called an ambulance.

The hospital staff pumped my stomach three times, but I don't remember any of that. I do remember lifting out of my body and watching the doctors doing everything to get me to breathe, to have a heartbeat. I didn't cooperate. They pronounced me dead. I watched them pull the sheet over my head.

Once I was out of body, I felt good for the first time. Love surrounded me. I ascended through a tunnel. This felt like the reverse of when I descended into my mother's womb. Light and love increased. Such a welcoming, a feeling of freedom. I felt a brilliant divine presence. It seemed like it was everywhere and everything. I was more conscious than I could ever remember. I heard telepathic imprints, like thoughts in my head, and received huge amounts of information. I understood everything.

I don't know how long my NDE lasted. There is no time there. But they wouldn't let me get very far: "You must return. You can't leave until you do what you set out to accomplish." I felt angry, abandoned, rejected. I didn't want to be in my body. I was fighting the whole time. A pressure pushed me back down. I had no option.

A profound incident occurred during Lania's three days of unconsciousness.

I didn't want to wake up. I had IVs in my arm, and nurses walked me around the halls, one under each arm, hoping to wake me up. I wasn't cooperative. When I finally came to normal awareness, I was sitting on a bench in a hallway, leaning up against a nurse who was slapping me and pouring water over my body.

During the three days of unconsciousness, I was strapped to the bed so I wouldn't fall out. I recall a nurse trying to wake me up and shaking my feet. She kept asking, "Lania, do you know this man?" Someone was standing near my bedside. He placed his hand on my left shoulder. I opened my eyes and saw Jack, blurry as he was.

It touched me that Jack had come. He was somebody I cared about. I had taken care of him after his wife's nervous breakdown and suicide attempt. Jack had been distraught and almost incapacitated. I helped Jack for several months. Then we lost touch with each other.

Jack gave me words of encouragement: "I had a profoundly sad feeling and knew it had to do with you. I visited your home and a neighbor explained what had happened. I came to tell you that my wife Sara is no longer in the mental hospital. She is back home and doing well. Lania, if Sara can do it, so can you."

Jack's message reminded me of why I had come into form. I paid attention.

There is something curious about Jack's visit.

No one else saw Jack. The hospital had no record of any visitors. Jack even promised to leave me some cigarettes, but the nurse couldn't find them. The hospital didn't acknowledge that I was in a recovery room where Jack had visited me. I don't know how Jack found me. None of my neighbors talked to him. Yet, Jack delivered that message. I didn't imagine it. His visit is vivid in my mind. He may have been an angel in disguise.

Lania felt so inspired following the NDE that she regenerated her organs in four years and three months. The surprised doctors found no trace of ulcerative colitis. They diagnosed her as being anorexic from the age of five due to her mother's abuse.

Lania explains how the healing began.

After recuperating for several months, I attended a party where my friend John introduced me to his brother Mark. It was love at first sight for both of us. I had been missing that my entire life. This man shifted my consciousness, frame of reference, and perception of myself. I felt protected, loved, and accepted in a way I had never felt before. Mark's love gave me the reason to stay on this planet. The power of that love healed me.

One time Mark drove me to the doctor when I thought I had a lump in my breast. The doctor recommended a mammogram. On the way back home, Mark said, "It is okay, you don't need to worry about the lump. It's gone now." I believed him so completely that I never had the mammogram and the lump disappeared.

Mother's Script

*Why did Lania's mother physically and
emotionally abuse her own child?*

Lania has a thought-provoking answer to this question.

The answer really depends upon how you view being physical.
If you see life as being real – then it makes no sense. However, if you
recognize life as an illusion – like a movie that you create and then
step into – it makes perfect sense.

From that perspective, these were things that I had set up before I
came into this body. I set up the hurdles that I needed to jump over in
order to learn how to validate myself, trust others, speak out, and know
that I was only responsible for myself. I wanted to come back to Truth.

I knew that I would go through hell before I came into this
lifetime. I chose my mother for that reason. As my primary caretaker,
she tried to destroy me, wanted to shut me up. But think about it.
Didn't my mother do the greatest thing for me? If that woman
tortured me and couldn't stop me, who could?

If I blamed my mother for playing the role I asked her to play,
wouldn't I do myself a disservice and keep myself in bondage?

As easy as that sounds, Lania didn't just "forgive my mother and
let her off the hook." First, Lania needed to release the anger, rage,
and hurt before going beyond it. She did a lot of inner work to
remember who her mother really was. The healing process opened
up other realities.

That is what I came to do. It was my responsibility to resolve these
issues and move forward. So I had to find the inner strength. Having
my angels and guides surrounding me from such an early age and
having them make their presence known helped keep me on track.

Lania sought help at a child guidance clinic after her son's birth
triggered the fear that she would do to him what her mother had
done to her.

I talked to therapists twice a week for four years. My mother died while I was in therapy. I couldn't yell at her, but there were deeper ways to deal with it. Even though she wasn't alive, that didn't mean her consciousness wasn't here.

I came to appreciate what my mother did for me. Who did my mother have to be in order that I might accomplish what I came here to do? Sure, she was the villain. But is that who she really is? From another perspective, wasn't she the greatest angel that ever lived for me?

Why? Because my mother was the taskmaster, the baddest of the bad. She put me through a torture camp from the time I was born. Hitler didn't do any worse … and still I love. I love people. My work is about compassion and non-judgment.

Did Lania's mother incur negative karma for abusing Lania?

She would have incurred karma if she hadn't played the role. We had something to resolve. It would only get resolved if my mother played her role. The better she portrayed her role, the more ability it unlocked in me. It took tremendous strength and determination, but my mother held her role in place like the finest actress.

My mother gave me the greatest gift. I learned to transcend her abuse. I learned how to move through anything that came to me. She gave me a core of steel. Now no one can stop me from bringing forth the conversation that I am here to bring. And what was the overriding factor that allowed me to do that? Love. I was able to find the love. Love is at the core essence of all that is. Love has been the message of all spiritual teachers – Jesus, Moses, Muhammad, Buddha, Krishna. And the lack of love has held all this torture and torment in place.

Lania had a special dream after she had resolved these issues with her mother. Following a serious car accident, Lania stayed home from work and felt depressed. She cried and put out a call for help.

That night my mother appeared in my dream. She told me, "Lania, if you had not done all the work to forgive me, it wouldn't have been possible for me to come to you tonight. I want you to realize that we set all of this up prior to your birth.

"You asked me to play this role. I didn't want you to think that that was who I really am. It was the role I played so that you could resolve the conflicts that stood in your way. I want you now to see who I really am."

Then, she proceeded to reveal herself as one of the most glorious, radiant beings. She brought me to her and enfolded me in her all-encompassing love. I was shocked at her loving presence.

I woke up crying. The dream changed my perception of who we are, what we are here for, how we interact with each other, as well as how we can resolve and overcome conflict, and restore our personal dignity in the process. Underneath it all, I realized that human experience has nothing to do with what is Real. However, it gives us the opportunity to discover that, in our own time and in our own way.

Memories of the In-Between

Lania recalls how she formulated this life and saw what was needed to ensure total success.

When I was setting up this incarnation, I wanted to get the most gusto out of this lifetime. For that, I needed certain components. Just as when we cook a pot roast dinner, we need the proper ingredients. We can't use apples and strawberries.

I wanted this lifetime to make a big impact on me. My goal was to learn about self-validation. I decided to experience the human condition from a horrendous perspective, doom and gloom, atrocities. Then, if I found my way back to Wholeness from that total annihilation of self, look what I would have accomplished. If I could make it, anybody could.

That is why Lania didn't chose a mediocre life.

Human experience works like a pendulum. If I had picked an easy "ho-hum" life, the pendulum wouldn't swing very far. Those experiences don't give a big evolutionary push. If I had a mediocre life, how motivated would I have been to do something about it?

I wanted the pendulum to swing over to the other side and possibly break through. I knew that if something was tearing me from limb to limb, I would either crumble, retreat, or get my act together and move through them.

Pre-Birth Agreements in Previous Life Times

During the pre-birth prelude, Lania reflected on what beliefs, attitudes, concepts, and traditions had kept her forgetting who she really was in former lives.

Before I came into form, I looked back and realized, "Well, it didn't work in that life. Or I accomplished a little bit doing it this way in another life. Or I maneuvered it around a little this other way."

In one lifetime, for example, I had been born as an only child to loving parents. They left me in the care of someone else one day while they went on a trip. To make a long story short, they suffered a fatal accident.

I went to live with my uncle who wasn't a kind man. He didn't like children and had no idea what little girls needed. He became angry that he had been saddled with taking care of this little girl. He abused me. As I grew up, I became bitter and couldn't function. I lost the love I had inside of me. I became sinister.

Lania recalls why she had planned to be with her uncle as that little girl.

Prior to my life as that little girl, I made an agreement. There was a man who had lost the woman he loved in a devastating occurrence. His heart had been broken. I told him, "I will manage to be with you in your next life in order to open your heart back up." The man agreed, "Yes, of course. I want my heart to be healed. What better way to do it than to be with a little girl who just wants love?"

But, as we see, I couldn't follow through on our agreement. The stage had been set. We had an opportunity to shift things around, but I lost the power to materialize that. When I was in the in-between, I had forgotten how intense it is to be in physical form. I didn't realize how much focus it would take to turn my uncle's heart around. It was too much, too big of a slice.

Pre-Birth Agreements

In planning her present life, Lania made certain that she had "enough help to pull me through, the proper players."

I laid out the whole plan prior to entering human form. I literally did a role call, a screening, to see if all the components were there. I made sure I had the support – the reminders, as well as the villains – the devastation, the heartache – to motivate me. It was like making a movie that required specific roles.

Then we practiced our lines, preparing for our parts, seeing how it played out. We looked to see if there were any missing players. We were setting the stage, making sure everything was in place. Of course, once I came through the tunnel, and came into form, I jumped in and forgot so that I could do it. That is the game, one of the rules I agreed to.

Pre-birth agreements involved other souls who stayed in spirit form.

We agreed that once I came into form, some of my soul family in the other dimension would remind me of my strength, of who I really am, of what I wanted to achieve. And they were diligent. Those were the thoughts and guidance I heard even as a child. They knew my optimum. When my mother was abusive, they said, "Give it to us. We will take care of it." In other words, "Don't hold onto the anger." Then, like a boomerang, as soon as I let go, I watched my mother experience the consequences of her own behavior.

My soul family kept me on line. I planned that these influences would come at specific junctions so that I could regain my strength, not lose it, not forget it. They kept reminding me: "Lania, are you still on track?"

This connection was there unless I turned away. And for many years, I did just that because of the way I was raised. I denied my abilities for fear of the repercussions.

Prior to birth, Lania volunteered to join a collective effort with like-minded souls to "see through the original plan" for humanity.

This group is like a mother who rings a dinner bell for children playing outdoors. In the midst of the game, the children become absorbed in the excitement and forget to come in and eat. They need a reminder. In a similar manner, many souls chose to awaken people from the dream, the illusion of this physical reality. We chose to call the others back in and wake them up: "You have been playing out there long enough."

We volunteered to bring back what was always supposed to have been on Earth. The spiritual consciousness of humanity had descended into the depths eons ago. I recall how beings who didn't have emotion came to this physical dimension. They experimented with physicality much like a child pulls the wings off a fly to see what the fly will do without wings. They did horrendous experimentation with humans and created fear, doubt, and an arena where there was no safety.

I knew the only way to uplift the spiritual consciousness of mankind was to transcend those similar conditions. I volunteered because I knew I was strong enough to hold these energies at this particular point in time.

A Mystical Land of Enchantment

*Lania remembers her real Home "at the
other end of the spectrum in consciousness."*

Where I am from, we always feel good. People love, trust, and
care for each other. Everyone is honored and nurtured. A vibrancy
and excitement pervades everything, drawing people forward to
create more joy.

Everyone there is already whole, so everything is manifested with
excellence. They communicate telepathically with thought-impressions.
There is no competition, only trust, safety, and harmony. The catalyst
for growth is to contribute towards expansion of the whole. To fulfill
the greater good is the goal of the collective.

Each feels that fulfilling their part is vital. And there is a synergy
effect. Each one receives more than what they came with – like
adding colored dyes to water, one after another, and watching
what happens as they mingle.

In that world, there is immense elegance and beauty. Vibrant
colors. Exquisite fragrances. Laughter and joy. Laughter is the music
of the spheres. Ecstasy is everywhere – in the beauty of color, in scent,
in sound. The tones, the frequencies, are magnified a million times
over. We can only handle a small watered-down version of that here.

Lania recalls hundreds of previous lives. Each in-between is
different.

Why would I want to do the same thing? There are so many
realms. Why stick with one? There is such a vastness of experiences
that we choose from between lifetimes. It is infinite. Star Trek does
not even come close.

One "in-between" activity Lania particularly enjoys is "bringing
things into creation that have never been – using thought." She
recognizes what frequencies are needed, determines how to
manifest them, and goes through a down-step process to bring
them into form, much like taking water and condensing it into ice.

Souls Waiting in the Wings for Birth

Lania's favorite inter-life region is the brightest star in the sky, the vortex of Sirius. She explains that everything that comes in and goes out of the physical dimension of reality must pass through that vortex of energy – including planets, galaxies, universes. We likewise enter the illusion through that vortex.

Lania sometimes chooses to go out beyond the physical.

There are dimensions that the human brain cannot conceive of beyond this physical one. Imagine that all the light in our dimension is a pinprick in the fabric of being. All the stars, planets, and vortexes are pinpricks of the fabric of this illusion. I have passed through the vortex of the Sun, one of the pinpricks in the fabric of being. It is not hot, by the way. What is on the other side? How do I describe it? I can experience it, but it is difficult to translate. There are colors that we don't have and a brightness factor that would disintegrate the physical body because it is so intense. However I can't translate the shapes, fragrances, or sounds because they don't exist here.

Lania goes back into Truth each time she leaves physical form.

Our belief systems determine the nature of the in-between experience. Whatever illusion we have created about where we will go, that is where we go – we go to our next illusion. We get exactly what we believe we are entitled to. It is our creation. If people believe they will go to Heaven, they go into an in-between that looks like the illusion they created when they had a body – streets of gold, etc.

When I leave the illusion, I go back to what always is, a huge vastness of love, harmony, balance, dignity, integrity. I go back to where I belong: Wholeness. There is nothing but Wholeness. We have just created this game we call physicality for our amusement.

When I go back into Wholeness, everything is right. There is no judgment. No reason for it. The human experience seems like a dream and fades away quickly. It no longer has meaning because in Wholeness there is no such thing as separation.

This is my last physical incarnation and I didn't need to do this one. I volunteered to help bring back what was supposed to be here all along.

Lania no longer goes in and out of remembering.

I came into physical form in order to overcome the illusion of separation and to remember who I really am. The story I am playing out here is the only way I can find myself and remember what brings me ultimate joy.

So I couldn't integrate what I came to do until I embodied who I really was. Once I did, I was in alignment with God's Will. All there is now is love, joy, expansion, and being present in my Self. I am awake in the dream, play in the dream, and watch myself create, instantly at will, by choice.

Lania serves as a role model. She teaches others to remember who they are via the "Reality Creation" process. She believes "everyone is a master."

I needed to match people toe to toe, to have identical experiences in my physiology. Then, no one can claim that I am an exception. So although I had all this wisdom, I didn't come in like a Pollyanna. Like everyone else, I experienced the forgetful state – separation, duality, believing I was disconnected from God, believing I could be bad or wrong. And just as I teach others, I transcended the negativity in my life and remembered wholeness, what is Home to me. And from my perspective, if I can find my way back Home, anyone can.

Souls Waiting in the Wings for Birth

*Individuals who have gifted memory
recall planning the scripts for earthly life.*

Chapter 34
Angels in the
Never-Ending Schoolhouse

**Now, she who knows is "one who can recollect
the beginning ... one who has become
contemporaneous with the birth of the world,
when existence and Time first became manifest."[1]**

– Mircea Eliade

*Beverly Anderson calls the soul's evolutionary
journey an open-ended schoolhouse program of
remembering who and what we are so that we can
experience ourselves as the little god that we are.*

Beverly Anderson is a mother, clairaudient, clairvoyant, and spiritual healer. She hears and talks with angels and sees visions of the past and future. Beverly's memory and consciousness extend back long before conception. In fact, Beverly recalls previous human lives as well as the heavenly life between each earthly life.

> People tell me to call myself a mystic, but that is a big word for somebody who I think is so ordinary. I am a Mom who pays bills, goes grocery shopping, gets my teeth filled just like everyone else. I am just a being who is living the most of me I know how and I haven't even got warmed up yet. Nor have most of us on the planet, but we are working on it.

Beverly's "continuous conscious memory" extends back to the moment when she was created as an individual spark of God. Her soul then became "encapsulated in different human forms, cultures, times, and places" in order to learn different lessons of perception and awareness. She has always been the same person with the same consciousness, personality, insecurities, and confidences who has simply matured "like a child growing up."

And I remember the in-betweens. They are just as tangible as the "heres" [earthly lives]. They are another form of being that is not squashed together in such a small package. Because when you are "there" and not currently occupying a shell, a package – I call it the kleenexes because they come and go – we do not lose or change anything about ourselves except our fear. Fear is a function of survival incorporated in the humanness of our bodies.

Awakening in Childhood

Beverly was born with certain memories,
but full memory did not flick on until the age of nine.
Since then, she has been on a quest to understand and share
her gifts. This has led to over thirty years of study on the
meaning and effects of karma, past lives, Tarot, as well
as modern and ancient mystic orders and religions.

Beverly experienced feelings and memories that made no sense to her conscious mind throughout childhood.

I remembered being a warrior. And I often dreamed that I was a Persian girl and woke up feeling stunned that I was a little girl in a white body. I thought, "This is weird! Why am I female and Anglo? I am used to being dark. I have always been dark. It makes no sense. Why am I in this life? I am so confused."

I can tell countless stories of lying in bed and feeling frustrated that I had no servants. "Don't they know I am the queen? They are supposed to bring me what I want." I thought, "Why do I feel that way? I was aggravated that nobody knew who I was. I was ticked-off. And I did not know how to express it.

Memories were brewing in Beverly's superconscious mind, nagging at her, poking at her – until the Universe arranged an NDE to bring back more "down-loaded information" to her consciousness. Beverly was nine years old.

When I walked back through the veil into this molecular vibration, I brought back memory of all of me: memories of all the in-between times and all of the times here. My brain was allowed – by the Grace of God – to access more of my memory of the All and being allowed to access other people's memories of the All.

To ask, "How do I remember?" is like asking, "How do I breathe?" There is no difference. There is no stop in time and space for me. And the veil is not really there. It is our brain's perceiving the veil as existing that cuts us off from our superconscious memory, our true higher self – other than the little piece of us here that we are trying to school right now.

So I don't like the phrase "the other side of the veil" because there is no veil. Heaven is simply there and our minds obscure it. Our mind is designed to sense sight, sound, smell, taste, and touch, and is so preoccupied with maintaining and protecting the body, that it tends to be a good cap on accessing collective consciousness.

I know and I am at ease with the angels. They are also children of God, but are on a different level of tone, perception, of being, of resonance, of soul, than we are. They are doing their karmic duty with joy and pride and are learning and growing, similar to us. Eventually we become angels – when our perception is broad enough and our fear small enough.

As a child, Beverly's cosmic memories seemed natural. She was only a kid and did not know any better. On the other hand, Beverly did not share memories with her parents.

Pre-cognitive skills run in the family, but my parents are also Southern Baptist and Roman Catholic. So one thing I could not broach with my mother was reincarnation. There was one life and then we go to Heaven. My mother has changed since then, I might add. Recently her consciousness welled up. I never thought I would see it happen.

Even though Beverly could not converse with her parents about her memories, God put some protective measures in her life.

By the time I tried to understand who I was, let alone get a grip on why I was here, I was given the gift of my teacher in the form of my brother Jim. We agreed prior to birth to be born to the same parents. He chose to be my big brother, with enough span between us in years where he could have some education on some topics that would help me. Jim was a Zen Buddhist studying martial arts. We talked, explored, and exchanged … and we have all of our lives. Jim has probably been my teacher before. He is very precious.

A Projectile of Light

Beverly remembers when God initially spun her on her merry way and said: "Have a good time. Come back when you are all done."

Beverly's soul journey began at the Source.

I remember before I left as a spark of God – I remember my spark and Him. And the profound limitless power of that makes me a little nervous. He is in the major leagues and we are in the minor leagues. But talent grows, evolves, and matures, and we will get there, too. But I will be fine doing the minor leagues for awhile. I am not ready to do that format yet. I do not respect it enough. I will, with time, as will all of us.

It is difficult to verbalize what happened when Beverly's soul became individuated.

I remember coming from the "All That Is," as a projectile of light. I remember being spat out, pushed out like a projectile and I was screaming through the universe as a spark of light, like a little star. I knew that I was going somewhere, but I did not know where. There was no fear, just a feeling of sheer exhilaration.

I clearly remember stars whizzing by, but there was no sensation of movement as we know it as humans. There was no density, no up or down, no left or right, no time, no sensations of colors, sound, or heat. You just were. It was pure energy. You were surrounded by comfort and ease. It was wonderful.

I haven't a clue as to "when" that was. There was no time associated with that because there was no space. Space did not mean anything. You just were. So that is the best human description I can give.

When science says that space travel is impossible because of space-time dimensionality, I know they are wrong. Oh yes, you can – if you are working beyond the quantum laws which the Creator is. He molds them to His Will.

Our soul's journey is an open-ended schoolhouse of remembering "the little god that we are."

God gave birth to us. He did not need to. He gave us life, gave us existence to share love with. He did not want to be alone. And we may be slightly errant or naughty children, but eventually all children grow up and mellow out. Even most humans go through wild, crazy phases and screw up a lot. Then, they get their shit glued together in their 40s or 50s.

We are similar for Him. We are His children. Occasionally we may be wild and do stupid things, but He loves us nonetheless. And look at how many little god-beings He gave birth to. Does not He do good work? Ain't it cool?

Some people are frustrated because they are not finding God. They try to wrap their brains around concepts that their brains are incapable of comprehending. Instead of looking out there, look inside. It is already there.

The parameters of His limitlessness give Beverly profound joy because the all-powerful, all-mighty Being at the basis of the universe, "our most wondrous Lord," is also evolving.

In His joyous exuberance of life and giving forth manifested life, He is learning and growing, too. His giving birth to us is part of His process of growing.

So the next time I see God, I will ask, "Where did you come from?" I know He is going to answer that He is part of a wholeness, too. The ad infinitum is beyond comprehension. My brain cannot go that far, but my soul can. We cannot wrap our brains around the end of our growth which makes me go, "Yeh, hah!" If the game gets more interesting than this, I want to play.

God chose an overriding lesson plan for our soul – genetics, predispositions, all the talents that we carry.

Each life force on this plane is unique. The lesson plan for each spark of life is also one of a kind, but incredibly interactive, so much fun. Our most wondrous Creator is one heck of a multi-tasker. He simultaneously juggles minutia and dimensions without even breaking a sweat, not even thinking about it ... just breathes it and it is.

The Creator is a loving, patient, joyful gardener. All He wants is for us to discover our uniqueness, revel in it, be proud of it, and live it effortlessly, without fear, worry, or shame. When we do that, we evolve into the seed of the godling that we are. It takes a while, but as we go along, we begin to know that we are good at some things and not good at others. We know we are supposed to be doing this and not doing that.

Souls Waiting in the Wings for Birth

Each spark of God, our speck of uniqueness, is just as precious as all the others. Each spark is like one of the elements in the table of elements. Each element reacts differently with the others. Beverly's overriding lesson plan is to understand her function as a catalyst.

I am like the oxygen molecule that has a correct molecular structure, tone of being, or energy dynamics, that can interact with lots of other elements and make things change. My lesson plan has been to understand that there is no power but the "All that is" and I am but a piece of that. Therefore how can I be more proud of myself than anyone else? How can I be more special than anyone else? Yes, I am unique, but each molecular structure has a function and a purpose that is to be regarded with the utmost respect.

People often tell me,"You are so amazing, so special." I look at them and say, "So are you!" I thank God for every soul who comes to me. I learn something from each of them, that I would not find anywhere else in the universe. So how can anybody tell me that they are more or less than anyone else? I do not buy that.

I disagree with human categorizing into levels of maturity and worthiness. Does it make the child who grows up first any more special than the little child who is to come behind him? We are all equally cherished and loved by the Love source. There is no better or worse soul.

The universe is like a choir.

Each soul in the choir has a unique voice, color, range, talent. Each soul has melodies it enjoys, as well as melodies it dislikes or feels comfortable singing. But that is okay. God created the whole choir, not just one voice.

So each voice is magnificent in its own way. But we need all the voices to make the music. So, yes, some are more or less than others. However, what is important is learning to appreciate and encourage each soul's voice, abundance, to manifest. That is what God is trying to teach us. Until we learn that, we will not be grown up enough to be little gods. We will be warring with each other and making a mess of the universe. So we are still children who have much to learn, but we are loved every step of the way.

God even loves the being that once was close to God whom the Bible calls Lucifer. God may be a little disappointed with Lucifer right now, but God will not even give up on him. And eventually God will win him Home.

There is no one who is better than another. Some are living their God-source better than others, but eventually everyone realizes the big picture.

Movies in Heaven

*God is so merciful. He gives us free will to
teach ourselves what we need to know – just like
a little child learns how to walk on his own.*

Beverly recalls the step-by-step events between one earthly life
and the next. The other side of the veil is as real as this side.

When I die, when my body quits functioning electrically, I am
liberated from up and down, forward and back, left and right,
beginning and end. I become a free entity unencumbered by time
and space. Within a short span of time, my angel encases me in her
protectiveness – she wraps herself around me to give me a cocoon.
She floats me for awhile until I adjust. It doesn't take long. I know
her well. She is always with me.

Some people are so frightened by that event that they don't allow the
cocooning to happen. They are afraid of the limitlessness of themselves.
They assume they are not worthy enough to simultaneously face their
god-self and God. Instead, they panic and flow through time and space
and are quickly reborn in order to feel safe again.

Beverly's angel takes her through the Light into Heaven.

Heaven is a gas. It is delightful. Heaven is being all that I can be. It
is the limitlessness of myself in an energy platform, spatial
dimensionality that is unencumbered by physical form, hunger, cold,
or fear. I am in front of my limitlessness, facing my god-self and God
at the same time.

Beverly points out some pros and cons of heavenly life.

The in-between zones are more instantaneous and responsive.
There we breathe a thought or a need and it manifests. Here we
breathe a thought, and unless we are really focused, it takes time to
manifest. We must work at it. There we need no help of angels. We
are angels, at whatever level of expression we are allowing that to be.

Heaven is wonderful; however there are things that we do not
experience there. Heaven does not give the satisfaction earthly life

does. There we do not have to try hard. There is no toning to the mettle of our character, to our being. There is no furnace to test our mettle. There is little satisfaction in accomplishing something which is effortless. And we do not learn when things are so wonderful. We just hang out. So even though earthly life is slow, dense, sticky, and kind of a pain in the ass, human life is important, or we would not bother with it.

Profundity of balance characterizes earthly existence.

I have all knowledge, information, resources available to me when I am in the in-between zones. I am like a kid in a candy shop. I get any information instantly – with none of this, "No, you are not supposed to have that information right now." That frustrates me because I know the knowledge exists. "Why don't you tell me? I know you know."

"No, you don't need all that information now. You are human and it will overload your circuits. You must respect that. It is not a good set of parameters for you to operate under. It is not healthy." And I know what my angels are talking about when they tell me that.

Heaven is a wonderful place, but ... so is earthly existence.

We cannot exist without them and they cannot exist without us. We cannot have there without here. There is balance in the universe, yin and yang, dark and light. Some people say, "When I die, I am going to Heaven and never coming back." I challenge that. Heaven is wonderful, but it gets boring after a while.

God gave birth to this plane of reality in order to add a base note to His reality, a bit of a deep tone, a slower dynamic to the parameter of the universe. The problem with this place is people do not slow down and listen to the tone and experience how delicious this tone is. Even angels are occasionally jealous because there are aspects of this level of reality that are unique: this place is Heaven ... if we live it like that, but most people don't. They live it as Hell. And that's what they get.

Setting the Stage

Heaven is where Beverly sets the stage for her next life on Earth.

I can do and be anything my heart desires, to prepare me for, to let me experiment with myself to realize what I need to figure out about myself next, so I can grow a bit more. I can go anywhere, learn anything, and hang with anyone I want to be with, including myself.

The other side of the veil is more relevant than earthly life because it is a continuation of a lesson plan.

I go there to check in to see how I am doing. I have a general overview of what I am supposed to be working on in my growth process, and it is obvious what I am lacking – what I have left on my overall lesson plan that I have not done yet. There is nothing forbidden for me to know. I scan what I did in past lives, and I look at the stuff I need to do eight or nine lives ahead.

When Beverly dwells in the in-between, a discussion, a "pow-pow," takes place between her soul and her angel group, her soul group.

I tend to be hyper-critical of my acting job and hold myself up to account: "Damn, I did not get that right." Or "Boy, I wish I had done that differently." And the angels say, "No, you did fine. It was lovely, wonderful. You learned this and you learned that." But I always pick the one thing I did not hit. And they keep telling me, "Don't be so upset about that. Look at the big picture, the whole pie, not that tiny speck that did not turn out perfect."

Beverly's angels encourage her to be gentle with herself, but the golden rule of the universe is free will.

Each of us is an expression of God. And since we are, our angels cannot tell us how to do that. They can only assist us in its expression. So there are different tones of souls. Some are slow and easy. Others are perfectionistic. Each soul is precious and unique. I am a screamingly high-pitched tone. I want the most out of everything because I know it is available.

Beverly's angels reassure her that she did well and ask, "Okay, what do you want to do this time to get it better, to do it righter, to do you wholer?"

I answer, "Well, I don't know. Do you have any suggestions?" So they show me movies. I am not joking. They show me spectrums of potentialities. It is like looking at a movie screen and picking the movie we want to be in out of three, four, or five movies of the future. (The angels are already working on having the events transpire.)

I love the movies. (My husband calls me a ham because I like drama and interesting things.) They are cool because I can pick time zone, culture, economic situation, topography, climate, a comedy or a drama, and I can mix and match the characters. I have a selection of actors that are currently available to be on my stage. I also correlate my productions with those whom I am most tightly bonded so that we can be born together again.

Souls Waiting in the Wings for Birth

If we are paying attention at all, we can "cook up a real interesting movie."

> As I sit and watch the movies, I think, "Well, that looks interesting. I could do that. That might work right there." The angels then let me jump into the format that seems most appropriate.

Occasionally selections can be agonizing, particularly if Beverly regrets some previous actions.

> If I did not do a good job on a previous lesson plan, I can get between a rock and a hard place and select unfortunate experiences in order that I get the point the next time. The angels urge me to be more gentle: "You really don't need to be that harsh with yourself," or "You don't need the lesson that strong, do you?" But I am strong-willed and strong-minded and they cannot talk me out of what my heart and mind are set on. They do not interfere. The angels just do their best to support me while I am in the process of living my lesson plans.

Many people pick easy lessons first. Beverly does not recommend that option. It can wear people out and stretch them pretty thin, if they get the hard core lessons all in a row. That is when people really get bent out of shape.

"I Saw All My Costumes"

*Beverly remembers pieces of thirty earthly lives –
beginning with the Garden of Eden. Of these life histories,
she has pristine memories of eleven lifetimes, including what
she ate and how she dressed. These dramatic lifetimes
affected her the most deeply and carried "karma lessons."
She recalls how and why she planned each life.*

Beverly's NDE, at age nine, gave her a perspective of who she really is.

> When I walked through the veil, I saw all my costumes. They looked like different clothes that I had put on.

Beverly has the most memory of the lives when she was practicing mysticism or some healing art. She saw how she impacted other peoples' growth and what not to do with her present abilities.

> I think I know why the angels let me bring back a large body of my memory: to explain why I am who I am. To let me know that what I am doing here is appropriate. And that I am saner than the average fellow, because sanity is not whether you are right or wrong, but sanity is a clear perspective of things.

Beverly is more than any or all of the faces she has worn.

> People associate brain with personality, but our brain is an electrical unit that helps us eat, sleep, run away, and store information. Our personality, essence, identity is eternal and the only part of us that is real. That is different from the faces we put on it. How we express ourselves changes in different formats for the various lessons we wish to learn. Otherwise, if we don't change our costume and the setting, the play will be the same over and over again.

Garden of Eden

Beverly's memories include an earthly life during a time when human beings had not yet lost the connection with their origins. She lived in the Christian Garden of Eden. The Greeks refers to this period as the Golden Age. In India, they knew it as *Satyuga*, the age of Truth.

There did exist a real time called Eden on this planet, but the Garden of Eden is not exactly as the Christian Bible paints it. The Bible version fails to mention the profundity of the balance and makes the Garden of Eden sound childlike, not as full in depth as it really was. The Garden of Eden was not the cartoonish expression of God totally providing for Adam and Eve – rather there was a total balance in the ecosystem which means great abundance and people living in harmony and balance with Earth.

The Christian Bible fails to explain why Adam and Eve were at peace.

The Garden of Eden was not a place. It was a time and space when men and women were incredibly awake, what we call "psychic." Human beings were in the fullness of the presence of the super-conscious mind. They had the "psychic gifts" that all great masters are still trying to redevelop which lead to peace, serenity, and bliss. And when you have all of that, you have no need for aggression.

Beverly recalls living in the Garden of Eden, but has no idea of "when." Because it was so long ago, she remembers it like we recall a dream.

In the Garden of Eden, I recall being a little child, between six to nine years old. Because we were very awake, everything was easy and everything we thought of appeared. Everything was lush and green, total abundance. We communicated with animals and plants because our higher consciousness connected to the life force within everything. We were also telekinetic – we moved things with our minds. We felt weather patterns change and predicted what crops would grow best.

There was no fear which means no violence, no aggression. There was huge community sharing in spirit. There was the feeling of community even when alone because you were never alone. The people were a people of oneness, instead of separate individuals full of fear. There was no selfishness, greed, coveting your neighbor's property, or lust because there was no need to. People shared freely. All the commandments, "Thou shalt not kill; Thou shalt not covet" – were unspoken because that behavior did not happen. There was no need for rules. There was only balance, bliss and peace. It was Eden, Heaven on Earth.

Memories of Eden inspire Beverly's spiritual counseling.

I have been other beings in other places ... but I believe my first human experience was one of balance, in the Garden of Eden.

Because I can remember it so well, I am at peace. I remember that we can do this. I know how this world is supposed to be. It is the motivation for my spiritual work.

I know that human beings can live in balance and the balance has been forgotten. That is why I teach people to discover their balance. Without balance, we remain aggressive and violent. As soon as we find balance within ourselves and open ourselves up to the super-conscious mind – which every religion calls different things, but we will call it God – then there is no fear, because we know we are not alone. We feel eternity. We feel time differently. I literally pray for all people to remember that time.

The dark time was started by fear, not because God created it to be difficult here.

We lost what the Christians call a state of Grace, or being "awake," due to "the deceleration" – what Christians call evil. Something clouded the consciousness and people felt alone. When the veil slipped over them and they felt alone, the immediate reaction was fear, and the root chakra developments of territoriality, violence, aggression, and hostility.

I like the Christian interpretation and symbology of the serpent, the wise one, knowledge, and the symbology of the decelerator – evil – as the devil who decelerated human evolution. The symbology is accurate. That they blamed humanity's Fall on women was a patriarchal observation. And that they blamed the agony of childbirth as a sin on women's indulgence in this knowledge is also inaccurate. That is just a biological function.

People ask Beverly, "How can you be so patient and not be frustrated with everyone?" She answers:

How can I not be anything but patient when I know the superconsciousness, the Christ consciousness, is motivating us to remember ourselves. That is when the 1,000 years of peace will come, when we really remember. Despite the extreme planetary imbalances going on, I feel encouraged. Sometime you must rock the boat pretty hard to get people's attention.

Shaman Hunter-Gatherer – 3060 BC

Beverly's present karma cycle started 5,000 years ago in the Tibetan flats of Asia.

That was a natural life, tied to the land, the mountains, and the holy places. It was effortless. I got a focus of balance, of the power of this planet within my resonance. I had distinct pre-cognitions and dreams of future lives.

Egyptian Priestess – 2380 BC

Beverly then jumped into "an arrogant, overly-bureaucratic society," to see whether she was mature enough to bring some balance to that level of sophistication.

That didn't turn out to be a good idea. I was a priestess and a royal in one body. I was the living god. I was an arrogant blue blood: beautiful, tall, imposing, eerie looking, scary ju-ju power coming out. I became wrapped up in my lovely brain and its curiosities and turned out being a royal witch. I was a terror. I did stupid and childish things. I was a stinker, a pain in the ass, a spoiled brat. I did not appreciate my abundant resources. I was disrespectful of my station and its responsibilities. That was the least positive manifestation of my skills and gifts.

Persian Princess – 1812 BC

Melding church and state did not work in the Egyptian life because Beverly did not appreciate who she really was. In the next life, she chose a different expression, a Persian princess in the true Samarian Persian culture prior to the Greek influence.

People have no idea of the expectations of behavior on the Egyptian royals and how confining it was. Even though I had been the ultimate power, the living god, I could not slip out of character. I was a living slave. So in the next life, I chose sensuality and hedonism, to roll around in humanness and have fun.

I learned the art of sexuality, the pleasures of the body and the senses, and how delicious it was to be human, but I did some of that at other people's expense. I was voluptuous, loud, and outrageous in my femininity. It was unmistakable and I used it like a sword. I was spoiled, bratty, and did not appreciate my station in life and the responsibilities attached to it.

On the other hand, I had learned enough about love and appreciated compassion and the healing gifts that I had love in that life. So I worked that one out.

Persian Warrior-Prince – 1336 BC

Beverly gained maturity as she went along. She learned to relax with her authority and not to be such "a pain in the ass." So, in the next life, she protected the kingdom and her duties and honor with greater responsibility.

That was an interesting, difficult life. I was warlike, but had a mystical side and healing powers. I was greatly torn between duty and responsibility and my aggressive wanting to lead.

My mysticism was seen as a gift because it made me an effective general-warrior. I could out-think the enemy. I knew what was coming. That life taught me that I can be in charge and make decisions: "I am right. Don't argue with me. Just get after it. It will save your ass. Do it now."

That was a good life, except I had a lot of macho stuff going on about my yang, active self. I was a bit of a pain-in-the-butt chauvinist. I picked being male so I could have all the women I wanted. I enjoyed a voluptuous, sexual-oriented life style. I was good at it. But I enjoyed my maleness so much that I took the feminine expression for granted.

Celtic Shaman/Chieftain – 1173 to 1118 BC

The next life was wonderful and fascinating. Beverly started to get her act together even more.

Sometimes viewing the movies takes a little longer. The longest one was prior to my Celtic life. I spent 700 years settling upon the culture and physical form. But 700 years seemed like a blink of an eye. I didn't really notice it as any longer until I was born again.

The Celts let women be their leaders and I picked a tall, strong, shaman. So I was female yin, but yang in my leadership abilities. I was like the living god, but I knew the living god was not me. The living god was all of us and it was to be respected and honored and to be used to heal and not to harm. My lustiness also stayed with me. I learned a lot in Persia.

Soothsayers, Oracles, Wise Women, Counsels – Middle Ages

Beverly recalls a cluster of four lives as a "witch" during the Dark Ages.

It is hard to hide me. I am clairvoyant and clairaudient. I feel and know things that other people do not. I reach out and try to help them. I affect things when I do not even try. When I operated on this level during the Middle Ages, it cost me my life.

People lived in "the deepest, darkest fear" during the Middle Ages. And when people are in fear, they react violently and aggressively. That is when the word "witch" became a negative word. Witch is a derivative of the Celtic word, wicca, the original soothsayers, oracles, wise women, or counsels.

> For thousands of years, we had been called wise women and counsels. No king would go into court without a wise woman standing right behind him, counseling him as to what was going to happen in a situation and whether someone was telling the truth.

Beverly's punishment for knowing what people were thinking and feeling – "not for practicing the black arts" – cost her life again and again. Her current phobias originate from being branded as a witch.

- *Fear of fire* – I was burned alive at seventeen.
- *Fear of standing in an elevator with a door closed* – I was buried alive and tried to claw out of the box. People were laughing and clapping and singing as they dropped dirt on the box.
- *Fear of the sea and drowning* – I was dropped off a boat with a rock around my ankles with my mouth bound and hands tied. I was a dark-haired Irish witch.
- *Fear of heights* – I was dropped from a parapet of a castle to the rocks below and plunged to my death.

Prior to each lifetime, Beverly's angels advised her that this was an age when fear was in control and she was beating her head against the wall by trying to make a difference. Yet Beverly was persistent and stubborn, and refused to surrender to deceleration.

> I am aware that these lives were a futile exercise, but at least I tried to shift the flow. I should have skipped that zone altogether. But then again, I meet fellow brothers and sisters from those lives and understand their phobias. So it was beneficial even though I did not have to do it so many times.

Appalachian Woman – 1860 to 1902

Prior to Beverly's lifetime in the Appalachian Mountains, she selected the appropriate lessons, even if they involved physical suffering.

> We carry with ourselves judgment about ourselves, even beyond this dimensionality – what we did wrong and what we did right. And even when we touch the all-consuming and all-encompassing love source of ourselves and God, we do not let go of the feeling of "could have," "would have," "should have."

Beverly carried some perception of debt, shame, and self-judgment as reflected by her thoughts in the inter-life period.

> I have had it easy. I have been blueblood so many lives. I have
> no respect for surviving on will alone. I have been arrogant in my
> assumptions that I understand where people are coming from that
> have not been born with so much abundance. I have had attractive,
> beautiful, powerful, dominant, charismatic-like bodies. I have had
> everything I wanted. Perhaps I should say, "Thank you for everything"
> and appreciate and acknowledge from whence it comes, instead of
> thinking I am the biggest, baddest thing walking around.

Being the person that Beverly is, she got after it with gusto. She carefully and consciously selected a less open-ended format: an illiterate woman born during the Civil War in the 1860s.

> That life brought me right down to the ground and landed me
> on my butt. I was born into abject poverty. My husband left me with
> a bunch of children. We lived in a shanty cabin with a dirt floor in
> the Appalachian Mountains. I was frightened and alone. I had no
> resources to supply my family with food and clothing. There was
> sickness everywhere. I watched some of my children starve to death
> in the cold winters. There was nothing I could do because I was born
> with a fragile body. I learned the preciousness of the vitality that I
> had previously been given. I died at age forty-two.

> That life was not a piece of cake. And I did not need to do that for
> Heaven, for God, or for the angels. I was not proving anything for
> them. But I needed to do it for me. Boy, did I come out of that life
> with some appreciation for the gifts of God! I only needed to do
> that once. I got the point.

The period between the Appalachian life and rebirth was "a quickie" – fifty-two years. Beverly was in a hurry to return in 1954 because there was a lot happening down here.

A Contemporary Mystic

*All of those lives led Beverly to this life where
she retains all of her memory including
precognitions of four future lives.*

Beverly's soul development did not need this life, and yet God
needed her for His overall scheme … and she is aware of whom she
works for.

> Actually I was jumping up and down and saying, "The party
> looks cool over here in this movie. Can I do that?" So I volunteered,
> "Okey-dokey. It looks interesting, but make sure that you give me
> enough tools. I am not going down unless you arm me up real well.
> I don't want to get hurt. Remember my frustration during the Middle
> Ages when I didn't make a difference. I don't want to do that again."
> So they gave me my tools when I walked back through the veil after
> my NDE. They honored the deal.

> What I do with my tools is up to me. I must admit that there have
> been some growth processes for me to become a more sophisticated
> operator of the tools. And the angels had explained that I would go
> through some trials and tribulations in order to get me to up to speed
> for what I needed to do. So I have had a variety of profound
> experiences to keep me continually growing.

Beverly selected her mother prior to conception, while her father
was "a karma lesson," something they agreed to learn together.
Her brother and sister volunteered to be siblings. Beverly carefully
picked a small female body.

> This is my least imposing physical form. So often I have been big,
> strong, and bold. I consciously did that so that I would not threaten
> people. It seems to be working fine.

Sojourn through the Amniotic Darkness

Beverly recalls the moment of conception.

Cosmic Cradle

I was perturbed and annoyed about how and why my parents conceived me. Let us say that it happened in less than favorable circumstances and I was a big surprise. But I was insistent on being born so I take responsibility for my part of the deal.

Beverly's mother nearly miscarried in the third month because Beverly was being "pouty" about the circumstances of conception.

I knew that if I did not eventually fall into my body there would be nobody there to fill up the container and it would be time to get rid of the fetus. So for awhile I was being stubborn about going in, but my mother's body did not reject the fetus and my body stuck. So I thought, "Oh, what the hell." I landed in the fourth month.

Beverly remained fully conscious throughout the pregnancy.

I remember hearing the sound of life. I hear space. It is an odd memory, like looking with no eyes. After I was a born, I recognized people, things, and places that I had become familiar with before birth.

Beverly "broke into this space/time continuum and disrupted things" at the time of birth.

My mother was in labor twenty-six hours. I remember the tone of panic and commotion, and a horrendous noise of machines and agitated doctors and running around the room. It was not gentle. I did not understand until my mother explained that she had a difficult time and, in effect, "died" on the table. The doctors zapped her heart to get it beating again. My mother told me, "You were just too much for my body to handle."

When I was born, I saw the doctors in doctor's garb and was shocked by the brilliant light. I felt cold and everyone was yelling. It was not a real chilled-out zone to come into.

Looking back, Beverly has been the same being, like a little child gradually growing up.

To this day I still look in the mirror and I am stunned by what I see. Is that my face? I have been packing around this package for forty years. But I regularly wake up and feel I am a man or big. Then, I get out of bed and I am this little bitty thing.

But my soul has not changed. I can be the smallest person in the room and I get everybody to do what I want them to do because I remember being in charge. I remember it very well.

Through this series of human births, Beverly has learned that there is no need "to beat herself up to get the point."

Souls Waiting in the Wings for Birth

There is all eternity. This is not a hurry-up program. There is not a budget in this flick. It is eternal. God's love and ability to create this format for us is limitless. The more I enjoy each lesson plan, the more abundant and effortless is my journey. I will still get all the lessons, both the high and low notes. So I am no longer a headstrong, impetuous child that I was millennia ago. I am starting to chill. And that is why they let me bring back so much of my collective memory. I respect it more.

Future Lives and the Thousand Years of Peace

I am absolutely certain that the human race will survive because I know lives that are to come. And I am definitely in a human body. How we live and how we use energy and how we treat one another change dramatically. And there's a lot less of us on the planet. I am talking scarce, as in clusters, communities.

I have glimpses of four future lives … . And the life (2075 AD) that I find the most delightful is because I feel a triumphantness. I know I will retain all of this. And I am born into a time of peace. The 1,000 years of peace is for real. It is a very different world: quiet, whole, and pristine again. And we have respect for Mother Earth and her power and how alive she is. And a lot of us remember who we are. This is the maturation of collective consciousness that has been promised. I will not be an uncommon item. Lots of people will be walking around remembering all of this. Boy, does that make people a whole lot easier to get along with … .

Recipes for Pre-Conception

**Every event, past, present, or future ...
exists now somewhere, in an eternal present,
and being existent, it is possible ...
to become conscious of events
in what we term the future ....[1]**

– J.W. Brodie-Innes

*The higher transcendent nature from which this
information comes is part of our human essence, according
to psychologist Abraham Maslow. For this reason Roman
philosopher Plotinus, among others, was able to teach
people to experience "Ecstasy," a state of consciousness
which enabled individuals to perceive what was previously
hidden from awareness.[2] In ancient India, the sage
Patanjali* (Yoga Sutras) *referred to such special
abilities as "siddhis," meaning "perfections."*

When people hear about pre-conception experiences, they usually want to have them, too. The dreams, visions, and memories in this book arose spontaneously. But all it takes is a little training and attentiveness to make them likely to happen for us.

This is because anything is possible with a human nervous system. "Peak-experiences" are within everyone's reach. Anyone can learn to communicate with their coming children and recall their own pre-conception memories – it just may not occur overnight.

However, when a person's consciousness is adept enough, receptive enough, pre-conception dreams and gifted memories spontaneously pop out of the unconscious during quiet times: sleep, relaxation, meditation, prayer, or intuitive moments.

The more interest we have and the more positive our attitude, the greater the potential for communication. Souls hovering around will know that their prospective parents are seeking to make contact, and, as the hundred-some cases presented here illustrate, communication is far more frequent than previously suspected.

Here are some recipes which culture the ability to have pre-conception experiences. Even if you do only one of these recommendations, or one from each category, you will be richer in your awareness for the effort.

"KNOW THYSELF, AND YOU WILL KNOW THE UNIVERSE AND THE GODS."

Inscription on the Temple of Delphi

1. Caring for the Subtle Self

*All individuals, whether born with sensitive awareness
or not, can unfold and fine-tune their consciousness.*

Journal of Dreams, Intuitions, and Hunches

One easy method to encourage and track pre-conception experiences is recording them in a diary or journal because years may pass before they come true. So, record it, even if it is only a hunch, feeling, intuition, faint thought, or unusual dream. Initial contact is often construed as wishful thinking and dismissed as a wandering mind.

You may recall that Francois Gilot, wife of Pablo Picasso, recorded her pre-conception dream in a journal, but did not appreciate its full meaning until a few years later after the birth of her first child. Without her journal, Francois might have forgotten the dream and subsequently its hidden message.

Daily Meditation

Consistent meditation is a powerful way to enhance unborn soul contact. It stills the mind and calms the body, both of which are necessary for awareness of subtle experiences.

Meditation helps us transcend the consciousness of mortality. As Pythagoras, the ancient Greek philosopher, advised, "Learn to be silent. Let your quiet mind listen and absorb."[3]

A daily meditation routine is ideal since it accustoms the mind and body to deep and silent activity. A high percentage of people interviewed for this book enjoyed regular meditation.[4]

Meditation techniques have been handed down from teacher to student over thousands of years, and are best learned from a trained teacher who is an experienced practitioner. This is vital because subtle nuances are too difficult to glean from a book or from an untrained person.

Regular Prayer

Prayer is an effective way of encouraging soul communications. History records that pre-conception visions spontaneously arise while praying. Martha, mother of the Byzantine saint Daniel, prayed for a divine answer to overcome her infertility. On the same night two great circular lights descended from Heaven and rested near her. She conceived her son shortly afterwards. A similar experience happened after Annapurnamba, mother of saint Karunamayi, witnessed a vision while praying in an Indian temple of the Mother Goddess.

Pray with all the emotions of your heart. Jesus gave us the powerful and beautiful Lord's Prayer. The Hail Mary is another beautiful Christian prayer. And the prayer of St. Francis of Assisi (1182 to 1226) helps us recall that we are spiritual beings inhabiting physical form.

> Lord, make me an instrument of Your Peace.
> Where there is hatred, let me bring love;
> Where there is injury, forgiveness;
> Where there is doubt, faith;
> Where there is despair, hope;
> Where there is discord, harmony;
> Where there are shadows, light;
> And where there is sadness, joy.
> O Divine Master, grant that I may seek
>   to console rather than be consoled;
> To understand rather than be understood;
> To love rather than be loved.
> For it is in giving that we receive;
> It is in forgiving that we are forgiven;
> It is in self-forgetting that we find;
> And it is in serving others that we awaken to Eternal Light.

Here is a famous prayer from ancient India:

> May Truth be our Religion. May Service be our Worship.
> May Knowledge be our Breath. May the World be our Family .... .
> May our eyes see happy and noble things.
> May our ears hear happy and truthful words.

Souls Waiting in the Wings for Birth

May our tongues be sweet and truthful.
May our bodies be Divine instruments.
May noble thoughts come to us from all corners of the universe.
May we never leave God. May God never leave us.[5]

Spiritual Teachings and Affirmations

The world's spiritual traditions created formulas for personal transformation and for awakening our memory of immortality. Memorize an affirmation to redefine who you think you are. If we believe that we are merely a physical body and mind, we are operating with only a partial answer. We have been locked up in mortal human bodies for so long that we tend to say, "I am no good." "I am a sinner." "That person is better than me." "I am far from God." Such negative thoughts shrink us.

Our Higher Self is beyond the body and our limited ego. We are created in God's image, but we wear imperfections as long as we identify with the ego and physical body. Affirmations like the one below taught by Dr. Deepak Chopra help remind us of our divine heritage.

I am not my atoms, they come and go.
I am not my thoughts, they come and go.
I am not my ego, my self-image changes.
I am above and beyond these; I am the witness, the interpreter, the
    Self beyond the self-image. This Self is ageless and timeless.[6]

Silently repeat the affirmation before bedtime. It erases old impressions and remolds the subconscious memory patterns of the mind in a positive way. As Hazrat Inayat Khan, the 20th century founder of the Sufi order in the West, said, "What is it that the initiator teaches the initiated one? He tells the initiated one the truth of his own being. He does not tell him something new or different. He tells him something which his soul already knows but which his mind has forgotten."[7]

The Company of Spiritual Individuals to Fulfill Desires for a Child and Making Contact

One infertile Indian woman sought blessings to have a child from saint Sai Baba of Shirdi and received an answer in a dream. The saint appeared saying, "Eat this coconut and you will birth a son." The woman awoke the next morning to find a real coconut in her bed. A year later, she presented her newborn son to Sai Baba. Similar accounts are reported from those who sought blessings from women saints, such as Amritananda Mayi and others, who travel yearly to the USA, allowing public contact and personal requests, such as help with infertility.

Day of Silence Once a Week

By observing silence, we are able to listen to the voice of our soul. Peace and quietness encourage receptivity and increase alertness to communications with the unborn soul.

Some suggestions for enhancing the silence:

Stay in seclusion if possible and attend
only to your essential work.
Have a light diet or juice fast.
Meditate and pray.
Memorize beautiful passages of
spiritual wisdom.
Write in your spiritual diary.
Avoid television, radio, and newspapers.

This develops the art of inner listening. The more often silence is practiced, the clearer perception becomes. As Blaise Pascal, the French philosopher and scientist, wrote: "All man's miseries derive from not being able to sit quietly in a room alone."[8]

Sharing the Pre-Conception Information with Friends and Family

Sharing experiences is a social method to support their perpetuation. It encourages a broader discussion and acceptance of the pre-conception phenomena in our culture. The subtle world of unborn souls is more tuned in to our realm than we think. They sense changes in our social attitudes within a family and culture.

Young children sense what they can talk about concerning where they came from and invisible angelic playmates. Do not stifle their memories.

Inspirational Music

Listen to inspirational music you enjoy, be it religious, gospel, classical, new age, or contemporary peaceful sounds. The Sufis and the ancient Pythagoreans enlisted music to elevate consciousness and awaken reminiscences of melodies heard in Paradise.[9] Refined music produces higher vibrations attractive to souls seeking birth.

Peaceful and Positive Thinking

Control of the mind and heart are important for contact. Unborn souls are least attracted, if at all, to anyone producing anger, jealousy, negative thoughts, greed, or hostility. Violence is to be totally avoided. Inner peace and hearts of selfless love are vital for inspiring the unborn souls to visit one's attractive environment.

I must first know myself ... to be curious about that which is not my concern while I am still in ignorance of my own self would be ridiculuos.

– *Socrates*

2. Caring for the House of the Soul

*Honor your physical body. Don't neglect
or poison it. The body is the temple of the soul
and it is through caring for the body that
we ascend the ladder of consciousness.*

Individuals are unique because they possess different genetics and physiologies. Some people are more resilient to stresses and others are more sensitive. Therefore, the applicability of these guidelines vary from person to person.

Take Regular and Plentiful Rest

Sleep enough at night to feel fresh in the morning. Minimize fatigue, and physical and mental exhaustion. Tiredness decreases receptivity and sensitivity. Efforts from the higher side to communicate may be missed altogether if we are burned out.

Fasting for Brief Periods

Fasting purifies the mind and body, preparing it for subtle communications. An angel announced the conception and birth of the Virgin Mary to her father after he had prayed and fasted for forty days in the desert. In a similar effort, Bhuvaneshwari fasted and prayed every Monday for one year, and had a pre-conception dream announcing the birth of her son, the Indian saint Vivekananda. Likewise, the Irish King Sena and Queen Eithne beseeched God for a worthy son by regular fasting, abstinence, and charitable acts. During one fast, they experienced simultaneous visions announcing the conception of the Christian Saint Mochoemog.

Avoid Non-Prescription Drugs, Alcohol, Cigarettes, Second-hand Smoke, and Generally All Mood Altering Substances

Certain substances tend to dull the mind and nervous system since they easily disrupt the biochemical balance of the mind and body. This results in the presence of toxins that poison vital life processes. Chemical abuse interferes with soul contact.

Eat Pure or Organically Grown Foods – Do Not Consume Processed Foods, Chemically Treated Foods, Genetically Engineered Foods, Irradiated Foods, or Microwaved Foods

Foreign substances and toxins may enter the body through these foods which may induce unintended consequences, such as dulling our senses and attentiveness to subtle impulses. For example, hydrogenated fats and oils, usually soy, canola, and cottonseed, are implicated in breast cancer and heart disease, and they suppress the immune system and cause photo-immuno suppression which leads to melanomas and skin cancer. Instead use extra virgin olive oil, palm oil, and organic butter.

Genetically engineered foods from transgenic crops are inadequately tested as to their safety. Transgenic foods contain unethical DNA, antibiotic resistance marker genes, and other genes spliced into them from bacterial and viral DNA, and insect DNA. Indications are that the process itself may be dangerous to health. Avoid non-organic soy, corn, russet potatoes, tomato products, and dough conditioner. Do not eat canola or cottonseed oil, whether organic or not. Avoid non-organic dairy which is likely to contain rBGH which increases cancer risk in humans.

Recent research shows that microwave oven-cooked food suffers severe molecular damage. When eaten, it causes abnormal changes in human blood and immune systems.[10]

Avoid Artificial Products, such as Aspartame in Foods, Vitamins, and Medicines.

A common artificial sweetener, called aspartame (Equal, Nutrasweet, Spoonful) is approved for use in restaurants and in up to 5,000 processed food products, including vitamins and medicines. 90% of the symptoms of aspartame have to do with the brain, such as, headaches, dizziness, blindness and other vision problems, epileptic-like seizures, depression, mental retardation in babies, death, and reports are pointing to multiple sclerosis and lupus.

Aspartame breaks down into several toxic compounds, including methyl alcohol, aspartic acid, and DKP (aspartylphenylalanine diketopiperazine), which are known to interfere with mental processes, attack the nervous system, and damage internal organs. In the human body, methyl alcohol (wood alcohol) is converted to formaldehyde (poisonous preservative used in embalming fluid) which has been shown to cause immune system damage and genetic damage at exceptionally low doses.

Instead use Stevia – a South American plant sweeter than sugar. Stevia is more than just a non-caloric sweetener. Clinical studies document Stevia's ability to lower and balance blood sugar levels, support pancreas and digestive system, protect liver, and combat infectious microorganisms.

Drink Pure Water without Chemical Residues

Public drinking water today is often treated with chemicals such as chlorine and fluoride in addition to likely containing traces of toxic pesticides, herbicides, pharmaceuticals, and other harmful chemicals. Microbial contamination is an increasing public health concern. Ensure that you are drinking purer water than urban tap water by purchasing filtered water cleaned up by a responsible source, install a water filter on your tap, or use clean well water.

Avoid Consuming Heavy Foods, like Beef and Pork, and Overeating Fatty Foods

Indulging in heavy foods tends to make the body sluggish, since such products may have been grown with hormones, antibiotics, and synthetic chemicals. Cut down on fat consumption – so many dangerous environmental chemicals are lipophilic (fat soluble) and they bio-accumulate in fatty tissues. We are at the top of the food chain, so harmful exposure is greater for us.

Health Care Products Free of Harmful Chemicals

Some health care products possess substances that produce unwanted side effects on the brain and nervous system. Avoid health care products containing substances that interfere with and poison bodily systems and functions: sodium laurel (laureth/TEA) sulfate in soaps, shampoos, toothpastes (sodium laurel sulfate is an engine de-greaser, foaming agent causing eye damage in children, premature hair loss, and scalp disorders); propylene glycol in beauty creams (causes liver abnormalities, kidney damage, and premature skin aging); and mineral oil (suffocates skin).

Release Tensions and Avoid Stress

Deep relaxation is more difficult when a person is stressed and under too much tension. Learn yoga from a teacher or a video that teaches physical postures for bringing the body into a balanced state. The Tibetans also have an ancient set of easy-to-do dynamic exercises called "The Five Tibetans."[11]

He who knoweth others is clever, but he who knoweth himself is enlightened.
— Lao-Tzu

3. Living Environment

Our cities have become noisy, dirty,
crowded places retarding our spirituality.

Beautiful Scenery and Sights of Mother Nature

Take a nature walk or spend an extended period enjoying the perfection of Mother Nature. Listen to the wind and waves, sounds of birds and animals, and rustle of leaves. Watch a beautiful sunset. Walk barefoot on the Earth.

Plato taught how earthly beauty resonates with the Beauty of the upper realms and elevates us to recall the "True Beauty" of the world we fell from. (Plato's *Phaedrus* 250) The English poet, John Keats, emphasized, "Beauty is truth, truth beauty, that is all ye know on earth and all ye need to know." American philosophers similarly encouraged the enjoyment of beautiful sights. Ralph Waldo Emerson referred to Beauty as "God's handwriting – a wayside sacrament."[12]

The rejuvenating powers of the wilderness were inspiringly proven to John Muir. As father of the National Parks and founder of the Sierra Club in 1892, he prepared the social ground for ecological consciousness through his nature writings. Muir encountered an overwhelming mystical sensation upon arriving at the Sierra foothills:

> We are now in the mountains and they are in us, kindling enthusiasm, making every nerve quiver, filling every pore and cell of us. Our flesh-and-bone tabernacle seems transparent as glass to the beauty about us, as if truly an inseparable part of it, thrilling with the air and trees, streams and rocks, in the waves of the sun, – a part of all nature, neither old nor young, sick nor well, but immortal.[13]

Clean Air

Urban environments contain airborne pollutants and many have adverse effects on exposed individuals. A lot of outdoor air pollution enters the home environment and workplace contributing to indoor air pollution. Air filters and purifiers can aid in cleaning the indoor air of undesirable substances.

Quiet Environment

Avoid disruptive vibrations such as loud music, rap, and rock and roll are to be avoided. They distract one from soul communications.

Keep Your Living Environment Free of Toxic Chemicals

Numerous individuals report sensitivity to chemical exposures, such as pesticides, household chemicals, solvents, air fresheners. These exposures need to be minimized. The effects of exposure are cumulative and can bring about chemical sensitivity in most anyone.

Glossary

Amnesia (spiritual) – a temporary state of forgetfulness about the soul's true nature while it inhabits a human body.

Clairaudience – "clear-hearing." The ability to hear the inner currents of the nervous system, mystic tones, and the words of angels.

Clairvoyance – "clear-seeing." The ability to look into the inner worlds, into the present, past, or future.

Cognition – knowledge reached through intuitive, superconscious faculties rather than intellect.

Consciousness – the condition or power of perception, awareness, apprehension. There are myriad gradations of consciousness. Five classical states of awareness are discussed in ancient Indian scriptures: wakefulness, dream, deep sleep, superconsciousness, and the utterly transcendent state.

Cosmic Contract – pre-birth agreements prescribing a person's life plan for each lifetime on Earth. The blueprint one chose before entering this world, a pattern believed by many as bestowed upon us by God.

Death – the soul's detaching itself from the physical body and continuing on in the subtle body with the same desires, aspirations, and occupations as when it lived in a physical body.

Enlightenment – the ultimate attainment of consciousness. Enlightenment comes when an individual resolves his earthly karma, fulfills his destiny, and realizes the Self which exists beyond time, form, and space.

Evolution of the Soul – evolution is the result of experience and the lessons derived from it. There are young souls just beginning to evolve, and old souls nearing the end of their earthly sojourn. Old souls are recognized by their compassion and wisdom.

Fate – God's plan that brings sweet and sour events to teach our souls. Fate is merely a mirror which reflects what is before it. Fate does not bind us. It tells the story of our lives.

Gifted Memory – memory of pre-conception experiences occurring prior to development of a physical brain for storing information.

Intuition – the sixth sense; direct understanding or cognition, which bypasses the process of reason. Knowledge derived immediately and spontaneously from the soul rather than from the imperfect medium of the five senses or from reason. Intuition is a superior source of knowing, but it does not contradict reason.

Karma – the natural law of cause and effect. The sum of all an individual's deeds, which sooner or later return upon the doer. What we sow, we shall reap. Each person by his thoughts and actions becomes the molder of his destiny. Positive karma can be increased and negative karma eliminated through meditation and the practice of virtue. Understanding karma as the law of justice frees the mind from resentment against God and mind. According to the context, karma can be translated as destiny (results of past actions) or duty (actions intended to produce good results in the future).

Land of Hidden Beginnings – subtle universe of light composed of finer-than-atomic forces.

Mantra – sacred sounds and energies endowed with special power, usually drawn from scripture. To be truly effective, such mantras must be given by a teacher. Mantras are used in meditation and recitation as a means of spiritual awakening.

Mysticism – spirituality; the pursuit of direct spiritual or religious experience. Characterized by the belief that Truth transcends intellectual processes and must be attained through various transcendental means, such as meditation or contemplation.

Nirvana – the final state of peace and everlasting bliss, transcendence of suffering, into which Buddhists enter when they are no longer bound by the consciousness of an illusory ego. "The Unbecome, the Unborn, the Unmade, the Unformed." A state associated with Liberation from cyclic existence. Opposite of *Samsara*.

Origen – early Christian Church Father and main exponent of the pre-existence of the soul before conception. The Fifth Ecumenical Council of Constantinople (553 AD) condemned Origen's doctrine of pre-existence and, by implication, reincarnation, as incompatible with Christian belief.

Plato (428 to 348 BC) – Greek philosopher and disciple of Socrates who taught the doctrine of the soul's pre-existence.

Plotinus (205 to 270 AD) – Egyptian-born philosopher, religious genius, and great mystic responsible for revival of Platonism in the Roman Empire (Neoplatonism). Plotinus taught the doctrine of the soul's pre-existence, nonviolence, vegetarianism, karma, reincarnation and belief in a immanent and transcendent Supreme Being. His writings, in six volumes, are called the *Enneads*.

Pre-Conception – the time prior to the biological conception of the soul seeking human birth.

Pre-Conception Communications – dreams, visions, and intuitions of the soul seeking human birth prior to biological conception.

Pythagoras (560 BC) – Greek philosopher who taught the doctrine of the soul's pre-existence, vegetarianism, and yoga. In addition, he formulated many of the principles of mathematics and music.

Reincarnation – theory that human souls return again and again to Earth due to being entangled in a web of unfulfilled desires.

Souls Waiting in the Wings for Birth

Sacred Scriptures – Christianity: *Holy Bible* (200 AD); Judaism: *Torah* (2000 BC); Islam: *Koran* (600 AD); Zoroastrianism: *Zend Avesta* (600 BC); Buddhism: *Tripakata, Anguttara-Nikaya, Dhammapada, Sutta-Nipatta, Samyatta-Nikaya*; Sikhism (1400 AD): *Adi Granth*; Taoism: *Tao-te-Ching*; Confucianism: *Analects, Doctrine of the Mean, Great Learning, Mencius*; and Hinduism: *Vedas* (6000 BC).

Samadhi – a theoretical state of superconsciousness attained by following techniques developed millennia ago by enlightened sages.

Soul – our innermost, unchanging being, as distinguished from our body, mind, and emotions. The soul is a radiant, self-effulgent, human-like, super-intelligent being. It is the finest of subatomic forms on the quantum level which science is so far unable to detect or measure.

Subconscious Mind – the part of mind beneath the conscious mind, the storehouse or recorder of all experience whether remembered consciously or not.

Veil – a type of temporary amnesia about the soul's origin and true celestial home that the soul agrees to accept while living on Earth. Some people have thin veils. Others have thick veils.

Credits

Grateful thanks are extended to the following authors, publishers, and/or copyright holders for granting permission to use illustrations and excerpts from the works indicated:

Figure 1:

Ajit Mookerjee Collection, photo by Jeff Teasdale.. From: *The Art of Tantra* by Philip Rawson, published by Thames and Hudson, London and New York.

Part One:

Anne Loader McGee. *The Star Baby* (Northridge, California: Tarsus Productions; copyright 1994).

Part One illustration:

René Coudris, Austria. *Diary of an Unborn Child, an Unborn Baby Speaks to its Mother*, (Gateway Books, Bath, U.K.; copyright 1992).

Part Two illustration:

Hollym International Corporation, Elizabeth, New Jersey. *Oriental Birth Dreams* by Fred Jeremy Seligson; copyright 1990.

Part Three illustration:

Himalayan Academy, Hawaii. *Dancing with Shiva* by Satguru Sivaya Subramuniyaswami; copyright 1993.

Figure 5:

American Museum of Natural History, New York. *Anthropological Papers of the American Museum of Natural History*, volume XIII, 1, "Social Life and Ceremonial Bundles of Menomini Indians" by Alanson Skinner; copyright 1913.

Figure 6:

Element Books Limited of Shaftesbury, Dorset, U.K. *Aborigine Tradition* by James C. Cowan; copyright 1992.

Figure 8:

American Museum of Natural History, New York. *Memoir of the American Museum of Natural History*, "Jesup North Pacific Expedition," volume VI, by Waldemar Jochelson; copyright 1905.

Figure 9:

Jonathan Shear. *The Inner Dimension: Philosophy and the Experience of Consciousness* (New York: Peter Lang, copyright 1990).

Chapter 35 (affirmation):

Harmony Books/Crown Publishers, Inc., New York. *Ageless Body, Timeless Mind* by Deepak Chopra; copyright 1993.

Illustrations by Gustav Doré:

Gustav Doré's (1832 to 1883) illustrations of Dante's *Paradiso* are on pages 322, 339, 351, 477, 495, 537, 581, and 627. One of Doré's illustrations from Milton's *Paradise Lost* appears on page 356. Doré was a prolific French illustrator, painter, and sculptor. All of his illustrations are in the public domain.

Footnotes and References

Details of published works appear in the Bibliography.
For the sake of brevity, these will be omitted in the Notes,
reference being only to the author, date, and page.

Introductory quote

[1] Harburg, E.Y., "Over the Rainbow," Metro-Goldwyn-Mayer, Inc.; 1967.

The Azure Palace

[1] The Azure Palace is adapted from *The Blue Bird*, written by Maurice Maeterlinck, who earned the Nobel Prize for literature in 1911. The play was Maeterlinck's most successful stage work – the "Peter Pan" of his time.

Chapter 1
Souls Waiting in the Wings for Birth

[1] Shaykh Muhammad al-Jamal ar-Rifa'i as-Shadhili, 1994, p. 197.

[2] Cosmic contract: a term coined by Lorenzo Caravella, *Mouth of God: Your Cosmic Contract* (1999) meaning that we plan the details of our life before birth.

[3,4] Thurman, 1994, p. 11.

[5] Hillman, 1996, p. 63.

[6] Fingarette, 1963, p. 234.

[7] Myer, 1888, p. 397, quoting *Book of Solomon*.

[8] Hinze, 1997, p. 9.

[9] Seligson, 1990, p. 170

[10] *Ibid*, p. 68.

[11] Malinowski, 1927, p. 36.

[12] Seligson, p. 125.

[13] Spier, 1933.

[14] Montagu, 1974, p. 178-179, quoting Daisy M. Bates.

[15] Eliade, 1973, p. 70, quoting Lommel.

[16] Corda, 1987.

[17] Berg, 1984.

[18] Walker, 1965, p. 187; Head and Cranston, 1977, p. 125, quoting *Jewish War*.

[19] Head & Cranston, 1967, p. 89, quoting Philo of Alexandria, *De Somniis* I:22A.

[20] Mathers, 1912, p. 29-30.

[21] Robinson, 1988, p. 132, Logion 5; Berman, 1996, p. 101.

[22] Hastings, Volume 11, 1920, p. 744-745.

[23] Corda, 1987, p. 12.

[24] Hartland, 1909, p. 222.

[25] Lockwood, 1970, p. 151.

[26] Eadie, 1992.

[27] Kapleau, 1971, p. 6, quoting Apollonius of Tyana, philosopher-reformer.

[28] Mead, 1966, p. 150, quoting Apollonius of Tyana, 1st century Greece.

[29] Northrup, 1921, p. 65-66, quoting Carlyle's *Sartor Resartus*.

[30] Mead, 1967.

[31] Head and Cranston, 1977, p. 280, quoting *Faust* – Act I, Scene 2.

[32] Head and Cranston, 1961, p. 107, quoting Thomas Taylor's *Introduction to Works of Plato*.

[33] Kingsland, 1937, p. 36.

[34] Kamala, 1979, p. 144.

[35] Emerson, 1909, p. 341; Head & Cranston, 1977, p. 310, quoting Emerson's *Journals* for 1830.

[36] Jonas, 1963, p. 55.

[37] Hill, 1950, p. 4, quoting Brigham Young.

[38] Rawson, 1978, p. 152.

[39] MacKendrick, 1952, p. 348.

[40] Plotinus's *Enneads*, II. 3, 15.

[41] Armstrong, 1953, p. 132, quoting *Enneads*, IV, 3, 12-13.

[42] Chu, 1972, p. 80-81.

[43] Corbin, 1977, p. 244.

[44] Maeterlinck, 1961.

[45] Satchidananda, 1987, September 18.

[46] Singer, Vol X, 1905, p. 182, quoting *Hanina, Hul.* 7b; Hastings, 1912, p. 793.

[47] Singer, Vol XI, 1905, p. 472, quoting *Wisdom* viii. 19 *et seq*, R.V.

[48] Khan, 1968, volume I, p. 181.

[49] Edwards, 1933, p. 128.

Souls Waiting in the Wings for Birth

50 Forke, 1962, p. 139.

51 Holck, 1974, p. 212.

52 Hinze, p. 35.

53 Chamberlain, Spring 1990.

54 Turnbull, 1948, p. 231, quoting Plato's *Phaedrus*, 250.

55 Plotinus is the philosopher who revived Plato's theories.

56 Crouzel, 1989, p. 207.

57 Breuer, 1984, p. 258, #1081.

58 Hira, p. 67.

59 Sorensen and Willmore, 1990, p. 89-91; also Lundahl, 1997, p. 48.

60 Lenz, 1979, p. 104.

61 *Ibid*, p. 92.

62 Paulsen, 1984, p. 3.

63 Corbin, 1980, p. 182-183.

64 Verny, 1981, p. 20, quoting Dr. Michael Lieberman.

65 Fetal sensitivity discoveries inspired a new field of study – the psychology of the child in the womb and immediately at birth. Pre- and Perinatal Psychology has its own professional, peer-reviewed journal *(Pre- and Perinatal Psychology Journal)* and international and North American societies.

66 Verification of pre-third-trimester womb memories – Chamberlain, 1990, citing research of Hubbard, 1950; Laing, 1982; Lake, 1978; Grof, 1985; Farrant, 1986; Earnshaw, 1983; Feldmar, 1979.

67 Chamberlain, 1990. See *www.net-connect.net/~jspeyrer/memory.html*; Sheldrake, 1981, 1987, 1988; Stevenson, 1983; Pert and colleagues, 1985; Lashley, 1950; Sabom, 1982.

68,69 Chamberlain, 1990.

70 Hartmann, 1896, p. x, preface.

71 Shaykh Muhammad al-Jamal ar-Rifa'i as-Shadhili, 1994. p. 139.

72 Jowett, 1937, p. 254, quoting *Phaedrus* 250.

73 Keshavadas, 1976, p. 78.

74 Yogananda, 1992, p. 4.

75 Watson, 1964, p. 97.

76 Buber, 1991, p. 4.

77 Paramhansa Yogananda.

78 Shear, 1990, p. 4-5.

79 Akishige, 1968.

80 Akishige, 1968; Allison, 1970; Anand et al, 1961; Gellhorn, 1943 and 1957.

[81] Gellhorn, 1943 and 1957.

[82] Wallace, 1970; Wallace, Benson and Wilson, 1971, Wallace and Benson, 1972.

[83] Wallace, 1970, p. 1751 (quoting Maharishi Mahesh Yogi), cited in Orme-Johnson, 1976, p. 38

[84] Wallace, 1970.

[85,86] Wallace, Benson and Wilson, 1971.

[87] Farrow, John T., Physiological changes associated with transcendental consciousness, the state of least excitation of consciousness, *Collected Papers* Vol. I, p. 108-133, 1976; Hebert, J. Russell, Periodic suspension of respiration during the transcendental meditation technique, *Collected Papers* Vol. I, p. 134-136, 1976. Also see research articles published in *Collected Papers* Volumes II-V.

[88] Levine, P.H., 1976; Haynes, C.T., 1976.

[89] Wallace, R.K. and Benson, H, 1972.; Banquet, J.P., 1972; Westcott, M., 1973; Kras, D., 1976; Levine, P.H., 1976; Haynes, C.T., 1976.

[90] *Ibid.*

[91] *Ibid.*

[92] Wallace, 1986.

[93] *Ibid.*

[94] Wallace, R.K. and Benson, H, 1972.; Banquet, J.P, 1972.; Westcott, M., 1973; Kras, D, 1976.; Levine, P.H., 1976; Haynes, C.T., 1976.

PART ONE
Voices Preparing the Womb

[1] McGee, 1994.

[2] Ring, 1985, p. 208, quoting Danah Zohar.

Chapter 2
Pre-Conception Communications: Waking Visions

[1] Vissell, 1989, p. 14.

[2] Coxhead, 197-, p. 8, quoting Old Testament.

[3] Stewart, 1960, p. 331.

[4] Zaleski, 1987.

[5] Skeat, 1900, p. 47.

[6,7] Fraser, 1959, p. 179.

[8] Hultkrantz, 1953, p. 244, 256-257, 265, 389.

[9] *Karma* – The moral principle of cause and effect, action and reaction. Positive *karma* is increased and negative *karma* eliminated through meditation and

virtuous actions. "*Karma* is a natural law of the mind, just as gravity is a law of matter." (Subramuniyaswami, 1993, p. 93)

[10] Hodson, 1955

[11] Ford, 1945.

[12] Stahl, 1952, p. 146.

[13] Krakovsky, 1970, p. 104.

[14-18] Zaleski, *ibid.*

[19] Hultkrantz, *ibid*, p. 260-261.

Chapter 3
Dreaming the Future

[1] Lewis, 1995, p. 135.

[2] Gibb, 1958, p. 57.

[3] Shear, 1990, p. 224, quoting Plato's *Republic* 571d-572b.

[4] Jowett, p. 280-81, quoting Plato's *Republic* IX, 571-572.

[5] Gibb, *ibid.*

[6] Mpier, 1992.

[7] Tishby, 1989, p. 827, quoting *Zohar* I, 183a-b.

Chapter 4
Pre-Conception Intuition

[1] Vissel, 1989, p. 14.

[2] *Ecclesiastes* 3: 1-2.

[3] Ptolemy I (c. 367 to 283 BC), one of Alexander the Great's leading Macedonian generals, established the greatest Greek library in the museum at Alexandria, Egypt. History records the destruction of the academy and its library in the 4th century.

Chapter 5
Souls Lining Up for Birth: Katarina Meets Her Children

[1] Baker, 1986.

[2] See Katarina's story, "Falling to Earth" in *Part Five – Footprints in Heaven.*

[3] Dr. Deepak Chopra – *Quantum Healing; Unconditional Life; Ageless Body, Timeless Mind.*

[4] The mind-body-soul connection provides a hidden message about a full-term pregnancy. Women who want children but are unable to carry them full-term, perhaps need to assess their mental, emotional and physiological states, since these influence the embryo growing inside. This is a delicate issue since it

reveals that we can positively influence our body's physiology as well as affect it disharmoniously. The mind-body-soul connection implies women need to be in tune with their whole being and avoid sending messages of disharmony and negativity into their body chemistry.

Chapter 6
Dancing in Two Worlds: Miscarriage Within the Greater Plan

1 Frank, 1947.

2 Formaldehyde is a common toxic component utilized in manufacturing numerous everyday products. Until recent years, carpet backing contained higher levels of formaldehyde, but health complaints and a recognition of its toxic nature have led to reductions in the amount today in carpet backing and certain products.

Chapter 7
Conversations with My Unborn Child

1 Star, 1986, p. 84.

Chapter 8
Golden Messages: Uncovering the Hidden Meanings in Dreams

1 Spiegelman, 1991, p. 135.

2-4 Lincoln, 1935, p. 121.

5 Seligson, 1990, p. 128.

6 Ibid, p. 119.

7 Ibid, p. 53, quoting Wieger, A History of Religious Beliefs in China.

8 Von Grunebaum, 1966, p. 357.

9 Seligson, p. 47; Confucius (551 to 479 BC).

10 Lincoln, ibid, p. 309.

11 Boas, 1925, p. 51; Lincoln, ibid, p. 319.

12 Talbot, 1967, p. 327.

13 Seligson, ibid, p. 155.

14 Gilot and Lake, 1964.

15 Rees, 1853, p. 403.

16 Seligson, ibid, p. 16-17.

17 Ibid, p. 154.

18 Ibid, p. 97.

19 Ibid, p. 216-17.

20 Ginzberg, 1913, p. 254.

Souls Waiting in the Wings for Birth

Chapter 9
The Time Before Time Began: Spirit-Children Down Under

1   Lawlor, 1991, p. 122.
2   Kaberry, 1935-6, p. 394.
3   Montagu, 1949, p. 99.
4,5 Montagu, 1974, p. 63.
6   Montagu, *ibid*, p. 60, quoting Spencer and Gillen.
7   Cowan, 1992, p. 25. Cowan is a contemporary author and anthropologist.
8   Cowan, *ibid*, p. 25, quoting Mountford in Montagu, 1974.
9   Kaberry, 1939, p. 42.
10 Spencer and Gillen, 1968.
11 Spencer and Gillen, 1966, p. 363; also Montagu, 1974, p. 61.
12,13 Lawlor, 1991, p. 50.
14 Goodale, 1971, p. 140.
15 *Ibid*, p. 138.
16 *Ibid*, p. 141.
17 *Ibid*, p. 141; also quoted by Montagu, *ibid*, p. 113.
18 Mountford, 1958, p. 147.
19 Goodale, 1971, p. 142.
20 Lommel, 1949-50, p. 162.
21 Elkin, 1933; also Montagu, *ibid*, p. 180.
22 Corda, 1987, p. 17.
23 Lawlor, 1991, p. 160.
24 Kaberry, 1935-36, p. 395.
25 *Ibid*, p. 394.
26 Lommel, 1949-50, p. 162.
27 McConnel, 1931, p. 16.
28 Stanner, 1936, p. 186-216.
29,30 Warner, 1937, p. 21.
31 Bates, 1940, p. 27; also Montagu, *ibid*, p. 178-179; 369.
32 Montagu, *ibid*, p. 117, quoting Douglas.
33 Kaberry, *ibid*, p. 394-400.
34 Montagu, *ibid*, p. 182.
35 Montagu, *ibid*, p. 181.
36 Hernandez, March 1941, p. 219; also Montagu, *ibid*.
37 Warner, *ibid*, p. 22.

38 Mountford, *ibid*, p. 147.

39 Elkin, *ibid*.

40 This is not the first time modern research underestimated ancient peoples. Although Upper Paleolithic cave art implied high mental development scientists initially rejected this possibility and withheld the evidence from the public because it ran counter to evolutionary theory.

41 Parker, 1905.

42 Lawlor, *ibid*, p. 51.

43 Lommel, 1950-51, pp. 14-21. See also Lommel, 1949-1950, pp. 158-164.

44 *Ibid*.

45 Berndt, 1952, p. 98.

46 Montagu, *ibid*, p. 392.

47 Lommel, *ibid*, p. 18,

48 Lawlor, *ibid*, p. 373.

49 Cowan, 1991, p. xiii.

50 Jochelson, 1926, p. 157.

51 Jung, 1965, p. 265.

52 Best, 1952, p. 8.

53 Otorohanga, 1928, p. 42.

54 Lockwood, 1970, p. 66-67.

Chapter 10
Near-Death Visions of Souls Seeking Birth

1 Cooper, 1947, p. 75.

2 Gaster, 1969, p. 214.

3 Cooper, *ibid*, p. 75, quoting Plato's *Apology*.

4 Kapleau, 1989, p. 309, quoting Stoddard, *Hospice Movement: A Better Way to Care for the Dying*.

5 Poteat, 1950, p. 359.

6 Poteat, *ibid*, p. 359 – as recorded by Posidonius (135 to 51 BC).

7 Dyer, 1883. p. 341.

8 Gaster, 1969, p. 214, quoting *Merchant of Venice*.

9 Gaster, *ibid*, p. 214, quoting *King Richard the Second*.

10 Finlay, 1979, p. 186.

11 Eadie, 1992; Hinze, 1997; Lundahl, 1997, p. 37; Gibson, 1992, p. 214-5.

12 Wallace, 1994.

13 Nelson, Volume I, 1988, p. 39.

[14] Lundahl, 1997, p. 38.

[15] Crowther, 1967, p. 39; Lundahl, *ibid*, p. 33.

[16] Morse and Perry, 1990, p. 6-9; Moody, 1988, p. 104-105.

[17] Nelson, 1988, p. 105-109.

[18] Sorensen and Willmore, 1990, p. 90.

[19] Gibson, 1992, p. 170-176.

[20] Inge, Volume I, 1918, p. 256.

[21] Cranston and Williams, 1984, p. 187, quoting *Zohar*.

[22] Tishby, 1989, p. 683.

[23] McCurdy, 1906, p. 50.

[24] Inge, 1948, p. 107.

[25] Danielou, 1955, p. 216.

[26] Turnbull, 1948, p. 260, "The Retreat."

[27] Stewart, 1960, p. 395.

[28] Turnbull, *ibid*, p. 189, quoting Plotinus, *Enneads*, "Return of the Soul," VI, v, 7.

[29] Mead, 1914, p. xix.

[30] Head and Cranston, 1977, p. 336-7.

[31] Shunjo, 1925, p. 635.

[32] Guerry, 1975.

[33] Skinner, 1925, p. 290-314; also Skinner, 1913, p. 40.

[34] Heinberg, 1989, p. 34.

Chapter 11
Light Attracts Light: Meeting a Saint Prior to Conception

[1] Subramuniyaswami, 1993, p. 823.

[2] Walters, 1990, p. 73.

[3] Apurvananda, 1961, p. 169.

[4] Mullin, 1994, p. 44, quoting Second Dalai Lama's *Autobiography*.

[5] Rao, 1989, p. 95.

[6] Murugan, 1997, p. 24.

[7] Blackman, 1997, p. 13.

[8] Budge, 1961, p. 631.

[9] *Ibid*, p. 681.

[10] Schepps, 1979, p. 25, quoting *Protoevangelium of James*, Chapter I, verse 7.

[11] Budge, *Ibid*.

[12-14] *Ibid*, p. 662.

[15] O'Grady, 1892.

[16] Hartland, 1909.

[17,18] Thompson, 1985, p. 46.

[19] Thurston, Volume I, p. 252.

[20] Finlay, 1979, p. 186.

[21] Keshavadas, 1978, p. 121-122. Meaning: "May that Eternal God, our Creator, independent Reality, one who has no beginning, light of wisdom, and Truth. That Lord who manifests through the Sun, propitiated by the highest gods, one who bestows wisdom, bliss, and everlasting life. We meditate on that Light. May our intellect be illumined by that Light of God. One who protects us from the waters of karma, the Light of all the lights, the essence of everything, one who bestows immortality. May that all-pervading almighty God bless us with enlightenment."

[22] Saraswati, 1997, p. 14.

[23,24] Personal communication with Shree Maa 4/12/99.

[25] Saraswati, 1997, p. 14; 31.

[26] *Ibid*, p. 136.

[27] Blackman, 1997, p. 107.

[28] Seligson, 1990, p. 174-175.

[29] Khanolkar, 1978, p. 1.

[30-32] Khanolkar, *ibid*, p. 6.

[33] Sholapurkar, 1992, p. 182.

[34] Vittal asked the pundits how he could atone for his wrongs. The Brahmins suggested he and his wife drown themselves in the river. Thinking that the children were old enough to be on their own and that it was the best way to release their children from the curse, the parents undertook a pilgrimage with the intention of voluntarily putting an end to their lives. This practice of self-immolation by drowning oneself or by burying oneself alive in the state of *samadhi*, is favorably regarded in this part of India. Accordingly the parents committed themselves to a watery grave at the sacred confluence of the Ganges and Yamuna Rivers at Prayag (present-day Allahabad). This place was considered a particularly auspicious location to end one's life.

[35] Khanolkar, 1978, p. 11.

[36] *Ibid*, p. 36.

[37] Rolland, 1965, p. 11.

[38-40] *Ibid*, p. 8.

[41] Isherwood, 1965, p. 20-21.

[42,43] Gupta, *The Life of M. and Sri Sri Ramakrishna Kathamrita*, Sri Ma Trust, Chandigarh, India, p. 317.

44 Bucke, 1969, p. 313.

45 Johnsen, 1994, p. 36.

46 Bucke, *ibid*, p. 313

47 Mahadevan, 1971, p. 113.

48 Isherwood, 1965, p. 148

Chapter 12
Children Born of Prayer

1 Dhar, 1975, p. 15, volume I.

2 Child, 1855, volume I, p. 321.

3 Talbot, 1967, p. 149.

4 Hastings, 1912, volume V, p. 36.

5 Crowther, 1967, p. 39.

6 Schneemelcher, 1963, p. 375.

7 Rigopoulos, 1993, p. 46, quoting *Sai Satcharita*.

8 Kamath, 1991, p. 134.

9 Fanibunda, 1978, p. 17.

10 Gomes, 1911, p. 161.

11 Hastings, 1912, p. 31; Gaster, 1969, p.183; Child, 1855, p. 322. This Temple was one of the most impressive monuments of Greek civilization. The sanctuary functioned as an international healing spa from the 5th century BC through Roman times. The sanctuary included temples, colonnades, hospitals, hotels, gymnasia, and the best-preserved theater of Greece, which has seating for 14,000 and nearly perfect acoustics.

12 Kamath, *ibid*, p. 148, quoting *Mount Sadhu in Meditation*.

13 Plummer, 1922, p. 184.

14 *Ibid*, p. 182.

15 Dawes and Baynes, 1948, p. 8.

16 Thurston, 1930, p. 96.

17 Dhar, *ibid*, p. 15.

18 Nara, 1985, p. 2.

19 Deora, 1989, p. 10.

20 Sholapurkar, 1992.

21 Singh, Kirpal, 1949, p. 15.

22-24 *Ibid*, p. 72.

25 Amritaswarupananda, 1991, p. 225.

26 *Ibid*, p. 231.

[27] *Ibid*, p. 232.

Chapter 13
Lodge of the Great Manitou

[1] Hultkrantz, 1953, frontispiece.

[2] Hallowell, 1940.

[3] Hultkrantz, 1953, p. 419.

[4] Swanton, 1911, p. 181.

[5] Hultkrantz, *ibid*.

[6] Ray, 1938, p. 67.

[7] Voegelin, 1937; Hirschfelder and Molin, 1992, p. 204.

[8] Powers, 1986, p. 53.

[9] Chapman, 1921, p. 302; Hultkrantz, *ibid*, p. 417.

[10] Underhill, 1945, p. 128.

[11] Hartland, 1909, p. 245.

[12] Dunham, 1993, p. 10.

[13] Speck, 1935, p. 48.

[14] Hudson, 1902, p. 106.

[15] Hartland, *ibid*, p. 244.

[16] Fewkes, 1901, p. 86; Haeberlin, 1916, p. 28, note 3.

[17] Fewkes, 1896, p. 162.

[18] Hirschfelder and Molin, *ibid*, p. 263.

[19] Cushing, 1892, p. 50-51.

[20] Boas, 1925, p. 47-49.

[21] Voegelin, 1936, p. 5.

[22] Hultkrantz, 1957, p. 79.

[23] Coomaraswamy, 1946, p. 466.

[24] *Ibid*, p. 470.

[25] Eliade, 1960, p.105; Eliade, 1964, p. 479.

[26] Butterworth, 1970, p. 5.

[27] *Ibid*, p. 6.

[28] *Ibid*, p. 4.

[29] Hatt, 1949.

[30] Gifford, 1933; Hultkrantz, *ibid*, p. 420.

[31] Hilger, 1952.

[32] Devereux, 1937, p. 417; Hultkrantz, *ibid*.

[33,34] Hultkrantz, *ibid.*

[35] Dorsey, 1889.

[36] Hultkrantz, *ibid.*

[37] Gifford, 1933.

[38,39] Gifford-Lowie, 1928, p. 343.

[40] Jones, 1939; Linton, 1940, p. 273.

[41,42] Hultkrantz, *ibid*, p. 419.

[43] Skinner, 1913, p. 74.

[44] *Ibid*, p. 37.

[45] *Ibid*, p. 76.

[46] *Ibid*, p. 77.

Chapter 14
Land of the Boomerang

[1] Montagu, 1974, p. 101.

[2] Mountford, 1951, p. 112.

[3] Hartland, 1909, p. 242.

[4] Kaberry, 1939; Montagu, 1974, p. 196-7; Kaberry, 1935-36, p. 394-400.

[5] Hartland, 1909, p. 245.

[6] *Ibid*, p. 240.

[7] Spencer and Gillen, 1966, p. 358.

[8] *Ibid*, p. 355.

[9] Cowan, 1992, p. 47.

[10] Montagu, *ibid*, p. 101, point 29; Spencer and Gillen, *ibid*, p. 116.

[11] Cowan, *ibid*, p. 46.

[12] *Ibid*, p. 48.

[13] *Ibid*, p. 46-48.

[14] Montagu, *ibid*, p. 30.

Chapter 15
The Great Mother's Maternity Ward

[1] Myer, 1888, p. 13.

[2] Gebbie, 1981, p. 341, quoting Berndt and McCarthy, *Sexual Behavior in Arnhem Land.*

[3] Neumann, 1955, p. 87.

[4] Montagu, 1974, p. 174.

5 McConnel, 1931, p. 15.

6 Montagu, *ibid*, p. 211-212.

7 Montagu, *ibid*, p. 212.

8 Mountford, 1951, p. 159; Montagu, *ibid*.

9 Montagu, *ibid*.

10 Montagu, *ibid*.

11 Taplin, 1879, p. 88 – first report on Aborigines' procreative beliefs; Montagu, *ibid*, p. 213.

12 Burkert, 1972, p. 367 note 90.

13 Montagu, *ibid*, p. 219-20.

14 Parker, 1905; Montagu, *ibid*.

15 Montagu, *ibid*, p. 220.

16 Mountford, 1951, p. 158; Montagu, *ibid*, p. 211.

17 Holmberg, 1927, p. 260.

18 Holmberg, *ibid*, p. 260, p. 415.

19 Mountford, 1965, p. 152.

20 Neumann, *ibid*, p. 263.

21 Butterworth, 1970, p. 2.

22 Eliade, 1991, p. 14.

23 Eliade, 1974, p. 267.

24 Butterworth, *ibid*, p. 2.

25 Eliade, 1974, p. 267.

26 Eliade, *ibid*, p. 16.

27 Mountford and Harvey, 1941.

Chapter 16
Travellers from the Light

1 Hinze, 1997, p. 96.

2 Schure, 1923, p. 108.

3 Cranston and Head, 1977, p. 21.

4 Schure, 1923, p. 160.

5 Eliot, 1909, quoting Marcus Tullius Cicero's *On Old Age*, 74. Cicero was a political leader (106 BC to 43 BC).

6 Head and Cranston, 1961, p. 92, quoting Apuleius' *The God of Socrates*.

7 Head and Cranston, 1967, p. 90, quoting Philo's *De Gigantes, 2 et seq*.

8 Corbin, 1980, p. 19, quoting *Epistle of the Towers*.

9   Corbin, 1980, p. 180, quoting *Manichaean Psalter*; Manichaeism is a Gnostic religion.

10 Corbin, 1980, p. 45.

11 Hopper and Lahey, 1960, quoting John Webster, *Duchess of Malfi*.

12 Head and Cranston, 1967, p. 268, quoting Goethe.

13 Waite, 1919, p. 46, quoting Thomas Vaughan.

14 Martin, 1981, p. 6, quoting Laurence Binyon's "Unsated Memory."

15 Martin, 1981, p. 8, quoting "Ode on the Intimations of Immortality."

16 Cranston and Head, 1977, p. 273, quoting Kant's *Critique of Pure Reason*.

17 Alexander, 1964, p. 117.

18 Maeterlinck, 1961, p. 218-219.

19 Cranston and Head, 1977, p. 267.

20 Alcott, 1872, p. 83-84. Alcott was an educator and father of Louisa May Alcott.

21 Kingsland, 1937, p. 141.

22 Bregman, 1982, p. 102.

23 Mead, 1967, p. 58, quoting *Phaedrus* 250c.

24 Jowett, 1937, p. 254, quoting *Phaedrus* 250c.

25 Schure, *ibid*, p. 114.

26 Inge, 1918, p. 4-5; Wright, 1981, p. 270; fragment 115.

27 Subramuniyaswami, 1993, p. 5. (*Sukla Yajur Veda; Brihadaranyaka Upanishad*, 4.4.18)

28,29 Yogananda, 1992, p. 216.

30 Rao, 1989, *ibid*, p. 29.

31 Head and Cranston, 1977, p. 89, quoting the 14th century Zen Buddhist, Bassui Tokusho.

32 Berman, 1996, p. 160, quoting Buddhist mystic Sen T'sen.

33 Shaykh Muhammad al-Jamal ar-Rifa'i as-Shadhili, 1994, p. 140.

34 *Ibid*, p. 217.

35 Smith, 1973, p. 201.

36 Corbin, 1980, p. 27.

37 Nicholson, 1963, p. 117.

38 Crookal, 1969, p. 121.

39 Eadie, 1992, p. 49, 97.

40 Walker, 1965, p. 187, quoting Josephus, *Jewish War*, Book 2, chapter 8, nos. 10-11.

41 Walker, *ibid*, p. 188; Head and Cranston 1967, p. 90, quoting *De Gigantes, 2 et seq.*

42,43 Myer, 1888, p. 196.

44 Krakovsky, 1970, p. 104.

45,46 Tishby, 1989, p. 701, quoting *Zohar* III, 303 b, *Hashmatot*.

47 Tishby, *ibid*, p. 743-44, quoting *Zohar* I, 90 b-91a, referring to *Psalm* 139:15-16.

48 Tishby, *ibid*, p. 702.

49 Ginzberg, 1913, p. 32.

50 Tishby, *ibid*, p. 744.

51 Berg, 1984, p. 81.

52 *Ibid*, p. 80.

53 Crouzel, 1989, p. 207, quoting Father Origen.

54 Sanford, 1991, p. 102.

55 Walker, *ibid*, p. 88, quoting Professor William Knight, *Fortnightly Review*, September 1878.

56 Head and Cranston, 1967, p. 124.

57 Walker, *ibid*, p. 81, quoting Soame Jenyns, *Disquisition of a Preexistent State*; Head and Cranston, 1961, p. 196.

58 Smith, 1973, p. 50; Head and Cranston, 1967, p. 98 (Clement's "Exhortation to the Pagans").

59 Walker, *ibid*, p. 214, quoting *Saint Jerome's Epistle to Avitus*.

60 Bregman, *ibid*, p. 155, quoting *Ep.* 105, 1485A-1488B.

61 Bregman, *ibid*, p. 157.

62 Kingsland, 1937, p. 138, quoting *De Principiis*, 3, 1, 20, 21.

63 Dechow, 1988, p. 18.

64 Kingsland, *ibid*, p. 138, quoting *Princ.* 3, 1, 20, 21.

65 Chadwick, 1966, p. 166, quoting *Comm. in John* xiii, 50.

66-69 Walker, *ibid*, p. 212, quoting Origen's *De Principiis*.

70 Danielou, 1955, p. viii.

71 Sanford, *ibid*, p. 55.

72 Sanford, *ibid*, p. 144, quoting Ludwig Ott, *Fundamentals of Catholic Dogma*, p. 100.

73 Lundwall, p. 24.

74,75 *Ibid*, p. 23, quoting Joseph Smith.

76 Hill, 1950, p. 5.

77 Gibson, 1992, p. 285, quoting *Pearl of Great Price*, p. 65.

78 Lundwall, *ibid*, p. 146-47; Crowther, 1967, p. 41.

79 Turnbull, 1948, p. 186, quoting Plotinus' *Enneads* VI, iv, 14.

80 Walker, *ibid*, p. 206.

81 Armstrong, 1953, p. 132, quoting *Enneads* IV, 3, 12-13.

82 Mead, 1914, p. xliii.

[83] Turnbull, *ibid*, p. 219, quoting *Enneads* VI, ix, 9.

[84] Sullivan, 1989, p. 274.

[85] Jonas, *ibid*, p. 55.

[86] *Ibid*, p. 44.

[87] Schmidt, 1978, p. 23-24.

[88] Robinson, 1988, p. 132, quoting Logion 5.

[89,90] Robinson, *ibid*, p. 265-266, quoting *Apocryphon of James* 34.17-18.

[91] Sugrue, 1973, p. 364.

[92] *Ibid*, p. 368.

[93] Heinberg, 1989.

[94,95] Atwater, 1994, p. 50.

[96] Lundahl, 1997, p. 164.

[97] Butterworth, 1970, p. 1.

[98] Neumann, 1955, p. 247 quoting *Book of Bahir*.

[99] Hatt, 1949, p. 34.

[100] Eliade, 1974, p. 272.

[101] *Ibid*, p. 273.

[102] Corda, 1987, p. 12, quoting Hazrat Inayat Khan.

Chapter 17
Circle of Life – Buddhist and Yogic Inter-life Realms

[1] Kapleau, 1971, p. 5.

[2] Keshavadas, 1988, p. 12.

[3] *Samsara* – the process of birth and death, impermanence, constant change. The correct date of Adi Shankara's life has not been definitively arrived at and is still a matter of controversy. Dates assigned to him vary from 6th century BC to 8th century AD.

[4] Asahara, 1993, p. 52.

[5,6] *Ibid*, p. 54.

[7,8] Kapleau, 1989, p. 261.

[9] Chaudhuri, 1976, p. 132; Hastings, Vol. VII, 1914, p. 186; Besides *gandharva*, Buddha uses the terms *manomaya*, *sambhavaisin*, and *nirvrtti*.

[10] Hastings, *ibid*.

[11] Evans-Wentz, 1973, p. xxxvi.

[12] Chang, 1963, p. 105 – the Gurus of the Succession and the Commentary on the Tantra of Kalacakra.

[13] Asangha brothers.

14 David-Neel, 1985, p. 39.

15 Chang, *ibid*, p. 106.

16 Kapleau, 1989, p. 257, quoting Zen master Yasutani.

17 Hsu, 1948, p. 173.

18 Keshavadas, *ibid*, p. 12.

19 Sullivan, 1989, p. 171, quoting *Agni Purana*, chapter 340 and 342.

20 Subramuniyaswami, 1993, p. 155, 729.

21 *Ibid*, p. 155.

22-24 Keshavadas, *ibid*, p. 12.

25 Venkateswarulu,Vol. V, 1985.

26 Keshavadas, 1976, p. 32-32.

27 Chaudhuri, 1976.

28 Kloetzli, 1989, p. 113, quoting Buddha's discourse *Samyutta Nikaya* (xv. 5,6).

Chapter 18
Soul's Orbit

1 Mead, 1966, p. 149.

2 Emerson, 1909; Head and Cranston, 1977, p. 310-11; from Emerson's journal quoting Pythagoras.

3 Plato's *Republic*.

4 McIntyre, 1903, p. 312.

5 Macrobius's *Commentary on the Dream of Scipio*.

6 Head & Cranston, 1977, p. 272, quoting Kant's "General History of Nature."

7 Figuier, 1893, p. 310.

8 Head & Cranston, 1977, p. 535.

9 Plato's *Phaedo* (107D to 115A).

10 Page, 1938, p. 515.

11 *Ibid*, p. 515-517.

12,13 Highbarger, 1940, p. 73.

14 *Ibid*, p. 74.

15 Fitzgerald, 1983, lines 631-657.

16 Highbarger, *ibid*, p. 93.

17 Fitzgerald, *ibid*.

18 *Ibid*, lines 657-684.

19-21 *Ibid*, lines 684-713.

22,23 *Ibid*, lines 713-735.

[24] *Ibid*, lines 713-765.

[25] *Ibid*, lines 736-765.

[26] Gayley, 1911, p. 360.

[27] Fitzgerald, *ibid*, lines 736-793.

[28] *Ibid*, lines 868-896.

[29] *Ibid*, lines 736-793.

[30] *Ibid*, lines 868-896.

[31] Highbarger, *Ibid*, p. 106.

[32] Steiner, 1968, p. 53.

[33] *Ibid*, p. 223.

[34] Chu, 1972, p. 55.

[35] *Ibid*, p. 66.

[36] *Ibid*, p. 70.

[37] Steiner, *ibid*, p. 73.

[38] *Ibid*, p. 69.

[39] *Ibid*, p. 44

[40,41] *Ibid*, p. 257.

[42,43] Goodwin, 187-?, p. 286-287.

[44] Guthrie, 1935, p. 186, quoting Virgil's *Aeneid*.

[45] Schure, 1923, p. 121-122, quoting Virgil and Homer.

[46] Goodwin, *ibid*, p. 286, "On the Face appearing within the Orb of the Moon."

[47] Schure, 1923, p. 121-122, according to Orphic Mysteries and Pythagoreans.

[48] Head and Cranston, 1961, p. 20.

[49] O'Flaherty, 1980, p. 252.

[50] Taylor, 1980 (1875), p. 79.

[51] Rhys, 1931, p. 192, quoting *Phaedo* 107.

[52] Turnbull, 1948, p. 226, *Phaedo* 83D.

[53] Corda, 1987, p. 13.

[54] Van Praagh, 1997, p. 100.

[55] *Ibid*, p. 101.

[56] *Ibid*, p. 102.

[57,58] Talbot, 1926, p. 148, p. 267-268.

Chapter 19
Indigenous Journeys

[1] Cott, 1983, p. 191.

[2] Garvan, 1964.

[3] Jochelson, Volume 10, 1905.

[4] Porteous, 1928, p. 215.

[5] Sullivan, 1989, p. 254.

[6,7] Doniger, 1991.

[8] Eliade, 1974, p. 480.

[9] Grimm, 1888, p. 828.

[10] Gaster, 1969, p. 851.

[11] Campbell, 1964, p. 334.

[12] Jones, 1968, p. 375; Brewer, 1934, p. 109, 459; 6th century Saint Medard, 2nd century Saint Polycarp, 5th century Saint Julia, 6th century British Saint Briocus.

[13] Cirlot, 1962, p. 27, quoting *Mirach*; Hastings, Vol. XI, 1920, p. 745.

[14] Jobes, 1962, p. 104, quoting *Zohar* 28 b.

[15] Grimm, *ibid*.

[16,17] Zaleski, 1987.

[18] Hultkrantz, 1953, p. 266-267.

[19] Erny, 1981, p. 25.

[20] Erny, 1973, p. 110.

[21] Malinowski, 1916.

[22] Malinowski, 1987, p. 146.

[23] Bowen, 1927, p. 550.

[24] Jochelson, *ibid*.

[25] Corda, 1987, p. 12.

Chapter 20
Bridge of Angel Hair

[1] Eliade, 1958, p. 232.

[2] Hatt, 1949, p. 50.

[3] *Ibid*, p. 62.

[4] Hartland, 1909, p. 22.

[5] Doane, 1882, p. 45.

[6] *Ibid*, p. 45.

[7] Sullivan, 1989, p. 112.

[8] Roberts and Donaldson, 1890, p. 583, Book VI, Chapter XXII; Dupuis, 1984, p. 344. Ladder is located in an initiation cave of Mithras.

[9] *Chandogya Upanishad* 4.15.5; 5.10.1.

10 Hopper and Lahey, 1960, p. 171; quoting British dramatist John Webster.

11 Hudson, 1902, p. 104-106.

12 Sullivan, *ibid*, p. 108. *Iatros*, "healer," and *mantis*, seer.

13 800 BC to 500 BC: Empedocles of Acragas, Pythagoras of Samos, Abaris, Aristeas of Proconnesus, and Hermotimos.

14 Stewart, 1960, p. 176.

15 Murphet, 1978, p. 22.

16 Larson, 1979, p. 277.

17 *Ibid*, p. 278.

18 Plutarch, On the Delayed Revenge of the Gods.

19 Stewart, *ibid*, p. 331.

20 Mead, 1967, p. 41.

21 Stewart, *ibid*, p. 331.

22 Sullivan, 1989, p. 110.

23 IStewart, *ibid*, p. 332.

24 De Lacy and Einarson, 1959, p. 291.

25-28 *Ibid*, p. 285.

29 David-Neel, 1985, p. 29.

30 Drolma, 1995.

31 Shear, 1990, p. 233, appendix.

PART FOUR
Cosmic Contracts

1 Personal communication with James O'Non, PhD, professor of physics.

Chapter 21
Souls Signing their Cosmic Contracts

1 Hallett, 1995, p. 159.

2 Murphet, 1979, p. 112.

3 Stewart, 1960, p. 176.

4 MacKendrick, 1952, p. 348.

5 Abimbola, 1976, p. 125.

6 Beier, 1980, p. 4.

7 Dhar, 1975, p. 678.

8 *Ibid*, p. 15.

9 Ford, 1945, p. 190.

10 Uchendu, 1965.

[11] Parker, 1905; Hartland, 1909, p. 243.

[12] Hartland, *ibid*.

[13] *Ibid*, p. 220.

[14] Priya, 1992, p. 7.

[15] Keshavadas, 1988, p.13.

[16] Crowther, 1967, p. 37.

[17] O'Dea, 1957, p. 128.

[18] Crowther, *ibid*.

[19] *Ibid*, quoting President Joseph F. Smith.

[20] Wallace, 1994, p. 106-7.

[21] Pond, 1889, p. 238.

[22,23] Schoolcraft, 1851-57, VI, p. 652.

[24] Wallis, 1919, p. 323; Wallis, 1947, p. 82.

[25] Skinner, 1913, p. 37; also see *Chapter 13 – Lodge of Great Manitou*.

[26] Hennecke and Schneemelcher, p. 1963, p. 252.

[27-29] Mead, 1906, p. 461.

[30,31] Hennecke and Schneemelcher, *ibid*, p. 402-403.

[32] Head & Cranston, 1967, p. 111.

[33] Robinson, 1988, p. 223, quoting *Sophia of Jesus Christ*; Hennecke and Schneemelcher, *ibid*.

[34] Warneck, 1909, p. 107.

[35] MacDougall, 1907.

Chapter 22
Golden Books of Destiny

[1] Hinze, 1997, p. 150.

[2] O'Flaherty, 1980, quoting *Garuda Purana, Uttara Khanda* 22, p. 70-72.

[3] Edwards, 1933, p. 194.

[4] Gibb, 1958, p. 35. This tradition fixes the time the decrees were written, "but not the origin of the decrees, for this is a thing of eternity, without a beginning." (Wensinck, 1965, p. 54).

[5] Safeer, 1983, p. 26, quoting Guru Gobind Singh, 10th Sikh Master.

[6] Schmidt, 1978, p. 232-24.

[7] Gibson, 1992, p. 285, quoting *Pearl of Great Price*, p. 65.

[8] Watt, 1948, p. 18, quoting the *Qadar*; Wensinck, 1965, p. 54.

[9] Pickthall, 1959, p. 73, quoting *Koran, Surah* III, verse 143.

[10,11] Singer, 1905, p. 182, quoting *Hanina, Hul.* 7b; Hastings, 1912, p. 793.

Souls Waiting in the Wings for Birth

[12] Birnbaum, 1964, p. 77, quoting Maimonides, 12th century Jewish philosopher.

[13] Hinze, *ibid*, p. 30, quoting *Psalms* 139:15-16. This book is distinct from the scroll in which someone's deeds are recorded as described in *Psalms* 69:28.

[14] Gaster, 1950, p. 348-349.

[15] Gaster, 1969, p. 764.

[16] Gaster, 1950.

[17] Holmberg, 1927, p. 260, p. 415.

[18] Talbot, 1926, p. 291. Also Talbot, 1967, p. 24.

[19] *Ibid*, p. 288.

[20,21] *Hinduism Today*, October 1998, p. 45.

[22] Porteous, 1928, p. 252.

[23] Dodds, 1951, p. 28, quoting Homer's *Iliad*.

[24] Lattimore, 1959, p. 209, quoting *Iliad* Chapter 9, 410-416.

[25] Fitzgerald, 1974, p. 477, quoting *Iliad* Book Twenty, lines 75-135.

[26] Briffault, 1963, p. 303.

[27] Cox, 1883, p. 267.

[28] Coomaraswamy, A., K., 1946, p. 476, quoting *Rig Veda*, II. 32.4.

[29] Briffault, *ibid*, p. 624.

[30] Halevi, 1995, p. 86.

[31] Miller, 1917, p. 515, 980-996 quoting Seneca's *Oedipus*. Seneca – 4 BC to AD 65.

[32] Singh, 1966, p. 383, quoting Maharaj Charan Singh.

[33] Grimm, 1888, p. 1402.

[34] Satchidananda, 1987, Feb. 11.

[35] Kamala, 1979, p. 111.

[36] Edwards, 1933, p. 194.

[37] Woods, 1947, p. 134.

[38] Jochelson, 1905.

[39] Brandon, 1962, p. 165, quoting Homer's *Iliad* XXIV, 109-110.

[40] Hodson, S. in Schultz, 1984.

[41] Scholem, 1987, p. 159.

[42] Ginzberg, 1925, p. 82.

[43,44] Newhouse, 1955, p. 41.

[45] Newhouse, 1966, p. 67-68.

[46] Newhouse, 1955, p. 43.

[47-49] Beier, 1966, p. 40-41.

[50] Gardner, 1960, p. 293.

[51] Hodson, G. in Schultz, 1984, p. 155.

[52] Coomaraswamy, 1941, p. 98, quoting Plato's *Laws* 644-45, 803-4; Saunders, 1975, p.74.

[53] Edwards, *ibid*, p. 193.

[54] Walker, 1965, p. 323, quoting *Enneads* III, 2, 17.

[55] Gaskell, 1930, p. 465, quoting Phillips Brooks' sermon, "The Pattern in the Mount."

[56] Myer, 1888, p. 115, quoting Rev. John Gregorie.

[57] Armstrong, A.H., 1965, p. 125.

[58] Paulsen, 1984, p. 205-6, quoting Paramahansa Yogananda's *Autobiography of a Yogi*.

[59] Das, 1990, p. 335.

[60] Cheney, 1972, p. 32.

[61] Spiegelman, 1991, p. 109.

[62] Coomaraswamy, 1941, p. 98.

Chapter 23
The Path of Suffering

[1] Gibson, 1993, p. 122; Gibson, 1994, p. 125.

[2] Spiegelman, 1991, p. 91 quoting *Koran, Sura* XVIII, Al-Kahf or The Cave.

[3] Sullivan, 1989, p. 5.

[4] Eadie, 1992, p. 94-95.

[5] Subramuniyaswami, 1993, p. 161.

[6] *Ibid*, 1993, p. 161, quoting *Tirukural*.

[7] Subramuniyaswami, 1993, p. 437.

[8] *Ibid*, p. 595.

[9] Das, 1990, p. 183.

[10] Gibson, 1993, p. 122; Gibson, 1994, p. 125.

[11] Sanford, 1991, p. 120, quoting Meister Eckhart.

[12] Gibson, 1993, p. 71; Lundahl, 1997, p. 30-31.

[13] Gibson, 1993, p. 71; Lundahl, *ibid*.

[14-16] Lambert, 1914, p. 21.

[17] Patchen, 1989, p. 308.

[18] Whitton, 1986, p. 80.

[19] Johnsen, 1994, p. 89.

[20] Subramuniyaswami, *ibid*, p. 151.

[21] Eadie, *ibid*, p. 67.

Chapter 24
Souls in Training: Free Will and Karmic Lessons

1. Cranston & Williams, 1984, p. 194, quoting *The Dybbuk*.
2. Schure, 1923, p. 127-128.
3,4. Walters, 1990, p. 73.
5. Malinowski, 1916; See *Chapter 19 – Indigenous Journeys*.
6. Taylor, 1980 (1875).
7. Jonas, 1963, p. 63.
8. Boas, 1889.
9. Talbot, 1926, p. 268.
10. Head and Cranston, 1967, p. 89 quoting Philo of Alexandria's *De Somniis* I:22A.
11. Bordow, 1986, p. 3.
12. Kapleau, 1989, p. 261.
13. Bowen, 1927.
14. Radin, 1945, p. 8; See *Chapter 32 – Cosmic Memory*.
15. Walters, 1977, p. 344.
16. Newhouse, 1966, p. 67.
17. Walters, 1977, p. 343, quoting *Sha'ar Hatsiyune*, letter 6*vav*.
18. Kapleau, 1989, p. 253.
19. Turnbull, 1948, p. 169.
20. Nicholson, 1963, p. 117.
21. Sayer, 1887, p. 210, quoting *The Banquet*. Dante, 1265-1321.
22. Subramuniyaswami, 1993, p. 718.
23. Cranston & Williams, p. 187, quoting *Zohar*.
24. Khan, 1968, p. 190.
25. Subramuniyaswami, *ibid*, p. 823.
26. *Ibid*, p.7, citing *Krishna Yajur Veda; Maitreya Upanishad* 4.3.
27. Martin, 1981, p. 35.
28. Sullivan, 1989, p. 143.
29. Sparrow, 1995, p. 92.
30. Sugrue, 1973, p. 373.
31. Head and Cranston, 1977, p. 543.
32. *Ibid*, p. 544.
33. *Ibid*, p. 544-545.
34. *Ibid*, p. 547.
35. Subramuniyaswami, *ibid*, p. 796.

36 Holck, 1974, p. 177, quoting Sri Aurobindo, the 20th century philosopher.

37 Subramuniyaswami, *ibid*, p. 990.

38 Jiyu-Kennett and MacPhillamy, 1979, p. 11.

39 *Ibid*, p. 11-12.

40 Uchendu, 1965.

41 Cott, 1983, p. 189.

42 Sullivan, 1989, p. 236.

43 Martin, 1981, p. 39.

44 Blackman, 1997, p. 16.

45 Keshavadas, Sant, "Healing Mantras of the East," audio cassette.

46 Kapleau, 1989, p. 273-274, quoting V. F. Gunaratna.

47 Rinpochay, 1979, p. 110, according to the XIV Dalai Lama.

48 Walters, 1990, p. 73.

49 Head and Cranston, 1967, p. 90, quoting Philo of Alexandria, *De Gigantes, 2 et seq.*

50 Das, 1947, p. 288.

51 Blackman, *ibid*, p. 12.

52 Head and Cranston, 1967, p. 144.

53 Cranston & Williams, *ibid*, p. 176.

54 Das, *ibid*, p. 285-286.

55 Bowen, *ibid*, p. 551.

56 Pond, 1889, p. 239.

57 Mackenzie, 1996, p. 89.

58 Hicks, 1984, p. 3.

59 Mullin, 1994, p. 255.

Chapter 25
Alternate Destinies

1 Das, 1990, p. 697, as recounted in the *Mahabharata*.

2 Shri Dileepji Pathak, disciple of Dhyanyogiji. Personal communication 11/25/98.

3 Corbin, 1980, p. 234.

4 Ventakeswarulu, 1981, p. 186-189, quoting *Padmapurana Uttarakhanda*.

5 Subramuniyaswami, 1993, p. 723; Maha-Mrityunjaya Mantra: "We adore the fragrant three-eyed one who promotes prosperity. May we be freed from the bondage of death as a cucumber from its stalk… ."

6,7 Zimmer, 1946, p. 37.

8 Dhyanyogi, 1979, p. 23.

9   A similar tradition exists within the Sikh religion where it is believed that Guru Nanak (1469 to 1539) would carry out his mission in ten different incarnations.

10   Mullin, 1994, p. 15.

11,12   Dhondup, 1986, p. 145.

13   Mullin, *ibid*, p. 15.

14   *Ibid*, p. 14.

15   Das, 1992, p. xxiii.

16   Goodman, 1986, p. 5.

17   Malik, 1984, p. 112.

PART FIVE
Gifted Memory: Pre-Conception Remembrances

1   Chamberlain, 1990.

Chapter 26
The Illusion of Forgetfulness

1   Seligson, 1990, p. 161.

2   Stewart, 1960, p. 288.

3   *Ibid*, p. 287.

4   Jonas, 1963, p. 63.

5   Schure, 1923, p. 129.

6   Hill, 1950, p. 198, quoting Elder Parley P. Pratt.

7   Shaykh Muhammad al-Jamal ar-Rifa'i as-Shadhili, 1994, p. 199.

8   Head and Cranston, 1967, p. 263, quoting Lessing, a German dramatist and critic.

9   Imerti, 1964, p. 94-95.

10   Hedge, 1877, p. 358; Unitarian Minister.

11   Buber, 1961, p. 96, volume I.

12   Abimbola, 1976, p. 113.

13   Hill, 1950, p. 15, quoting Elder Parley P. Pratt, *Key to Theology*, p. 53.

14   Schure, 1923, p. 127-129; Martin, 1981, p. 237.

15   Walker, 1965, p. 49; Guthrie, 1919, p. 432, quoting *Enneads*, IV. 3, 26.

16   Myer, 1888, p. 196, quoting Solomon ben Yehudah Ibn Gebirol, aka Avicebrol, Avicebron and Avicembron, (1021-1070); *Zohar* III, 61a-61b.

17   Slater, 1983, p. 27.

18   Nicholson, 1963, p. 15; Gairdner, 1980, p. 14.

19   Walker, 1965, p. 236-237.

[20] Stewart, 1960, p. 321.

[21] Govinda, 1970, p. 116.

[22] Freemantle, 1975, p. 2.

[23] Kamala, 1979, p. 151.

[24] Rao, 1989, p. 75. *Annamaya, pranamaya, manomaya, vijnanamaya,* and *anandamaya koshas;* quoting *Taittiriya Upanishad.*

[25] Kamala, 1979, p. 151.

[26] Head and Cranston, 1977, p. 171.

[27-29] Jonas, 1963, p. 158, quoting *In somn, Scipio* II. 11.

[30] Head and Cranston, 1967, p. 222.

[31] Mead, 1914, p. xxv-xxvii, quoting Adi Shankara's treatise, *Tattvabodha.*

[32] Mead, 1907, p. 96.

[33] Mead, 1914, p. xxvi.

[34] Sugrue, 1973, p. 370.

[35] Plato's *Republic,* Myth of Er.

[36] Jowett, 1937, *Meno* 81.

[37] Fitzergerald, 1983, lines 684-713.

[38] Head and Cranston, 1967, p. 209.

[39] Plutarch, *On the Delayed Revenge of the Gods.*

[40] De Lacy, 1959, p. 285.

[41] Yogananda, 1992, p. 66.

[42] Muktananda, 1983, p. 42-23, quoting *Garbha Upanishad.*

[43,44] Yogananda, *ibid,* p. 64.

[45] Subramuniyaswami, 1993, p. 797.

[46] Pargiter, 1904, p. 70, quoting *Markandeya Purana,* Canto XI, verse 14.

[47] *Ibid,* Canto XI, verse 17.

[48] *Ibid,* Canto XI, verse 18.

[49] *Ibid,* Canto XI, verse 19.

[50] Baba, 1955, p. 66.

[51] Buber, 1961, p. 144.

Chapter 27
Piercing the Veils of Light

[1] Walker, 1965, frontispiece.

[2] Wheelwright, 1959, p. 58, referring to Greek philosopher Heraclitus, c. 480 BC.

[3] Stewart, 1960, p. 286.

[4] Stevenson, 1983, p. 7.

[5,6] Head and Cranston, 1967, p. 111, quoting *Pistis Sophia*.

[7] Sullivan, 1989, p. 271.

[8] Macrobius's *Commentary on the Dream of Scipio*.

[9] Beier, 1966.

[10] Stewart, *ibid*, p. 161.

[11] Jowett, 1937, *Meno* 81.

[12] Alcott, 1868, p. 202.

[13] Edwards, 1933.

[14] Jonas, 1963, p. 162, quoting *Die Ssabier*.

[15] *Ibid*, p. 83, quoting *Das Iranische Erlosungsmysterium – Abridged Mass of the Dead*.

[16] Hill, 1950, p. 15, quoting *Gospel Doctrine*, p. 15-16.

[17] Blackman, 1997, p. 56.

[18] Kamala, 1979, p. 149.

[19] Spiegelman, 1991, p. 57.

[20] Jonas, 1963, p. 45, quoting *Excerpts from Theodotus* 78.2.

[21] Lundwall, p. 146-47; Crowther, 1967, p. 41.

[22] Gibb, 1958, p. 57.

[23] Gibson, 1993, p. 55.

[24] Lenz, 1979, p. 108.

[25] Taylor, 1980 (1875), p. 51 and 103.

[26] Stewart, *ibid*, p. 287.

[27] Cheney, 1972, p. 111, quoting Plato's *Phaedrus* 250.

[28] Stewart, *ibid*, p. 286.

[29] Hill, 1950, p. 19.

[30] William Wordsworth, "Ode on the Intimations of Immortality."

[31] Corbin, 1980, p. 182-183.

[32] Wagner, 1970, p. 127.

[33,34] *Ibid*, p. 129.

[35] Corbin, *ibid*, p. 182-183.

[36-38] Wagner, *ibid*, p. 129.

[39] Corbin, *ibid*, p. 182-183.

[40] Jonas, 1963, p. 113.

[41] Happold, 1964, p. 178.

[42] *Ibid*, p. 179-180.

[43] *Ibid*, p. 180-181.

[44] Jonas, *ibid*, p. 114.

[45] Happold, p. 179-180.

[46] Jonas, 1963, p. 114.

[47] Halevi, 1995, p. 19.

[48] Edgar, 1984, p. 153.

[49] Eastern and Western Disciples, Vol I, 1979, p. 19.

[50] Hixon, 1992, p. 114.

[51] *Ibid*, p. 115.

[52] Ananyananda, 1983, p. 254.

[53] Vivekananda, Vol IV, 1970-1973, front cover inside.

[54] Caravella, 1999.

Chapter 28
Footprints in Heaven: Contemporary Gifted Memory

[1] Head and Cranston, 1977, p. 351.

[2] Chamberlain, Spring 1990.

[3] Head & Cranston, *ibid*, p. 76, quoting *Sangiti Sutta* (paraphrase)

Chapter 29
Children As Messengers: Contemporary and Historical Accounts

[1] Cott, 1983, p. 191, "Chinua Achebe: At the Crossroads."

[2] Chamberlain, 1988, p. 193.

[3] Walker, 1965, p. 43, quoting *Penn Monthly*, September 1875.

[4] Stevenson, 1987.

[5] Atwater, P. M. H., 1994, p. 177.

[6] Hinze, 1997, p. 91.

[7] Mahadevan, 1971, p. 65.

[8] Jochelson, 1926, p. 161.

[9] Stevenson, 1987, p. 68-71.

[10] Stevenson, 1983, p. 36.

[11] Stevenson, *ibid*.

[12] Gibson, 1992, p. 87.

[13] Gibson, 1992, p. 87; Lundahl, 1997, p. 35.

[14] Ruff, 1963, p. 61; Hinze, *ibid*, p. 43.

[15] Lundahl, 1997, p. 36, quoting Hinze, Sarah, *Life Before Life*.

[16] Hearn, 1923.

[17-19] *The American Magazine,* July 1915.

[20] Ray, 1938.

[21] Boas, 1894.

[22] Stevenson, 1983, p. 196.

[23,24] Stevenson, 1987.

[25] Colgrave, 1940, p. 157.

[26] Cruz, 1977, p. 302.

[27] Mullin, 1994, p. 10.

[28-34] *Ibid,* p. 47-52.

[35,36] *Ibid,* p. 61.

[37] *Ibid,* p. xv.

[38] *Ibid,* p. 111.

[39] *Ibid,* p. 113.

Chapter 30
Gifted Memory and Higher Consciousness

[1] Shaykh Muhammad al-Jamal ar-Rifa'i as-Shadhili, 1994, p. 139.

[2] Eliade, 1968, p. 122.

[3] Inge, 1918, volume I, p. 4-5; Wright, 1981, p. 270; fragment 115.

[4] Head and Cranston, 1967, p. 90, quoting Philo of Alexandria's *De Gigantes, 2 et seq.*

[5] Turnbull, 1958, p. 146.

[6] Walters, 1977, p. 344.

[7] Meera, 1991, p. 19.

[8] Yogananda, 1972, p. 4.

[9] Yogananda, 1992, p. 215.

[10] Steiner, 1968, p. 222.

[11] Paulsen, 1984, p. 11.

[12] Brains, 1976, p. 239.

[13] Banerjee, 1974, p. 87.

[14] Stevenson, 1983, p. 249.

[15] Dr. Ian Stevenson investigated 230 reincarnation cases in Burma. Forty-seven percent (107) of the parents having children who remember previous lives dreamed of their child prior to birth. Sayadaw's story is more rare because the monk recalls appearing in the dreams of two people.

[16] See Guru Gobind Singh's autobiographical poem, *Bachitra Natak,* "The Wondrous Drama." Singh and Singh, 1976; Seetal,1968; Safeer, 1983; Nara, 1985; Deora, 1989; Johar, 1987; Johar, 1979; Kohli, 1986; Singh, 1992, Singh,

1976; Singh, Gopal, 1978; Singh, Gopal, 1966; Singh, Harbans, 1966; Singh and Suneet, 1970; Singh, Puran, 1966; Singh, Trilochan, 1968.

[17] Anna, p. 65, ISBN 81-7120-378-7.

[18,19] Paulsen, 1984, p. 1.

[20-28] *Ibid*, p. 2-4.

[29] Malik, p. 1984.

[30] Hallett, 1995, p. 159.

[31] Dhar, 1975, volume I, p. 18.

[32] Hixon, 1992, p. 301.

[33-35] *Ibid*, p. 115.

[36] Chidatmananda, 1964, p. 336.

[37] Hixon, *ibid*, p. 115.

[38] Chidatmananda, 1964, *ibid*, p. 336.

[39] Anna, *ibid*, p. 81.

Chapter 31
Native American Seers

[1] Andrews, 1962, p. 46

[2] Wallis, 1947, p. 82.

[3,4] Hultkrantz, 1953, p. 231.

[5] Brinton, 1896, p. 305.

[6] Eliade, 1960, p. 73.

[7] Andrews, *ibid*, p. 45.

[8] O'Bryan, 1956.

[9] Hultkrantz, 1953, p. 418-419.

[10] Osgood, 1932, p. 84.

[11] Hultkrantz, 1953, p. 418.

[12] Wallis, 1919, p. 324.

[13] Wallis, 1947, p. 82.

[14,15] Wallis, 1919, p. 323.

[16,17] Wallis, 1947, p. 82.

[18] Skinner, 1925, Volume 38, No. 150, p. 479.

[19] Nerburn, 1993, p. 42.

[20] Radin, 1923, p. 270-271.

[21] Boas, 1889.

Chapter 32
Cosmic Memory

[1] Stahl, p. 135-136.

[2,3] Eliade, 1968, p. 123.

[4] Kapleau, 1989, p. 278.

[5] Spiegelman, *ibid*, p. 35.

[6] Das, 1947, p. 152.

[7] Eliade, 1982, p. 193, quoting Apollonius Rhodius, *Argonautica* 1. 642 ff.

[8] Scholem, 1973, p. 241.

[9] Head and Cranston, 1977, p. 282.

[10] Yogananda's poem, "Cosmic Creation."

[11] Eliade, 1960, p. 50-51; Eliade, 1968, p. 91.

[12] Eliade, 1968, p. 120, quoting Hesiod's *Theogony* 32, 38.

[13] Head and Cranston, 1967, p. 147.

[14] Smith, 1973, p. 232.

[15] Schure, 1923, p. 14.

[16] Eliade, 1968, p. 122, quoting *Fragments* 129.

[17] Eliade, 1982, p. 193.

[18] Eliade, 1968, p. 121.

[19] Lincoln, 1935, p. 196-7, quoting Harrington, *Journal of American Folklore*, volume 21, p. 326-7, 1908.

[20] Kroeber, 1925, p. 754.

[21] Hartland, 1909, p. 222.

[22] Sarkar, 1987; Chatterji, 1978.

[23] Chatterji, *ibid*.

[24,25] *Ibid*, p. 111.

[26] Scholem, *ibid*, p. 415.

[27,28] Buber, 1945, p. 5.

[29-31] *Ibid*, p. 65.

[32] bid, p. 66.

[33] This is a summation of Radin's various write-ups of Thunder-Cloud's story – 1913, 1914, 1923, and 1945.

[34] Radin, 1945, p. 2.

[35] *Ibid*, 1945, p. 7.

[36] Radin, 1923, p. 315.

[37] *Ibid*, p. 270.

38-41 *Ibid*, p. 315-316.

42,43 *Ibid*, p. 270-271.

44 Radin, 1913, p. 304.

45 Radin, 1913, p. 306-307; Radin, 1923, p. 275.

46 Radin, 1923, p. 271.

47 Radin, 1923, p. 307-308.

48 Radin, 1913, p. 307.

49 A difference of opinion exists about the dates of Buddha's life. Southern Buddhists put the dates back to 624 to 564 BC, and Chinese Buddhists set it at 1000 BC.

50 Ghosh, 1987, p. 35.

51 Hixon, *ibid*, p. 236.

52 Hardy, 1967, p. 141; Martin, 1981, p. 42.

53 Prabhavananda, 1980, p. 171.

54 Eastern and Western Disciples, Vol I, 1979, p. 175.

55 Sivananda, 1993, p. 35.

56 Banerjee and Osler, 1974, p. 89.

57 Dhar, volume I, p. 680.

58 Coomaraswamy, 1946, p. 481, quoting Vaughn.

Chapter 33
Overcoming Spiritual Amnesia

1 Martin, 1981, p. 5.

Chapter 34
Angels in the Never-Ending Schoolhouse

1 Eliade, 1960, p. 51.

Recipes for Pre-Conception Experiences

1 Woods, 1947, p. 330.

2 Mead, 1914, p. xxxiv.

3 Dyer, 1998, p. 1.

4 Eastern Meditation techniques are taught by Transcendental Meditation Centers of Maharishi Mahesh Yogi, Dr. Deepak Chopra, Ma Yoga Shakti, Karunamayi, Shree Maa, Anandi Ma, and Amritanandamayi, to name a few. Ron Roth, a former Catholic priest, teaches Christian meditation.

5 Ma Yoga Shakti, *Meditation* Audio Tape.

6 Chopra, 1993, p. 47.

7 Spiegelman, 1991, p. 57.

8 Dyer, *ibid.*

9 Nicholson, 1963, p. 64.

10 NEXUS Magazine, Vol. 2, #25, Apr/May '95. Originally printed from the April 1994 edition of Acres, USA. Also see *www.all-natural.com/microva1*.

11 Kaye, 1999.

12 Dyer, *ibid.*

13 Smith, 1965, p. 66.

Bibliography

Abimbola, 'Wande, *Ifa*, Oxford Univ. Press, Nigeria, Africa; 1976.

Akishige, Y., "A historical survey of the psychological studies in Zen." *Kyushu Psychological Studies, V, Bulletin of the Faculty of Literature of the Kyushu University* 11: 1-56; 1968.

Alcott, Amos Bronson, *Tablets*, Roberts Brothers, Boston, MA; 1868.

Alcott, Amos Bronson, *Concord Days*, Roberts Brothers, Boston, MA; 1872.

Alexander, Hartley Burr, *Mythology of All Races – North American*, Cooper Square Publishers, New York, NY; 1964.

Allison, J., "Respiratory changes during Transcendental Meditation," *Lancet* 1(7651): 833; 1970.

American Magazine, "The Most Extraordinary Coincidence I know of; Was it Reincarnation?"; July 1915.

Amritasvarupananda, Swami, *Mata Amritanandamayi*, M.A. Centers, CA; 1991.

Anand, B.K, Chhina, G.S. and Singh, B., "Some aspects of electroencephalographic studies on yogis," *Electroencephalography and Clinical Neurophysiology* 13: 452-456; 1961.

Ananyananda, Swami, *Life of Ramakrishna*, Advaita Ashram, Calcutta, India; 1983.

Andrews, Ralph W., *Curtis' Western Indians*, Superior Publishing, Seattle, WA; 1962.

Anna, *Saints of India*, Sri Ramakrishna Math, India; ISBN 81-7120-378-7.

Apurvananda, Swami, *Ramakrishna and Sarada Devi*, Sri Ramakrishna Math, India; 1961.

Armstrong, A.H., *An Introduction to Ancient Philosophy*, Beacon Press, Boston, MA; 1965.

Armstrong, A.H., *Plotinus*, George Allen & Unwin LTD, London, England; 1953.

Asahara, Shoko, *Beyond Life and Death, The Spirit of Truth*, Aum Publishing Co., Japan; 1993.

Atwater, P.M.H., *Beyond the Light*, Carol Publishing Group, New York, NY; 1994.

Baba, Meyer, *God Speaks*, Dodd, Mead and Co., New York, NY; 1955.

Baker, Jeannine Parvati and Baker, F., *Conscious Conception*, Freestone Publishing, Berkeley, CA; 1986.

Banerjee, H.N. and Oursler, William, *Lives Unlimited*, Doubleday, Garden City, NY; 1974.

Banquet, Jean-Paul, "Spectral analysis of the EEG in meditation," *Electroencephalography and Clinical Neurophysiology* 35: 143-151; 1973.

Banquet, Jean-Paul, "EEG and Meditation," *Electroencephalography and Clinical Neurophysiology* 33: 454; Abstract; 1972.

Bates, Daisy, C.B.E., *Passing of the Aborigines, A Lifetime Spent...* John Murray, London, England; 1940.

Beal, Samuel, *The Romantic Legend of Sakya Buddha*, Trubner & Co., London, England; 1875.

Beier, Ulli, *Yoruba Myths*, Cambridge Univ. Press, Cambridge, England; 1980.

Beier, Ulli, *Origin of Life and Death, African Creation Myths*, Heinemann, London, England; 1966.

Berg, Philip S., *Wheels of a Soul*, Research Centre of Kabbalah, Jerusalem; 1984.

Berman, Phillip, L., *The Journey Home*, Pocket Books, New York, NY; 1996.

Berndt, Ronald M. and Berndt, Catherine, *First Australians*, Ure Smith Publication, Sydney, Australia; 1952.

Best, Elsdon, *The Maori as He Was*, R.E. Owen Government Printer, Wellington, New Zealand; 1952.

Birnbaum, Philip, *A Book of Jewish Concepts*, Hebrew Publishing Co., New York, NY; 1964.

Blackman, Sushila, *Graceful Exits, How Great Beings Die*, Weatherhill, New York, NY; 1997.

Boas, Franz, "First General Report on the Indians of British Columbia." *Report of the Fifty-Ninth Meeting of the British Association for the Advancement of Science*; 1889.

Boas, Franz, *Contributions to the Ethnology of the Kwakiutl*, Volume III, Columbia Univ. Press, New York, NY; 1925.

Boas, Franz, "Chinook Texts," *Smithsonian Institution Bureau of Ethnology*, No. 14-20; 1894.

Bohm, David, *Wholeness and the Implicate Order*, Routledge, London, England; 1995.

Bonnefoy, Ives, *Asian Mythologies*, Univ. of Chicago Press, Chicago, IL; 1993.

Bordow, Sita, *Sri Swami Satchidananda*, Integral Yoga Publications, Yogaville, Virginia; 1986.

Bowen, Patrick G., "The Ancient Wisdom in Africa," *The Theosophist*, Madras, India; August 1927.

Brains, Robert, *Friends and Lovers*, Basic Books, New York, NY; 1976.

Brandon, Samuel George Frederick, *Man and his Destiny in the Great Religions*, Manchester Univ. Press, England; 1962.

Bregman, Jay, *Synesius of Cyrene*, Univ. of California Press, Berkeley, CA; 1982.

Breuer, Hans-Peter, *The Note-Books of Samuel Butler*, Volume I, Univ. Press of America, Maryland; 1984.

Souls Waiting in the Wings for Birth

Brewer, E. Cobham, Rev., *Dictionary of Miracles*, J.B. Lippincott, Philadelphia, PA; 1934.

Briffault, Robert, *The Mothers*, Grosset & Dunlap, New York, NY; 1963.

Brinton, Daniel Garrison, *Myths of the New World*, David McKay, Philadelphia, PA; 1896.

Buber, Martin, *Chinese Tales*, Humanities Press International, Inc., New Jersey; 1991.

Buber, Martin, *Tales of the Hasidim, The Early Masters*, Schocken Books, New York, NY; 1961.

Buber, Martin, *For the Sake of Heaven*, Jewish Publication Society of America, Philadelphia, PA; 1945.

Bucke, Richard Maurice, *Cosmic Consciousness*, E.P. Dutton, New York, NY; 1969.

Budge, Sir Ernest A.T.W., *Amulets And Talismans*, Univ. Books, New York, NY; 1961.

Budge, Sir Ernest A.T.W., *Miscellaneous Coptic Texts*, Longmans and Co., London, England; 1915.

Burkert, W., *Lore and Science in Ancient Pythagoreanism*, Harvard Univ. Press, Cambridge; 1972.

Butterworth, E.A.S., *The Tree at the Navel of the Earth*, Walter De Gruyter & Co., Berlin, Germany; 1970.

Campbell, Joseph, The Masks of God: *Occidental Mythology*, Viking Press, New York, NY; 1964.

Capra, Fritjof, *The Tao of Physics*, Shambhala, Berkeley, CA; 1975.

Caravella, Lorenzo, *Mouth of God: Your Cosmic Contract*, Sunstar, Fairfield, Iowa; 1999.

Chadwick, Henry, *Early Christian Thought and the Classical Tradition, Studies in Justin, Clement, and Origen*, Oxford at the Clarendon Press, London, England; 1966.

Chamberlain, David, PhD, *Pre- and Perinatal Psychology Journal*; 4 (3), p. 171-189; Spring 1990.

Chamberlain, David, PhD, *Babies Remember Birth*, Jeremy P. Tarcher, Los Angeles, CA; 1988.

Chang, G.C.C., *Six Yogas of Naropa and Teachings on Mahamudra*, Snow Lion, New York, NY; 1963.

Chapman, Reverend John W., "Tinneh Animism," *American Anthropologist*, Volume 23, 1921.

Chatterji, Krishnalal, *The Guiding Light, A Treatise on Thakur Sree Sree Anukul Chandra*, Indian Progressive Publishing, Calcutta; 1978.

Chaudhuri, Sukomal, *Analytical Study of the Abhidharmakosa*, Sanskrit College, Calcutta, India; 1976.

Cheney, Sheldon, *Men who Walked with God*, Dell Publishing, New York, NY; 1972.

Chevalier, Haakon M., (trans.), *Secret Life of Salvador Dali*, Dial Press, New York, NY; 1961.

COSMIC CRADLE

Chidatmananda, Swami, *Life of Ramakrishna*, Advaita Ashrama, Calcutta, India; 1964.

Child, L. Maria, *Progress of Religious Ideas*, Volume I, C. S. Francis & Co., New York, NY; 1855.

Chopra, Deepak, *Ageless Body, Timeless Mind*, Harmony Books, New York, NY; 1993.

Chu, Paul E., *Life Before Birth, Life on Earth, Life After Death*, World View Press, New Jersey; 1976.

Cirlot, Juan E., *A Dictionary of Symbols*, Philosophical Library, New York, NY; 1962.

Cohen, J., *The Origins and Evolution of the Moses Nativity Story*, E.J. Brill, Netherlands; 1993.

Colgrave, Bertram, *Two Lives of Saint Cuthbert*, Cambridge Univ. Press, Great Britain; 1940.

Coomaraswamy, Ananda K., "Symplegades," in Montagu, Ashley (ed.), *Studies and Essays in the History of Science and Learning in Honor of George Sarton*, 31 August 1944, Henry Schuman, New York, NY; 1946.

Coomaraswamy, Ananda K., "Lila" in *Journal of American Oriental Society*, #61; New Haven, CT; 1941.

Cooper, L., *Plato, On the Trial and Death of Socrates*; Cornell Univ. Press, Ithaca, NY; 1947.

Corbin, Henry, *Avicenna and the Visionary Recital*, Spring Publications, Univ. of Dallas, TX; 1980.

Corbin, Henry, *Spiritual Body and Celestial Earth*, Princeton Univ. Press, Princeton, NJ; 1977.

Corda, Murshida Vera Justin, *Cradle of Heaven*, Omega Press, Lebanon Springs, New York, NY; 1987.

Cott, Jonathan, *Pipers at the Gates of Dawn*, Random House, New York, NY; 1983.

Cowan, James G., *The Aborigine Tradition*, Element, Rockport, Massachusetts; 1992. (Also published by Element Books Limited, Shaftesbury, Dorset, UK; 1992.)

Cowan, James G., *Letters from a Wild State*, Bell Tower, New York, NY; 1991.

Cox, George, W., *Introduction to the Science of Comparative Mythology and Folklore*, Kegan Paul, Trench & Co, London, England; 1883.

Coxhead, David, and Hiller, S., *Dreams: Visions of the Night*, Thames and Hudson, London, England.

Cranston, Sylvia, and Williams, C., *Reincarnation, a New Horizon in Science, Religion and Society*, Julian Press, New York, NY; 1984.

Crawley, Alfred, *Idea of Soul*, Adam and Charles Black, London, England; 1909.

Crookal, R., *Interpretation of Cosmic and Mystical Experiences*, James Clarke & Co., England; 1969.

Crouzel, Henri, *Origen*, Harper & Row, San Francisco, CA; 1989.

Crowther, Duane S., *Life Everlasting*, Bookcraft, Salt Lake City, UT; 1967.

Cruz, Joan Carroll, *The Incorruptibles*, Tan Books and Publishers, Rockford, Illinois; 1977.

Curtis, Vesta Sarkhosh, *Persian Myths*, Univ. of Texas Press, Austin, TX; 1998.

Cushing, Frank Hamilton, "A Zuni Folk-Tale of the Underworld," *Journal of American Folklore*, 5, p. 50-51; 1892.

Danielou, Jean, *Origen*, Sheed and Ward, New York, NY; 1955.

Das, Bhagavan, *Essential Unity of All Religions*, Ananda Publishing House, Benares, India; 1947.

Das, Surya, *The Snow Lion's Turquoise Mane*, Harper Collins, San Francisco, CA; 1992.

David-Neel, Alexandra, *Magic and Mystery in Tibet*, New Age Publishers, Delhi, India; 1985.

Dawes, Elizabeth, and Baynes, Norman H., *Three Byzantine Saints*, Basil Blackwell, Oxford, England; 1948.

Dechow, Jon F., *Dogma and Mysticism in Early Christianity*, Mercer Univ. Press, Georgia; 1988.

De Lacy, P.H., and Einarson, B., *Plutarch's Moralia*, Volume VII, Wm. Heinemann Ltd., London, England; 1959.

Deora, Man Singh, *Guru Gobind Singh*, Anmol Publications, New Delhi, India; 1989.

Devereux, George, "Mohave Soul Concepts," *American Anthropologist*, January-March 1937.

Dhar, S., *A Comprehensive Biography of Swami Vivekananda*, Volume I, Vivekananda Prakashan Kendra, Madras; 1975.

Dhondup, K., *The Water-Bird and Other Years, A History of the Thirteenth Dalai Lama and After*, Rangwang Publishers, New Delhi; 1986.

Dhyanyogi, Madhusudandasji, *Death, Dying and Beyond*, Dhyanyoga Centers, CA; 1979.

Doabia, Harbans, Singh, *Gobind Singh Ji Maharaj*, New Chandigarh Printing Press, India.

Doane, Thomas William, *Bible Myths and Their Parallels in Other Religions*, Commonwealth Co., New York, NY; 1882.

Dodds, E.R., *The Greeks and the Irrational*, Univ. of California Press, Berkeley and Los Angeles, CA; 1951.

Doniger, Wendy, *Mythologies*, Univ. of Chicago Press, Chicago, IL; 1991.

Dorsey, James Owen, "Teton Folk-Lore," *American Anthropologist*, Old Series, Volume I; 1889.

Drolma, D.D., *Delog, Journey to Realms Beyond Death*, Padma Publ., Junction City, CA; 1995.

Dunham, Carroll, et al, *Mamomato*, Penquin Books, New York, NY; 1993.

Dupuis, Charles F., *Origin of All Religious Worship*, Garland Publishing, New York, NY; 1984.

COSMIC CRADLE

Dyer, Thomas F. Thiselton, *Folk-Lore of Shakespeare*, Corner House, Williamstown, Mass.; 1978.

Dyer, Thomas F. Thiselton, *Folk Lore of Shakespeare*, Griffith & Farran, London, England; 1883.

Dyer, Wayne, *Wisdom of the Ages*, Harper Collins, New York, NY; 1998.

Eadie, Betty, *Embraced by the Light*, Gold Leaf Press, Placerville, CA; 1992.

Eastern and Western Disciples, *Life of Swami Vivekananda*, Volume I, Advaita Ashrama, Calcutta, India; 1979–.

Edgar, Neill, "Mystery Teachings Through the Ages," in *Theosophical Guide for Parents* by Schultz, Karen, Parents Theosophical Research Group, Ojai, CA; 1984.

Edwards, Tryon, *Useful Quotations*, Grosset & Dunlap, New York, NY; 1933.

Eliade, Mircea, *Myth of the Eternal Return*, Princeton Univ. Press, Princeton, NJ; 1991.

Eliade, Mircea, *A History of Religious Ideas*, Univ. of Chicago Press, Chicago, IL; 1982.

Eliade, Mircea, *Shamanism, Archaic Techniques of Ecstasy*, Princeton Univ. Press, Princeton, NJ; 1974.

Eliade, Mircea, *Australian Religions*, Cornell Univ. Press, London, England; 1973.

Eliade, Mircea, *Myth and Reality*, Harper & Row, New York, NY; 1968.

Eliade, Mircea, *Myths, Dreams and Mysteries*, Harvill Press, London, England; 1960.

Eliade, Mircea, *Patterns in Comparative Religion*, Sheed and Ward, New York, NY; 1958.

Eliot, Charles W., "On Old Age," *Harvard Classics*, Volume 9, P.F. Collier & Son, New York, NY; 1909.

Elkin, A.P., "Totemism in North-Western Australia," *Oceania*, Volume III; 1933.

Ellis, Alfred Burton, *Ewe-Speaking Peoples*, Chapman and Hall, London, England; 1890.

Emerson, Edward Waldo (ed.), *Journals of Emerson*, Houghton Mifflin, Boston, MA; 1909.

Erny, Pierre, *The Child and His Environment in Black Africa*, Oxford Univ. Press; Nairobi, Kenya; 1981.

Erny, Pierre, *Childhood and Cosmos*, New Perspectives, Washington; 1973.

Evans-Wentz, Walter Yeeling, *The Tibetan Book of the Dead*, Causeway Books, New York, NY; 1973.

Fanibunda, E.B., *Vision of the Divine*, Shri Sathya Sai Education & Public Foundation, Bombay, India; 1978.

Farrow, John T., "Physiological changes associated with transcendental consciousness, the state of least excitation of consciousness," in David W. Orme-Johnson, John T. Farrow (Eds.): *Scientific Research on the Transcendental Meditation Program: Collected Papers*, Volume 1, p. 108-133, MERU Press, West Germany; 1976.

Fewkes, J. Walter, "An Interpretation of Katcina Worship," *Journal of American Folklore*, Volume XIV, April-June, 1901.

Souls Waiting in the Wings for Birth

Fewkes, J. Walter, "The Prehistoric Culture of Tusayan," *American Anthropologist*, Old Series, Volume IX, No. 5, Washington, DC; 1896.

Figuier, Louis, *The To-Morrow of Death*, Roberts Brothers, Boston, MA; 1893.

Fingarette, Herbert, *The Self in Transformation*, Basic Books, New York, NY; 1963.

Finlay, Ian, *Columba*, Victor Gollancz, London, England; 1979.

Fitzgerald, Robert, *The Aeneid*, Random House, New York, NY; 1983.

Fitzgerald, Robert, *The Iliad*, Doubleday & Co., New York, NY; 1974.

Ford, Clellan S., *Comprehensive Study of Human Reproduction*; 1945.

Forde, C. Darryll, "Ethnography of the Yuma Indians," *University of California Publication in American Archaeology and Ethnology*, Berkeley, Volume 28, No. 4; 1931.

Forke, Alfred, *Lun-Heng, Philosophical Essays of Wang Ch'ung*, Paragon Book Gallery, New York, NY; 1962.

Forlong, J.G.R., *Short Studies in the Science of Comparative Religions*, Bernard Quaritch; 1897.

Frank, Philip, *Einstein, His Life and Times*, A.A. Knopf, New York, NY; 1947.

Frazer, Sir James George, *The Golden Bough*, MacMillan & Co., London, England; 1959.

Freemantle, F. and Trungpa, Chogyam, *Tibetan Book of the Dead*, Shambhala, Boulder, CO; 1975.

Gabriel, Michael and Marie, *Voices from the Womb*, Anslan Publishing, Lower Lake, CA; 1992.

Gairdner, Canon W.H.T., *Theories, Practices and Training Systems of a Sufi School*, Society for Sufi Studies, London, England; 1980.

Gardner, Martin, *The Annotated Alice*, Bramhall House, New York, NY; 1960.

Garvan, John M., *The Negritos of the Philippines*, Verlag Ferdinand Berger, Austria; 1964.

Gaskell, George Arthur, *Dictionary of Sacred Language of all Scriptures and Myths*, Lucis, New York, NY; 1930.

Gaster, Theodor Herzl, *Myth, Legend, and Custom in the Old Testament*, Harper & Row, New York, NY; 1969.

Gaster, Theodor Herzl, *Thespis, Ritual, Myth and Drama in the Ancient Near East*, H. Schuman, New York, NY; 1950.

Gayley, Charles Mills, *The Classic Myths in English Literature and in Art*, Ginn & Co., Boston, MA; 1911.

Gebbie, Donald, A. M., *Reproductive Anthropology*, John Wiley & Sons, New York, NY; 1981.

Gellhorn, Ernst, *Autonomic imbalance and the hypothalamus*, Minneapolis: Univ. of Minnesota Press; 1957.

Gellhorn, Ernst, *Autonomic Regulations*, Interscience Publishers; 1943.

Ghosh, B., "Buddha Dipankara, Twenty-fourth Predecessor of Gautama," *Bulletin of Tibetology*, No. 2, July 1987; Sikkim Research Institute of Tibetology; Gangtok, India.

Gibb, Elias J.W., *A History of Ottoman Poetry*, Volume I, Luzac and Co., London, England; 1958.

Gibran, Kahlil, *Sand and Foam*, Heinemaun, London, England; 1954.

Gibson, Arvin S. "Near-Death Experience Patterns From Research in the Salt Lake City Region," *Journal of Near-Death Studies*, Volume 13, Number 2; Winter 1994.

Gibson, Arvin S., *Echoes From Eternity*, Horizon Publishers & Distributors, Bountiful, UT; 1993.

Gibson, Arvin S., *Glimpses of Eternity*, Horizon Publishers, Bountiful, UT; 1992.

Gifford, E.W., "The Cocopa," *University of California Publications in American Archeology and Ethnology*, Volume 31: 5; 1933.

Gifford-Lowie, "The Awal'ala Indians of Lower California," *University of California Publications in American Archeology and Ethnology*, Volume 23: 7; 1928.

Gilot, Francoise and Lake, Carlton, *Life with Picasso*, McGraw-Hill, New York, NY; 1964.

Ginzberg, Louis, *Legends of the Jews*, Volume V, Jewish Publication Society of America, Philadelphia, PA; 1925.

Ginzberg, Louis, *Legends of the Jews*, Volume II, Jewish Publication Society, Philadelphia, PA; 1913.

Gomes, Edwin H., *Seventeen Years Among the Sea Dyaks of Borneo*, Seeley & Co., London, England; 1911.

Goodale, Jane C., *Tiwi Wives*, Univ. of Washington Press; 1971.

Goodman, Michael Harris, *The Last Dalai Lama*, Shambhala, Boston, MA; 1986.

Goodwin, William W., *Plutarch's Morals*, Volume V, 28, Athanaeum Press, London, England; 187-?.

Govinda, Lama Anagarika, *The Way of the White Clouds*, Shambhala, Berkeley, CA; 1970.

Grimm, Jacob, *Teutonic Mythology*, Volume IV, George Bell & Sons, London, England; 1888.

Guerry, Vincent, *Life with the Baoule*, Three Continents Press, Washington DC; 1975.

Gupta, *The Life of M. and Sri Sri Ramakrishna Kathamrita*, Sri Ma Trust, Chandigarh, India.

Guthrie, William Keith Chambers, *Orpheus and Greek Religion*, Methuen & Co., London, England; 1935.

Guthrie, Kenneth Sylvan, *Plotinos*, Volume II, Platonist Press, New Jersey; 1919.

Haeberlin, H. K., "The Idea of Fertilization in the Culture of the Pueblo Indians," *Memoirs of the American Anthropological Association*, 3:1, p. 27-30; 1916.

Souls Waiting in the Wings for Birth

Halevi, Z'ev ben Shimon, *Kabbalah*, Thames and Hudson; 1995.

Haley, Alex, *Roots*, Doubleday, New York, NY; 1976.

Hallett, Elisabeth, *Soul Trek, Meeting Our Children on the Way to Birth*, Light Hearts Publishing, Hamilton, Montana; 1995.

Hallowell, A. Irving, PhD, "The Spirits of the Dead in Saulteaux Life and Thought," *Journal of Royal Anthropological Institute of Great Britain and Ireland*, 70:1; 1940.

Happold, Frederick C., *Mysticism*, Penguin Books, Baltimore, MD; 1964.

Hara, Minoru, "Birth of Extraordinary Persons: The Buddha's Case," in Werner, Karel, *The Yogi and the Mystic*, Durham Indological Series No. 1, Curzon Press, Riverdale Co.; 1989.

Harburg, Edgar Yipsel, "Over the Rainbow," Metro-Goldwyn-Mayer, Inc.; 1967.

Hardy, R. Spence, *Manual of Buddhism*, Chowkhamba Sanskrit Series, Varanasi, India; 1967.

Hartland, Edwin Sidney, *Primitive Paternity*, Volume I, David Nutt, London, England; 1909.

Hartmann, Franz, *The Life of Phillippus Theophrastus Bombast of Hohenheim Known by the Name of Paracelsus*, Kegan Paul, Trench, Trubner, and Co., London, England; 1896.

Hastings, James, *Encyclopedia of Religion and Ethics*, Volume V, T. & T. Clark, Edinburgh, England; 1912.

Hastings, James, *Encyclopedia of Religion and Ethics*, Volume VII, T. & T. Clark, Edinburgh, England; 1914.

Hastings, James, *Encyclopedia of Religion and Ethics*, Volume XI, T. & T. Clark, Edinburgh, England; 1920.

Hatt, Gudmund, *Asiatic Influences in American Folklore*, Bianco Lunos Bogtrykkeri, Denmark; 1949.

Haynes, Christopher T., Hebert, J. Russell, Reber, William, and Orme-Johnson, David W., "The psychophysiology of advanced participants in the Transcendental Meditation program: Correlations of EEG Coherence, creativity, H-reflex recovery, and experience of transcendental consciousness," in David W. Orme-Johnson, John T. Farrow (Eds.): *Scientific Research on the Transcendental Meditation Program: Collected Papers*, Volume 1, p. 208-212, MERU Press, West Germany; 1976.

Head, Joseph and Cranston, Sylvia L., *Reincarnation, The Phoenix Fire Mystery*, Julian Press, New York, NY; 1977.

Head, Joseph and Cranston, Sylvia L., *Reincarnation in World Thought*, Julian Press, New York, NY; 1967.

Head, Joseph and Cranston, Sylvia L., *Reincarnation, An East-West Anthology*, Julian Press, New York, NY; 1961.

Hearn, Lafcadio, *Gleanings in Buddha Fields*, Houghton Mifflin Co., Boston, MA; 1923.

Hebert, J. Russell, "Periodic suspension of respiration during the transcendental meditation technique," in David W. Orme-Johnson, John T. Farrow (Eds.): *Scientific Research on the Transcendental Meditation Program: Collected Papers*, Volume 1, p. 134-136, MERU Press, West Germany; 1976.

Hedge, Frederic Henry, *Ways of the Spirit*, Roberts Brothers, Boston, MA; 1877.

Heinberg, Richard, *Memories and Visions of Paradise*, Jeremy P. Tarcher, Los Angeles, CA: 1989.

Hennecke, Edgar and Schneemelcher, W., *New Testament Apocrypha*, Westminster Press, Philadelphia; 1963.

Hernandez, Theodore, "Social Organization of the Drysdale River Tribes, North-West Australia, *Oceania*, Volume XI, No. 3, pp. 211-221; March 1941.

Hicks, Roger and Chogyam Ngakpa, *Great Ocean, An Authorized Biography of the Buddhist Monk Tenzin Gyatso, His Holiness the Fourteenth Dalai Lama*, Penguin Books, London, England; 1984.

Hicks, R.D., *Diogenes Laertius, Lives of Eminent Philosophers*, Volume II, London, England; 1931.

Highbarger, Ernest Leslie, *Gate of Dreams*, John Hopkins Press, Baltimore, MD; 1940.

Hilger, Sister M. Inez, "Chippewa Child Life and its Cultural Background," *Bureau of American Ethnology*, 146; 1952.

Hill, George Richard, *Saviors on Mount Zion*, Deseret News Press, Salt Lake City, UT; 1950.

Hillman, James, *The Soul's Code*, Warner Books, New York, NY; 1996.

Hinduism Today, Himalayan Academy, Kapaa, Hawaii; October 1998.

Hinze, Sarah, *Coming From the Light*, Pocket Books, New York, NY; 1997.

Hira, Bhagat Singh, *The Great Sikh Saints*, National Book Shop, Delhi, India.

Hirschfelder, A. and Molin, P., *Encyclopedia of Native American Religions, Facts on File*, New York, NY; 1992.

Hixon, Lex, *Great Swan, Meetings with Ramakrishna*, Shambhala Publications, Boston, MA; 1992.

Hodson, Geoffrey, *Occult Powers in Nature and in Man*, Theosophical Publishing House, India; 1955.

Hodson, Geoffrey, "The Symbology of Alice in Wonderland," in *Theosophical Guide for Parents* by Schultz, Karen, Ojai, CA; 1984.

Hodson, Geoffrey, *Reincarnation, Fact or Fallacy?*, Theosophical Publishing House, Wheaton, Illinois; 1967.

Hodson, S., "Theosophy and Family Life," in *Theosophical Guide for Parents* by Schultz, Karen, Ojai, CA; 1984.

Holck, Frederick H., *Death and Eastern Thought*, Abingdon Press, Nashville, Tennessee; 1974.

Holmberg, Uno, *The Mythology of All Races, Volume IV, Finno-Ugric, Siberian*, Archaeological Institute of America, Marshall Jones Co., Boston, MA; 1927.

Hopper, Vincent F. and Lahey, G.B., *The Duchess of Malfi*, Barron's Educational Series, New York, NY; 1960.

Hsu, Francis L.K., *Under the Ancestors' Shadow*, Columbia Univ. Press, New York, NY; 1948.

Hudson, J.W., "An Indian Myth of the San Joaquin Basin," *Journal of American Folk-Lore*, Volume XV, p. 104-106; 1902.

Hultkrantz, Ake, *The North American Indian Orpheus Tradition*, The Ethnographical Museum of Sweden, Stockholm, Sweden; 1957.

Hultkrantz, Ake, *Conceptions of the Soul Among North American Indians*, Caslon Press, Stockholm, Sweden; 1953.

Imerti, Arthur D., *Expulsion of the Triumphant Beast, Giordano Bruno*, Rutgers Univ. Press, New Brunswick, NJ; 1964.

Inge, William Ralph, *Christian Mysticism*, Methuen & Co. LTD, London, England; 1948.

Inge, William Ralph, *The Philosophy of Plotinus*, Volume I, Longmans, Green and Co., London, England; 1918.

Isherwood, Christopher, *Ramakrishna and His Disciples*, Simon and Schuster, New York, NY; 1965.

Jiyu-Kennett, Roshi and Mac Phillamy, Daizui, *The Book of Life*, Shasta Abbey Press, CA; 1979.

Jobes, Gertrude, *Dictionary of Mythology, Folklore and Symbols*, Scarecrow Press, New York, NY; 1962.

Jochelson, Waldemar, "The Yukaghir and the Yukaghirized Tungus," Jesup North Pacific Expedition, *Memoir of the American Museum of Natural History*, Volume IX; 1926.

Jochelson, Waldemar, "Jesup North Pacific Expedition," *Memoir of the American Museum of Natural History,*Volume VI; 1905.

Johar, Surinder Singh, *Guru Gobind Singh*, Enkay Publishers, New Delhi, India; 1987.

Johar, Surinder Singh, *Guru Gobind Singh*, A Study, Marwah Publications, New Delhi, India; 1979.

Johnsen, Linda, *Daughters of the Goddess*, Yes International Publishers, St. Paul, Minnesota; 1994.

Jonas, Hans, *The Gnostic Religion*, Beacon Press, Boston, MA; 1963.

Jones, William, *Credulities Past and Present*, Singing Tree Press, Detroit, Michigan; 1968.

Jones, William, "Ethnology of the Fox Indians," *Bureau of American Ethnology*, Bulletin 123; 1939.

Jowett, B., *The Dialogues of Plato*, Random House, New York, NY; 1937.

Jowett, B., *Republic of Plato*, Clarendon Press, Oxford, England; 1888.

Jung, Carl G., *Memories, Dreams, Reflections*, Vintage Books, New York, NY; 1965.

Kaberry, Phyllis M., *Aboriginal Woman*, Blakiston Co., Philadelphia, PA; 1939.

Kaberry, Phyllis M., "Spirit Children and Spirit-Centres of the North Kimberley Division, West Australia," Oceania, Volume 6, pp. 394-400; 1935-36.

Kamala, *Priceless Precepts*, Oakland, CA; 1979.

Kamath, M.V. and Kher, V.B., *Sai Baba of Shirdi*, Jaico Publishing House, Bombay, India; 1991.

Kapleau, Philip, *The Wheel of Life and Death*, Doubleday, New York, NY; 1989.

Kapleau, Philip, *The Wheel of Death*, Harper & Row, New York, NY; 1971.

Kaye, E., *Fountain of Youth*, Warner Books, New York, NY; 1999.

Keshavadas, Sadguru Sant, *Lord Ganesh*, Vishwa Dharma Publications, Oakland, CA; 1988.

Keshavadas, Sadguru Sant, *Gayatri, The Highest Meditation*, Motilal Banaarsidass, India; 1978.

Keshavadas, Sadguru Sant, *Liberation from Karma and Rebirth*, Colonial, Virginia Beach, VA; 1976.

Khan, Hazrat Inayat, *The Sufi Message of Hazrat Inayat*,Volume I, Barrie and Rockliff, London, England; 1968.

Khanolkar, Savitribai, *Saints of Maharashtra*, Bharatiya Vidya Bhavan, Bombay, India; 1978.

Kingsland, Wm., *Gnosis or Ancient Wisdom in the Christian Scriptures*, George Allen & Unwin, London, England; 1937.

Kloetzli, Randy, *Buddhist Cosmology*, Motilal Banarsidass, Delhi, India; 1989.

Kohli, S. Singh, *Life and Ideals of Guru Gobind Singh*, Munshiram Manoharlat Publishers, New Delhi; 1986.

Krakovsky, Rabbi Levi Isaac, *Kabbalah*, Research Centre of Kabbalah, Israel; 1970.

Kras, D.J., "The Transcendental Meditation technique and EEG alpha activity," in David W. Orme-Johnson, John T. Farrow (Eds.): *Scientific Research on the Transcendental Meditation Program: Collected Papers*, Volume 1, p. 173-181, MERU Press, West Germany; 1976.

Kroeber, Alfred, "Mohave: Dream Life," *Handbook of the Indians of California, Bulletin of American Ethnology*, No. 78; 1925.

Lambert, George C., *Treasures in Heaven*, Salt Lake City, UT; 1914.

Larson, Raymond, *Plato, The Republic*, AHM Publishing Corp., Arlington Heights, Illinois; 1979.

Lattimore, Richmond, *Hesiod*, Univ. of Michigan Press, Ann Arbor, Michigan; 1959.

Lawlor, Robert, *Voices of the First Day*, Inner Traditions, Rochester, Vermont; 1991.

Leeming, David, *Mythology: The Voyage of the Hero*, Oxford Univ. Press, New York, NY; 1998.

Souls Waiting in the Wings for Birth

Lenz, Frederick, *Lifetimes, True Accounts of Reincarnation*, Bobbs-Merrill Co., Indianapolis, IN; 1979.

Levine, Paul H., "The coherence spectral array (COSPAR) and its application to the study of spatial ordering in the EEG," *Proceedings of the San Diego Bio-Medical Symposium* 15: 237-247; 1976.

Levine, Paul H., Hebert, J. Russel, Haynes, Christopher T., Strobel, Urs, "EEG coherence during the Transcendental Meditation Technique," in David W. Orme-Johnson, John T. Farrow (Eds.): *Scientific Research on the Transcendental Meditation Program: Collected Papers*, Volume 1, p. 187, 207, 247; Maharishi International Univ. Press, Fairfield, IA; 1975.

Lewis, James R., *The Dream Encyclopedia*, Visible Ink Press, Detroit, Michigan; 1995.

Lincoln, Jackson S., *The Dream in Primitive Cultures*, William and Wilkins, Baltimore, MD; 1935.

Linton, Ralph, (ed.) *Acculturation in Seven American Indian Tribes*, D. Appleton-Century Co., New York, NY; 1940.

Lockwood, D., *I, The Aboriginal*, Meridian Books, World Publishing Co., Cleveland, Ohio; 1970.

Lommel, Andreas, "Modern Culture Influences on the Aborigines," *Oceania*, Volume 21; Sept-June 1950-51.

Lommel, Andreas, "Notes on Sexual Behaviour and Initiation, Wunambal Tribe, North-Western Australia, *Oceania*, Volume 20, p. 158-164; Sept-June 1949-1950.

Lundahl, Craig, *Eternal Journey*, Warner Books, New York, NY; 1997.

Lundwall, N.B., *The Vision or The Degrees of Glory*, Bookcraft Publishing Co, Salt Lake City, UT.

MacDougall, Duncan , MD, "Hypothesis Concerning Soul Substance Together with Experimental Evidence of The Existence of Such Substance," *American Medicine*; 1907.

MacKendrick, Paul L. and Howe, Herbert M. (editors), *Classics in Translation, Volume I: Greek Literature*, Univ. of Wisconsin Press, Madison, WI; 1952.

Mackenzie, Vicki, *Reborn in the West*, Marlowe & Co., New York, NY; 1996.

Maeterlinck, Maurice, *The Blue Bird*, Dodd, Mead and Co., New York, NY; 1961.

Mahadevan, T.M.P., *Ten Saints of India*, Bharatiya Vidya Bhavan, Bombay, India; 1971.

Malik, Inder, L., *Dalai Lamas of Tibet, Succession of Births*, New Delhi, India; 1984.

Malinowski, Bronislaw, *Sexual Life of Savages in North-Western Melanesia*, Beacon Press, Boston, MA; 1987.

Malinowski, Bronislaw, *The Father in Primitive Psychology*, W.W. Norton & Co., New York, NY; 1927.

Malinowski, Bronislaw, "Baloma; the Spirits of the Dead in the Trobriand Island," *Journal of the Royal Anthropological Institute of Great Britain and Ireland*, Volume 46; 1916.

Martin, Eva, *The Ring of Return*, Sun Publishing Co., Albuquerque, NM; 1981.

Mathers, S.L. MacGregor, *Kabbalah Unveiled*, Theosophical Publishing Co., New York, NY; 1912.

McConnel, U., "A Moon Legend from the Bloomfield River, N. Queensland," *Oceania*, Volume II; 1931.

McCurdy, Edward, *Leonardo Da Vinci's Note-Books*, Charles Scribner's Sons, New York, NY; 1906.

McGee, Anne Loader, *The Star Baby*, Tarsus Productions, Northridge, CA; 1994.

McIntyre, J. Lewis, *Giordano Bruno*, MacMillan and Co., London, England; 1903.

Mead, George Robert Stow, *Doctrine of the Subtle Body in Western Tradition*, Theosophical Publishing House, Wheaton, Illinois; 1967.

Mead, George Robert Stow, *Apollonius of Tyana*, University Books, New Hyde Park, New York, NY; 1966.

Mead, George Robert Stow, *Plotinus, Select Works* (Thomas Taylor's trans.), G. Bell & Sons, London, England; 1914.

Mead, George Robert Stow, *The World Mystery*, Theosophical Publishing Society, London, England; 1907.

Mead, George Robert Stow, *Fragments of a Faith Forgotten*, Theosophical Publishing Society, London, England; 1906.

Meera, Mother, *Mother Meera*, Meeramma Publications, Ithaca, New York, NY; 1991.

Memoirs of the Historical Society of Pennsylvania, Volume XII, Philadelphia; 1881.

Miller, Frank Justus, *Seneca's Tragedies*, G.P. Putnam's Sons, New York, NY; 1917.

Montagu, Ashley, *Coming Into Being Among the Australian Aborigines*, Routedge & Kegan Paul, London, England and Boston, MA; 1974.

Montagu, Ashley, "Embryological Beliefs of Primitive Peoples," *Ciba Symposia*; Jan.-Feb. 1949.

Moody, Raymond A., Jr., MD, *The Light Beyond*, Bantam, New York, NY; 1988.

Morse, Melvin, MD, *Closer to the Light*, Villard Books, New York, NY; 1990.

Mountford, Charles, P., *Ayers Rock, Its People*, East-West Center Press, Honolulu, HA; 1965.

Mountford, Charles, P., *The Tiwi, Their Art, Myth and Ceremony*, Phoenix House, London, England; 1958.

Mountford, Charles P., *Brown Men and Red Sand*, Robertson and Mullens, Melbourne, Australia; 1951.

Mountford, Charles, P., and Harvey, A., "Women of the Adnjamatana Tribe of the Northern Flinders Ranges, South Australia," *Oceania*, Volume 12, p. 155-163; 1941.

Mpier, M.M., "Dreams among the Yansi" in *Dreaming, Religion and Society in Africa*, E.J. Brill, Netherlands; 1992.

Souls Waiting in the Wings for Birth

Muktananda, Swami, *I Am That, The Science of Hamsa from the Vijnana Bhairava*, SYDA Foundation, South Fallsburg, New York, NY; 1983.

Mullin, Glenn H., *Mystical Verses of a Mad Dalai Lama*, Theosophical Publishing House, Wheaton, IL; 1994.

Murphet, Howard, *Sai Baba Avatar*, MacMillan Co. of India; 1978.

Murugan, *Karunamayi*, Sri Mathru Devi Viswa Shanti Ashram Trust, Bangalore, India; 1997.

Myer, Isaac, *Qabbalah, The Philosophical Writings of Solomon Ben Yehudah Ibn Gebirol or Avicebron*, MacCalla & Co., Philadelphia; 1888.

Nara, Giani Ishar Singh, *Safarnama and Zafarnama*, Nara Publications, New Delhi, India; 1985.

Nelson, Lee, *Beyond the Veil*, Volume I, Cedar Fort, Orem, UT; 1988.

Nerburn, Kent, *The Soul of an Indian*, New World Library, San Rafael, CA; 1993.

Neumann, Erich, *The Great Mother*, Princeton Univ. Press, Princeton, NJ; 1955.

Newhouse, Flower A., *Rediscovering the Angels*, Christward Ministry, Escondido, CA; 1966.

Newhouse, Flower A., *Shining Ones*, Christward Ministry, Escondido, CA; 1955.

Nicholson, Reynold Alleyne, *The Mystics of Islam*, Routledge and Kegan Paul Ltd, London, England; 1963.

Northrup, Clark S., *Sartor Resartus by Thomas Carlyle*, Harcourt, Brace and Co., New York, NY; 1921.

O'Bryan, Aileen, "The Dine: Origin Myths of the Navaho Indians," *Smithsonian Institution Bureau of American Ethnology*, Bulletin 163; 1956.

O'Dea, Thomas F., *The Mormons*, The Univ. of Chicago Press, Chicago, IL; 1957

O'Flaherty, W.D., *Karma and Rebirth in Classical Indian Traditions*, Univ. of California Press, Berkeley and Los Angeles, CA; 1980.

O'Grady, S.H., *Silva Gadelica (I.-XXXI.) A Collection of Tales in Irish*, Williams and Norgate, London, England; 1892.

Orme-Johnson, David W., and John T. Farrow (Eds.): *Scientific Research on the Transcendental Meditation Program: Collected Papers*, Volume 1, MERU Press, West Germany; 1976.

Osgood, Cornelius, "The Ethnography of the Great Bear Lake Indians," *Bulletins (and Annual Reports) of the Canada Department of Mines*, 70, National Museum of Canada; 1932.

Otorohanga, W.B., *Where the White Man Treads*, Wilson and Horton, New Zealand; 1928.

Page, Thomas Etherbert, *Virgil*, Volume I, Loeb Classical Library; 1938.

Pargiter, F. Eden, *Markandeye Purana*, Asiatic Society, India; 1904.

Parker, K. Langloh, *Euahlayi Tribe*, Archibald Constable and Co., LTD., London, England; 1905.

COSMIC CRADLE

Patchen, Nancy, *Journey of a Master: Swami Chinmayananda*, Asian Humanities Press, Berkeley, Calif.; 1989.

Paulsen, Norman, *Christ Consciousness*, Builders Publishing Co., Salt Lake City, UT; 1984.

Pickthall, Mohammed Marmaduke, *The Glorious Koran*, New American Library, New York, NY; 1959.

Plummer, Charles, *Lives of Irish Saints*, Oxford Univ. Press; 1922.

Pond, Rev., Gideon H., "Dakota Superstitions," *Collections of the Minnesota Historical Society*, Volume II; (1860-67), Reprint 1889.

Porteous, Alexander, *Forest Folklore, Mythology and Romance*, MacMillan, New York, NY; 1928.

Poteat, Hubert M. (trans.), *Marcus Tullius Cicero*, Univ. of Chicago Press, Chicago, IL; 1950.

Powers, Marla N., *Oglala Women*, Univ. of Chicago Press, Chicago, IL; 1986.

Priya, Jacqueline Vincent, *Birth Traditions*, Element, Rockport, MA; 1992

Prabhavananda, Swami, *Spiritual Heritage of India*, Vedanta Press, Hollywood, CA; 1980.

Radin, Paul, *The Road of Life and Death*, Pantheon Books, New York, NY; 1945.

Radin, Paul, "Winnebago Tribe," *Annual Reports of Bureau of American Ethnology*, Volume 37; 1923.

Radin, Paul, "Religion of the North American Indians," *Journal of American Folk-Lore*, Volume 27; 1914.

Radin, Paul, "Personal Reminiscences of a Winnebago Indian," *Journal of American Folk-Lore*, Volume 26; Oct.-Dec., 1913.

Rao, Polamuri Sampatha, *Message of Bhagwan Balayogi*, P. Divya Kiran, India; 1989.

Ray, Verne F., "Lower Chinook Ethnology Notes," *Univ. of Washington Publications in Anthropology*, Volume 7; 1938.

Rhys, Ernest (ed.), *Five Dialogues of Plato*, J. M. Dent & Sons, London, England; 1931.

Rigopoulos, A., *Life and Teachings of Sai Baba of Shirdi*, State Univ. of New York Press, New York, NY; 1993.

Ring, Kenneth, *Heading Toward Omega*, William Morrow, New York, NY; 1985.

Rinpochay, L. and Hopkins, J., *Death, Intermediate State and Rebirth*, Snow Lion, Ithaca, NY; 1979.

Roberts, A. and Donaldson, J., *Ante-Nicene Fathers*, Volume IV, Christiana Literature Co., New York, NY; 1890.

Robinson, James M., Editor, *The Nag Hammadi Library in English*, Harper & Row, New York, NY; 1988.

Rolland, Romain, *Life of Ramakrishna*, Advaita Ashram, Calcutta, India; 1965.

Ruff, Betty Clark, "My Toddler Taught Me About Death," *Instructor*; February 1963.

Souls Waiting in the Wings for Birth

Safeer, Pritam Singh, *The Tenth Master*, Guru Nanak Foundation, New Delhi, India; 1983.

Sanford, John A., *Soul Journey*, Crossroad, New York, NY; 1991.

Saraswati, Swami Satyananda, *Shree Maa, The Life of a Saint*, Sunstar, Fairfield, IA; 1997.

Sarkar, Rabindra Nath, *Latest Revelation in the East*, Sanskrit Pustak Bhandar, Calcutta, India; 1987.

Satchidananda, Sri Swami, *Golden Present*, Integral Yoga Publications, Virginia; 1987.

Saunders, Trevor J., *Plato, The Laws*, Penguin Books, Middlesex, England; 1975.

Sayer, Elizabeth P., *The Banquet of Dante Alighieri*, George Routledge and Sons, London, England; 1887.

Schaya, Leo, *The Universal Meaning of the Kabbalah*, Penguin Books, Inc, Baltimore, MD; 1973.

Schepps, Solomon J., *Lost Books of the Bible*, Bell Publishing, New York, NY; 1979.

Schmidt, Carl (ed.), *Pistis Sophia*, E.J. Brill, Leiden, Netherlands; 1978.

Scholem, Gershom G., *Origins of the Kabbalah*, Princeton Univ. Press, Princeton, NJ; 1987.

Scholem, Gershom G., *Major Trends in Jewish Mysticism*, Schocken Books, New York, NY; 1973.

Schoolcraft, Henry Rowe, *Historical and Statistical Information Respecting The History, Condition and Prospects of the Indian Tribes of the United States*, Volume VI, Philadelphia, PA; 1851-1857.

Schultz, Karen, *A Theosophical Guide for Parents*, Parents Theosophical Research Group, Ojai, CA; 1984.

Schure, E., *Pythagoras and the Delphic Mysteries*, William Rider & Son, Limited, London, England; 1923.

Seetal, Sohan Singh, *Guru Gobind Singh*, Lyall Book Depot, Ludhiana, India; 1968.

Seligson, Fred Jeremy, *Oriental Birth Dreams*, Holly, Elizabeth, NJ; 1990.

Shandler, Nina, *Yoga for Pregnancy and Birth*, Schocken Books, New York, NY; 1979.

Shaykh Muhammad al-Jamal ar-Rifa'i as-Shadhili, *Music of the Soul, Sufi Teachings*, Sidi Muhammad Press, Petaluma, CA; 1994.

Shea, David and Troyer, Anthony, (trans.), *Oriental Literature or Dabistan Al-Madhahib*, Triple Stars Printing Press, Lahore, Pakistan; 1973.

Shear, Jonathan, *The Inner Dimension, Philosophy and the Experience of Consciousness*, Peter Lang Publishing, New York, NY; 1990.

Sholapurkar, G.R., *Saints and Sages of India*, Bharatiya Vidya Prakashan, India; 1992.

Shunjo, Honen, the *Buddhist Saint: His Life and Teaching*, Chionin, Kyoto, Japan; 1925.

Singer, Isodore, (ed.), *The Jewish Encyclopedia*, Volume X and Volume XI, Funk & Wagnalls, New York, NY; 1905.

Singh, Dalip, *Guru Gobind Singh and Khalsa Discipline*, Singh Brothers, Amritsar, India; 1992.

Singh, Gobind M. & Singh, S.K., *Guru Gobind Singh*, Hemkunt Press, New Delhi, India; 1976.

Singh, Gopal, *Thus Spake the Tenth Master*, Punjabi Univ., Calcutta, India; 1978.

Singh, Gopal, *Guru Govind Singh*, National Book Trust, New Delhi, India; 1966.

Singh, Harbans, *Guru Gobind Singh*, Guru Gobind Singh Foundation, Chandigarh, India; 1966.

Singh, Khushwant and Suneet Vir, *Guru Gobind Singh*, Jaico Publishing House, Bombay, India; 1970.

Singh, Kirpal, *A Great Saint Baba Jaimal Singh*, Rohini Sat Singh, Anaheim, CA; 1949.

Singh, Maharaj Charan, *The Master Answers*, Radha Aoami Satsang Beas, Punjab, India; 1966.

Singh, Puran, *Guru Gobind Singh*, Guru Gobind Singh Foundation, New Delhi, India; 1966.

Singh, Trilochan, *Guru Gobind Singh*, Gurdwara Parbandhak Committee, Delhi, India; 1968.

Sivananda, Sri Swami, *Lives of Saints*, Divine Life Society, India; 1993.

Skeat, Walter William, *Malay Magic*, MacMillan and Co., London, England; 1900.

Skinner, Alanson, "Songs of the Menomini Medicine Ceremony," *American Anthropologist*, 27, p. 290-314; 1925.

Skinner, Alanson, "Traditions of the Iowa Indians," *Journal of American Folklore*, Volume 38, No. 150; 1925.

Skinner, Alanson, "Social Life and Ceremonial Bundles of the Menomini Indians," *Anthropological Papers of the American Museum of Natural History*, 13;1; 1913.

Slater, Joseph, *Collected Works of Ralph Waldo Emerson*, Volume III, Essays: 2nd Series, Belknap Press of Harvard Univ. Press, Cambridge, MA; 1983.

Smith, Herbert F., *John Muir*, Twayne Publishers, New York, NY; 1965.

Smith, Margaret, *Studies in Early Mysticism in the Near and Middle East*, Philo Press, Amsterdam; 1973.

Soifer, Deborah A., *Myths of Narasimha and Vamana*, Sri Satguru Publications, Delhi, India; 1991.

Sorensen, M.R. and Willmore D.R., *The Journey Beyond Life*, Volume I, Family Affair Books, Sounds of Zion, Midvale, UT; 1990.

Sparrow, Lynn Elwell, *Reincarnation*, St. Martin's Press; 1995.

Speck, Frank Gouldsmith, "Penobscot Tales and Religious Beliefs," *Journal of American Folklore*, 50; 1935.

Spencer, Sir Baldwin and Gillen, F.J., *Native Tribes of Central Australia*, Dover, New York, NY; 1968.

Souls Waiting in the Wings for Birth

Spencer, Sir Baldwin and Gillen, F.J., *Arunta*, Anthropological Publications, Macmillan & Co., Netherlands; 1966.

Spiegelman, J. Marvin, *Sufism, Islam and Jungian Psychology*, New Falcon Publications, Scottsdale, AZ; 1991.

Spier, Leslie, *Yuman Tribes of the Gila River*, Univ. of Chicago Press, Chicago, IL; 1933.

Stahl, William, H., *Macrobius' Commentary on the Dream of Scipio*, Columbia Univ. Press, New York, NY; 1952.

Stanner, W.E.H., "Murinbata Kinship and Totemism," *Oceania*, Volume 7, p. 186-216; 1936.

Star, Rima Beth, *The Healing Power of Birth*, Star Publishing, Austin, TX; 1986.

Steiner, Rudolf, *Life Between Death and Rebirth*, Anthroposophic Press, Hudson, NY; 1968.

Stevenson, Ian, MD, *Children Who Remember Previous Lives*, Univ. Press of Virginia, Charlottesville, VA; l987.

Stevenson, Ian, MD, *Cases of the Reincarnation Type*, Volume IV, Univ. Press of Virginia, Charlottesville, VA; 1983.

Stewart, J.A., *The Myths of Plato*, Southern Illinois Univ. Press, Carbondale, IL; 1960.

Sugrue, Thomas, *There is a River, The Story of Edgar Cayce*, Holt and Co., New York, NY; 1973.

Sullivan, Lawrence E. (ed), *Death, Afterlife, and the Soul*, Macmillan, New York, NY; 1989.

Swanton, John R., "Indian Tribes of the Lower Mississippi Valley and Adjacent Coast of the Gulf of Mexico," *Bureau of American Ethnology*, 43; 1911.

Talbot, P. Amaury, *Tribes of the Niger Delta*, Barnes & Noble, New York, NY; 1967.

Talbot, P. Amaury, *The Peoples of Southern Nigeria*, Oxford Univ. Press, London, England; 1926.

Talmage, James E., *The Vitality of Mormonism*, Gorham Press, Boston, MA; 1919.

Taplin, Rev. G., *The Folklore, Manners, Customs, and Languages of the South Australian Aborigines*, Johnson Reprint Corporation, Adelaide, Australia; 1879.

Taylor, Thomas, *Eleusinian and Bacchic Mysteries*, J.W. Bouton, New York, NY; 1980 (1875).

Thompson, E.A., *Who Was Saint Patrick?*, Boydell Press, Great Britain; 1985.

Thurman, Robert A.F., *The Tibetan Book of the Dead*, Bantam Books, New York, NY; 1994.

Thurston, Herbert, *The Lives of the Saints*, Volume I, Burns Oates & Washbourne, London, England; 1937.

Thurston, Herbert, *The Lives of the Saints*, Volume II, Burns Oates & Washbourne, London, England; 1930.

Thurston, Herbert, *The Lives of the Saints*, Volume III, Burns Oates & Washbourne, London, England; 1931.

Tigunait, Pandit Rajmani, *From Death to Birth*, Himalayan Institute Press, Honesdale, PA; 1997.

Tishby, Isaiah, *The Wisdom of the Zohar*, Volume II, Oxford Univ. Press, New York, NY; 1989.

Turnbull, Grace H., *The Essence of Plotinus*, Oxford Univ. Press, New York, NY; 1948.

Uchendu, Victor C., *The Igbo of Southeast Nigeria*, Holt, Rinehart and Winston, New York, NY; 1965.

Underhill, Ruth, *Indians of the Pacific Northwest*, Bureau of Indian Affairs, Washington, DC; 1945.

Van Praagh, James, *Talking to Heaven*, Dutton Book, New York, NY; 1997.

Venkateswarulu, Bulusu, *Lives of Ancient Indian Saints*, Volume V, Kakinada, India; 1985.

Verny, Thomas, MD, and John Kelly, *The Secret Life of the Unborn Child*, Dell Publishing, New York, NY; 1981.

Vissell, Barry and Joyce, *Risk to be Healed*, Ramira Publishing, Aptos, CA; 1989.

Vivekananda, Swami, *Complete Works of Swami Vivekananda*, Volume IV, Advaita Ashram, Calcutta, India; 1970-1973.

Voegelin, Charles Frederick, "Shawnee Female Deity," *Yale University Publications in Anthropology*, 10, New Haven, CT; 1936.

Wagner, Geoffrey A., *Gerard de Nerval*, Univ. of Michigan Press, Ann Arbor, MI; 1970.

Waite, A.E., *The Works of Thomas Vaughan*, Theosophical Publishing House, London, England; 1919.

Walker, E.D., *Reincarnation*, Univ. Books, New Hyde Park, New York, NY; 1965.

Wallace, RaNelle, *The Burning Within*, Gold Leaf Press, Carson City, NV; 1994.

Wallace, Robert Keith, *The Neurophysiology of Enlightenment*, Maharishi International Univ. Press, Fairfield, IA; 1986.

Wallace, Robert Keith and Benson, Herbert, "Is the meditative state that is achieved by yogis and other far eastern mystics accompanied by distinct physiological changes? A study of volunteer subjects in the U.S. indicates that it is." *Scientific American*, Volume 226, 84-90; 1972.

Wallace, Robert Keith, Benson, Herbert, and Wilson, Archie F., "A wakeful hypometabolic state," *American Journal of Physiology*, Volume 221, 795-799; 1971.

Wallace, Robert Keith, "The Physiological Effects of Transcendental Meditation: a proposed fourth major state of consciousness," doctoral dissertation submitted to the Univ. of California at Los Angeles, Department of Physiology, School of Medicine; 1970.

Wallace, Robert Keith, "Physiological effects of Transcendental Meditation," *Science*, Volume 167, 1751-1754, 1970.

Souls Waiting in the Wings for Birth

Wallis, Wilson D., "The Sun Dance of the Canadian Dakota," *Anthropological Papers of the American Museum of Natural History*, Volume XVI, Part IV; 1919.

Wallis, Wilson D., "The Canadian Dakota," *Anthropological Papers, American Museum of Natural History*, Volume 41:1; 1947.

Walters, Donald (Kriyananda), *The Essence of Self-Realization*, Crystal Clarity, Nevada City, CA; 1990.

Walters, Donald (Kriyananda), *The Path*, Ananda Publications, Nevada City, CA; 1977.

Warneck, Johann, *The Living Christ and Dying Heathenism*, Fleming H. Revell Co.; New York, NY; 1909.

Warner, W. Lloyd, *A Black Civilization*, Harper & Brothers, New York, NY; 1937.

Watson, Burton, Complete Works of Chuang Tzu, Columbia Univ. Press, New York, NY; 1968.

Watson, Burton, *Chuang Tzu*, Columbia Univ. Press, New York, NY; 1964.

Watt, William M., *Free Will and Predestination in Early Islam*, Luzac & Co., London, England; 1948.

Wensinck, Arent Jan, *The Muslim Creed: its genesis and historical development*, Frank Cass & Co., London, England; 1965.

Westcott, Mark, "Hemispheric symmetry of the EEG during the Transcendental Meditation technique," in David W. Orme-Johnson, John T. Farrow (Eds.): *Scientific Research on the Transcendental Meditation Program: Collected Papers*, Volume 1, p. 160-164, MERU Press, West Germany; 1976.

Wheelwright, Philip E., *Heraclitus*, Princeton Univ. Press, Princeton, NJ; 1959.

Whitton, Joel L., and Fisher, Joe, *Life Between Life, Scientific Explorations into the Void Separating One Incarnation from the Next*, Warner Books, New York, NY; 1986.

Woods, Ralph L. (ed), *The World of Dreams, An Anthology*, Random House, New York, NY; 1947.

Wright, M.R., *Empedocles: The Extant Fragments*, Yale Univ. Press, New Haven, CT; 1981.

Yogananda, Paramahansa, *Man's Eternal Quest*, Self Realization Fellowship, Los Angeles, CA; 1992.

Yogananda, Paramahansa, *Autobiography of a Yogi*, Self Realization Fellowship, Los Angeles, CA; 1972.

Zimmer, Heinrich, *Myths and Symbols in Indian Art and Civilization*, Harper & Brothers; 1946.

Index

About the Authors

ELIZABETH CARMAN has enjoyed a life-long passion to study the human mind and our full potential. Elizabeth earned a BA in psychology with honors from Michigan State University and later on an MA in Interdisciplinary Studies from Maharishi International University. She served as a social worker in Chicago. Elizabeth has devoted more than thirty years researching consciousness, including long-term consciousness development courses and advanced programs at Maharishi European Research University and Maharishi Vedic University in North America, Europe, and Asia. She has taught numerous meditation and personal growth workshops and served on faculty at Maharishi International University. Elizabeth is a native of the Upper Peninsula of Michigan on Lake Superior and lives in Austin, Texas, where she enjoys the great outdoors with her husband Neil.

NEIL CARMAN has a love for nature, graduating with a BS and MS in botany from the State University of Iowa and a PhD in botany from the University of Texas at Austin where he served as an assistant professor teaching biology, botany and comparative studies, including a course on the scientific basis of consciousness. Environmental interests led him to serve as a state air pollution investigator with the Texas Air Control Board. Neil was responsible for the investigation leading to the largest air pollution lawsuit and fine paid by an industrial plant in Texas history (General Tire & Rubber Co.); but only after the company pressured the agency to cover-up violations and Neil became a whistleblower in order to protect a poor minority neighborhood near the plant. Currently he works for the Sierra Club on air quality in Texas and as a technical advisor to Houston residents on air toxics and smog. Neil often serves as a pro bono technical resource for citizens across the US. He has received awards for his state environmental work and for community projects with the Sierra Club. He has spent more than thirty years investigating the field of consciousness. He is a native of Iowa City, Iowa, and lives in Austin, Texas, with his wife Elizabeth.